W9-BVZ-334

THE COLLECTED WORKS OF
SAMUEL TAYLOR COLERIDGE · 3

ESSAYS ON HIS TIMES

General Editor: Kathleen Coburn

Associate Editor: Bart Winer

THE COLLECTED WORKS

1. LECTURES 1795: ON POLITICS AND RELIGION
2. THE WATCHMAN
3. ESSAYS ON HIS TIMES
4. THE FRIEND
5. LECTURES 1808–1819: ON LITERATURE
6. LAY SERMONS
7. BIOGRAPHIA LITERARIA
8. LECTURES 1818–1819: ON THE HISTORY OF PHILOSOPHY
9. AIDS TO REFLECTION
10. ON THE CONSTITUTION OF THE CHURCH AND STATE
11. SHORTER WORKS AND FRAGMENTS
12. MARGINALIA
13. LOGIC
14. TABLE TALK
15. OPUS MAXIMUM
16. POETICAL WORKS

The Morning Post and Gazetteer

No. 9776. FRIDAY, JANUARY 10, 1800. Price in 1783, - - 3d. | Taxed by Mr. PITT, 3d. | Price 6d.

1. A typical front page of the four-page *Morning Post* (10 Jan 1800). Note price, doubled because "*Taxed by Mr.* PITT". From a copy in the British Library

THE COLLECTED WORKS OF

Samuel Taylor Coleridge

Essays on His Times

IN

The Morning Post

AND

The Courier

I

EDITED BY

David V. Erdman

ROUTLEDGE & KEGAN PAUL

BOLLINGEN SERIES LXXV
PRINCETON UNIVERSITY PRESS

The Collected Works, sponsored by Bollingen Foundation, is published in Great Britain by Routledge & Kegan Paul Ltd Broadway House, 68–74 Carter Lane, London EC4V 5EL ISBN 0–7100–7902–8 and in the United States of America by Princeton University Press, Princeton, New Jersey ISBN 0–691–09871–9 LCC 68–10210 The Collected Works constitutes the seventy-fifth publication in Bollingen Series

The present work, number 3 of the Collected Works, is in 3 volumes, this being 3: I

Designed by Richard Garnett
Printed in the United States of America
by Princeton University Press

THIS EDITION

OF THE WORKS OF

SAMUEL TAYLOR COLERIDGE

IS DEDICATED

IN GRATITUDE TO

THE FAMILY EDITORS

IN EACH GENERATION

Either they condemned action and so advocated. . . negotiations for peace in time of war; or they condemned inaction and so advocated war, for idealistic reasons, in time of peace. Both were Dissenting attitudes, both—confusingly—sometimes held by the same person.

A. J. P. Taylor *The Trouble Makers: Dissent over Foreign Policy 1792–1939*

CONTENTS

I

III

APPENDIXES

The Courier

LIST OF ILLUSTRATIONS

I

II

III

ACKNOWLEDGMENTS

For assistance amounting at times to collaboration I am indebted to Charlotte Woods Glickfield, in the early stages of gathering clues and searching files; to Carl R. Woodring, during fifteen years' exchange of information and ideas that has made these volumes and his Coleridge book interlocking enterprises; to Lucyle Werkmeister, historian of the newspapers and voluminous correspondent; and in the last few years to Bart Winer, whose editorial scholarship has extended the scope of this collection and immensely improved the accuracy of the annotation. To the last three named and to Kathleen Coburn, John Colmer, and Max F. Schulz I am indebted for patient, critical reading of the manuscript in various stages. For the application of professional classicism to the Latin and Greek quotations and allusions we are all indebted to Lorna Arnold.

For extensive assistance and general encouragement I am grateful to Morchard Bishop, the late Edward E. Bostetter, Northrop Frye, James R. MacGillivray, the late Charles G. Osgood, Lewis Patton, the late Abbie F. Potts, Thomas M. Raysor, Elisabeth Schneider, Milton Teichman, E. P. Thompson, and Robert S. Woof. I am indebted to Dulany Terrett for generous permission to cite and quote his dissertation on Coleridge's politics. For a variety of particular favours I am grateful to Paul A. Arbucho, the late R. C. Bald, F. W. Bateson, Betty Bennett, Gerald E. Bentley, Jr, Cynthia Bowling, U. Bredehorn, the late Wallace Brockway, Howard O. Brogan, Kenneth Neill Cameron, Kenneth Curry, the late Helen Darbishire, Tom Dargan, Richard Gollin, Earl Leslie Griggs, Jerome Landfield, Carol Landon, the late Thomas Ollive Mabbott, Kenneth MacLean, the late H. M. Margoliouth, Robert Mayo, Mary Moorman, Martin K. Nurmi, Warren U. Ober, Conor Cruise O'Brien, Stephen M. Parrish, Burton R. Pollin, Herman Ramras, Ruth Reavey, Fernand G. and Anne Renier, Barbara E. Rooke, Ben Syfu, William Dean Vanech, Eugene B. Vest, William S. Ward, George Watson, Sir John Wedgwood, George Whalley, the late R. J. White, Carol Wolf, Elin Wolfe, and Paul M. Zall.

For encouragement and assistance in many ways I am grateful

to my colleagues at The New York Public Library. Edward G. Freehafer and John M. Cory, successive Directors, and Harald Ostvold and James W. Henderson, successive Chiefs of the Research Libraries, have been particularly generous and sympathetic. For help in the expedition of research I have been indebted to Saro J. Riccardi of the Newspaper Division, to Lola L. Szladits and the late John D. Gordan of the Berg Collection, and to David H. Stam, William L. Coakley, and Marilan Lund, Editorial Assistants; also to the librarians of Princeton University, of Duke University, of the University of Minnesota, of the State University of New York, of the Newberry Library, and of the New-York Historical Society; of the Pierpont Morgan Library, especially Herbert S. Cahoon; of the Library of Congress, especially Frederick R. Goff; of the British Museum, the Bodleian Library, the Cambridge University Library, and the Public Libraries of Bath, Bristol, Norwich, and Shrewsbury.

I am grateful to the John Simon Guggenheim Memorial Foundation for a Fellowship in 1954, to the Research Foundation of the State University of New York for a Fellowship in 1971, to the Bollingen Foundation for grants of assistance as well as for the large material support which is making possible so extensive and editorially ample an edition of the works of Coleridge. All of those engaged in this series are immeasurably indebted to Kathleen Coburn and Rupert Hart-Davis for their inspiration and pantisocratic dedication to the yoking of our collaborative energies, and to numerous graduate students who formally and informally have kept the intellectual exchanges open over the years.

For immediate critical advice at critical moments and for never permitting research to become unnaturally abstruse I am most happily indebted to my wife and daughters and neighbourly friends. Tory and Lissalotte of the youngest generation relieved with merriment the drudgery of the final revisions.

DAVID V. ERDMAN

Crane Neck Point
September 1973

PRINCIPLES OF ATTRIBUTION

ASCERTAINING the authorship of newspaper paragraphs, almost always unsigned, has been a major editorial task. Sara Coleridge based her edition of her father's newspaper essays (*EOT* 3 vols 1850) largely on a file of clippings he had kept and evidently signed or initialled. The file has not survived but some of her working notes have (in the Victoria College Library), and her grouping of certain and probable attributions preserves the record of her reliance on signed evidence for the first group and circumstantial and "strong internal evidence of both style and matter" for the other. Very few scraps of manuscript evidence survive from the actual writing of published essays (see Appendix B), but a good deal of general and particular evidence can be found in Coleridge's correspondence, notebooks, and published works; so most of Sara's "probable" attributions are now confirmed, and most of the new discoveries rest on a combination of external and internal proofs. In the course of familiarising myself with Coleridge's journalism and of learning to assign the authorship of the few essays whose attribution to Coleridge rests almost entirely on their style, I have published several extended demonstrations of method (Erdman 1957, 1957–8, 1959a, 1959b, and, with a revision of the latter, an anthology *Evidence for Authorship: Essays on Problems of Attribution*, edited with E. G. Fogel in 1966). I have now applied the test of style to all the essays that have been proposed as Coleridge's, with special attention to those for which the external clues are ambiguous.

In the present volumes the basis for each attribution is summarised or referred to in its headnote. Essays or briefer paragraphs for which the evidence is inconclusive—or which were certainly or probably written in collaboration—are given in Appendix A.

Of Sara Coleridge's "probable" attributions of *Morning Post* essays I have rejected only one, more out of caution than from any firm conviction that it is *not* by Coleridge. It is the essay of 21 April 1800 (*EOT* II 403–8), one of the six she accepted out of twenty-five *Morning Post* essays listed in her notebook under "Conjectured". When she wrote that "there are few that do not contain sentences or phrases to be found elsewhere in his writings, *or* some other special marks of his style", I take her to have been very uncertain about such neutral essays as this one. As *Essays on His Own Times* went to press, Sara herself put queries upon the two that she called the "most dubious of the *conjecturals*" from the *Courier* (1811). These did not pass the test of *style*, and in questioning them she put her finger on a special problem of conjecturing the authorship of pieces of journalism: "They contain my Father's opinions, but, I now think, may not have been from his pen."

By and large it is my own impression that, for the whole period of his writing for the *Morning Post*, the opinions of Coleridge are the opinions of the newspaper—and vice versa. These opinions vary and even threaten at times to separate. But in any debatable case of attribution, the opinions expressed are insufficient indication of authorship—though the idiosyncratic choice and arrangement of "matter" may lead us to external parallels that make the case. On the other hand, in some of his writing for the *Courier*—for example, in his attempt to mend Street's obituary on Fox in 1806 or in his sympathetic comment on Byron's Separation poems in 1816—the clue to Coleridgian authorship or interference is a *difference* of opinions. It is, however, the *manner* of their expression that we find distinctive. Sara was confident that, in her father's case at least (*EOT* I lxxxv–lxxxvii), "there is a *countenance* in an author's mode of expression...clearly recognizable by those well acquainted with his mental idiosyncrasy". She conceded that there are authors "who can assume different persons as well as different costumes" but put her father in a class with Spenser, Shakespeare, Milton, and Dante as far as original genius and strongly individualised products are concerned.

My Father's genius was never hidden in the different forms it assumed or modes in which it was manifested. The identity was more impressive than the diversity in all that proceeded from his mind. In his prose writings the union of ardour with precision is one of the most general characteristics of his manner; and another is the combination of learning with imaginativeness. He was wont to illustrate a subject by images borrowed from the realm of Faëry [i.e. romance; she might have added necromancy, medicine, chemistry, meteorology, navigation]...and the deep treasury of Scripture. ...His prose was that of a poet, yet possessed the appropriate prosaic rhythm; and this is the most general mark....Perhaps there are few *good* styles, such as are not encrusted with icy mannerisms, but pure and free and flowing, like a mountain stream in April, which are so recognizable as my Father's....

"Except in one or two doubtful cases", declares a modern critic, "it would be quite possible to identify Coleridge's contributions simply by singling out those items which have a genuinely individual quirkiness of flavour." (Anonymous reviewer of *Omniana* in *TLS* 5 Aug 1969 p 496.) Sara nevertheless declared the possibility of having been mistaken "in some of my few conjectural attributions"—a wording that, again, indicates that she considered only a fraction of her "probable" attributions really "conjectural".

Coleridge himself, in *Confessions of an Inquiring Spirit*, Letter III, defended the validity of resting the case for authenticity on internal evidence (combined with sufficiently limiting external evidence) when dealing with the work of an original genius. Not only "its characteristic features, but...its surpassing excellence" would render "the chances of its having had any other author than the giant-mind, to whom the biographer ascribes it, small indeed!" When, within the chronological limits of Coleridge's known or inferable availability and obligation to the editors of the *Morning Post* and, subsequently, the *Courier*, we discover dozens of editorial essays and leading paragraphs comparable in spirit, rhythm, and quirkiness to other essays and paragraphs indubitably by Coleridge, what are the chances of the unsigned essays' having had any other author? Of the limiting factors, let us consider first the implications of journalistic publication.

Editorial paragraphs appearing under the masthead (leaders or leading paragraphs, without titles) spoke directly for the newspaper and were presumably written by the editor or by someone hired by him (e.g. Coleridge when he was formally a member of the staff, as in 1800 or 1811); consultation usually preceded or accompanied their composition—and the result might often be collaborative. Many of the new attributions are in this category, and most of the essays printed in Appendix A are editorial collaborations—here treated as conjectural whenever the Coleridgian share of the work seems less than major. A good many of the new attributions are in the category of special articles, placed separately under independent headlines such as "Our Future Prospects", "The Keswick Impostor", "America", or addressed as Letters to the Editor and signed pseudonymously, as are the letters or series of letters by "Humanitas", "ΕΣΤΗΣΕ", "A Lover of 'Universal Toleration'", and "Plato". Theoretically, anyone might contribute such essays with or without invitation; sometimes they were reprinted or translated from another journal, with or without acknowledgment. On the other hand, some were clearly mere overflowings from the leading-paragraph area. Of the *Morning Post* essays of this sort now added to the canon, two are quite independent, in a period when Coleridge was not writing leaders, but signed by his Greek pseudonym; two are signed by place, "Keswick"; most are written in an editorial "we" by a person who identifies himself with and speaks for the newspaper and its policies. Several of the new attributions are unsigned obituaries.

Each of the ostensibly independent contributions needs to be considered as a special case, but for the paragraphs ostensibly written by members of the editorial family we need to find out who these members were, how gigantic their minds, how distinctive their styles. For the *Morning Post* our information is fairly precise. We know that Daniel Stuart wrote many of his own editorials and that he was assisted by his handyman, George Lane, who was good at gossip and epigrams and news stories but had no mind for the political department. There is enough of a canon of Stuart's political writing (notably the series signed "X. Y." in the *Courier*) to familiarise us with his workmanlike but essentially unsoaring style. Over the years there are occasional runs of editorial matter different in style from the usual Lane or Stuart variety, some by a user of clichés in French whom I suspect to be T. G. Street, editor of Stuart's evening paper the *Courier*, whose style in later years (when Stuart and Coleridge joined him on the *Courier*) seems easy to distinguish. And then there is the legend, evidently correct but imprecisely dated, that Stuart was assisted at times by his brother-in-law, James Mackintosh—for whom Coleridge developed an especial loathing not wholly unrelated to the rivalry in their relation to Stuart. Fortunately, the style of Mackintosh, the mechanics of his mind and rhetoric, cannot easily be mistaken for the style of Coleridge—as Coleridge himself was rather intensely aware. The problem thus reduces itself, mainly, to the differentiation of Coleridgian from Mackintoshian rhetoric and from Stuartian horizontality of intellectual stature. Fortunately, Burke was not alive and his writings were not of the right political orientation to have entered the pages of Stuart's paper in Coleridge's day. If differentiation from Burke's eloquence had to be attempted, decisions might be immensely more subtle and difficult.

Coleridge's contributions to the *Courier* in 1804, as pointed to in his correspondence, are mainly collaborative with Stuart, and do not seem to involve Street. Later, in 1806 and again in 1811 and after, our editorial problem is primarily to sort out the various and shifting parts played by Coleridge, Stuart, and Street in the writing, revising, imitating, or borrowing of paragraphs and passages and word coinages inspired and sometimes written out by Coleridge but often appearing at one or two removes. During this same period several other contributors are to be reckoned with—Mackintosh and Croker and, after 1817, William Mudford, editorial successor to Street—but there is little likelihood of our mistaking any of their work for Coleridge's, except in the case of Mudford. His style, modelled on the styles of Wordsworth and Coleridge, quite lacks the Coleridgian quirkiness, but perhaps a flat piece of Coleridge's writing might be mistaken for Mudford's.

The saving fact is that Coleridge is a writer who can seldom proceed any distance incognito without being provoked into some ironic comment, some gesticulation of metaphor, or some metaphysical outcry that gives him away. Sometimes it is a single word: "sequaciousness", "weather-wisdom", "fugacious" ("a temporising, fugacious policy"), "unadding" ("with as obstinate and *unadding* a fidelity" as a parrot), "humanness" (a word he uses in 1806 in a letter as a conscious coinage, which is cited in *OED* from a letter of his of 1802, and which appears in italics in one of the newly attributed essays of 1800 on Washington), or "lengthy" (a word he holds at arm's length as an Americanism—and which Street borrows again and again until the mirth is beaten out of it). It may be a phrase: "the impolite obstinacy of events"; "the panic of property" (a favourite, used all his life); "the labyrinthine and improgressive steps of [Bonaparte's] tiresome figure-dance"; "enthusiasm and imagination, mutually feeding each other"; "the chasmy and incoherent accounts" of the French Constitution. The mind at work in such expressions rapidly and nimbly outdistances the minds of Street and Stuart and Mackintosh. Their declamation distinguishes itself from Coleridge's eloquence by its lack of the intellectual quality Coleridge distinguished in Burke's: "It seems characteristic of true eloquence," he said in *Watchman* No 1, "to reason *in* metaphors; of declamation, to argue *by* metaphors."

To reason in metaphors is to analyse their implications and employ them purposefully. "Assumed opinions...become real ones; the *suspension* of a tenet is a fainting-fit, that precedes its death." Efforts at free thought in France may be "as transient and void of immediate effect, as bubbles....Yet still they prove the existence of a vital principle; they are the bubbles of a fountain, not such as rise seldom and silent on the muddy and stagnant pools of despotism". In Coleridge's hands the metaphor is a precision instrument. He was acutely sensitive to the difference between good writing, in which "every phrase, every metaphor, every personification, should have its justifying cause", and writing "vicious in the figures and contexture of its style". Alert to structural and postural tensions, he would say of the French Constitution that it exhibits "a metaphysical posture-master's dexterity in balancing"; of an unimpressive argument: "How will it fly up, and strike against the beam, when we put in the counter-weights!"; but of the assertion that Jacobinism and Royalism completely counteract each other, that it is "a childish application of mechanics to the subject, in which even as metaphors, the phrases have scarcely any intelligible sense".

The probability of Coleridge's authorship of the essays collected here has been established by external clues of many kinds and varying degrees of probative force, from claims and allusions in letters, to serial linking, to self-borrowings. But only when I have found an intelligible, mature application of mechanics throughout the reasoned length of an essay or, to be more exact, a precise accommodation of vehicle to tenor and a nice consistency in the progression of the vehicle, have I felt completely certain of Coleridge's authorship of the whole. (In the flatter portions, especially of the more ephemeral paragraphs, it is always possible that we may be hearing not Coleridge in an uninspired moment but the amplifying or revisory locutions of his editors.) "Nevertheless", to borrow the cautionary words of the editor who was his own daughter, "as men are sometimes deceived in their physiognomical divinations, indubitable as it is that mind does shine through the vizor of clay, and even, in some measure, mould it, I may have been mistaken in some of my few conjectural attributions, and I shall be thankful to any one, who will give me information on the subject, or point out to me any errors... in this...edition..." (*EOT* I lxxxvii–lxxxviii).

EDITORIAL PRACTICE, SYMBOLS, AND ABBREVIATIONS

THE texts reprinted from the *Morning Post* and *Courier* preserve the original spelling and even the punctuation, except when the punctuation (which may be the compositor's) obscures meaning and except for the correction of obvious printer's errors. But liberties have been taken with the paragraphing and in the invention of titles, since most newspaper "paragraphs" lack them altogether—and in the addition of subtitles when they serve to indicate that the successive paragraphs of a given Paragraph deal with separate subjects and were perhaps intended to be thought of as independent Paragraphs (a distinction often deducible from the discourse but not from the typography). The newspaper practice, irregularly observed, of printing proper names in italics or small capitals has been ignored, but the varying spellings of such names as "Suwarrow/Suwarow" and "Bonaparte/Buonaparte" have been kept in the text, though in the introduction and notes the most usual spelling has been maintained. The occasional square or ornamental brackets occurring in the newspaper have been changed to parentheses; square brackets enclose editorial interpolations—including some made by Sara Coleridge, as noted.

Most of the extant runs of the *Morning Post* and the *Courier* (the former in the British Museum and the Newberry Library, the latter in the New-York Historical Society, the New York Public Library, the British Museum, and the London Guildhall) have been consulted and, selectively, collated. Errors in one copy are often not found in the others, for it was the compositors' practice to set two or more copies of each day's issue for printing from several presses simultaneously. Theoretically, the first setting could be inferred, but any run of collected issues would represent a random assortment of printings. The *Courier*, an evening paper, often issued a "Second Edition" with something new in its leading paragraph; the extant runs quite often lack any example of the first.

Editorial announcements of forthcoming articles by Coleridge, which appeared over the masthead on p 2 or 3 of the *Morning Post* or the *Courier*, are printed in chronological sequence among the essays but are not listed in the table of contents. They are printed in italics and indented slightly.

The editor's headnote gives the date of the article, its original title (if any), and the location in *EOT* or a summary of the reasons for attributing it to Coleridge.

Coleridge's footnotes are indicated by symbols (*, †, etc) and are printed full measure. The editor's footnotes are numbered and (when not too brief) printed in double columns. The order of the editor's footnotes follows (perhaps Coleridgian) logic; i.e. it is assumed that when the text contains an asterisk or a dagger the reader then turns from text to note and then goes back again. The editor's footnotes, which are sometimes notes on Coleridge's footnotes, follow that order. Thus the footnote indicators within the text may leap from 1 to 5, notes 2–4 being notes on Coleridge's footnotes.

Textual notes ([a–b], etc) at the foot of the page, preceding the editor's footnotes, indicate all changes in or questions about the texts. Textual notes on certain articles indicate collation with earlier or later versions, and textual notes on speeches recorded by Coleridge indicate what is unique in his reporting.

The editions referred to in the editor's footnotes are, when they are known, those Coleridge used; "see" before the work indicates that it is not necessarily the edition Coleridge cites or quotes (though it may be one he is known to have used).

Coleridge manuscripts, when quoted, are printed literatim, including cancellations, except that "it's", "its'", "your's", and "yours'" have been standardised to "its" and "yours". The following symbols are also used in quoting from manuscript (with "wild" as an example):

[wild]	A reading supplied by the editor.
[? wild]	An uncertain reading.
[? wild/world]	Possible alternative readings.
⌈wild⌉	A tentative reading (owing to obliterations, torn paper, etc).
[. . .]	An illegible word or phrase.
⟨wild⟩	A later insertion by Coleridge.

Strokes, dashes, and other symbols are Coleridge's.

ABBREVIATIONS

(In the works listed, place of publication is London, unless otherwise noted)

AA	*The Annual Anthology* [ed Robert Southey] (2 vols Bristol 1799–1800).
A-J	*The Anti-Jacobin, or Weekly Examiner* (1797–8).
Allsop	[Thomas Allsop] *Letters, Conversations and Recollections of S. T. Coleridge* (2 vols 1836).
Answer	C. T. S. [S. T. Coleridge] *An Answer to "A Letter to Edward Long Fox, M.D."*.
AR (1825)	S. T. Coleridge *Aids to Reflection* (1825).
A Reg	*The Annual Register* (1758–).
Aspinall	Arthur Aspinall *Politics and the Press c. 1780–1850* (1949).
Barnes	Donald Grove Barnes *George III and William Pitt, 1783–1806* (Stanford 1939).
BCWL	*Blake, Coleridge, Wordsworth, Lamb, Etc. Being Selections from the Remains of Henry Crabb Robinson* ed Edith J. Morley (Manchester 1922).
BE	*Biographia Epistolaris* ed A. Turnbull (2 vols 1911).
Beer	J. B. Beer *Coleridge the Visionary* (1959).
Bisset	Robert Bisset *The History of the Reign of George III* (6 vols 1820).
BL (1817)	S. T. Coleridge *Biographia Literaria* (2 vols 1817).
BL (1847)	S. T. Coleridge *Biographia Literaria* ed H. N. and Sara Coleridge (2 vols 1847).
BL (1907)	S. T. Coleridge *Biographia Literaria* ed John Shawcross (2 vols Oxford 1907).
BM	British Museum
BNYPL	*New York Public Library. Bulletin* (New York 1897–).
Bourne	H. R. Fox-Bourne *English Newspapers* (2 vols 1887).
B Poets	*The Works of the British Poets* ed Robert Anderson (13 vols Edinburgh 1792–5; vol XIV 1807).
Braekman and Devolder	W. Braekman and A. Devolder "Three Hitherto Unpublished Letters of S. T. Coleridge to J. J. Morgan" *Studia Gandensia* IV (1962) 203–23.
Bruun	Geoffrey Bruun *Europe and the French Imperium, 1799–1814* (New York and London 1938).
Byron *L&J*	*Works of Lord Byron: Letters and Journals* ed Rowland E. Prothero (6 vols 1898–1901).
C	Samuel Taylor Coleridge

C&S	S. T. Coleridge *On the Constitution of the Church and State* (1830).
CC	*The Collected Works of Samuel Taylor Coleridge* (London and Princeton, N.J. 1969–).
CIS	S. T. Coleridge *Confessions of an Inquiring Spirit* ed G. St J. Hart (1956).
CL	*Collected Letters of Samuel Taylor Coleridge* ed Earl Leslie Griggs (6 vols Oxford and New York 1956–71).
C Life (G)	James Gillman *The Life of Samuel Taylor Coleridge* (1838).
C Life (H)	Lawrence Hanson *The Life of Samuel Taylor Coleridge, the Early Years* (1938).
CM	S. T. Coleridge *Marginalia* ed George Whalley (in ms). *The Collected Works of Samuel Taylor Coleridge* XII.
CN	*The Notebooks of Samuel Taylor Coleridge* ed Kathleen Coburn (New York, Princeton, N.J., and London 1957–).
Colmer	John Colmer *Coleridge: Critic of Society* (Oxford 1959).
Conciones	S. T. Coleridge *Conciones ad Populum. Or Addresses to the People* (Bristol 1795).
Cottle *E Rec*	Joseph Cottle *Early Recollections; Chiefly Relating to the Late Samuel Taylor Coleridge, During His Long Residence in Bristol* (2 vols 1837).
Cottle *Rem*	Joseph Cottle *Reminiscences of Samuel Taylor Coleridge and Robert Southey* (1847).
CRB	*Henry Crabb Robinson on Books and Their Writers* ed Edith J. Morley (3 vols 1938).
CRC	*The Correspondence of Henry Crabb Robinson with the Wordsworth Circle* ed Edith J. Morley (2 vols Oxford 1927).
C Rev	*The Critical Review; or, Annals of Literature* (1756–1817).
C 17th C	*Coleridge on the Seventeenth Century* ed R. F. Brinkley (Durham, N.C. 1955).
DC	Derwent Coleridge
DCL	Dove Cottage Library, Grasmere
Debrett	*The Parliamentary Register; or History of the . . . Debates of the House of Commons* (*and House of Lords*) [ed John Almon] (pub Debrett 112 vols 1774–1813).
De Q	Thomas De Quincey
Deutsch	Harold C. Deutsch *The Genesis of Napoleonic Imperialism* (Cambridge, Mass. 1938).
DNB	*Dictionary of National Biography* (1885–).
Dropmore MSS	*The Manuscripts of J. B. Fortescue, Esq., Preserved at Dropmore* (10 vols 1892–1927).
DW	Dorothy Wordsworth

DWJ	*Journals of Dorothy Wordsworth* ed Ernest de Selincourt (2 vols Oxford 1941).
EB	*Encyclopaedia Britannica* (11th ed 29 vols Cambridge 1910–11).
Ed Rev	*The Edinburgh Review* (Edinburgh and London 1802–1929).
EHC	Ernest Hartley Coleridge
EM	*Encyclopaedia Metropolitana* (29 vols 1817–45).
EOT	S. T. Coleridge *Essays on His Own Times* ed Sara Coleridge (3 vols 1850).
Erdman (1956)	David V. Erdman "Coleridge, Wordsworth, and the Wedgwood Fund" *BNYPL* LX (1956) 425–43, 487–506.
Erdman (1957)	David V. Erdman "Coleridge on George Washington" *BNYPL* LXI (1957) 81–97.
Erdman (1957–8)	David V. Erdman "Newspaper Sonnets Put to the Concordance Test" *BNYPL* LXI (1957) 508–17, 611–20; LXII (1958) 46–9.
Erdman (1958)	David V. Erdman "Coleridge as Nehemiah Higginbottom" *Modern Language Notes* LXXIII (1958) 569–80.
Erdman (1959a)	David V. Erdman "The Signature of Style" *BNYPL* LXIII (1959) 88–109.
Erdman (1959b)	David V. Erdman "The Extent of Coleridge's Contributions to the *Critical Review*" *BNYPL* LXIII 433–54, 515–30, 575–87.
Erdman (1960)	David V. Erdman "Coleridge in Lilliput..." *Speech Monographs* XXVII (1960) 33–62.
Erdman (1961a)	David V. Erdman "Coleridge on Coleridge" *SIR* (1961) I 47–64.
Erdman (1961b)	David V. Erdman "Lost Poem Found" *BNYPL* LXV (1961) 249–68.
Erdman (1975)	David V. Erdman "Coleridge and the 'Review Business'" *The Wordsworth Circle* VI (1975) 3–50.
Erdman and Zall	David V. Erdman and Paul M. Zall "Coleridge and Jeffrey in Controversy" *Studies in Romanticism* XIV (1975) 78–83.
Farington	Joseph Farington *The Farington Diaries* ed James Greig (8 vols 1922–8).
Farrer	James Anson Farrer *The War for Monarchy, 1793–1815* (1920).
Fox *Corres*	*Memorials and Correspondence of Charles James Fox* ed Lord John Russell (2 vols 1853).
Friend (1809–10)	S. T. Coleridge *The Friend* ([Penrith] 1809–10).
Friend (1818)	S. T. Coleridge *The Friend* (3 vols 1818).

Friend (*CC*)	S. T. Coleridge *The Friend* ed Barbara E. Rooke (London and Princeton, N.J. 1969). *The Collected Works of Samuel Taylor Coleridge* IV.
George *Catalogue*	Mary Dorothy George *Catalogue of Political and Personal Satires... in... the British Museum* (vols V–XI, 1935–54).
Glickfield	Charlotte Glickfield "Coleridge's Prose Contributions to the *Morning Post*" *PMLA* LXIX (1954) 681–5.
G Mag	*The Gentleman's Magazine* (1731–1907).
Grant	James Grant "Past Metropolitan Papers... The 'Courier'" *Once a Week* VII (1871) 522–57.
Grounds... Peel's Bill	S. T. Coleridge *The Grounds of Sir Robert Peel's Bill Vindicated* (1818).
Hansard	*The Parliamentary Debates from the Year 1803 to the Present Time...* pub under superintendence of T. C. Hansard (41 vols 1812–20).
Hazlitt	William Hazlitt *Political Essays* (1819).
HC	Hartley Coleridge
HCR	Henry Crabb Robinson
HCR *Rem*	Henry Crabb Robinson *Diary, Reminiscences, and Correspondence* ed T. Sadler (3 vols 1869).
Hindle	Wilfrid Hindle *The Morning Post* (1937).
HLQ	*The Henry E. Huntington Library Quarterly* (San Marino, Cal. 1937–).
HNC	Henry Nelson Coleridge
IS	*Inquiring Spirit, a New Presentation of Coleridge from His Published and Unpublished Prose Writings* ed Kathleen Coburn (1951).
L	*Letters of Samuel Taylor Coleridge* ed E. H. Coleridge (2 vols 1895).
Lady Holland	*The Journal of Elizabeth Lady Holland (1791–1811)* ed Earl of Ilchester (2 vols 1908).
LB (1798)	[William Wordsworth and S. T. Coleridge] *Lyrical Ballads with a Few Other Poems* (Bristol and London 1798).
LCL	Loeb Classical Library
Lects 1795 (*CC*)	S. T. Coleridge *Lectures 1795: On Politics and Religion* ed Lewis Patton and Peter Mann (London and Princeton, N.J. 1971). *The Collected Works of Samuel Taylor Coleridge* I.
Litchfield	R. B. Litchfield *Tom Wedgwood, the First Photographer* (1903).
LL	*The Letters of Charles Lamb to Which Are Added Those of His Sister Mary Lamb* ed E. V. Lucas (3 vols 1935).
LLP	*Letters from the Lake Poets to Daniel Stuart* [ed Mary Stuart and E. H. Coleridge] (1889).

LR	*The Literary Remains of Samuel Taylor Coleridge* ed H. N. Coleridge (4 vols 1836–9).
LRR	S. T. Coleridge "Six Lectures on Revealed Religion, Its Corruption and Political Views" ms transcript by E. H. Coleridge.
LS (1817)	S. T. Coleridge *A Lay Sermon* (1817).
LS (*CC*)	S. T. Coleridge *A Lay Sermon* ed R. J. White (London and Princeton, N.J. 1972). In S. T. Coleridge *Lay Sermons: The Collected Works of Samuel Taylor Coleridge* VI.
L Works	*The Works of Charles and Mary Lamb* ed E. V. Lucas (6 vols 1912).
Maccoby	Simon Maccoby *English Radicalism, 1786–1832* (1955).
M Chron	*The Morning Chronicle* (1769–1862).
Migne *PL*	*Patriologiae cursus completus... Series Latina* ed J. P. Migne (221 vols Paris 1844–64).
Misc C	*Coleridge's Miscellaneous Criticism* ed T. M. Raysor (Cambridge, Mass. 1936).
MLR	*Modern Language Review* (Cambridge 1905–).
M Mag	*The Monthly Magazine* (1796–1843).
MPL	S. T. Coleridge *A Moral and Political Lecture* (Bristol [1795]).
M Post	*The Morning Post* (1772–1937).
M Rev	*The Monthly Review* (1749–1845).
Mrs C	Sara (Fricker) Coleridge
N&Q	*Notes and Queries* (1849–).
NYPL	The New York Public Library
OED	*The Oxford English Dictionary* (13 vols Oxford 1933).
Omniana	*Omniana, or Horae Otiosiores* ed Robert Southey with articles by S. T. Coleridge (2 vols 1812).
Parl Deb	*Cobbett's Parliamentary Debates* (22 vols 1803–12).
Parl Hist	*The Parliamentary History of England* ed William Cobbett and John Wright (36 vols 1806–20).
PD	S. T. Coleridge *The Plot Discovered* (Bristol 1795).
Phil Trans	*Philosophical Transactions of the Royal Society* (1665–1886).
P Lects (1949)	*The Philosophical Lectures of Samuel Taylor Coleridge* ed Kathleen Coburn (London and New York 1949).
PML	Pierpont Morgan Library, New York
PMLA	*Publications of the Modern Language Association* (Baltimore 1886–).
Poole	M. E. Sandford *Thomas Poole and His Friends* (2 vols 1888).

PW (EHC)	*The Complete Poetical Works of Samuel Taylor Coleridge* ed E. H. Coleridge (2 vols Oxford 1912).
QR	*The Quarterly Review* (1809–1952).
Rolo	Paul Jacques Victor Rolo *George Canning* (1965).
RS	Robert Southey
RX	John Livingston Lowes *The Road to Xanadu* (rev ed 1930).
SB	*Studies in Bibliography* (1948–).
SC	Sara (Coleridge) Coleridge
SCB	*Southey's Common-Place Book* ed J. W. Warter (4 vols 1849–51).
SH	Sara Hutchinson
Sh C	*Coleridge's Shakespearean Criticism* ed T. M. Raysor (2 vols 1930).
SIR	*Studies in Romanticism* (Boston 1961–)
SL	S. T. Coleridge *Sibylline Leaves* (1817).
S Letters (Curry)	*New Letters of Robert Southey* ed Kenneth Curry (2 vols New York and London 1965).
S Life (CS)	*Life and Correspondence of Robert Southey* ed C. C. Southey (6 vols 1849–50).
SM (1816)	S. T. Coleridge *The Statesman's Manual* (1816).
SM (*CC*)	S. T. Coleridge *The Statesman's Manual* ed R. J. White (London and Princeton, N.J. 1972). In S. T. Coleridge *Lay Sermons: The Collected Works of Samuel Taylor Coleridge* VI.
SP	*Studies in Philology* (Chapel Hill, N.C. 1906–).
Stuart	Daniel Stuart "Anecdotes of the Poet Coleridge" *G Mag* n.s. IX, X (1838), reprinted in *BE*.
Sultana	Donald Sultana *Samuel Taylor Coleridge in Malta and Italy* (Oxford 1969).
Terrett	Dulany Terrett "Coleridge's Politics, 1789–1810" (diss Northwestern University 1941).
Thibaudeau	Antoine Claire Thibaudeau *Bonaparte and the Consulate* tr and ed G. K. Fortescue (1908).
Thompson	E. P. Thompson *The Making of the English Working Class* (1963).
Trans RS Canada	*Transactions of the Royal Society of Canada* (Ottawa 1882–).
Trevelyan	George Macaulay Trevelyan *Lord Grey of the Reform Bill* (1929).
TT	*Specimens of the Table Talk of the Late Samuel Taylor Coleridge* ed H. N. Coleridge (2nd ed 1836).
UTQ	*University of Toronto Quarterly* (Toronto 1931–).

Variants (1958)	David V. Erdman "Unrecorded Coleridge Variants" *SB* xi (1958) 143–62.
Variants (1961)	David V. Erdman, Lucyle Werkmeister, and R. S. Woof "Unrecorded Coleridge Variants" *SB* xiv (1961) 236–45.
VCL	Victoria College Library, University of Toronto
W&C	H. M. Margoliouth *Wordsworth and Coleridge, 1795–1834* (London and New York 1953).
Watchman	S. T. Coleridge *The Watchman* (Bristol 1796).
Watchman (*CC*)	S. T. Coleridge *The Watchman* ed Lewis Patton (London and Princeton, N.J. 1970). *The Collected Works of Samuel Taylor Coleridge* ii.
Werkmeister (1963)	Lucyle Werkmeister *The London Daily Press 1772–1792* (1963).
Werkmeister (1967)	Lucyle Werkmeister *A Newspaper History of England 1792–1793* (1967).
Windham Papers	*The Windham Papers: The Life and Correspondence of William Windham, 1750–1810* (2 vols 1913).
WL (*E* rev)	*The Letters of William and Dorothy Wordsworth: the Early Years 1787–1805* ed Ernest de Selincourt rev Chester L. Shaver (Oxford 1967).
WL (*M* rev)	*The Letters of William and Dorothy Wordsworth: the Middle Years 1806–1820* ed Ernest de Selincourt rev Mary Moorman and Alan G. Hill (2 vols Oxford 1969–71).
W Life (M)	Mary Moorman *William Wordsworth* (2 vols Oxford 1965).
Woodring	Carl R. Woodring *Politics in the Poetry of Coleridge* (Madison Wis. 1961).
Woof (1962)	R. S. Woof "Wordsworth's Poetry and Stuart's Newspapers: 1797–1803" *SB* xv (1962) 149–89.
W Prose	*The Prose Works of William Wordsworth* ed W. J. B. Owen and Jane Worthington Smyser (3 vols Oxford 1974).
WPW	*The Poetical Works of William Wordsworth* ed Ernest de Selincourt and Helen Darbishire (5 vols Oxford 1940–9).
WW	William Wordsworth
WW LC	Wordsworth Library Catalogue (ms).
WW *SC*	*Catalogue of the...Library of...William Wordsworth* (Preston 1859).

CHRONOLOGICAL TABLE
1772–1834

(public events to the end of 1818, the year C's last essay appeared in the *Courier*)

1772	(21 Oct) C b at Ottery St Mary, Devonshire, to the Rev John and Ann (Bowdon) Coleridge, youngest of their 10 children	George III king (1760–1820) Wordsworth 2 years old Scott 1 year old *M Post* began
1774		Southey b
1775		American War of Independence C. Lamb b
1776		Adam Smith *Wealth of Nations* Gibbon *Decline and Fall*
1778		Hazlitt b Rousseau and Voltaire d
1781	(Oct) Death of C's father	Kant *Kritik der reinen Vernunft* Schiller Die *Räuber*
1782	(Jul) Enrolled at Christ's Hospital preparatory school for girls and boys, Hertford (Sept) Christ's Hospital School, London, with C. Lamb, G. Dyer, T. F. Middleton, Robert Allen, J. M. Gutch, Le Grice brothers; met Evans family	Priestley *Corruptions of Christianity* Rousseau *Confessions*
1783		Pitt's first ministry (–1801)
1784		Samuel Johnson d
1785		De Quincey b Paley *Principles of Moral and Political Philosophy*
1789		(14 Jul) French Revolution Blake *Songs of Innocence* Bowles *Sonnets*
1790		Burke *Reflections on the Revolution in France*
1791	(Sept) Jesus College, Cambridge, Exhibitioner, Sizar, Rustat Scholar; met S. Butler, Frend, Porson, C. Wordsworth, Wrangham	(Mar) John Wesley d Paine *Rights of Man* pt I (pt II 1792) Boswell *Life of Johnson* Pitt obtains vote from Parliament to arm against Russia

		Henry Dundas in Pitt's cabinet as home secretary Anti-Jacobin riots at Birmingham
1792	(3 Jul) *Encaenia*, C's prize-winning Greek Sapphic *Ode on the Slave-Trade*	Pitt's attack on the slave-trade Fox's Libel Bill Cornwallis's victory near Seringapatam
1793	(May) Attended Cambridge trial of Frend (15 Jul) First poem in *Morning Chronicle* (2 Dec) Enlisted in 15th Light Dragoons as Silas Tomkyn Comberbache	Arthur Young appointed secretary to the new Board of Agriculture Stuart succeeds Mackintosh as secretary of the Foxite "Friends of the People" (21 Jan) Louis XVI executed (1 Feb) France declares war on England and Holland (Mar–Dec) Revolt of La Vendée (16 Oct) Marie Antoinette executed; John Hunter d Godwin *Political Justice* WW *An Evening Walk* and *Descriptive Sketches*
1794	(7–10 Apr) Back at Cambridge (Jun) Poems in *Cambridge Intelligencer*; set out with Joseph Hucks to Oxford (met Southey), pantisocracy hatched; Welsh tour (Aug–Sept) Met Thomas Poole; engaged to Sara Fricker (Sept) With RS published *The Fall of Robespierre* (Cambridge); *Monody on Chatterton* published with *Rowley Poems* (Cambridge) (Dec) Left Cambridge; sonnets in *M Chron* (24 Dec) Began *Religious Musings*	Sir William Windham enters Pitt's cabinet with Portland and other Whigs (17 May) Suspension of Habeas Corpus Robespierre executed, end of the Terror (Oct–Dec) State Trials: Tooke and Thelwall acquitted of charge of treason (–1795) Paine *Age of Reason* Paley *Evidences of Christianity* Stuart *Peace and Reform, Against War and Corruption*
1795	(Jan) Bristol lodgings with George Burnett, RS (Feb) Political lectures (May–Jun) Lectures on Revealed Religion (16 Jun) Lecture on the Slave-Trade (Aug–Sept) Quarrel with RS, pantisocracy abandoned (4 Oct) Marries Sara Fricker (26 Nov) Lecture on the Two Bills (3 Dec) *Conciones ad Populum* published (Dec) *An Answer to "A Letter to Edward Long Fox"* and *Plot Discovered* published; *Watchman* planned	(Jun–Jul) Quiberon expedition (Aug) Stuart becomes editor and proprietor of the *Morning Post* (Aug) Constitution of the Year III (26 Sept) WW and DW at Racedown (Nov) Directory begins (6 Nov) Treason and Convention Bills introduced (18 Dec) Two Acts put into effect Lewis *Ambrosio, or the Monk*

1796	C's *Religious Musings* completed (9 Jan–13 Feb) Tour to Midlands to sell *The Watchman*; met Erasmus Darwin, Joseph Wright (painter) (1 Mar–13 May) *The Watchman* in ten numbers (16 Apr) *Poems on Various Subjects* (19 Sept) Hartley b; reconciliation with RS (31 Dec) *Ode on the Departing Year* in *Cambridge Intelligencer*; move to Nether Stowey	Napoleon general-in-chief of the French army of Italy (–1797) George Canning under-secretary for foreign affairs (–1799) Sir Francis Burdett enters Parliament (Jul) Robert Burns d (Sept) Mary Lamb's violent illness (Nov) Catherine of Russia d England treating for peace with France Threats of invasion of England Jenner performs first smallpox vaccination Burke *Letters on a Regicide Peace* Dr Thomas Beddoes *Essay on the Public Merits of Mr Pitt*
1797	(Mar) WW at Stowey (5 Jun) At Racedown (Jul) DW, WW, and Lamb at Stowey; DW and WW in Alfoxden House (16 Oct) *Osorio* finished; *Poems, to Which Are Now Added, Poems by Charles Lamb and Charles Lloyd* (Nov) C is engaged by *M Post* (13–16 Nov) C's and WW's walk to Lynton and *Ancient Mariner* begun (12 Dec) C's *Melancholy. A Fragment* in *M Post* (26 Dec) C's *The Visions of the Maid of Orleans, a Fragment* in *M Post* (30 Dec) C's stanzas *To Sir John Sinclair, Alderman Lushington, and the whole Troop of Parliamentary Oscillators* in *M Post*	Pitt, as Chancellor of the Exchequer, proposes to finance the renewed war against France by increasing taxes Negotiations at Lisle (Feb) Bank of England suspends cash payments (Mar) Stuart acquires copyright of *Telegraph* (Apr–Jun) Mutinies in the British Navy (26 May) Grey's motion for Parliamentary Reform defeated; Fox and Grey lead a Whig secession from attendance in Parliament (9 Jul) Burke d (4 Sept) Coup of 18 Fructidor (20 Sept) Stuart acquires *Gazetteer* (17 Oct) France and Austria sign peace treaty (Nov) Frederick William II of Prussia d; Frederick William III begins rule (20 Nov) *Anti-Jacobin, or Weekly Examiner* begins Erskine *View of the Present War with France*
1798	(2 Jan) First prose that is definitely C's appears in *M Post* (Jan) C's Unitarian sermons at Shrewsbury; Wedgwood annuity £150 accepted; C's *Fire, Famine, and Slaughter* in *M Post* (Mar) *Ancient Mariner* completed (5 Mar) Wordworths have received notice that their lease of Alfoxden will not be renewed	Charles Cornwallis Lord Lieutenant of Ireland (–1801) (Feb–Oct) Irish Rebellion (7 Feb) Duke of Norfolk dismissed (2 Mar) French Swiss decree (22 Mar) House of Lords orders Perry to Newgate for three months for "constitutional" libel (Apr) Helvetic Republic

	(8 Mar) WW–C poem *The Old Man of the Alps* in *M Post* (9 Mar) C's last prose of year in *M Post* (10 Mar) C's *The Raven* in *M Post* (11 Mar) C and the Wordsworths decide to go to Germany for a year (Apr) *Fears in Solitude*; *Recantation: an Ode* (16 Apr); RS engaged to supply "occasional verses, without a signature" for *M Post* (18 Apr) RS's first poem in *M Post*, *Lover's Rock* (22 Jun) RS's *Ode to Silence, alias Unanimity* in *M Post* (18 Sept) *Lyrical Ballads* published; WW, DW, and C to Hamburg (Oct) C to Ratzeburg	(3 Apr) Motion in Commons against the slave-trade lost by four votes (May) Bonaparte sent to invade Egypt (12 Jun) Malta taken by French (Jul) Bonaparte invades Egypt (9 Jul) *Anti-Jacobin* last number (1–2 Aug) Nelson's victory in Battle of the Nile Lloyd *Edmund Oliver* Bell introduces Madras system of education in England
1799	C goes to Cassel to see the King and Queen Louise Stuart buys *Courier* (Apr) C had news of death of Berkeley; C at University of Göttingen (May) Ascent of Brocken (29 Jul) In Stowey again (Aug–Dec) Sixteen "epigrams" by C in *M Post* (6 Sept) RS and C's *The Devil's Thoughts* in *M Post* (Sept–Oct) Devon walking tour with RS; met Humphry Davy in Bristol; experiments with nitrous oxide (Oct–Nov) First Lakes tour, with WW (26 Oct) Met Sara Hutchinson (10 Nov) C receives Stuart's offer to come to London on full salary (27 Nov) Arrives in London to accept *M Post* offer (Dec) DW and WW at Town End (later Dove Cottage) (4 Dec) C and Davy visit Godwin (7 Dec) Series on the French Constitution begun in *M Post* (9 Dec) C's *Maiden* and *To a Young Lady* in *M Post* (24 Dec) C's *Ode to the Duchess of Devonshire* appears; writes	Lord Robert Hobart joins House of Commons (Jan) First attempt at a vote for Union defeated in the Irish Parliament (Apr) Newspaper Act (May) Sir Sidney Smith repulses the French at Acre (25 Jul) Bonaparte drives Turks from Aboukir (29 Aug) Pope Pius VI d as a prisoner at Valence, France (8 Oct) Bonaparte suddenly appears in France (9 Nov) Bonaparte first consul under new constitution Schiller *Die Piccolomini* and *Wallensteins Tod* published Royal Institution founded

	almost constantly for *M Post* (–15 Jan 1800) (29 Dec) Dines with Francis Burdett and Godwin at Tooke's	
1800	(Jan–16 Apr) *M Post* reporter and leader-writer; translating *Wallenstein* at Lamb's (27 Jan) C's obituary of George Washington in *M Post* (4–18 Feb) Parliamentary reporting (2 Mar) Mrs C leaves London (Mar) C at Pentonville with Lamb; offered proprietary share in *M Post*, declines offer (Apr) To Grasmere and WW (May–Jun) In Stowey and Bristol (24 Jul) Move to Greta Hall, Keswick (Sept–Oct) Superintends printing of *Lyrical Ballads* (2nd ed) (Oct) C and Poole defend Monopolists (4 Dec) *Skeltoniad* against Mackintosh	(18 Jan) Debate over Union in Dublin (3 Feb) Fox returns to Parliament (Feb) Bill for Union passed (18 Feb) Louis de Frotté, general of the royalist army, shot on orders from Napoleon (Mar–Apr) Pius VII Pope (Apr) Commons approves bill for Union (25 Apr) Cowper d (14 Jun) Battle of Marengo Burns *Works* ed Currie Union of Great Britain and Ireland (5 Sept) Malta after long siege falls to English Mary Darby Robinson *Lyrical Tales*
1801	(Jan) *Lyrical Ballads* (1800) published; prolonged illnesses (21 Jan) C returns to London (May) C reads William Herschel's *Theometric Spectrum* (27 May, 22 June) Odes in *M Post* (Jul–Aug) With SH at Stockton; writes *Tranquillity* ode (15 Sept) Returns to *M Post* with *Ode after Bathing* (15 Nov) In London (27 Nov) Series on cabinet changes begun in *M Post* (4 Dec) Stuart prints C's *Tranquillity, an Ode* Christmas at Stowey	Davy lecturer at Royal Institution (Jan) Evangelicals begin monthly *Christian Observer* (Feb) Pitt, Grenville, and Windham resign (Mar) Addington ministry (–1804) Southey *Thalaba* Sir Alexander Mackenzie *Voyages on the River St Lawrence*
1802	(25 Jan) Returns to London with Poole; under care of Stuart and the Howells (23 Feb) Conclusion of cabinet series (22 Mar) "Mr. Addington's Administration" (Mar–Nov) In Lakes, severe domestic discord (4 Apr) *A Letter to* — [Sara Hutchinson]... (Jul) Translates part of Gessner's *Erste Schiffer*	Henri Benjamin Constant de Rebecque eliminated from Tribunate Cornwallis appointed to negotiate treaty of Amiens (25 Mar) Peace of Amiens (18 Apr) Erasmus Darwin d (8 May) Bonaparte life consul (15 May) News of Bonaparte's consulship reaches England (2 Oct) WW marries Mary Hutchinson (Oct) French army enters Switzerland

	(Aug) Scafell climb; visit of the Lambs (Sept–Nov) Writing for *M Post* (4 Oct) *Dejection* ode in *M Post* (11 Oct–31 Dec) Articles in *M Post* on the impostor Hatfield and Mary of Buttermere (14 Oct) *France. An Ode* in *M Post*, revision of *Recantation* (Nov) Three-day visit to London; tour of South Wales with Tom and Sally Wedgwood (23 Dec) Sara C b	Fox encounters Bonaparte at his levée in Paris *Edinburgh Review* founded Cobbett's *Weekly Political Register* founded Malcolm Laing *History of Scotland* Paley *Natural Theology* Spinoza *Opera* ed Paulus (1802–3)
1803	(Jan–Feb) In Somerset with Wedgwoods, Poole; with Lamb in London; makes his will (6 Jan) "Our Future Prospects" in *M Post* (Jun) *Poems* (1803) (summer) Visits by Hazlitt, Beaumonts, and S. Rogers to Lakes; Hazlitt's portrait of C (Jul–Aug) "The Men and the Times" in *M Post* (15–29 Aug) Scottish tour with DW and WW (Aug or Sept) Stuart sells and leaves *M Post*; C stops writing for it (30 Aug–15 Sept) Scottish tour alone (15 Sept) Return to Keswick	(Jan) Charles Erskine elected cardinal (Feb) Act of Mediation in Switzerland; Col Despard, one of the United Englishmen, hanged as an organiser of sedition (Mar) English troops leave Egypt (8 Mar) Royal message on the war (30 Apr) Louisiana bought by U.S. from France (May) Khusrau Pasha of Egypt deposed by a Mameluke and Albanian force led by Muhammed Ali (18 May) Official declaration of the war with France (25 May) Emerson b (Sept) Emmet's execution in Ireland (22 Nov) Mackintosh offered recordership of Bombay Cobbett *Parliamentary Debates* (later Hansard) Hayley *Life and Posthumous Writings of Cowper* Chatterton *Works* ed RS and Cottle Malthus *Principles of Population* (2nd ed)
1804	(Jan) Ill at Grasmere; portrait by Northcote (24 Jan) To London (Feb–Mar) C writes for *Courier* on Sheridan and Addington and the Volunteers (27 Mar) Stuart introduces C to Sheridan; C leaves London (9 Apr) In convoy to Malta (Jul) As private secretary to Alexander Ball, British High Commissioner at Malta, C drafts "Observations on Egypt" and other papers, some versions intended for *Courier*	British and Foreign Bible Society formed (Feb) Muhammed Bey el-Elfi returns to Egypt from England (8 Feb) Volunteer Bill introduced (12 Feb) Kant d (14 Feb) King George becomes "ill" (20 Feb) Sheridan is offered office of receiver-general of the Duchy of Cornwall (Mar) Code Napoléon (Apr) 2nd Pitt ministry (–1806); collapse of Addington's administration

	(Aug–Nov) Sicily, two ascents of Etna; stays with G. F. Leckie	(15 Apr) Charles Pichegru d, Paris, strangled while awaiting trial for treason (May) Ahmad Pasha al-Jazzar d; John Wesley Wright, navy commander, captured at Quiberon Bay, imprisoned at Paris (18 May) Napoleon made emperor (June) Sir John Stuart knighted for services in Egyptian campaign (12 Dec) Spain declares war on Britain
1805	(Jan) Appointed Acting Public Secretary in Malta; news of loss of John Wordsworth on *Abergavenny* (Jan, Mar) Brief items in *Courier* (Sept–Dec) In Sicily (Dec) To Naples and Rome	Henry Addington becomes Viscount Sidmouth France transfers rule of Tirol from Austria to Bavaria (Apr) Third Coalition against France (9 May) Schiller d (26 May) Napoleon King of Italy (17 Oct) Napoleon's victory at Ulm (21 Oct) Nelson's victory at Trafalgar (27 Oct) John Wesley Wright commits suicide (murdered?)
1806	(Jan) In Rome, meets Washington Allston, the Humboldts, L. Tieck, and Schlegel; to Florence, Pisa (Mar) Meets Angelica Catalani (23 Jun) Sails from Leghorn (17 Aug) Lands in England; London, job-hunting; Parndon with the Clarksons and to Cambridge (15 Sept) C tries to modify editor T. G. Street's obituary on Fox (26 Oct) In Kendal (Nov) Keswick, determined on separation from Mrs C (Dec) At Coleorton with WW and SH, crisis of jealous disillusionment with them	(Jan) Pitt d, "Ministry of All the Talents" (spring) Rate of income tax raised from 6¼% to 10% (Jul) Small British force under Sir John Stuart defeats French at Maida in Calabria (6 Aug) Holy Roman Empire ends (26 Aug) Palm executed (13 Sept) Fox d British blockade (Oct) Austerlitz (Prussians defeated) (14 Oct) Jena (Nov) Berlin Decree and Continental System Angelica Catalani makes her first appearance in London Arndt *Geist der Zeit* Hazlitt *Free Thoughts on Public Affairs*
1807	Coleorton; hears WW read *Prelude* and writes *Lines to William Wordsworth* (Jun) With C family at Stowey (Aug) Meets De Quincey; in Bristol (Nov) In London	French seize the Ionian Islands Burdett chosen by electors of Westminster in Middlesex Election (Feb) Napoleon fights Russia (Mar) Portland ministry (–1809) (25 Mar) Abolition of slave-trade (25 May) Sir Francis Burdett—address to the Electors of Westminster

		(Jun) Napoleon fights Russia again (Jul) Peace of Tilsit (Aug) Truce between Russia and Turkey (2 Sept) Bombardment of Copenhagen by British fleet (Dec) Peninsular War begins Davy and oxymuriatic acid WW *Poems in Two Volumes* RS *Letters from England by Don Espriella; Specimens of the Later English Poets* C. and M. Lamb *Tales from Shakespeare*
1808	C translates and revises *Geist der Zeit* (15 Jan–Jun) In rooms at *Courier* office, Strand; lectures at Royal Institution on Poetry and Principles of Taste; illnesses, Bury St Edmunds (Jun–Aug) Bristol, Leeds, Keswick (Jul) Review of Clarkson's *History of the Abolition of the Slave-Trade* in *Ed Rev* (1 Sept) Arrives Allan Bank, Grasmere (Nov) First Prospectus of *The Friend*; Kendal (27 Dec) First instalment of WW's Cintra Letters in *Courier*	American Non-Intercourse Act Bell–Lancaster controversy Sir Arthur Wellesley to Portugal Crabb Robinson *Times* correspondent in Peninsula Joseph Bonaparte made king in Spain Distillation from grain prohibited (Distillery Bill) (Apr) Sir John Moore's correspondence published in *Courier* (1 May) Hazlitt marries Sarah Stoddart (Jul) Palafox, leading Saragossa townspeople, fights off French (21 Aug) Wellesley defeats Junot at Vimiera (14 Nov) Arrival of British troops under Moore in Salamanca (23 Nov) All of the Spanish armies routed (Dec) Palafox and Saragossa townspeople again fight off French; Dr T. Beddoes d (4 Dec) Madrid reoccupied by French Dalton *New System of Chemical Philosophy* and publication of atomic theory Lamb *Specimens of English Dramatic Poets* Scott *Marmion* John and Leigh Hunt's *Examiner* begins Goethe *Faust* pt I Thomas Ashe *Travels in America*
1809	(13 Jan) C's rewriting of a Cintra Letter in *Courier* (1 Jun) *The Friend* No 1 published	Lord Erskine's bill for the prevention of cruelty to animals Tirolean patriot Andreas Hofer

(8 Jun) *Friend* No 2
(10 Aug) *Friend* No 3
(7 Sept) *Friend* No 4
(14 Sept) *Friend* No 5
(21 Sept) *Friend* No 6
(28 Sept) *Friend* No 7
(5 Oct) *Friend* No 8
(12 Oct) *Friend* No 9
(19 Oct) *Friend* No 10
(26 Oct) *Friend* No 11; C publishes WW's sonnets to Hofer and Tirolese in *Friend*, also a refutation of charges of Jacobinism
(4 Nov) C's mother d
(9 Nov) *Friend* No 12
(16 Nov) *Friend* No 13
(23 Nov) *Friend* No 14
(30 Nov) *Friend* No 15
(1 Dec) News of Cortes' proclamation in *Courier*
(7 Dec) *Friend* No 16
(7 Dec–20 Jan 1810) "Letters on the Spaniards" in *Courier*
(14 Dec) *Friend* No 17
(21 Dec) *Friend* No 18
(28 Dec) *Friend* No 19

drives out Bavarians twice and Austrians twice
(Jan) Sir John Moore d; victories in the Peninsula; Duke of York–Mrs Clarke scandal
(Feb) *Quarterly Review* founded
(9 Mar) Byron *English Bards and Scotch Reviewers*
(Mar) Revolution in Sweden
(Mar–Apr) Revolt in the Tirol
(11 Apr) Cochrane destroys French fleet at Aix
(May) Napoleon's capture of Vienna and his excommunication; Pius VII imprisoned
WW *Convention of Cintra* pamphlet
(27 Jul) Battle of Talavera
(Jul–Nov) Walcheren expedition
(Aug) Attack on Flushing
(Sept) Wellington defeats French under Masséna at Busaco
(21 Sept) Canning–Castlereagh duel
(Oct) Perceval ministry (–1812)
(14 Oct) Peace of Schönbrunn
(20 Oct) Alexander Ball d in Malta
(3 Nov) Cortes proclamation, Seville
(19 Nov) Defeat of Spanish army under Areizaga at Ocaña
(10 Dec) Garrison at Gerona surrenders to French
Schlegel *Über dramatische Kunst und Literatur*

1810 (4 Jan) *Friend* No 20
(11 Jan) *Friend* supernumerary
(25 Jan) *Friend* No 21
(31 Jan) *Friend* No 22
(8 Feb) *Friend* No 23
(15 Feb) *Friend* No 24
(22 Feb) *Friend* No 25
(1 Mar) *Friend* No 26
(Mar) SH leaves for Wales
(15 Mar) *The Friend* No 27, last number
(3 Apr) Writes on "Parties" in *Courier*
(Oct) To London; Montagu precipitates WW–C quarrel; with Morgans in Hammersmith
(Nov) Personal association with H. Crabb Robinson begins

Louis Bonaparte deposed as King of Holland; Bernadotte elected as successor to Swedish throne; French driven from Portugal
(Feb) Hofer shot on orders from Napoleon
(23 Feb) Petitions concerning the Catholic leaders presented to the House of Commons (–1 Mar)
(Mar) Battle over admission of press to House of Commons
(12 Mar) Burdett speech moving discharge of Gale Jones from Newgate
(Apr) Burdett arrested
(May) First reform bill since 1797 introduced
(21 Jun) Burdett released from Tower
(Jul) Napoleon annexes Holland

		(Sept) Commons committee publishes report recommending resumption of cash payments by Bank of England within two years (Dec) King George's insanity generally conceded WW *Guide to the Lakes* Mme de Staël *De l'Allemagne* Scott *Lady of the Lake* RS *Curse of Kehama* C. W. Pasley *Essay on the Military Policy and Institutions of the British Empire*
1811	(21 Mar) C's (?) poem *Lovers' Quarrels* in *Courier* (Mar–Apr) Miniature painted by M. Betham; meets Grattan (19 Apr) C prints "The Regent and Mr. Perceval" in *Courier*—its signature makes public announcement of his joining the staff (20 Apr) First *Table Talk* recorded by John Taylor Coleridge (May–Sept) Regular contributions to *Courier* (30 Aug) C's poem *The Hour-Glass* in *Courier* (4 Sept) C publishes attack on Hibern-Anglus in *Courier* (18 Nov–27 Jan 1812) Lectures on Shakespeare and Milton at Scot's Corporation Hall, Collier, Byron, Rogers, Robinson attending (Dec) George Dawe bust of C	(5 Feb) Prince of Wales made Regent (20 Mar) Cardinal Charles Erskine d (5 May) Victory over Masséna (16 May) Debate on Grattan's petition to restore former rate of duty on spirits (18 May) British victory at Albuera over French under Marshal Soult (21 May) Lord Sidmouth's Dissenting Ministers Bill negotiated in the House of Lords without a division (25 May) Duke of York's reappointment as army commander announced (27 May) Petition concerning Catholic leaders presented by the Marquess of Downshire to the House of Lords (31 May) Patrick Duigenan opposes Grattan's motion for a committee on the Roman Catholic petitions (Jun) Lord King threatens to demand rent payments in gold (1 Jun) Papers admit an "alarming increase" in the King's "illness" (7 Jun) Perceval (in Commons) presents "thanks of the House" to Major-Gen Beresford for "distinguished ability" displayed at Albuera (18 Jun) Debate on Catholic Emancipation ("Catholic claims"); Downshire's petition voted down (24 Jun) House of Lords debates the assassination of Bonaparte (27 Jun) Lord Stanhope introduces a bill to make bank-notes legal tender

		(12 Jul) Samuel Romilly presents petition in the Court of Chancery concerning regulations of Christ's Hospital (19 Jul) Lord Stanhope's bill passed (30 Jul) Lord Lieutenant and Privy Council of Ireland present a proclamation against the activities of the Catholic Committee (Aug) Comet appears (9 Aug) Irish government arrests five Catholic delegates in Dublin (Nov) Bread riots in Nottingham (Nov to 1815) Luddite uprisings (25 Nov) Dr Marsh delivers address to University of Cambridge, concerning the Bible Society Shelley *Necessity of Atheism* Sir John Joseph Dillon *The Letters of Hibern-Anglus*
1812	(Jan–May) Essays in *Courier* (Feb–Mar) Last journey to the Lakes to collect copies of *Friend* (Apr) With the Morgans, Berners Street, Soho (May–Aug) Lectures on drama in Willis's Rooms; portrait by Dawe (May) Lamb and HCR patch WW quarrel (14 May) C writes obituary on Perceval for *Courier* (Jun) Catherine Wordsworth d; *The Friend* reissued (3 Nov–26 Jan 1813) Shakespeare lectures in Surrey Institution (Nov) Half Wedgwood annuity withdrawn; RS and C *Omniana* (Dec) Thomas Wordsworth d	Burdett re-elected (Jan) Wellington captures Ciudad Rodrigo (11 Feb) Meeting of the Court of Common Council to consider a grant of £500 to the National Institution for the Instruction of the Children of the Poor according to the Principles of the Church of England—the Council refuses to give support (18 Feb) Restrictions on the Regency expire (Mar) Wellington captures Badajoz (11 May) Spencer Perceval assassinated in the House of Commons by John Bellingham (Jun) Lord Liverpool forms a cabinet with his former colleagues in the last Perceval administration (18 Jun) U.S. declares war on Great Britain (22 Jun) Napoleon opens war on Russia (Oct–Dec) The retreat from Moscow (18 Dec) Napoleon reaches Paris and issues the 29th Bulletin of the Grand Army Combe *Tour of Dr Syntax in Search of the Picturesque*

1813	(23 Jan) *Remorse* opened at Drury Lane (2 Sept) Meets Mme de Staël (Oct–Nov) Bristol lectures on Shakespeare and education; with Morgans at Ashley (2 Oct) C's last article in *Courier* until 4 Jan 1814 (Dec) Illness	Sir William Garrow attorney-general (–1817) (Jul–Aug) Peace Congress at Prague a failure (10 Aug) Austria declares war on Napoleon (Sept) Sir Walter Scott declines laureateship; RS becomes poet laureate (Autumn) Wellington successful in Peninsula; Switzerland, Holland, Italy, Rhineland, Spain, Trieste, Dalmatia freed of French rule (Dec) Austria's accession to Allies' force RS *Life of Nelson* Northcote *Memoirs of Reynolds* Leigh Hunt imprisoned for libel (1813–15)
1814	(Jan) Illness (5 Apr) Lectures at Bristol on Milton, Cervantes, Taste; lecture on French Revolution and Napoleon; under medical care of Dr Daniel for addiction and suicidal depression (3 May) Charles Danvers d (1 Aug) *Remorse* performed in Bristol (Aug–Sept) Allston portrait of C; Allston's exhibition of paintings; essays "On the Principles of Genial Criticism" published in *Felix Farley's Bristol Journal* (Sept) At Ashley with the Morgans (20 Sept–10 Dec) Letters "To Mr. Justice Fletcher" in *Courier*	(1 Jan) Invasion of France by Allies (Jan) Byron *The Siege of Corinth* (Mar) Allied forces reach Paris (9 Mar) Castlereagh obtains four-power pact against separate negotiations (22 Mar) Ministers decide against further negotiation with Bonaparte (31 Mar) Inhabitants of Paris invited to choose what kind of government France should have (2 Apr) Senate declares the Emperor deposed (6 Apr) Napoleon's abdication (May) First Treaty of Paris; Napoleon exiled to Elba; restoration of the Bourbons (8–9 Jun) Cochrane perjury trial (Sept–Jun 1815) Congress of Vienna (24 Dec) Peace of Ghent signed by Britain and U.S. Inquisition re-established in Spain WW *Excursion* Scott *Waverley* Cary's *Dante* completed
1815	(Mar) At Calne with the Morgans (Jun) *Remorse* performed at Calne (Jul–Sept) Dictating *Biographia Literaria* (Aug–Sept) *Sibylline Leaves* and *Biographia Literaria* sent for publication in Bristol	(Mar–Jun) The Hundred Days: Napoleon escapes from Elba, returns to France (6 Apr) Allies mobilise vs Napoleon (Jun) Sir Robert Peel introduces bill to improve an act of 1802 concerning child labour in factories (18 Jun) Waterloo

		Restoration of Louis XVIII Napoleon from Plymouth to St Helena (20 Nov) Second Treaty of Paris WW *Poems* of 1815; *The White Doe of Rylstone* Scott *Guy Mannering*
1816	(Feb) Grant from Literary Fund, also from Byron (Mar) London: illness (10 Apr) Sends *Zapolya* to Byron (15 Apr) Accepted as patient and house-mate by Dr Gillman, Moreton House, Highgate (May–Jun) *Christabel* published (three editions); renews acquaintance with Hookham Frere (25 Jul) Article on "golden side" of war in *Courier* (29 Aug–11 Sept) Letters on Maturin's *Bertram* in *Courier* (Dec) *Statesman's Manual* published; Hazlitt's antagonistic reviews in *Examiner* (Jun, Sept, Dec) and *Edinburgh Review* (Dec)	Michael Angelo Taylor's act concerning the libel of newspaper reporters in Commons (14 Apr) Byron's *Fare Thee Well* published in *Champion* (24 Apr) Byron's departure from England (21 Jun) Motion for relief of Roman Catholics rejected in the Lords (7 Jul) Sheridan d Parliamentary Committee on Education of the Poor (30 Sept) Report by the Drury-Lane Committee of Management read at a General Assembly of the Proprietors; re-elected members are the Earl of Essex, Lord Byron, George Lambe, Richard Wilson; newly elected, Col Douglas and Robert Walpole (2 Dec) Spa Fields Riot Shelley *Alastor and Other Poems* Peacock *Headlong Hall* Maturin *Bertram* J. H. Frere ms tr of Aristophanes
1817	(17 Mar–2 Apr) Articles in *Courier* in defence of RS's *Wat Tyler* (25 Mar) Reviews own Second *Lay Sermon* (14 Apr) *Remorse* revived (Jul) *Biographia Literaria*, *Sibylline Leaves* published (summer) Meets J. H. Green (Sept) Meets Henry Cary (Nov) *Zapolya* published; C's tr of Hurwitz's *Hebrew Dirge* for Princess Charlotte; Tieck visits C	(Feb) Privy Council grants warrants for arrest of several Spencean Philanthropists (13 Feb) RS *Wat Tyler* pirated (4 Mar) Habeas Corpus suspended; Cobbett's *Political Register* reduces price to 2d (8 Mar) Maturin's tragedy *Manuel* first performed (27 Mar) Sidmouth Circular on libels (Apr) *Blackwood's Magazine* founded as *Edinburgh Monthly Magazine* (6 Nov) Death of Princess Charlotte Elgin Marbles purchased by government and put in BM Keats *Poems* Hazlitt *The Characters of Shakespeare's Plays* Moore *Lalla Rookh*

		Ricardo *Principles of Political Economy* Cuvier *Le Règne animal*
1818	(Jan) "Treatise on Method" in *Encyclopaedia Metropolitana* published (Jan–Mar) Lectures on poetry and drama (Jan) Meets T. Allsop (31 Mar) "Plato's" article on children in cotton factories in *Courier* (Apr) Pamphlets supporting Peel's Bill against exploitation of child-labour (Nov) *The Friend* (3-vol edition) (Dec) Lectures on the History of Philosophy (Dec–Mar 1819); literary lectures (Dec–Mar 1819)	(28 Jan) Habeas Corpus restored and never again suspended (19 Feb) Peel introduces new factory-worker bill, covering children only (27 Apr) House of Commons passes Peel's revised bill (bill later killed in House of Lords) (1 Jun) Parliamentary motion for universal suffrage and annual parliaments defeated (Jun) Westmorland election Keats *Endymion* (Aug) *Blackwood's* and *Quarterly* attacks on Keats Hallam *Middle Ages* Hazlitt *Lectures on the English Poets* Lamb *Collected Works* (dedicated to C) Peacock *Nightmare Abbey*

1819 (Mar) Financial losses in bankruptcy of Rest Fenner, C's publisher
(29 Mar) Lectures end
(Apr) Meets Keats in Millfield Lane; HC elected Fellow of Oriel; revives interest in chemistry; occasional contributions to *Blackwood's* (to 1822)

1820 (May) HC deprived of his Oriel Fellowship
(Oct) DC to St John's, Cambridge

1821 (Jul) Reunion with brother Rev George C
(autumn) Refuses invitation to lecture in Dublin

1822 (spring) C's "Thursday-evening class" begins; SC's tr of Martin Dobrizhoffer *An Account of the Abipones, an Equestrian People of Paraguay*
(Nov–Feb 1823) Wife and daughter visit C, Highgate
(29 Dec) HNC begins recording his *Table Talk*
Edward Irving's first visit
DC leaves Cambridge prematurely

1823 (Sept) *Youth and Age* begun
(Dec) Gillmans and C move to 3, The Grove

1824 (Mar) Elected FRSL, annuity of £100
(Jun) Carlyle and Gabriele Rossetti call at Highgate
DC B.A. Cambridge

1825 (May) *Aids to Reflection* published
(18 May) RSL essay "On the *Prometheus* of Aeschylus"
Proposes three lectures on projected London University
DC ordained

1827 (10 May) Thomas Chalmers calls at Highgate; C's serious illness: his first communion since Cambridge; visit from Poole
DC marries Mary Pridham
Sir George Beaumont d, leaving £100 to Mrs C

1828 (22 Apr) Fenimore Cooper meets C
(21 Jun–7 Aug) Netherlands and Rhine tour with Dora and WW
(Aug) *Poetical Works* (3 vols); John Sterling calls at Highgate

1829 *Poetical Works* (2nd ed)
Poetical Works of Coleridge, Shelley, and Keats (Galignani, Paris)
(Sept) SC marries cousin HNC; Lady Beaumont left C £50; Poole visits Highgate
(Dec) *On the Constitution of the Church and State*

1830 *On the Constitution of the Church and State* (2nd ed)
(Jun) HNC and SC settle in Hampstead
(Jul) C makes his will
Republication of *The Devil's Walk* "by Professor Porson"

1831 Last meetings with WW; *Aids to Reflection* (2nd ed)

1832 Legacy of £300 from Steinmetz
Harriet Martineau visits him

1833 HC's *Poems* dedicated to C
(24–9 Jun) To Cambridge for meetings of British Association
(5 Aug) Emerson calls at Highgate
HC's *Biographia Borealis*

1834 (Jul) Proofs of *Poetical Works* (3rd ed)
(25 Jul) Death at Highgate

EDITOR'S INTRODUCTION

1. COLERIDGE AND *THE MORNING POST*

. . . he was a Protestant, because it enabled him to lash about to the Right & the Left—& *without a motive* to say better things for the Papists than they could say for themselves. Oh! it was the Impulse of a purse-proud Opulence of innate Power!

—Coleridge on Donne[1]

IN November 1797, for a very "small" but desperately needed stipend, Coleridge engaged to supply "verses or political Essays" to the London *Morning Post and Gazetteer* edited by Daniel Stuart.[2] In the same month he began writing *The Rime of the Ancyent Marinere*, with some initial help from Wordsworth. During the next five months, though the composition of a volume of *Lyrical Ballads* to go with the *Rime* absorbed much of the poets' attention, Coleridge kept up a considerable and lively flow of newspaper poetry and prose—some of the poems and all the prose quite unknown until recently. His contributions then ceased, perhaps at the term of an original commitment to "four or five months" such as we know he made for a season two years later, except for some making up of arrears with a slight poem in May, borrowed and emended from Wordsworth's notebook, and a belated political ballad at the end of July. A year of silence, the year in Germany, followed.

The political essays and short paragraphs of this first season represent in their intensity and irony, and in the "English Jacobinism" of their themes, a recrudescence of the political fervour of Coleridge's Bristol lectures of 1795 and the early numbers of his *Watchman* of 1796. The poems include two he liked well enough to sign and several

[1] Annotation on Donne *Poems* (1669): *Misc C* 137 (corrected from *CM* ms).

[2] See *CL* I 360. The offer (prompted by C's friend Dr Beddoes) came through James Mackintosh, Stuart's brother-in-law, who recommended the paper's "political tone" and expressed his and Stuart's acquaintance with C's "Character & talents". The "pittance" of a guinea a week was for a minimum of contributions (which C did not exceed until 1799). He had recently let pass an opportunity for full-time employment writing the "heavy articles" for the *Morning Chronicle* (see *LL* I 35, *CL* I 222, 226, Bourne I 261, 263).

topical and more or less timely political essays in verse. With those in prose they constitute, for Coleridge and for the Opposition press, a significant enunciation of the logical and emotional reasons for resisting Pitt's war or—when the political barometer fell rapidly in March and April—for disengaging from opposition and going into political retirement or "secession". Read closely, the message of the famous Ode of April 1798 is not really *Recantation* (its title) but disengagement. By 11 March Coleridge and the Wordsworths had made up their minds to withdraw to Germany for a year or two, outside the zone of war.

While in Germany, Coleridge evidently neglected the *Morning Post* entirely. In February 1799 the editor inquired forlornly of Mrs Coleridge: "Do you think I have any reason to hope for communication from him?"[1] In August, home again, he resumed the contribution of topical and epigrammatic verses and possibly some bits of prose. Shortly thereafter Napoleon moved into the centre of world politics, and Coleridge moved to London to pursue him in the leading paragraphs of the *Post*—so effectively that by March 1800 a proprietary share in the paper was his if he wanted it. He declined the offer and the responsibility but continued irregularly—that is, with four half-year breaks during the next three and a half years—to contribute prose and verse through a cycle of peace and renewed war until the autumn of 1803. The paper was then sold to new proprietors; Coleridge moved tentatively to Stuart's other newspaper, the evening *Courier*, in 1804; and then he sailed for Malta. Later he served an almost uninterrupted two-year stint on the *Courier* in 1811–12 and was its valuable Correspondent to some effect each year from 1809 to 1818. But the two London papers, one for the morning, one of the evening, and Coleridge's relations to them were as different as their different times; it is advisable to treat them separately in this Introduction, though simple chronology sufficiently separates the texts of his contributions.

THE QUESTION OF POLITICAL CONSISTENCY

Before joining the *Morning Post* Coleridge had played many journalistic parts and had contemplated others, not with unmixed enthusiasm. He could be righteous in defence of the newspaper as a necessity of political life—and dismiss it as a useless, if relatively innocent, means of gaining a livelihood.[2] In 1797, at the age of

1 See App B for Stuart's letter.

2 Cf *Watchman* No 1 (*CC*) 10–11 (1 Mar 1796) and *CL* I 376 (19 Jan 1798).

twenty-five, he considered himself and was considered by others primarily a "poet and religionist".[1] Yet the lodestone of his poetry was political Liberty; the lodestar of his religion "the republic of God's own making".[2] His *Religious Musings* (1796) concerned what "fraternises man"; his sermons, *Conciones ad Populum, or Addresses to the People* (1795), concerned the price of bread, the war with France, and the culpability of the government—i.e. the ministry of William Pitt. His nightmares were of *Fire, Famine, and Slaughter* (the title of one of his first contributions to the *Morning Post*), and he woke throbbing with feelings of personal responsibility for the "guilt" of his nation and of all mankind.[3] If need drove him to journalism, an abiding absorption in the drama of events, a state-physician's interest in (especially) the sequelae of the French Revolution, gave more than "hireling" intensity to his odes and paragraphs.

A political enthusiast more than a political thinker, especially in his *Morning Post* years, Coleridge was even less a consistent partisan. He remarked his own "precipitance in praise", and we sometimes find him equally precipitant the other way. Carrying sympathetic identification to imaginative extremes, he could at one moment feel himself a soldier "on the war-field...among heaps of dead" yet, in the next, recoil into a state of "blest self-content" miraculously cleansed of all participation in "the evil thing".[4] His first response to the Revolution—or rather to the allegedly "just and necessary War" against it—had been the characteristic project of Pantisocracy and "aspheterism", a project simultaneously calculated to press the ideals of Equality and Fraternity and Christianity into immediate practice and to justify a complete and precipitate retirement from the entire Eastern Hemisphere, "wisely forgetful" of all its "shame and anguish".[5]

Coleridge was a poetical shaman or "greenland Wizard"[6] meeting each crisis of his tribe with a personal combat with the spirit of Evil. He entered the political maze of Woes and Joys "with no unholy madness",[7] he believed; yet he developed a glittering eye and he inextricably entangled himself in the spectral webs he was endeavouring to exorcise. To the shame and anguish of the moment he responded

[1] Letter of Thomas Wedgwood to Godwin, published in Erdman (1956) 431.

[2] *L* I 235n; cf *CN* I 1073.

[3] *PW* (EHC) I 237, and 166 (*Ode on the Departing Year* st 6).

[4] Sts 6 and 9.

[5] *Pantisocracy*: *PW* (EHC) I 68.

[6] *The Destiny of Nations* line 98: *PW* (EHC) I 135.

[7] *Ode* st 1: *PW* (EHC) I 161.

with an abandon coupled with a movement of noble detachment that made him a natural "news commentator" and reviewer of controversial matter, if not a good controversialist.

In sober prose, he said he supposed that his "daily & hourly Thoughts" *ought* to be given mainly to "private & personal" matters; "that the dedication of much hope & fear to subjects which are perhaps disproportionate to our faculties & powers, is a disease. But", he continued in 1800, "I have had this disease so long. . . that I know not how to get rid of it; or even to wish to get rid of it. Life were so flat a thing without Enthusiasm [he had been wishing that Sieyès and Bonaparte might hang]—that if for a moment it leave me, I have a sort of stomach-sensation attached to all my Thoughts, like those which succeed to the pleasurable operation of a dose of Opium".[1] Though he looked down on "the Press as a Trade" and said he preferred "the Country, & the lazy reading of Old Folios",[2] he seldom managed to stay long in any place of retirement or to confine his attention to abstruse research. When he chose he could write powerful editorial essays, in prose or verse, and although he often desisted, he really did not want *not* to "cry the State of the political Atmosphere" with his eye on the storm-clouds and his pen at the service "Of Science, Freedom, and the Truth in Christ".[3]

Inevitably his conversational flow upon the current subjects of event and debate was the sort to delight a newspaper proprietor, less concerned with long-range consistency than with forcefulness of response to new issues and with ingenuity in the analysis of political motives. To tap that flow was the ambition of more than one publisher, as Coleridge knew. "At a dinner-party, Sir Richard Phillips, the bookseller, being present, Coleridge held forth with his usual splendour, when Sir Richard, who had been listening with delight, came round behind his chair, and, tapping him on the shoulder, said, 'I wish I had you in a garret without a coat to your back.'"[4] This story Coleridge often told with glee, according to Daniel Stuart. The latter retold it as a definition of "something like" their relationship when Stuart was proprietor of the *Morning Post* and Coleridge was its "leader writer". "My practice", said Stuart, "was to call on him

[1] *CL* I 558 (2 Jan 1800); cf II 902, also II 722 and *Poole* II 163.

[2] *CL* I 372 (16 Jan 1798), 582 (21 Mar 1800).

[3] *On Having Left a Place of Retirement: PW* (EHC) I 108.

[4] Stuart IX 487–8. Cf X 25: "I recollect a conversation at that time [1802–3] with Mr. Perry, of the Morning Chronicle, in the smoking room of the House of Commons, in which Perry described Coleridge's writings as poetry in prose."

in the middle of the day, talk over the news, and project a leading paragraph for the next morning. In conversation he would make a brilliant display." The display did not always materialise into copy for the printer. But Stuart, writing almost forty years afterwards in a state of offended pride and enfeebled memory, greatly exaggerated the poet's reluctance to "write daily on the occurrences of the day". As the present collection of contributions to both of Stuart's newspapers bears witness, he achieved more than one sustained series of editorial essays on the men and the times and numerous brilliant paragraphs on current or imminent events, as well as several ironic satirical pieces in verse and prose that somehow failed to get into the 1850 collection.[1]

Coleridge had offended Stuart by seeming to claim more than his due of credit for the editorial policy of the *Morning Post* and for its phenomenal increase in circulation and to insinuate that his own labours had made Stuart rich while adding nothing to his own fortune or reputation.[2] Stuart in turn—by pooh-poohing Coleridge's claim to have insisted upon "fixed and announced principles" as the condition of his joining the *Morning Post* and by rating Coleridge's contributions as not "more than one hundredth part of the cause" of the paper's success[3]—roused Sara Coleridge to write in her father's defence, first in her edition of the *Biographia Literaria* (1847) and then in her collection of his *Essays on His Own Times* (1850). Her recovery of many of his contributions, her examination of Stuart's "pieces of bad construing, dictated by resentment",[4] and her extensive introductory interpretation and extrapolation of her father's political ideas served to correct the record. It is not surprising that she did some faulty construing of her own, dictated by filial

[1] Poems such as the annotated Odes of 27 May and 22 Jun 1801, not even listed by SC, were probably lacking from her clipping-file. But some of the jesting, Swiftian essays, the "Modest Proposals" of 1 Apr 1812 and 31 Mar 1818, or the pseudo "Plan" of 30 Nov 1811, may have offended her taste. Conceivably political disapproval, on her part or on C's in the first instance, may account for the absence of the 1798 prose and the alarmist articles of 1812 and 1815 in defence of the Church Establishment. She avowedly excluded pieces considered ephemeral.

[2] C's claims were made in 1817, in *BL* ch 10, and in posthumously published *Table Talk*. Earlier, when C was angry at Stuart's failure to rescue *The Friend* in 1809, he told his brother that Stuart owed "a very large fortune not indeed *exclusively* to my efforts but so far that without them he could have done nothing...". *CL* III 238. Stuart's letter to C 29 Sept 1802 (see App B, below) gives early authoritative support to C's claim.

[3] Stuart IX 487. For Stuart's statement of fixed principles, however, see notice of 27 Jan 1800, quoted below, I xciii n 1.

[4] *BE* I 87.

devotion. For example, to bear out her conviction that Coleridge had insisted on an independent policy before granting his services to the *Post* or, later, the *Courier*, she cited what she took to be a statement of the terms on which he had proposed to write for the latter paper. It was, actually, a proud set of conditions, drawn up while he was writing for the *Courier* on terms of miserable dependency, for presentation to *The Times*, whose editor he fondly hoped might accept a more independent arrangement.[1]

Nevertheless, it was well for Sara Coleridge to call attention to her father's "virtual consistency" in all his political writings and to single out "the character and conduct of Napoleon" as "the plank or bridge, whereon Mr. Coleridge and the *Morning Post* crossed over from warm interest in the cause of the French nation to decided Anti-Gallicanism, from earnest demands for peace to vigorous defence of renewed and continued war", from Opposition to a "firm and serviceable, though unfettered support of Government" even while she found it necessary to "guess darkly...how my Father may have differenced the earlier from the later stage of the war in his own mind".[2]

In the *Morning Post* essays we see Coleridge frequently on that plank or bridge, running back and forth or pausing uncertainly in the middle. It is valid to recognise an over-all consistency in Coleridge's thinking—if we understand that the consistency is virtual or ideal, not actual; that it is his own desideratum, so that even while he speaks boldly on one side of a question he keeps a longing (or a roving) eye on the other sides of it. For example, while vigorously *opposing* a movement for Reform, "he carefully recorded his protest in favour of reform, conducted judiciously...". This is Sara's illustration of her conclusion that "the spirit of his teaching was ever the same amid all the variations and corrections of the letter".[3] Indeed for some interpreters of Coleridge's thought, "the most striking feature...is its unity..."[4]—perhaps because the most unexpected.

It is the unity not of a straight line but of an S-curve. Just when we are ready to conclude that the author of *The Friend* of 1818 has changed completely from the young Jacobin who wrote *Addresses to the People* in 1795, we find him reprinting in *The Friend* one of those youthful addresses in order to demonstrate that "I was never myself,

1 Cf *EOT* I lxxi and *BCWL* 42.
2 *EOT* I xxi, xxviii–xxxi.
3 *EOT* I xxv.
4 R. J. White *The Political Thought of Samuel Taylor Coleridge* (1938) 23.

at any period of my life, a convert to the [Jacobinical] system".[1] Yet, if we are not so easily convinced by this demonstration as was his editorial daughter, and turn to compare the reprinted with the original address, we discover that Coleridge has silently omitted from his reprinting just those passages which *would* have been taken as "proof of [his] former Jacobinism"! For a moment, confronted with "all the variations and corrections" indeed, our belief in the unity vanishes. But then we note that even the original author of Addresses *to* the People insisted in his text that "we...should plead *for* the Oppressed, not *to* them".[2] So we must smile at ourselves as well as at "S. T. C." and conclude that he is in truth "ever the same" in the sense that he is never single-sided or single-minded but always both Jacobin and anti-Jacobin, Radical and Tory, poet and moralist, intermingled. All his behaviour flows from the same well-spring. All his writing is dipped more or less deeply in the same Coleridgian dye—that dye of "another colour" which fades and changes under scrutiny, varies with the weather, yet can be recognised in the deserts of Arabia.

"Recantation" is a term Coleridge uses for himself, more than once, but it is less accurate than "oscillation", a term he prefers to use for others. We are amused at his anecdote in the *Biographia* of the strange words that came from his mouth when, on his tour to solicit subscriptions to his political periodical *The Watchman*, he solemnly declared that he was "far from convinced, that a christian is permitted to read either newspapers or any other works of merely political and temporary interest".[3] The remark "produced an involuntary and general burst of laughter", says Coleridge, amongst the audience of potential subscribers. And the anecdote has served to laugh out of court any serious question of the author's youthful political seriousness. Yet we do not find it quite so amusing to read *in The Watchman*, a paper established partly to resist the new "gagging bills", an argument in support of the wisdom of the state in gagging seditious writers—such as one might construe the Watchman himself to be.[4]

[1] *Friend* (*CC*) I 223 (II 146). Cf John Thelwall's comment in the margins of a copy of *BL* (at I 177): "Stowey 1797. I visited and found him a decided Leveller—abusing the democrats for *moderation*...". This is to agree that C was not a committed Jacobin (democrat)—but a critic from the left, from the position of the rejection of property, "aspheterism". But Thelwall, whose remarks blend recollection and interpretation, would even insist (I 174) that C's being "a down right zealous leveller" was equivalent to his being "a man of blood" from the "violence and sanguinary Tendency of some of his doctrines".

[2] *Conciones: Lects 1795* (*CC*) 43.

[3] *BL* ch 10 (1907) I 118.

[4] *Watchman* No 10 (*CC*) 343.

He often doubted his cause because he doubted himself, and *vice versa.* He consequently often lost the possibility of effective irony. Neither a Milton nor a Shelley in intellectual self-discipline or in dedication to a cause, he was almost Byronic in his ability to see the romantic extravagance of his own positive assertions. But he lacked Byron's kind of humorous detachment that could turn the romantic to burlesque. (When Coleridge makes fun of himself, it is like Lamb hissing his own farce: the victim makes haste to throw the first stone at himself, in *assumed* detachment.) Also, maturing in the 1790's, he lacked the later Byron's external source of buoyancy in the rise of popular radicalism. Both poets were animated by the career of Napoleon, but in different phases. For Byron, Napoleon was a youthful idol who fell but was succeeded by the upsurge of "the people" in Italy, Greece, and his own England and Scotland. Coleridge was a young man during the French Revolution, and for him the ensuing years, despite the momentary "Greek fire" of Bonaparte's first ascendancy, were in England a political Ice Age, forcing the "Friend of Freedom" increasingly back upon his own resources—and thus arousing his basic self-mistrust.

Hence the loud assertions of "I myself I", generally kept out of the leaders but coming forward in some of the poems and in the paragraphs that I have entitled "Apologia"—though his *chef-d'oeuvre* in this genre is the "Apologetic Preface to *Fire, Famine, and Slaughter*" written for *Sibylline Leaves.*[1] Hence too the fact that his most impassioned editorials are often the most ambiguous, as for example "The War Not a Crusade" of 1800. Sara Coleridge is right that their attractiveness often lies in the reference to "general principles"[2]—but the principles do not really emerge. Like the conclusion of *Christabel,* they are only promissory; the political principle that ultimately makes its appearance is the no-principle, Expediency—a term that glides with uneasy motion in Coleridge's usage from the older Burkean meaning of action suiting occasion to the newer pejorative meaning akin to "opportunism". Coleridge's most sober writing is in the tradition of Junius: focused not on long-range goals—though

[1] Reprinted in *PW* (EHC) II 1097–1108.

[2] "I am disposed indeed to think that there must be an enduring use in articles which relate to the history of our country at an important period... and in which the opinions expressed are constantly referred to general principles, and if the collection were likely to be useful hereafter to historian, biographer or essayist, I should not be discouraged by any prospect of a cold reception from the reading public at large." SC to Archdeacon Bailey 18 Jun 1849, from a ms letter in the Cornell University Library, quoted by permission.

assuming humanitarian ones—but on present issues, with "acuteness" and elegant "freshness". Stuart grants this only of the few things Coleridge wrote with "the printer's devil at his elbow", but he does grant it.[1]

COLERIDGE AND STUART

With this general evaluation, it makes less sense to study Coleridge's "political thought" in its scheme and theory than to study his political writings in their oscillation in the daily context of the journalist's natural element, which was always more or less to Coleridge a familiar element. The notes in the present edition are designed to supply some of the journalistic as well as the political and biographical background for such study. A true history of the *Morning Post* and its sources of influence and support during this period would be invaluable; what little we do know, of Stuart's means and methods and of the official and unofficial pressures upon the English newspapers particularly in 1798 and in the Amiens period, can afford at least some points of orientation for the modern reader of these ephemera.[2]

Everyone knew, what Stuart's foes never forgot, that in 1796 he had been compelled to pay damages to the London *Telegraph* for having gulled it with a forged French newspaper purporting to contain the preliminaries for peace between Austria and France, to influence the price of stocks. Once in later years Crabb Robinson "put some awkward questions" to Coleridge about Stuart concerning the ethics of his business and (perhaps) his political conduct. "Why, if I'm pressed as to Dan's strict honesty," said Coleridge, "which I don't wish to be, I shd. say: Dan's a Scotchman who is content to get rid of the itch when he can afford to wear clean linen."[3] It would

[1] "To write the leading paragraph of a newspaper I would prefer him to Mackintosh, Burke, or any man I ever heard of. His observations not only were confirmed by good sense, but displayed extensive knowledge, deep thought and well-grounded foresight; they were so brilliantly ornamented, so classically delightful. They were the writings of a Scholar, a Gentleman and a Statesman, without personal sarcasm or illiberality of any kind. But when Coleridge wrote in his study without being pressed, he wandered and lost himself." Stuart to HNC, *BL* (1847) II 395.

[2] Hindle (1937) supplies very little information that can be relied on. Werkmeister (1963) ch 2 and (1967) 332–41 concludes with Stuart's purchase of half the proprietary in 1795; but she has supplied further information in correspondence.

[3] *BCWL* 48 and a ms letter of HCR to Thomas Robinson, 25 Nov 1848, in Dr Williams's Library, Gordon Square, London. Robinson thinks of "Stuart's desertion of the popular

be interesting to know whether Coleridge thought him clean of unethical practices during the period 1797–1803, for there is reason to believe that various forms of stock-jobbing continued to be a regular Stuartian perquisite of journalism—and that, ironically enough, income from such sources enabled him during this period to keep his morning paper free from political venality, if not from political opportunism.[1]

Tradition has been courteous to the reputation of Coleridge's editor. Sara Coleridge knew and somewhat shared Robinson's opinion of Stuart as "a very slippery fellow, indeed a bad character" but felt it advisable to dwell on his generous appreciation of "a mind different in kind from his own" and to suppress her father's satirical comments on his "Scotchiness".[2] Charles Lamb's portrait (in "Newspapers Thirty-five Years Ago") is rather obviously calculated to deny the

cause" as having occurred before his undergoing "the suspicion of being involved in a famous stock-jobbing forgery of the *Eclair*...", i.e. before 1796. In 1815 with WW, Robinson called on Stuart and did not think the "splendour" of his living could be "the fair and mere mercantile produce" of "newspaper writing and editing". *CRB* I 170.

[1] Lucyle Werkmeister, who has been making an exhaustive survey of the extant newspapers of this period, finds that Stuart was involved in many forgeries and other stock-jobbing schemes besides the *Eclair* business. His frequent jesting about the stock exchange must have been Freudian. For the slightly earlier period see Werkmeister (1963) 67–8 and Werkmeister (1967) 144, 176, 337–8.

[2] HCR to T. Robinson 25 Nov 1848; SC to HCR 15 Jul 1849, ms letters in Dr Williams's Library. To quote SC more fully: "Stuart was from first to last the great link between my father and all newspaper employment, and a volume or volumes containing his *journaleer* political writings,—as many as can be ascertained and collected—must of necessity refer to him as the Proximate Cause of all he performed in that way. A grievous pity it was, for his own sake, (Stuart's I mean), that he did not content himself with private communications to my husband and myself on the subject of the pecuniary transactions and relations between him and my father. Had he left the matter to me, every good deed, every money aid on his part could have been fully and faithfully stated; all my father's partial & grateful expressions respecting him recorded, while the satirical remarks from which he could not refrain even when he felt most warmly toward him, on his *Scotchiness*, suffered to remain in oblivion,—which indeed as far as it depends on me, they still shall. He would have gone down to all future readers of my father's work and biography...as a most kind, generous, and faithful friend of a man of literary genius, one who in a very extraordinary manner appreciated a mind different in kind from his own, or at least, by some means or other, had a *sense* of its superiority. Now, from what he has written in the Gentleman's Magazine & elsewhere [only the *G Mag* series of 1848 is known to me—DVE], it will be seen that there was a great vein of coarseness and a great deal of vanity and self consequence mingled with his better qualities." Nevertheless, Stuart "was a serviceable friend for many years, and deserves from me no small share of gratitude in the form of moderation".

imputations of "Scotchman": "frank, plain, and English all over"; but we may certainly accept the addition: "one of the finest-tempered of Editors" and one of the most successful.[1] Before 1799 Coleridge knew him only in correspondence and print.

Born in 1766 in Edinburgh, Daniel Stuart at twelve went to London, according to tradition, to work at the printing-house of his brothers Charles and Peter. Yet they do not seem to have had a press of their own, although Daniel and Charles are alternately and irregularly listed as "printer" of the *Morning Post* from 1782 to 1788. By 1789 Daniel Stuart was the "publisher" of this leading daily, which had a circulation then of about 2100.[2] In that year his sister married James Mackintosh, whose *Vindiciae Gallicae* two years later was the erudite answer to Burke, alongside Tom Paine's more popular *Rights of Man*. In 1793 Stuart succeeded Mackintosh as secretary of the Foxite (or radical Whig) "Friends of the People", and in 1794 he wrote his own pamphlet on *Peace and Reform, against War and Corruption*. Since 1789 the newspaper had been in the pay of the Prince of Wales and an Opposition paper, for "Prinny" was a political Prince Hal until he attained the throne. But bad management (not apparently Stuart's) and a costly libel suit caused the circulation to dwindle to a mere 350 copies by August 1795—whereupon Stuart conveniently acquired both copyright and office[3] for the nominal sum of £600, becoming editor and half proprietor.[4]

The *Morning Post* after this transaction became more independent, if never perhaps as "democratical" as the *Telegraph* or the early *Courier*. It was willing to give "an early and conspicuous place" to communications from the London Corresponding Society even late in 1797 (e.g., 28 April and 2 November).[5] It disliked the *coup d'état*

[1] *L Works* II 250.

[2] See Werkmeister (1963) 62–5, 79, 93, 106–7 et passim—succinctly summarised in Werkmeister (1967) 339–41. Werkmeister's full account of the Stuarts' activities largely supplants the fragmentary, though usually exact, information in Aspinall (1949) and the impressionistic account in Hindle (1937).

[3] Evidently also the editor's residence. See Stuart to C 20 Sept 1802 (App B, below).

[4] The silent half-owner was John Fuller. But accounts are unclear. Cf Werkmeister (1967) 339–41.

[5] Though he may long since have deserted "the popular cause" (see HCR's suspicion cited above), Stuart was competing for the readership of the radical papers, or seeking to hold the readers he had acquired through absorption of such rivals: in 1797 he acquired the copyrights of the expiring *Telegraph* (sold at Christie's 14 Mar; latest extant copy 18 Mar) and of the "oldest established Morning Newspaper in London", the *Gazetteer*; he had absorbed the *World* in 1794. L. Werkmeister has discovered that the *Telegraph* and *Courier* were closely related in 1796 and 1797 and believes

of Fructidor, however, and by 28 December was expressing detestation of "the Liberty of the Directory" as well as of "the Liberty of the British Cabinet", as the *Anti-Jacobin* noted with glee.[1] It is significant if not unambiguous that Mackintosh felt he could endorse its "political tone" to Coleridge in November. Mackintosh had recanted "prematurely" the year before, confessing his Jacobin sins at the bedside of the dying Edmund Burke; thereafter he lectured privately and publicly against the sins of his former political associates, and he would not have endorsed the tone of a consistently Jacobinical paper. Stuart nevertheless continued strongly to oppose Pitt and the war, even though he went to considerable pains to supply his columns with copious war correspondence so that readers could exult both in British victories, when they occurred, and in those of Napoleon and the French generals. While endorsing Coleridge's "recantation" in April 1798, he kept the paper flexibly anti-ministerial until the fall of Pitt in 1801, and anti-war until the autumn of 1802, when the swing of circulation figures and the arguments of Coleridge persuaded him to attack Fox and the peace. He and

---

that when Stuart acquired the *Telegraph* he also bought shares in the *Courier*, for the latter paper was immediately moved into the old *Telegraph* office at 159 Fleet St. The old *Courier* office was then used to house Thomas Hardy, and both *M Post* and *Courier* supported Hardy during the riots of Oct 1797.

Stuart's co-proprietor J. Fuller stated, a month after purchase of the *Telegraph*, that the *M Post* had "kept about half" the circulation of 310 (of the day before the purchase), and he assumed that it would keep half the *Gazetteer*'s circulation, estimated at between 300 and 600. Letter of Apr 1797 in Robert L. Haig *The Gazetteer 1735–1797* (Carbondale 1960) 258–9.

In *M Post* 3 Dec 1802 Stuart surveyed the slow but steady growth in circulation as having been "six years in rising from 400 to 2100 per day" by the autumn of 1801. He then ascribed the more rapid climb to 3500 per day by the end of 1802 to the *Post*'s political views' being more realistic and more popular than those of rival papers—from which we may deduce that Coleridge with his political essays and poems had served Stuart very well. Stuart indeed admits as much in his letter of 29 Sept 1802 (App B, below). On New Year's Day 1803 Stuart defined the circulation as "now 700 or 1000 higher than that of any other daily": "...after a struggle of seven years, having raised this Paper from the lowest to the most high in circulation and character: we feel this an occasion...to return Thanks to the Public. We make no promises, no boast; we have performed....On Monday...it will be printed on a BEAUTIFUL TYPE, ENTIRELY NEW, cast purposely by Messrs. Fry and Steele. The Title will thenceforward be only *The Morning Post*"—dropping "*and Gazetteer*". Alluding to this time Stuart (x 26) says that the booksellers who set up the *British Press* (or *Morning Literary Advertiser* 1 Jan 1803–22) took from him "my chief assistant George Lane", adding sourly, "But they never thought of Coleridge!!!" At the time, Stuart must have rejoiced at that.

[1] *A-J* 8 Jan 1798.

Coleridge then supported the Addington ministry, or rather urged it in the direction of renewing the war. The more consistently liberal *Morning Chronicle* was also more partisan and was opposed to the war even out of season, with Fox.

The sale of the *Morning Post* in the autumn of 1803 only dramatised the end of an era for both Stuart and Coleridge. Napoleon, as a bridge, had collapsed; there would be no return to the days of Opposition or, as it proved, to the days of Independence. Sides were taken, commitments made; when Coleridge followed Stuart into the editorial office of the *Courier* in 1804, that paper had already become at least a quasi-ministerial journal.[1]

The point here is that the virtues of the *Morning Post* in its best years were elasticity and variety, not consistency; and that these were Coleridge's virtues too, including a brilliant ambiguity and a skill in what he called, in another connection, "motive-mongering".[2] In the *Post* he could write, for example, about Bonaparte in such a way as to share with English Jacobins their dislike of Bonaparte's anti-Jacobinism, with anti-Jacobins their dislike of his anti-Bourbonism, and with various other sorts their more or less sneaking admiration of his Commanding Genius. There was also the virtue or limitation (contrast the intricacy of his notebook styles!) of having more or less to pursue a single topic and to keep in mind the point of view not of the poet or the abstruse researcher but of the political "public" who ruled England—for Coleridge recognised that the paper was dependent "[poss]ibly...in a great degree [on] the tastes of [Lon]don Coffee house men & breakfast-table People of Quality".[3]

THE QUESTION OF INFLUENCE

The influence of the *Morning Post* on the course of events is a question that Coleridge himself raised in so exaggerated a form as to cast doubt on the reliability of any of his own assertions about it. Evidently he and Stuart sometimes engaged in the newspaperman's game of detecting in the evening's speeches the fine arguments of the morning's leading paragraphs, a game in which high scores could be made if one forgot that most of the arguments had been common property

[1] C's first assignment (see headnote 27 Feb 1804) was to write a defence of Addington, to which he referred, with a private irony Stuart would understand, by the Mackintoshian title "Vindiciae Addingtonianae".

[2] An annotation on *Hamlet* III iii 73–96: *Sh C* I 33.

[3] To Stuart c 30 Sept 1800: *CL* I 627.

since the debate began. There are times when Coleridge seems to take general allusions to "the press" as pointed citations of his own particular paragraphs. The most famous instance is his protestation in the *Biographia Literaria* at the "hyperbole" of Fox's (alleged) charge that the *Morning Post* had produced the war of 1803. In the *Biographia* he also claims, retrospectively, that the *Post* had all along been "a far more useful ally to the Government in its most important objects...than if it had been the avowed eulogist of Mr. Pitt"—forgetful that during most of his years on the *Post* he would have strongly disapproved of being useful to Pitt.[1] Certainly the author of "Lord Moira's Letter" and *Fire, Famine, and Slaughter* in January 1798 would, despite later apologetics, have scorned the insinuation that his attacks were merely a matter of "loyal opposition".

What both Coleridge and Stuart had intended most of the time had been to keep abreast of the political impulses of the "Coffee house men". As Coleridge put it when writing privately to Stuart in 1816, their editorial policy had had "one main guide, a sympathizing Tact for the real Sense, Feeling, and Impulses of the *respectable* Part of the English Nation".[2] It was this public and its opinion to which they made their humble recommendations. In the *Biographia* Coleridge claimed for himself—in the letter to Stuart he gave entirely to Stuart (his doing both almost simultaneously may illustrate his elasticity)—all credit for "the Tone first given & then consistently kept up by the plain *un*ministerial, anti-opposition, anti-jacobin, anti-gallican, anti-Napoleonic Spirit" of the *Morning Post*.[3] If "first given" refers to the period before April 1798, then the "Tone" is inaccurately defined. The term "anti-opposition" is patently incorrect for that period. And even for April a stronger term than "*un*ministerial" seems to be called for. Coleridge put the emphasis this way to fend off allegations of ministerial *influence*—and we will do well to take his remark as opening rather than dismissing the question. But before turning to the implications of this language, we can perhaps put the question of *Coleridge's* influence into truer perspective by considering the very small scale of the eighteenth-century newspaper and the paucity of editorial comment from an editor like Stuart. Even when we have accepted most of Sara Coleridge's refutations of Stuart's depreciations of her father's rôle, we

[1] *BL* ch 10 (1907) I 144. See below, I lxxxiii.

[2] *CL* IV 638.

[3] *CL* IV 639. C is making the point that the *Courier* of 1816, lacking even the appearance of independence, lacks much of its potential utility to Government.

may be imposed upon by Stuart's argument that it was news coverage that built the circulation of the paper and that "an occasional essay or two could produce little effect". But in 1797–8 the very infrequency of any serious comment must have secured for the few vigorous essays—and topical verses—a maximum effect. On most days, two and a half of the paper's four pages were taken up by advertisements and notices. The editorial paragraphs under the masthead often consisted of a digest of "intelligence" without commentary. Those rare moments when a voice does speak out to the reader in a paragraph of opinion and argument—or in such verses as *Parliamentary Oscillators*, the "War Eclogue", *Recantation*, and, in a later year, the Ode to Addington—must have stood out as moments of unique personal impact.[1] If we take verse as well as prose into account, it was Coleridge who gave the *Post* its strongest voice even in the first five months, when he was contributing merely by mail.[2] In 1802, when Coleridge resumed in September after a lapse of half a year, it took only two strong essays and a peppering of epigrams to set the town talking and reverse a decline in circulation.[3]

From Stuart's editorial notices his interest in the "Poetical Department" as an adjunct to the leading paragraphs is manifest. Often he hailed the poems of Coleridge (by name or pseudonym) and, later, Wordsworth as important political pronouncements—or as affording timely relief *from* the vexing politics of the day.[4] Coleridge's hiring in 1797 coincided in fact with Stuart's fresh attention to this neglected department. And although he was at first overshadowed in acclaim as well as in flamboyance and productiveness by the novelist and poet Mary "Perdita" Robinson, also just engaged, and was soon surpassed in dependability by Robert Southey, engaged in April to supply "occasional verses, without a signature",[5] it was Coleridge

[1] These conditions account for some of our confidence about the identification of C's contributions and should be borne in mind when considering the conjectural attributions of App A. There were few voices speaking in the paragraphs of the *M Post*; among them C's is usually easily singled out.

[2] That C could then cease, leaving Stuart to pursue the consequences during an iron time, may in part account for Stuart's final, ungrateful impression. The later contributions also came in uncompleted cycles.

[3] See Stuart to C 29 Sept 1802 (App B, below).

[4] See notices of 13, 16 Apr 1798, 14 Oct 1802, 13, 29 Jan 1803.

[5] *S Life* (CS) I 329. Stuart in 1838 was mistaken in his recollection that RS had simply come forward to supply "the deficiency" in C's contract: RS could show friends "the chairs and tables into which [he] had transmuted bad verses". His *M Post* contributions run from 18 Apr to the end of 1797 and from Jul 1799 to the end of 1800 (though by 3 Feb 1800 he was threatening to give up "rhyming, a guinea's

whose first "Lines by Albert" received the heading "ORIGINAL POETRY (*Exclusively for the* MORNING POST)". Both Mrs Robinson and Coleridge, in their own names and a variety of pseudonyms, were published with considerable editorial fanfare, but it was "S. T. COLERIDGE" who supplied the readers with a political Christmas tale of Joan of Arc as a sansculotte—a "*Fragment*" of 148 lines (from a poem to be "entitled The Progress of Liberty—or the Visions of the maid of Orleans") in which a parallel acceptable to English Jacobin readers (probably at that date the *Post*'s main readership) is implied between modern France, now attempting to invade Ireland or England, and the France of "that warrior-maid" who had properly "scourged" the invading *English*. It was he in January 1798 who, pseudonymously, lifted the Opposition banner in highest defiance of Pitt, with his "War Eclogue" of *Fire, Famine, and Slaughter*. And it was his enabling Stuart to announce on 13 April that "Mr. Coleridge has honoured us with an Ode..." that inspired Stuart to give proud notice on the 17th that the poetry of the *Morning Post* would "in future be critically select". But it was also the political change of course from Eclogue to Ode that brought invaluable relief to a newspaper editor recently closely questioned by the Privy Council on his Jacobin associations.[1]

MINISTERIAL PRESSURE

The occasion of the *Recantation* Ode was the "French invasion of Switzerland", not the ministerial pressure on Stuart; yet in the history of the oscillations of Coleridge and the *Morning Post* the latter perhaps warrants the greater attention. For Stuart the questioning itself, for Coleridge the anti-Jacobin alarm preceding it, served to remind editor and writer that Pitt's acts of December 1795 against liberty of press and assembly had erected "a vast aviary" (as Coleridge had defined it) within which "all the honest" were still "incaged".[2] With the passage of time the cage had come to seem roomy. In December 1797 the tide of popular opposition to the

worth a week"). In Dec 1801 he talked of being "about to write verses once more for the *Morning Post*"; in Jan 1803 he repeated the idea; but his only known contributions in these later years are a ballad on 1 Sept 1803 and a poem on Emmet submitted the same month but not published before the paper changed owners. Cf *S Letters* (Curry) I 264, 267, 306, 314, 327, 330, 331.

[1] For verse contributions cited in this paragraph see listing in App D, below.

[2] *PD: Lects 1795* (*CC*) 315.

Assessed Taxes buoyed politicians and journalists with renewed Jacobinism of tone. The best essay that Stuart received from Coleridge in January 1798 endorsed Radical Reform as the essential precondition for peace, national solvency, and justice for Ireland, and Stuart "kept [it] up as a *bon bouche*"[1] till the 20th, the Saturday before the celebration of Fox's birthday, when Opposition would shape into slogans its resumption of Parliamentary Reform as a party aim. The essay does not exactly endorse Fox's morals in saying they "are totally unlike" Pitt's. Coleridge does leave open the possibility that what is "highly flattering to Mr. Fox", the inseparability of Fox and Reform, is not necessarily ideal for the nation.[2] Yet he minces no part of his endorsement of Reform, and he leaves only drivellers and sharpers to believe in, or *wish* the nation to place confidence in, the present Ministry.

For Coleridge this represented the extreme "Yea" in his "arc of oscillation".[3] During January and February 1798 the *Morning Post* confidently continued to move on its accustomed republican course—or to drift, for the "Parliamentary Oscillators" of Pitt's party had not, after all, joined Opposition, and the coffeehouse men had felt no irresistible tide. Stuart boldly ignored attacks from the *Anti-Jacobin* as "too contemptible for notice" (27 January) and was unimpressed by "Ministers' sudden alarm at invasion", which seemed only "designed to smother murmurs at the passing of the Triple Assessment Bill" (12 January). He even defended as "a measure of retributive justice" the French Directory's seizure of neutral ships touching at English ports: "We shall be told, perhaps, that we are stepping out of our way to defend the conduct of the French. We deny it. We are only shewing how impractically shallow the politics

[1] See App B, Stuart to C, below.

[2] The political position of Fox was often C's own position, but he seldom liked to say so. In 1793 he came short of committing himself in reporting that "Mr. Fox's letter to the Westminster Electors...is quite the *political Go* at Cambridge, and has converted many souls to the Foxite Faith" (*CL* I 51), and in 1817 he would accuse Fox of having led RS (not mentioning himself) into "visionary hopes" of the French Revolution (below, II 476). His "Sonnets on Eminent Characters" conspicuously omit Fox, and he seems always to have identified Fox with tendencies he feared in himself, sensuality and indolence, and to have distrusted him as a *party* man. C's faith might more accurately be called Sheridanite, signifying an inclination to political flexibility and sudden *démarches*.

[3] In *CIS* (1956) 48 (Letter III) C offers "Yea, and Nay, but as an attempt to delineate an arc of oscillation" in his state of mind. The "Yea" in his political psychology is the essay's justification of the passion of "patriotic indignation", as in *Watchman* No 1.

of Administration have been" (18 January). And he issued no cautions to Coleridge when requesting more of his "excellent" pieces: something "on the approaching downfall of the Pope"—a request that brought the rather hackneyed article on "Rome" (8 March but announced 2 March) and, as by-product, the atmospheric essay of 24 February—also "a poetical piece" on "Pitt's Air Castle of conquering France;—of making Ireland happy by coercion;—of paying off the national debt &c &c".

Blithe in private and in public, the editor did not sense that events were moving to a crisis. On 30 January a leader on "The Swiss Confederacy" shows little sympathy for the Swiss aristocracies. A leader of 7 February on the dismissal of the Duke of Norfolk is a routine protest, but is preceded (6 February) by a severely indignant communication signed "Harmodius". On 12 February Stuart printed, without disclaimer, an evidently French report on "Revolution in Switzerland"—on the need for a revolution there and on the fallacy of confusing attacks on the Swiss Oligarchy with attacks on the People. The paragraphs in February grow fewer and briefer; there is an appreciable loss of momentum, but not admittedly of direction.

Stuart was not the only editor who was grateful, nevertheless, when Coleridge sent in a reflective essay defining this barometric fall and viewing it as ominous (24 February). Stuart and Perry, who promptly reprinted the piece in the *Morning Chronicle*,[1] doubtless read it in simple Opposition terms. They could relish the indictment of "the political wisdom of Mr. Pitt" and the mock-alarm at "the torrent of Democracy" without being troubled by the Burke-like veneration of "the most ancient and established Governments of Europe" or the implication that more effective action than Pitt's should be taken against "the armies of France". In context, the ostensible editorial goal is still a Peace Cabinet—though as to invasion there could not be two opinions among Englishmen (as Fox would say). The writer himself, however, while putting the onus for current political apathy on the Gentry and Proprietors, is washing his hands of the evil thing—as readers of his *Ode on the Departing Year* can recognise: we have reached the ambivalent centre of indifference between the Yea and Nay of Coleridge's arc.

[1] Perry's reprinting C's essay (as "Reflections on the State of Europe") enabled Stuart (in the *Post* 10 Mar 1798) to jeer at the *Courier* for having alleged that the *M Chron* was "the *only* Paper to which we should look for Political Remarks!"

On 1 March three pawns fell into the hands of Pitt and his Home Secretary, Portland. One was John Binns, an organiser for the London Corresponding Society. The other two were United Irishmen, Rev James Coigley and Arthur O'Connor, editor of the Dublin *Press*, an ally of the London *Courier*. In Coigley's pocket a paper was found that would hang him—an address from a Secret Committee in Ireland to the Directory of France recommending the proclamation of "distinct republicks" in the British islands and the arming of those who joined the invading forces. Arrested at Margate, where the Irishmen had sought passage to France, the three were brought before the Privy Council and sent to the Tower with great to-do. Binns and O'Connor were acquitted of treason, but not before enough alarm had been worked up to rouse the Gentry and Proprietors to vote the suspension of Habeas Corpus: whereupon the acquitted and other suspected Democrats and Reformers could be jailed without indictment or trial. In the wake of the arrests, "insolent and indecent liberties" began "to be taken throughout the kingdom with the characters of those persons who [had] forborne to support the Minister in his mad and merciless career", the *Courier* charged (8 March).[1] Coleridge felt it advisable to explain to his conservative brother George (once again) that he had snapped his "squeaking baby-trumpet of Sedition"[2] and that, while he had chiefly blamed "the present ministers" for the increase of such "fiery & undisciplined spirits" (as he himself might have been), he conceded that "the Ministers may have had in their possession [presumably during the interrogation of Binns and the others] facts which may alter the whole state of the argument".[3]

Two years earlier Coleridge had expressed alarm at Binns's first arrest and had followed the case in *The Watchman*.[4] We have no

[1] By 5 Mar the Wordsworths, under surveillance as "a sett of violent Democrats", had received notice that their lease of Alfoxden would not be renewed.

[2] We must recognise some irony of allusion in this phrase; as Woodring notes (p 22), C is "applying to himself the denunciation of Priestley in Gibbon's autobiography...".

[3] *CL* I 397, c 10 Mar. Cf Stuart's leader of 5 Mar: "We understand that in a few days a motion will be made... for suspending the *Habeas Corpus Act*, founded, as it is said, on facts that have recently transpired.—Ministers having seen their error in suspending this Act once before, without reason, will now, we presume, have good grounds for their conduct, before they take the step; and if they have good grounds, we hope they will proceed with alacrity." (Among Privy Council papers connected with the 1 Mar arrests the "good grounds" appear to be some printed forms of a constitution and by-laws for a society of United Englishmen.)

[4] *CL* I 191; *Watchman* (*CC*) 127–30, 160–2, 191, 199–201, 266–8.

record of his response to Binns's second arrest, in 1797. Binns was each time acquitted, but this third time he was nevertheless promptly sent off to jail (under the suspension of Habeas Corpus) until Pitt's fall in 1801. Coleridge's response may be deduced from his paragraph of 9 March.

Stuart's was such that he received the particular attentions of Pitt and Portland. On 2 March he filled three columns with the Binns–O'Connor arrests; he was then himself summoned before the Privy Council to explain how he had come into possession of "so particular an account" of the arrests and the probable charges. The next day he published an account of the interrogation, evidently carefully selective, which he chose to "leave it to the reader" to evaluate. His own conduct and that of ministers are represented as above reproach, and in the next days he understandably declines to print paragraphs and letters received on the subject. "The King's Ministers treated the Editor with great politeness, and he is determined to make no unfavourable allusions to them respecting his examination" (5 March). For a moment in effect, however, Stuart endorses the domestic policy he would normally castigate: "...if they have good grounds [for suspending Habeas Corpus], we hope they will proceed with alacrity" (5 March). Four days later he prints a more lugubrious (and Coleridgian) prophecy that when ministers do act upon a different system, the change "will NOT be favourable to freedom" (see "Euthanasia of the Constitution", 9 March).

From this time forward the *Morning Post* can be seen to grow increasingly, if unevenly, "independent". On most days its Opposition principles seem as firm as ever, with occasional justification of the Directory and vilification of ministers. But when arrests are made in Manchester, of something like United Irishmen, Stuart no longer thinks it "proper at this time to lay before the Public all the particulars" as he would have done. He straddles the alarmist and anti-alarmist positions: the country is "menaced at home by too many (few indeed, but still too many)", who are disposed to favour the designs of France (14 April). And when the *Courier* (now partly under Stuart's ownership but not yet under his editorial control) chooses still to "palliate the unprincipled proceedings of the French" in Switzerland, the *Morning Post* disputes the undertaking of "so bad a cause" and even scolds the evening paper for jeopardising "the freedom of the Press" (2 April). The rebuke implies the new ministerial system unfavourable to that freedom: our masters will take it away from us if we exercise it now.[1] Indeed, on 22 March the House of Lords had ordered Perry and his printer to Newgate for three months for an allegedly "constitutional" libel in their *Morning Chronicle*—i.e., for bringing into ridicule the Bishop of Durham's solemn warning, in that House, that female dancers sent from sensual France might destroy England in "a more subtle and alarming warfare" than that of French gunboats.[2] On 4 April the Attorney General (Sir John Scott, later Lord Eldon) brought in a bill "for preventing the mischiefs arising from the printing and publishing newspapers", calling for registration of printers and publishers, partly on the pretext that the editor and printers of the *Courier* were escaping indictment because he was unable to find their names on record.[3] This time Stuart remained silent (unless he said something in the *Post* of 5 April, an issue no longer extant). And his morning paper remained exempt from prosecution.

For Coleridge certainly, and for Stuart possibly, it required nothing more than these indirect menaces to bring about the observable change of tone. And now that suspected English Jacobins were being jailed without trial, by political paralogic the *Morning Post* could look back at Fructidor and righteously condemn the Directory—especially for the heinous imprisonment of opponents without trial (14 April 1798). Now "utmost indignation" could be bestowed equally upon the French as exporters of revolution to Switzerland, and the Pitt government as "prime authors of our present calamities" (also 14 April). Yet the change took place in two stages, the first after the arrest of Binns and the United Irishmen, the second after 19 March, when the French Swiss decree of 2 March first reached London. During the first phase, Freedom was still mainly menaced at home and by "military excesses in Ireland" (15 March). Readers

[1] For an early note of caution see *CL* I 386 (13 Feb 1798): "I have sent you Payne's Letter to Erskine—it was sent to me privately by the Editor of the Morning Post—for they do not venture to *publish* it."

[2] Debrett v (1798) 327–8; see also 350–1, 354. Pitt branded the paragraph as no trifle but "impudent malignity" and as "one of a chain of experiments made to try what their Lordships would bear", and his followers seized upon it as ground for punitive measures against editors who "praised the enemies of the country...and endeavoured to render the friends of the Constitution contemptible".

[3] Debrett v 576–96. The intemperate remarks of Earl Temple and Windham indicate a wish to suppress the *Courier* for its general "Jacobinism" with little knowledge of that paper beyond the *Anti-Jacobin*'s account. Half a year later, with the Newspaper Act in force, the proprietor, printer, and publisher of the *Courier* were taken in the act of calling the Emperor of Russia "obnoxious" and "ridiculous" and were jailed and fined.

could take *The Old Man of the Alps*, a Wordsworth–Coleridge poem treating of grief in a Swiss family caused by violence in France (in 1790) as vaguely topical; but on the same page of the 8 March *Post* they would find paragraphs treating of grief in English families threatened by arbitrary arrest. In the paragraphs of 9 March 1798 dealing with popular apathy and the duty of British preachers we seem to see Coleridge preparing the ground for recantation.[1] On 10 March his bitter parable of vengeance and destruction, later entitled *The Raven*, served as a purgation of some of the "antisocial passions" that he must now regulate. He had written the poem a year earlier; a week later he might not have wanted it published. Shortly after sending it to the newspaper he wrote a letter to his brother George announcing his withdrawal from politics to set his affections "in right tune": "I think the present ministry weak & perhaps unprincipled men; but I could not with a safe conscience vote for their removal; for I could point out no substitutes." Fox and the Reformers? "The Opposition & the Democrats are not only vicious—they wear the *filthy garments* of vice....I am no Whig, no Reformist, no Republican...".[2] For his conservative brother's benefit he allowed his expression to reach the extreme Nay of its oscillation, but not in a public utterance.

The second phase began on 19 March, when Stuart, printing the French declaration against the Swiss aristocracies, found it "impossible to reflect, without the utmost indignation, on the conduct of the French". Three days later the Whig Duke of Bedford in the House of Lords, "unaw'd...amid a slavish band" (to borrow the poet's words) or (as he is reported to have said himself) one of the "few...unawed by clamour" who had "opposed the presumptuous boasts of the Minister" from the beginning, made a motion for the removal of ministers, for peace and reform, on which the vote was 13 against 100.[3] On 3 April in the House of Commons a motion against the slave-trade, with the ministers divided, was lost by four votes. By the 13th Stuart had received Coleridge's *Recantation*. For the next day's editorial Stuart wrote his own, overreading his lines (but he would swing back) both as supplied by the Whigs—"as the

[1] Woodring (p 181) observes that in *France: an Ode* and *Fears in Solitude* "Coleridge had to charge the British with impiety and their clergy with indolent hypocrisy as a political transition to his patriotic rejection of French blasphemy."

[2] *CL* I 396–7. Even on principle his object now was not to go to this extreme but rather "to destroy the bad passions...by keeping them in inaction".

[3] Debrett v 357.

Duke of Bedford so nobly intimated, we should adjourn our domestic disputes till the Enemy is defeated" (an adjournment Bedford had granted only in case of actual invasion)—and as supplied by Coleridge: "...are we to be told that we have recanted our former sentiments? No, we follow them up...we applauded the French Revolution...a great people breaking their chains upon the heads of their oppressors..." and so on. Here he claimed (more than Coleridge implied) to have condemned everything since 18th Fructidor; then he roundly condemned the oppressive ministers of Great Britain, emasculators of the Constitution—but not to be driven from office until we "resist and repel the French". The poet balked at such an issue: "Shall I with *these* my patriot zeal combine? |...no! they stand before my ken | Loath'd as th' Hyaenas".[1] But then the poet and his friends had made up their minds, some time between 6 and 11 March,[2] to depart for the universities of Germany "for the two ensuing years". The editor was obliged to stay in London and keep publishing a newspaper that might not too easily be found inflammatory.

RECANTATION OR OSCILLATION?

Both editor and poet, in their different ways, recanted while saying that they did not, and oscillated more than they recanted. Stuart had been at least since December vowing equal detestation of French and British "Liberty": one of the graces of good journalism is the ability to arrive freshly again and again at the same new position. It is instructive to study Coleridge's political utterances in chronological order, but we are observing a weathervane, not a magnetic needle. In his earlier retirement ode, on the *Departing Year*, he had similarly thrown up his hands at a nation "enslav'd and vile" from ambitious policy (a judgment softened only much later to "Not yet enslaved, not wholly vile"). In *Recantation* he moved from the proposition that Pitt's England is vile to the proposition that England and France are both vile. When he revised the poem for Stuart's editorial use again, in October 1802, he would say, mainly, that France is vile.[3] (The ultimate proposition, that England is *not* vile, he rarely expressed without qualification.)

[1] Lines 85–7. *PW* (EHC) I 247n. Cf *CL* I 121 for C's equivalence of Ministers and Hyaenas.

[2] See *WL* (*E* rev) 211–14. This was before news of the invasion of Switzerland.

[3] Woodring (p 181) notes a still further aspect of C's withdrawal: "In March, when the annuity from the Wedgwoods had made his detachment from ephemeral quarrels possible and morally necessary, his letters had begun

In the spring of 1798 the threat of French attack was officially made the grounds of British policy and accepted as such even by the Whigs—not that it was imminent but that it was likely enough to call for mobilisation. On 20 April both Houses unanimously approved an Address for embodying the cavalry and additional militia and for measures against the "disaffected". To the debate on this Address, Coleridge contributed (but did not at the time publish) another poem of recantation, *Fears in Solitude*, in argument comparable to the Whig speeches on this occasion, particularly Sheridan's. In supporting the Address, Sheridan urged all to tremble at the real peril of invasion but continued to blame ministers for misrule and reiterated his approval of the French Revolution and his disbelief in the existence of an English Jacobin conspiracy. Yet his remarks (and his vote) meant a shelving of opposition, and Pitt interpreted them as reflecting a real "change in [Sheridan's] sentiments".[1] His colleague George Tierney actually voted for suspension of Habeas Corpus, for Sheridan's reasons, though Sheridan himself would not follow their logic so far. Coleridge wrote a satiric ballad to the effect "That Tierney votes for Mister Pitt, | And Sheridan's *recanted*!"—but before it got into the *Morning Post* the Whigs' brief flirtation with ministers had ended and hostility between Tierney and Pitt had taken the sensational form of a verbal insult followed by a duel, 25 May.[2]

Stuart swung momentarily to the extreme of castigating the *Courier* for criticising Sheridan and Tierney and for disapproving "the arrest of those who would favour France" (23 April). But both the defecting Whigs and the *Morning Post* saw that to support defensive war (the alarms now subsiding) would be to encourage Pitt's dream of a new coalition and a new offensive war. What actually came next was the Irish Rebellion, stirring the Whigs, including Fox himself, to vociferous opposition—much of it kept from publication by frequent clearings of reporters from the House. Stuart, who seems to

---

to argue the importance of moral, independent action by individual citizens and the unimportance of party leaders and the governments they misshaped (*CL* [I] 395)."

[1] Debrett VI 4, 16.

[2] C's satire *Recantation Illustrated in the Story of the Mad Ox* (title of the version printed in *AA* 1800) was written when "Mr. Sheridan and Mr. Tierney were absurdly represented as having *recanted*" (*PW*—EHC—I 299n), i.e. in the newspapers of 20–1 Apr 1798, though it harks back to a famous speech by Sheridan in 1794 (which probably accounts for the mistaken date for the poem in *EOT* III 963). A badly patched version, ending with the duel instead of the recanting, finally appeared in the *M Post* 30 Jul 1798 (see notice in App D). The 1800 text must represent at least a partial restoration of the original version.

have received the article he had asked Coleridge to write on Ireland[1] but to have held it too long, found room for very little comment on the Rebellion.

Coleridge, if he had not stopped writing on political subjects, could not have maintained the tone of recantation. Even his ballad of Tierney and Sheridan in its first version must have been too much for Stuart, must have had too much mockery in its defence of the Whigs' oscillation. Nevertheless, we can date from this April the effect Coleridge describes in reference to 1799 and after: "...that the *Morning Post* proved a far more useful ally to the Government in its most important objects, in consequence of its being generally considered as moderately anti-ministerial...".[2] Neither Coleridge nor the *Morning Post* ever returned to the *strongly* anti-ministerial expressions of January 1798. That phase has almost been lost to history except for the reinterpretation of it in the "Apologetic Preface" and for a sinister profile of the *Morning Post* that survives in the distorting mirror of the weekly *Anti-Jacobin*.[3]

A YEAR OF SILENCE

The French invasion, against which *Recantation* and *Fears in Solitude* were to arouse sinning but beloved England, never came. The scene shifted to the eastern Mediterranean, where Napoleon's fleet was destroyed in the Battle of the Nile, September 1798. That month Coleridge before sailing for Germany made arrangements to preserve his connexions with the *Morning Post* by contributing essays on the state of German literature,[4] but nothing of his appears in the newspaper until August 1799, after his return. By that time Britain and her allies were the invaders, in the Alps and in Holland, and the war had become one of increasing carnage. The alliance with Russia meant an embrace of General Suvorov, hero of the massacres of Ismail and Warsaw[5]—an embrace at which the *Morning Post* balked (12 July 1799) and Coleridge and his friends, privately, seethed. Still worse, for the erstwhile Friends of Freedom, was the dismaying fact that triumphant ministers accompanied their rejoicing in victories won or anticipated against France not with a relaxation of anti-Jacobinism at home but with a programme of coercive legislation

[1] See 2 Mar announcement, and Stuart's letter of 20 Jan 1798 (App B, below).

[2] *BL* ch 10 (1907) I 144.

[3] See App C, "The Lash of the *Anti-Jacobin*", below.

[4] See *CL* I 417–20.

[5] See *PW* (EHC) I 162n.

more sweeping and more elaborately supervisory, especially of handbill and newspaper printing, than any "gagging acts" hitherto attempted. The bitter spirit of the time was eloquently expressed in the title of Southey's grim poem in the *Post* of 22 June 1799: *Ode to Silence, alias Unanimity*.[1]

In this savage season, influenced by the spirit (at least) of ministerial coercion, and seizing the opportunity presented by the imprisonment of the proprietor, printer, and publisher of the *Courier* (for a libel calling the Emperor of Russia "obnoxious" and "ridiculous"), Stuart promptly acquired control of the paper he had joined the *Anti-Jacobin* in abusing, and freed it from "...the violent politics, that is, 'the independent Principles'...which had rendered the paper obnoxious" (the word had stuck).[2] It was now to be, like the *Morning Post*, neither "the tool of a despotic administration" *nor* "the instrument of a party", though the new editor (T. G. Street) did not feel ready to make a public declaration until the paper had been "in the possession of new Proprietors" for a year (*Courier*, 20 August 1800).[3] It is a sign of Street's or Stuart's caution, but also a sign of the times, that the change-over between May and August 1799 is hardly perceptible, so silent had the once Jacobinical *Courier* become even before its old proprietors were driven *hors de combat* by heavy fines and imprisonment.[4] The greatest change in policy—and the one

[1] Anyone who has wondered about C's interest in Spinoza in a time of spies and fears and has pondered the congruence of C's double track of necessitarian meliorism and abstruse retirement with Spinoza's doubling of social science and quietism will be struck by the pertinence of some of the chapters in Lewis Samuel Feuer *Spinoza and the Rise of Liberalism* (Boston 1958), e.g. "Revolutionist in Mystic Withdrawal", and especially the section headed "Determinism and Social Science: the Guide to Action and the Apotheosis of Acquiescence" (pp 82–6). Spinoza "wished to devise a reliable anodyne for the defeat of political and personal hopes which was always on the horizon. He provided a philosophy for applied social science, but he was always in spirit prepared to retreat from The Hague to Rijnsburg, to renounce political participation in favor of withdrawal."

[2] *Courier* 20 Aug 1800. In their salad days both Stuart and Street had been editorially and proprietorily involved in the *Courier*, L. Werkmeister discovers, and she deduces that Stuart may have retained a silent partnership during the regime of George Ross and John Parry.

[3] One rare consequence of the sworn statement in the *Courier* of 20 Aug 1800 (sworn "before me, H. C. Combe, Mayor") is its giving us the names of the printers: "We, Edward Brize, Joseph Carter, Robert Vickers, Thomas Westhill, being the Pressmen, and Thomas George Street, being the Publisher...". Four true pressmen: the figure supports James Grant's statement that several presses were used, printing from several settings of each day's paper.

[4] Hereafter the *Courier* and *Morning Post* were closely allied (and many of C's essays were printed in both papers,

most useful to Pitt—was from sympathy with the rebellious Irish to support of the ministers' new patent remedy, Union. Yet the chief contribution made by both of Stuart's papers in this period was a general avoidance of political discussion, with an occasional reminder that Liberty had friends and that ministers were still "bad".[1]

A suitably ambivalent support of the war, with minor sniping and some cynicism about purposes and allies, may be found in the poems and epigrams Coleridge contributed to the *Morning Post* in August and September 1799, although in his private correspondence he expresses only the cynicism without the support—as in his ironic pleasure at the "retrograde Majesty" of Suvorov's announced "Victory at Novi" but actual retreat.[2] Indeed some of his published verses seem inspired by an irresistible impulse to renew allegiance with the devil's party, not only in ironic "devil's thoughts" but even in the expression of positive hopes for peace and the "amelioration of mankind".[3] Yet the hand of censorship is visible upon these verses, apparently guided by the poet himself without waiting for Stuart's blue pencil. In this ebb season he could even descend to such hack writing as the manuscript sermon on which he inscribed: "...Written for whom I neither know or care as a College Commemoration Sermon—Oct 6th 1799".[4] To be sure, the elements of Coleridge's later ("mature") political philosophy may be discovered in it;[5] but his own comment on this piece of anti-Jacobinism, two days after writing it, was: "The one Side is all too hugely beangel'd, the other all too desperately bedevil'd; yet spite of the Flattery, and spite of the Caricature both are *likenesses*." Able to flatter or caricature both sides, in this dreary time he could have faith in neither. On September 2 and 3 his Epigrams express almost equal contempt for the "vipers" of Pitt and the viperous United Irishmen.

---

as noted passim), but Street was more cautious and therefore more demagogic than Stuart—as we see in connexion with the Poole–Coleridge defence of monopolists in Oct 1800.

[1] E.g. *M Post* 20 Mar 1799: "The friends of Liberty, as well as the advocates of bad Ministers, will regret to find that the report of the successes of the Austrians [against the French] is completely contradicted."

[2] C's pun about Suvorov's coming off with "Eclat—i.e. A *claw*!" (*CL* I 529) derives from some wit in the Jan 1799 *M Post*.

[3] Contributions of 6, 19, and 24 Sept 1799. See App D, below.

[4] BM Add MSS 35343 f 33, an attack on the new philosophy composed, at George Coleridge's request, for someone too lazy to write his own.

[5] John Colmer, who partly transcribes this document in *N&Q* v (Apr 1958) 150–2, makes this point; but of course the political elements lay at hand for use whenever C chose to join Pitt and Windham.

COLERIDGE AND NAPOLEON

Then abruptly the political atmosphere was electrified by the sudden dramatic appearance of Napoleon in France (on 8 October) out of the obscurity of apparent eclipse in Egypt, and by the concurrent disaster of the "Secret Expedition" of British and Russian armies in the Netherlands, as well as Masséna's defeat of the Russians under Korsakov in Zurich. In Nether Stowey the fire of old Jacobin sympathies and even Gallican sympathies kindled again, despite all declarations of recantation and fears, and with it the impulse to thumb the nose at Pitt. The counter-revolutionary weather might yet change; a friend of Freedom might again sing *ça ira* ("it *grows out again*"). "...What say you of the Resurrection & Glorification of the Saviour of the East after his Tryals in the Wilderness?" exclaimed Coleridge to Southey. "...Buonaparte—! Buonaparte! dear dear DEAR Buonaparte!—It would be no bad fun to hear the Clerk of the Privy Council read this paragraph before Pitt &c...."[1] If Napoleon cleaned out the corruptions of the French Directory, if he proved as able a statesman as general, might he bring peace? Was it possible the people of England might at last jettison the system of Pitt and Grenville? Coleridge could laugh at the "Glorification" and at the simple enthusiasm of his friend Poole. Yet his own imagination, fired by the power of the risen Bonaparte, now drew him into the political department of the *Morning Post*, and it would keep him there long after his friend Southey had returned to the pre-October cynicism.[2] Hoping that Wordsworth would now write the great poem to save their generation from sinking into "contempt for visionary *philosophes*", Coleridge welcomed for himself "the absolute necessity of scribbling prose".[3] Bonaparte had re-awakened the newspapers and would bring the Opposition back to their benches. In a new mood of wary hopefulness, exuberant in spirit yet divided in mind, Coleridge was ready to flow in any of several rills at once to compose paragraphs that would be provocative, illuminating, dialectical, and sometimes (to Stuart's joy) "a sensation".

By 10 November he had received Stuart's invitation to come to London on full salary. For "the next four or five months" he was to have "*all*" his expenses paid, "let them be what they will", including

[1] To RS 15 Oct 1799: *CL* I 539.

[2] See *S Life* (CS) II 44, 46, but also Carnall 55.

[3] To WW c 10 Sept 1799: *CL* I 527; to RS 10 Nov [1799]: *CL* I 545.

the cost of having his family with him.[1] And he did not hesitate to accept, though he continued what he was doing—exploring the Lakes with Wordsworth—for another week or so and then, quite evidently in an elated mood, travelled by way of Sockburn, where he lingered several days to complete the rapid process of falling in love with Sara Hutchinson. At midnight 27/28 November he arrived in London, and by 19 December he and his family were settled at 21 Buckingham Street, Strand, in an "airy" and "healthful Place" that he hoped the Southeys would share with them.[2] Nearby was the newspaper office, topped in front with a gilded globe (it had been the office of the *World*)[3] and furnished with rosewood desks and silver inkstands, as Lamb remembered thirty-five years later.[4] Meanwhile Napoleon

[1] *CL* I 545, 552, 559. Cf Stuart IX 487: "I agreed to allow him my largest salary". But there was no advance payment, for C had at first to borrow £25 "to pay my Wife's travelling expences & al[so] my first expences in London". *CL* I 559. The terms of C's engagement are not difficult to reconstruct. All expenses paid by Stuart; a cash reserve to be gained by translations and other hack-work for booksellers: he would work "from I-rise to I-set—i.e. from 9 in the morning to 12 at night. . . Mornings to Booksellers' Compilations—after dinner to Stewart". He would leave London "by the first of April". *CL* I 552; see 545, 548.

He did by April 1800 translate two of the three Wallenstein plays he had bargained for, and for the stipulated four months he supplied Stuart an average of six columns of prose a week, not counting three tries at parliamentary reporting and several poems and epigrams. This would seem an ample fulfilment of contract, for in the following September when he offered to "recommence my old occupation", he defined it as "binding myself down to send you six columns a week". *CL* I 628. The average was achieved only with some fluctuation, perhaps displeasing to Stuart, for C added: "any week in which I do not send at least five Columns I should consent to be counted as nothing". He fell below five columns on only six of his nineteen weeks. Here is the tally of columns per week, beginning with the week ending Saturday, 7 Dec 1799: 3⅔, 1⅔, ½, 7, 11¾, 10, 5¾, 10, 5¾ (plus report of Pitt's speech), 12½, 7½, 10½, 1 (plus report of Sheridan's speech), 5⅓ (plus report of Pitt's speech), 4⅓, 1⅓, 7, 5, 6½.

[2] *CN* I 590; *CL* I 550. C probably stayed at first with John and James Tobin at 7 Barnard's Inn. R. S. Woof "Coleridge and Thomasina Dennis" *UTQ* XXXII (1962) 49.

[3] Stuart, however, described it as topped with "Balls & Mercury": to C 20 Sept 1802 (App B, below).

[4] Still later, S. C. Hall, the editor of the *Amulet*, recalled the memory he cherished most of C: "It was in the Strand: he pointed out to me the window of a room in the office of the *Morning Post* where he had consumed much midnight oil; and then for half an hour he talked of the sorrowful joy he had often felt when, leaving the office as day was dawning, he heard the song of a caged lark that sung his orisons from the lattice of an artisan who was rising to begin his labour as the poet was pacing homewards to rest after his work all night." *A Book of Memories* (1871) 43. By dawn the fruit of C's labour was already in the hands of the news-boys; "any number of papers" might be obtained until "the types were broken up", at "eleven o'clock, every fore-noon". *M Post* 8 Jan 1800.

had overturned the Directory and promulgated a new Constitution, increasing Stuart's need for an able commentator.

The desperation of the *Morning Post* toward the end of November is manifest. An essay "On the Revolution" was prepared, for Tuesday the 26th, by a writer so insensitive to word-play as to say, not in jest, that Bonaparte was sweeping the body politic from the face of France. There was a promise of more "To-morrow, perhaps", and again on Wednesday and Thursday of "Observations on the late Revolution in Paris, to-morrow" and "to-morrow, certainly". Coleridge arrived by that Wednesday. As soon as a copy of the new Constitution was received from Paris he came to the rescue, 7 December, with an impressive set of observations upon it.

Stuart may have thought he simply needed an able writer; what he obtained was political guidance as well. In October, with the British and Russians in retreat, the *Morning Post* saw merely the end of bipartisanship and the end of Pitt's cabinet approaching. Fox could be mentioned again, indeed must be insisted upon: to suppose that the "quibbling" ministers would make peace, when a monarchy in France was their real object, was to be their dupe; it remained "with the people...to decide whether they will have Mr. Pitt and a war...or Mr. Fox and a peace..." (6 November). Yet the *Post* held that nothing had changed in France, even after Bonaparte's *coup d'état* of 18 Brumaire. Its government was still Jacobin; the "new" men were "all the same men, professing the same principles, and only divided into the Government and Anti-government factions" (4 December). Indeed the new government's "character of Jacobinism" seemed to Stuart plain enough to "dispel all present hopes of a termination of the war with this country" (4 December). George Rose could hardly have pointed out a more useful position for the Opposition press to take.

Coleridge at first did not depart emphatically from this view, but his own assumption gradually prevailed that Jacobinism was really defunct in France. More immediately his insight enlarged the *Morning Post*'s understanding of the real change effected by the *coup*, even granting that the Constitution was an insubstantial façade, and of the commanding genius of Bonaparte. Only after Coleridge's arrival did the *Post* take any stock in the notion that Bonaparte's regime was inspiring "enthusiasm in France" and might produce "very different" results, whether in prosecuting the war or in consolidating a peace, from those achieved by "the corrupt" Directory (17 December). Often Coleridge would return to the mood of February 1798, sighing, "alas! explosion has succeeded explosion so rapidly, that novelty itself ceases to appear new".[1] If the "detestable Villainy" of the new Constitution could fool the French, it was because they were children who deserved no better and it was "an infirmity to hope or fear concerning them", he wrote at the end of the year.[2] Yet he himself entertained the infirmity. On 12 December in an essay of "Advice to the Friends of Freedom" he offered little comfort to those who trod the narrow path between "the resignation of despair" and tantalising hopes for "better states of society"; these hopes we must not entrust to the new hero of France, and in England the wisest still accept "the present Ministry...from fear of worse men"—yet it is now assumed, without names named, that "our" side knows of a viable alternative of "good men" for bad. By 24 December Coleridge *will* have some hopes, and he calls on the Whig leaders, Fox and Sheridan, to inspire them. Not only because of the British reverses but because the new French Government may sincerely "wish for peace", an active minority might now rally public opinion against further bloodshed under consecrated banners. Fox is reminded that in 1791 Pitt had been compelled to pull back from the brink of war despite "firm and overflowing majorities".

Fox's and Grey's secession from Parliament in 1797 and the more oscillatory secessions of Coleridge from "active life" had reflected similar fears for the nation. Grey, who had begun the secession, would remain away as long as the specific measure of Parliamentary Reform lay dormant. For the Irish Opposition, who had in fact inspired the English secession in the first place, the next step had been rebellion—and defeat. Fox, of the English, had intended to retire from politics altogether—to "literature, and especially the metaphysics of grammar, and the cultivation of his plants".[3] Coleridge had similarly from time to time announced his retirement to literature, gardening, and "metaphysicizing". It may have seemed to him that each had snapped his trumpet for the same reason, that the people had become "too violently heated"—or too apathetic. But now the nation out of doors seemed ready to listen to reason once more—from Fox, and Coleridge. Perhaps even to change the "*existing circumstances*"[4] within doors, i.e. Pitt's majorities. On 3 February 1800 Fox's return to Parliament was a sensation, and Coleridge felt that the eloquence of the "great orator" met all his "pre-formed" expectations—even

1 21 Dec 1799, below.
2 To RS [28 Dec 1799]: *CL* I 554.
3 *Lady Holland* I 149.
4 24 Dec 1799 (first paragraph), below.

his test of moral integrity: "Fox possesses all the full & overflowing Eloquence of a man of clear head, clean heart, & impetuous feelings".[1] With French Jacobinism "dying a natural death"[2] and fear of the "owlet Atheism" forgotten along with disdain of the aristocratic dissipations (not to mention the "*filthy garments*")[3] of Fox and Sheridan, the new enthusiasm—as well as the editorial policy—of this dramatic winter could accept the essential purity of all denizens of Devonshire House, where perhaps the spirit of Liberty was still alive.[4]

Coleridge would continue to veer about—privately, in his feelings about Fox and Sheridan, and publicly in his view of Bonaparte as a master of expediency—if not in his criticism of ministers for their rigidity. In his analysis of the French Constitution he concluded that the arrival of a despot and the demise of revolutionary Jacobinism, while distressing to lovers of liberty, had made nonsense of the British war aim, to destroy Jacobinism and restore despotism. The *Morning Post* on Coleridgian days (when its views were less hesitant than on non-Coleridgian days such as 30 December) was willing to suppose Bonaparte's regime strong enough to maintain itself, in war or peace, and thus also willing—at least ironically—to regard peace overtures as genuine. When they came it led Opposition papers, with Coleridge sturdily wielding both prose and verse, in the sport of ridiculing an embarrassed ministry and in the protestation that peace was worth bargaining for. In essays beginning 2 January Coleridge put forward a view still attractive to historians and cogent enough to cause at the time "no ordinary sensation" (8 January). While looking upon the motives of Bonaparte as less pacific than strategic, he increasingly placed the onus on his own government. The arrogance and confidence of Lord Grenville, based on the assumption that France was on the run, and of the Austrian archduke Charles, who supposed that a bit more fighting would bring the

[1] To Josiah Wedgwood [4 Feb 1800]: *CL* I 568.

[2] 24 Dec 1799, below.

[3] To George Coleridge [c 10 Mar 1798]: *CL* I 396; the "owlet" is in *Fears in Solitude* line 82.

[4] On 24 Dec 1799 C's extravagant Ode to the Duchess of Devonshire, the Whigs' "faery queen", appeared in response to an old poem of hers, now topically interesting as describing the scene where Masséna had defeated Suvorov, just published in *Courier*, *Post*, and *Chronicle*. C, singling out her lines in praise of William Tell for redirecting the arrow to "the tyrant's heart" (note the implications for Suvorov and Pitt), redirected the praise to hers in four swelling strophes. If approval of Swiss Liberty made the Duchess an unspoiled genius, by the same token Fox himself had remained essentially clean of heart.

allies more spoils, led them into a basic miscalculation of the political and military situation—a miscalculation that, as we know, gave Europe another decade and a half of war. To Coleridge the underestimation of both the genius and the popularity of the First Consul appeared natural in minds whose best answer to the failures in the Netherlands and Switzerland was a new campaign. His anticipation of "no favourable results" either from negotiations or from new campaigns was not so much a piece of pessimism as an argument for a change of ministers. He could easily predict the failure of rivalrous allied armies against Napoleonic planning. He could foresee, and even justify on the ground of expediency, the acceptance in France "even [by] the lovers of liberty" of Napoleon's constitution and dictatorship, with Pitt ultimately to blame for rejecting negotiation.[1]

During January and early February 1800, when he was at times writing all the editorial paragraphs in the *Morning Post*, he worked up immense respect for Napoleon and contempt for Pitt. Dismissing as academic the question of Bonaparte's rise to power—"Revolution! a change of Ministry in England could be accompanied with no less convulsion"—he insisted upon the reality of the French ruler's "political sagacity and moderation". Gathering momentum in paper after paper, his critical disintegration of the ministry crested in his most formidable critique since January 1798 of the whole Pitt–Burke position, giving attention to the entire range of components of the unstable amalgam called government, from supercilious "King's Friends" to rabid alarmists, "Mr. Windham, &c. who are so panic-struck from Jacobinism and atheism, that they do not *think*".[2]

During this heat, the journalist's impulse to expose sham and fraud rode high on the (pretended) discovery that Lord Grenville's replies to Tallyrand were written by Windham—and the even more improbable discovery that the whole "Intercepted Correspondence" purportedly of French officers writing homesick letters from Egypt was a ministerial concoction. At the same time in dead earnest, in often impassioned prose, he now turned to the enormous question of fixing the guilt for the war begun in 1793. In his essay of 25 January Coleridge writes with the fervour of the author of the *Ode on the Departing Year* but in a maturer voice.

At this juncture a crisis occurred in his relations with Stuart. Writing to Southey on the 25th Coleridge said he had "discovered

[1] 2 Jan 1800 "On Peace", below.

[2] See 22, 23, 24, 25, 28 Jan 1800, below.

so scoundrelly an act of Sheridan's & so dastardly a one of Stuart's" that he was "half-inclined to withdraw...", Stuart having received from Sheridan two completely contradictory accounts of a disturbance at Norwich in which Tom Sheridan was involved, and having printed the atrociously false one, which "breathed the spirit of the most foul & sanguinary Aristocracy—".[1] The lies in the story were, apparently, insinuations that a brawl among drunken soldiery was due to the "antipathy" of the local "Democratic party" to troops who had pulled down Thelwall's lecture-room there in 1797. Coleridge's personal loathing of the Foxites erupted for the moment: "depend upon it, Sheridan is a thorough-paced *bad man*!"; "the Jacobins as men are heroes in virtue, compared with Mr. Fox and his party".[2] Yet he did not withdraw. The spirit of the times had so seized him that in the next weeks he could respond, as we have seen, to the "clean heart, & impetuous feelings" of Fox and report the anti-ministerial wit of Sheridan[3] with equanimity. Did he simply oscillate back to the "honest cause" and swallow the "profligate and unprincipled" goings-on? There are indications that before resuming work for the newspaper he had some kind of show-down with Stuart and won from him certain concessions, meaningless perhaps but spelled out in print.

In the *Biographia* he says that soon after his return from Germany he accepted "the literary and political department in the Morning Post...on the condition that the paper should thenceforwards be conducted on certain fixed and announced principles, and that I should neither be obliged nor requested to deviate from them in favour of any party or any event".[4] Stuart in 1838 replied: "Whether he made any stipulations about the politics or tone of the paper, I cannot now say; but it would [have been] unnecessary...".[5] Coleridge in November or December might have felt it unnecessary, but after Stuart's "dastardly meanness" in printing lies to serve party men, he evidently laid down the law to his employer. For the next Monday, 27 January, Stuart printed a statement that can most easily be accounted for as an attempt to satisfy Coleridge's demand for an announcement of fixed principles even while shielding such Public Characters as Sheridan: "But to state principles, fixed, reasonable, and practical, to judge of men and measures entirely according to

[1] *CL* I 564.

[2] Ibid; to William Taylor 25 Jan 1800: *CL* I 565.

[3] *CL* I 568, quoted above, a private opinion expressed in a letter. C reported a Sheridan speech on 11 Feb; he gave judicious excerpts from Fox's speech 6 Feb.

[4] *BL* ch 10 (1907) I 141–2.

[5] Stuart IX 484.

their agreement or deviation from these principles, is indeed difficult, and makes necessary an unceasing intention of mind [Stuart may not be sure he can do it]—especially when to this determination is added a respect for all Public Characters...".[1] The announcement is wrapped in boasts about type, paper, circulation, and new departments, but these do not conceal the agonised squirming.

One of the departments to be improved was the reporting of parliamentary debates, and Coleridge may in part have been resisting Stuart's plan to put him in charge and involve him in some part of the reporting. In February he reported two speeches by Pitt and one by Sheridan, more than competently, and pursued the topics of debate in leading paragraphs. Even within the first week he would groan that "this Newspaper Business...is too, too fatiguing",[2]

[1] *M Post* 27 Jan 1800. Readers are reminded of the new type, of a circulation "more than *trebled*" in four years, of efforts "to make our Paper respectable in respect of literary merit", and new improvements are promised in a regular department of New Fashions and Fashionable Life and in parliamentary reporting.

Some journalists, we are told, "have stepped forward to pledge themselves more particularly on the score of their Parliamentary Reports"; we know that C was one of these, reluctant, but possibly thus yielding Stuart a *quid pro quo*. For the paragraph leads on to the Editor's pledge about principles: "...we shall attempt, what no other Paper attempts, to make our observations on every public event strictly impartial. We are aware that we here pledge ourselves for the performance of no easy task. To abuse one party indiscriminately, and as indiscriminately defend the measures of another, and to be restrained from excess of praise or censure, not by a sense of right or wrong, but merely by a prudent calculation on what the public temper will bear, may call forth some ingenuity, and demands a considerable portion of confidence, but requires neither steady reflection or comprehensive views. But to state principles, fixed, reasonable, and practical, to judge of men and measures entirely according to their agreement or deviation from these principles, is indeed difficult, and makes necessary an unceasing intention of mind—especially when to this determination is added a respect for all Public Characters, as far as they have been deemed worthy to occupy a station in the public confidence or public hope. This is genuine impartiality, and for the adherence to this we pledge ourselves solemnly. But we will not purchase a character for impartiality by a sacrifice of all principle, by traducing Mr. Fox in one paragraph, and Mr. Pitt in the next, without sense or reason. Ours shall not be an impartiality of abuse of all public men, a disregard of right or wrong, by which some have obtained from the thoughtless multitude a character for impartiality. Such a conduct is of the most pernicious kind. We know how to listen to the arguments of party writers, and in the conflict between them we may discover the truth. Such a conflict is useful, it is necessary to the public; but of a most dangerous nature is that which, from disappointment and hatred of both parties, equally abuses both, steals into the confidence of the people, and obtains a character for candour, by degrading all that is free, honest, or independent in a country, which is indebted for all its enjoyments to the freedom of its constitution, the honesty, and independent spirit of its inhabitants."

[2] To RS 12 Feb 1800: *CL* I 569.

though despite fatigue he felt happier than a wine merchant. He was really in the thick of a sensation partly of his own creating:

> We Newspaper scribes are true Galley-Slaves.... Yet it is not unflattering to a man's Vanity to reflect that what he writes at 12 at night will before 12 hours is over have perhaps 5 or 6000 Readers! To trace a happy phrase, good image, or new argument running thro' the Town, & sliding into all the papers! Few Wine merchants can boast of creating more sensation....[1]

He not only heard some "favorite & often urged" arguments repeated in Parliament almost in his "own particular phrases", but he now had something to do with perpetuating them in his own phrases. In his report of Pitt's "Security" speech of 17 February he recovered many more of Pitt's actual terms than did his nearest rivals, while at the same time making many more creative improvements upon the speech. It was indeed partly thanks to Coleridge that Pitt's remarks not only presented Pitt's own position memorably but also expressed the opposing arguments more eloquently than he can have desired.

Yet a week after his third bout of reporting Coleridge declared that he was "Stowey-sick": "Stewart won't let me go, but I don't do much for him".[2] He did continue to do a great deal, but with an increasingly dominant note of pessimism, whether in commenting on the parliamentary debates (English and Irish) or on the diplomacy. Hope for political liberty had "died of a dead palsy" (27 February); Pitt's "financial phlebotomy" had "already touched an artery" (26 February); and as for the bribery and corruption attendant on the bringing in of Irish Union—which Coleridge now supported as a wartime necessity—one's sarcasm seemed hardly worth articulating.

A further complication of his political feelings, perhaps not yet near the surface of consciousness, was the fact (as he later saw it) that his approval of Union as a wise measure was painfully at odds with his contempt of Pitt, its author: what he later appeared to forget was his contempt of the means the author employed.[3]

In Coleridge's mind he had committed himself to the *Morning Post* for only four months, and he stuck to his resolve to leave London by April. Though he contributed heavily in March, we see from his letters that he felt guilty about not doing more and that he felt pressed by Stuart, not at first realising that Stuart was pursuing him only to draw up a larger contract. Coleridge was determined

[1] To Wedgwood [4 Feb 1800]: *CL* I 569.

[2] To Poole [25 Feb 1800]: *CL* I 574.

[3] See *CN* I 1606, 21–2 Oct 1803, in which, analysing his feeling about Pitt as "Author of the Irish Union, deemed by me a great & wise measure", C leaves out of account the effect on his feeling, at the time, of his scorn of the dishonest means Pitt used.

merely to fulfil the old. "*After* these, if it be worth your while, I will do what I can—only not for any regular *Stipend.*—That harrasses me—".[1] His major contributions of March have the quality of a casting up of his account, not only of his winter's employment but of the winter's posturing of Pitt and Bonaparte on the world stage.

In the end he did slide away, with an uncomfortable feeling that he had failed to settle accounts with Stuart or Bonaparte—or even Pitt. But from his correspondence one gets the impression that it was the "fagging" bore of translating Schiller, a side employment that intruded upon his journalism, that wearied him, and that he did not really wish to make a clean break. "Newspaper writing is comparative extacy", he wrote on the day his last essay of the season was printed; "—I do not despair of making Bonaparte as good as *Pitt*—but there is a 2nd Part of Pitt to come—& a Review of a curious Pamphlet connected with it...".[2] The extant part of "Pitt" had "made a sensation". As Poole had too candidly observed, Coleridge had begun to feel his own power.—"Truly and in simple verity, my dear Tom, I feel not an atom more power than I have ever done, except the power of gaining a few more paltry guineas than I had supposed."[3]

When he at last discovered what Stuart was after him for, it was this latter, exceptional power that he felt; yet he found in himself the strength to say no and to opt for the "lazy reading of Old Folios". His "Pitt" had reached Stuart on 17 or 18 March and appeared on the 19th. Two days later he told Poole secretly what Stuart was proposing: "half shares in the two Papers, the M.P. & Courier, if I would devote myself with him to them".[4] When Cole-

[1] To Stuart [1 Mar 1800]: *CL* I 578–9.

[2] To Samuel Purkis 27 Mar, the day C's review of Young's pamphlet appeared: *CL* I 583. The short comment of 16 Apr, hardly counting as an essay, was probably written beforehand, though it could have been sent to Stuart in a letter—as he evidently later sent the note of 23 Jun 1801.

[3] To Poole 31 Mar 1800: *CL* I 584–5.

[4] *CL* I 582; see *CRB* 234. The term "half shares" can hardly be taken to mean half ownership of each paper; perhaps it meant something like half the main editorial salary of each. But proprietary arrangements varied widely. When Topham took Charles Este into the editorship of the *World* in 1787 (a roughly comparable situation, for Este advanced no capital) he was given three of the paper's twelve shares. Werkmeister (1963) 159. When in 1790 the proprietors of the *Gazetteer* (owned in sixteen shares) failed to give one half-share, valued at £100, to the editor (in addition to his salary of £200 a year) he seems to have been discouraged. Haig *The Gazetteer* 210–17. If Stuart still owned half the *M Post* (as he did in 1796) he may have offered to divide that—and perhaps whatever share of the *Courier* he owned. In 1780, when the *M Post* had a daily circulation of 3000, its twenty-five shares were valued at £350 each but sold at nearly

ridge confessed preferring the country and books to the "real Evil" of an almost certain "2000£ a year"[1] or even "two Thousand Times two thousand Pound", Stuart could only stare; "for such Ideas are not animals indigenous in the Longitudes & Latitudes of a Scotchman's Soul". What he had hoped his stint with Stuart had earned him was a free-lance status.

The summarising essays must have restored readers' faith in the political sagacity of the *Morning Post*. The summing up of "Bonaparte, in his Relations to France", and "in his Relations to England", climaxing in "Pitt and Bonaparte. Pitt", are more than usually stately and judicious, giving the impression of history's being slowed down for its portrait. The situation and the protagonists are these and these—and the author may now retire to his garden and his reading. Applying historical insight to what has happened and what ought to happen rather than to what the obstinacy of real events may bring, our historian is not unlike those he describes as guided by the torch of a blind cupid. Bonaparte now has the fate of Europe in his hands. Bonaparte seriously desires peace. Therefore he shall attain it; there cannot be, because there must not be, another bloody conflict. Coleridge feels the Napoleonic power but miscalculates the inertia of its impediments—which are, in the immediate future, the obstinacy and optimism of the Austrian Emperor, with Pitt's subsidies behind him.

At the end of the month, one thing that prevented Coleridge from writing his final essay "of Bonaparte" was the fact that Bonaparte marched off to war, Austria having proved as stubborn as Grenville.

In his parting essay of the season, 27 March, Coleridge turned his attention, once again, to the connexion between slaughter and famine, in a vociferous review of Arthur Young's *The Question of Scarcity Plainly Stated and Remedies Considered*. Pitt had inveighed against

---

£800 each; by 1783, with circulation down to 1650, its twenty-four shares were worth only £200 each. Werkmeister (1963) 79.

From statements in *M Post* 3 Dec 1802 the circulation can be deduced to have been under 1500 when C went to London in Nov 1799 and to have risen to 2000 or more during his four months' editorship—a rise sufficient to impress the Stuart of 1800 (who for a while in January bragged of a "tripling" of sales), even though the Stuart of 1838 would roundly assert (IX 486–7) that C "wrote nothing that I remember, and consequently nothing that is worth remembering in the Morning Post during the first six or eight months of his engagement, except [the essays of 22 Jan and 19 Mar 1800 and] the poem of 'The Devil's Thoughts,' which I think came by post from Dorsetshire". Stuart altogether forgot 1798.

[1] Conceivably C was offered *shares* worth £2000. But their annual yield would be only a fraction of that.

irritating the populace by falsely linking the scarcity with the war. Now the price of grain was soaring, with the resumption of war, and Coleridge indicated that a better way to overcome scarcity would be to make peace with France and learn from her some agrarian lessons. For Coleridge at this date the politics of this review are remarkable in two particulars: a reminder of "the blessings" gained by the French "from the destruction of Feudalism" during their revolution, and a resounding attack on Young's "recantation" from sympathy with that revolution—a recantation seeming to differ from Coleridge's chiefly in its "permanence" (which Coleridge attributes to its having been rewarded by a government pension).

THE PEACE WITHOUT A FULCRUM

Here Coleridge's term of active service halted for several months—and so did the political department of the *Morning Post*. Bonaparte and his adversaries supplied news of troop movements and battles, and brief leaders were written about these, but there was not another political essay of any length or quality until Coleridge once more, from Keswick, supplied an essay for 6 August—again defending the French Revolution for having turned "waste and neglected land" into cultivated farms.

This essay found welcome in both of Stuart's newspapers, though by this time Stuart had acquired a fairly competent writer for a series of leaders on the rumoured armistice between France and Austria (5, 6, 8, 14 August) and, later, a series on "The Policy of Bonaparte" (23, 24, 29 October, 11 November).[1] For another journalistic sensation, however, he again had Coleridge to thank—a series of agricultural letters amplified from drafts by Thomas Poole, fanning a controversy that raged several months on whether the soaring prices were due to bad harvests or to hoarding—a debate in which Coleridge's defence of "Farmers and Monopolists" became too unpopular to suit the *Courier* and was firmly balanced in the *Morning Post* by letters on the other side. Coleridge, conceding a major point and in somewhat flustered retreat in his last printed Letter, 14 October 1800, begged Poole for a final clinching essay that would "come up in the Rear like the Roman Triarii, on whom alone. . .depended the Stress of the Battle, and the Hope of the Victory",[2] but none came.

[1] One might suppose Mackintosh to have contributed these (see below), but their style does not suggest his authorship.

[2] [c 11 Oct 1800]: *CL* I 634.

Coleridge's retirement from the political department was now complete and continued another seven months. The summer of 1800 was for Coleridge a period of drastic devaluation of his own merits. His "labor-pangs" with *Christabel* seemed to be holding up the *Lyrical Ballads*, and he felt ready to "abandon Poetry altogether".[1] To a suggestion that he gather his political essays into a book he answered, "There is no thought of ever collecting my Morning Post Essays—they are not worth it."[2] He did send Stuart a few "facetious" poems in October—including a scatalogical inscription "of remorseless animosity" directed against James Mackintosh, which suggests that he suspected (or knew) that Mackintosh had been called in to aid Stuart on his own failure to return.[3] He suffered a wretched winter. But even in mid-February when his health was somewhat recovered and he was reading in the newspapers of the resignation of Pitt, Grenville, Windham, and the rest—the King having refused to honour Pitt's promises of political relief to Catholics—Coleridge's comment to Poole was: "Change of Ministry interests *me* not—I turn at times half reluctantly from Leibnitz or Kant even to read a smoking new newspaper...".[4]

More seriously, he was "oppressed at times with a true heart-gnawing melancholy" from contemplating "the state of my poor oppressed Country".[5] The scarcity had been and continued real enough, as far as the poor were concerned. If he wrote now for Stuart it would be hard to maintain the supercilious tone of a newspaper written for coffeehouse gentlemen. "So many miserable Beings" came begging at his door "with half-famished children...that when I received the Newspaper, I could scarcely read the Debates; my heart swelled so within me at the brutal Ignorance & Hardheartedness of all Parties alike—Add to this, I was affected by a Rheumatism in the back part of my head...". Besides, the Poole–Coleridge defence of monopolising farmers had not been so clever. "The Farmers in these Northern Counties", he concluded to Poole, "are getting rich. Their Crops last year were [not scarce but] excellent; but the County itself is starving."[6]

By the middle of May (1801), on Stuart's urging, he expressed

[1] To James Tobin 17 Sept 1800: *CL* I 623.

[2] Ibid.

[3] William Jerdan *Autobiography* (4 vols 1852) III 312 thus describes C's *Skeltoniad* of 4 Dec 1800. See *CL* I 636, and, for suspicion of Mackintosh's authorship (which seems probable) of a review of Godwin's *Antonio* in *M Post* 15 Dec, *CL* I 657.

[4] 13 Feb 1801: *CL* II 676.

[5] To Poole [23 Mar 1801]: *CL* II 709.

[6] 24 Mar 1801: *CL* II 710–13.

willingness "to do any thing for you off hand with great pleasure" upon suggested topics.[1] It must have surprised—and surely delighted—Stuart to receive for publication 27 May a baker's dozen of prose notes on everything topical from insurrections in Lancashire to owls, to rumoured negotiation of "a treaty, offensive and defensive, highly honourable to Great Britain, and the Republic of Algiers"—all attached as footnotes to a saucily introduced *Expostulatory and Panegyrical Ode, Addressed to the R. H. H. A–d––g––n* of twenty-three six-line stanzas. Less mordant than the railings of Thersites, yet more cynical than his essays had been—about "tremblingly" ambitious Addington, the "illustrious statesmen" of the old and new administrations, their respect for "Fox's speech" yet their owlish pursuit of war (by "burning Copenhagen", hiring "congenial cheap allies", and quack recipes of hope)—this *tour de force* expresses in grim jest much that Coleridge no longer allowed himself to think in prose. It cocks a snook at public characters, pledges of high principle, and the fine anti-Jacobin honesty and independent spirit of "all true Britons":

> "Rule, Britannia! rule the waves!"
> Blacken your sugar isles with slaves,
>   Speak mercy, preach devotion;
> On foaming billows rear your throne...

Following this with a "Philosophical" Ode addressed to the chief justice, on the chemistry and morality of love, that could be emblazoned in the gospel of Women's Liberation,[2] Coleridge eloquently declared his mental holiday from journalism for coffeehouse men. During the summer he appeased Stuart with this and a brief letter-paragraph 23 June. In August a bath in the "gladsome Ocean" inspired a few lines, which he sent at once to Southey and shortly afterward to Stuart "as a symptom of convalescence". But "*Do not write for Stuart*" he advised Southey in the same letter.[3]

In September, only half applying the advice to himself, he offered to return[4] to the *Morning Post* with some simple verses over his own Punic (punning) signature, Ἔστησε. Stuart, responding with a remittance of £30 (13 guineas of it for Southey), asked for prose too. But Coleridge postponed any "attempt to write some good prose

[1] *CL* II 729.

[2] Published 22 Jun, but timeless. See App D, below.

[3] [12] Aug 1801: *CL* II 751–2.

[4] In a letter not extant but referred to in that of 19 Sept (*CL* II 759) and presumably containing the verses, which Stuart announced on 12 Sept.

for you" until he had given "*the Poetics* a compleat *Jog*".[1] Nothing as sustained as the spring Odes was forthcoming, only three slight pieces including a Song Against the New Philosophy called *Drinking versus Thinking* (22, 25, 26 September).

Coleridge now spoke of possibly coming "up to London" but supposed it to be "of no great importance" to Stuart how soon he came.[2] On 3 October it became of great importance, for the leading paragraph announced "that the PRELIMINARIES OF PEACE are SIGNED between FRANCE and BRITAIN!—contrary to the general expectation."

Drinking versus Thinking had seemed an appropriate philosophy during the first months of the Addington ministry, whose measures at home and toward Ireland continued the Pittian system (see the 27 May ode) and whose negotiations with France were conducted in profound secrecy. In his *Tranquillity* ode, written in late summer and out of date by the time Stuart printed it in December, Coleridge had spelled out the politics of holding aloof from "The present works of present man" and concentrating on the "dreamlike" aspect of "distant Fights, and Treaties crude": "What Statesmen scheme, and Soldiers work...Disturb not me!" In August and October the treaties were signed—between France and Bavaria, between France and Naples, Spain and Portugal, between France and Portugal, between France and the Ottoman Porte, and between France and Prussia. But a treaty that included England quickly induced sobriety.

Parliament met at the end of October 1801 and adjourned from 15 December to 2 February; Coleridge arrived 15 November, staying until the day after Christmas and returning again 21 January. Sara Coleridge found only two essays of this period, both on the state of parties in relation to the peace, 27 November and 3 December, the latter focusing on rumours of negotiation between Addington and the followers of Fox. Three more essays, in December, February, and March, round out the discussion and make clear that Coleridge's views remained pacific, and even Foxite, before he began in the closing months of 1802 to reverse them—and then, in the telling, to predate the reversal.

It is possible that during this period he made several briefer contributions—such as the defence of Quakers on 18 December—insufficiently marked by his style to be identified, but his application was nothing like the full campaign of his previous winter in London. It must have been of this time that Stuart was thinking when he

[1] *CL* II 759.

[2] 22, c 27 Sept 1801: *CL* II 762, 763.

remembered Coleridge as generally ill and unable to "write daily on the occurrences of the day". It was now, not earlier, that Stuart "took a first floor for him in King Street, Covent Garden, at my tailor's, Howell's, whose wife was a cheerful good housewife, of middle age, who I knew would nurse Coleridge as kindly as if he were her son...". And to this period must belong the anecdote of a leading paragraph which Coleridge, "on the sofa groaning with pain", had not written, agreed to let Stuart write, and then declined to correct or decorate with "graceful touches".[1]

In 1802 and 1803 Coleridge would tell a story of his shocked disappointment at Fox's response to the announcement of peace terms in October 1801—a story resting on misquotation of Fox's words and distortion of Fox's views. But in his writings of 1801 Coleridge seems almost to canonise Fox and is able to present as his own a view of the peace that is essentially consistent with Fox's.[2] That autumn the absorbing question was what changes might transform the Addington administration into—or replace it by—an effective peace ministry, and the focus was upon Fox because the most obvious solution would have been a Fox cabinet. But Fox was excluded by King George's "prejudices" (to use a tame and palliative word, as Coleridge puts it, 3 December). Indeed George would not even take back Pitt (who, submissive in crises, made a promise never to bring up Catholic Emancipation again—and was chagrined not to be recalled at once) as long as the more entirely tractable Addington could hold on. The alternative, then, would be the entrance into Addington's cabinet of a sufficient majority of Foxites to make it firm against the restoration of Pitt and against the nation's being once again "plunged into a war *of principles*" (this is the language of *Coleridge* in 1801, 3 December).

Coleridge was overlooking this whole series of essays when he declared in the *Biographia Literaria* that "From the commencement of the Addington administration" everything he had written in the *Morning Post* had been "in defence or furtherance of the measures of Government".[3] But he knew, even at the time, that a road that seemed smooth and easy might prove treacherous and insecure and lead "by labyrinthine windings to the very den of the monster, from which we all wish to escape".[4] In these essays he speaks out boldly to warn members of the Old Opposition against the venom of a

1 Stuart IX 478.

2 3 Dec 1801, third paragraph, below.

3 *BL* ch 10 (1907) I 144–5.

4 3 Dec 1801, below.

deadly poison that (it would seem) he himself was unconsciously imbibing. At one time he speaks in the words of a state-physician, analysing the chemistry of the expected political changes, seeking antidotes against the Pittian venom, advising a bitter pill. At another he speaks of the Foxites themselves as "the skilful and honest physicians of the state" who must not degenerate into quacks administering opium (sic) but apply "the knife and the cautery" against the "foam of a mad faction", the war party of Grenville and Windham.[1]

The details of coquetting between Addington and the Whigs are amply supplied in the five essays—indeed more amply than in surviving memorials of the politicians concerned. As early as midsummer Addington had given Grey's father a peerage (of dubious advantage to Grey), and soon after the peace he invited into the cabinet Grey and Bedford, who declined to enter without Fox and without any pledge of support for Parliamentary Reform. In December Erskine asked for office. In January Sheridan spoke out, in the vein of Coleridge's remarks against deserters, and Grey took offence, though Fox insisted that it was not he but Tierney who was being scolded.[2] Then Fox himself uttered public warnings. Ultimately it was Tierney and Sheridan (and Coleridge) who grew warlike and Addingtonian, though Addington's early nod at praise from Tierney only gained him a furious scolding from Pitt. By November 1802 Fox observed that Addington might now, if he still seriously wanted peace, seriously need Grey and the rest, in which case an accommodation would mean a real change and be "desirable and practicable".

Napoleon's increasing strength provided the external pressure—peace having removed only the dramatic paraphernalia of war from the stage of his successes, which had been all along essentially diplomatic.[3] Fox certainly minimised and perhaps underestimated the probability that Napoleon would resort again to the means of war; yet if Fox had been foreign minister, he might have been able to keep the struggle diplomatic. When, after no changes at all, war was resumed, Fox agitated for a system of defence (Windham's) that would drastically depart from the Pittian, and for a strategy that would not, like Pitt's dependence on coalitions, make for further French aggrandisement (as Coleridge observes in the *Biographia*,

1 11 Dec 1801, below.

2 Yet the belief at Holland House was that "Grey gave up Fox with a quibble". *Lady Holland* II 147.

3 As Deutsch points out, it was Napoleon's career that suggested to Clausewitz the observation about war as a continuation of diplomacy. Deutsch's whole Chapter 7, "The Collapse of the Amiens Settlement", is highly relevant.

without naming Fox).[1] On this line of accommodation the new wartime Opposition to Addington (and Pitt) would be the working alliance of Fox and, of all old enemies, Grenville, who turned to him by January 1804.

Between October 1801 and March 1802 the *Morning Post*, like Coleridge, was generally aligned with the Old Opposition, supporting the Peace but critical of Addington's weakness against Pitt and Grenville. All the same, Stuart was shrewd enough to avoid identification with Fox, especially in the area of his open anti-Bourbonism and his apparent approval of Bonaparte. The opportunism of Stuart's policy is often disarmingly transparent, as when the *Post* praises Fox in a backhanded manner "to give to the Ministerial Papers an example of independence, to shew them that our tone is not 'decided' by that of any public man".[2]

The definitive Treaty of Amiens was signed 27 March 1802, about three weeks after Coleridge left London. During the ensuing twelvemonth of official tranquillity, one of his first acts was the writing of an ode in the form of "A Letter to —— [Sara Hutchinson] April 4, 1802" that, though not political in theme, reflected the era in its images.[3] A storm wind, carrying such "tragic Sounds" as "the Rushing of an Host in Rout" and the groaning of wounded men, is momentarily stilled to "a Trance of deepest Silence". Moreover, the poem announces, not too hopefully, a treaty of emotional tranquillity conducive to the production of poetry. In his next extant letter (to Poole, 7 May) he considers the possibility of devoting the year to "a long poem" and inquires about "the price of provisions & house rent in the South of France".[4]

By October the ode, published in the *Morning Post*, was entitled *Dejection*, and Coleridge was writing for Stuart the kind of political prose that later could be seen to have added fuel to the renewing British hostility to Napoleon. By January 1803 he was predicting a new coalition against France. Yet his personal plans still assumed an enduring peace, and he was thunderstruck in March when, just as he was getting "fitted...out with clothes" for a Continental tour, "lo! pounce down [came] the King's Message, & a *War*!"[5]

[1] *BL* ch 10 (1907) I 142.

[2] *M Post* 15 Oct 1801. As late as 23 Jul 1802 the ministerial *True Briton* could call it "the *Jacobin Post*" and accuse it of advancing "impudent Falsehoods daily" against Government.

[3] *CL* II 790–8.

[4] *CL* II 800.

[5] To Poole 13 Mar 1803: *CL* II 938, referring to royal message of 8 Mar; the official declaration of war came 16 May.

During this time Coleridge kept away from London, except for a three-day visit in early November, but from 6 September 1802 to 6 January 1803 he contributed verse and prose on a scale approaching that of 1800, assisting Stuart when he was responding with some hesitation to the general turning of the tide of opinion and was particularly sensitive to fluctuations in circulation.[1] What with the experimental nature of the peace, the temporary character of the ministry, and the rumoured and actual regrouping of parties, the tone of the *Morning Post* gave it an advantage over papers more partisan in habit or reputation. By December Stuart boasted that his paper alone was soaring in circulation, because it alone was now consistently both anti-consular and independent of Fox.[2] He could have added that not only the drift of events but a firm shove on the tiller by Coleridge, in his November letters to Fox, had carried it to that position.[3]

Stuart's predicament is first expressed in a sober editorial of 20 May 1802 on "The Parliamentary Debates on the Definitive Treaty":

> Why the old Opposition did not urge their triumph, why Mr. Fox did not attend...are questions....The discussion has been abandoned to the war faction, divided for a moment indeed, by a temporary schism, about peace; and those who have uniformly been the enemies of the war, are left in amazement, on finding, as they suppose, that peace cannot be had; and in danger of joining the war faction from an honest indignation, at the restless ambition of France, without considering that to the conduct of the late and present Ministers...we owe that spirit of ambition and those dangers with which we are too seriously threatened....

Why Coleridge did not assist Stuart until September is also a question, one answer being that political as well as personal Dejection

[1] See reports in *M Post* 31 May, 21 Sept, 3, 6 Dec 1802, and 1 Jan 1803. Cf *EOT* I xc, where 2090 should read 2990. Some representative figures for daily sales are: for 1801: low, in Sept, 2097; fair average (winter) 2425; for 1802: May average 3290; low, 3 Sept, 2797; 1 Oct, 2910; 5 Nov, 3195; 1 Dec, 3505.

[2] Stuart claimed by Jan 1803 to be selling 700 to 1000 more copies than any other daily paper. In Sept 1802 he put the daily sales of his rivals at: *Morning Herald*, 2400; *Times*, 2240; *M Chron*, 1650. On 6 Dec he stated that *M Chron* was "the only one of these three that [had] advanced (from about 1500 to nearly 2000 daily).... Because, in speaking of the misconduct of France, it not only has agreed with The Morning Post, but it exceeded this paper in the warmth of its indignation, till snubbed by such speeches as those of Mr. Fox", to whom it was still committed.

[3] Stuart's letters to C of 20–3 and 29 Sept 1802 (App B, below) acknowledge the wonderful effect on circulation of C's new righteousness against Bonaparte, and they show Stuart responding gladly to urgings from C to let him "abuse" the Whigs who display "adoration" of Bonaparte—even Fox, even the *Post*'s own Mackintosh.

would take six months to ripen. April news of the "wretched Business" of the French Concordat, which "first occasioned [Coleridge] to think accurately & with consecutive Logic on the force & meaning of the word *Established* Church",[1] was quickly followed by news, reaching England 15 May, of Bonaparte's election as first consul for ten years, soon to be extended to life, with power to name his successor. There are some Coleridge notebook jottings in May probably intended for newspaper paragraphs, a memorandum on "the chattering of the Geese that saved the Capitol" that should have engendered a "little Essay of mine justifying the writing in a Newspaper", and a query—"What are the Likenesses & what the Differences between France under Bonaparte & Rome under Augustus" or "Greece. . .under Alexander"—which his essays of September and October would attempt to answer.[2] But his first response to the elevation of Bonaparte was the fascinated, ambivalent memorandum: "A *Throne* the Δος πoυ στω of Archimedes— Poet Bonaparte—Layer out of a World-garden—".[3]

The Greek words ("Give me a fulcrum [and I will move the world]") evidently apply, as Kathleen Coburn observes, to Bonaparte's ambitions, but the next part of the note develops the concept of the commanding genius as poet—with a striking empathic equivalence of Bonaparte to Coleridge. A suitable gloss comes from an exercise in self-observation made by Coleridge a bit later when he was "sitting by the Eskdale side" looking at lonely mountain tarns: "O for wealth to *wood* these Tarns. . . . Bear witness for me, what thoughts I wandered about with—if ever I imagined myself a conqueror, it was always to bring peace—but mostly turned away from these thoughts to more humane & peaceable Dreams".[4]

What world-gardening a Coleridge–Bonaparte might have decreed! It is tempting to speculate the derivation from this Archimedean standing-place, πoυ στῶ, of the new Coleridge signature announced three months later as a motto of non-apostasy: "῎Εστησε signifies—*He hath stood*—which in these times of apostacy from the principles

[1] To George Coleridge 3 Jun 1802: *CL* II 803.

[2] *CN* I 1170, 1171, 1174, 1186, 1191, 1195. The note on the Geese is dated Apr–May by Kathleen Coburn; the essay is mentioned 20 Oct (*CL* II 876). What he had in mind can be seen in *Friend* No 4 (*CC*) II 62–3, where the image of the geese as newspaper writers is related to the concept of Bonaparte as the emperor (Charlemagne now) to be warned against. The geese must chatter, even though, for example, every "Paragraph in the Morning Post during the Peace of Amiens. . .warning the Nation. . .was a punishable Libel", i.e. upon Napoleon.

[3] *CN* I 1166.

[4] *CN* I 1214.

of Freedom, or of Religion in this country, & from both by the same persons [i.e. Bonaparte and followers] in France, is no unmeaning Signature, if subscribed with humility, & in the remembrance of, Let him that stands take heed lest he fall—."[1]

In September Coleridge returned to the editorial pages, heralded by a sunrise hymn and love poems, and a rapid fire of epigrams. In a series of essays in late September and on 2 October he formulated the hazards of the uneasy peace by comparing the Roman and French Republics and depicting Bonaparte as having changed from an Augustus to a Julius Caesar with touches of a Tiberius. Here Coleridge writes not as one taking heed lest he fall but as one viewing with alarm. The anxiety expressed in the recent series on Addington, lest the British Friends of Freedom descend the slippery path of accommodation to anti-Jacobinism, is replaced by anxiety about the menace of French philosophy.[2] It is not so much that Coleridge's view of Bonaparte changed: the appearance of Bonaparte also changed, as the emergent reality of French power looked very different from the fond image of a France subsiding into commercial and political insignificance. It is that Coleridge now drew more reactionary conclusions from the reappraisal. Fox and Sheridan, remaining much firmer against anti-Jacobinism, moved toward support of an effective war of defence. Coleridge, while scorning Fox for allying with Grenville, moved toward Pitt—and Addington.

Coleridge was emboldened rather than disturbed by praise of his Comparison essays from the extremist Peltier. Coupled with enthusiasm from Stuart and admiration from the inescapable Mackintosh "and many others you dont know" (including a gentleman at the Attorney General's table who told Mackintosh "there had been much true old English Spirit in the M. Post of late") it convinced him that he was speaking for "men of all parties".[3] "These are almost *your own* words", Stuart exclaimed, and Coleridge moved swiftly to cross his Rubicon. In the first of two essays (5 and 9 October) probing the transiency of Bonaparte's military despotism, he argued in favour of Royalism in "the language of...an artful Royalist"; in the second he seemed himself to speak as the Royalist, urging the advantages of family pride and hereditary nobility (the aristocratic implications of "I griev'd for Bonaparte"). Between these

[1] To William Sotheby 10 Sept 1802: *CL* II 867. C had begun using the signature in 1801.

[2] See esp 25 Sept 1802, below.

[3] Stuart to C 23, 29 Sept 1802 (App B, below); C to RS [8] Jan 1803: *CL* II 912.

essays he spelled out calmly (8 October) the circumstances favouring "Mr. Pitt's Return to Office" in due time. He turned next to the circumstances favouring a "Return of the Bourbons at the Present Time" (12 October), promising vaguely to get around some day to the *dis*advantages. Instead, on 14 October, he supplied a revised version of his ode of recantation, now titled *France*, and the war-whoop passages from his *Fears in Solitude*.

These he followed a week later with a definitive essay on Jacobinisms and on his own brand of anti-Jacobinism. And by this time he had wrought his public indignation to the pitch of Burke's a decade earlier and was ready to unleash it upon Fox in two letters signed in his bold new signature. These Stuart had begged him to write, yet was "afraid to publish" until Coleridge allowed him to soften "the reprehensory parts" with "a few conciliatory Passages".[1] From then on the parties and the nations proceeded to accelerate their verbal warfare and to convert it to military conflict with little further public assistance from the Watchman who had Stood.

The writer of these paragraphs was determined, nevertheless, to consider all matters in a purely "speculative point of view" (6 January 1803). War, Mr Pitt's return, the accomplishment of a Bourbon restoration—these were simply eventualities "too probable" to admit of much doubt. Had Bonaparte (that commanding genius) "played an unwise game" after all? Although the dictatorship had failed to "die away into a free Republic", was it nevertheless proving to be "as transient as that of Rome was durable"? The hopes of the essays of 1799–1800 were now disowned as "speculations" that had "formed no part of *our* hopes"; the fears were claimed as prophecies now "fully verified" by the course of events.

Gone, however, was the old refrain that French fury would subside if left alone. Despite the judicious tone of the October essays, there is a battle hymn in their "speculations". The writer who pictures Bonaparte's empire as swiftly tumbling and who predicts that the restored monarchy will "necessarily" be pacific and "magnanimous" (9 October) is in effect tempting his English readers to interfere in the process rather than resign themselves to a peace now daily ridiculed. The reporter of "speculations" upon Pitt's return (8 October) seems to have settled in his own mind for Pitt as the necessary man of the coming hour: he explains very convincingly the wisdom of avoiding all precipitancy—of appearances. Napoleon

1 "...only a few conciliatory Passages [are] Stuartian, but all the reprehensory parts *I myself I*—" C declared to RS. Ibid.

must be permitted to take the fatal step by himself; yet *goading him* is now recommended, and turning away from Fox and peace is all but stipulated.

In all these essays there is a lapse of precise memory about earlier hopes and avowals, and there is an appearance of candour in the raising of serious questions *con* as well as *pro*—combined with postponement and evasion of all the cautionary questions. Nevertheless, or perhaps consequently, these essays are full of vigour. Throwing caution to the winds was a heady activity; Coleridge now wrote easily, swiftly, *con brio*, never with surer power. "I dedicate three days in the week to the Morning Post", he reported proudly to Tom Wedgwood, "and shall hereafter write for the far greater part such things as will be of as permanent Interest, as any thing I can hope to write.... My Comparison of the French with the Roman Empire was very favorably received."[1] On his thirtieth birthday he recorded "...great columns of misty Sunshine travelling along the lake.... No clouds on the tops of the mountains—I meditating on Switzerland, & writing the Letters to Mr Fox—Eleven in the morning—".[2]

Although he continued to indicate the *expediency* of supporting Addington, his positive attention now shifted to Pitt (a dramatic peripeteia managed so quietly that Sara Coleridge did not notice it), whom he now credited with abilities and with a purposive detachment that reveal where Coleridge's bets—if not his deepest sympathies—were now placed. He now accepted without much trace of irony Pitt's definition of Bonaparte as child of Jacobinism, and he approved, for a second war, Pitt's previously scarified aims of reducing France "within due bounds" and restoring the Bourbons. When French military pressure on the new Helvetian Republic made it a good time to republish the Ode in which groans from "bleak Helvetia's icy caverns" reverse the poet's sympathies, his revisions transforming *Recantation* to *France: An Ode* included elimination of the already truncated fifth stanza, with its allusion to "the present Ministry and their supporters" as creatures "Loath'd as th' Hyaenas". Pitt's ministry had fallen, but the poem's original balance could have been preserved by some form of declaration that the friend of Liberty refused to "combine" with the war party. Instead a general condemnation of rebels was substituted, applicable to English as well as French Jacobins.[3]

In the *Morning Post* of 14 October, immediately after the Ode, an

[1] 20 Oct 1802: *CL* II 876.

[2] *CN* I 1252.

[3] The four lines beginning "The Sensual and the Dark rebel in vain".

excerpt from *Fears in Solitude*, somewhat revised, urged Englishmen to hurl the invading foe into the sea and then repent having stung him to frenzy: a most curious message for a time of peace, and from the *Morning Post*, which this autumn seemed, more cautiously than Peltier and Cobbett but as pointedly, intent on stinging Bonaparte to a new frenzy expected to culminate in a new invasion. Anti-Jacobins of England and of France must now unite to topple the Jacobin tyrant, and in this connexion the immediate purpose of Coleridge's threshold-passing essay "Once a Jacobin Always a Jacobin" was to support the major assumption that the recantation now required of former English and French Jacobins was really possible. This cleared the way for his fierce "Letters to Mr Fox", calculated to convert, or to isolate, the chief representative of English Jacobinism (according to the second definition in "Once a Jacobin").

Before printing these, Stuart published, on 30 October, a *Sonnet to Mr. Coleridge, on reading, in The Morning Post, his beautiful and affecting ode, entitled, "France"*—a tribute signed by "Hafiz" (Stott), Stuart's most faithful poetaster. The sonnet is marked by the paper's increasingly hypocritical approval of the peace. Coleridge's "Tremendous Minstrelsy" was soul-piercing and inflammatory, said the sonneteer, and "it had no dying fall"; but "no!—great Minstrel, cease!" This was not a time to sing songs "to rouse the world": the French were submissive to the yoke and would not fight for their own or Helvetian freedom. Hafiz transparently implied that the French and Swiss *ought* to be rising to throw off the yoke and that such stirring minstrelsy as Coleridge's ought not to be wasted, as the official peace compelled it to be.

The double letter to Mr. Fox is called a "letter of hysterical anger" by one of Fox's biographers and has been compared in its shock effect to *The Watchman* essays on Fasts and on Modern Patriotism. But there is no reason to suppose Coleridge either hysterical or angry in his decision to administer an unpleasant but strategically necessary shock to the Friends of Freedom by a frontal attack on their long-revered leader, who seemed committed to peace at any price. Debates in the newly elected Parliament would begin toward the end of November, and the time was ripe to set forth the conclusions toward which Coleridge's essays of August and September and Stuart's paragraphs (especially of 8, 10, and 18 September) had been driving: the repudiation of peace and Fox, who now bore the taint of a conciliatory visit to Napoleon in Paris. The attack was needed to facilitate the transition from peace to war by the Addington administration—and the change from ridicule to vindication of that administration by the *Morning Post* and such independent Foxites as the *Post*'s most congenial political hero and adviser, Sheridan. Stuart had responded, with his paper's circulation, to Coleridge's initial salvoes in this campaign. Yet he truly did not wish to "go to Newgate", and his letter of 29 September shows him softening "Tyrant" to "Despot", "considering" every passage with alerted prudence, and keeping in touch with Sheridan and Attorney General Perceval for the day's definition of "the Liberty of the Press". Coleridge may exaggerate the length of time Stuart kept the Letters, "afraid to publish them".[1] But Stuart may have resisted efforts to draw all his editorial forces into the same exposed position as that invested by ΕΣΤΗΣΕ. Afterward he made considerable further use of Coleridge's arguments; yet he found it necessary to write a series of lengthy apologetics (beginning 27 November) to deny having said irritating things of France or having attacked Fox ("we have said nothing in regard to France which we were not bound to state upon the principles Mr. Fox has inculcated")—and to deny that his paragraphs were serving the interests of a war party, with a saucy suggestion (13 December) that Fox's friends ought to patronise the *Morning Post* now if only to show that "they can *endure* the Liberty of the Press as well as applaud its adulation".

Charles Lamb, who had looked forward to "S. T. C.'s letter to Mr. Fox" and was dismayed by its combination of humble expressions and arrogant charges,[2] represents the *Morning Post* reader who had not felt moved to recantation. There was, indeed, an embarrassed and embarrassing tortuosity about some of the argument. At one point all political action is defined as Jacobinism, yet Fox is scolded for having failed to be militant as well as vigilant against English Jacobinism all along: Fox should have taken active steps to suppress the Societies before declaring them harmless. But Fox's greatest failure is represented as his not having noticed that the Revolution was *French*. At the root of this charge is Coleridge's now utter detestation and devaluation of Bonaparte, no longer a genius but only a provincial upstart.

In redefining his own position Coleridge draws upon his past experience of political ideas and men, his own associations with "the

[1] Stuart "kept them 3 weeks—afraid to publish them", C told RS (*CL* II 912). But C was still "writing the Letters" 20 Oct, while Stuart began announcing publication 1 Nov and published the first letter 4 Nov.

[2] *LL* I 329, 331–2.

associated Jacobins", but somehow recaptures only the moments when he was at odds with those who thought him a fellow-radical, selecting only a few negative instances out of a general context of positives. And in his presentation of arguments about the relations of France and England that he suggests Fox *ought* to have uttered, he somehow makes the new arguments up out of things that Fox and he himself *did* say, aimed the other way round.

Fox was soon told of Coleridge's attack but declined to read it. In the opening debate in the new Parliament, in late November, he asserted that "the cry for war" was "not the real cry of the people of England" and deplored the tendency of newspaper publishers of both countries to inflame England and France into a state of war "for the purpose of selling their papers, or to raise the merit of their journals". He conceded that a war of newspapers was better than a war of armies: "Let the Moniteur and the Morning Post, the Times, and the Argus, go on in their hostile language, it is easier to be endured than a war of bayonets." The reporter for the *Morning Post*, or its editor, however, narrowed the reference, quoting Fox as saying: "let paper contend with paper, let the *Moniteur* fight it out with *The Morning Post*...". Indeed, from the *Post*'s tendency throughout the year to assume credit for the lion's share of the verbal war effort, it was almost inevitable that Coleridge should suppose that Fox alluded exclusively to the *Morning Post* when, in the final debate on a declaration of war in May 1803, Fox reiterated his criticism of the "violent abuse" in the journals for having largely accelerated the present crisis. Ultimately Coleridge would have it that, on the one side, Fox held him personally responsible for the war and, on the other, Bonaparte sought his arrest when he incautiously travelled into his dominions in 1806.[1]

Coleridge left it to Stuart to continue the paper war, but in "Our Future Prospects", a New Year's prophecy, 6 January 1803, in a series of metaphors of dynamics and balance he put a keystone into the arch his essays of the previous season had been constructing. We have observed his interest in the fulcrum by which a poet or a Bonaparte might move the world—and in his own, precarious, power to stand while others fell. In an image deceptive with the modesty of the journalist who feels his power as imponderable but real and who can variously estimate it as decisive in a vast balance or as nil, Coleridge stands as the gentian daring to grow within a few steps of the glacier, a glacier of "never-melted ice" that yet, when melting,

[1] Cf *WL* (*M* rev) I 52, and see below, 9 Nov 1802 n 12.

sends torrents rushing into the Valley (*Hymn Before Sunrise*, 11 September 1802). The gentian-journalist's rôle is that of "venturing near, and...leaning over the brink of the grave", now usually the brink of war. Innocent enough—though consider the poppy beside the skull in *Osorio* v 33. But less innocent is the grain of sand (or the shouting voice) that precipitates an avalanche. An image-cluster of fulcrum, melting snow, and avalanche is functional in most of the political essays of 1802 and climactic in "Our Future Prospects". Coleridge is fascinated by the incredible notion that his nearly weightless words may tip the teetering balance.

The potential avalanche is at first Napoleonic France, which he probes for the possibilities of swift shifts of mass ("Affairs of France" 5, 9 October) after having made comparison to the slower dynamics of Roman empires ("Comparison" 21 September–2 October). France has been "precipitated" into a slavery that in turn will "undermine her false power". The genius of English freedom, watching with "calm and dreadful" force in the "eye" (somewhat gentian-like, taking its bright spot of blue as an eye), has somehow blown up Bonaparte's navy "into the air", and with "a few squibs" England's newspapers can keep the First Consul in great alarm. The precariousness of the balance gives the squib enough power to be an effective "infernal machine" (29 September). In another image Bonaparte's precarious position is that of "an isthmus of Darien, beat upon by the two oceans of Royalism and Republicanism" (2 October). And there is frequent reference to the "foundations" of power, to power "evenly balanced", and to apparent force and potential "counterpoise".

Fortunes at the lowest ebb can return "in a head, and like a wall of waters". The French might have a king "and yet not lose a grain of sand from the weight of [their] present influence". But the French government is built on wind as against one built "on social rights, that is, hereditary rank, property". Since property is the "grand basis" of power, the English (unless they "stumble at the threshold") may easily stand forth and repel the French (if they do invade). In the essays of October and the letters to Fox, the appeal is to the English to exert decisive influence upon the dynamics of France chiefly by refusing to accept its "stupendous" appearance as truly monumental.

The author of "Our Future Prospects" does not wish to incur "the charge of wishing to accelerate the renewal of hostilities"; yet nations (and journalists) cannot "continue always quiet and unconcerned spectators". Within Coleridge's own "sagacity" there is a struggle over the crucial difference between the merely watching eye (of the gentian) and the voice, capable, however small, of swelling the war-whoop.

Nations cannot continue quiet, because France has weakened the balance of nations: "What she removed from the scale against her, she has applied to augment her own preponderance...". Yet, while he points to the "resources for restoration of [the] balance", a coalition of nations "to arrest the progress" of France, Coleridge does not suggest putting in these counter-weights. A simple "gust of Jacobinism was sufficient to overthrow the stupendous monument" of the first Constitution (4 November), and other gusts may now topple Bonaparte. Coleridge is the quiet eye watching the inevitable processes of gravitation: "The mis-shapen mass of snow...accumulating and accelerating in its progress" reaches a "limit". "The same law that hurried it from its elevated situation...conducts it to the spot where its impelling force is to be exhausted" and it *does* melt "before a milder temperature".

Reasoning in this kind of metaphor, Coleridge and his opponent Charles Fox might have been in full agreement. Let the genial eye of England stay the ambition of France. Indeed, Coleridge ends on the note of the sagacious observer surveying "with wonder and admiration" but not "terror and dismay" the terminating effects of "a political eruption". Nevertheless, the metaphor is overruled by the argument—that "tame submission" must itself have limits; that even "cautious powers" cannot for ever keep "aloof from the horrors and operations of war". Since war is horrible, the writer shrinks from hastening its renewal; yet that wish appears to lie behind the whole composition.

WAR WITHOUT QUARTER

At the end of May 1803 England went to war with France. In the preceding months Stuart had moved about rather uncertainly, now in the van of those calling for firm measures and for support of the men who, at the hour, happened to be in the ministry; now ridiculing Addington; now righteously opposing war (over Malta); now vigorously pushing for war (over Egypt). At the breakdown of peace he could boast of having anticipated it: to think that last October "this Paper was accused of calling for war, because we spoke with indignation of the ambition and aggrandisements of Bonaparte"!

(25 March). But in general his paragraphs descended to the usual squabbling manner of the *Morning Post* without Coleridge, accompanied by a more craven sort of back-tracking than his, under fire.

The renewal of hostilities finally crystallised Stuart's position. It must also have led him to appeal to Coleridge and others for help, but from March to the end of June there was a dearth of serious political writing in the *Morning Post*. In July Stuart began a series of anonymous papers on the invasion supposedly threatened by France—which he must have been happy to interrupt on the 18th by the first essay of a signed series by Coleridge on "The Men and the Times".[1]

In a three-hour speech on 24 May, Fox had made a last-ditch effort to turn a vote of congratulation to ministers for going to war into a vote urging them to make peace.[2] It was a powerful speech that raised serious doubts that the war could be justified in terms of national defence. Indeed most of the offences and insults officially charged in evidence of French hostility had been trumped up: what the Grenvilles censured ministers for was that, during the Peace, they had failed to accumulate a sufficient tale of French offences to make a good *casus belli*. Napoleon, far from intending to push toward war with England, had been as surprised as Coleridge when the King's message came pounce down in March. What he had done in Switzerland, what seemed to be his "designs against Egypt, Syria, and the Greek islands", did not directly endanger Britain, Fox insisted. But these things signified the expansion of the French Empire, and the choice of what today would be called "preventive" war was made to destroy that empire before it grew still larger. It was this imbalance that Britain viewed with alarm.

It was the disparity between official and unofficial definitions of the crisis that led Coleridge in his July essay to stress "political" as well as "moral" reasons, that made him recognise Fox's speech as "the most powerful attack on the moral and political justice of the war", and that led him into the use of devices of debate that postponed the confrontation of Fox's bill of particulars—except in notes that were never used. In the second essay (20 August) he proposed to take up Fox's arguments "fairly" in his next—meanwhile briefly

[1] Announced 1 Jul, "a Series of Papers" headed "The Invasion" began with Nos I–IV on 2, 5, 7, 9 Jul; on 18 Jul "The Men and the Times" took precedence ("The Articles on the invasion shall be continued To-morrow"). On 8 Aug, however, the *M Post* was promising *both* "No. VI. of 'The Invasion', and No. II. of 'The Men and The Times'"; the "hard" line of the Invasion series was not being abandoned.

[2] Debrett (1803) III 379–82.

anticipating "the result of the whole" by casting his vote for war, careless "How ugly my Physician's face may be".[1]

His second essay must have been written before his walking tour of August. His never writing a third may be owing in part to Stuart's long delay in finding room for the second (the four-page newspaper was not designed to cope with a session of Parliament so extended as that of the summer of 1803) and in part to Stuart's having "sold and finally left the Morning Post in August"—or September.[2] Coleridge, returning to Keswick from his Scottish tour by 15 September, heard nothing from Stuart but soon noticed an alarming change in the newspaper. The leading paragraphs of 6 and 7 October predicted—and then recommended—"the principle of no quarter" to invading French armies, and even "indiscriminate slaughter" of the prisoners then in English jails if they should grow "turbulent".

Coleridge, profoundly shocked, expressed to Poole, who had asked for "more of the Men and the Times", his indignation and frustration at the turn things had taken:

> I have been, to use a mild word, agitated by two INFAMOUS atrocious Paragraphs in the Morning Post of Thursday & Friday last—I believe them to be Mackintosh's—*O that they were!* I would hunt him into Infamy.—I am now exerting myself to the utmost on this Subject.... Do write instantly on the subject of this *No Quarter*!———I have written twice to Stuart who still, I believe, superintends the paper in part—& can get no answer from him....[3]

It had been one thing to predict the return of the Bourbons and argue that Bonaparte must be fought in the name of humanity and on the principle of national expediency. It was another to be silenced and yet held responsible for bellicose editorials that brushed aside his basic moral assumptions of humane interest. "Many articles in the M. P. not mine are attributed to me. Very probably, those infamous articles may [be]...".

He had already been thought capable of the earlier series on "the

[1] The quotation from Suckling squints at two physicians, war and "Doctor" Addington.

[2] Stuart IX 488; cf *BL* ch 10 (1907) I 145.

[3] 14 Oct 1803: *CL* II 1016. One reader of the "unnatural and sanguinary suggestions" in the *M Post* sent a Swiss historian's "Character of the Empress Elizabeth of Austria" to Kirby's *Wonderful Museum* (later an outlet for C's articles on the Keswick Impostor) as the nearest historical precedent for "the temper and disposition which that paper inculcates" (I 402–6, probably the October issue; letter dated 10 Oct). This reader, signing as "A Lover of Mercy" (C himself perhaps?), focused, as C did, upon the person writing rather than on the newspaper, and sent his "Character" of the empress to the *Museum* as "a receptacle of *Remarkable Characters*...".

Invasion". (On 12 September Southey assured John Rickman, and himself: "Those vile 'Invasion' papers were not Coleridges, thank God!"[1]) The much fiercer, slaughter-proposing articles "really made Coleridge ill with vexation and anger. He is preparing", Southey reported, "an answer"—a project perhaps abandoned when Coleridge learned that the author was not Mackintosh.[2] The latter's replacement of Coleridge as the paper's political voice would indeed have been a bitter pill. By 9 August space was being given to a warlike speech by Mackintosh, and there were apparently good grounds to suspect that his influence on the *Morning Post* was increasing and was ministerial.[3] In the 1834 *Life of Mackintosh* (by William Wallace)[4]

[1] *S Letters* (Curry) I 328.

[2] RS to Charles Danvers, Wednesday [14 or, more probably, 21 Oct 1803]: *S Letters* (Curry) I 331. By the time of this letter C had discovered (and must soon have told RS) the author of the "damnable articles", presumably the new *M Post* editor, Dennis O'Bryen (1755–1832), on whose earlier career as a radical friend of Sheridan see Werkmeister (1967) passim. RS only hints at "the secret history of this mystery of iniquity. The author is Irish—there is reason to believe a rebel in his heart, hence a cursed and devilish manifesto designed to please and irritate the people here and to be actually serviceable to France." Two sentences later RS does not necessarily imply that he is speaking of the same person when he alludes to "the new Editor" of the *M Post* as lacking the "interest or liberality" to print "the poem I wrote upon poor Emmet". But then O'Bryen was not openly the editor in any case. See below, I cxvii/n 1.

It may be worth noting that Mackintosh himself, in a review of O'Bryen's pamphlet *Utrum Horum? The Government; or, the Country?* (1796) in *M Rev* XXI (Dec 1796) 403–14 (attribution by Wallace, and Nangle), had taken pains to suppress the rebel in O'Bryen. Toward the end of the review Mackintosh took upon himself "our peculiar duty, in reviewing the publications of the Friends of Liberty, to warn them against dishonouring their noble cause by any attempts at justifying, or even at palliating, those detestable enormities which have been perpetrated in its name [in the French Revolution]. It is from the Friends of Liberty that the strongest abhorrence of such enormities is naturally to be expected and justly to be required". It is the expected political irony that O'Bryen and Mackintosh should now have joined forces in advocating enormities in the name of national liberty.

[3] A year earlier, in Stuart's letters to C of Sept 1802 (App B), although he puts Mackintosh among the "coxcombs" paying adoration to Bonaparte, and although he is careful to indicate that Mackintosh examined C's article only *after* publication, one gets an uncomfortable impression that Mackintosh is concerning himself very closely with the political tone of the *M Post*, that Stuart through Mackintosh is keeping closely posted on the conversation at the Attorney General's table—and that C is meant to receive this impression.

[4] Wallace edited, and wrote the biographical notice in, the posthumous edition of Mackintosh's *History of the Revolution in England...with notices of the Life, Writings, and Speeches of Sir James Mackintosh*. See pp lvii–lviii. Nothing in the vaguer and wholly laudatory account by Mackintosh's son would contradict this tale, except the moral tone. The dates of appointment and knighting are found in *A Reg* for 1803.

it is asserted that Mackintosh "became a shareholder in the property of the Morning Post, and engaged to write in it at a yearly salary", presumably soon after his second marriage in 1798; that Pitt on going out of office in 1801 made "a written request or memorandum to the new Minister to provide for Mackintosh", at the request of Canning (who would have been in charge of relations with the press); that Addington "did not immediately comply" but that when hostilities were renewed in 1803 "the war and its policy were vindicated by Mackintosh in the columns of the Morning Post; and the Minister, now more sensible of his merit, offered him the vacant recordership of Bombay". He received the appointment on 22 November and "the honour of knighthood" a month later. But the whole transaction is clothed in mystery. As early as 7 October word reached Joseph Farington the diarist "that Stewart...informed Kemble that Government had purchased that paper...".[1] Stuart in 1838 admitted that "in the summer of 1803" Addington had sent him "a message of thanks...offering any thing I wished". And while stating "I declined the offer", Stuart continued cryptically: "The particulars of this affair are curious, important and honourable to all parties." It is striking that in another instalment of his remarks, apropos of claims that had been made for Mackintosh as responsible for the success of the *Morning Post*, "though with less reason even than for Coleridge", Stuart used the same language, as though hinting at another part of the same story: "Some day I may make a statement on that point; which, if I do, it will be curious, interesting, and honourable to Sir James."[2]

[1] Farington II 158. Later (II 250, 9 Jun 1804) Farington heard that "Cadell & Davis purchased the Morning Post from Stewart in 1803 for Mr. Addington" and that Dennis O'Bryen "now writes in that paper". This is as close as we get to the identification of the new editor; the only other new name, N. Byrne, is that of the printer.

The *M Post* had been in the pay of the Prince in the 1780's, and perhaps he had continued to keep some kind of hand on it, as he could have done through Sheridan or, as we might guess, through the mysterious "James Nott" whose name appears on the colophon as "publisher" as early as 1799. Up to 20 Sept 1803 the imprint reads "Printed by D. Stuart, and Published by J. Nott, 335 Strand". Beginning 21 Sept it reads "Printed by N. Byrne, and Published by J. Nott, No. 335, Strand".

[2] Stuart IX 578, X 126. As for Mackintosh's ultra-patriotism, C may have noticed the report in *M Post* 9 Aug 1803 of his speech to a corps of Volunteers: "They came forward to ...stand the foremost *in the imminent deadly breach*, to oppose their breasts, for a wall of defence, before all that was dear...all the zeal of the religion of patriotism...not a man among them who did not...the darling passion of his soul, actually to die for his country...By the blood of... Wallace and with Bruce...".

Half a year later C made note of a

Since we know that the new *Morning Post* almost immediately became, what *Punch* would later call it, "The Fawning Post", rhapsodic in appreciation of the "sublimity" of the Prince of Wales and dedicated to impressing the British nation with his qualifications for a military command,[1] we must assume that some sort of curious and honourable accommodation was arranged that satisfied the Prime Minister's desire for uncritical press support and the Prince's desire for a personal organ. The money was found to buy Stuart's retirement to the *Courier*—not very much, it seemed to Coleridge: "Stuart has sold the paper for 15000£—he netted 8000£ a year—it was scarcely 2 years' purchase"[2]—but the assumption was probably fallacious that Stuart had been netting anything like £8000 a year from advertising and daily sales: neither Crabb Robinson then nor Stuart's historian today, Lucyle Werkmeister, can believe that he grew rich on "the fair and mere mercantile produce of" journalism.[3] If his income was derived chiefly from stock-jobbery and other dealings unrelated to daily circulation, his shifting his base of operations to the *Courier* need not have meant a serious diminution in his annual "purchase". But it would, since the *Courier* was already competently edited by Street, have meant a great diminution in his need for Coleridge.[4]

---

further instance of Mackintosh's bloody-mindedness: "Duellists...true Assassins! Confute...Mackintosh's Defence of Duelling, as if it prevented Assassination". *CN* II 1971 (Mar 1804).

1 Addington could not satisfy Prinny's desire for a military command, but he could secure him leading paragraphs such as those headed "The Present Crisis" in *M Post* 3 Nov 1803, lauding first the "exemplary" conduct of King George, then, as "nearly of as much public importance", that of the "beloved Prince" "restricted to the simple military station of a Colonel of Dragoons" by "motives of State necessity" yet capable, in that capacity, of reminding "us of Caesar" and more: placing "himself on the point most exposed to attack, with his single regiment....His white plume, like that of Henry IV...a rallying point...".

2 To Poole 14 Oct 1803: *CL* II 1016, repeated in 1809, *CL* III 238. See also Werkmeister (1967) 339. I do not know where Hindle (p 84) picks up the figure of £25,000—perhaps out of thin air.

3 *CRB* I 170.

4 Stuart appears to have begun talking of selling the *M Post* in the autumn of 1802, for George Lane his assistant, in *G Mag* x 275–6, tells of turning down an invitation to edit the *British Press* and *Globe*, then learning "the very next day" that "Mr. Stuart was desirous to dispose of his paper". This was "nearly two months" before Lane accepted a second invitation, evidently some time before the launching of the new papers in Jan 1803. Werkmeister (1967) 339 seems to assume 1802 as the date of sale but gives no evidence.

GUILT AND WOE

In 1804 Stuart was helpful to Coleridge in London, persuaded him to write for the *Courier* some essays defending Addington against the coalition of the New and Old Oppositions, and finally introduced him to Sheridan—who "really did intend to take & introduce me to Addington"[1]—and possibly to the great man himself, for in 1807 Coleridge recalled that Addington had told him how valuable his *Morning Post* essays had been in 1801–3.[2] But the great Coleridgian ship, which had been ready in the essays of July and August 1803 "to embark on this stormy Sea of Politics", never received the editorial command to leave port.

Upon loss of access to the *Morning Post* he tried for a while to "whip & spur" himself to finish his work as a book. In his "birthday" memorandum of October 1803 he adjured himself not to allow Christmas to "pass without some thing having been done/—at all events to finish The Men & the Times, & to collect them & all my Newspaper Essays into one Volume...".[3] And in November he headed a list of "the Works that I have planned, in the order in which I wish to execute them", with: "The Men and the Times: & then absolutely to have done with all newspaper writing."[4] But despondency, night terrors, and a new variety of "gout" intensified by domestic strains laid him low.

That Coleridge would recoil from the bloody consequences of his recent advocacy of war, when their reality confronted him, was almost absolutely predictable. Yet there seemed no available alternative position to recoil toward.[5] An early reflection upon the war's renewal

[1] To RS 28 Mar 1804: *CL* II 1111–12. In London C was resolved to make use of any interest that could secure him a place in a warm Mediterranean island. He even "called on Sir James Mackintosh who offered me his endeavors to procure me a place under him in India" but retreated when Sir James assured C "*on his Honor—on his Soul!!!* (N.B. HIS Honor!!) (N.B. *HIS* Soul!!) that he was sincere." *CL* II 1041. Yet it was Mackintosh who put into C's head (*CL* II 1087) the idea of getting "some little place or other" at Malta by making use of "any sort of Interest with the Governor", Sir Alexander Ball.

[2] "I had Mr. Addington's Suffrage, as to the good produced by the Essays written in the Morning Post...together with my two letters to Mr. Fox". To Mary Cruikshank Sept 1807: *CL* III 27. The channel would have been Sheridan.

[3] *CN* I 1577.

[4] *CN* I 1646.

[5] Thelwall, visiting C and RS in Nov 1803, joined in an unenthusiastic discussion of "the *second* war", which "S. expressly stated, & C. tacitly admitted ...was only the *rump*, or necessary consequence of the first...". Marginal note on *BL* (1817) I 207. Burton R. Pollin and Redmond Burke "John Thelwall's Marginalia in a Copy of Coleridge's *Biographia Literaria*" *BNYPL* LXXIV (1970) 82.

was this notebook entry in the spring of 1803: "Tell Adam, the day after Abel's Death, in 4 square leagues 700,000 men shall be assembled. Possible?—and to murder each other!"[1] The summer's Scottish tour, with the Wordsworths and then alone, bore reminders that, on the one hand, the common people could still talk "of the French and the present times" in language that "most people would call Jacobinical",[2] but that, on the other, from the traumatic episode of his being "taken up for a spy & clapped into Fort Augustus", a writer's interest in fortifications was incongruous and suspect.[3] From dreams in which he was the victim of confused "Horror, Guilt & Woe, | My own or others", he would awake screaming to protest his mistaken identity:

> ...O wherefore this on *me*?
> Frail is my Soul...
> But free from Hate, & sensual Folly!
> To live belov'd is all I need...[4]

In the autumn he was a man ripe for oscillation—in a political climate that was hostile even to the entertainment of moral doubts about the slaying of prisoners. Coleridge might have succumbed to the purely physical and psychological impact of opium withdrawal symptoms in another harsh winter, but his moral sensitivity to the pressures of Duty during what seemed at last a *real* threat of French invasion was excruciatingly acute. In October the execution of Robert Emmet elicited a wild apologia, in a letter to his new aristocratic friends the Beaumonts, because in Emmet's career he thought he saw what his own might have been, extrapolating from 1795. Recollecting "the unwise & unchristian feelings, with which at poor Emmett's Age *I* contemplated all persons of *your* rank in Society", he confessed that while he had always "detested Revolutions in my calmer moments" he had often "aided the Jacobins, by witty sarcasms & subtle reasonings & declamations full of genuine feeling against all Rulers & against all established Forms!" "Poor young Emmett", being the same sort, had seized this agitating moment of renewed war to attempt a rebellion—and had been hanged! "O if our Ministers had saved him...for the next 10 years of his Life, we *might* have had in him a sublimely great man, we assuredly sh[ould] have had in him a good man, & heart & soul an *Englishman*!"[5] Coleridge was also

[1] *CN* I 1372.
[2] *DWJ* 267; see *CL* I 1469 and n.
[3] To RS [11] Sept 1803: *CL* II 982; see *CN* I 1491.
[4] To RS [11] Sept 1803: *CL* II 984.
[5] 1 Oct 1803: *CL* II 1000–3.

pained by the question of shouldering a musket. Wordsworth, back from Scotland, at once enrolled in the Grasmere Volunteers. But it was Coleridge's "deepest conviction", he confessed to Sir George Beaumont, that there was "no real Danger that threatens G. Britain as an Empire". Napoleon would indeed invade: "the Miscreant" was so "mad with Hatred of Englishmen as Englishmen" that he would disgorge what troops he could to spread "Bloodshed & pitiless Devastation over particular Tracts" even though hopeless of conquest. Coleridge, with his "eyes ever & anon on the Map", allowed himself to be "haunted with anxieties concerning" Beaumont's personal safety, and thus by a subtle extension concerning his own. Persons who were not "possessed of military Science" ought to keep away from the more dangerous Tracts. If, after all, the French *did* prove a real danger, he trusted that he "should not be found in my Study if the French remained even 10 days on British Ground. But merely to place one's self close by the Sluice-gate of the Stream, with no chance of doing any good that ten thousand cannot do better than you, 10,000 men, who can do nothing else, on whom their Country have no other Call, and Posterity no Claims——but I write in pain—my nature turns away with Terror from the Idea of appearing obtrusive or presumptuous to you."[1]

Little wonder that "Guilt & Woe" filled his dreams; that he felt he ought to spur himself to do something that he alone could do, for his Country and for Posterity; and that as his "Illnesses" increased and he became increasingly desperate at "their strange dependence on the state of my moral Feelings and the State of the Atmosphere conjointly", he should stake everything on an escape to Madeira or, as it turned out, to Malta (curiously symbolic as having been the *casus belli*) in "a Persuasion, strong as Fate, that from 12 to 18 months' Residence & perfect Tranquillity in a genial Climate would send me back to dear old England, a sample of the first Resurrection".[2] Like Bonaparte's in 1799, Coleridge's resurrection took the prospective form of a return from the Mediterranean. His flight to it, however, was a recoil from Duty and from Journalism—to say nothing of abstruse research or the unfinished *Christabel.* He was not in a mood conducive to actual progress in the completion of "The Men & the Times"—or in the desirable project of collecting all his Newspaper Essays into a Volume.

1 [17] Oct 1803: *CL* II 1016–17.

2 To Matthew Coates 5 Dec 1803: *CL* II 1021.

2. COLERIDGE AND *THE COURIER*

What I most desiderate in the Courier, in [truth], is steadiness & consistency.—It is an immense [tru]st—& we are morally answerable in proportion. I certa[inly] would always *lean* toward the Government for m[any] reasons besides the aversion, we both have, to their only effectual Rivals or possible Substitutes—

—Coleridge to Stuart [18 January 1809][1]

COLERIDGE'S 140-odd contributions to the *Courier* span fourteen years, from February 1804 to March 1818. There might have been hundreds more—full ninety of these fall within one five-month period in 1811—had access to its pages been as free to Coleridge as he wished. For if he promised more than he wrote, he wrote or at least drafted many more articles than were printed; and if he sometimes felt private dismay at its "venal" reputation, he usually leaned in the direction of its editorial policy. If this leaning impressed Hunt and Hazlitt and Cobbett as servility, his inclination to think things out (and at length) appeared to the managing editor to be a luxury the *Courier* could seldom afford. The proprietary editor found it simpler, for a while, to help Coleridge print his own philosophising political journal than to make room for him on the *Courier* staff, though when *The Friend* failed he did that for a season. Before and after 1811–12 Coleridge's identifiable assistance to the paper consisted of a few essays, scattered occasional paragraphs, and four series of Letters (in 1809, 1814, 1816, and 1817).

COLERIDGE AND THE MALTA YEARS

When Daniel Stuart, in the autumn of 1803, yielded his proprietorship in the *Morning Post* by the "honourable" and mysterious arrangement whereby it became a government paper attentive to the Prince of Wales,[2] he turned his attention to his evening paper, the once Jacobin *Courier*,[3] and obtained Coleridge's assistance as soon as he could enlist it, early in 1804. Coleridge then spent some time at the *Courier* office, and although his chief purpose in London was to seek a restorative post abroad, he seems to have assisted Stuart

[1] BM Add MS 34046 f 69; torn, but with decipherable remnants hitherto inaccurately or incompletely transcribed; cf *CL* III 168.

[2] See above, I cxvii–cxviii.

[3] See above, I lxix and lxxxiv. By 1805 RS considered the *Courier* "abominably ministerial" and Stuart to have all but "sold body and soul to the Devil". *S Letters* (Curry) I 391.

with half a dozen editorial paragraphs[1] and to have written as many more himself, including one in praise of Sheridan and three in vindication of the Addington administration (not without giving these privately a somewhat mocking designation).[2] He also seems to have helped Stuart with materials for a sequel to his 1802 Letters to Fox (six Letters signed Sidney beginning 22 March).[3] And he wrote one of the "Volunteer Essays" he promised.[4]

When Coleridge sailed for Malta, with assistance from Stuart,[5] it must have been understood between them that he was to send intelligence and comment from the Mediterranean. His first letter (Gibraltar 21 April) was chiefly personal, but he promised subsequent letters "better worth the postage"[6] and asked to "have Cobbett & the Courier sent" to him, perhaps already thinking of a series of Letters attacking Cobbett as "A Political Harlequin" such as those launched the following winter.[7] His second, from Malta 6 July, written when he had recovered health and spirits, expressed a desire for the editor's opinion about the fall of Addington and the return of Pitt and enclosed "some Sybilline Leaves" for Stuart's use. In confidence, Coleridge was now in service to the *de facto* Governor of Malta, Sir Alexander Ball, as "a sort of diplomatic Understrapper".[8] His first assignment was to "dilate and dress" for the ministry in London (1) "A Political Sketch of the Views of the French in the Mediterranean" from materials supplied by Ball and other associates.[9] The "Leaves" hastily transcribed for Stuart had been written "for Sir A. B." but could be taken as "*my Ideas*" if put into other words. They took almost three months to reach London.[10]

1 See App A, below.

2 "Vindiciae Addingtonianae", suggesting the despised Mackintosh's *Vindiciae Gallicae*. See above. Was it perhaps for these that Stuart said Sheridan intended to introduce C to Addington? See C to RS 28 Mar 1804: *CL* II 1112.

3 See App A, below.

4 To Rickman [15 Feb 1804], [28 Feb 1804]: *CL* II 1063, 1075.

5 Stuart put credit at C's disposal and took care of his affairs in England. *CL* II 1114, 1144, 1168, 1174.

6 *CL* II 1135. Sultana (pp 125, 148) interprets this letter as transmitting to Stuart "particulars of" some naval accidents reported in the *Courier* of 24 May; but the *Courier* particulars, attributed to "Philadelphia Papers", are not in C's letter. (Neither is the report Sultana cites of "a rupture between England and Spain".)

7 See 8 Jan 1805, App A, below.

8 *CL* II 1146; see Sultana pp 159ff for the story of C's employment by Ball.

9 Sultana p 159, quoting a letter of 4 Jul 1804 from Ball to Granville Penn. Sultana's work enables us to recover much of C's Mediterranean years and to locate some of the surviving fragments of his official and journalistic papers. Apparently no copy of "A Political Sketch" survives, but Sultana (p 164) finds what must have been its leading ideas in Ball's letter to Penn.

10 *CL* II 1146.

Meanwhile Coleridge prepared three more papers for Ball in July: (2) a paper on relations with Algiers,[1] (3) a sequel to Ball's earlier "Political Sketch", concentrating on the importance of Malta,[2] and (4) a sequel to that, on the importance of Egypt.[3] In October he prepared a paper (5) on the importance of Sicily.[4] For Stuart he seems to have prepared variant drafts of all but the Algiers paper, apparently as series of Letters, which he refers to as "Letters to you on Sicily and Egypt" and as a "not unimportant packet respecting Sicily, Egypt, and Africa, directed to you, & after your perusal, to Sir G. Beaumont".[5]

Stuart, on receipt of the July letter and its "Sybilline Leaves" in late September, printed a personal notice of Coleridge's health and (discreetly) his "visit to Sir A. Ball", and seems to have begun to put their "Ideas" into his own words. On 4 October he echoed editorially the Ball–Coleridge view of the importance of Malta and spoke of an article "we had prepared" on British policy in the Mediterranean. But news of a naval victory forced a postponement "till to-morrow", actually for ever.[6]

Six months later Stuart salvaged a witticism from a letter of Cole-

[1] See Sultana pp 160–1, 187n. C kept the original draft, a ms in the hands of Ball and his departing private secretary, Francis Laing, with C's "interlinear and marginal revisions"—now VCL F 14.2. See App B, below. We can see that C did "dress" and trim the account but only once "dilate" it, slightly and not substantively. As it stands, the Algiers paper would scarcely have served the *Courier* in any case.

[2] Written 13 Jul 1804; Sultana pp 170–1, 216. C's own draft was used in *Friend* No 27; see below, I cxxix/3.

[3] Sultana (pp 174–5) refers confusingly to four papers as "it": the original memorial written for Ball, which is lost; a "version of it", which Sultana has valuably traced, in the Nelson papers (BM Add MS 34932 ff 239ff); a version in letter form for the *Courier*, now lost; and C's rough ms "Observations on Egypt" (BM Egerton MS 2800 ff 118–24), long known to Coleridgians, double the length of the Nelson version but not in letter form. See App B, below.

[4] Sultana (pp 195, 207–9) identifies as C's notes for this paper the two pages edited as *CN* II 2261; he dates them c 10 Oct 1804, from echoes of a paper by G. F. Leckie here and in C's first letter home on return to Malta from Syracuse and Leckie; the physical facts of the notebook make a November date more probable. The Sicily ms among C's Malta papers (VCL F 14.4) is identified by Sultana (p 222 nn 11, 12) as drafted in 1801 or 1802 by Leckie and in his hand; the conjectural inscription on a flyleaf "?A despatch of Sir A. Ball's in part composed by S. T. C. while acting as Public Sec. at Malta" is apparently mistaken on all counts.

[5] 30 Apr and 1 May 1805: *CL* II 1165, 1167. On 22 Oct 1804 (*CL* II 1149–50) C had described "the Pacquet" as letters Stuart might publish; in retrospect C seems to lump together his political letters for Stuart and "my fine Travels addressed to Sir George Beaumont" (*CL* II 1159–60); perhaps both were meant for publication, at least in pamphlet form.

[6] See editorial notices of 24 Sept and 4 Oct 1804 (below), discovered by Sultana.

ridge to Southey, for the *Courier* of 28 March 1805.[1] But by 30 April Coleridge learned that his "large, and (forgive my vanity!) rather important" packet of Letters had been destroyed in quarantine at Gibraltar, because the bearer had died of the plague, and another set had been "thrown over board from the Arrow...on being close chaced".[2] These losses from the fortunes of war have obscured the extent and assiduity of Coleridge's journalistic activities during his first months in Malta. Some notes and drafts survive but have never been published, while a further series of Letters, drafted by Charles William Pasley but bearing unmistakable signs of Coleridge's dilating and dressing, a series of four Letters opposing the idea of relinquishing Malta for the tiny island of Lampedusa, did get published in the *Courier*, in August 1805, but have only recently been recognised.[3]

The political ideas transmitted as his own were somewhat new to Coleridge; yet he did not modify his Malta views when he printed in *The Friend* of 1810 his draft of Ball's third paper, the sequel to the first.[4] The evidence supports Sultana's interpretation that Coleridge left England with a sense only of the negative importance of Malta and Egypt, as strategically dangerous in French hands, and that he acquired from Ball and G. F. Leckie, English consul at Syracuse, the idea of their political importance for British conquest and colonisation. The fourth paper survives in an early, prolix rough draft and a later, polished version that was sent to Ball's friend Lord Nelson, plus an Appendix and some tangential Notes that Coleridge retained.[5] In the first draft, the official paper advocates preventing and, ultimately, pre-empting the French occupation of Egypt. Economically the argument is for turning to the cheap labour of Egypt to feed Europe, just as the Romans were fed by the ancestors of the present Egyptian peasantry, and in preference to the more hazardous economy of the "Slave-Colonies" of the West Indies. Coleridge detested slavery, but the calculations of the "Observations on Egypt" are

[1] See *CL* II 1164 (2 Feb 1805) and text, 28 Mar 1805, below; Sultana's discovery.

[2] To Stuart 30 Apr 1805: *CL* II 1165.

[3] See App A, 10 Aug 1804, below.

[4] *Friend* Nos 22 and 27 (*CC*) II 304–8, 368–9; see Sultana (though his references are confusing) 171, 216. Other Malta items in *The Friend* that C may have intended originally for the *Courier* are "A Letter...from an American Officer..." in No 15 (*CC*) II 202–5 (I 254–8 and 254n) and the "Anecdote of Buonaparte" that follows it in each edition, (*CC*) I 205 (II 258–9). Items among C's surviving Malta papers in VCL that Sultana suggests as possibly intended for Stuart are copies that C made (in Jan 1805) of two letters from Robert Lamb of 28 Oct and 30 Nov 1804 (pp 262–3) and a copy made in Aug 1805 of a deposition of alleged corruption in a Malta dockyard (p 353).

[5] See below, App B.

those of a master-race economist. The fellaheen, "docile even to lameness wherever Power is firmly and at the same time humanely exercised. . . might be induced to perform. . . all the work of the colonial Slaves without the expence of their yearly importation" (f 243). The profits of this humane firmness, "a much clearer surplus", a "more rapid and regular return of Capital", would support a standing army, as those from less docile and better clothed and housed European labour would not. But why a standing army, abhorrent to freeborn Englishmen? Obviously to hold Egypt and—the thought slips out parenthetically—to bring in quickly "all the fruitful parts" of Arabia.[1]

Presumably the lost version intended for Stuart, or the fuller and more soberly reasoned one promised him in 1806, would have made a similar advocacy. Yet the deduction Sultana makes, that "as a political journalist" Coleridge "was now committed to the cause of imperialism. . .",[2] neglects the coil of resistance lurking in any Coleridgian commitment. And Sultana looks for Coleridge's own ideas in the passages that are unique in the early draft, closest to Ball's dictation (having mistaken it for a later), instead of in the

[1] The possibly Coleridgian enthusiasm of this seizure of oases appears in his Appendix to "Observations on Egypt" (see App B, below). Perhaps to speak of C's imperialism is only a harsher way of saying, "Politically he came to believe in an enlightened but expansionist colonial policy for Britain, based on the economic and cultural development of territories colonized" (Kathleen Coburn "Poet into Public Servant" *Trans RS of Canada* 3rd ser LIV—1960—9). Yet it is well to have the details. The Mediterranean colonists (and surely those of the East as well as West Indies) were to be primarily overseers and men of capital. The enlightened view was that slaves, being "degraded Savages", must not be given the freedom of "enlightened" men but kept in hand by "adscription to the soil" (see "Observations" [*O*] footnote). Expansion meant seizing sources of corn and fruit; cultural development allowed some legal rights but continuance of economic inequality: the "productive labour [of the Egyptian Peasantry] giving a much clearer surplus than can possibly be drawn from that of an European" the game would be up if Egyptian peasants developed a taste for the "Dress, Houses and Utensils" of the European.

[2] See below, App B, "Observations on Egypt": Appendix, and Sultana pp 128–9, 174, 177–8; also 308, in which C's "imperialist ideas" are found echoed by RS: "This country [Britain] is strong enough to conquer, and populous enough to colonise." Sultana (p 200) describes Leckie as "a ruthless and unscrupulous imperialist with a passion for Machiavelli" with an aim of annexing Sicily "to England in the teeth of the official policy"; on p 258 he further defines C's "new role of propagandist for imperialism".

Sultana unfortunately gets the two extant drafts of "Observations on Egypt" (one previously unknown) in reverse of chronological order and also confuses them with missing and hypothetical drafts. An attempt is made below (App B) to unscramble these matters.

corrective Appendix and Notes, which Coleridge could have drawn upon in 1806 and in which are to be found *both* the embrace of all fruitful Arab lands *and* an insistence that the only "genuine" colony is a population of free men—and that attentive perusal of history will refute the stupid notion "that Slavery ⟨in general⟩ is not incompatible with domestic security or vigour in war".[1] Even in 1809 Coleridge would draw back from the implications of armed imperialism, and in later years, thinking back, he would confess (to a later editor of the *Courier*) that he had "sometimes wished that the Mediterranean Coasts of Africa might be given up" to French ambition—if only to keep them away from British interests "in the East Indies".[2]

Writing these papers did not give him high spirits. At times he seems to have felt himself once again enlisted and in uniform, Comberbache once more (see the *déjà vu* anecdote in *CN* II 2290, "reality bursting on me. . .in the 15th of Light Dragoons"). And any attempts he made to introduce moral considerations into these minutes of advice to policy-makers encountered Ball's frank cynicism: "For fear, for fear, for fear—now of Russia—now of this—now that—but all for fear. The same day he said—no moral feeling—the Cabinet would laugh aloud at such an idea/we are none of us in these things actuated by any notion of right or Justice, & we know it!!—".[3] With what conviction did Coleridge write that Englishmen must "not be suffered to forget, that Greatness and Safety are with us Words of one meaning"? The image of the "Prize-harvest", the multitude of enemy ships seized in "the first months of any war" (in 1804 a matter of rivalry between Nelson and the adjacent admiral and of envy on the part of Ball, who coveted an admiralship and at whose prize-court in Malta Coleridge was given some duties), seems morally revealing when, after the literal reference just cited, it reappears as a metaphor to describe Egypt as booty, "a precious Wreck without an Owner" that must be captured to prevent its

[1] Ms note on Henry P. Brougham *An Inquiry into the Colonial Policy of the European Powers* (2 vols Edinburgh 1802) I 69: BM Egerton MS 2800 f 108. C regards the economic assumptions of advocates of colonial subordination as idiotic.

[2] To Richard Sharp 10 Oct 1809: "But I suspect, that to combine a government altogether fitted for tranquillity, legal freedom, & commercial activity *at home* with the causes and conditions of that individual Greatness and that selection, in every department, of the very man for the very place, which are requisite for maintaining our *external* empire, and the splendor of our Arms *abroad*, is a state-riddle which yet remains to be solved." *CL* III 240–1. And to William Mudford 9 Feb 1819: *CL* IV 920.

[3] *CN* II 2295, Dec 1804.

"drifting into our enemy's Port"—I quote the early draft. Is the stripping away of the adjective "precious" in the final draft a sign of Coleridgian morality?

RETURN TO ENGLAND

When Coleridge returned to England in the summer of 1806, he reported to Stuart that before his "political papers" had been thrown overboard he had perused them "with attention" and that "the contents, tho' not the language", were "fresh in...memory"[1]—a strong hint that they could be written out again if wanted. "If Coleridge left Malta and Sicily with one positive hope for his own future it was that he might interpret for the people of England chiefly through the press, their place in world affairs."[2] And Stuart invited him to Margate to talk things over. More urgent than Letters on Mediterranean policy, however, was the crisis of leadership brought about by the recent death of Fox, eight months after the death of Pitt. When Coleridge left Stuart for London, he set out full of resolution to "institute & carry on [an] enquiry into the characters of Mr Pitt and Mr Fox".[3] For a moment Stuart must have felt that his patient encouragement was to be rewarded. Nothing was more to Coleridge's political taste than an inquiry of such moral and dramatic scope, leading inevitably into the ministerial needs and negotiations of the present. But as soon as he arrived at the *Courier* office, alas, he discovered that the effectual ruler was Stuart's more active partner and managing editor, Thomas George Street, a shallow man and a corruptible, if not already corrupt, journalist.[4] Street himself had drafted a glib obituary panegyric on Fox and would incorporate only a few suggestions from Coleridge—who found the

[1] To Stuart [22 Aug 1806]: *CL* II 1177–8. C has moved the true story of the throwing overboard of papers from the *Arrow* in early 1805 (Sultana, p 288 and n, cites official documents)—at which C was not present—to an apparently imaginary occasion during his return home on the *Gosport* in midsummer 1806; he could thus claim to have perused the documents recently.

[2] Coburn "Poet into Public Servant" 10.

[3] To Stuart [15 Sept 1806]: *CL* II 1179.

[4] In view of government interest in the transformation of the *Courier* in 1799 that put Street in charge (see above, I lxxxiv) and in the light of Street's subsequent career (see below, I cliv n 4), it stretches credibility to suppose him the innocent and unrewarded servant of successive Tory governments until December 1809, when Canning discovered that he had by then received an estimated £2000 from the Treasury (Aspinall 89, 206–17; the sum may have represented payments since 1807).
See Werkmeister (1963) 378–9. Street came to notice in 1788 as author of *Aura; or, The Slave, a Poem*. In 1792 he was an assistant to the Rev Charles Este, editor of the *Courier*.

result outrageously false in manner and matter and Street so "satisfied" with it that he could not be persuaded to do more than "add a note of amendment: as it was too late to alter the article itself".[1] Coleridge, now fearing "that what I shall write for tomorrow's Courier, may involve a kind of Contradiction", told Stuart that Street's "asthmatic" style was a sign of "no expenditure of Logic", that as editorial strategist he did not make intelligent use of "the political position occupied by the Courier"—and withdrew.[2] The one Essay he had "contrived to preserve", his "valuable paper on the present state of Egypt much fuller of facts & more sober reasoning, than the one written for Sir A. B. to be sent to the ministry", remained in manuscript.[3]

In the winter of 1807–8, when Coleridge returned to London to give lectures at the Royal Institution, he lodged in "a nice suite of Rooms...and a quiet Bedroom" that Stuart provided for him at the *Courier* office "without expence".[4] He knew he must repay Stuart for this and other favours "either by Obligation or by past services or both".[5] In February 1808 we find him writing (to Beaumont) from the *Courier* office of an essay in "moral & political Defence of the Copenhagen Business" (of 1807) as finished but for "a concluding Paragraph",[6] but no such defence appeared in the *Courier*.[7] Stuart

[1] *CL* II 1179–80. For a part of the text, and C's amendment, see below, App A, 15 Sept 1806.

[2] C did not write—at least Street did not print—the morrow's article. For announcements of revised and new Characters of Pitt, Fox, and other "eminent men" five years later, see 19 Sept and 5 Oct 1811, below. For C on "asthmatic sentences" cf *Friend* (*CC*) I 20, 26.

[3] To Stuart [22 Aug 1806]: *CL* II 1178; see "Observations on Egypt" in App B, below. If encouraged, C might have used, to aid his memory, the various drafts and fragments of papers numbered 2 through 5, above. An article on Sicily (for which C had a mere fragment, no 5) might have been most to the point in the autumn of 1806, for Napoleon had just bargained for it and been turned down by Fox. Yet Fox was now dead; the British were seizing colonies and treasure in South Africa and Argentina; and Trafalgar had basically altered the shape of policy and possibilities. Fresh, pertinent journalism could have been founded on C's knowledge of the Mediterranean; the time for his packets of Letters of 1804 was gone, as far as the *Courier* was concerned.

[4] To the Morgans [23 Nov 1807]: *CL* III 37. By February C was complaining of "the Noises of the Pressmen at between 4 & 5 in the morning, & continued till 8—the continual running up stairs by my door to the Editor's room, which is above me". To the Morgans [17 Feb 1808]: *CL* III 73. To call his "old woman" who dwelt in the basement, he had to shout down three or four flights of stairs. *CL* III 50 n 3.

[5] To WW [21 May 1808]: *CL* III 109.

[6] *CL* III 75–6.

[7] The essay in *Friend* No 24 (*CC*) II 321–33 two years later may have been drafted at this time.

and Street may have obtained some assistance from Coleridge in conversation, but for a time his illness and his lecturing seem to have taken most of his energy.

POETRY AND PUFFING

In the literary department as well as the political, the *Courier* under Street's management was a different journal from Stuart's *Morning Post*. Stuart had catered avowedly to "the Literati" and had featured "Original Poetry" by Mary Robinson, Coleridge, Southey (always anonymously), and Wordsworth. Although Street had "Shakespeare and Burke ever ready at his finger ends" to adorn editorial platitudes, and loved "sumptuous and gay" living,[1] his *Courier* was normally barren of original or even reprinted poetry, and years could go by without the notice of a single literary work. The exceptions stand out: a sprinkling of poems by Coleridge;[2] a rich assortment of poems from Wordsworth's 1807 volume and, later, selections from *The Excursion* and *The White Doe*; two long excerpts from Southey's *Letters from England by Espriella* in 1807; three shorter ones from Wordsworth's *Cintra* pamphlet and eight from *The Friend* in 1809–10, and clusters of reviews in 1814–17, possibly at Coleridge's instigation.

Most of these reprintings belong under the head of puffing, a practice Street understood well enough; but the authors puffed were primarily Stuart's and Coleridge's friends, and the initiative appears to have come chiefly from Stuart, sometimes from Coleridge. The array of twelve Wordsworth selections in July and November 1807 gave a wider circulation to certain of his new poems than has been noted by literary historians.[3] The laudatory presentation of two long

[1] Jerdan *Autobiography* I 92.

[2] See App D, below, for list of poems by or probably by C.

[3] The *Courier* reprinting of WW's poems has not been fully tallied. For 1807 there are *Alice Fell* (2 Jul), *The Sailor's Mother* (4 Jul), *Anticipation—October 1803* (7 Jul), "Another year!—another deadly blow!" (8 Jul, at the end of an editorial against hoping for peace), "It is not to be thought of that the flood" (17 Jul), *The Solitary Reaper* (18 Jul), *Sonnet, Written in October 1803* ("When looking...") (28 Oct), *The Seven Sisters* (4 Nov), *The King of Sweden* (5 Nov), and *The Seven Sisters* (repeated, 19 Nov). WW's *Sonnet, Suggested by the Efforts of the Tyrolese* was reprinted 18 Nov 1809 "From Mr. Coleridge's Friend" and signed "W. W.". His sonnet *Lines Composed in 1809* ("Brave Schill! by death deliver'd take thy flight"), hitherto thought first published in 1815, appeared unsigned 20 Feb 1813. An editorial of 28 Sept 1813 concludes with the sonnet "High deeds, O Germans, are to come from you!" signed "Wordsworth—1807" (but with a variant first recorded for 1820). Also signed "W. W." is the *Sonnet* ("Now that all hearts are glad...") 1 Jan 1814 (mistakenly reported in *CRB* 848 as c Jan 1813, now located by R. S. Woof

quotations from "Espriella" on 17 and 20 November—a "Description of Birmingham" and a "Description of Manchester"—delighted Southey, who thanked Stuart "for the lift...given Espriella" because "one newspaper will do more for a book than two Reviews".[1] Southey assumed that he had also Coleridge to thank and later urged him to "puff" the receipts of a second edition into his pocket and, again, to "puff Espriella, in the Courier, as the best guide to the Lakes".[2] Yet Coleridge, according to his own account, had "bitterly reprobated" the Birmingham passage to Stuart.[3]

Street in his society notes never alluded to Coleridge or his works—as he did occasionally to the project of an important advertiser or an eminent dinner acquaintance. And so little did Coleridge's propinquity to the "Editor's room" serve him when he was lecturing in 1808 "on the Distinguished English Poets, in Illustration of the general Principles of Poetry" that his lectures were given no notice beyond the mere listing in two meagre and belated advertisements supplied by the Royal Institution.[4] We might now have more than a few fragmentary reports if he had been encouraged to quote from these lectures or to review them in his own newspaper, or if either editor had been interested, as William Mudford later was, in literature. Lacking such encouragement, Coleridge was driven by the accumulation of memoranda in his commonplace books, he said, to undertake the publication of an independent "Weekly Essay", *The Friend*, which he announced as a defiant flight *from* "Personal

"Wordsworth's Poetry and Stuart's Newspapers: 1797–1803" *SB* xv—1962—189). For puffs of *The Excursion* and *White Doe*, see below. The 1807 selections are nearly all presented as "By Wordsworth" or "From Wordsworth's Poems".

[1] *LLP* 394–6. RS promised to have Longman, his publisher, "follow it up by advertising". It is amusing to compare in Espriella's 56th Letter the satiric account of puffing.

[2] C to the Morgans [23 Nov 1807]: *CL* III 36; *S Life* (CS) III 134, 151. See also *S Letters* (Curry) I 463.

[3] To Stuart [8 Jan 1809]: *CL* III 165. But that was for its possible offensiveness to *Friend* subscribers in Birmingham; five years later C might see no harm in its being reprinted in the *Courier*.

[4] See notices of 25 Jan and 9 Mar 1808, App E, below. The Institution's series included thirteen lecturers. Humphry Davy, whose lectures in chemistry were the main attraction, became ill and the whole series was postponed from Dec 1807 to Jan 1808 and then C's were further put off to 12 Mar. Since attendance was by subscription, the managers gave slight attention to newspaper notices. See Bence Jones *The Royal Institution* (1871) 276–85, 342. Raysor (*Sh C* II 6–20) deduces that C lectured 15 Jan, 5 Feb, and approximately sixteen more times by 13 Jun, when, violently ill, he withdrew, receiving £100 for that part of the "five courses of five lectures" he had contracted to deliver at £140.

and Party politics, and the events of the day", though intended to have the impact of "a newspaper".[1]

This flight easily led back to the *Courier*, however. For Stuart was quite willing (and Street could have no positive objection) to puff *The Friend* with excerpts (along with a few advertisements, for which Coleridge was charged) as well as to supply direct material assistance in the form of credit for stamped paper. And when *The Friend* descended, as it inevitably did, from large general principles to some personal footnotes and asides on the politics of the day, these were sent to Street to serve both as puffs and as samples of Coleridge's political writing. By October 1809 Coleridge was prepared to let *The Friend* overflow into the *Courier* whenever he found himself writing on "subjects too much connected with persons & immediate Events to fit them for my own work".[2]

It would seem that neither his puffs nor his overflowings were accommodated, however, except when Stuart himself intervened. The truth was that Street did not relish Coleridge's kind of editorial essay, partly because it was long and "Street always preferr[ed] news, and a short notice of it in a leading paragraph to any writing however brilliant"[3]—but also because it was apt to be critical of the powers that Street aimed to please. Street was by now blatantly and slavishly pro-ministerial, even on so unpopular a matter as the Convention of Cintra (so called). But the policy as well as the proprietorship of the *Courier* was divided. Stuart, no longer in charge of leading paragraphs, was yet able to publish a series of ostensibly independent editorials, signed "X. Y.", attacking both the *Edinburgh* Whigs for their cynicism about the war in Spain and the Tories for their complacency.[4] Coleridge, writing to Street 7 December 1808, must certainly have irritated him when he praised "the independence truly honourable to you" of "X Y's admirable Letters", yet took "the privilege of an old friend" to profess himself "sadly grieved

[1] Thus announced in advertisements 5 Apr and 30 Jun 1809 and on the original title-page.

[2] To Stuart 2 Oct 1809: *CL* III 230. "...Street will see from the Article sent...how far I should be likely to serve the paper". A few weeks earlier C had sent materials from Pasley to Stuart (*CL* III 221, 226) not apparently for publication but for information ("...you will be so good as to shew [the letter] to no one"). Similar "secret" material of 1809, on the 1806 battle of Maida (*CN* III 3582), is interpreted by Sultana (p 405) as intended for publication in the *Courier* to expose Sidney Smith's conduct at Maida, but it seems not to have been used.

[3] Stuart, quoted in *BE* II 83.

[4] The eleven Letters ran from 8 Nov to 22 Dec 1808; on 16 Dec Stuart admitted authorship; C in reply 28 Dec claimed to have guessed it only on 26 Dec, when rereading them. See *CL* III 142, 152.

by three or four Paragraphs written in your own editorial character; especia[l]ly that defence of the Duke of Portland, assuredly the most unprincipled and rapacious State-Invalid, that ever disgraced an Administration".[1] Did Coleridge, with many *Courier* readers, entertain the fairly obvious suspicion that Street was the Tory duke's hireling? Was he issuing a warning—too late—[2] against that temptation? "I cannot exactly decypher the exact tone", Coleridge complained, "you wish the Courier to have, respecting the Cintra Convention and Court of Enquiry...".[3] While respecting Street's formal attachment to the "glorious Constitution" without "any reform", he pleaded that "it were blindness not to perceive...a heaving and a fermentation" among the people that would not tolerate ministers who were "absolute Menials of the Royal *Person*"[4]

1 *CL* III 137.

2 Street's commitment to the Tory cabinet of the Duke of Portland probably began shortly after its installation in early 1807. For Street's secret payments from the Treasury, see above, I cxxviii n 4.

3 To Street [7] Dec 1808: *CL* III 136–7. The burden of a long article on "The Portland Administration" in the *Courier* 12 Nov 1808 was that "though the Marquis Wellesley is an able Statesman, it does not follow that the Duke of Portland is unfit for office". On Cintra Street's "tone" was at first to report and even echo some of the expressions of universal disgust and indignation (e.g. 20, 22, 27 Sept: the "disgraceful Convention" did have "black and hideous features" —yet it must be fulfilled); then to emphasise that "one of the hideous features" (letting the French carry off their plunder) was to be "softened"— and to complain that criticism "begun in patriotism" was "degenerating into party": blame of the generals was not to be construed as an attack on ministers (29 Sept); then to give space to a correspondent ("Junio" 5 Oct) who had at first "thought with" those around him but now saw "reason to change his opinion"; and always to create the impression that His Majesty and His Majesty's ministers were at one with the people against the generals—or at least in wishing an enquiry—though a court-martial that could punish the generals, if guilty, was preferable to an enquiry, which could be turned against ministers (22 Nov). C disliked a Court of Enquiry for very different reasons—because it could "*kill* the Quicksilver of popular feeling by the Saliva of Drivellers" (*CL* III 137). When the Board of Enquiry finally reported a decision "not unfavourable" to the three generals, Street reported the fact with exclamation marks (30 Dec) and thereafter dropped the subject. For Stuart's strong views on Cintra, see his letter of 16 Dec 1808 to C, in *Friend* (*CC*) II 476.

4 *CL* III 137. C as usual tempers his language to his recipient's expectations. To Street he expresses pleasure that the English are not only "uniform in their contentment with" their Constitution but "are not even earnest about any reform in its shape" (if only ministers will act *responsibly*). To RS, earlier in the week, C refers to the same "stirring and heaving in the mind of the People" as affording "Hope for a Reform in Parliament, imperfect, and meagre as any Act-of-Parliament Reform would be" and explains specifically that he means electoral reform that would produce "20 additional honest Senators [who] would do the work of Giants...". *CL* III 130.

—nor, Street could infer, editors who were absolute menials of such ministers. Jealous for the paper's independence, Coleridge was unable "not to feel just the same Interest in the Courier, as if it were at once my own property and of my own writing".[1]

WORDSWORTH, COLERIDGE, AND CINTRA

Coleridge was both remonstrating and testing the ground, for his immediate aim was to open the *Courier* to Wordsworth's "series of most masterly Essays on the affairs of Portugal & Spain", which he took care to mention to Stuart as well as to Street and to send via Stuart.[2] The latter responded with alacrity, getting the first instalment of Wordsworth's tract into the *Courier* 27 December, almost as soon as it reached him, and undertaking to find a publisher for the complete pamphlet.[3] For Stuart, former secretary of the Friends of the People, as well as for Wordsworth and Southey and Coleridge, the resistance of the Spanish people to Napoleon stirred embers of the sympathy they had once felt for the French and, retrospectively, for the Americans. Having heretofore supported the war with mixed feelings, they easily romanticised the *popular* character of a national revolution under British Tory auspices[4] and minimised the foreseeable betrayal of the Spanish populace, even while fiercely impatient now with military and ministerial want of "steady PRINCIPLES" as flagrantly illustrated by Cintra.[5]

[1] *CL* III 137.

[2] To Stuart [c 6 Dec 1808]: *CL* III 134; to Street [7] Dec 1808: "...and I shall send the two first to Mr. Stuart by the next post". *CL* III 137.

[3] See John Edwin Wells "The Story of Wordsworth's 'Cintra'" *SP* XVIII (1921) 15–76, esp 24–5, 30; also *CL* III 160 (3 Jan 1809, misdated 27 Dec 1808 by Wells).

[4] Somehow the "heaving and... fermentation" C now felt among "the *People* of England, not the *Populace*", was respectably "different from the vulgar seditions of corresponding Societies and Manchester clubs"—in its respect for King and Constitution. To Street [7] Dec 1808: *CL* III 137. And of course a *national* revolution in Spain could remain purely national. Colmer (124–5) points to C's "clear recognition of the difference between the spirit of a genuine nationalism and that of an artificial internationalism..."; yet we must remember that the English had had similar illusions about the French nation in 1790—and that C was quite in favour of anti-Napoleonic internationalism, however artificially stoked it might need to be by Britain.

[5] This is WW's central charge (see his tract passim); yet: "from the moment of the rising of the people of the Pyrenean peninsula, there was a mighty change; we were instantaneously animated; and, from that moment, the contest assumed the dignity...from that moment 'this corruptible put on incorruption'..." (first essay). See also RS: the British general "has abandoned our vantage ground, betrayed the cause...degrading into a common and petty war

Street was thus unhappily confronted by an aroused "independence" on the part of Stuart, Coleridge, Wordsworth, and Southey (who threatened to write on Cintra if Wordsworth did not) just at a time when his masters needed an organ of support. He did not openly resist; his first open defiance of Stuart's "advice...on such subjects" occurred a year later.[1] But the first Wordsworth instalment was printed with no notice of more to follow. And the second instalment suffered "an accidental loss" at the printing-house, and then, after it was resupplied (partly "re-written...and in some parts recomposed" by Coleridge),[2] suffered another delay of about a week.[3] By that time Street was in the clear, for shortly the deluge of parliamentary debates began, and he could not be expected to find room for the third and fourth parts (which had been in his hands all along) or for what Coleridge himself offered to supply, two essays that should form a sequel since Wordsworth in any case must now withdraw the rest of his to make the pamphlet Stuart had arranged to print.[4]

Wordsworth had responded to the *Courier* delays by making further revisions, causing still further delay. Coleridge was delayed by the rewriting and recomposing, by preparations for *The Friend*, and by mumps, but in April he told Stuart he *had* written his "parallelism" between the Spanish and Belgic revolutions (i.e. his "Letters on the Spaniards"); on 27 September he reported that Miss Hutchinson was copying it out "for the Courier"; and by 2 October he had sent it to Street's desk. There it languished another two months.[5]

On Stuart's initiative the *Courier* of 5 April 1809 had devoted a column and a half to the Prospectus of *The Friend*, signed February 2

between soldier and soldier, that which [nevertheless] is the struggle of a nation...a business of natural life and death, a war of virtue against vice, light against darkness...". *S Life* (CS) III 175.

1 According to Stuart, as quoted by Canning in a letter of 1 Jan 1810. Aspinall 208.

2 To Stuart [8 Jan 1809]: *CL* III 164; see also C's letter to Poole 3 Feb 1809: *CL* III 174.

3 The second part fills almost five columns, 13 Jan 1809, with a note "*To be continued*". For C's contribution see App A, 13 Jan 1809, below.

4 The instalments were published over the initial "G" (for Grasmere); C in his additions to the second began a train of thought he would continue; C's own first "Letter on the Spaniards" (7 Dec 1809) picks up the theme of WW's final paragraph, "the grounds of hope and fear in the present effort of liberty against oppression", and in C's sixth (21 Dec 1809) he declares himself "proud to consider these Letters as an Appendix" to WW's pamphlet.

5 To Stuart [c 4 Apr], 27 Sept, 30 Sept, 2 Oct 1809 ("Street will see from the Article sent to him"): *CL* III 189, 225, 227, 230. As early as 3 Feb C was alerting Poole to look for two essays of his on Spain in the *Courier* "soon": *CL* III 174.

but announcing a first number "on the first or second Saturday of May".[1] Coleridge was grateful, but no further notice was taken, either of the non-appearance in May or of the actual appearance in June of the first and second numbers.[2] Stuart, aware of delays in paper supply and other difficulties with the launching of *The Friend*, evidently hesitated to urge its promotion; Street meanwhile in his editorial paragraphs gave flattering notice to "an entire new work, *Le Beau Monde, and Monthly Register*" to which "the Literary and Fashionable World" were said to be looking forward (29 April) and to "Ackermann's promise of a Poetical Magazine for the present month" (1 May).[3] An advertisement of *The Friend* No 3, as "On the CONSTITUTION of GREAT BRITAIN as it actually exists, and on the Principles and Motives by which our judgments and wishes concerning it ought to be guided and modified", drafted apparently by Coleridge himself, did finally appear in the *Courier* 30 June—but the number itself (not "On the Constitution" but "On the Communication of Truth" and liberty of the press) did not appear until 10 August.[4] Wordsworth's pamphlet meanwhile, about which Stuart was most enthusiastic, was off the press and assiduously advertised and puffed in the *Courier* until Stuart left town.[5]

[1] Stuart had printed additional copies of the Prospectus for C in Feb, promising the first number "on the first or second Saturday of March". See *Friend* (*CC*) I liii and n 9; lvi and n 1.

[2] On 4 Apr (posted 7 Apr) C thanked Stuart for his "kindness" (*CL* III 188); c 12 Apr he spoke of this as an advertisement "at full in the Courier" (to George Coleridge: *CL* III 193). On 15 Apr and again 24 Apr he asked Stuart for "once at least more a short advertisement" (III 196, 201); on 2 May he specified an advertisement "in the Saturday's Courier" (6 May), "announcing it for Saturday, 13 May" (III 206–7). Neither *Friend* No 1 nor the announcement was forthcoming. By 4 Jun C realised a bit tardily that Stuart's "Patience was quite exhausted by my frequent applications...concerning the Friend ...", particularly over difficulties in details of supply of stamped paper and printing arrangements (III 209).

[3] See also cordial puffs of Ackermann's *European Magazine*, 29 Apr, 24 May, 27 Jun—but Ackermann was paying for formal advertisements at the same time. C was finally billed for "Friend advt in Cou[rier] 10/–[;] [Morning] Post 12/–[;] [Morning] Chronicle 11/–. £1.13.–" (BM Add MS 34046 f 119)—a mere token charge as far as the *Courier* notices were concerned.

[4] Stuart was apparently not delighted with the first numbers, for C was "not a little anxious" for his opinion of the third. To Stuart 13 Jun 1809: *CL* III 214.

[5] Advertisements: 27, 29 May, 1, 22, 28 Jun; puffs: 5 Jun (a warm recommendation headed "Mr. Wordsworth's Pamphlet" and a short excerpt on the "justice of the cause of the Spaniards"), 15 Jun (three quarters of a column headed "Universal Peace"), 21 Jul (half column, from C's part, oddly enough, of the excerpt of 13 Jan). Wells ("The Story of Wordsworth's 'Cintra'") notes only the first three advertisements.

In September, beginning with No 4 on the 7th, *The Friend* achieved steady weekly publication. An advertisement of that number, together with a puff of half a column excerpting "part of a note, from the 4th No. of Mr. Coleridge's excellent periodical Work, the *Friend*", appeared in the *Courier* of 12 September. It was a note perfectly acceptable to either proprietor, comparing Buonaparte to Charlemagne in reference to the "perilous designs and unsleeping ambition of our neighbour the mimic and caricaturist of Charlemagne".[1] Yet Nos 5 and 6 were unnoticed; on 27 September, the day before publication of No 7, Coleridge felt he had to beg Stuart to be "so good as to have the next Number advertised in the Courier, & some one other paper...";[2] and the puff appeared, somewhat tardily, on 16 October, a full column from No 7 concerning discipline on board a man-of-war, headed "*Conscience—that makes Cowards—aye, and Heroes of us all*".

By this time, not without several parleys with his conscience, Coleridge had urged Stuart to let him give the *Courier* "a little *brightening up*", had sent in his first article on Spain, from which he wished Street to judge "how far I should be likely to serve the paper", and had asked Stuart to ask Street whether he would be able to use "two Columns twice a week for the next 12 weeks" from a person with "principles as Anti-jacobin, Anti-buonaparte &c as his own, but with a dread & contempt of the present Ministry only less than that of the last...". Obviously the answer must have been that Street could use the anti-Jacobinism but not the contempt of the ministry. Coleridge felt that he "could not write in any strict harmony with the tone predominant in the leading paragraphs of late", yet rightly and sadly surmised that Street would be even less interested in "literary assistance".[3]

This October appeal to Stuart, recently married and in semi-retirement, was the culmination of a good deal of Coleridgian attention to the *Courier* and its divided editors in previous months, to which Stuart and even Street had replied with some encouragement.[4] In January 1809 Coleridge had offered to send Stuart, if not "full

[1] This must have been sent to the *Courier* in ms (though published after a week or so of delay), for as printed in *The Friend* it ran over from No 4 to No 5, not published till 14 Sept. Nos "3.4.& 5" reached Stuart only "a few days" before 25 Sept, according to his letter of that date (*Friend—CC*—II 491). Street on 5 Oct promised "the remainder" of the note "soon" (DCL Letters Concerning *The Friend* Folder D), but see below.

[2] *CL* III 227.

[3] To Stuart 20 Oct 1809: *CL* III 230.

[4] Street replied 5 Oct (*CL* III 228n), but see below, I cxxxix nn 4, 5.

and orderly" essays, at least "the substance of my reflections, irregularly & in hints", stemming from his deep interest "in the American Affairs". He found himself "very warmly" admiring a recent article and pleased by "many things in the latter papers"; he could share Stuart's inclination to "*lean* toward the Government" (overlooking the rapacious and unprincipled Duke of Portland—see above)—if the paper could develop responsible "steadiness & consistency".[1] In March, after flattering Stuart with reporting "how universally the conduct of the Courier was extolled" for its behaviour during the trial of the Duke of York, he sketched out and offered to put together "the fragments" of an essay on patronage and "the effect of the military principle".[2] And throughout the gestation of *The Friend* he kept reminding Stuart of the fact that "for an hour daily after the receipt of the Courier" he was filled with Thoughts and Emotions (suitable for Paragraphs).[3] On 15 April he wrote expressing shock at the absence of any leading paragraph in a recent *Courier* and sketching the material for lively paragraphs on news items he saw in *Couriers* of the 12th and 13th.[4] "Out of your Letter", Stuart promptly replied, "I have written a paragraph or two",[5] and indeed Coleridge's letter was quoted almost verbatim in a leading paragraph of 20 April. Thus encouraged he began writing a "very long Letter... suggested by some of the last Couriers...on the state of parties" and "the question of Reform in the Representation"[6]—a topic even Stuart would hardly regard as welcome to the *Courier*. Coleridge, however, with growing confidence ventured on 5 May some cautious criticism of "the two last Couriers" for the manner in which they attacked Sir Francis Burdett (the writing, he presumed, of Stuart himself); demonstrated how he would have made almost the same attack but more plausibly; then implied that what might be thought "coarse & inveterate" in the first paragraph must be the responsibility of Street.[7] Nothing came of this, though Stuart appears to have

1 *CL* III 168.

2 *CL* III 185. Later C would draft and almost get into the *Courier* (in Jul 1811) such an essay, on the reappointment of the Duke of York. See below, III 220ff.

3 18 Apr 1809: *CL* III 201.

4 *CL* III 195. "Your observation about the want of a leading paragraph made me laugh", said Stuart, claiming to have been "as much surprized" himself—but to have seen that late news had "squeezed out" the leader, and so to have refrained from speaking to Street about it. Stuart to C 19 Apr 1809: *Friend* (*CC*) II 488.

5 Ibid.

6 To Stuart [24 Apr 1809]: *CL* III 201.

7 *CL* III 207–8; after saying this C immediately expresses disagreement "with Street" on another paragraph (on Lord Auckland's Divorce Bill). See C's editorial in the *M Post* of 16 Apr 1800, below. Did Auckland try again?

made two excerpts from Coleridge's letter of 4 June, his usual way of sending in paragraph material to Street. When Stuart left London in July, Coleridge had not yet prepared in final form or sent to Stuart or Street his series on Spain.[1]

On 11 September he sent Stuart some excerpts from letters from C. W. Pasley to correct an unjust "tendency in the Courier" to throw too much blame on the Earl of Chatham for reverses in the siege of Flushing. Stuart on 25 September and 5 October thanked Coleridge for these extracts as containing "precisely" his own opinions on the expedition but intimated that his own disgust with government policy could not be communicated in public: to Street he had "abused the Expedition from the beginning"—to no avail.[2] By this time the difficulties enmeshing Coleridge and Stuart arising from the arrangements for *The Friend* exploded into "a sort of quarrel";[3] in October it was Street who responded promptly to Coleridge's need for more stamped paper for *The Friend* and who looked forward to his promised article on Spain "with Impatience".[4] Nevertheless, said article, when it reached Street's desk, rotted for three months[5] and was not readied for publication in the *Courier* until Stuart resumed authority in mid-November.

The Friend had been given one excerpt in September and one in

[1] Stuart's "absence from town of more than four months" began c 25 Jul and was uninterrupted till c 3 Nov, according to Stuart's letters of 25 Sept and 10 Nov; in the latter he speaks of returning to Cheltenham in a week. *Friend* (*CC*) II 491, 494.

[2] *CL* III 222 and Stuart's letters, *Friend* (*CC*) II 492, 493. It may have been at this time that C supplied Stuart with a ms of criticism of British generalship in actions of 4 and 12 Jul 1806 (the battle of Maida) marked "*secret*" (perhaps because libellous) yet concluding (perhaps ironically): "All this for the Newspapers—and the good People of England". *CN* III 3582, dated 1809/10. Sultana (p 405) is confident the information was "for publication by Stuart in the *Courier* with a view to exposing the allegedly scandalous conduct of Sir Sidney Smith", commander at the time of the battle. But no use in the *Courier* has been found.

[3] To RS [Nov 1809]: See *CL* III 259. The fact that no letters from C to Stuart are extant from Oct 1809 to Mar 1811 or from Stuart to C after 10–13 Nov 1809 does not signify there were none. Long before Mar 1811 C must have corresponded about the co-operation with Stuart then in progress.

[4] *CL* III 228n (Street to C, 5 Oct 1809; see App B, below). Griggs overlooks the failure to publish C's article till 7 Dec and quotes Street's letter as seeming "to disprove a misleading sentence of Stuart's in...1838: 'In the Courier Mr. Street...did not require or encourage his [C's] services.'" Street's encouragement in 1817 will make a stronger exception, but Stuart's remark stands as a general definition of the case.

[5] Cf C to Stuart 4 Jun 1811 (*CL* III 333): "A Newspaper is a market for flowers & vegetables, rather than a Granary or Conservatory—and the Drawer of its Editor a common Burial-ground...".

October. It was now puffed twice a week; a half column 13 November, "Bonaparte's Tribute to Great Britain (From the twelfth number of Mr. Coleridge's Friend [9 November])"; two columns from the same number on 15 November, "The Oppression of Taxes", in which Mr. Coleridge "so admirably puts down the vulgar clamourers against Taxation and the National Debt, that we feel it our duty, to lay it before our Readers, strongly recommending them to peruse the whole of the Number"—genuine praise from Stuart's heart;[1] a sonnet of Wordsworth's on 18 November "From the 14th [actually 13th] Number"; and on the 25th nearly two columns of "Bonaparte and Charlemagne", a more extended reprinting of the passage first excerpted in the *Courier* in September.[2]

Coleridge's rounding upon Bonaparte—as safe an object of abuse as sin—was no doubt a comfort to both editors after the epistolary rumblings that threatened to descend in criticism of "the present state of men & measures", of, for example, the Canning–Castlereagh duel—Stuart's sympathies being with the younger man, Street's (bought) against him, whereas Coleridge would have wished a condemnation of both. "Good God! what a disgrace to the nation...!!" he had written to Stuart. "And not a Breathing of its hideous Vulgarity & Immorality in any one of the Papers!"[3] There was also a tactical reason for reprinting the "Note" at the end of November, a reason that occurred to the journalist's mind of Stuart (or of Street, giving in),[4] as the *Courier* was now opening its columns

[1] Stuart thought it "a most brilliant one. I shall make a long extract from it in the Courier and another in the Morning Post". Letter to C 10 Nov 1809; *Friend* (*CC*) II 494. Is it possible that Stuart continued to own a share in the *M Post*, or was there merely a sort of reciprocity in puffing?

[2] See 7 Dec 1809 n 2, below.

[3] 27 Sept 1809: *CL* III 227. The excisions at the end of this letter may indicate Stuart's sending possible matter on to Street, but if on this topic it was unlikely to be used. Until Canning's duel with Castlereagh in September and his fall from the cabinet, the paper had been "Canning's *Courier*". See in the *Courier* of 11 Oct 1808 a jovial protest against being called by the *M Chron* "Mr. Canning's Paper". Street's switch to abuse of Canning, first evident 2 Oct 1809, was crude, obvious—and subsidised (see Aspinall 207–8). It ceased with Stuart's return to London.

For C's view see *CL* III 195, also 260: "And Mr. Canning was one of Stuart's Statesmen of real Ability—in what? and what proof?—These are things, that perplex me in a man of Stuart's consummate good sense."

[4] Street on 5 Oct, responding to a lost letter from C, had promised to "quote soon in the Courier" the "remainder" of the Note. *CL* III 228n. A month later C complained (in a lost letter) to Stuart, who replied: "I have spoken to Street about the extract respecting Charlemagne. He says he could not find the part you mean. On such occasions the best way is to prepare the extract for the press yourself and send it up in a letter. In the whirlwind of business in which an Editor is involved he forgets or post-

to Letters from S. T. Coleridge, Grasmere. Letter I, shelved in October, begins with an involved allusion to the *Courier*'s having extracted "from *The Friend* the parallel of Charlemagne and Bonaparte".[1] As an allusion to the puff of 12 September, this would reveal the delay of the Letter. But a fresh puff of the Charlemagne–Bonaparte parallel had the effect of refreshing the allusion. The *Courier* of 5 December could then contemporaneously announce: "We have received three very able Essays from Mr. Coleridge.—The first of which it is our intention to insert to-morrow." The morrow came 7 December; Letters II and III were published 8 and 9 December; and four more by the 22nd. Coleridge himself delayed writing the eighth (and last) Letter another month. In it he promised another, in which he would take issue with a recent editorial paragraph—a promise Street cannot have urged him to fulfil.[2]

THE HIRELING *COURIER*

That Coleridge gave some credence to the general suspicion of Street's venality, while accepting the image of independence that Stuart's letters and paragraphs had established, appears from a letter to Samuel Purkis of 11 October 1809 calling attention to recent and coming contributions. Coleridge does not wish his friend to think him ". . . an Approver of the Courier—on the contrary, I can scarcely persuade myself, that it is not a *venal* print—tho' I am sure, that if it be, Mr Stuart (the half-proprietor) is not aware of it. But it has manfully fought the good fight for Spain & against Peace-men—or rather your manufacturers of *Truces* . . .".[3] It is noteworthy that Canning, when he did not suspect but knew of "the *peculiar* hold which the Treasury has upon the *conductor* of the *Courier*", likewise supposed it "probably" unknown to Stuart.[4]

---

pones such things as are not pressed on him by the day." To C 10–13 Nov 1809. *Friend* (*CC*) II 494.

1 7 Dec 1809. Two more puffs appeared, 5 and 6 Jan 1810: "Sir Alexander Ball (From the 19th Number of Coleridge's Friend)" (over a column), and "Christmas Out of Doors (—Coleridge's *Friend*)" (half a column). On the "great Service to the Circulation" of *The Friend* of such extracts in the *Courier* see William Wray to C, *Friend* (*CC*) II 501.

2 See *CL* III 272 and Letter VIII (20 Jan 1810), below. C also promised an "orderly conclusion". For a draft of a sequel see App B, 1810, "Letters on the Spaniards. IX".

3 *CL* III 245. C expects the first three "Letters on the Spaniards" to appear "shortly". The pun probably alludes to Paine; see below, 25 Jul 1816 n 18.

4 Aspinall 207–8 (30 Dec 1809). Canning knew Street to have been in the pay of Charles Arbuthnot, Secretary of the Treasury, and he could

Though the secret became every day a more open one, the division of editorial and proprietorial responsibility must have been expedient for all concerned. Stuart in a recent letter (25 September) had made clear to Coleridge that his only way of expressing his disgust with "the whole of our military plans" and "public affairs" generally had been not to write "a Line these six months". To criticise would have meant to pursue a hint from Coleridge that "the root of all the evil is the Kings Will, to which all factions of any weight in the State equally bow for the Sake of place & power".[1] It would be the menace of royal power to which Coleridge two years later objected in the reappointment of the Duke of York as commander-in-chief—and its effect on the press, which he felt in Street's zeal, and Stuart's acquiescence, in the suppression of his remarks. He now explained to his upright brother George that he was to earn "five guineas an Essay" by writing for "a party Newspaper", although he could "hardly reconcile it to [his] Conscience".[2] His own writing would be "in the spirit of Sincerity & Good will"; nevertheless he would be "wittingly assisting with all my powers the sale & influence of what I do not approve on the whole—and I cannot at all reconcile it to my feelings...".[3] He was reluctant to give up the illusion that "his" newspaper was "at once my own property and of my own writing".[4] If not Street, then Stuart must be credited with "an independence truly honourable".

Like Stuart's letters signed "X. Y.", Coleridge's Letters on Spain

not believe the latter's claim that the Treasury, even when supported by remonstrances from Stuart, was unable to control Street. Arbuthnot "...as patronage secretary to the treasury was primarily responsible for controlling the ministerial papers", as Denis Gray puts it. *Spencer Perceval* (Manchester 1963) 134.

1 Stuart to C 25 Sept 1809: *Friend* (*CC*) II 492. Earlier (to C 14 Feb 1809) Stuart had feared that the trial of the Duke of York might "be the death of the King" or "occupy the attention of Ministers to the exclusion of the affairs of Spain &c"—yet considered it "most fortunate in itself, that such a millstone about our neck as the Duke of York should be got rid of". Ibid II 486–7.

2 9 Oct 1809: *CL* III 240. This price would work out to £42 for the eight "Letters on the Spaniards"; hence E. L. Griggs (*CL* III 233n) suggests that their contribution cancelled C's indebtedness to Stuart for stamped paper for *The Friend*, i.e. the "Balance due £44. 15*s*. 11*d*." quoted from the *Courier* account in BM Add MS 34046 ff 80–1. Yet further notations by Stuart, also quoted, indicate that he did not credit the articles to this account, and it seems probable that C collected cash for them. (In the same letter to his brother, C expresses the feeling that it was really Stuart who was the debtor, having acquired "a very large fortune" partly through C's labours for the *M Post*. *CL* III 238.)

3 *CL* III 240.

4 To Street [7] Dec 1808: *CL* III 137, quoted above.

addressed *to* the editor could stand on their own sincerity, and their publication could be considered a demonstration of the moral power of his own writing. They would pay off some of his obligation to Stuart, which he acknowledged despite mixed feelings;[1] they would strengthen the circulation of *The Friend,* to which the first and seventh Letters call emphatic attention; they would also strengthen Stuart's position in the *Courier* by singling out (in Letters II and VIII) the wisdom of "X. Y.";[2] and they would advertise Wordsworth's *Cintra* pamphlet (in Letters V and VI). Their being signed "S. T. Coleridge, Grasmere" would serve to mark the distinction between the independent author and the venal print.[3]

When *The Friend* expired in March 1810 Coleridge did not at once turn to the *Courier,* except for supplying a characteristic and vigorous essay on "Parties" for 3 April and, possibly, three months later a flailing of Francis Burdett, 4 July, something he had long wished to write.[4] Eventually, when he moved to London at the end of October to put himself under medical care, he got in touch with Stuart and told his friends that he was writing for the *Courier* on the question of the moment, paper against gold, in opposition to the report of the Bullion Committee ("these Scholars of the Edinburgh Review").[5] He did not do so until May 1811, unless two long excerpts 7 and 8 December 1810 from Huskisson's defence of the bullionist position represent a contribution of a sort.[6] But word spread quickly and unpleasant publicity was soon given to his intended course by the Jacobins of the new age, who saw in the Perceval ministry a

[1] C expected from Stuart immediate cash or credit to keep *The Friend* going (to Poole 12 Jan 1810: *CL* III 272), but he felt a moral obligation to make up for articles promised and not supplied.

[2] Stuart still wrote an occasional "X. Y." letter, e.g. 18 and 28 Sept 1809 (in support of the new theatre prices).

[3] Never before or after did C fully sign any newspaper essays, except his trial piece of 19 Apr 1811, the literary essays of 30 and 31 Aug 1811 in the *Courier,* and the series on art in the *Bristol Journal* in 1814.

[4] See App A, below. C also supplied a note for 20 Sept 1810 denying the authorship of a letter to the editor 15 Sept signed "S. T. C." that had accused Walter Scott of plagiarism.

[5] On 14 Nov 1810 C wrote to Rickman for another copy of the "Report of the Bullion Committee", having missed a copy that (presumably) Stuart had sent. *CL* III 299. On 28 Nov Lamb told Hazlitt that C was in town and "writing or going to write in the Courier against Cobbet & in favor of Paper Money". *LL* II 112.

[6] "Mr. Huskisson and his Pamphlet" (i.e. *The Question Concerning the Depreciation of Our Currency Stated and Examined*) *Courier* 7 and 8 Dec 1810. The brief introduction is not Coleridgian in style; the most one can suppose is that C made the selections, the topic having been undertaken as his.

continuation of court-supported Toryism, in the *Courier* its most flagrant hireling (while Stuart and Coleridge remained offstage, they were quite right), and now found their suspicions of *The Friend* apparently confirmed.

"EXTREMES MEET", announced the *Examiner* of 25 November 1810: "Mr. Coleridge, once a republican and a follower of Tom Paine, is now a courtier and a follower of Spencer Parcival [sic]. Not succeeding in persuading the public to read the crampt and courtly metaphysics of his lately deceased paper, the *Friend*, he now takes his revenge by writing against the popular judgment in the hireling daily prints.—But even here he is as harmless as ever; for what with the general distaste to such writings, and what with the difficulty of getting at Mr. Coleridge's meaning, he obtains but very few readers." Objecting to this "sneer", the editor of the Staffordshire *Advertiser* considered "Mr. Coleridge's ability as the best pledge of his integrity" and argued that his "late letters to the *Courier*" had expressed "his own peculiar feelings and principles" and had been free of the paper's ministerial taint.[1]

The expectation that Coleridge would be able to take a firmly independent line in the *Courier* of 1811 was unrealistic, however. At the beginning of the year the paper faced its critics with a full-page editorial headed "Newspaper Corruption", denying categorically that it was "venal" (11 January 1811).[2] But it proceeded to demon-

[1] On 9 Dec 1810 the *Examiner* printed without comment this paragraph from the *Advertiser:* "Mr. Coleridge, it appears, has discontinued the publication of 'The Friend', and arrived in London, where, it is said, he is to commence political writer. The *Examiner* in a sneer at his circumlocutory style and metaphysical distinctions, has put him down as a proper and probable ministerial advocate. The Editor has not, we conceive, in this instance, decided with his usual fairness of judgment. If he argue on Mr. Coleridge's late letters to the *Courier*, we have only to add, that they are written on those enlarged principles which cannot be said to embrace any side or party. It would be as just to consider all the advertisements in the *Morning Post* as possessing the crooked and time-serving properties of that notorious print, as to conclude that Mr. Coleridge was a ministerialist, because he availed himself of the extensive sale of the *Courier* to make public his own peculiar feelings and principles, on which he justified the war of Spain. The *Examiner* itself owes too much to its own just claims to render it necessary to fling thus the obscurations of ill-nature and surmise on the fair claims of others. We consider Mr. Coleridge's ability as the best pledge of his integrity."

[2] Daniel Lovell in the *Statesman* 12 and 27 Dec 1810 (partly reported in *Courier* 11 Jan 1811) singled out *M Post* and *Courier* as the most conspicuous of "several morning and evening newspapers in the pay of the present Ministers, hired for the purpose of propagating false-hood and calumny, with a view to mislead the public and draw their attention from the dangers which surround the

strate that it was the partisan of the Perceval ministry on the regency question, on the question of military flogging, and on the question of condemning the critics of such flogging as "mutinous libellers". Nine months earlier the *Courier* had, for a moment, uttered bold protest against the arbitrary jailing of John Gale Jones for having published a criticism of a slur upon newspapers made in the House of Commons. "Upon the same law of [Parliamentary] privilege there is not a Proprietor nor Editor...belonging to any Newspaper, who might not be dragged from their homes", the *Courier* had fumed (2 April 1810). But Jacobinical demonstrations had soon contaminated such "defence of the liberty of the subject"; the *Courier* had prudently deleted "all strong passages" from a "long and forcible article" already set in type (13 April); and by June, when Jones was released from Newgate, the *Courier* had become so notoriously opposed to *popular* defence of the liberty of the subject that "the mob stopped before our office and hissed and groaned".[1]

By February 1811 Jones was in prison again for political libel, this time in the Cold Bath Fields "Bastille", which Coleridge in 1799 cited as giving the devil ideas for prisons in hell (*The Devil's Thoughts* stanza IX). Cobbett was writing his weekly *Register* from Newgate, on a two-year sentence for an article against excessive flogging, based on a newspaper account of an officer sentenced to one thousand lashes. John and Leigh Hunt were to be tried for reprinting in the *Examiner* an article (Drakard of the Stamford *News*, the original writer, would be tried in March) that outdid Cobbett by citing "in a mass" a number of newspaper accounts of flogging—and offended the attorney general by quoting (out of context, he would protest) a brutal remark he had made at the Cobbett trial.[2] On 16 February Lords Holland and Folkestone announced motions in the two Houses on the new use of "informations *ex officio*" by the attorney general. Cobbett hoped for a full discussion of "the State of the Press...that the public may, in time, see how *they* will be affected by the *freedom* or *slavery* of this great political and moral engine" (23 February). It was at this point that the *Courier*, responding to Lord Holland's

Country." The *Courier* asserts in reply that since 1799 it "has been conducted upon one steady uniform principle... equally condemning the tyranny of the French Government, the seditious anarchy of the Burdett mob, and the selfish jobbing politics of the Opposition...hence it has many enemies, bitter, slandering, lying, rancorous enemies; but...many steady zealous friends among the best men of the community...".

1 Noted in *Courier* 18 Feb 1811.

2 Cf T. B. Howell *Complete...State Trials* (1823) XXXI 370.

notice, acquitted the attorney general and the administration, in advance of any inquiry, while yet restating its disapproval of severe punishments for public libel (16 and 21 February). It announced it would shortly discuss the treatment of John Gale Jones in Cold Bath Fields. If as severe as reported in "a Sunday Newspaper" (the *Independent Whig*), it called for "investigation and redress"; "if not, for instant contradiction, in circumstantial detail, by authority" (18 February). According to Stuart, "Coleridge came to me and said 'This is most atrocious. If it be true, the Government should be attacked and exposed for permitting it,'—(and this he knew I should be ready to do in the *Courier*:) 'but if not true, the Public should be undeceived.' He proposed that I should go and make inspection. I said I would if he would go with me. He agreed."[1]

The consequence was a three-part article (4, 7, and 12 March) "The Abuse of Prisons", describing the sanitary and humane conditions in the House of Correction, reporting an interview with Gale Jones (which contrasted his stubborn protest "on principle" against prison rules prohibiting books and writing material with the warden's willingness to ignore the rules). This article, written by Stuart, once directly quoting Coleridge, is not slavish in tone,[2] it reaffirms the *Courier*'s disapproval of the jailing of libellers of public men; but it served to deflate the protest against such jailing; and it quite flew in the face of evidence on record in the assertion (on the mere word of the warden apparently) that the mutineers of '97 (whose mistreatment had been notorious when Coleridge was of the devil's party) had really been as gently treated as Jones was now.[3]

Meanwhile on 22 February the Hunt brothers were tried and acquitted of their libel charge; whereupon the *Courier*, on the 25th,

[1] Stuart to HNC, quoted in *EOT* III 1032–3. With C thus co-operating with Stuart it is plausible to look for contributions in the *Courier* at this time, but there seem to be none. SC supposed (*EOT* III 1033) she detected her father's influence in an article of 16 Feb 1811 acquitting the attorney general of harshness in prosecutions for libel and "disclaiming any thought of accusing the administration of severer conduct with regard to the public press than their opponents", yet protesting the too-great hostility to the press among *all* public men and declaring that the punishment of persons convicted of libels was too severe. (There is a transcript of this article, in an unknown hand, in VCL MS LT 84.) But within the context of general support of the ministry's hostility to the Opposition press, this sort of protestation frequently suited the editor's purpose.

[2] The nature of the quotation (7 Mar) shows that C accompanied Stuart. This was perhaps Stuart's last energetic effort to "take the trouble of conducting the Paper" (see *CL* IV 640n, quoted below, cliii).

[3] See *EOT* III 1033–4 (but SC fails to note the third part). SC made a summary of the article of 4 Mar, quoting a few passages. VCL MS LT 84.

published what Cobbett justly called "a most atrocious article" (transparently Street's) accusing the jury of having found a false verdict, accusing the *Examiner* of having intended to stir up mutiny in the army, and arguing that since soldiers are "out of the pale of the constitution" it is not legitimate for a newspaper to criticise military punishment. John Drakard of the Stamford *News* immediately protested that the *Courier*'s calling his article a "detestable and mutinous libel" would prejudice his own trial, which was pending; and the *Courier* professed it "would have abstained from aggravating the case of a brother journalist under prosecution, had it known" (1 March). Cobbett, ripping the "venal" essay to shreds, professed to detect "a hand superior to that which is generally employed in that paper" and implied (by stressing that "the venal man, or, rather, his coadjutor upon this occasion" was avowedly "departing from *his usual practice* with regard to prosecutions for libel") that Coleridge, the superior coadjutor, was responsible for the *Courier*'s *more* vindictive tone.[1] The *Examiner* (3 March) responded to the charge that its "Mutinous Libels" sprang from defect of character by hinting at the character defects of the three writers of the *Courier:*

> We shall not even examine which it is of the writers in the *Courier* that has thus subjected himself to the danger of exposition—whether it is the same person who advocated the cause of reform in another paper, now rendered infamous by corruption [Coleridge in the *Morning Post*]; whether it is the author of a notorious and unprincipled imposition practised some years ago upon the Public, for the vile purposes of stock-jobbing [Stuart, who forged a copy of the *Éclair*];—or lastly, whether it is that gentlest and most maudlin of metaphysicians [this is of course Street], who descants with so much propriety, over the turbot and silver plate, on the folly of ardent principle and the optimism of corruption. It is enough for us, that this charge is a good specimen of his consistency. . . . Retire, retire, Gentlemen, for decency's sake,—or if not for decency's, for your own,—to your patrons and a bottle; and there, calling for white handkerchiefs and pouring out libations to the departed *Friend*, lament over the shocking increase of humanity and public spirit, so fatal to selfishness and public corruption.

A week later the *Examiner* had received a disclaimer (10 March): "Mr. Coleridge has requested the Editor to state, that he is not the author of the article in the *Courier* quoted at the head of this Paper last week: and the Editor accordingly states it with great pleasure. Mr. C. will hear further from him on this subject." (Did anyone notice at this juncture that a pathetic *Epitaph on an Infant* was sent

[1] *Political Register* 27 Feb, 2 and 20 Mar 1811.

to the *Courier*, 20 March, by one signing himself "Aphilos", i.e. *Friend*less?)[1] Coleridge was not the author of the atrocious article—nor did he have the power to stay its sequel, a full-page screed "On Military Punishments" 21 March, published as soon as Drakard had been tried and convicted, and insisting that both Drakard and the Hunts had published "seditious libel" in "inflammatory language" and merited the worst severities. Continuing the attack on the *Examiner* and "other weekly papers", just as the *Anti-Jacobin* had once harried the *Morning Chronicle* and *Courier* and *Morning Post*, a further article on 1 April warned these papers written "for the corruption of the lower class" that far from being *persecuted* they were "just very *lucky*" to be let off so lightly, considering how full they were of sedition.

AUXILIARY EDITOR

Such was the *Courier* of 1811,[2] which Coleridge joined—not, as he wished, to be the continuer and improver of the independent voice of Stuart, but as the censored subordinate of Street. Superficially fulfilling the premature characterisations of the *Examiner*, Coleridge's trial editorial of 19 April on "The Regent and Mr. Perceval", signed with his initials, could all too easily be read, not only by Street but by the public, as a voucher of the willingness of "S. T. C." to serve both Perceval and his Treasurer's hireling. It was a long and principled defence of "state patronage" (a delicate yet an obligatory topic for a ministerial paper),[3] in which he scolded the *Edinburgh* "reformers", invoked the shades of Lord Nelson and Sir Alexander Ball, and congratulated "the whole navigable ocean" on its joint subjection to the moon and British commercial and naval power. Coleridge was prepared to build a severe critique on this foundation, but would soon discover his mistake.

Nine days later, negotiating *with Stuart*, he offered to attend the *Courier* office daily "from 9 to 2", to scan the morning papers, write the leading Paragraph when Mr. Street was busy, and fill "whatever room there was" with "small paragraphs, poems etc," as well as

[1] As in *PW* (EHC) I 417.

[2] In circulation the *Courier* had reached about 7500 daily. See below, I cliv/2.

[3] The *Courier*'s first defence of Perceval's rôle in this place-jobbery had been on the level of mud-slinging (5 Apr: see Cobbett's gleeful critique 10 Apr). C lifts the discussion to the realm of political philosophy—but it remains a defence of the purchase of votes with places.

Two years earlier, C seems to have intended a rather different treatment of the patronage question in his essay proposed to Stuart in *CL* III 185 [28 Mar 1809]. See above, I cxxxviii.

"a series" of longer articles. He asked for "a month's Trial". By Sunday, 5 May, he had "particularized" his proposal to Street "and found a full, and in all appearance a warm, assent". "As to weekly Salary" nothing was said, but he would start early Monday morning.[1] And the evidence is that he attended fairly steadily from 6 May to 14 June, supplying from four to eleven acceptable paragraphs a week, anonymously, and doubtless being of various unrecorded service.[2]

By the end of the first week he was pointing out to Stuart how much more efficiently he could have organised the day's paper (10 May) than Street was doing.[3] After another two weeks, talking with Crabb Robinson, he gave the impression that he would be giving the *Courier* a more liberal complexion but for "a prudent and shrewd man (Street)...always at his elbow" who knew "sometimes how to make use of his talent, but more frequently reject[ed] it as not suiting his purpose".[4] The policy continued to be, as epitomised in the words of the *Examiner* (31 March), "defence of the cat-o'-nine-tails and humanity". At the end of his trial month (4 June) Coleridge wrote to Stuart urging him either to get him "settled" on some "weekly or monthly" wage—or to put him "in the way of some other Paper". He could report that "Mr. Street seems highly pleased with what I have written this morning on the Battle" of Albuera (a battle that required a careful interpretation of dispatches to make it acceptable), but he still did not know where he stood "as candidate for the place of *Auxiliary*".[5] He continued to write a steady quantity of short

[1] On 26 Mar C refers to "a job... offered me to day" (probably a preliminary agreement with Stuart and Street); the offer to attend daily is in C's letter to Stuart 28 Apr; on 3 May C speaks of it as settled; on 5 May he writes to Stuart of Street's assent. *CL* III 314, 319, 326, 326–7.

[2] During the twenty-one weeks from 6 May to 27 Sept, C published 95 prose contributions—of which 45 were collected in *EOT* (not counting the suppressed one on the Duke of York)—plus at least three poems. And C may have been responsible for the brief puff and long quotation of Pasley's admired book on 30 Sept (see *CL* III 330).

[3] *CL* III 328–31. In his next letter, 4 Jun, C professes to be "most cautious & shy in recommending any thing" to Street (*CL* III 332), but one wonders.

[4] *CRB* I 33 (28 May 1811). C may have been hinting at an early negative from Street on the Duke of York article, but did not specify.

[5] *CL* III 332–5 (4 Jun: C had already submitted the York article). Stuart seems to have wanted to consider some of C's current work as payment for past obligations; C insists that he must be paid currently. He will save on coach hire by walking *back* to his room in Hammersmith, but "to walk in...would take off all the blossom & fresh fruits of my Spirits". To others C would soon complain that Stuart, "a *Maecenas* worth 50,000£", had refused to treat him "with common humanity" in the matter of debt incurred for *The Friend*. To J. J. Morgan [12 Oct 1811]: *CL* III 338.

paragraphs, with only a ten-day break in mid-June. But he chafed under the conviction that the best of his writing and thinking was destined to rot in that "common Burial-ground", the drawer of the Editor.[1]

STREET AT HIS ELBOW

Coleridge had been prepared "to compress, or rather to select, my thoughts, so as to make them more frequently admissable".[2] He had even been willing to compromise (he thought) by prudential silences: "...I will never write what, or for what, I do not think right—all that Prudence can justify, is *not* to write what at certain times one may yet think".[3] But he had underestimated the rigour of Street's adherence to ministers. On 11 and 12 June Coleridge was approached by Crabb Robinson for information about the venality of an early editor of the *Morning Post*, one John Benjafield, who had received Treasury money and then blackmailed the Prince of Wales for an annuity (in 1789), about which gossip had recently arisen.[4] The conversation got around to Street, and Coleridge read aloud to Robinson "a very beautiful essay" that demonstrated both his own incorruptibility and the sort of thing Street was refusing to print. This was a trenchant criticism, written in May, of the reappointment of the Duke of York to command of the army, two years after his disgrace in the Mrs Clarke inquiry.[5] Coleridge's principles, placing parliamentary above royal "interest", might have suited the Perceval ministry four months earlier, but since "Prinny" on becoming Regent had abandoned the Whigs it had become particularly expedient to exalt the royal family.[6]

In July Street finally yielded, or pretended to yield, and had it set in type for the *Courier* of 5 (or 14?) July—but only, it would seem, after having given the wink to his paymaster, Arbuthnot of the

[1] The phrase is in the letter of 4 Jun to Stuart: *CL* III 333.

[2] To Stuart [10 May 1811]: *CL* III 328.

[3] To Stuart 4 Jun 1811: *CL* III 334. But he knew that this was "but a more artful way of telling a lie" (to quote his own description in a letter to James Perry in 1818: see below, I clxxv/2n).

[4] *CRB* I 34–5; Aspinall 274–6; for details, including Stuart's bland deposition, see Werkmeister (1963) 106 et seq.

[5] C to Stuart 4 Jun 1811 (*CL* III 332) speaks of it as in Street's hands and already growing out of date; he had hinted about it in his essay on Lord Milton's Motion, 28 May (q.v.); HCR understood it had been "promised long since" (quoted in III 332n).

[6] For C's and Stuart's view of the Duke as "a millstone about our neck" see Stuart to C 14 Feb 1809 in *Friend* (*CC*) II 486–7.

Treasury, who called on Stuart and with some difficulty persuaded him to stop the press and destroy the copies already printed.[1] It may be that this episode helped Street to tighten his grasp on the government purse and on the reins of the *Courier*. It was a demonstration of power that upset Coleridge badly—especially the display of "Stuart's laziness, and not choosing to quarrel with Street"—and he asked Crabb Robinson to recommend him to Walter of *The Times*. He even drew up a statement of "what service he was willing to give; such as attending 6 hrs a day & writing so many articles per week"—details Robinson thought too mean to particularise—and of the political guarantee he hoped for: "always supposing the paper to be truly independent (1st) of the Administration (2) of the Palace Yard [i.e. of the popular demonstrations][2]—& that its fundamental principle is, the due proportion of political power to Property [freely allowed to circulate and not assisted in] its natural tendency to accumulate in large & growing masses".[3] But there was no opening on *The Times*, and Coleridge swallowed his pride. On through the summer he kept up in the *Courier* "a constant Fire"[4] on the daily topics of Bonaparte, Bullion, Wellington and Soult, the Catholic leaders and their Petition, America, the Comet, and the

[1] For the three surviving fragments of C's article, see App B, below. One appears to be part of an article actually printed; the other two constitute an apologetic preamble and a draft article, neither in fair-copy state.

Robinson's account gives the copies printed and destroyed as 2000—an improbability, for the first thousand or so would have been on the streets before the stop-press order and could not have been destroyed. (The few surviving copies of the 5 and 14 Jul issues lack C's essay but are too few to make a fair sample.)

[2] For this meaning of Palace Yard see my "Byron and 'The New Force of the People'" *Keats–Shelley Journal* XI (1962) 58. C's ms reads "the Populace"; see *CL* III 334n. See also below, App B, 1818, "The Character of Queen Charlotte" (at n 3)

[3] *CRB* I 37. HCR somewhat freely paraphrases the first part of C's proposal, which is in VCL MS Fl. 6 (transcribed in *CL* III 334n). SC misquotes and misapplies it (*EOT* I lxxx–lxxxi) as evidence of terms dictated to Street! But the moment of C's returning to the *Courier* despite the suppressed edition is just not the time to insist that C maintained "his connection with public journals" in an "elevated spirit" and a "high and firm moral tone".

The details of editorial service spelled out in C's document are instructive: He would put in "any six hours of the Day" at the office, between 8 A.M. and 8 P.M. when nothing occurred "of paramount interest after 8 o/[clock] in the Evening" to hold him later; he would daily supply "any number required of small Paragraphs or the *leading* Paragraph"; in addition he would supply "two Essays a week, on the great Interests of the Time, of from two to three Columns: still letting these in busy & crowded times accumulate, according as their Subjects are less temporary, to keep up a constant Fire from the Paper in more open & leisure Months".

[4] See preceding note.

Price of Grain. At the end of August he supplied a bonus of two literary essays (one of them sixteen years old), signed, and two small poems, unsigned. At the end of September he ceased for two months, probably feeling that his term was concluded, since in April he had asked for "the next half year".[1]

The trial of his serving as "Auxiliary" editor (if he could live with having "*not* to write" what he might sometimes think) might seem to have succeeded. Indeed when he reappeared in the *Courier* office on 5 October, what he had been spending "near a week" doing was reading, at Westminster Library, in "Irish Eloquence" for the purpose of comparing Flood, Curran, and Grattan with Fox, Pitt, and Windham. On his way up to his room "to finish an Essay on this Subject" he handed to Street (or left on his desk) a declaration that he had "finished Pitt, Buonaparte, Fox, and Sir A. Ball"[2]—characters of eminent men, which he had persuaded Street to announce in the paper on 19 September in large italic type above the masthead: ". . . drawn by the same hand that sketched some masterly Outlines of Public Characters in the Morning Post about ten years ago". (The announcement offered Wellington, Melville, and Wilberforce as well.) His apprenticeship having been served, he would now rise above topical journalism with a gallery of grand portraits, also an introductory Letter "on the nature and uses of character-writing". This introduction he promised to deliver "on Monday Morning by a quarter after nine, together with Pitt's & Fox's" Characters.[3] Street was not only co-operative; he was ready to make room at once, and he announced the "general introduction" for Monday and "The character of Buonaparte on Thursday".[4] This, the fifth public announcement of "To-morrow Buonaparte", was a magnificent gesture.

But nothing happened. Were both men bluffing? Not one of the portraits ever appeared, and none survive in manuscript.[5] Nor did Coleridge run away. Under two months later he was back in the auxiliary editor's chair with a satiric prose exposé (on 30 November) of what could be called the "Irish Eloquence" and empty-headedness of the Parliamentary Opposition, and in January 1812 he held forth on

[1] To Stuart [28 Apr 1811]: *CL* III 319.

[2] To Godwin 5 Oct 1811, to Street [5 Oct]: *CL* III 335–6.

[3] *CL* III 336.

[4] See editorial notices Sept, Oct 1811.

[5] Yet C may have been able to show sheaves of work in progress, even a recent draft (far from the full portrait promised) of "Buonaparte" (see App B, 1810, below).

the topic that calls for his later title, "Is the Church in Danger?", leading up to an April Fool's day "Modest Proposal, for Abolishing the Church of England".[1] Two March contributions resume the standard Coleridgian analysis of party politics.

It is clear that Coleridge fully intended to fulfil his promise. Ten months later he would be offering to Stuart the "alas, long promised Characters" "which I have in a more or less fragmentary form by me".[2] Perhaps he had been hammering on Street's door so long (though not with these, which Street would at any time have welcomed) that he was stunned when it opened. In 1816 he explained to Stuart that ever since the suppression of the Duke of York essay he had been unable to look on the conduct of the *Courier* "without some pain". It had "gradually lost that sanctifying Spirit, which was the Life of its Life", he felt. "For had the Paper maintained & asserted not only its independence, but its *appearance* of it, it is true that Mr. Street might not have had Mr. Croker to dine with him, or received as many Nods & Shakes of the Hand from Lord This or That; but at least equally true, that the Ministry would have been far more effectually served, and that (I speak *now* from Facts) both the Paper & its Conductor would have been held by the Adherents of Ministers in far higher respect—. And after all, Ministers do not *love* Newspapers in their hearts, not even those that support them".[3] Stuart did not obey Coleridge's injunction to burn this letter; he answered it and later appended a summary of his reply, to the effect "that as long as I actively interfered, the Paper was conducted on the independent Principles alluded to by Coleridge".[4]

There is a curious *double entendre* in what both men say about the appearance of independence. With Stuart it was frankly a matter of "keeping on terms with the Ministers" by disagreeing with them occasionally "in the most friendly way" and then offsetting one criticism with two endorsements ("if we thought one thing wrong, we placed forward two that were right"). "But this course required great delicacy of management; the slightest mistake spoiled the Plan. These mistakes Street fell into & embarrassed himself with the

1 For the title see a letter to Stuart 7 Aug 1812: *CL* III 415–16.

2 Ibid.

3 8 May 1816: *CL* IV 639–40. Cf Cobbett *Political Register* 20 Jan 1811: "They despise the *Courier*...but, it keeps them in countenance; they are gratified to see in print what even they would be ashamed to utter" etc. And see Jerdan *Autobiography* I 92: "... the most distinguished characters of all ranks and professions, feasted at [Street's] plenteous board, and yet, in the end, suffered the stricken man to slink into...obscurity...".

4 *CL* IV 640n.

Ministers." But it was clearly a matter not simply of error but of calculation; Stuart's tale reveals that he strove for apparent independence while Street sought to demonstrate authoritative dependence. "I found it better therefore from the year 1810 or 1811 to leave Street entirely to his own course, as I would not take the trouble of conducting the Paper. So it gradually slid into a mere...Instrument of the Treasury, Street making it acquire the reputation even of being official. This best served his purposes [N.B.]; but from the year 1816 I resolved gradually to withdraw[1] from the Paper altogether [more completely or finally than in 1811, apparently]. The Paper acquired a very high character for being official and a great circulation[2] but it became very ~~obnoxious~~ odious to the Mob."[3]

Apparently for Street's purposes the more openly he dined with government agents the better.[4] He probably appreciated the value of

[1] Here a deleted passage in the ms reads "and at the end of that year applied to Watts as my Locum tenens Deputy, and to be a Proprietor". BM Add MS 34046 f 164.

[2] The average daily sale in 1808 was over 6000, by Jul 1809 over 6500 (claimed to be as much as any two other papers), near 7000 by 1810, reaching 9000 in 1814. *Courier* 23 Nov 1810, 3 Jan 1814; cf 17 Feb 1810. RS in 1808 gave the daily printing as 5000 and the readership, counting four persons to each paper, as 20,000. *S Letters* (Curry) I 475. James Grant *The Newspaper Press* (1871) 346–67 gives wildly improbable figures (if accurate, the *Courier*'s own boasts would have been higher) of "about 12,000 copies" during the war (i.e. before 1815) with 16,500 copies "on one occasion".

[3] BM Add MS 34046 f 164. Stuart's note on C's letter of 8 May 1816, summarising his reply. Given incompletely in *CL* IV 640n.

[4] The liaison man was John Wilson Croker (1780–1857), a member of John Murray's literary group, defender of the Duke of York against Wardle's charges in 1809. Stuart and C would know that something was going on when he dined with Street. In 1811, for example, Croker persuaded John Walter of *The Times* to give partial support to Perceval in return for favours and "comments" (tips or hand-outs). Stuart must have been familiar with such trafficking. But Street worked closer to sources of power, and on levels perhaps beneath Croker's ken. His developing the *Courier* into the principal ministerial paper (see Aspinall 91 and 185) gave him a base for his more secret service to persons described as "respectable individuals of the High Tory party, not members of the Government" (to adapt a quotation in Aspinall 222) and to the Home Office. In Dec 1816, when government spies, notoriously John Castle, injected revolutionary bluster into the talk of the organisers of popular demonstrations in Spa Fields (see Thompson 632–6), Street collaborated with the Home Office, through John Beckett and his informer Dowling "the Spectacle Spy", in preparing the *Courier* report of "the speeches of the Watsons" from Dowling's notes, improved by "various hints...tending to prove the extended system [i.e. revolutionary conspiracy] in which the late tumults had their origin" (report quoted in Aspinall 406; see also 84). (Dowling in turn gave evidence at the elder Watson's trial for high treason.) Street could resist instructions from the Treasury when they meant "risking the popularity of his paper", as Arbuthnot

attacks on "the venal *Courier*" as advertising. But he certainly made it difficult for Stuart and Coleridge to keep from *knowing* that the term was accurate. As a former butt of the *Anti-Jacobin*, Coleridge cannot have relished the raven croak of Cobbett at the *Courier*'s serving "all the old blood-sucking Anti-Jacobin crew",[1] even though after March 1811, when the rumour of Coleridge's joining the *Courier* had been premature, Cobbett did not attempt further allusions to the "coadjutor" beside the "venal man" but kept the tone of his dissections of *Courier* articles impersonal.[2] Coleridge, in one of the last contributions (21 September) of his trial term, jested about an encounter with one of Cobbett's readers:

> A fellow in rags, who had held my horse for the few moments that I had occasion to dismount, expressed his thanks for a shilling, in these words:—"Bless your honour! I have not had a pint of beer, or seen the *Register*, for a week past." "The *Register*?" quoth I—"Aye," replies he, with a grin, "Cobbett's the man, Sir! He has *Ideas*—A man's nothing without Ideas."

---

complained in 1813 (Aspinall 216) and evidently knew he had the backing to offend the parvenue Canning even when in the cabinet and despite Stuart (see ibid passim). When the ultra Tories went into opposition to Canning's own ministry in 1827, Arbuthnot sought out Street, "sure that he of all men would be the most useful" (ibid 326). He commanded large fees. Consider the implications of Beckett's wry note to Lord Lowther, c 1818, and his approving that Lowther "acquiesce": "Street's letter [mentions] that the Big Wigs hereabouts [either Home Office or Lowther's committee for managing the press] had pressed him to give a helping hand at the *Courier*—but he seems flat about himself." Street has made a request to Lowther, unexplained by either to Beckett, who shrugs: "Surely it can't be poverty!" (ibid 212–13).

Street was their man for emergencies, as when Lowther wanted a London expert to guide WW and De Q in launching the *Westmoreland Gazette* (ibid 358–9, 361). But he ran his own enterprise; he "knew well" the smugglers of Continental news—and thus obtained direct as well as indirect access to official sources; he made international connexions: in 1822 he wrote a hypocritically loyal letter to Canning offering "to place the *Courier* entirely at your command" even while, as Canning later discovered, "the villain...took his lessons partly from the French Embassy here and partly from our own ultras" (ibid 214).

On Croker see also Myron F. Brightfield *John Wilson Croker* (Berkeley, Cal. 1940) 26, 156, 165–6.

[1] *Political Register* 30 Jan 1811 p 226. Worse, but perhaps mercifully unknown to C, were his friends' laments at the "prostitution" of his genius. See DW to Catherine Clarkson 16 Jun 1811, evidently recognising as C's the essay of 28 May, on "poor Coleridge's late writings in the Courier" as showing "the same sad weakness of moral constitution" as she felt tainted "his intercourse with his private Friends....They are as much the work of a party-spirit, as if he were writing for a place—servile adulations of the Wellesleys". *WL* (*M* rev) I 494.

[2] For Cobbett's attacks on articles in the *Courier* (by Street and C) see App C 2, below.

A defiant parting shot—or a remark that cut two ways?[1] Embarrassment at Street's insistence on visible dependency may partly explain why, after the auxiliary half year—during which, it is understood, Coleridge's mind, if not his desk drawer, accumulated essays the managing editor would not accept—his main contributions were either jesting *performances* (not to be mistaken for official editorial thought) or series of indignant Letters forced, as it were, upon the editor: the Letters to Judge Fletcher by "An Irish Protestant", "The Present Crisis" by one Junius Brutus, the review of *Bertram* by "L", or the *Wat Tyler* articles purportedly "Rejected" from an imaginary journal.

LECTURES AND TWOPENNY LETTERS

In November 1811 Coleridge returned to lecturing, his main public employment for the next three years.[2] Once again it is regrettable that his newspaper was not sufficiently his or not sufficiently literary to report his lectures. Crabb Robinson managed "to conciliate Mr. Walter's good will" (as Coleridge asked him to do) only sufficiently to get *The Times* to carry a report of the first lecture. Coleridge had ingeniously suggested paying for a puff "by sending occasional articles to the Times, prose or verse", but Walter had at first resisted even an announcement unless it were "cold & dry".[3] (Robinson's

[1] One implication of this mounted arrogance is that Cobbett's readers are ignorant journeymen who have the *Register* read to them in taverns, the *Courier* readers being respectable coffeehouse men. Cf C's report to RS [12 May 1812] of the "really shocking" tap-room sentiments at the assassination of Perceval. *CL* III 410.

[2] Cf HCR to Mrs Clarkson 29 Nov 1811 (ms Dr Williams's Library): "...certainly C. would never have roused him[self] to this effort, if he had not felt an immediate want that impelled him to make it. He has left the *Courier* some weeks...". C's steady run of contributions concluded 27 Sept, but a *tour de force* on the Whigs' "Plan of the Ensuing Campaign" appeared 30 Nov. A letter of 27 Sept (to Dr Edward Jenner: *CL* VI 1025–7) even on the day of his last regular contribution indicates his having hit upon an unexceptionable topic. The *Courier*, he said, was now "open and prepared for a series of essays on this subject" (the history of smallpox vaccination). We do not know whether Dr Jenner responded with materials, but no such series appeared in the newspaper. In justifying the *Courier* as outlet, C described it to Jenner as "the paper of the widest circulation, and, as an evening paper, both more read in the country, and read at more leisure than the morning papers".

[3] To HCR 6, 8, 18 Nov 1811: *CL* III 342–4, 347–8; *CRB* I 51–2. C's stung response contains two striking confessions, each perhaps only partly true, for the history of his journalism. He speaks of having in hand only one "prose Essay" (still to be polished "a little")—this despite the declarations of recent months (and perhaps this Essay is the Bonaparte); and he declares

diary, two days after the first lecture, records that Fraser of *The Times* believed that "Stuart has tried to influence Walter's mind against Coleridge".[1]) Robinson and the Colliers managed to get brief reports into the *Morning Chronicle* of the first, third, fourth, seventh, and eighth lectures (of the first seventeen); and two of these were copied by the *Courier*—a day and a half late, an index of the coolness of relations.[2] The *Courier* further, on 11 May 1812, printed the prospectus of his second series of "Lectures on the Drama" but did not report any of these.

Nevertheless, on the day of Perceval's assassination, Coleridge, appalled at "the atrocious sentiments universal among the Populace" rejoicing at a prime minister's death, went round to the *Courier* office "to offer my services if I could do any thing for them on this occasion".[3] An obituary article was the result. And again silence. But the following August he called at the office, hoping to see Stuart, and left a letter offering to supply twenty articles on politics, "all of which I have in a more or less fragmentary form by me...".[4] Coleridge put the *alternative* to the purchase of twenty articles as a loan "for eight days". Stuart notes that he simply "sent 20£".[5] The proposal in any event was badly timed: never did more space-filling news whelm London editors than in the autumn of 1812. Salamanca, the capture of Fort Detroit...Wellington in Spain and Napoleon in Russia...this was scarcely the time for more of "Is the Church in

---

that he has "always thought & written in the same Tone of Feeling" as *The Times*, has found it twice quoting "sentences which I myself wrote", and considers it "incomparably the best Journal" of Great Britain and "the only one which without impudence can dare call itself independent or impartial". *CL* III 347–8.

[1] *CRB* I 51–2. Presumably to force C to stay with the *Courier*, Stuart not quite leaving Street alone if it involved losing C. And perhaps *The Times* (influenced by Croker despite its independence) shied away from C for his opposition to Perceval's strengthening the royal family.

[2] The fourth was advertised in *M Chron* 29 Nov, in *Courier* 30 Nov; the eighth in *M Chron* 13 Dec, in *Courier* 14 Dec (this lecture HCR thought the "worst" [*CRB* I 55]—it dealt with incest).

The first lecture series ran from 18 Nov 1811 to 27 Jan 1812; the second from 19 May to 5 Jun 1812; the third from 3 Nov 1812 to 26 Jan 1813. The *Courier* did run advertisements (not noted in *Sh C*) of the first lecture on 14, 15, 16, 18 Nov 1811; of the sixth on 5 Dec; of the seventh on 9 Dec.

[3] To RS [12 May 1812, referring to 11 May]; *CL* II 410.

[4] To Stuart 7 Aug 1812: *CL* III 415. The inconsistency with his remark five months earlier that he had in hand only one essay, unpolished, may be more apparent than real. Writing for *The Times* would have meant starting a fresh line; supplying paragraphs for Stuart would mean continuing in a familiar vein and turning to account a long accumulation of notes and ideas.

[5] *CL* III 416n.

Danger?"[1] Street would, however, accept in December one of those comparisons he had always liked, this one of "Buonaparte and the Emperor Julian". Two days later (28 December) at the news of Napoleon's desertion from his own army "a muffled fugitive", Coleridge seized the opportunity to rejoice at an "aera...in the modern world" and in "the history of mind".

In January 1813 when Coleridge's "German" drama (*Osorio* changed to *Remorse*) was finally produced at Drury Lane, a handsome review appeared in the *Courier*—reprinted without acknowledgment from the *Morning Chronicle* of the same day, and without Coleridge's knowing it.[2] Probably Stuart was responsible, as he may also have been for the publication of a political sonnet by Wordsworth on 20 February, from manuscript.[3] For most of the year 1813 Coleridge was in London, sharing poverty and expectations with the Morgans. His extant correspondence ceases for six months after March (during which period there is no evidence for or indication

[1] One of the twenty articles proposed was "Is the Church in Danger?... N.B. The Bible Society—Egyptian Hall! VANSITTART!!!"—a response to a report in the *Courier* of 7 Aug of a Bible Society meeting "yesterday...in the Egyptian Hall, at the Mansion House", at which Nicholas Vansittart, chancellor of the exchequer since May, had been added to the Society's vice-presidents.

And C's first proposal, "Two articles on America in relation to G.B.—and on Maddison's Proclamation" (C had written on Madison for Stuart 5 Dec 1811), was highly relevant, the *Courier* of 30 Jul having announced President Madison's declaration of war of 18 Jun. But Street did not find space for discussion even of that until 3 Sept!

As for Bonaparte, however, C was too late; an un-Coleridgian "Inquiry into the...pretension of Napoleon Buonaparte to the appellation of 'great'" had begun on 5 Aug, to conclude on 8 Aug. The next we hear of C's Character of Bonaparte is its announcement as a lecture topic in the *Bristol Gazette* of 14 Apr 1814. *Sh C* II 57.

[2] 25 Jan 1813, Monday. By "Monday Night" C had not yet seen the *M Chron* review (but had heard that it was by Hazlitt and contained a sneer). To Rickman 25 Jan: *CL* III 427–9. Apparently when C did see it (as he must have done, in the *Courier* at least) he did not think it Hazlitt's nor think it sneering; he omits it from comment in his remarks on hostile reviews in his letters of 27 Jan and 8 Feb 1813. *CL* III 430, 432. P. P. Howe, in his *Life of Hazlitt* (1922; Penguin 1949 p 167), considers it not by Hazlitt but possibly by his predecessor, William Mudford (on whom, see below).

[3] *Lines Composed in 1809* ("Brave Schill! by Death deliver'd take thy flight"), unsigned. In *WPW* III 113 listed as first published 1815. At this stage of the rift and uneasy truce between WW and C, the former seems to have been trying harder than the latter to mend matters. The anonymity of this newspaper sonnet suits either (a) the possibility that WW sent it to Stuart directly but hesitated to force the printed poem on C's attention with a signature or (b) the possibility that WW sent it for the *Courier* to C, who delivered it without attaching WW's name. Consider the perhaps not accidental sequence, in the autumn, of a Stuart editorial quoting WW followed by a C editorial quoting himself (but anonymously). See below.

of any contributions to the *Courier*), and when it resumes he is writing to Stuart and Street about articles that "might be written".[1]

On 28 September, three days after his letter to Stuart, a leading editorial carried out, in part, his suggestion for an article refuting the notion that "the Emperor of Austria [ought] to persevere in the terms offered to his Son in Law [Napoleon] in his frenzy of Power, even tho' he should be beaten to the Dust".[2] This leader rises appreciably above the shallow rhetoric of Street, borne up, I believe, by the more sensible earnestness of Stuart; the peroration is a confection of Streetian clichés—but it concludes with a Wordsworth sonnet! This odd reunion of collaborators was obviously impelled by the letter to Stuart, but Coleridge's hand does not appear in its composition. Five days later, however (2 October), a brief but completely Coleridgian article, even quoting himself, appears—and then no more until January 1814.[3]

Also on 2 October he wrote to Street, carrying further the discussion of the "present expediency" of writing on "the subject of an Armistice" and, briefly, expressing nausea at the *Morning Chronicle*'s faith in the superiority of French intelligence—and embarrassment at putting Street to the expense of frequent twopenny letters.[4] Two days later Street did take up the cudgels against the Opposition's "faith in the immense superiority of French intellect and French resources", but the style shows that he had not allowed Coleridge to write his own piece—nor can the more elaborate themes of Coleridge's letter be found anywhere in the *Courier*. The twopenny letters were welcome as prods, but not otherwise.[5]

[1] To Stuart 25 Sept 1813: *CL* III 441–2; to Street 2 Oct 1813, partly quoted in App B, below.

[2] *CL* III 441; see App A, *Courier* 28 Sept 1813, below. Careful study of this long editorial, in the context of preceding weeks of editorial writing on the war, in which Street's characteristic flippancy and dashing syntax establish a recognisable range of effects, makes me think that Stuart composed the main argument and straightforward passages (with suggestions by C) and supplied the apt sonnet from WW ("High deeds, O Germans, are to come from you!") but let Street concoct the peroration, with quotations from *Othello* and Bonaparte that he had been using all season.

The last line of the sonnet reads "a sacred" (as texts of 1820–32) rather than "her sacred" (1807, 1815), on which rather slender reed I rest the conclusion that the poem was supplied in ms.

[3] Unmistakably C's throughout, the essay of 2 Oct 1813 is based on a paragraph in the *Courier* of the previous day; it represents an effort on C's part to be immediately useful.

[4] Letter cited above, n1.

[5] Perhaps Street was unwilling to encourage C's offer to write (disturbingly) about the Church in danger or

In the winter of 1813–14, when his Bristol lectures were reported in local papers, several of these reports were reprinted in the *Courier*.[1] And a New Year's "crisis" Letter signed "Junius Brutus" was accepted that urged the relentless completion of Napoleon's defeat without a compromise settlement that would leave him on the throne (4 January 1814). At length in the autumn of 1814 he laid successful siege to the political department, with the help of Stuart, who admitted a series of six Letters "To Mr. Justice Fletcher" signed "An Irish Protestant", beginning 20 September.[2] Meanwhile Coleridge called attention to a kind of influence that gave him at least sardonic comfort: "The Courier for the last 2 years has been repeating me with a thousandfold Echo in it's leading §§s"; moreover, "it might be proved, that no small number of fine Speeches in the House of Commons & elsewhere originated directly or indirectly in my Essays & Conversations".[3] The verbal clues, at least, of such echoing can be demonstrated in one seminal and one peripheral example. His definition of an *imperium in imperio* could be heard to reverberate in Parliament and in the newspapers, as in the Stuartian essay on the Catholics as seeking "a Government within a Government" in the *Courier* of 22 June 1813; when he took it up again in 1814 Coleridge could seem to be reclaiming his own. Or, at the level of amusement at provincial language, in 1811 he had written of a "*lengthy* gentleman" and asked to be excused "an Americanism"; eleven days later Street had picked it up, and again twice in March 1813, and then, draping it in heavy pedantry, in October: "*lengthy*, as their friends the Americans—*longus in narrationibus; tarde commovetur, raro incalescit*". Coleridge took it back lightly in July 1816.[4]

---

the Bible Society or Roman Catholicism just because he wished the *Courier* to appeal more to loyal clergymen than to coffeehouse philosophers. As a Tory organ, says James Grant (III 556), the *Courier* devoted itself "to the special support of Church and State", and "the clergy everywhere not only became its patrons by 'taking it in,' as the phrase is, but sounded its praise from the pulpit as well as in private". In figures that we must halve (as we must halve his figure of a daily sale of 16,500 at one time during the war), Grant passes along the statement "that at one time no fewer than five thousand clergymen were subscribers to it". Also just because of this, C must have felt particularly frustrated at the exclusion of so much of his own thinking about Church and State.

[1] The second lecture 19 Nov, the first 17 Dec, part of the sixth 20 Dec 1813. See *Sh C* II 254.

[2] On Stuart's mediation at this time, read between the lines of C's letters to him of Sept and Oct 1814: *CL* III 529–40.

[3] To J. J. Morgan [16 Jun 1814], to Stuart 12 Sept: *CL* III 510, 531.

[4] C in *Courier* 16 Sept 1811, 25 Jul 1816; Street 27 Sept 1811; 15 and 25 Mar, 16 Oct 1813. This pattern suggests the ambiguity of neologisms as evi-

In the autumn of 1814 it required evidently a considerable tussle to persuade Street to accept the "Fletcher" Letters, which were superficially ministerial yet incautiously fierce in their opposition to leniency toward conspiratorial Irish Catholicism. While the first two were in Street's hands, Coleridge in a long apologia to Stuart (12 September) referred to several other essays "on Ireland & Catholic Emancipation", offered presumably in 1811 or 1813, as "unfortunately remain[ing] for the greater part in Manuscript, Mr. Street not relishing them".[1] With a foot once more in the door he proceeded to offer "a series of Essays on the Principles of *genial* criticism concerning the Fine Arts, especially those of Statuary and Painting". Four of these had already been printed in August in *Felix Farley's Bristol Journal* "to serve poor [Washington] Allston", an artist who was "exhibiting his Pictures at Bristol", and to counter an attack on Allston in the London *Sun*.[2] Mr Street was to be asked whether "this Series, purified from all accidental, local, or personal references", and extended to sixteen or twenty essays "containing animated descriptions of all the *best* pictures of the great Masters in England, with characteristics of the great Masters from Giotto to Correggio", would "suit or serve the Courier in the present Dearth" (between sessions of Parliament). With every two of these, Coleridge would supply "one political Essay".[3] Despite a very "flattering" response from Stuart,[4] Street evidently rejected this package sight unseen. A month later Coleridge, sending in his third Fletcher Letter, again offered via Stuart "one political and one critical Essay, weekly—after I have finished the Fletcher Letters—which (if Mr. Street should chuse) I should carry on into a full & fair view of the whole Relations of Ireland to Great Britain, including the Catholic Question—Should it be convenient to you to send me, as soon as possible, a few Pounds, I should be served by them especially".[5]

---

dence of authorship; yet "goodiness", perhaps because it involved a moral concept that Street did not absorb, remained C's own.

[1] *CL* III 531. Apparently the essay of Jan 1812 and the "Modest Proposal" of April were but the lesser part of what C had in manuscript—or in gestation—upon this subject.

[2] To Stuart 12 Sept 1814: *CL* III 534–5. These were reprinted in Cottle *E Rec* II 201–40. C asked Stuart to use his influence with Taylor of the *Sun* to stop its attack.

[3] To Stuart 12 Sept 1814: *CL* III 535.

[4] 16 Oct 1814: *CL* III 535.

[5] 16 Oct 1814: *CL* III 536; C was earnest about both the wish to write and the need for funds.

A VIEW OF IRELAND

Politically our "Irish Protestant" was again moving into hotter water than the conductor of a Government print might like. Coleridge's own view in later years was that he had been, in giving himself the *nom de plume* of "An Irish Protestant", guilty of "self-calumniation"—yet also that he had omitted an important circumstance which, "in truth and candor...should be [stated], that the Working Classes did not substitute Rights for Duties...till the higher Classes ...had subordinated *Persons* to *Things*...".[1] Stuart somewhat disapproved of the third Letter (though he did not hold it up), for what Coleridge interpreted as its mistiness:[2] probably its too generalised castigation of Jacobinism among journalists, barristers, and "Committee Parliaments". After the fourth Letter, 2 November, Street delayed printing the fifth and sixth.[3] On 23 November Coleridge promised two more to make up "8 distinct Letters" (the fifth and sixth having been double) and further proposed a political series on Ireland and the Catholic Question as well as something on America, for which he had prepared himself by "the painful & disgusting task of reading the Quarterly & Edingburgh reviews for the last year".[4] The two more Letters did not get into print, nor anything else in this offer; and here the extant correspondence lapses for a year. There arises a question whether Street vetoed all proposals or whether Coleridge in some other way managed to repay Stuart's latest "*Loan*...by...following articles".[5] In March 1815 he told Cottle, somewhat ambiguously, that he had been "having to turn off every week from" his grand projects "to some mean Subject for the Newspapers", though his actual accomplishment had been "*little*".[6] Perhaps he was referring to efforts that March to publicise his aroused hostility to the Corn Bill.[7] Or possibly he had something to do with the unusual bustle in the literary department of the *Courier* that winter, a series of book reviews: of Lucien Bonaparte's epic *Charlemagne*, 13 December 1814; of Southey's *Roderick*, 20 December; of Charles Lloyd's translation of Alfieri's *Tragedies*, 7 January

[1] See below, 29 Sept 1814 n 1, 2 Nov 1814, C's added footnote.

[2] To Stuart [29 Oct 1814]: *CL* III 537.

[3] They had been in Street's hand some time when C inquired of Stuart, 23 Nov, hoping the delay was due simply to "the Press of Parliamentary & American Matter"—"for if there had been any thing offensive in them, I should have heard from Mr Street". *CL* III 542–3.

[4] Ibid.

[5] *CL* III 544; it is not clear whether he always intended to pay off loans with articles.

[6] *CL* IV 546.

[7] See below, I clxv.

1815; of Wordsworth's *Excursion*, 12 January; of Walter Scott's *Lord of the Isles*, 13 January; and of the *Travels of Lewis and Clarke*, 9 February.[1] So much reviewing was quite unusual for the *Courier*, nor did it fail to attract the attention of its chief beneficiary, Wordsworth, who thanked Stuart "for the notice of the Excursion", observing that his columns had "lately given more space to Literature than heretofore: and very properly".[2]

These reviews can be seen at a glance not to be Coleridge's own writing; yet he had renewed his efforts to sell something literary to the *Courier*, and there remains the possibility that these reviews were of his procuring. Their style, and the circumstances, suggest that they could have been written, with some suggestions from Coleridge, by his amanuensis-*cum*-collaborator John Morgan. Economically the Morgan and Coleridge fortunes had become interdependent; every ten pounds from Stuart staved off common poverty.[3] And in some of the work emanating, in Morgan's handwriting, from the Morgan–Coleridge household, the metaphorical style as well as the thought of Coleridge is evident—in the *Bertram* Letters, for example.[4] In some of it, the manuscript review of *Christabel* for instance, little of his style but something of his presence is felt.[5] In style and general tone these *Courier* reviews seem in the latter category. Coleridge had been discussing the need to oppose the bludgeon-work of the

[1] The RS review was preceded by one puff (an extract 6 Dec) and the WW by three (a notice 18 Aug of "Mr. Wordsworth's Poem" quoting the dedicatory sonnet; 21 Oct "The following passage from Mr. Wordsworth's Poem of the *Excursion* [bk IV lines 576–98], just published, will be read with pleasure for its truth and simple yet dignified language"; 17 Dec "The Country Funeral. From Wordsworth's Excursion"—an excerpt of forty-seven lines). There were advertisements 2, 26 Sept; 19 Oct; 21 Dec.

[2] *WL* (*M* rev) II 198. WW wished to recommend to Stuart "a *remarkably* able" new writer, Mr De Quincey, who was "preparing a short series of Letters" on "the stupidities, the ignorance, and the dishonesties of the Edinburgh Review; and principally as it relates to myself...". But the Letters were never finished. See *WL* (*M* rev) II 198–9.

[3] C had lived with the Morgans in London from Nov 1810 to early 1813, when family business failures overtook them (and C pawned some of his books to help out). Letters to Morgans 29 Feb 1812, Sept 1813 (Pforzheimer collection). Morgan to escape debtors' prison went to Ireland for a while, then joined his wife and sister-in-law in May 1814 in Ashley, near Bath. C was with them again from Sept 1814 to the spring of 1816. The reviews of Dec 1814–Feb 1815 come at a likely time for a joint writing project.

[4] On the long review of Maturin's *Bertram*, see below, *Courier* 29 Aug 1816.

[5] On the Coleridge–Morgan review of *Christabel* see *W&C* 174–91. In *CL* III 542 C indicates that Morgan worked with him on the Fletcher Letters.

Edinburgh Review with constructive reviews of just this sort, workmanlike and appreciative and largely given to quotations of the work in question.[1] Such reviews would refrain from personality; these reflect just about the amount of personal reference Coleridge would approve of (though he might not manage to hold *himself* to it). Wordsworth is treated with respect; in the review of Lloyd's *Alfieri*, in which the comment on imaginative control in drama is not un-Coleridgian, the silence about Lloyd as translator would suit Coleridge's feeling of continued love of Lloyd mixed with "unfeigned Horror".[2] The generous notices of Southey and Scott would have had Coleridge's approval—also the high praise of *The Excursion*, despite his private expression of "*comparative* censure" in response to Wordsworth's prodding.[3] We might have expected Wordsworth to credit Coleridge with some responsibility for laudatory notice in the *Courier*, but at this time such bitterness existed between them that Wordsworth could communicate to Stuart his pleasure at these puffs but to Coleridge only his displeasure at their slight imperfection.[4] In May, seeing a puff of *The White Doe of Rylstone*, a quotation without comment of the sixty-four "Lines Prefixed to 'The White Doe,' A Poem, By William Wordsworth", he expressed to Coleridge no gratitude but only annoyance that "Some prefatory Lines have found their way into the Courier, much to my regret, and printed with vile incorrectness".[5] At this point the *Courier*'s increased interest in literature ceased as suddenly as it had begun.[6]

As for the political department, in Coleridge's correspondence we see his mind turning against reaction and toward Parliamentary

[1] Recently (20 Oct 1814: *CL* III 538–9) C had urged on Stuart a plan "to blow up this Magazine of Mischief" with a series of counter-reviews in the *Courier*. It was an ambitious scheme calling for the aid of some six or eight of "the cleverest literary characters" known to C and his literary neighbour Bowles. Did it materialise, more modestly, in this group of six reviews by (apparently) one or two moderately clever characters (say Morgan and Bowles)?

[2] To RS [9] Feb 1808: *CL* III 59.

[3] *WL* (*M* rev) II 238. What C had to say in *BL* is also more elaborately critical than this brief sympathetic notice in the *Courier*.

[4] The notice of *The Excursion*, WW told Stuart, would "serve the Book". "I owe the Editor a bit of grudge for having *appeared* to join in . . . the vulgar clamour against me; but I forgive him." *WL* (*M* rev) II 199. What WW called a joining in was simply there viewer's gambit of granting that in some of WW's poems many saw "peculiarities" that obscured his" excellencies".

[5] *WL* (*M* rev) II 238 (22 May 1815). The *Courier* text varies from the first edition in a single word, "early" for "earnest" in line 16, which is incorrect but makes a kind of sense and is scarcely *vile*. It is hard to avoid the conclusion that WW was simply being irritable.

[6] For a fuller account see Erdman (1975).

Reform in such a way that he could not have written paragraphs suitable for a Treasury paper on very many of the major topics of the immediate postwar years. He disliked the "pantomime Trick of pretending to give a British Constitution" to the French; he felt the behaviour of the British Parliament itself to be "mad or ideotic": "The Corn Law Debates are more disgraceful than even the Bullion"; and on exactly these subjects the papers preserved "a profound silence".[1] "It must be uncomfortable for the Courier, except on great points, to express dissatisfaction with Ministers—but really...". To refrain from exposing the Treasury's "Apostatism to the Retrenchers, Banks &c" was (he protested to Stuart) to accept great humiliation.[2]

NECESSARY AND URGENT TRUTHS

In March 1815 Coleridge found himself, as twenty years earlier, plunged once more into addressing the public in opposition, this time to the monstrous Corn Bill, "a Commutation of the War & Property Taxes for a Poll-Tax...pressing heavier, the lower it descends...".[3] He drew up the petition to be voted upon at a "public meeting in the market-place at Calne" and at the meeting "mounted on the Butcher's Table made a butcherly sort of Speech of an hour long to a very ragged but not butcherly audience: for by their pale faces few of them seemed to have had more than a very occasional acquaintance with Butcher's Meat. Loud were the Huzzas!—and if it depended on the Inhabitants at large, I believe they would send me up to Parliament."[4] The Corn Bill and the pale faces "haunted" him, as did the feebleness of the opposition in Parliament. "I have hitherto in the Friend, in the M. Post and the Courier, and in conversation, opposed the so called Parliament Reformers—I have not altered my *principles*—yet now I must join in pleading for Reform."[5] This was strong talk; he saw, now, his assumptions false about "the Ideal of a Legislature"; he saw "the historical cause too".[6] And yet

[1] To Morgan 23 May 1814: *CL* III 497.

[2] To Stuart [29 Oct 1814]: *CL* III 540; but the reading "Vansittart's Assentation" in *CL* is a mistake for "Vansittart's Apostatism" in the BM ms.

[3] To R. H. Brabant [10 Mar 1815]: *CL* IV 549–50. The *Courier* on the Corn Bill was—silent.

[4] *CL* IV 549. C had not done this sort of exhorting since his more avowedly republican days at Bristol in 1795. (He and the Morgans had moved to Calne early in 1815.)

[5] To Brabant [13 Mar 1815]: *CL* IV 553–4.

[6] Ibid.

the other side of his sympathy for the hungry, a dread of their rising like lions on being roused, was a confirmation of his anti-Jacobin alarms as expressed in the Fletcher Letters: he assured Lady Beaumont that the Letters gave "no exaggerated picture of the predominance of Jacobinism. In this small town of Calne 500 Volunteers were raised in the last War—I am persuaded, that 5 could not be raised now" (especially, he might have added, after his petition and oration).[1]

And yet Coleridge himself remained one of the poor, convinced that he must starve unless people could be persuaded to subsidise his serious work, he declared to Stuart, "for at present there is nothing to do for the Newspapers, and since the Courier is so entirely devoted to the Government for the time being, there is no Paper in which I could write without offence to my own Mind".[2] The Government for the time being was that of Liverpool and Castlereagh; the increased devotion of the *Courier* was particularly manifest in a series of almost daily squibs and verses attacking Opposition leaders, modelled on the *Anti-Jacobin* and supplied by Croker.[3]

In May 1816, shortly after Coleridge retired to Highgate under the care of James Gillman—he had visited the *Courier* office on the way and clashed with Street by taking a sympathetic view of Byron's Separation poems[4]—Stuart paid him a call and encouraged him to write a series on the Catholic Question, the continuation of the Fletcher series he had wanted to do. After "reflecting a great deal on the subject...and somewhat on the Courier in general" (for he now heard it "most authoritatively uttered" that Stuart himself was "under Bond & Seal to the present Ministry") he wrote a long letter to Stuart, received a long reply, and wrote again.[5] If he wrote on the

[1] 3 Apr 1815: *CL* IV 565.

[2] 7 Oct 1815: *CL* IV 592. "In other words, there does not exist a single London Paper conducted on determined Principles, or that would admit a series of Articles conducted on Principles. No wonder! Is it not even so in the political World at large?" In C's remark later in the month, to Byron, that he is "almost compelled to write...on the Duke of Wellington, Mr —— Picture Gallery, & the Lord knows what, in order to procure 15£..." (*CL* IV 605), the operative word is "almost".

[3] Croker's series, begun Feb 1815, continued for three years and in critical times appeared daily. Brightfield *Croker* 166. RS called them "capital ...some of the best things of their kind". *S Letters* (Curry) II 123 (16 May 1815).

[4] See *Courier* 18 Apr 1816, below.

[5] 8–13 May 1816: *CL* IV 638–43; Stuart's reply in 640n. Note Henry White's assumption about Stuart when, in a letter to the Princess of Wales 10 Jul 1814 (Aspinall 311), White said that in extremity he could sell his paper to the Government, which "would at once buy it through the medium of Daniel Stuart of the *Courier*, Goldsmith of the

Catholic Question he "must be allowed to express the Truth & the whole Truth concerning the impudent avowal of Lord Castlereagh that it was not to be a *Government Question*".[1] On this condition he would "write immediately a Tract" that Mr Street could divide "into 10 or 20 Essays or Leading Paragraphs".[2]

Even so, he lamented the paper's loss of sanctity "under Mr Street". Comparing the *Courier* to a tree, often for Coleridge an image of himself, he felt that there was "no longer any *Root*" in it. Outwardly it was the old tree still, but "barked round above the root, tho' the circular Decortication is so small and so neatly filled up and colored as to be scarcely visible but in its total effects—Excellent Fruits still at times hang on the Boughs: but they are tied on by threads & hairs."[3] Stuart's reply (quoted above)[4] temporarily reassured him, putting all the blame on Street for making the *Courier* "acquire the reputation" that made it "odious to the Mob"; Coleridge replied that he still preferred the *Courier* "with all its faults" to any other: it was still "the best & most effective Vehicle of what I deem most necessary & urgent Truths"; now that Stuart had in effect commended the Catholic essays, "From this Hour I sit down to it, tooth and nail—& shall not turn to the Right or Left till I have finished it." Should they be in the form of "Letters, addressed to Lord Liverpool"?[5] On 4 June the *Courier* published an excellent review of *Christabel* (reprinted from *The Times* of 20 May), probably by Charles Lamb.[6]

Coleridge had not been reading the *Courier* recently; it was now sent him "every evening", and before the end of June he was "really so shocked at the damnable immorality of the principles supported in that paper, which is now little less than a systematic advocate of the Slave-trade and all its West-India Abominations, besides every other mode of Despotism & Ministerial Folly, that I have resolved myself never to let an article of mine contribute to the *sale* of that paper—Besides, they are playing false, as well as their

---

Anti-Gallican, John Walter of *The Times*, or some other of their 'literary hirelings'" (Aspinall, paraphrasing).

1 *CL* IV 640.

2 Ibid.

3 *CL* IV 639.

4 See above, I cliv and n 3.

5 *CL* IV 642–3. No such Letters appeared in the *Courier*, but fourteen months later C did send a long letter *to* Liverpool (with copies of the freshly published *BL* and *SL*) appealing to "the wise and temperate measures of your Lordship, and your Lordship's coadjutors in the British Cabinet...". *CL* IV 757–63.

6 See L. M. Schwartz in *SIR* IX (1970) 114–24 and Erdman (1958) 53–60.

Masters, with the Catholic Question—& Street will never let my Essays be published, even if I did not (as I shall do) retract them".[1] Coleridge seems to refer to Catholic essays written and in Street's hands and to be withdrawn.[2] The context of this splendid outburst, however, is a report to Morgan of a two-hour talk with Stuart, in which Coleridge had tried without success to persuade Stuart to publish a "Critique" having to do with "the fine Arts, and...public places"[3] and had been advised instead that his friend might qualify for a regular job with the *Courier*, earning as much as twelve pounds a week. If Morgan were to commit himself to that sort of job, Coleridge felt, it should be with the *Morning Chronicle*, not the *Courier*, and without waiting for Morgan's answer, he wrote to recommend him to James Perry, the *Chronicle* editor. It sounds rather as though Coleridge were expecting to be an active collaborator in his friend Morgan's journalism; it is noteworthy that he now leaned less toward Government than toward the Opposition—but nothing finally came of the proposal.

What did follow, only a month after Coleridge's resolve "never to let an article of mine contribute to the *sale*" of the *Courier*, was the first of what promised to be a series on the "golden side" of the late war![4] That the second instalment petered out in the opening paragraph, a surviving manuscript attests, but the reason for such

[1] C to Morgan 24 Jun 1816: *CL* VI 1041 (Braekman and Devolder 218). "They" would seem to include both proprietor and editor, but it is Street primarily that C feels "has had his Cue from Castlerag and Carlton House" (ministers and Regent) to squelch C's essays. For another witness to the *Courier*'s increasingly inhumane "tone" this year, there is an unsigned letter to the *Edinburgh Christian Instructor* XIII (Dec 1816) 404–5 that describes both *Courier* and *Times* as "journals stamped with the characters of venality and falsehood" but singles out the *Courier* as having changed its tone and "been superlatively wicked and perverse" on the subject of "the Persecution of the Protestants in the South of France".

[2] On 17 Sept C tells Hugh J. Rose "There will soon appear in the Courier some *Anti Emancipation* Essays" (*CL* IV 671). On 24 Sept he instructs Gillman's assistant to bring him some papers from "the Drawing Room Table Drawers" including "the Letter to Lord Liverpool (Letter the third, *I believe*) on the Catholic Emancipation" (IV 683). It is tempting to deduce that Street did receive, and hold, two Letters; blew hot and cold when C sought to retract them, and even seemed receptive to a third; then let them rot in the Editor's drawer. (The various fragments on Catholic Emancipation in BM Egerton MS 2800 ff 109–10, 112–13, 115 are of later date, as watermarks show; can they be fresh starts or attempts to recall from memory the earlier Letters?)

[3] *CL* VI 1040 (Braekman and Devolder 218). Braekman supposes this to refer to the *Bertram* review, but it sounds more like the "Essays on the Fine Arts" offered to Stuart 12 Sept 1814: *CL* III 534.

[4] See *Courier* 25 Jul 1816, below.

rapid loss of momentum is not apparent.[1] And though nothing came of the "Critique" that Coleridge spoke of as Morgan's, a critical review of Maturin's gothic drama *Bertram*, which was partly Coleridge's and partly Morgan's, did appear a month later. Coleridge had long nurtured the idea that one or the other of Stuart's daily papers might make its fourth page available to some sort of regular literary reviewing. Stuart's position had been that newspapers, especially evening papers, were not designed for such a purpose. Yet even as Stuart professedly withdrew from the management, and as Coleridge's political momentum appeared to subside, room was somehow found for the long *Bertram* review, running to five sizable Letters, in August and September 1816, with a brief sequel on Maturin's *Manuel* the following March.[2]

Coleridge's next contributions to the *Courier* were also in the form of reviews—but their content was strongly political. And they were welcomed for their politics, directly by Mr Street. It was now March 1817, the month when the Manchester Blanketeers attempted to march to (upon!) London with their demand for food and Reform. In Coleridge the fear of English Jacobinism rose to coincidence with the perennial anti-Jacobinism of Street and the Treasury. Now putting his political prophetics into pamphlets that he chose to call Lay Sermons, Coleridge was out with his "second Lay-sermon (a most unfortunate name)"[3] in early March—and Street drew heavily upon it in a leading paragraph approving passage of the Bill for the Prevention of Seditious Meetings, 21 March. Street fulminated against the Blanketeers and the revolutionary "Faction" and then added:

> Of these demagogues, and of their views and conduct, we had intended to have drawn a picture ourselves—But it is done for us by such an abler hand—it is drawn with such vigour and truth of colouring—that we relinquish at once our intention, and adopt and exhibit to our readers Mr. Coleridge's picture of them in his *Second Lay Sermon* just published.

Here Street quoted several pages of warning against incendiary and mischievous misleaders of the people, a harangue against the "harangues of our reigning demagogues" that, though so close upon Coleridge's anti-Corn Bill harangue to the people of Calne, represents

[1] See App B, 1816, below. C that summer was suffering acute agonies from opium withdrawal.

[2] See notes on text 29 Aug 1816, below. Such things (according to Stuart) were "never inserted...but to oblige some individual". *CL* VI 1040–1. C on the other hand obliged the *Courier* with a report (3 Oct) on the recent "Report of the Drury-Lane Committee".

[3] To John Murray 27 Feb 1817: *CL* IV 706.

the ultraconservative climax of his lifelong discrimination between speaking *for* the people and speaking *to* them. Now he favoured clamping Lord Sidmouth's Six Acts upon the nation to protect the people from being spoken *to*. And yet at the same time Coleridge supplied humane matter for Street's opposite number and one of the objects of the Six Acts, the editor of *Hone's Reformists' Register*. Hone would "most unexpectedly find some passages, from which I select one or two for those whom *he*, perhaps, would call the *lower* classes"—especially "Mr. Coleridge's Description of Land-Graspers and 'Christian Mammonists'".[1]

The *Courier*, for once, had been opened to his message of alarm even before he asked. And he was thus encouraged to ask again. He wrote at once to Street: "I thank you for your handsome mention of me, & the part from the Sermon is perhaps as well as any." But Coleridge wanted to correct a false impression given by the *Times* reviewer (and not exactly dealt with by the *Courier*), which lay in a failure to note that although his first Lay Sermon had been written in a difficult style, his second was plain and comprehensible by "the general Reader" on first reading. In short, he asked Street to promise to insert "a short Review of my second Sermon"; and Street did so on 25 March.[2] The review was supplied ostensibly by "a friend" (Morgan), but even in describing it to Street, Coleridge made pretty clear that he was responsible for everything but the pen and ink.[3]

Meanwhile Street had begun publishing Coleridge's defence of his old friend Southey, in the form, at first, of a political critique of Southey's *Wat Tyler*, a long-forgotten closet drama written in the days of Pantisocracy and now (13 February 1817) piratically published by the Radical Reformers (the acknowledged publisher of a second edition being William Hone). In the *Quarterly Review* Southey had recently been viewing the mobile populace with alarm and calling for suppression of the Radical press. In the House of Commons a Whig acquaintance, William Smith of Norwich,[4] asked ironically why the

[1] *Hone's Reformists' Register* I (Saturday, 19 Apr 1817) 386, 408; also II (26 Jul 1817) 14. C had addressed his first Lay Sermon (*SM*) "to the Higher Classes", the second (*LS*) "to the Higher and Middle Classes". Aspinall (p 29) cites the view of RS that "repressive laws would be altogether nugatory so long as papers like *Cobbett's Register* and *Hone's Register* were 'read aloud in every ale-house' and wherever Soldiers met together" (RS to Lord Liverpool 1817). One can imagine the nugatory effect of C's words' being read with approbation "to the mob" in taverns.

[2] [22 Mar 1817]: *CL* IV 712–14.

[3] See Erdman (1961a) 58–60; for the text, see below, *Courier* 25 Mar 1817.

[4] For notes on William Smith see 17 and 18 Mar 1817, below.

Quarterly's (and the Government's) view of "venomous" works that carried "poison to the unsuspicious reader" (he was quoting Southey) had not been applied to "a poem recently published" containing passages "exhorting to general anarchy" ("Ye are all equal. . . Equality is your birthright": he was quoting Southey's play). "Why. . . had not those who thought it necessary to suspend the Habeas Corpus Act taken notice of this poem?"[1] Southey responded with cool righteousness in two brief letters to the *Courier* (naturally) in early March. Coleridge rushed in with four essays in vindication of "Mr. Southey and Wat Tyler" (17 March to 2 April 1817). And then Southey prepared what Wordsworth called a "rod" for Mr Smith, a pamphlet *Letter to Wm. Smith*, which the *Courier* reprinted on the day of publication, 26 April, with a brief editorial, probably by Street, reluctantly bringing "an end to our article"[2] prematurely, for Coleridge had a sequel ready in July.

Coleridge's four essays, with Street's appendage, while serving the cause of suppression, constitute more directly a salvo in the Battle of Reviews, for both Southey and Coleridge rise in defence of the *Quarterly*, resenting not only Smith's slur but his disregard of its sacred anonymity. Since Coleridge himself had recently received something like the *Wat Tyler* treatment (his "beautiful *Fire, Famine, and Slaughter*, written in his Jacobinical days", having been "reprinted to his annoyance by Hunt in the *Examiner*")[3] he could easily identify himself with Southey—or Job (see the second essay)—as the victim of "an old acquaintance" now leading the pack of "Jeffrieses, Cobbetts, Hunts, and all these creatures" toward whom he entertained "a feeling more like Hatred than I ever bore to other Flesh and Blood".[4] Purporting to defend Freedom, they were "Liberticides" who would end in "the suspension of Freedom of all

[1] Extract in *S Life* (CS) IV 367–9. The Radicals and Radical Whigs were collaborating in this *reductio ad absurdum* of political censorship. Brougham had begun the attack in February. Smith spoke 14 Mar. The *M Chron* and *Examiner* preceded and followed. The Preface to Hone's "new edition" of the play came after C's and RS's defences and played off the *M Chron* against the *Courier*. Hazlitt's attacks of 9 and 30 Mar and 4, 11, 18 May in the *Examiner* fill pp 190–241 in Hone's edition of Hazlitt's *Political Essays* (1819).

[2] Most accounts confuse the several RS letters on and to Smith (e.g. *WL—M* rev—II 378). The "rod" is reprinted in *S Life* (CS) IV 370f.

[3] *CRB* I 198. C's poem had, of course, been printed and reprinted by C himself; his current edition, with elaborate "Apologetic Preface" (awaiting publication in *Sibylline Leaves*), was in effect calculated to forestall or draw the teeth of the Radicals' use of it.

[4] To Street [22 Mar 1817]: *CL* IV 714. "Hunts, Hazlitts, and Cobbets" is the list in the second essay.

kinds". And the worst villains were Smith and other "Foxites" who "fostered the vipers".[1] "Since a Quarterly Reviewer has thus been courageously unmasked", declares Coleridge in the first essay, with pious irony, "...Who knows but the apostasy, even of the *Courier*, may be proved in the House of Commons to the heart's content of the deluded multitude."[2] For cheek, "even of the *Courier*" was courageous indeed.

For the third and fourth essays Coleridge invented a "Westminster or Parliamentary Review" edited by "the Youths in the Deaf and Dumb Institution", from which his *Courier* papers purported to be "rejected Reviews". But the invention, no doubt suggested by the famous *Rejected Addresses*, was not successfully exploited. The relief afforded to the Rejected Reviewer is evident enough, but there is more ire than mirth in his descent to mimic stutterings and his devious allusion to stable-droppings. In a letter to Street, Coleridge defiantly professed to "see no possible Objection to the Third" essay, while admitting that the second "was (I feared) an *edge-tool*".[3] "If I were in Southey's place", wrote Dorothy Wordsworth to Catherine Clarkson, "I sho[uld] be far more afraid of my injudicious defen[ders] than my open enemies. Coleridge, for instance, has taken up the Cudgels; and of injudicious defenders he is surely the Master Leader". She particularly disliked "his praise of the '*Man*' Southey in contradistinction to the '*Boy*' who wrote 'Wat Tyler'".[4] In the fourth essay, presenting a brief for the *man* as innocent of the crime of *publishing* the "school-boy's arrow", Coleridge not only insists on a moral distinction between Smith and Southey as scheming politician and detached poet, but he feels so secure in Southey's rectitude that he makes a violent affirmation that even when it was written *Wat Tyler* would have been "as a *publication*...a *seditious* and *inflammatory Brochure*". (Southey would admit its *present* publication to be "mischievous" but "not seditious".[5]) Also, in the first essay,

[1] Ibid.

[2] 17 Mar 1817. It is worth noting that one of the incidental psychological gains C obtained by his speech to the "ragged" multitude of Calne, in 1815, was the chance to clear his political conscience—and record: "I was not sorry to have an opportunity of shewing that I had not supported Government so strenuously from the Treaty of Amiens to the present Year from any interested motive, but from conscience." To Brabant [10 Mar 1815]: *CL* IV 549.

[3] [23 Mar 1817]: *CL* IV 715.

[4] *WL* (*M* rev) II 379.

[5] C's "Apologetic Preface" to *Fire, Famine and Slaughter* does not admit his own work to have been seditious or inflammatory. It must be recalled that when C himself was charged with youthful Jacobinism, he would issue a softened and abridged text of one of his Jacobinical speeches as evidence. See also *CL* IV 798.

since Smith had criticised "the settled, determined malignity of a renegade", Coleridge must insist "that it is natural and necessary for a renegade, as he calls him, to be more violent than another man". Southey personally, however, was not perturbed. To the attacks he responded "gaily", appreciating their publicity value. To Coleridge's "very excellent paper" his reaction was that he was glad to see his old comrade "called forth" to battle; it might even lead to his rejoining the family circle at Keswick.[1]

For these essays Coleridge asked to be paid two guineas a column, and, asking Stuart to send him "any pamphlets worth reading", he intended to go on writing.[2] Yet the *Wat Tyler* series appears to have been his last extensive contribution, though he may have supplied the materials for a digest and endorsement 24 September 1817 of his attack on the *Edinburgh Review* in the *Biographia Literaria*,[3] and on the death of Princess Charlotte in November he sent in a brief obituary paragraph (7 November). In the latter part of 1817 Stuart moved to a rural estate; Street was demoted, apparently because his violent Toryism (abetted by Coleridge's tirades against "the Foxites" and Roman Catholics) was proving impolitic in postwar years; and a new managing editor arose.[4]

[1] RS's letter, quoted variantly in Cottle *Rem* 176 and in Earl Leslie Griggs *HLQ* VIII (1945) 86. Hazlitt's anonymous preface to Hone's *Wat Tyler* focuses on C (pp vi–vii): "Had Mr. Robert Southey made up his mind to revel only in the 'sweet sin of Poesy,' at his retreat in Cumberland, perhaps no ghost had risen...but, to indulge his wayward fancy, injudicious friends sent him the *Courier* newspaper, which, ever and anon, terrified his imagination with strange and marvellous relations; and one Mr. Coleridge, a person residing at Bristol, and subject to similar delusions, being so served likewise, the two poor gentlemen blew responsive notes, and increased each other's alarm, until the one wrote nonsense verse and prose, and the other nonsense prose only." RS's "paroxysm" in the *QR* not having laid the spirit, C "preached lay sermons in the *Courier*, to prove to all the world that Mr. Robert Southey, as an old Poet, and a young Laureate, had a right to a pension, and...to '*a sort of squint in the understanding*.'" The preface proceeds to quote Hazlitt's anonymous *M Chron* series on C's embarrassing defence of his friend the "Stripling Bard".

[2] *CL* IV 712, 719. Letter No 1047 (pp 710–12) should be dated 29 Mar, not 15; it refers to the article that appeared 2 Apr; see below, n 1 to that article. Letter 1052 (pp 718–19) should precede No 1047; it alludes to the *Examiner* not of 30 Mar but of 23 Mar, on the present distresses.

In Letter 1052, writing to Stuart while Street was out of town, C "candidly" expressed his need, offered "a succession of Articles for a quarter of a year or four months", and assured Stuart that he "should prefer writing for the Courier" even at a reduced salary. *CL* IV 719.

[3] See text, App A, below.

[4] *LLP* xi; Aspinall 212. In 1818 Street was one of Lord Lowther's "small committee which managed the Press" and may have visited WW to help set up the *Westmoreland Gazette* (see

A NEW *COURIER*: MUDFORD AND "PLATO"

The passing of the old *Courier* was perhaps also hastened by the ruthless, merry, and reductive anti-anti-Jacobinism of the Hazlitts, Hunts, and Hones, who filled Opposition dailies and weeklies and pamphlets with gibes at "the Typhon of the Courier office" and "the Croker of the Courier" and with Hazlitt's ridicule of Coleridge's defence of "the Stripling Bard". The latter appeared in the *Morning Chronicle*, the *Examiner*, and the preface to Hone's piracy of *Wat Tyler*.[1] The former may be sampled in a letter in T. J. Wooler's *Black Dwarf* for 5 November 1817, addressed to the attorney general Samuel Shepherd: ". . . let me ask you, Sir Samuel, what could induce you to venture an assertion so *singular*, as that the Courier was not under the influence of the administration. . . ? If *you do not know* that this same Courier is only a vane fixed on the pivot of ministerial policy, you know nothing whatever of the politics of the day".[2] Croker continued and perhaps even increased the Government's attention to the *Courier*—but especially to its sophistication and its appearance of independence; he would later boast of having persuaded prime and cabinet ministers secretly to write leaders and special articles.[3] The new editor, William Mudford, whose style Coleridge told him was like Wordsworth's,[4] had got his training as a parliamentary reporter for the *Morning Chronicle*, somewhat reopened the *Courier* to literary matters, and responded to Coleridge in time[5] to take the wind out of overtures Coleridge had begun making to Perry, the *Chronicle* editor.[6] Mainly to get his new Shakespeare

above, I cliv n 4). In Mar Lowther wanted him to spend some time in Westmorland as "an experiment to see how he takes. He will fill up his time very well with Wordsworth or going to see Southey. At all events it might be a visit to them, with whom he is very intimate." Lonsdale MSS, quoted in Aspinall 359.

[1] See App C, below.

[2] Can these remarks in the *Black Dwarf* be also traced to Hazlitt? See *CL* IV 668n. C was also ridiculed in the *Yellow Dwarf* No 1 (3 Jan 1818) 4–5: "The Press—Coleridge, Southey, Wordsworth, and Bentham" (quoting C's *Zapolya*).

[3] Brightfield *Croker* 167.

[4] *CL* IV 813.

[5] By 18 Feb 1818 (see *CL* IV 838), possibly before 2 Feb (see ibid 825).

[6] William Mudford (1782–1848) had published several sprightly pieces of hackwork, including an illustrated book on Waterloo and other battles of the 1815 campaign; as an editor he was said to have "none of Street's force, character, or talent". Aspinall 104, 214, 222n. He became acquainted with C through C's admiration (expressed in an open letter to Street or Stuart passed along to Mudford) of an unsigned review in the *Courier* (3, 5, 10, 15, 22, 26 Jan 1818) of the posthumous *Anecdotes of the Life of Richard Watson, Bishop of Llandaff*.

lectures puffed, Coleridge had written a fulsome letter to Perry, not hiding his criticism of Opposition mistakes and his detestation of Jacobinism but expressing, with Opposition epithets, his utter disapproval of "the Sidmouth Sect" and "the Castlereagh Gang" and, sweepingly, the whole spirit of the Government's domestic and foreign policies.[1] In a second letter he confided warmly to the editor of "the only one of the influencive and (as it were) *authentic* papers which had maintained a literary tone" that he had stopped writing for the *Courier* as not open to the whole truth.[2] Might he, with encouragement, have returned after twenty-four years to the *Morning Chronicle*? His recalling 1794, he told Perry, made him blush. But soon a warm and intimate correspondence sprang up between Coleridge and Mudford, and in January and February 1818 the *Courier* gave Coleridge's Shakespeare lectures the kind of active support his earlier series had quite lacked. To quote T. M. Raysor:

> The *Courier* printed seven announcements (not advertisements) of Coleridge's lectures in February,[3] when help was most needed; the *New Times* (Stoddart's paper) and the *Morning Chronicle* followed the example of the *Courier* four or five times. And Coleridge used two of his poems to give further publicity to his lectures, publishing "Fancy in Nubibus" in the *Courier*, January 30, and "The Solitary Date Tree," in the *New Times* on January 31. After receiving [a cordial letter from Coleridge], Mudford increased his efforts for Coleridge and published on February 9 a brief report of the lecture of February 6...following this on February 13 with a little article presenting Coleridge's claims of priority to Schlegel, very much in the words of Coleridge's letter.

(To Perry 25 Jan 1818: *CL* IV 813–14.) Three epigrams on Watson, inspired by Mudford's first two instalments, were published 9 Jan; I suspect C's hand (see App D, below). For the conjecture that Mudford reviewed C's *Remorse* see above, I clviii n 2. Under Mudford the *Courier* occasionally ran a column on p 4 headed "Literature" that was a survey of book advertisements and brief puffs.

[1] 25 Jan 1818: *CL* IV 815. Only six months earlier C had written a letter of praise for his policies to Lord Liverpool! See *CL* IV 757–63.

[2] [5 Feb 1818]: *CL* IV 829. "...thinking that to tell truth *all on one side* was but a more artful way of telling a lie, I withdrew from all *periodical* political writing as soon as I found the *whole truth* not admitted". To Perry 25 Jan 1818: *CL* IV 814. Retrospectively, this is not unnaturally how the 1811 experience would appear to C; he would forget that at the time he had been prepared to write "all on one side". See above, I cl n 3.

[3] *Sh C* II 307. Actually nine separate notes on eight days in Feb, preceded by an editorial notice 24 Jan "drawing the public attention to Mr. Coleridge's Lectures" (plus an advertisement) and a notice 29 Jan of the second lecture; followed by an eighteen-line notice 3 Mar. Raysor observes: "In the early nineteenth century, when newspapers were limited to four pages...any attention to matters of literary interest might be regarded as an act of infinite condescension and personal kindness on the part of the editor."

In the spring of 1818 the new editor's receptiveness to Coleridge and his principles is further reflected in a series of Letters in the *Courier* in behalf of a "Bill for the Relief of the Children employed in Cotton Factories". For three or four months, encouraged by his Swedenborgian friend C. A. Tulk, Coleridge engaged in passionate agitation to secure passage of Sir Robert Peel's factory bill, seeking out facts, stirring up sympathisers, and—according to his letters to Tulk, Mudford, and Crabb Robinson—doing his best to secure the bill's passage by causing the children's plight to be "*ding-donged* on the public Ear—in Papers, Magazine, and 3 penny pamphlets"[1] and even, perhaps, leaflets for members of Parliament on their "entering the house".[2] In the *Courier* two Letters to the Editor that Coleridge seems to have inspired and may have assisted in are followed and culminated by a powerfully ironic essay in his best Swiftian mode, signed "Plato" (31 March 1818).[3] In this last known contribution to journalism Coleridge reverts to his earliest sarcasms upon Lord Mayor's feasts,[4] champions living children against machinery, and endeavours to "laugh men out of their prejudices" and "open the public eye" to concern for "the health, comfort, and moral condition" of the children *and* their employers and legislators.

[1] To Tulk 21 Feb 1818: *CL* IV 843. Griggs revises to "Magazine[s]", but C may have had a single magazine in mind (not located), though he probably enlisted more than one newspaper (see second note following).

[2] To Green 30 Apr IV 853. And see headnote 31 Mar 1818. In May (to H. J. Rose *CL* IV 857) C refers to "Three of the circular papers—which I have written (that is of the *printed* papers)" as though more than three had been printed (two such pamphlets survive, one signed but one anonymous, as perhaps all the others were: reprinted in *C Life*—G—and *IS*) and as though he had written other *kinds* of appeals, perhaps letters to MPs. The existence of another printed pamphlet is attested by a transcription made by EHC (now in the collection of Kathleen Coburn) of some part of it. The surviving transcript begins: "p 3. of Pamphlet. p. 37 of Report *after* line 20." It ends with the date "London, 15th May, 1818" without signature but with the copy of an imprint, "Printed by W. Clowes, Northumberland - Court, Strand". Passages of a report of some kind cited in the essay or speech (for the whole *may* be a reprint of someone's speech, only presumably got to the press by C) are cited by page number but not quoted, as also a quotation from "pages 374, 375 of the minutes of the evidence before the Select Committee of the House of Commons in 1818", said to contain an "admission of the Master Spinners themselves".

[3] That C and Mudford rewrote, if they did not concoct, the two Letters is a possibility; see 31 Mar headnote. Likewise C could have had something to do with two anonymous articles published in the ministerial morning *Sun* on 1 and 6 Mar 1819, when discussion of the Bill resumed, headed "Sir Robert Peel's Bill" and "Cotton Factories" respectively. A clipping of the latter somehow ended up in SC's clipping file with the query "Coleridge, S. T.?" (VCL E). Neither of these is Coleridgian in style or spirit, however.

[4] See verses of 2 Jan 1798 listed in App E, below; also, probably, the paragraph of 17 Jan 1798 in App A.

One side effect of this agitation seems to have been Tulk's lending him a copy of Blake's *Songs of Innocence and of Experience*—in which Coleridge (most highly pleased and unreservedly rejoicing in *The Little Black Boy*) found a "wild poem", *The Little Vagabond*, so audacious in defence of children neglected and morally exploited by adults as to shock and, simultaneously, delight our essayist and lead him to imagine with relish the upraised "whites of his Eyes" the poem's impact would effect in one of the hypocritical "*modern Saints*" of false eleemosynary pretensions. It is a temptation the present editor cannot resist to imagine that what Coleridge called Blake's "mood of mind in this wild poem", read in February, contributed to Coleridge's wild mood of mind as "Plato" in March.[1]

The mood to which he subsided when it became evident that his ding-donging on the public ear had been in vain is expressed in the following notebook entry: "Feby 25, 1819. Highgate: after reperusal of my inefficient yet not feeble Efforts in behalf of the poor little white slaves in the Cotton Factories.—But *still* are we not better than the other Nations of Christendom? Yes—perhaps—I don't know—I dare not affirm it. Better than the French, certainly! Mammon versus Moloch and Belial. But Sweden, Norway, Germany, *the Tyrol?*—No."[2]

EPILOGUE

In November 1818 Coleridge sent in part of an essay of a "column or more on the character of the late Queen" (Charlotte, who died on 17 November) and on "a restless overweening conceit of Rights independent of Duties" lying at the root of the "characteristics of the Age". But a page of the manuscript was missing and two more pages were to come, and Mudford waited for them in vain. Coleridge at the same time offered to supply occasional paragraphs "which I might as well write as talk".[3] And possibly he did so. Mudford sounds like the sort who could draw out copy. But if any of his paragraphs derive substance from Coleridge's written or spoken conversations,

[1] See C's "rude scrawl" on "Blake's Poems" sent to Tulk with his letter of 12 Feb (*CL* IV 836–8). In his next letter to Tulk (21 Feb: IV 841–4) he refers to "this affair of the poor Children" as a mutual and not a new concern, and proceeds to outline the three points of the Master Manufacturers' arguments to which his Essay should feelingly reply—precisely the arguments to which his Plato essay does, ironically, reply.

[2] *CN* III 4482.

[3] To Mudford [c 4 Dec 1818]: *CL* IV 890–1; cf *CL* IV 896. A draft that supplies the matter of the missing page has now been found, but the conclusion was probably never written. See App B, below.

they bear no discernible indications of his style.[1] The Queen's death, 17 November, it may be noted, caused a postponement of Coleridge's "historical and biographical" (i.e. philosophical) lectures, which Mudford announced at the end of his publication 2 December of Coleridge's Prospectus.[2] Though counting on Mudford, Coleridge was uneasy lest Street should still exercise some veto power: "I hope, that Mr Street will...let my Prospectus appear."[3] He was apparently assured that Mudford now managed the paper. Late in December he asked him for a *tête à tête* to learn "what the Tone in domestic Politics is which the Courier wishes to adopt", and he listed seven headings for discussion—the seventh with finesse: "7. (*Should it be again forced upon your attention*) the Catholic Question".[4] Apparently he soon submitted some actual drafts on the latter subject; a fortnight later he wrote: "If the two or three Letters on the Catholic Question are likely to be of no use to the Courier, even tho' they were compleated...I should like to have them back."[5] In the next sentence, undaunted, Coleridge suggested a reply to some letters in *The Times* on the Bank of England and cash payments, warning that his tone would be that of "a Cassandra on this point", too.[6] In the event, Mudford proved no more receptive than Street; he preferred neutrality on the Catholic question[7] and seems to have been moderate, even Whiggish, on cash payments.[8]

In an aside to Godwin, Coleridge confessed that although reading the Opposition press tempted him to Toryism he could not read "the Quarterly Review (Southey's Articles by no means excepted) without downright whispers of the Devil to be a Rebel".[9]

In 1822 Street was again prominent in the *Courier*, dropping out of sight once more until 1828, when he replaced Mudford as editor for a brief period.[10] Stuart, contrary to his daughter's belief that he had

1 Thomas J. Wise thought he saw several Coleridgian things in the *Courier* of 1818–19, but felt it would exceed his bibliographer's responsibility to make note of them.

2 The Prospectus (see App E) fills two thirds of a column. Not noted in *Sh C*, or *P Lects*, or *CL*.

3 *CL* IV 891 (date more probably 3 Dec than 4 Dec). Mudford continued to insert such notices as C supplied (directly: see *CL* IV 840, 901, 910; or indirectly: see *CL* IV 928) up to 27 Mar 1819, announcing "Monday his last". But few reports of these lectures were made (see list in App E, below); on 13 Mar C lamented no longer seeing Mudford in the audience. *CL* IV 928.

4 *CL* IV 900–1.

5 [c 8 Jan 1819]: *CL* IV 910.

6 *CL* IV 910; see ibid n 3.

7 *CL* VI 1037–8 [19 Jan 1819] (mistakenly printed as two letters in *CL* IV 896, 912).

8 I take C to be responding to Mudford's views in *CL* IV 920 (9 Feb 1819).

9 30 Dec 1818: *CL* IV 902.

10 Street was put in to oblige the new Wellington ministry, as Mudford explained in a signed statement dated

sold out in 1822, continued to hold a third of the shares and occasionally to wield his influence.[1] In 1823 Coleridge made some jottings that show him tempted to venture in a pamphlet or essay on the times a refutation of current Tory absurdities.[2] And in 1826 he wrote for Stuart's private amusement (but perhaps with the newspaper still vaguely in mind) an elaborate plan of a review article on the Waverley novels that was to compare them with the work of Shakespeare, Richardson, Smollett, Fielding, and Sterne and "to give the *Recipe* for the construction of these stories in Scott's novels". Private reviewing had the comfortable advantage that "in a letter to a friend, one is not forced to be on one's guard against the charge of envy [the charge made against him as reviewer of *Bertram*], and such like amiable dispositions".[3]

As late as November 1828, during Street's renewed editorship, we hear that Coleridge "must devote [time] to an article for a Newspaper, necessary for my immediate affairs—O how my soul shrinks from *Politics*...".[4] But the nature of the necessity or of the politics remains unknown.

30 Jan and reprinted in the *Courier* 31 Jan 1828 as "From a Morning Paper" (*M Chron* 31 Jan): "When Mr. Canning was placed, by the King, at the head of his Councils, he had the unsolicited support of the *Courier*. When the grave closed over [his] remains...it was conveyed to me, in no equivocal terms, that the support which I had given...to Mr. Canning...disqualified me from remaining the Editor of it, if the Paper was to continue the organ of the existing Government."

Street, in a long unsigned article on 28 Jan, announced that the editorship was returning to the hands "that conducted it for the long period of nearly twenty years (from 1799 to 1817)—from the close of the war that was terminated by the hollow peace of Amiens, to the end of that more stupendous contest which placed this country at the head of the world." The ensuing remarks, extravagantly praising the labours and "master mind" of Liverpool, convey the impression that that dazzlingly worthy successor to Pitt not only led the nation to the "glories of 1815" and guided it to a healing peace but in effect refreshed the *Courier* with daily inspiration while the Whigs fell silent and ashamed. Canning's rule, alas, spread such "doubt and perplexity" that it was not surprising "that the Journalist [i.e. Mudford] should not have been free from error". But now, "we trust we have again a Tory Administration, determined upon maintaining the Constitution, as it is established in Church and State—an Administration by which the principle of Parliamentary Reform will not be supported—nor the Catholic Question be conceded—nor the Test and Corporation Acts be repealed". But the Reform Bill loomed ahead, and the *Courier*, under a rapid succession of editors attempting to serve successive Whig and Tory administrations, declined abysmally. See Aspinall 222–44.

[1] Aspinall 214.

[2] See App B, 1823; also "The Thoughts of an Honest Tory, of 1821", App B, 1821.

[3] *LLP* 298. In 1827 the *Courier* became, to De Quincey, a "base rene-gado" for supporting the Whig–Tory coalition. *New Essays by De Quincey* ed Stuart Tave (1966) 127.

[4] To Sotheby 9 Nov 1828: *CL* VI 117.

ESSAYS ON HIS TIMES

ESSAYS IN
THE MORNING POST

1798

2 January–9 March

ON PEACE. I

INCOMPATIBLE CIRCUMSTANCES[1]

2 January 1798, Tuesday. New attribution; referred to in essay of 20 January; C's authorship confirmed by internal evidence.[2]

WE sincerely wish that the opposition to the Assessed Taxes may be as perseverant and vigorous, as it is wise.[3] They present to the eye of a calm observer all contrarieties of evil reconciled in ruin. With the injustice and cruelty of an *ex post facto criminal law*, they unite the indiscrimination which belongs to the nature of a prospective statute; and although they increase the burthens of the people, they will diminish the sum total of the revenue. But execrable as these Taxes appear, we ought not to forget that worse and heavier measures must take place, UNLESS THERE BE A PEACE.

Without a PEACE, folly may precipitate our destruction, but no human wisdom can prevent it. A skilful General, who has found reason to respect the talents of an enemy, by considering what in sound policy the enemy *ought not* to do, may conjecture with sufficient certainty what he *will not* do. If we pursue this method, we shall discover a *proof* of the truth of an assertion which has been often made, viz. *that the French Directory will not conclude a Treaty*

1 For poems contributed to the *M Post* beginning 7 Dec 1797 and for the editorial announcement of C's first poem, see App D, below. C's first prose contribution may have been a paragraph of 28 Dec 1797, "The Glory of Bonaparte", given in App A, below. See also the "Mock Advertisement" of 2 Jan 1798, conjecturally attributed to C, in App A, below.

2 Coleridgian terms and nuances, not found in other writing in the *M Post*, include "contrarieties of evil reconciled in ruin", "the indiscrimination...of a prospective statute", "the flush of oratorical courage". Clinching evidence is the appearance of C's favourite image, doubled, in the French distrust of the English "under the mask of Peace" viewed as an argument itself to be disrobed of "its rhetorical domino" (see C's letter of 23 Jan, *CL* I 379; his essays of 27 Dec 1799 and 21 Sept 1802, and *BL*—1907—I 146). See also the following nn.

3 On 24 Nov 1797 William Pitt, as Chancellor of the Exchequer, had proposed to finance the renewed war against France by tripling the taxes on male servants, horses, carriages, dogs, and watches and increasing the house and window duties. Under the public protestations that ensued, even some of Pitt's loyal followers wavered in their voting—the subject of C's satire on *Parliamentary Oscillators* (30 Dec). The formula of that poem—beginning with affirmation of Opposition wisdom, ending with doubt of Pitt's wisdom—is repeated in this editorial.

honourable to this Country with the present Ministers.[4] It is reasonable to suppose, that in their own mind they return this answer[5] to the

[4] It was a common argument that the Cabinet which had launched the war, in 1793, was committed to victory or a humbling peace. William Pitt (1759–1806), second son of William Pitt, Earl of Chatham, had been prime minister since 1783. Though now thought of as founder of the modern Tory party, he considered himself a Whig (of the Chatham–Shelburne group rather than the Newcastle–Rockingham–Portland magnates). His Cabinet in 1798 was composed of King's Friends, former followers of Lord North, and his own followers, all popularly called Tories, as well as (since 1794) Lord Portland and several of his followers. In common parlance the term "Whigs" was now generally reserved for the Opposition, led by Charles James Fox (see below), Richard Brinsley Sheridan (1751–1816), the playwright, and George Tierney (1761–1830), scion of a wealthy London merchant family who appointed himself Opposition leader during the secession of Grey and Fox.

[5] C's view of the Directory's stiffened attitude toward England after the coup of 18 Fructidor (4 Sept 1797), the view assumed in this and his 20 Jan article, was expressed in the *Courier* of 10 Oct in an article C cited to Thelwall as "a very sensible vindication of the conduct of the Directory" (*CL* I 351). The coup had consisted of an arrest and banishment to Guiana of royalists in the new Legislative Councils, among them Pichegru, a general discovered to be in the pay of Pitt. "T. B." (in the *Courier*) observes that the London friends of Liberty are divided but finds "*natural justice* and reason" on the side of the Directory: the purged Councils were using their law-making power to "overturn the Constitution"; the patriots, in a minority, "had nothing left for it but to sit still, and see the Constitution undermined and overthrown, or to violate the Constitution in order to save it". The only law "above the Government" is "the first law of Nature, '*Self-preservation.*'" The Directory, having force on its side, had been justified in using it.

"T. B." applies the argument to England in a way that sheds light on C's innuendoes about "patriotic indignation" in the essays of 20 Jan and later. Would Pitt, we are asked, be justified in seizing and banishing English Reformers? No, because they were not trying to overthrow the Constitution but to recover it; nor were they above the law, as the Councils were. But the King would be justified in seizing members of a Parliament that voted to destroy the Constitution and to take away his veto. "The question of Tyranny would depend upon the King's subsequent conduct...the subsequent conduct of the Directory shews no marks of Tyranny, or a desire for absolute power."

"T. B.'s" article was sent to the *Courier* as "an extract from a letter I wrote the other day to a friend in the Country", and it begins: "Strange things have taken place in the political world since you left Town; and it requires no small attention thoroughly to understand them. The late conduct of the Executive Directory creates great debate among those who attend to what is going on; and even they who profess the same principles of Liberty, differ very much as to the propriety of their conduct". I suggest that "T. B." may be Thomas Beddoes, his friend in the country Coleridge. C's mistaken reference (*CL* I 351) to the article as having appeared Thursday (instead of Tuesday) could mean that he had the original letter and was only guessing when it might have been published. Would he have called Thelwall's attention to it so obliquely? Quite possibly; Thelwall might be one who strongly differed "as to the propositions of our Negociators: "You propose to us Peace or War; and we chuse the former. We chuse a state of comparative Peace with the name of War, rather than a War which may be fatal to us, under the mask of Peace.—Infamous Liberticides![6] we penetrate into your design. You would disband your armies, you would dismantle your ships, that you might be able to extend the more ruinous War of corruption. We laugh at the Members of your Senate, when, in the flush of oratorical courage, they threaten to beard us in our metropolis; but we dread that revenue which gives force to your projects of disorganization; we dread the treachery of that Minister, 'who purchases and pays La Vendee, who buys commotions, who excites revolts, who foments conspiracies and agitations, who scatters every where distrust and disquietude, who rears scaffolds, and inundates them with French blood.'[7] If he can do these things *now*, what may he not effect when disembarrassed from all the expences of ordinary War? We are not yet purged from the leaven of the old system. The vices of perjury, fanaticism, and extreme selfishness, which during so many ages Superstition and Despotism had supplied with fuel, although they will be extinguished by the final influence of Freedom, yet burst forth into ten-fold fury at her first approach.[8] Many among us are yet open to corruption; many, who by their talents and lofty professions, may win their way into situations of the greatest trust. The War lessens your means of corrupting us. War, therefore, open War, is our best Peace with your present Ministers."

Disrobed of its rhetorical domino, the argument will appear thus: First, neither the Ministers or Ministerial writers have ever denied,

---

propriety"; it was a time for cautious identifications.

On Beddoes and his interests see Paul M. Zall "Dr Beddoes the Bristol Brunonian" *The Wordsworth Circle* II (1971) 67–73.

6 A Coleridgian word, possibly his coinage (though *OED* cites RS *Maid of Orleans* 1795 as earliest use). Cf *Watchman* (*CC*) 261; 31 Dec 1799, 1st paragraph, below; *SM* (*CC*) 60; *CL* IV 714.

7 Quotation not located, presumably from an English Opposition spokesman but possibly fabricated by C, who dramatises this indictment six days later in his *Fire, Famine, and Slaughter: A War Eclogue*. The Government's support of French royalist uprisings in the Vendée was no secret. For an ironic contrast between "Ireland and La Vendee" (article of 17 Jan, almost certainly C's), see App A, below.

8 This is C's way of speaking of the person of Freedom and of handling the metaphor of purgation and fire. Cf *PW* (EHC) I 65 and 245–7; *Watchman* No 1 (*CC*) 33. The substance and imagery reappear, with reversed emphasis, in the editorial note to C's *Lewti* of 13 Apr; see App D, below. For leaven as an ingredient of evil in the political dough, see C's essay of 20 Jan.

that English gold has been repeatedly employed in exciting and supporting a counter-revolutionary spirit in France. Secondly, our Ministers still retain their hatred of the present order of things in that Republic. Mr. Windham[9] professes, that every successive event has but contributed to deepen his abhorrence; and Mr. Pitt on the 5th ult. declared, that he ardently "wished the system to be subverted."[10] The present Ministers then avow themselves unalterably convinced, that the existence of morality, of religion, and of social order, depends on the overthrow of the present Government in France, and that intrigue and corruption are justifiable *means* of overthrowing it.

Peace cannot alter those *convictions*, and it will increase those *means*: and these are the only hostilities which the French nation find terrible or dangerous. The principle of self-defence, (and if we consider the pre-eminent horrors of a *civil* war, we may add that the principle of general humanity too)[11] justifies them in their refusal to conclude a Treaty with us, while such men possess the management of our revenues. That the French Negociators did not directly and officially assign [a]this reason[b] may be easily explained. They wisely abstained from furnishing to the partizans of despotism new pretexts for accusing the French Magistrates of an insolent and ambitious interference with the governments of other nations. Let us not deceive ourselves. Peace and the present Ministry are incompatible circumstances. We will grant, for a moment, that Mr. Pitt and his coadjutors possess all the talent, wisdom, and virtue which have been ascribed to them by their doubtless very *disinterested* advocates; and then entreat every man seriously to ask himself whether or no the People of England may not purchase their continuance in power at too high a price.

[a-b] *M Post*: this, reasons

[9] William Windham (1750–1810), Secretary at War, identified with British support of counter-revolution in France. See essays of 1800 passim. Windham had been a follower of Fox since 1783 but was won to Burke's view of the French Revolution and entered Pitt's Cabinet with Portland and other Whigs in 1794. But in *Watchman* No 3 (*CC*) 122 he is said to resemble Burke "as nearly as a stream of melted lead resembles the lava from Mount Vesuvius".

[10] Pitt is quoted in *M Post* 6 Dec 1797 as wishing peace for Europe "and for France itself; as an object of compassion, as a victim to the most devouring tyranny under which a nation ever struggled. It is for the repose of France that I wish for such a system to be subverted, and for happier principles to be adopted." The report in Debrett IV (1797–8) 377 is not so precise.

[11] On justification of Irish and English popular resistance to the Pitt government see 20 Jan; on the horrors of civil war cf 17 Jan (App A, below).

TRUCES

4 January 1798, Thursday. New attribution, on the evidence of style, especially the characteristic pun.

IT was remarked, during the time that Lord Malmesbury sneaked into the regicide,[1] and with the reliques of that smile which he had dressed up for the levee of his master, still flickering on his curled lips, presented the faded remains of his courtly graces, to meet the scornful, ferocious, sardonic grin of the bloody ruffian, who, while he was receiving his homage, measured him with his eye, and fitted to his size the slider of the guillotine! It was remarked, that there are no two words in our language more similar in sense and sound, than TRUCES and TRUSSES, for they both *suspend ruptures*, but very seldom are instrumental in healing them.[2]

QUERIES

9 January 1798, Tuesday; *M Post* title. Reprinted from *Watchman* No 3.[1]

1. WHETHER the wealth of the higher classes does not ultimately depend on the labour of the lower classes?

2. Whether the man who has been accustomed to love beef and

[1] Sir James Harris, 1st Earl of Malmesbury (1746–1820), had twice been sent to "regicide" France by "his master" Pitt or, more directly, Foreign Secretary Lord Grenville—in Oct 1796 and again in July 1797—to negotiate for peace. Malmesbury, nicknamed "the Lion" for his fine eyes and leonine white locks, was both times hampered by demands stipulated by Grenville, whom he lacked the courage to ignore, though fully empowered to treat on his own initiative. After the first failure, Burke commented to Windham: "This mongrel (Malmesbury) has been whipped back to the kennel yelping, with his tail between his legs." On the length of time it had taken "the Lion" to reach Paris, Burke observed that he had had to go there on his knees. Farrer 54, 57.

[2] Cf "...your manufacturers of *Truces*, or rather (excuse the pun) parchment *Trusses* for suspending incurable Ruptures". To Purkis [11 Oct 1809]: *CL* III 245. And see the pun revamped in *Courier* 25 Jul 1816, below, at n 18.

[1] At the end of his *Watchman* review of Dr Thomas Beddoes's *Letter to... Pitt, on the Means of Relieving the Present Scarcity and Preventing the Diseases That Arise from Meagre Food*, C proposes to overcome wealthy men's "slowness to good works" by addressing a few queries to their avarice and fears. The questions that follow differ from the *M Post* recension in some minor details as well as in the variants shown in the textual notes. Berkeley's *Querist* may have suggested the form of these remarks. See *Watchman* (*CC*) 102–3 and nn.

[a]cleanly raiment,[b] will not have stronger motives to labour[c] than the man who has used himself to exist without either?

3. Whether extreme poverty does not necessarily produce laziness?

4. Whether, therefore, to provide plentifully for the [d]swinish multitude[e] be not feeding the root,[2] the juices[f] from which will spring upwards into the branches, and cause the top to flourish?

5. When the root yieldeth insufficient nourishment, whether wise men would not wish to top the tree, in order to make the lower branches thrive?

6. Whether hungry cattle do not leap over bounds?[3]

7. Whether [g]there might not have been[h] suggested modes of employing two hundred millions of money to more beneficial purposes than to the murder of three[i] millions of our[j] fellow-creatures?[4]

COMMON SENSE[5]

a–b *Watchman*: clean linen c *Watchman*: labour, as well as greater ability,
d–e *Watchman*: poor f *M Post*: pieces
g–h *Watchman*: Dr. Beddoes, Dr. Priestley, Dr. Kirwan, Mr. Keir, and the Earl of Dundonald, might not have
i *Watchman*: two j *Watchman*: their

[2] Ironic identification of the lower classes as "the swinish multitude" had become, since Burke's reference to "Learning...trodden down under the hoofs of a swinish multitude" in his *Reflections on the Revolution in France* (1790) 117, a commonplace. On the sentiment of the passage cf the query of Blake's Duke of Orleans: "Is the body diseas'd when the members are healthful?...can Nobles be bound when the people are free...?" *French Revolution* lines 181–6.

[3] Here C omits a *Watchman* query, "whether it would not have been a wise law, which should have appropriated one week at least of every month in each session of Parliament to the discussion of schemes for the national benefit?"

[4] In *The Watchman* C concludes: "And whether to produce and make happy be not to imitate God; and to slaughter and desolate, and to take pleasure therein, be not practices very nearly resembling those of the Devil?"

[5] This pseudonym may be related to a jesting notice in the *Cambridge University Magazine* of 1 Mar 1795 announcing the expiration of that journal (with which C had had some connexion): "N.B. Messrs. *Wit*, *Common-Sense*, and *Grammar*, are totally unsuspected of knowing any thing about it." See *RX* 458 and cf 24 Jan 1800 (in App A, below).

LORD MOIRA'S LETTER

REFORM AND FOX[1]

20 January 1798, Saturday; entitled "Lord Moira's Letter". New attribution; acknowledged as C's in Stuart's letter of 20 Jan 1798 (App B, below); confirmed by evidence of style.

WE have condemned the means by which Lord Moira's letter was first given to the Public; but this letter has been commented on in the House of Commons, and it would be idle in us to affect a more scrupulous delicacy.[2] The information conveyed is briefly this: a large number of Senators were alarmed by the state of the country; they were prepared to co-operate in the removal of the present Ministers; but they made it an indispensible preliminary, that Mr. Fox[3] should be excluded totally and absolutely from the new administration. The reasons for this interdict, though not stated in that letter, are obvious. Mr. Fox has pledged himself to support a RADICAL REFORM:[4] and Sir W. Pulteney[5] and his friends well

[1] For nine conjectural contributions between 6 and 20 Jan see App A, below. For a list of C's five verse contributions in January, including *Fire, Famine, and Slaughter*, see App D, below.

[2] On 2 Jan the *Courier* had printed a letter dated 15 Jun 1797 that had circulated in "higher Political Circles" in "manuscript copies, for some months". It had been written by Francis Rawdon-Hastings, 2nd Earl of Moira (1754–1826), a distinguished soldier in the American war, who had been suggested as the possible head of a new coalition ministry to replace Pitt. Grenville and Windham were also to go, and the new ministers would make peace with France and modify the Government's unsuccessful fiscal and Irish policies. The letter implicated Henry Dundas (1742–1811), then secretary of state for war and the manager of patronage and votes behind Pitt, as a moving force in this scheme of organising a more neutral cabinet—implicated him not by name but by a stipulation that retained him in a cabinet purged of Pitt and Grenville. In a gloating comment in Parliament 4 Jan 1798, Dundas inadvertently confirmed the letter's authenticity. See Debrett IV 589–93.

[3] Charles James Fox (1749–1806), third son of Henry Fox, 1st Baron Holland, had entered Parliament in 1769 as supporter of the court and had held office in admiralty and treasury until 1774; thereafter he remained in Opposition except during an ill-starred coalition with Lord North in 1782–3 and for the few months he served as prime minister in 1806 before his death. Early in 1797 Fox and some of his followers announced their secession from a Parliament wholly under Government dictation, but the December agitation against the income-tax bill brought Fox and Sheridan to the House amid applauding crowds.

[4] See below, n 9.

[5] Sir William Pulteney (formerly Johnstone) (1729–1805), 5th bt, MP for Cromartyshire 1768–74, for Shrewsbury 1775–1805, had written a pamphlet in 1784 against Fox's East India Bill, but in Moira's letter Pulteney was proposed for Chancellor of the Exchequer. He was considered the richest commoner in the kingdom.

know, that if he were admitted into power, he neither would or could apostatize from his professions. His temper, his morals, his intellect, are totally unlike those of the present Premier; and the situations of the men are as dissimilar as their characters. Mr. Fox could plead for his apostacy neither his youth nor that mighty revolution in the affairs and opinions of mankind, which changing the circumstances might, it has been said, have caused and justified a change of principles.

Lord Moira was adverse to this exclusion of Mr. Fox, and appears to have felt its injustice and to have pointed out its impolicy; but at length his Lordship consented to place himself at the head of this party, proposing to himself as the result of their union—1. A peace with France—2. The removal of our financial embarrassments[6]—3. The establishment of a just and lenient government in Ireland.[7] We sincerely respect Lord Moira's talents and integrity, and therefore wonder that he should not have perceived that neither of these three purposes could have been effected without that radical reform, to the *prevention* of which so great a man was to have been sacrificed.

It must, we conceive, appear evident, that the second project depends for its success on the accomplishment of the first; at least, it is not easy to believe that Sir W. Pulteney would succeed where Mr. Pitt has failed. To prevent the national bankruptcy which has already begun, and the confusions which are not far distant, a speedy peace is absolutely necessary; and indeed the gentlemen who applied to Lord Moira appeared not unmindful of this truth.

The present Ministers have endeavoured to conclude a treaty with France, and have failed. This failure, as we have proved on a former day,[8] originated in their notorious and confessed antipathy to the principles of the French Government. The Directory read in the very countenance of our negociation, the pale and trembling fierceness of *exhausted powers* but *unsubdued hatred.* But have Sir W. Pulteney

6 Behind the new tax proposals lay Pitt's need to retard the unprecedented increase in the national debt. By Feb 1797 the metallic reserve of the Bank of England had been so depleted by subsidies to allies that a run on the bank, inspired by the collapse of peace negotiations in late December, began 20 Feb, became a rout at the news of a French landing in Wales 22 Feb, and was halted only by indefinite suspension of cash payments.

7 Since the recall in 1795 of a lord lieutenant of Ireland who had encouraged hope of Catholic Emancipation, the dynamics of Irish disaffection and official repression had been coursing toward the rebellion that was to erupt in May. Lord Moira had been severely criticising the violence that accompanied Government attempts to disarm the United Irishmen.

8 A reference to the essay of 2 Jan "On Peace".

and his friends avowed different sentiments? They have kneaded up less eloquence, less power of argument; but have they leavened the mass with less malignity? Certainly not. With what new advantages then would they open a new negociation? We should only have substituted owls for vultures. Both alike are birds of prey, and the former are the less respectable. But at least it will be said, the new Ministers will have the confidence of the People at home. What—of that People to whom they obstinately refuse any share in the election of its own legislators? They opposed Mr. Grey's motion[9] root and branch; and they have set the seal of their aversion on Mr. Fox, only because they are well acquainted with his determination to introduce and support some similar motion. Is not this to declare, that the householders of Great Britain are incapable of chusing their own agents with common prudence or common honesty; and that their agents so chosen will not promote the true peace and welfare of their constituents, unless they are bribed to their duty by the secret influence of the Crown?[10] Such are the tenets which they must needs entertain who oppose themselves so implacably to the cause of national reform and amelioration; and will the Nation place confidence in the men, who place no confidence in the Nation?[11] The man who believes it, must have the understanding of a driveller; the man who wishes it, must have the heart of a sharper.

But the third project is, if possible, still more absurd. While the feelings and opinions of the Irish Nation remain in their present

[9] Charles Grey (1764–1845), to become Viscount Howick (1806) and Earl Grey (1807), had been member for Northumberland since 1786. When his motion for Parliamentary Reform, 26 May 1797, was defeated by 256 to 91, he led the "secession" of the Foxite Whigs.

The movement for "reform in the representation of the people", begun in the 1760's by Whig landlords out of office and London merchants opposed to the Government's tax policy toward the Colonies and toward themselves, was still primarily directed against the power of the King's placemen and pensioners and the rising price of Parliament seats. But the revolutions in America and France were giving "representation" a more popular meaning. The speeches at Fox's birthday banquet, 24 Jan 1798, appealing to the example of George Washington and toasting "our Sovereign, the Majesty of the People", sounded alarmingly republican; the Duke of Norfolk, who gave the toast, was promptly dismissed from his lord-lieutenancy and his militia command. When Fox repeated it, he was dismissed from the Privy Council.

[10] In *Watchman* No 1 C describes "secret influence" (control of Parliament through pensions, places, etc) as an "enormous *wen*" on the head of the state. See *Watchman* (*CC*) 13–14 and n; see also *Conciones: Lects 1795* (*CC*) 69 and n 5.

[11] On "confidence" as the politicians' catchword, see Lecture on the Two Bills: *Lects 1795* (*CC*) 268 and n 2.

state, ordinary laws and ordinary measures must be ineffectual, either to remove or restrain the impulse of popular fury. Deeply do we deprecate all vindictive sentiments; but there are crimes so wide in their mischief, so foul in their complexion, that to forgive them, as *Citizens*, would generate in us such a deadness of the heart, as would destroy all that delicacy of moral feeling, by which we are impelled to forgive, as *individuals*. We approve not of that proud philosophy, which addresses itself to men as to beings of pure intellect, and would destroy their passions and their affections. It is unsuited to our nature, and must therefore be false and dangerous. Patriotic indignation is necessary to patriotic energy; and he who would suppress it, because it may hurry us to evil, choaks up the fountain of an hundred virtues, only because he fears that one virtue may overflow its banks.[12] Deeply do we deprecate all vindictive sentiments; but the hellish havock which certain men have let loose on Ireland, hallows vengeance; and we would prostrate ourselves before their scaffolds, as at an altar of mercy.[13] Does Lord Moira, who has made himself a witness of the unutterable atrocities which have been perpetrated by part of the English soldiery in Ireland, and palliated by Lord Grenville[14] in England—does Lord Moira imagine, that the Irish Nation will be reduced to consider that as a just and lenient Government, which neither gives them justice for the past, or security for the future? But did Sir W. Pulteney and his friends wish to do this? Would they have been able to do it? We will suppose for a moment that they had given that, less than which the Irish patriots would

12 This passage, beginning "We approve not...", is a reworking of *Conciones*: "Let us beware of that proud Philosophy...", which was an attack on Godwinism and itself a reworking of Lecture 3 of C's Lectures on Revealed Religion; see *Lects 1795* (*CC*) 46, 162–5. On C's view of the necessity of patriotic indignation, and on C's—and Joseph Gerrald's—use of the phrase "rebellion to tyrants is obedience to God", see ibid 145 n 1. Also cf the "Queries" of 9 Jan, above.

13 Cf the moral wrestling in one of the Irish manifestos, an *Appeal of the People of Ulster*, quoted in *M Post* 21 Apr 1797: "Our intentions...are to obtain the great objects of our pursuit, through the means of *calm discussion*. ...The common enemy...have practised upon us a system of reiterated aggression...for the purpose of goading us into *insurrection*, or driving us into *despair*. They have hitherto failed, and *they will still fail*....But, Countrymen! is there not a point beyond which forbearance becomes a crime, and human nature is incapable of enduring? Shall we be forced beyond that point? *If we should*, our poor and feeble oppressors would find, that UNITED IRELAND could, in an instant, trample them to the dust."

14 William Wyndham Grenville (1759–1834) held various offices under Pitt in the 1780's, was created Baron Grenville in 1790, and headed the foreign office until he resigned with Pitt in Feb 1801.

consider an[a] insult; that they had abolished the Test Acts[15] in Ireland, and given the Irish People a full, fair, and free representation in Parliament. The result is evident. No Ministers, we trust, would be sufficiently stupid or daring to give this to the Sister Kingdom, and continue to deny it at home. Surely we are equally enlightened, equally capable of the blessing. We have indeed manifested an almost saintly moderation and forbearance; but we have not yet lost all our human feelings; we could not long endure that Government, which should deny us freedom, only because by our patience and aversion from tumult we had shewn ourselves worthy of it. Sir W. Pulteney and his associators are alarmed by the war, the financial embarrassments, and the organized massacres in Ireland; yet they still cling to that system of corruption in our elections and legislature, which is the true source of all these evils. They resemble a beaten dog, that snaps at the stick and licks the hand that holds it. But surely it must be highly flattering to Mr. Fox to find that the grand scheme, on which the salvation of his Country depends, is consolidated with *his* name and influence; that their friends and enemies are common; that REFORM and FOX are political synonimes.[16]

VOLUNTARY SUBSCRIPTION

22 January 1798, Monday. New attribution, from the central image of the taper lighted "to make darkness visible", C's strong interest in the Assessed Taxes, and the seriousness about "a mockery".

AFTER five days of unsuccessful effort to promote subscriptions in support of the war,[1] the Treasury journals announced on Saturday morning, that the arrangements at the Bank were compleat, and that the subscription would *then* commence. It is well known that it commenced on Monday or Tuesday, but the ill success of the scheme made its promoters deny that it had begun. The public, however, could no longer be deceived, and it was formally announced

[a] *M Post*: as

[15] Religious tests that barred Roman Catholics from civil or military office, partially repealed by the Roman Catholic Relief Act of 1829. George III, throughout his reign, was adamant against "Catholic Emancipation".

[16] Also on 20 Jan appeared a brief squib probably by C. See "God and Mammon", App A, below.

[1] Supporters of Pitt's tax bill who conceded that an ungraduated tax was easy for the rich argued that the latter would make large voluntary contributions to the war budget. With some fanfare books for voluntary subscriptions were opened 15 Jan.

on Saturday, when Ministers gave their personal assistance to the undertaking. The following were the principal sums subscribed:

Mr. Pitt	— 2000	Mr. Dundas	— 2000
The Speaker	— 2000	Lord Bridport	— 2000
Lord Carrington	— 2000	Mr. Rose, sen.	— 1000
Lord Cremorne	— 1000	Mr. Rose, jun.	— 1000[2]

The above paltry subscriptions will impress the public with a just idea of the patriotism of the champions of the war; they will shew the *generosity* and *disinterestedness* of placemen and pensioners. Men receiving 20,000*l.* per ann. from the public, men who have amassed enormous, overgrown fortunes in the service of Government, give scarcely a tenth of their annual income to maintain the system by which they have acquired their wealth, tho' in an hour of the utmost exigency, and at a moment when example is essential to success.[3] Such contemptible subscriptions are a mockery of the people. The people overloaded and oppressed with taxes and other misfortunes are called upon to subscribe liberally in defence of their country, and the example set is that of miserable sums from men wallowing in the spoils of the public; men whom war pampers, and whose prosperity is commensurate with the general distress. The knowledge of the amount they have given must excite indignation.

[2] The Speaker of the House of Commons was Henry Addington, on whom see 27 May 1801 n 1, below. Robert Smith, 1st Baron Carrington (1752–1838), son of a banker, was a close friend of Pitt, who had created his barony in 1797 for political favours. Thomas Dawson, Viscount Cremorne (1725–1813), was owner of Irish estates said in 1799 to have been worth £8000 p.a. Henry Dundas (1742–1811), later Viscount Melville, Pitt's right-hand man, was in Pitt's cabinet as Home Secretary (1791) and Secretary of War (1794–1801); he was also treasurer of the Admiralty since 1782, chancellor of the University of St Andrews since 1788, Governor of the Bank of Scotland since 1790, president of the Board of Control for East India affairs since 1793, and Custos Rotulorum of Middlesex since 1793, to name his major sinecures. Alexander Hood, Baron (later Viscount) Bridport (1727–1814), admiral, had received a large fortune from his first marriage to a relation of the Grenvilles. George Rose, Sr (1744–1818), MP for Christchurch (1790–1818), Pitt's manager of the press and of elections, had been a secretary of the Treasury since 1782, Master of Pleas in the Court of Exchequer since 1784, verderer of New Forest since 1788, clerk of the Parliaments since 1788—not an exhaustive list. His son George Henry Rose (1771–1855) had held diplomatic posts beginning as secretary to the British Embassy at The Hague in 1792; MP for Southampton (1794–1813).

[3] Cf *PD: Lects 1795* (*CC*) 316: "...they expect to be rewarded...in order to which an infinity of pensions and places is necessary, to the great impoverishment of the honest and the laborious...". On pensions see *Watchman* passim.

It serves but to make darkness visible, like a taper lighted up in an immense gloom.[4]

In the true spirit which we have occasionally noticed, in the spirit and ambition by which alone Ministers are actuated, the Treasury journals have lately attacked His Majesty for not subscribing; they have attacked him with a virulence equalled only by their libels against those who would abolish sinecure places and pensions. Ministers pretending to be the champions of the Constitution, have destroyed its best parts; and with an unbounded zeal for the monarchy, they traduce the Monarch. They have repeatedly excited slander against the Prince of Wales, because his Royal Highness would not become their instrument; and now the King is attacked, because he will not lend himself to their views. They love the constitution only in proportion as it gives them power, and the Monarch, as he assists in filling their purses. We hope the King has refused to subscribe from a hatred of the war. He will render himself amiable to his people, by the closeness with which he holds his purse strings; and if it be from motives of opposition to the war, he will greatly diminish the unpopularity of suffering to remain in his Councils, men, who are involving the nation in ruin.

The voluntary subscription at the Bank must prove abortive. Admitting that both Houses of Parliament, and a great proportion of the public were to subscribe at the *very generous* rate of the placemen and pensioners we have already named, the whole sum would not amount to two millions. Out of this would be deducted the Assessed Taxes of the subscribers, and ultimately the sum actually arising would not be much more than one million. One million!—what a poor figure it would make in the Army Extraordinaries! It would not pay the "Candle ends" and "Cheese parings" of office![5]

The difference of the spirit displayed in the present subscription and at that of the Loyalty Loan, is very remarkable. Scarcely 20,000*l.* has been raised within the time in which 18,000,000*l.* was last year subscribed. Such is the nature of advancing money upon a prospect of gain, and advancing it with the simple view of supporting the war.—A Loan-jobber, by putting down 100*l.* can subscribe for 1000*l.* of a Loan, and have time to pay the remainder by installments.

[4] Cf e.g. *CL* I 277: "...the Light shall stream to a far distance from the taper in my cottage window...shew to mankind the...Idol...worshipped in Darkness!" And see *Friend* (*CC*) II Index under "taper".

[5] These terms, attributed to Windham in connexion with benefices, became constants in C's political vocabulary.

In fact it is not necessary he should be possessed of more than 100*l.* since he can immediately sell his bargain. Several persons went or wrote to the Bank, to put down their names, but on hearing they could not be put down unless they gave the money, they remained silent. This circumstance has induced the Minister, rather than strangle the plan in its infancy,[6] to receive the subscriptions by installments at six different periods.

In this proceeding we see copied the measure of Robespierre, so ridiculed and execrated in this country.[7] It is a *voluntary* subscription backed by *forced* loan. A person has the choice of *voluntarily* subscribing his assessed taxes at the Bank, or of being *forced* to pay them by the tax gatherer. The latter is the mode on which Government must depend for efficient assistance. A few Placemen, Pensioners, Contractors, and their dependents may subscribe voluntarily; but from the people the tax must be wrung by a hard hearted rigour. This measure will fully prove the hollowness of the pledges of the *life and fortune* men; it will shew to the world that Mr. Pitt is supported by *some other* means than public spirit.[8]

INSENSIBILITY OF THE PUBLIC TEMPER[1]

24 February 1798, Saturday. New attribution; composed by the author of "Rome" (8 March), an essay Stuart had solicited from C; closely related to C's essays of January and to *Fears in Solitude* and other April writings; confirmed by the nature of the allusions (see footnotes).

THE insensibility with which we now hear of the most extraordinary Revolutions is a very remarkable symptom of the public temper, and no unambiguous indication of the state of the times. We now read with listless unconcern of events which, but a very few years ago, would have filled all Europe with astonishment. To revolutionize half Europe now seems an affair of less difficulty and

[6] A typically Coleridgian phrase; for its complexity of allusion cf *Watchman* (*CC*) 10 n 1.

[7] The forced loans of revolutionary France were common horrors of English journalism. For C on forced loans see *Watchman* No 5 (*CC*) 182, 185.

[8] Implied pun; cf "God rest his body!" in the squib by "Pat. Pennyless" (probably C), 29 Jan (App A, below).

[1] For a conjectural paragraph of 29 Jan see App A, below. Between 29 Jan and 24 Feb, C contributed to the *M Post* two poems borrowed from WW—*Translation of a Celebrated Greek Song* and a Sonnet—and possibly the jesting Latin verses headed *De Papa*; see App D, below. He appears to have contributed no prose.

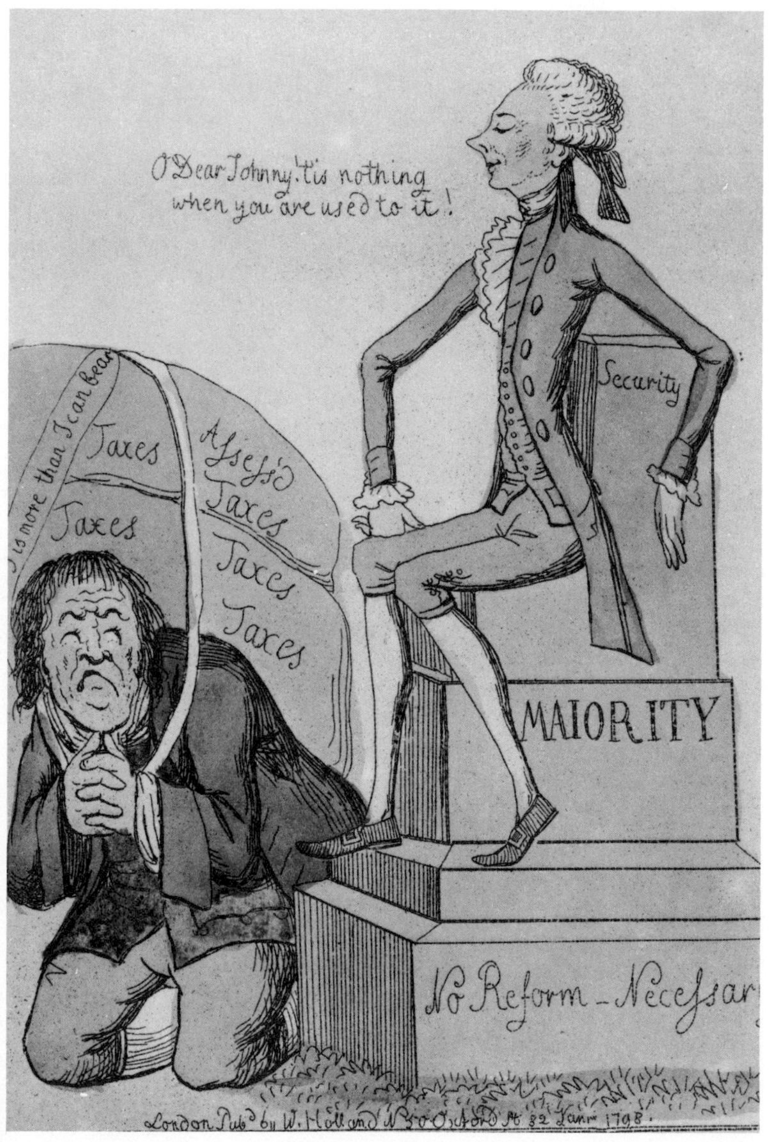

2. *Patience on a Monument, Smiling at Grief.*
Anonymous print (1 Jan 1798). Copy in the British Museum

No "Reform" is necessary for Pitt's "Security", but the Assess'd Taxes are more than John Bull can bear. Cf Coleridge's essays of 20 and 22 Jan 1798, also the conjectural attribution of 12 Jan (App A)

of less moment than an insurrection in a remote province would have appeared in the [year] 1789. The dying convulsions of the Swiss Republics,[2] the dissolution of the Germanic Confederacy,[3] to which the negotiations at Rastadt[4] manifestly and inevitably lead, and the consequent annihilation of the independence of all those Princes and States who reposed under the protection of that great Confederacy, are events now scarcely thought worthy of being a theme for Coffee-house conversation. Government after Government is daily swept away by the torrent of Democracy, and added to its force.[5] We read without emotion that the armies of France have entered the city of Rome; that city which, in ancient times, was the civil, and in modern times, the spiritual metropolis of Europe, which is endeared by so many recollections and associations to the statesman, the soldier, the admirer of the arts, and the man of letters; of which the name alone calls before our imagination every sort of literary and martial glory, and which in the eyes of many men[6] is still rendered august and venerable, by being the seat of the principal Minister of that religion, which has been for many ages professed by the majority of civilized nations. The entry of General Berthier into Rome[7] is now heard with almost as much indifference, as we

[2] The French had not yet invaded Switzerland; English radicals felt little sympathy for the Swiss aristocracies. On 12 Feb the *M Post* printed a French article on the need for a revolution of the Swiss People against their Oligarchy. Not until 19 Mar would news of a French ultimatum and invasion reverse the *M Post*'s—and C's—sympathies.

[3] Thinking of the facility of this dissolution, C scribbled on a scrap of paper: "German Empire—Not an Island, & too large to feel its common interests—why not the same of France? —Much to historical Events; yet still some thing is wanting—it was never conquered—That is perhaps the reason—". Langlais MS (watermarked 1796), Folder A, PML.

[4] Called for by the Treaty of Campo Formio of 17 Oct 1797 between France and Austria, "a congress had been opened at Rastadt between the various princes of the Germanic empire and the French republic, for the adjustment of their respective pretensions; but the settlements went on very slowly, and many differences were either found or made". Bisset II 634. In Apr 1799 two of the French ambassadors to the congress were waylaid and assassinated by a troop of Hussars (see 3 Feb 1800 n 12, below). It was disbanded that year.

[5] Cf 6 Jan 1803 on the force impelling an avalanche; 21 Sept 1802 on the "new deluge" of free men that will sweep away slaves and dwarfs.

[6] But not in C's eyes. At first reading, this passage on Rome as "spiritual metropolis" seems too sympathetic for C to have written it, with his strong dislike of Roman Catholicism; but he is simply being historical: in the recapitulation of this matter, which begins the essay of 8 Mar, the Coleridgian view, based on Gibbon's, is explicit: "kept them in awe by fraud".

[7] Early in 1797 Pope Pius VI had ceded Bonaparte the northern part of his states; in December a French general was killed in a scuffle in Rome, and Berthier, left in command after

should read of the entry of the *Seiks*, or the King of *Candahar* into *Samarcand*.[8] This familiarity with revolutions may perhaps one day be found to be fraught with the most important consequences. When nations have lost their horror at great changes; when they no longer hear of them with amazement and dread; the principal bulwarks of ancient institutions may be pronounced to be already destroyed.[9] What is familiar to the imagination ceases to be terrible; and what ceases to be terrible we no longer feel a strong inducement to resist.[10] When we hear with unconcern the crash of every Government around us tumbling to the ground, the strength of that principle which interests [us] in our own Government must already be impaired.

In the midst of these stupendous revolutions,[11] the Nobility, Gentry, and Proprietors of England, make no efforts to avert that ruin from their own heads, which they daily see falling on the same classes of men in neighbouring countries. Their infatuated zeal for the war and the Minister is indeed nearly extinguished; but infatuation is succeeded by supineness. Exhausted by the drunken delirium of 1792, they have sunk into languor and lethargy.[12] Few men continue believers in the political wisdom of Mr. Pitt. Those indeed must be sturdy believers who persist in that faith in the face of the last five years experience. But though most men have abandoned all confidence in the Minister, yet no man will bestir himself to rescue the

---

Bonaparte's departure, seized the opportunity to occupy the city. The Pope was taken to Tuscany and the Roman democrats proclaimed a republic on 15 Feb 1798.

[8] The Sikhs (spelled *Sic'hs* and *Seeks* in *Asiatic Researches*) were a militant theocracy in the Punjab whose actual forays had never carried them across the northern mountains into Samarkand. Nor had the somewhat Napoleonic King of Kandahar who caused some of "the revolutions of Persia" in earlier years, or the contemporary king of that name (d 1798), ever laid siege to that ancient capital of Tamerlane, which stood in the midst of a plain reported by Sir William Jones to be "one of the four paradises of Asia" (*Asiatic Researches*, as quoted by RS, *SCB* II 512). Tippoo Sahib had, however, once projected an invasion of British India *from* Kandahar (Bisset II 674).

On contemporary indifference to extraordinary revolutions, compare the somewhat bored response of Lady Holland to "the downfall of the detestable government of Rome" effected by mere "common intrigue" rather than "the effort of reason". *Lady Holland* I 174–5.

[9] C uses the same language in the *Courier* 29 Sept 1814, below.

[10] Cf *Watchman* No 4 (*CC*) 131; 11 Mar 1800, below; *Ode on the Departing Year*.

[11] Cf 21 Dec 1799, below.

[12] Cf "the stumbling and drunken tyranny of Robespierre"—words C puts into Pitt's mouth 18 Feb 1800. And cf C's poem of 19 Sept 1799; see App D, below.

Country which he is about to ruin, from his hands.—They see, every month, some of the most antient and established Governments of Europe perish the victims of his system of policy. They see almost the whole civilized world at length subjected (in a great measure by his incapacity) to the yoke of an irresistible and *imperial* Democracy. They see almost all the European States compelled to co-operate in the attempt to ruin Great Britain, some by active aid, some by connivance and collusion, and even the least unfriendly, by passive acquiescence. Not a single power ventures even to mediate between us and France. Not even the most trusted and favoured of our late allies dared to stipulate, when they made their own peace, that negotiation should be left open for us. All these things the body of Proprietors in England must see, and if they continue much longer to see them with patience, they will merit the fate which in that case infallibly awaits them.

[2 March 1798, Friday]

The excellent articles respecting Ireland and Rome[1]*—the Pittiad, &c. to-morrow certain.*

ROME

8 March 1798, Thursday; *M Post* title. New attribution; written evidently in response to Stuart's letter of 20 Jan (see App B). A byproduct, finished first, was the leader of 24 Feb.

THE fate of Rome is now sealed for ever,[1] and that city, upon which the patriotic pride of its inhabitants, and the testimonies of such a long line of illustrious Poets and Historians have bestowed the epithets of Divine, Imperial and Eternal; whose lot it has been to be twice mistress of the world, to have governed mankind by force, and, in a later period, to have kept them in awe by fraud; which civilized as she subdued, and introduced the arts into all the countries that had been conquered by her arms; whose Senators, not those tools who filled the senate under the Imperial line, the creatures and slaves of the Court, who were ambitious of the office

[1] For Rome see 8 Mar 1798, below. As for Ireland, C may have sent something, as Stuart had requested, but the piece may have been held too late, i.e. beyond 19 Mar, when the news from Switzerland caused editorial policy to swerve about.

[1] See 24 Feb 1798 n 7.

only that they might deserve places and pensions from the Crown, who (at least a large majority of whom) supported every Minister and every measure, who sacrificed and sold the rights and liberties of the people; not those servile instruments of despotism, but those Senators in the Republican times of Rome who are said to have been degraded rather than honoured by a comparison with Kings; that city, endeared to the recollection of the scholar and the statesman, the man of letters and the soldier, by so many ties, is doomed to be subservient, perhaps, to the Cis-alpine Republic.[2] Sad contrast to its former greatness and grandeur!

The Gauls were the first conquerors of Rome, the Gauls are the last; yet from Brennus to Berthier, upwards of twenty-one centuries have elapsed, and in that interval the city has successively fallen into the hands of Goths, Vandals, Moors, and Spaniards.

It was in the 363d year of the city, and 389th before Christ, that Brennus made his dreadful irruption into Rome, and massacred the citizens and destroyed the buildings.[3]

It was not till near eight centuries afterwards (A.D. 410) that Rome was again taken by the Goths, under Alaric, in the middle of the night. *Adest Alaricus*, says a Latin writer, *trepidam Romam obsidet, turbat, irrumpit*.[4]

The injury which the city sustained from Alaric was less than she had received from Brennus, though the wealth of Rome, the gold and jewels, the purple, the vases, and precious statues, were carried off to glut the avarice of the followers of Alaric. At the end of six days, however, the Goths evacuated the city.[5] It was again taken by Genseric, and his Moors and Vandals, in the year 455. After a pillage of fourteen days, the sacred and profane treasures of the city were carried to the vessels of Genseric.[6] The injuries of Carthage, says

[2] Note that this long sentence is an expanded variant of the sixth sentence of 24 Feb. Lombardy had been constituted by the French the Cisalpine Republic on 9 Jul 1797.

[3] According to Livy, the Galli (Celts from central Europe), under the leadership of Brennus, defeated a Roman army at Allia in 389 B.C. and sacked nearby Rome. Half a year later the Galli were driven north by the tremendously successful (if semi-legendary) dictator Marcus Furius Camillus, to whom C refers in his conclusion.

[4] Paulus Orosius *Adversos paganos historiarum libri septem* (418) VII 39. Tr I. W. Raymond (New York 1936): "Alaric appeared before trembling Rome, laid siege, spread confusion, and broke into the City." Edward Gibbon *Decline and Fall of the Roman Empire* ch 31 (6 vols 1777–88) III 236n, quoting Orosius in a footnote and also specifying "in the middle of the night" (from St Jerome), is probably C's immediate source—as for the rest of this article.

[5] Gibbon ch 31 III 244–5.

[6] Ibid ch 36 III 440. On Genseric see *Courier* 27 Apr 1804 (App A, below).

an elegant writer,[7] were revenged by the Moors, and the spoils of Rome reached in safety the port of Carthage.

It fell again a prey to a conqueror, and Recimer, the patrician, sacked it in the year 472.[8]

Belisarius entered it a conqueror in 536, but it was to deliver the city after 60 years servitude from the hands of the Barbarians.[9] Yet the vigour and valour of Belisarius were unable to preserve it from the invasion of Totila, who effected the conquest of it in the year 546. The glories and grandeur of Rome would have been extinguished for ever, if the decree of Totila for changing the city into a pasture for cattle had not been averted by the intervention of Belisarius. The year afterwards Rome was wrested by Belisarius from Totila, who took it again in 549.[10] For the recovery of it from the warlike Goths, Justinian was indebted to an Eunuch, Narses.[11] Having now reached the lowest period of her depression, her opulence and power exhausted, Rome contained no longer within herself the power of resistance or of defence. For her deliverance from the Lombards in 754, she was indebted to a King of the Franks;[12] and a fleet of Saracens in 846 would have taken and violated the former mistress of the world, but for the vigorous measures of Leo the 4th, and the fleets of the once contemptible states of Gayeta and Naples.[13] In 1084, Rome fell again into the hands of a conqueror, Henry the 3d, King of Germany and Italy.[14] From this period she remained for a long time free from any foreign attack, and still continuing to influence, and in many instances to direct, the civil as well as spiritual concerns of the Christian world. But at length Charles V. made himself the master of it, not without much difficulty; and for nine months, during which it remained in the possession of a Catholic Prince, the ravages and enormities of his troops were infinitely greater than all the cruelties and severity of Alaric, or any conqueror since Brennus.[15] From the time of Charles the 5th, to the establishment of a much more formidable power[16] than ever she encountered, the city of

[7] Gibbon ibid.

[8] Gibbon ch 36 III 489.

[9] Cf Gibbon's shoulder note ch 41 IV 175 and sentence about delivery "from the yoke of the barbarians".

[10] Gibbon ch 43 IV 284–94.

[11] Ibid IV 298ff.

[12] Gibbon ch 49 V 115. The "King of the Franks" is Pepin.

[13] Gibbon ch 52 V 438–40. It was the Saracen invasion of 849 that was repulsed with the help of Pope Leo IV.

[14] Gibbon ch 56 V 621–2.

[15] The comparison of Charles V and Alaric is Gibbon's; C has returned to ch 31 III 244–5.

[16] Napoleon Bonaparte (Buonaparte) (1769–1821), as general-in-chief of the French army of Italy 1796–7, had driven the Austrians from Italy, quelled insurrection at Rome, established two

Rome remained tranquil; a monument of decayed greatness, and existing an independent state, not by her own energies and resources, but by the sufferance and forbearance of her more powerful neighbours. As an independent state, however, she will be suffered to exist no longer; this last conquest by the Gauls will be fatal and final; for modern Rome, degenerate and degraded from all her former glory, has no Camillus to drive the conquering Gauls a second time from her walls.[17]

EUTHANASIA OF THE CONSTITUTION

9 March 1798, Friday. New attribution; a further extension of C's essay of 24 Feb, with a political mixture of Spinoza and Hume (repeated later: see n 1) that cannot have come from Stuart; followed immediately by the next paragraph, on the indolence of the clergy, the two perhaps meant as a single essay.

IT is sufficiently clear and certain, that the system upon which Ministers are acting, both with respect to England and Ireland, will soon be changed. The Government of the Empire must assume a form more favourable to freedom, or it will be shaped into an absolute monarchy. We have lost all our most valuable rights and liberties. The protection, vigour, and the guardian genius of our Constitution are gone. Soon shall we lose even the forms of freedom, for the experience of all ages has shewn, that no country ever long preserved even the shadow of liberty, after it had lost the substance.[1]

Italian republics on the model of the French Constitution, and carried the war into Austria to obtain a victor's peace in the Treaty of Campo Formio (17 Oct 1797). In May 1798 he would be sent to invade Egypt.

17 The materials for this article may have been assembled when C was devoting "much attention" to the subject of an intended lecture for 21 Apr 1795 "On the Rise, Progress and Decline of the Roman Empire". See *Lects 1795* (*CC*) Intro p xxxiv.

The *M Post* of 8 Mar also contains *The Old Man of the Alps*, C's poem apparently based on a Wordsworthian original; see App D, below.

1 The political psychology of this paragraph is implicit in many of C's utterances; he uses the same reading of Hume in *Courier* 19 Apr 1811, and an elaborate parallel lies in a late ms draft, BM Egerton MS 2800 ff 138–9 (watermark 1820): the ministers can shape their system of rule into an absolute monarchy because the citizens regulate their own conduct by expediency and selfish calculation; the nation's mind being thus indifferent to the moral principle that should guide public acts and measures, it "must anticipate as its fairest prospect the *euthanasy* of its political Freedom in the lenient Despotism of an Oligarchy formed by the alliance of individual *Wealths* with the vast Patronage-power of the Executive". Cf C's distinction between the shadows and substance of freedom, in *Watchman* Prospectus (*CC*) 5. For the pertinence of Spinoza see Introduction, above I lxxxiv n 1.

Our own opinion is, that the change, which it must be apparent to every man, will take place, will NOT be favourable to freedom. It will not, because the people have lost the spirit and relish of liberty. Every man seems to be impelled by the desire of acquiring wealth, and a sordid and selfish principle has introduced itself among us, which has been fatal to the cause of freedom. The change, we think, will be favourable to absolute monarchy, which Hume considers as the true *euthanasia* of the British Constitution, and which he goes even the length of saying, "It would have been happier for us to have established peaceably from the beginning."[2]

INDOLENCE OF THE CLERGY

9 March 1798, Friday. New attribution; possibly intended—as it is printed in *M Post*—as the immediate sequel of the previous paragraph, the question of increasing selfishness having suggested that of increasing irreligion.

ONE of the causes of the alleged increasing carelessness of the people in matters of religion, may be traced to the indolence of the Clergy themselves. Whatever may be their learning or their abilities, however pure their private conduct, yet they seem to think that the excellence and truth of the doctrines which they preach, are of themselves sufficiently manifest, and require no active exertions from them. Or, if they are prevailed upon to rouse from their inertness, it is to exert all their dexterity and argumentative faculties upon some difficult polemic point, which, as it cannot be made clear to common apprehension, does little service to the cause of religion. This dissolute and irreligious conduct of the people, Goldsmith, in one of his Essays,[1] imputes "to the vulgar being pretty much neglected

[2] Quotation, slightly out of context, from the penultimate paragraph of David Hume's Essay IX "Whether the British Government Inclines More to Absolute Monarchy, or to a Republic" *Essays, Moral, Political and Literary* (Edinburgh 1741) 102 (identical in the last ed revised by Hume, 1777). Hume's essay makes nothing of the spirit and relish of liberty; his argument is that a British republic would be unstable (and undesirable) so that either way the Constitution must terminate in an absolute monarchy—which, "therefore, is the easiest Death, the true *Euthanasia* of the *British* Constitution".

Strong evidence for C's authorship of this paragraph is the fact that it and the Egerton MS draft coincide in making quite un-Humean application of Hume's language. See also C in *Courier* 19 Apr 1811, below; also *CL* IV 711.

[1] From the third paragraph of Oliver Goldsmith Essay XVII *Essays* (2nd ed 1766) 141 (var). The mention of polemics is related to the last paragraph, pp 147–8.

in our exhortations from the pulpit. Our divines seldom stoop to their mean capacities; and they who want instruction most, find least in our religious assemblies."[2]

[2] C's further contributions this year, continuing through 30 Jul, were all poetical. See App D, below. Stuart treated *The Recantation* as a major statement of policy (see his notices of 13 and 16 Apr, given in App D), though the paper made a less decisive break with English Jacobinism than did C himself. The political climate was transformed by the arrest of United Irishmen 1 Mar, followed by suspension of Habeas Corpus (and, in May, by military rebellion and suppression in Ireland), and by French invasion of Switzerland (news that reached London 19 Mar). The hopes for Peace and Reform expressed in C's January paragraphs were sunk; Fox now resumed the theme of political retirement (until stirred from it by the rebellion); C's title signifies: if this be recantation, make the most of it. In September C departed with the Wordsworths for Germany, offering to send essays for the *M Post* on German literature but not actually contributing anything till Aug 1799.

1799

7–31 December

[27 November 1799, Wednesday][1]

Observations on the late Revolution in Paris, to-morrow.

[28 November 1799, Thursday]

Observations on the late Revolution in Paris, to-morrow, certainly.

ON THE FRENCH CONSTITUTION. I[1]

7 December 1799, Saturday; *M Post* title (without "I"). *EOT* II 330–8, in SC's group of "probable" attributions; corroborated by *CN* I 600 and *CL* I 552, 554—and by firm internal evidence. Most of the variants of text in *EOT* appear to be errors of transcription, but in one instance SC supplies an obvious omission.

YESTERDAY we gave from the French account the sketch of the new Constitution.[2] We have little doubt that this sketch will be discovered to be grossly inaccurate; yet, on a subject so deeply interesting, no man can wholly suspend his reasonings and opinions. Assuming, therefore (although as a mere hypothesis), that the French reports are true in the main points, we may pronounce this outline of their future Government a most interesting production, and in a high degree instructive, concerning the present opinions of the leading men in France. The prejudices of superstition, birth, and hereditary right, have been gradually declining during the four last centuries, and the empire of property as gradually establishing itself in their stead. Whether or no this too will not in a distant age submit to some more powerful principle, is, indeed, a subject fruitful in *dreams* to poetic philosophers, who amuse[a] themselves with reasonings on

[a] *EOT*: accuse

[1] C arrived in London this day.

[1] For C's verse contributions to the *M Post*, resumed 24 Aug—*The British Stripling's War Song*, *The Devil's Thoughts* (in collaboration with RS), *Lines Written in a Concert Room*, and numerous "Epigrams"—see App D, below. For what may possibly be C's first prose contribution of the season, in Oct, and for reasons why an essay "On Peace" 6 Nov cannot be his despite a recent attribution, see App A, below.

[2] On 6 Dec the *M Post* published an account, dated "Paris, Dec. 1", of the document framed by Abbé Sieyès and Bonaparte that was shortly to be promulgated as the Constitution of the Year VIII. C's immediate and lucid interpretation of what he rightly called the "chasmy and incoherent accounts of the French papers" gave the *M Post* an impressive lead over the rest of the London press.

unknown quantities; but to all present purposes it is a useless and impertinent speculation. For the present race of men Governments must be founded on property; that *Government is good in which property is secure and circulates*; that *Government the best, which, in the exactest ratio, makes each man's power proportionate to his property*.[3] In America, where the great mass of the people possess property, and where, by the exertion of industry, any man may possess it in its most permanent form, this principle may, perhaps, co-exist with universal suffrage; but not so in old and populous countries, in which land is of high value, and where the produce of individual labour can hardly be large enough to admit of considerable accumulation. Artificial power must be here balanced against physical power; and when the physical strength of a nation is in the poor, the Government must be in the hands of the rich.

These truths appear to have determined the present ruling faction in France, in the production of the new Constitution.[4] In England, power is taken from the multitude by absolute exclusion and legal incompetency; in France, the statesmen are endeavouring to realise the same effect more *complaisantly*, by a system of *filtration*;[5] for in this view only is the new Constitution intelligible. The original motion is, indeed, to be given to the people; but is modified so often by so many after impulses, that it is at last wholly swallowed up and

[3] Referred to in C's essay of 8 Jan 1800: "...we have contended zealously, that the security and circulation of property, with political power proportioned to property, constitute a good Government...". The "more powerful principle" alluded to in the previous sentence would have been aspheterism or pantisocracy, an escape from property and its exigencies. *The* "poetic philosopher" for C was Plato; see *Friend* (*CC*) I 472. For a statement of C's views on property close to the present passage, see *Friend* No 11 (*CC*) II 146.

[4] The old Constitution of the Year III (Aug 1795) establishing a representative republic had appeared to C, in more equalitarian days, to embody the positive values of the Revolution. But it had never been tried; before the first elections the Convention decreed the continuation of two thirds of its own members in the new legislature, dooming it to unpopularity and leading France finally to the collapse of representative government and the army-supported *coup d'état* of 4 Sept 1797 (18 Fructidor). That "revolution" had banished or driven into seclusion 200 constitutional deputies—including a deportation of the leaders to Cayenne, alluded to frequently below—and had left few "honourable or able" men in public life (Thibaudeau ix).

[5] C's term, a characteristic coinage (perhaps), for the process of election under the new Constitution whereby electors of each district (by universal suffrage) were to choose a tenth of their number, who in turn would choose a tenth to form a departmental list of "notables", from which the Senate was to nominate tribunes and legislators and even the consuls—at the end of their ten-year terms. London papers carried early accounts of the Constitution 5 and 6 Dec, the official text 25 Dec. Cf 26 Dec 1799, second paragraph, below.

3. *The French Consular Triumverate, Settling the New Constitution, with a Peep at the Constitutional Pigeon Holes of the Abbe Sẹịyes in the Back Ground*. Print by James Gillray (1 Jan 1800)

A peep under the table shows devils forging chains. Underline: "The above are true Likeness of Cambaceres,—Le Brun,—the Abbe Sẹịyes, and Buonaparte, drawn at Paris Novr. 1799". Cf Coleridge's series "On the French Constitution" (7, 26, 27, 31 Dec 1799)

lost. The multitude only throw in the shuttlecock; the rich men hold the battledores, and play the game, till in its due time the shuttlecock once more falls to the ground, and once again the multitude perform the same most *important* office! If this were possible, and if it had been well planned, we should have been foremost to have given it the suffrage of our approbation, as a system which stole away the artificial powers of the State from those who already possessed the physical strength, without, however, tearing from them the soothing idea of self-importance.[6] But to us it appears that the whole merit of the new Constitution consists in its general intention; the execution is most miserable. The plot is as perplexed as that of a Spanish comedy; and, like that, formed, it should seem, purposely to admit the greatest possible number of *intrigues*. To us, at least, it brings with it not the faintest promise of permanency.

We will subject it to a detailed examination. France, it seems, is to be divided into twenty-five prefectures, which are to be subdivided into cantons and districts. The inhabitants of these, in order to become active citizens, must pay twelve days' wages. If it were expected that the labouring poor[7] would really, from pure patriotism, and out of their own purses, pay this purchase-money, it were, indeed, a cruel and detestable tax. But we presume that it is hoped that a multitude will be thus excluded, and the others will be paid for by richer men; and thus the people rendered either inert, or subjected to the influence of the wealthy. Had Sieyès[8] been anxious to introduce a system of corruption among his fellow-citizens, it were not easy to conceive a more happy expedient. At the moment of a general election, will the vanity of a Frenchman suffer him to remain a mere looker-on? He will give his vote for pay, rather than declare his

[6] An intensification of terror had loomed before Bonaparte's return from Egypt and his coup of 9 Nov (18 Brumaire); the sequel must be either a further deterioration of government, leading to a return of the Bourbons, or an effective dictatorship admitting gradually some constitutional republicanism, necessarily at first more in form than in fact. C, recognising Bonaparte's genius and feeling "an Infusion of animal Spirits" (*CL* I 539) at his return, hoped for the latter development. It might not have surprised C to learn that the cynicism with which he viewed the Sieyès document, while accepting its expediency, was much like Napoleon's own.

[7] Cf 1 Feb 1800 and n 10, below.

[8] Emmanuel Joseph Sieyès (1748–1836), abbé and political theorist. Influential in the early days of the Revolution, he dissented from the Constitution of the Directory (1795). Elected a Director in May 1799, he was ready, after 18 Brumaire, with his perfect constitution—only to have it completely reshaped by Bonaparte. Made a provisional consul, he soon entered the silent Senate.

insignificance, by not giving his vote. If for a moment we dismiss this fear of bribery and *clientism*,[9] if the rich should not buy up the suffrages of the poor, what can be the result but turbulence and sedition? To pay the thirtieth part of their income to the privilege of giving a single vote, is an oppressive burthen; not to give their votes an intolerable exclusion; and thus the very first process of the Constitution creates a whole class enemies to it. The power is offered to them only the more insultingly to make them feel their impotence.

This we consider as applicable only to these times of agitation, when faction, novelty, terror, and extravagant hope, suffer no part of the French community to remain purely passive. If we could conceive of this constitution, as having survived its infancy, which we believe impossible; if we could conceive it sanctified by time, and in full possession of the power derived from the opinion of its power, it would still remain an objection, that it invited corruption. In peaceable aeras it does not need the repressing influence of a contribution to preserve the mass of legal voters in their natural inertness: the sole effect were this, that the same evil would be realized in France, which England sees in its pot-boiling Boroughs.—Votes would be collected for[a] the wealthy indeed, but only as far as they employed their wealth to the production of perjury and debauchery in the minds of those, whose morals are of more especial importance to the well-being of society.

So much for the ground work of the new Constitution. We must next suppose these active citizens met in the principal town of their canton, in order to reduce themselves to an hundred, and this hundred met once more to reduce themselves to ten. Milton has described the Pandemonium as a very orderly meeting;[10] and he has not transgressed against probability, for there was no *election* going forward. Those who know some of the boroughs of England will best estimate the consequences of a contested election on the morals of the voters. If it be found that habits of intoxication and proneness to riot have adhered to such places; if aversion from regular industry have distinguished the lower classes, and hereditary feuds the higher, and all this in a dispute whether A or B, with whose persons and characters a vast majority of the voters were utterly unacquainted, should deliver in to the Minister his yea, yea, and no word beside; if this be the result with us, in a people comparatively phlegmatic, and on an

[a] *EOT*: from

[9] Not in *OED*.

[10] Cf Milton *Paradise Lost* II 496–7: "Devil with Devil damn'd | Firm concord holds, men onely disagree...".

occasion almost ridiculously unimportant; what may we not anticipate of a contest in France, in which all the voters *may be* and many *must be*, at once voters and candidates. It is perhaps impossible for any body of men, who have *met together*, to preserve a perfect calmness of intellect, however remote the object of their meeting may be from their self-interests: so contagious is passion, so solitary a thing is reason! What then can we expect of a convention, in which personal envy, and personal vanity are superadded to the influences of corruption, love of change, and political dissention? We might almost as easily suppose the brute agitations of a chaos capable of arranging themselves into an organized world, as such a cluster of such assemblies capable of forming a wise legislature.

There are but two modes in which such assemblies can be conceived as subsisting; under the influence of military terror; or under the absolute universality of the most sordid corruption, in which votes should be openly considered as marketable articles, rising and falling, as at a Stock Exchange. But we will suppose this strong process completed, and 5,000 "picked and chosen" men the result. From these the Constitutional Jury of 80 are to elect the Executive and the Legislature; and after the election, to watch over their proceedings, fill up their vacancies, and, by a species of ostracism, to *absorb* any man of dangerous influence into its own body. Who is this Constitutional Jury? Are they to be elected? And by whom? Are they self-originated? Or, do the three Consuls assume the revolutionary privilege of giving the beginning to an order, which is afterwards to perpetuate itself? To these questions the chasmy and incoherent accounts of the French papers afford no solution; and it would be temerity to hazard a conjecture on the subject. We remember nothing analogous to such an order in antient or modern times, unless it may be supposed to bear some distant resemblance to the Ephori of Sparta. It has, indeed, all the originality of a monster. The power attached to it is strange and enormous. It is to do nothing; but they who are to do all are to be its creatures, and absolute dependants.

The division of the Legislature into the Senate and Tribunate, the latter for the purposes of discussion, the former invested with the power of decision, seems to have a mingled tendency. A Legislature of silent listeners may probably pass laws with greater calmness, and more prospective wisdom, than a body of men perpetually heated by disputation; for every man is in some measure prejudiced in favour of arguments which he himself has adduced. And even [the circumstance] of their voting by ballot may, to a certain degree, prove preventive of faction.[10] But, on the other hand, the individuals that compose it are too much withdrawn from that best and most salutary species of *ephorism*,[11] the opinion of the public; and the public speakers are degraded into mere advocates, the certain effect of which will be, to take all majesty from their eloquence, and thus injure and mutilate the most impressive organ of national instruction.[12] Public speaking is far, very far, from the meanest or least important utility of a Legislature. The debates of the House of Commons have educated the people of England in the science of politics more widely and fundamentally than all the works of all our writers.

Of the Executive, the accounts are so very imperfect, that it is scarcely possible to form a judgment of it. Whether the Grand Elector, the two Consuls, the six Members of the Council of State, and the nine Ministers, are to form one body; or, whether their powers are to be balanced against each other, is left[a] uncertain. It appears improbable to us, that this Constitution will be accepted by the French people, if their acceptance of it be considered as a necessary preliminary; or that it will continue, if imposed upon them without their assent. One error appears to us to pervade the whole, viz. the assumption, that checks and counter-checks can be produced in Legislative Bodies, merely by division of chambers and diversity of titles, where no real difference of interest exists in the Legislative, as individuals, except that transient one arising from their functions. It appears to us simply a skein of threads, tangled rather than divided. The public, however, will wait for more accurate information, nor pass sentence of absolute condemnation on so scanty a stock of facts: yet, we believe, that few are so wholly unacquainted with the nature of the human mind, as to expect very sanguinely a system productive of quietness from intriguers, or a constitution favourable to genuine liberty from a Commander in Chief.

[a] *EOT*: less

[10] In James Harrington's *Oceana* (1656) a bicameral legislature of voteless debaters and silent balloters was advocated. Thomas Poole, an admirer of the English Republican, was more impressed than C by the new Constitution, arguing that there was "more of *Harrington*" in it "than you seem aware of". *Poole* II 4.

[11] "Supervision", "controlling power", from the Spartan magistrates who controlled the kings.

[12] Cf 14 Jan 1800 at n 9, below.

[9 December 1799, Monday]
The Friends of Freedom shall receive sound advice in our Paper of to-morrow. The excellent article on this subject came to hand too late for this day's paper.

[11 December 1799, Wednesday]
"*Advice to the Friends of Freedom,*" *to-morrow certain.*

ADVICE TO THE FRIENDS OF FREEDOM[1]

12 December 1799, Thursday; *M Post* title. New attribution; acknowledgement in *CL* I 552 confirmed by strong internal evidence; listed by Glickfield; reprinted by Colmer 193–5.

THAT *the Gentlemen in the confidence of Government* should consider it as part of their occupation to abuse, with equal virulence, each successive ruling faction in France, is more natural than politic. For if the French Rulers have been indeed dishonest and ignorant, robbers, assassins, and blunderers, there still remains a justifiable hope, that this feculence, which has boiled up on the surface of the revolutionary cauldron, may at last be wholly scummed off;[2] that experience must have trained, and that some fortunate moment will bring into action a corps of wise and virtuous Statesmen; and that the evils which individual mismanagement has occasioned, individual talent may remove. But if the Leaders in France have been already as wise and virtuous as can be expected of men; if their measures, domestic and foreign, have risen out of necessity and the mere nature of the case, then it were to be feared that the case itself is untenable, and that that system which involves such necessity is unfit for France, unfit for human nature. Thus, in proportion as we diminished our disapprobation of the Leaders, we should increase our aversion from the Republic. We are not however surprised, that the hirelings of the Ministry do that which they can do most readily; personal invective is an easy trade; and they have been long apprenticed to it. These Gentlemen have long ago worn out, in all sober men, the power of being *surprised* at *their* blunders. All that they afford us is now and then an occasion of amusement.

But it makes, we confess, a different and most melancholy impression

[1] For C's "Epigrams" in the *M Post* of 7, 9, and 12 Dec, see App D.

[2] For the cauldron and its scum, see *CN* I 162; *PW* (EHC) II 1100, and cf *M Post* 30 Jan 1800 and n 3, below.

on our minds, that men, *who believe themselves* the friends of freedom,[3] should be so duped by the heat of the game as to play into their adversaries' hands: and that while the culprits in France are industriously criminating each other, the professed lovers of liberty in England should be employing every trick of sophistry in exculpating them all; incessant manufacturers of excuses for men, who have scarcely the impudence to attempt a definite excuse for themselves. What a rare *fluidity* must a man's PRINCIPLES possess, that can be emptied so rapidly from one mould into another, and assume, with such equal facility, the shape of each!

We recognize three distinct classes of these tenacious, though versatile, apologists. The first is composed of men who endeavour to make bad practices sit easy on them by the adoption of bad principles. *Humists* in opinion,[4] debauchees in conduct, they have lost all power of sympathising with whatever exists in society, and mistake for philosophy, and a love of freedom, that restlessness of mind and body which results from lewd habits and embarrassed circumstances. These men find, from each successive explosion in France, a stimulus so necessary and so pleasurable, that each in its turn is first palliated and finally justified. Their modes of justification are, indeed, laughably inconsistent with each other; but this forms no objection with men who love *fashions* in philosophy, and would deem it a proof of intellectual poverty to appear thrice together in the same habiliments. Of the comparative number of this first class we can form no opinion; a very few are much too many. In the second class we place those who, having dwelt with unfeigned benevolence on the mass of evils in society, associate with all who profess to heal them, feelings so ardent, that they do not suffer themselves to distinguish between physicians and empirics. They look upon the present Ministry not only as too completely occupied in the anxieties of self-defence, to be interested concerning the permanent well being of their fellow-subjects; but even as prosecuting a direct system of hostility against

[3] C typified three classes of Friends of Freedom in England, i.e. opponents of Pitt's policy of repression, in *MPL* and *Conciones: Lects 1795* (*CC*) 8–13, 37–40. See also *CL* I 395.

[4] Persons who act on the philosophical assumptions of David Hume's atomism: they view as virtuous "any action, sentiment, or character" that gives them pleasure, even (Hume as historian would have been outraged at the application) the successive revolutions in France. See *A Treatise of Human Nature* (1739), the last paragraph of Bk III Pt I Sec II "Of Morals". Cf Lamb's remark the following March: "None of the Damned philosophical Humeian indifference, so cold, and unnatural, and unhuman!" *LL* I 177. Cf also the last sentence of the present essay.

the hopes and comforts of the middle-ranks, and the amelioration, knowledge, and social affections of the lower classes.

As tending to this end, and not from any interested motives, they justly survey with abhorrence the taxes on incomes, the jealous provisions against popular discussion; but, above all, the heavy imposts on paper, newspapers, and letters. To France, some of these men are attached by their love of the Sciences, which more eminently flourish there, and which appear more decisively connected with the immediate good of mankind; while others, who have long amused themselves[5] with shaping out, in their own imaginations, better states of society, are seduced to an obstinacy of hope that they will be realized in France, only because they see no chance of their being realized elsewhere. The third class is far the most numerous, and comprises all who apologise for the French in direct and habitual opposition to the Minister; all who, with little extravagance and as little greatness of mind, are in the habits of personal dislike of Mr. Pitt and his party; who, fixing their feelings on men rather than measures, have made an ejection of the present Members from the Administration an object and a passion, and who will always find some excuse, even for the enemies of mankind, provided they happen at the same time to profess themselves the enemies of Mr. Pitt.

Passion makes men blind; and these men, by the alarm which their intemperate zeal, unfixed principles, and Gallican phraseology excite, form around the Minister a more effective phalanx of defence, than all his body-guard of Loan-jobbers, Contractors, Placemen and Pensioners, in and out of Parliament. But these are times in which those who love freedom should use all imaginable caution to love it wisely.[6] There exists a large number of men, in every sense of the word respectable, who remain attached to the present Ministry only from fear of worse men.[7] How shall they be induced to sympathise with our principles, unless they can be convinced that those principles impel us to sympathise with them in their abhorrence of men and measures, whose iniquity consists in their militation against all principles? Good men should now close in their ranks. Too much of

[5] Cf 7 Dec, fifth sentence, above.

[6] Cf "...those who have loved Freedom with wise ardor...". *Conciones: Lects 1795* (*CC*) 43.

[7] These respectable but cautious men are like the "Parliamentary Oscillators" of C's poem, but also like C in his recanting letter of Mar 1798: "I think the present ministry weak & perhaps unprincipled men; but... could point out no substitutes". *CL* I 396. The *M Post* had now, in other essays, resumed advocating Fox as substitute; the present essay assumes a viable alternative of "good men" for bad.

extravagant hope, too much of rash intolerance, have disgraced all parties: and facts, well adapted to discipline us all, have burst forth, even to superfluity. 'Twere surely wiser and better to sink at once voluntarily into the resignation of despair, than to tantalize ourselves with hopes which have no firmer foundations than Robespierre's, Tallien's, and Barras's.[8]

THE WAR OF THE CHOUANS

19 December 1799, Thursday. New attribution. The only leading paragraph "on...Peace" (see C's claim of 24 Dec[1]) that is manifestly in his style. Note the ironic "amusement" (cf 7 and 12 Dec), the heated imagination of Ministers (who are "heated in the game" 8 Jan 1800; cf 12 Dec 1799); the interest in the politics of weather. C, in Ratzeburg and Göttingen during "almost the whole of last winter", was more likely than Ministers to remember the freezing of the Elbe.

TWO Mails became due from Hamburgh yesterday, and, as the wind was fair, it is supposed they are detained by the frost, which may have blocked up the navigation of the Elbe. Ministers, who did not know that Holland was a wet and cold country, have probably forgotten that the Elbe was frozen up almost the whole of last winter.[2] As the Dutch expedition failed by the conspiracy of the elements,[3]

[8] Maximilien Robespierre (1758–94), egalitarian Rousseauist and leading Jacobin, who came to rely on the Terror and was overthrown and guillotined in Jul 1794 (Thermidor). Jean Lambert Tallien (1767–1820), ardent Jacobin publicist, who was president of the Convention when he opened the Thermidorian attack on Robespierre but made no subsequent positive contribution. Vicomte Paul François Nicolas de Barras (1755–1829), who as member of the Directory, 1795–9, built a career on the prestige of Bonaparte and prepared the way for Brumaire—after which his usefulness and career were over.

[1] "For Stewart I write often his leading Paragraphs, on Secession, Peace, Essay on the new French Constitution, Advice to Friends of Freedom...". To RS: *CL* I 552. Up to the date of writing, this list covers all the certainly identifiable prose: on Fox's "Secession" from Parliament (24 Dec), "On the French Constitution" (7 Dec), "Advice to the Friends of Freedom" (12 Dec), and the brief paragraph of 19 Dec, which glances at the announcement (in *M Post* 16 Dec) of a truce between the armies of Austria and France in Swabia. C may also have had a hand in leading paragraphs on peace of 17, 18, and 20 Dec, but the internal evidence is not strong.

[2] Cf "Even yet the Mouth of the Elbe is so much choked with Ice, that the Pacquets for England cannot set off." To Mrs C [10] Mar 1799: *CL* I 470.

[3] On the expedition see 24 Dec n 1, below. "All parties disclaim having projected it", recorded Lady Holland (II 35) on 10 Nov; "Pitt's friends say it was all Dundas's scheme; he again lays it to the Queen and Princess of Orange; and they to the *map-makers* for placing dry land where there ought to be swamps."

the negotiations of the British Cabinet may now be stopped by the *unexpected* misfortune of the freezing up of the Elbe; and before a Messenger can land on the Continent, the Court of Vienna may have concluded a peace; and Suwarrow[4] may be in St. Petersburgh! But all this will be the fault of the elements! Ministers never want foresight, nor do they ever neglect their duty.

Since the termination of the expedition to Holland, and the retreat of Suwarrow, the amusement of the day, in the Ministerial circles, is the war of the Chouans.[5] This is a happy subject. The intelligence from thence, true or false, cannot soon be contradicted, and partizans and victories multiply as the imagination is heated. It is said that the Chouans have sent for a Prince of the Blood to lead them to Paris. Perhaps they have: but where will they find him?

PRINCIPLES, NOT TITLES

19 December 1799, Thursday. New attribution, on strong evidence of style and theme: here is C's general political message about measures and principles above men and titles.

WE reverence the purity of intention which exists in the majority of the opposers of the present Administration; we fully believe that posterity will reverence the wisdom of their general purposes; it has been the habit of our conviction to fix on them our best hopes and expectations. Zealously, therefore, but with no unfriendly zeal,[1] we caution them against the false play into which their own ardour may seduce them; but, above all, against those who agree with them only in the assumption of the same general titles. Every age has had some favourite general term—Friends of Religion, Friends of Free-

[4] Count Aleksandr Vasilievich Suvorov (1729–1800), Russian field-marshal, victorious in the first part of 1799 (Cassano, Trebbia, Novi) but driven into winter quarters by Masséna's defeat of Korsakov at Zurich in Sept and a futile Alpine march. In Nov Paul I wrote to George III of his resolve to recall his forces from Switzerland and ordered Suvorov back to the Russian frontier.

[5] Chouans ("screech-owls"), the name given to bands of peasants, mainly smugglers and dealers in contraband salt, who rose in revolt in the west of France in 1793 and joined the royalists of La Vendée. In 1798 they had resumed activity, with the support of Pitt, but were soon discouraged by the arrival of troops in Oct 1799 led by Hédouville (see 1 Jan 1800, below). The "Prince of the Blood" would be the Comte d'Artois (later Charles X), whose nonappearance now and earlier in the Vendean uprising, despite his sabre-rattling words, made him a figure of fun.

[1] An echo of "with no friendly voice", Milton *Paradise Lost* IV 36.

dom, or Philosophers:[2] to these goodly phrases every man is self-eligible; they stand as open to the Factious as to the Patriot—to the mischievous Visionary as to the sober-minded Reasoner. Under the protection of these phrases bad men contrive to share the credit which their betters had gained, and thus yield to the hirelings of corruption only too plausible a pretext for involving all alike in one undistinguishing censure. It is in the nature of things that crimes and extravagance should arrest the attention of the public more forcibly than wise and virtuous exertions; and thus it happens that the follies of a few self-chosen associates may injure the good name of the purest patriots.

What then is to be done? We must declare our principles openly; and prove that they are PRINCIPLES,[3] by abjuring all connection with men the moment they act in opposition to them, however fair their professions may remain, and however long we may have been accustomed to look on them as friends and fellow-labourers.

TO THE EDITOR OF THE MORNING POST

21 December 1799, Saturday. Signed letter to Editor introducing the poem called *Introduction to the Tale of the Dark Ladie*; letter reprinted in *PW* (EHC) II 1052–3 and, more accurately, in *CL* I 550–1.

SIR,

THE following Poem is the Introduction to a somewhat longer one, for which I shall solicit insertion on your next open day.[1] The use of the Old Ballad word, *Ladie*, for Lady, is the only piece of obsoleteness in it; and as it is professedly a tale of antient times, I trust, that "the affectionate lovers of venerable antiquity" (as Cambden says)[2] will grant me their pardon, and perhaps may be induced to admit a force and propriety in it. A heavier objection may be adduced against the Author, that in these times of fear and expectation, when novelties *explode* around us in all directions, he

[2] Cf C to G. Coleridge, 10 Mar 1798: "...those men...who have modestly assumed to themselves the exclusive title/ Philosophers & Friends of Freedom". *CL* I 395. And see above, 12 Dec 1799, on "Friends of Freedom".

[3] See Introduction, above (I xcii), for C's insistence about this time that the *M Post* follow "fixed and announced principles".

[1] A ruse; there was to be no longer poem. The *Introduction*, the first "Asra" poem, was later called *Love*. Letter and poem were reprinted in the *Courier* on the same day.

[2] From William Camden's *Britannia* tr Philemon Holland (1610) 738. See *CN* I 612–13n.

should presume to offer to the public a silly tale of old fashioned love: and, five years ago, I own, I should have allowed and felt the force of this objection. But, alas! explosion has succeeded explosion so rapidly, that novelty itself ceases to appear new;[3] and it is possible that now, even a simple story, wholly unspiced[a] with politics or personality, may find some attention amid the hubbub of Revolutions, as to those who have remained a long time by the falls of Niagara, the lowest whispering becomes distinctly audible.

S. T. COLERIDGE

PARLIAMENT. I

SHERIDAN AND FOX

24 December 1799, Tuesday. Reprinted *EOT* II 338–41, in SC's "probable" group, but confirmed by style—if not by the reference to a leader on "Secession" in *CL* I 552, an ambiguous reference since there was also "the secession of Austria".

WE augur well from the pleasure so generally felt from the belief that Mr. Sheridan will not suffer the events of the late Expedition to lie wholly enwrapped in Ministerial mystery.[1] No man is more worthy the honourable task, than one who has shewn himself so eminently qualified to feel with reason, and to reason with feeling; while by the lighter, though not less fascinating, charm of his wit, he breaks the spell of sophistry, and exposes to scorn the low *cant* of those *poor creatures*, who style themselves after Jesus, for no better reason which we can discover, than that *the Disciples of Loyola* had done so before them; men, whose delicate religion is frightened into

[a] *M Post*: unspired [emendation by E. L. Griggs; cf "a *tang* of personality": *CL* I 365]

[3] Cf the Humeian indifference to revolutions, of Feb and Mar 1798.

[1] A "Secret" Expedition of 36,000 British and Russian allies, the former mustered in London with great fanfare—including C's "War Song" in the *M Post* 24 Aug (see App D, below)—invaded the French Netherlands in Aug 1799 but failed to inspire an expected Dutch uprising and withdrew in October under an armistice, after a loss of 16,000 men. The Duke of York, who marched 10,000 forward and back if not up and down, was a conscientious commander, but the bad intelligence and the campaign plans, on which he had not been consulted, were the responsibility of Pitt's Cabinet, and his chief general was the superannuated Abercromby, probably the "General ——" of C's *Devil's Thoughts*, published the day before the duke sailed to take over command (see App D, Sept 6, below). The general's advent is mistaken, by the devil's own faulty intelligence, for "General Conflagration". Sheridan did move an inquiry into the failure of the expedition 10 Feb 1800; see 11 Feb, below.

hysterics by the transient babble of Gallic infidelity, yet can contemplate with untrembling nerves ten thousand of their fellow-subjects sacrificed in a disastrous Expedition; as if our *consecrated banners*, like those of Mahomet,[2] gave immediate passports into Paradise to all who perished beneath them. We participate in the public pleasure; and are satisfied that every effect will be produced which splendid talents and undoubted integrity *can* produce under *existing circumstances*.[3] Yet there is something so awful and imposing in the actual union and visible co-operation of great minds, that we cannot but feel regret at the continued secession of Mr. Fox.

We have ever considered this as a delicate subject, on which the best and wisest men may be allowed to differ. Mr. Fox certainly did not retire, merely because his enlightened eloquence produced no immediate effect on an audience, with whom arguments will not always prove current coin, merely because they are unanswerable. The debates on the war with Russia established the fact, that a Minister, with firm and overflowing majorities, may yet be compelled to *retreat* from his purposes, when the arguments of his opponents have convinced a majority *out-doors*.[4] Besides, it is not Mr. Fox's excellence to amuse predisposed followers with lofty, well-compacted periods, that seem so much like sense, that they do as well. His is a rememberable eloquence: his arguments live in the minds even of those, over whose prejudices they cannot effect an immediate conquest, and operate for years, after they were first adduced with a liveliness, which only uniform professions and opinions the most definite can lay claim to. His speeches had always a solid worth,

[2] The frivolous aspects of ceremonies consecrating banners unfurled for Victory and Taxation were reported in the *M Post* in August and satirised in *The Devil's Thoughts*. C had been touching a generally sensitive nerve when he had preached, in Shrewsbury in 1798, against "those who had 'inscribed the cross of Christ on banners dripping with human gore'" (Hazlitt 138). As early as 1795 C had made a memorandum on a bishop's "consecrating D. of York's banners" (*CN* I 174). His fragment on *Mahomet* breaks off before mention of Mohammed's banners.

[3] The tribute to Sheridan as playwright, orator, and wit—Sheridan having remained, with Tierney, to lead the remnant of Opposition not seceding—is handsome in view of C's personal disappointment at his rather shabby treatment of *Osorio*. Within a month C was expressing private disgust with Sheridan as "a thorough-paced *bad man*" (*CL* I 564). An even more blandishing overture to the Whigs is publication, in this same issue of the *M Post*, of C's ode to Lady Georgiana, the Duchess of Devonshire.

[4] In 1791 Pitt, though he obtained a vote from Parliament to authorise him to arm against Russia, withdrew his ultimatum on seeing the strength of the opposition, especially outside Parliament. Cf *Answer: Lects 1795* (*CC*) 324.

which remained when the fashion and beauty were gone: and therefore, imperfectly as his sentiments were *reported*, he had still the nation at large for his audience. He retired, because that noblest audience was too violently heated and alarmed. He retired, and ceased to speak, in order that what he had spoken might be the more willingly recurred to, the more seriously reconsidered; but he retired, well knowing that national errors can never be permanent, and waiting for the symptoms of convalescence.

Mr. Fox cannot, he cannot wish to, deny himself to the nation for ever: the sole question is, have any events occurred which may render the present time auspicious for his re-appearance. With a diffidence and hesitation which we always feel when our opinions are in opposition to those of so great a man, we presume to think *that there have.* He would come forward at a time when proud threats and confident promises have been followed by results the most calamitous and degrading; when the truth, *that heavy charges must attach somewhere*, is too glaring to be *disbelieved* by any; when (for so it is rumoured) Ministry themselves meditate an escape by the poor intrigue of a half-submission: he would come forward, while yet the wound is bleeding beneath the public eye, and in that cause of humanity, of which our countrymen, with all their prejudices, have lost neither the sense nor the feeling. He would come forward at a time in which his well remembered predictions have received their fullest and most palpable accomplishment. The new Confederacy of Monarchs has proved more short-lived than the former; and experience of the past has been demonstrated to be (what Mr. Fox has always stated it) a poor and inefficient counter-balance to ambition, jealousies, and Court intrigues.[5] In the mean time, the absurd pretensions of French liberty, which alarmed us, as wholly unfit for our nature, and incompatible with the other Governments of Europe, are, for these very reasons, dying a natural death, and, therefore, proved to have been unfit subjects for alarm.[6] The nation begins now to be

[5] After nearly two years of peace, Pitt's Second Coalition, with Russia and Austria, opened a campaign in March that by autumn had driven France from most of Italy; but Bonaparte's return in October coincided with Masséna's defeat of the Russians in Zurich and the collapse of the Netherlands invasion; now Russia had withdrawn, and the Austrians were making peace. The bipartisan silence of the summer was now abandoned; the Whigs were calling for investigation of the Expedition; as early as 6 Nov the *M Post* was once more suggesting there was a choice of "Mr. Pitt and a war...or Mr. Fox and a peace...".

[6] This was C's view; it had not been Stuart's, who argued as late as 4 Dec that Brumaire had changed nothing and that the "character of Jacobinism"

sensible that French Atheism and French Anarchy will find a place only in the page of the historian, when the enormous debts which it incurred to prevent their propagation will be felt at every cottager's table, at every shop-keeper's fire-side. It begins to be sensible that, like a child, it has been running away from the yelping of a cur, and standing for security at the heels of a vicious horse.[7] In the mean time, it is more than it ever was plausible, at least, that the new French Government wish for peace; and that, if peace be not made with Austria, the exorbitancy of *French* ambition will not have been the only impediment. Amid these events (if we may be permitted to use a holy language) "we remember that he told us how these things should come to pass."[8] The Roman Senate, in its adversity, thanked their General, for that, he had not despaired of the Commonwealth:[9] and we cannot suppress our earnest wishes, that Mr. Fox may speedily find it wise to earn a similar suffrage from the English nation, and give them new hopes, by shewing that he ventured to hope himself.

ON THE FRENCH CONSTITUTION. II[1]

26 December 1799, Thursday. *EOT* I 179–83, in SC's group of certain attributions; see III 1006; claimed in *CL* I 554; clear internal evidence.

FROM the article in our yesterday's paper our readers have learnt that the new Constitution will be solemnly presented to the whole French Nation, for their acceptance or rejection.[2] On the first view, nothing can appear more bold and Republican than this preliminary measure; but it has the misfortune of stamping a character of absurdity on the whole Constitution, which is to be the object of their votes. The whole people, without exception, are called upon to judge, and of course supposed capable of judging, upon a Constitution complex almost to entanglement; a thing of checks and counter-

of the new Government of France must "dispel all present hopes of a termination of the war...".

7 C reused this comparison after a similar reference to "French Ambition" in *Friend* No 10 (*CC*) II 144 (I 220). In *The Friend* the reference is more openly to "a vicious War Horse".

8 The prophetic message suggests Isaiah, or Joseph interpreting Pharaoh's dream: Gen 41. 32.

9 The general was Gaius Terentius Varro in 216 B.C., for his opposing the forces of Hannibal. See Livy *Annals* 26. 61.

1 For C's *Christmas Carol*, in *M Post* 25 Dec, see App D, below.

2 The Christmas issue had presented "An Official Copy" of the new Constitution.

checks, that might almost seem intentionally formed to exhibit a metaphysical posture-master's dexterity in *balancing*. The whole people, without exception (both those who *can* sign their votes, and those who must "cause them to be signed"), are called upon to judge upon a Constitution, as momentous as it is intricate; a Constitution, which gives an influence vast and Kingly to the Chief Magistrate; transfers all responsibility from him to his own creatures; and confers upon him, at the same time, the more than Kingly prerogative of being the proposer of all possible laws, in a Government of which he and two inferior associates form the Executive; a Constitution which elevates the great Functionaries and Powers of the State into a separate order, never more to become one again with their fellow-citizens; Nobles for life, and Judges and Revisers of the acts of the 300 Legislators, whom they themselves had previously elected. On all this, and upon far more than all this, the whole nation is called upon to judge and decide by a Constitution, whose prime, leading, and fundamental principle it is, that the great mass of the nation have just virtue and wisdom enough to choose their *Constables*, and no more!

By this appeal to the universal suffrage, the sovereignty of the people is admitted in its widest extent; and the people are called upon to exercise it, as the suicide exercises his power over life, only to destroy it for ever. The indefeasible validity of *personal* rights is thus expressed as fully as the wildest Democracy could vote it; by a Constitution as Oligarchic as ever that of Venice was, and which pronounces the people at large a foul and unwholesome element, unfit to be employed in the simplest offices, without long processes of filtration. But this, however, we may, perhaps, pass over, as a Courtly grimace to amuse the Half-Jacobins; an act of pure tenderness to the genius of Democracy, now on its death-bed; and it would be too rigorous to expect consistency in a mere compliment. Sieyes and Buonaparte are, we presume, sufficiently assured of the affections of the soldiers, and the terrors and hopelessness of the nation, to know, that no real deliberation will be called forth, no actual power exercised by the people. Happy will it be for France, if the new Constitution involve no absurdities more pernicious.

This production of the Abbe's political science, in our humble opinion, carries with it few marks of wisdom; though it is strongly featured with cunning and personal ambition; yet it has such an imposing air of novelty, that we feel ourselves puzzled and perplexed, from what point we should first survey it. In countries where the favour of an hereditary Monarch, to whom obedience is secured by superstition, forms the predominating impulse of the State, we may expect to find a sense of honour, and all the dubious virtues that flow from pride tempered by chivalrous courtesies; in a Democracy, in which the continuance in the great public functions is short, and the elections depend immediately on the esteem and affections of the people, we might hope to meet with all that is graceful, shewy, and energetic in genius and intellect; and while[a] we believe such a state in its nature impermanent and unadapted to man, we are compelled to admit, that while it lasted it would be a *hot-bed* for individual talent and occasional heroism; in a Government founded in property, and in a nation among whom property was the ruling spirit, we might look with confidence for active industry, attachment to law and order, and aversion from innovation. We are fortunate enough to live in a country in which, with all its defects, the national character is made up, though in different quantities, by all these three principles, the influence of a Court, the popular spirit, and the predominance of property. We find ourselves of course disposed to hail with astonishment, but "with no friendly voice,"[3] a Constitution, in which all Legislative Functions are places of Government, Legislature itself a lucrative profession, and preferment in it to be expected neither from the honorary favour of an hereditary Monarch, or[b] from the privileges of rank, or[b] the influence of property, or[b] from popular favour; but, as it should seem, by secret intrigue in the palace of a military Dictator, or in the different Courts of the great all electing conservatory Senators, who are themselves that which they are by a species of organization, almost as mysterious as that of mushrooms and funguses. For who are to elect the Senate? Not the people, whose power of acquiescence we have shown to be a mere trick of French politeness—but the Committees! And who elected the Committees? Sieyes and Buonaparte. And here we must pause—we can rise no higher in this system of causation. These are self-elected—the power and the wisdom of France impersonated in an Abbe and a Commander in Chief.

On the following days we hope to employ more detailed investigation of this novelty. We have given our opinions, and shall continue to give them, not without that self-distrusting scepticism which our very imperfect acquaintance with the present state of the parties in France imposes on us. Convinced, too, that whatever Constitution

[a] *EOT*: though [b] *EOT*: nor

[3] Milton *Paradise Lost* IV 36; cf C's use of this allusion to Satan, above, 19 Dec 1799.

France may have at present cannot possibly be its Constitution ten years hence, we are disposed to hope more from the personal characters and talents of the immediate Functionaries under the most absurd form, than from the theoretical[a] excellency of the best code, considered in and for itself alone.[4] If Sieyes have virtue and penetration enough to place the legislative power of France in the hands of four or five hundred temperate men, not without talents, France will revere his memory as a nation, when only her *antiquaries* know any thing about his codes of[b] Constitutions.[c] *But we doubt*, and our faith cannot remove mountains.[5]

METAPOTHECARIES

26 December 1799, Thursday. New attribution, characteristically Coleridgian both in the pun and in the manner of presenting it.

A MINISTERIAL paper observed, some few days past, that the new French Constitution was wholly *metaphysical*. If the writer meant that it is unintelligible upon principles of common sense, we entirely coincide with him: and in this sense some future writer on the measures of the Allied Powers may perhaps style his work a *Treatise* on *Metaphysics*. An incurable punster once observed to us,[1] that these low mixers of intellectual drugs should be entitled, not *Metaphysicians*, but *Metapothecaries*.

ON THE FRENCH CONSTITUTION. III

27 December 1799, Friday; entitled "The French Constitution". *EOT* II 343–8, in SC's "probable" group; but claimed in *CL* I 554; firm internal evidence. The errors in *EOT* readings (see textual notes) suggest that SC was working from a worn or badly printed copy.

Ecce iterum crispinus![1] In the present dearth of foreign and domestic news, the Public find an interest even in a new French Constitution!

[a] *M Post*: re-actical [emendation from *EOT*] [b] perhaps a mistake for "or"
[c] *EOT*: constitution

[4] Cf C's doubts in 1814 at the "pantomime Trick of pretending to give a British Constitution" to the French. *CL* III 497.

[5] Matt 17. 20.

[1] C was the "incurable punster", but the word was RS's. Cf "Metaphysicians! Do, Southey, keep to your most excellent word...& always say—*Metapothecaries*." To RS 21 Oct 1801: *CL* II 767–8. C uses the word often.

[1] A tag from Juvenal 4. 1: "Here's Crispin yet again." Used by C as the beginning of a letter to Wedgwood 24 Feb 1801: *CL* II 685.

Our readers have learnt, that the candidates for all offices, national, departmental, and those of the sub-departments, are to be gradually obtained by a series of honourable *decimations*.[2] We have before objected to this system of election by primary, secondary, and tertiary assemblies (in all which the same persons are at once candidates and voters), from its pernicious *moral* tendency. We believed, and we still continue to believe, that such an arrangement must necessarily tend to exasperate those *political* agitations, so inseparable from important elections, by the super-addition of violent *personal* passions.[3] If this has been proved to have been the case in the Primary Assemblies under the former Constitutions,[a] if those were found to generate and diffuse the spirit of intrigue, and the disposition to innovation, the argument of course applies three fold against the present Constitution;—a Constitution, too, which makes such enormous sacrifices to the wish of producing stability and preventing innovation.

In favour of this arrangement it may be said, that it confirms and realises two opposite advantages, and both of the highest importance. It takes from the people the all-unsettling power of acting from immediate and momentary impulses, while, at the same time, by the stimulation of hope, and the sense of personal self-importance, it impels every individual to be a *Citizen*, suffers no man to remain dead to the public interest, and thus elevates the selfish into a social principle, without detriment to social peace. And truly, if (after the process of *filtration*[4] had been completed)[b] the persons thus chosen by the electing assemblies to be the candidates for the different functions, were once again presented to the people, and finally appointed by their individual votes, collected *without assemblage*, we should admit this to be an important improvement on the system of universal suffrage, and perhaps the best possible form of a representative system, not expressly founded on property. But the Conservatory Senate makes the final election; a circumstance which not only alters, but absolutely reverses the effect. To have been chosen by our fellow citizens and neighbours as a good and prudent man, and again

[a] *EOT*: constitution [b] *EOT*: compelled

[2] For the series of tenths, see above, 7 Dec 1799 n 5.

[3] The distinguishing of moral, political, and personal aspects is characteristic; cf 25 Mar 1800, below. On the harm of personal passions, cf "I am no...Reformist...fiery & undisciplined...I devote myself to such works as encroach not on the antisocial passions...to destroy the bad passions not by combating them, but by keeping them in inaction." To George Coleridge [c 10 Mar 1798]: *CL* I 397.

[4] See above, 7 Dec 1799 n 5.

re-chosen by them as best and wisest among the good and prudent, this were indeed a noble aim for the noblest ambition! But to receive a legislative appointment from a Senate of eighty Nobles, from a body excluded equally by its *paucity* and its *privileges* from all acquaintance and fellow-feeling with the competitors or their constituents; this none but intriguers could hope for, this no honest pride, no honourable ambition would desire.

A Constitution founded on such a basis seems to possess the unfortunate prerogative of combining the injustice of the most absolute with more than the insecurity of the most popular Governments. The despotisms of the world have hitherto endeavoured to keep their subjects in inaction;[5] they excite few hopes, and have therefore little to fear from the resentments of disappointment. In a Democracy every man may hope and struggle; but if he be disappointed, he must waste his anger on his rivals: for anger towards a populace is too ridiculous a thing to be often indulged, [a]and, when indulged,[b] too impotent to be dreaded; but a cabal of eighty Nobles is a fair and palpable object of hatred; a conspicuous target, to which the poorest aims may direct a successful shaft. In a nation of twenty-five millions, a nation characteristically enthusiastic and volatile, such a body must, and indeed ought to, become an object of jealousy and suspicion; and at every election may create such enemies, not only nine-tenths of the competitors (supposed the flower and pride of wealth or talent), but likewise all of the people who had wished or expected the choice to have fallen differently from the real event. The only argument, therefore, from which the justice or policy of such an order could deduce a shadow of justification, is fairly adducible against it; for from the common instincts of human nature, it militates against that permanence and security from change, to which alone it can appeal, as a sufficient reason for its existence.

A respectable Morning Paper has observed, that "the present plan, by which the Representative System is consecrated, narrows excessively the exercise of the Right of Election."[6] We should have chosen to express ourselves otherwise: we should have said—"the present plan, by which the Representative System is secretly assassinated, wholly takes away from the people the exercise of the *Power*

[a–b] *EOT* omits

[5] Cf "The cadaverous tranquillity of despotism..." in *PD: Lects 1795* (*CC*) 289.

[6] *M Chron* 26 Dec leader, somewhat misrepresented here, for it goes on to say that the present Constitution seeks to reduce the people "to absolute imbecility" etc, a point not very different from C's.

of Election, while most absurdly, or jesuitically, it pretends to admit the *Right*." A Senate elected by Buonaparte and Sieyes can only be considered as the accomplices of Buonaparte and Sieyes. We are justified, therefore, in considering the Executive Government and the Senate as one and the same body. This body possesses all the influence of France, appoints all the offices throughout all the nation, civil and military, legislative or judicial, lucrative or honourable. Supposing that this vast and enormous influence were only powerful enough to bring in one man in ten among the candidates returned by the successive Assemblies, a supposition absurd and incredible! yet this would be still sufficient. The Senate, by choosing the tenth part of the candidates, might constitute a Legislature entirely of its own creatures. The whole process of popular election is therefore a mere trick—a miserable masquerade domino, to throw around the nakedness of despotism.

The same respectable paper asserts, that "without providing in words, that property shall have exclusive advantages in the new *scheme*, it secures the fact. The list of *Eligibles* will contain all the men of eminence and property; and the Conservative Senate, amidst an ample choice, may select as members of the Legislature, the men distinguished for talents or influence. While none are excluded, the great must thus be necessarily preferred." Consistently with the talent and good sense, which in general pervade the opinions of our fellow-journalist, we are unable to understand this otherwise than as a trope of irony. Whom may these high-pensioned[a] eighty nobles select, but their own creatures? For surely the writer did not assume disinterestedness and clear-sighted patriotism, as postulates and axioms—ideas involved in the very notion of a self-elected, self-perpetuating senate of eighty nobles? If indeed the legislative and judicial functions become marketable articles, the richest man will of course be the buyer, provided they will return good interest for the money; and the rich man, without talent, pride, or principle, can consent to receive his absolute creators for his unconditional masters. Is it unknown to this writer, that in a country[7] celebrated far and wide for religion, gentlemanly honour, diffusion of property, and attachment to law, sequaciousness the most blind and unconditional has been commonly demanded from, and promised by, men of rank and property, previously to their being permitted to be *elected* into a legislative function? and for what one assignable reason

[a] *EOT*: high-passioned

[7] England.

are we to hope better things from the accomplices of Sieyes and Buonaparte? It appears to us that the men of property will be too wise to buy, at any heavy sum, places in a silent legislature, empowered only to decide on laws proposed to them by a Commander in Chief; their very decisions too annulable by the Senate, their creators. The men of property will rather buy laws of the Government *in prospectu*, and needy men will hire themselves as the mechanic-legislators, necessary in this business of Law-making to the Government, only as the bellows-blower is to the organist. The work *must* be done; but any fellow may do it.

The whole first chapter of the Constitution we do indeed consider as the mere ornamental outworks of a military despotism. No real power is left to the people.

We have dwelt on this first chapter long, but we trust not disproportionably, having considered all the following chapters (except that which relates to [a]judicial arrangements[b] and civil security) as containing nothing essential which is not involved in the consequences of the first. The first chapter brings forward the undeniable truth, that the Government of France is to be an oligarchy, supported, and only supportable, by the military, who are therefore placed entirely and absolutely under the command of the Chief Consul, Buonaparte; all which follows we regard as mere theatrical evolutions of a figure dance.[8] We shall, however, not leave any part of this most interesting production wholly unconsidered. Our Readers will not conceive of it as occupying too large a portion of our attention, if only they reflect on[c] the intimate connection in which the subject of the French Government stands with that of Peace. If the French people accept, or rather submit to, this Constitution, all danger from French principles is passed by; the volcano is burnt out, and the snow has fallen round the crater.[9]

a–b EOT: prejudicial arguments *c EOT*: *on*

[8] Image repeated 25 Sept 1802, below.

[9] See 6 Jan 1803, below. Cf Burke on 11 May 1792: "Old religious factions are volcanoes burnt out; on the lava and ashes, and squalid scoriae of old eruptions grow the peaceful olive, the cheering vine, and the sustaining corn." *Speeches* (4 vols 1816) IV 59.

ON THE FRENCH CONSTITUTION. IV

31 December 1799, Tuesday; *M Post* title (without "IV"). *EOT* I 183–9, in SC's group of certain attributions; concludes series.

A LEGISLATIVE Assembly, the elected Representatives of a mighty nation, is attacked and dissolved by a military faction. The Leaders of this faction assume the Supreme Power with all its Royal patronage and emoluments, and, not content with this, create moreover four or five hundred places with high salaries under the titles of Senate, Legislature, and Tribunate; partly to reward their immediate creatures, and partly from the same motives with which puppet-shewmen are hired by cut-purses, viz. to amuse the crowd while they are picking their pockets.[1] These enormities they modestly submit to the suffrages of the Great Nation, "proclaim them at the head of the military," and begging, like the mendicant in Gil Blas,[2] with levelled musquets, crave the Great Nation to call them a Constitution, and, as the last act of its indefeasible sovereignty, to vote itself enslaved for ever! The eighteenth century is now at its close—a century venerable for its discoveries, terrific in its events! This impudent offer of these mountebank Liberticides—was it to mortify human pride, that *this* is doomed to be the *last* incident of such a century? Is it to deaden the extravagance of human hope, that the general acceptance of it will probably be the *first* incident of the new age? Alas, poor human nature! Or rather, indeed, alas, poor Gallic nature! For Γραιοι αει παιδες:[3] the French are always children, and it is an infirmity of benevolence to wish, or dread aught concerning them.

The general detection of this gross imposture required little penetration; but in the more wearisome task of exposing the detail and minutiae, we may fairly lay claim to some degree of that patience, which we are obliged to solicit from our readers. The fourth article of the first chapter declares the right of Citizenship forfeited,

[1] C apparently thought of using this image in Nov 1802, when he wrote in a notebook: "Puppet-shew—crowned Heads—which the Pope? which a [?Lion] and which one pleases Gentlemen, which the Masses please". *CN* I 1280. He did write, in *M Post* 25 Sept 1802, in allusion to the French Constitution, that it could work only for "the very antithesis of Englishmen", who would never consent "to be *puppets*!"—a shift of the metaphor.

[2] In Bk I ch 2 of Alain René Lesage *Histoire de Gil Blas de Santillane*, doubtless known to C in Smollett's translation.

[3] From Plato *Timaeus* 22B; see *Friend* (*CC*) I 504 and n 2. "The Greeks [are] always children". Cf a letter to RS [28 Dec 1799]: *CL* I 554.

by affiliation with any foreign body, which supposes distinctions of birth. The second chapter begins by constituting, in effect, such a body in France; for it constitutes eighty unremovable Senators, privileged to fill up their own vacancies. Those among our readers who have made themselves acquainted with the ordinary course of succession to the Senatorial dignity in the Imperial towns of Germany[4] will perceive at once, that these Nobles for life would, if the order continued long enough, become in reality, if not in name, *hereditary* Nobles. But we need not travel so far for an analogy. What member of a self-elected Corporation in our Corporate Boroughs does not struggle to bring in his own nearest relative as Corporator? And as all have the same wish, mutual interest at length introduces mutual accommodation.

It is not here the place to discuss the advantages or disadvantages of privileged orders. Our Nobles in England, from the largeness of their landed estates, have an important stake in the immediate prosperity of their country; and, from the antiquity of their families, may be reasonably presumed likely to associate with it a more deeply-rooted and partial affection. By the more delicate superstition of ancestry they counteracted in former ages, and to a certain degree still counteract, the grosser superstition of wealth.[5] Let us not forget too, that by occasion of their younger children they were the original founders of an order of Gentlemen among us, into which order a liberal education and polished manners have at length the privilege of incorporating any man,[6] whatever his parental rank might have been: and thus, by the introduction of a greater *social* equality among us, they more than compensate to us for their *political* superiority. Meantime their Legislative capacity, which gives them dignity and public usefulness, excites no jealousy in the people, their power and *direct* influence being constitutionally less than that of the popular and representative branch. Of the Conservative Senators the number is not large enough to affect in any degree the manners of society; nor is it provided that they should be men of property; nor can the people possibly attach to their rank and origin

[4] As C had been doing earlier in the year. Cf his letters to Josiah Wedgwood and to Mrs C (*CL* I 464–70, 509).

[5] Cf *LS* (*CC*) 170 and textual notes.

[6] Cf *Friend* No 16 (*CC*) II 210–11. At times C expressed the very opposite view of "the Religion of the *Gentleman*" as "more blasting to real Virtue, real Utility...than all the Whoredoms & Impurities which this Gentlemanliness does most generally bring with it"—this on 1 Mar 1800 (*CL* I 577), scarce two months after the *M Post* paragraph. See also *LL* II 238.

those associations of splendid or venerable, which necessarily hang round a feudal nobility: meantime, in their political capacity, they are then only not idle when they exercise an enormous power, and that too robbed from the people, of whom exclusively it is the rightful attribute—the power of election. Still had eighty senators, so privileged, been nominated by the whole nation, if they had been selected and chosen by the free votes of their fellow-citizens, however pernicious the institution might be, yet the individuals would doubtless have possessed an origin at least as honourable, as the most adulatory herald dares attach to the most ancient nobility. But *these*, the creatures of a renegade Priest, himself the creature of a foreign mercenary—these, the stones which Buonaparte, the Deucalion of this new inundation, found beneath his feet, and flinging them behind him metamorphosed into senators[7]—what but fear, mingled with scorn, can attach to *these?*—But if their good or kind auspices are undiscoverable, not so their evil influences. To secure to their own relatives places of honour and emolument, each Senator becomes at once an intriguer, and a centre of intrigues: he to the Government, the Government to him, and all to each other.

Except that it is convenient for Buonaparte to have eighty places of a thousand a year each at his disposal, we remain wholly in the dark concerning the intention, or possible utility of this new Conservative. It *makes* the whole of the political machine, and it can suspend its operations. Other occupation it has none. Like the God of the mechanic materialists, it has no other attributes but those of creation and miracle.[8] The people have no promise or security that it will possess wisdom, talent, or integrity, and no appeal if it possess them not.

It were wasting our readers' attention to direct it particularly to the other branches of the Legislature, the hundred Tribunes who are to talk and do nothing, and the three hundred Legislators whom the Constitution orders to be silent. What a ludicrous purgatory for three hundred Frenchmen! The shamelessness of calling that a Legislature which can neither propose nor reason, and whose acts are annullable *ad arbitrium*, can only be equalled by the exquisite absurdity involved in the very notion of splitting the intellectual faculties, and subdividing the business of Thought, almost as curiously as that of a

[7] The tale of Deucalion, the Noah of Greek legend, who repeopled the earth by tossing stones behind him, is told in Ovid *Metamorphoses* 1, esp 1.381–415.

[8] C had in mind the mechanistic materialism of Hobbes and Descartes; see *Lects 1795* (*CC*) 98–102, and p 100 n 1.

pin manufactory. However, all these different law-manufacturers[9] are well salaried; yet not so as to place them out of the temptation of corruption. Even the Chief Consul must find it necessary to bribe high to secure his re-election, by influence, by promises, and not improbably by taking the pay of foreign Governments. Indeed, never was a Government framed which lay so open to corruption, both in itself, and from external powers! There exists no appearance of a preventive, in a nominal Legislature, for which no property is requisite, in which no talent can be exerted, and where no popularity can be gained. The whole Constitution betrays a rooted contempt of the people, and a distrust of human virtue in general, yet leaves to none, whom it invests with power, any of those common assistants to well doing which the most virtuous man does not profess to deem useless. It has indeed divisions and sub-divisions even to superfluity; but how, under any circumstances these could be a check on each other, or on the Consulate, no where appears. It is indeed mere fraud and mockery. Checks and counterpoises can only be produced by real diversity of interests, of interests existing independent of legislative functions; but these chambers are all alike filled with the creatures of the Dictator, by him chosen, feeding on his stipends, and acting under his controul. But it cannot last: for to what body of men or species of interest can it appeal for love or protection?[10] The property, the talent, the popular spirit, the prejudices of the Royalist, the Priest, and the Jacobin, are all injured, insulted, trodden under foot by it. And what are idle promises of individual liberty in a Constitution which recognises in the Chief Consul the right of suspending it *ad arbitrium*, and which does not recognise in the nation that which is worth a thousand Tribunates, that without which no nation can be free or happy under the wisest Government, the LIBERTY OF THE PRESS?

[9] In 1802 in the *M Post* C will describe constitution-maker Sieyès as "supplanted...in his own manufactory" (29 Sept) and Bonaparte as "master in the manufactory, in which [Fox is] head-journeyman, or foreign agent—the manufactory of this gloomy and ominous WAR PEACE" (9 Nov).

[10] Note that C does not predict the collapse of Bonaparte himself. Stuart's leaders of 28 and 30 Dec are less perspicuous; his analysis of "Paris Journals to the 23d", finding the Constitution unpopular, jumps to the conclusion "that Buonaparte and his Constitution will have but a short existence".

1800

1 January–14 October

FRANCE. I[1]

1 January 1800, Wednesday. *EOT* I 189–93, in SC's group of certain attributions.

FRENCH VICTORIES

YESTERDAY, at noon, we received by express the Paris Papers to the 28th ult. The installation of the new Government is consummated, and has been accompanied by the happy omen of a victory over the Austrians in the Genoese, which, however, is probably more important to the ruling faction, by its tendency to put the French people in good temper, than from any permanent advantage to be expected from it.

On the 14th ult. General Klenau, reinforced by a corps of Russians from Leghorn, advanced against General St. Cyr, in the eastern border of Genoa, while General Kray attacked General Watrin in the positions of Villageo and the Bochetta. Kray was repulsed, and, as the French accounts say, with great loss. Klenau appears at first to have been successful. The advanced posts of General St. Cyr fell back; but the General soon made dispositions to attack Klenau in his turn, which he did with full success, putting his army to complete rout.[2] The number of the slain is stated in the *Moniteur* at 2000; the French have taken 1800 prisoners and four pieces of cannon, and state their own loss at 200 men killed or wounded. These victories may suspend, perhaps, the fate of the Genoese, which, as well as the French army in their territory, are admitted to be labouring under the most cruel necessities. It is added, however, that eighty ships laden with provisions have entered the ports of Liguria, and that one hundred and fifty more were following them, and in sight.[3] The

[1] For an "Impromptu" in this day's *M Post* probably by C, see App D, below.

[2] These battles of midwinter counted as little more than skirmishes. The Austrians under Paul Kray von Krajova (1735–1804) and Johann von Klenau (1760–1819) would retreat into Bavaria until April, when Kray bore the brunt of the French spring campaign. Laurent Gouvion Saint-Cyr (1764–1830) was the French Governor of Genoa and temporarily commander of the Army of the Rhine. François Watrin (1772–1802) commanded the French.

[3] This day's *Times* calls the report "absolutely incredible". Blockaded by an English fleet, the army of Genoa and its citizens suffered a winter of acute privation.

capitulation of Coni on the 3d is confirmed, and the articles are given at length in the *Moniteur* of the 27th, but they have nothing remarkable that requires insertion.

Hedouville, General in Chief of the Army of England, in a Proclamation dated the 22d ult. announces that he has conceded to the Chouannese Insurgents,[4] that there shall be no requisitions of money until it shall be decided if a resumption of hostilities shall take place or not. At a time when the enormous power of deciding on the fate of all the persons exiled, or imprisoned by prior factions, is given to Buonaparte, under pretence of the danger which might follow from the re-admission of a few individuals affected to Royalism, these armistices and conciliations, and pacificatory overtures to the Chiefs of a Royalist banditti, actually in arms against the Government, have a most inconsistent and mysterious appearance. Are the French Government really so weak? Or are they only *finessing*?[5] Has the extirpation of Chouannerie been purposely procrastinated by each ruling faction, in order that there may always remain a pretext for keeping up a large standing army in the interior? Is the predatory warfare of these rebel banditti serviceable to the Republican cause, by alarming the men of landed property against Royalism? Or are they permitted to exist merely as decoy-birds that procure for the Republic arms, ammunition, and large sums of money from England, for which they return continual supplies of *hope* to our Secretary of War, and his young associates, towards their projected march to Paris?—A commerce, of which, it must be confessed, the balance is greatly in favour of France; or, lastly, are the counties[a] most tainted with Royalism secretly destined to be divided among the soldiery, on the realization of a peace with Austria? and is even the spread of Royalism beheld with a concealed satisfaction, as increasing the probable extent of the boon? It is not indeed impossible that each and all of these reasons have a share in the true causes of the phaenomenon.

[a] *M Post, EOT*: countries

[4] Gabriel Marie Théodore Joseph Hédouville (1755–1825) was in negotiation with the Chouan chieftains; they would agree to an armistice on 4 Jan 1800.

[5] Re-arming royalists in Britanny and Normandy amounted to 60,000 in November 1799. "Bonaparte saw that effectual as a force might be... conciliation was much more beneficial..." (Bisset II 708). Émigré royalists and constitutionalists were invited to return; even some estates were restored. The Chouans "still persisted in revolt, and cultivated a correspondence with the British fleet"; but by early spring a combination of "pacific measures" and "force and severity... crushed the insurrection".

FRANCE UNDER THE NEW CONSTITUTION

AMONG the contents of the Paris papers, the most immediately interesting is of course the account of the proceedings on the installation of the new Constitution. We have given them at large, with the proclamations of Buonaparte.[6] The first, to the French nation, is pure common-place; a confused bundle of puerile generalities, on order, justice, and moderation, which came with peculiar grace and modesty from the man who, after having entered the House of Legislature with a band of grenadiers, has erected a daring and unmodified despotism in that country, which had confided in him to dotage, which, with the effusion of its best blood, had earned all his laurels for him;—and which had done this, and more than all this, because they believed him an enthusiast for their liberty. The second proclamation, to the French soldiers, and the third to the army of Italy, are well-written, eloquent, and affecting; but to us chiefly interesting, as open denunciations that all hopes of peace are at an end. The Allies seem determined to press into France from all quarters, and the Chief Consul without noticing, retorts the menace. "Soldiers! it is no longer your frontiers that you must defend; it is the enemy's states that must be invaded."—Through all these proclamations the fierce confidence, and proud self-involution of a military despot, intoxicated with vanity, start out most obtrusively; and it is still more glaring and offensive in his letter to General St. Cyr, on the victory over the Austrians. This was written the day after his installation, and never did epistle from an Oriental Monarch to some slave he meant to honour, affront the principles of Equality with a more stately egotism. Let our readers turn to the letters of Paul the First to Cardinal Ruffo, and those to his victorious General, Suwarrow; and they will find the great *Autocrat* of all the Russias modest and humble in the comparison.[7] This insolence in the usurper

6 The Paris dispatch fills p 3 and half of p 4.

7 The letter of Paul I, Emperor of Russia, to Cardinal Ruffo, commander of allied forces in Naples, is on p 4 of the *M Post* of 31 Dec 1799 and is ornately cordial. Paul's letter to Suvorov of 29 Oct 1799, appointing him generalissimo, is on p 1 of the *M Post* of 10 Dec. Paul I (1754–1801), who succeeded Catherine II as tsar in 1796, reversed his mother's policies, partly freed the serfs, and seemed a "magnanimous prince" to Pitt (and the satirists). Fabrizio Ruffo (1744–1827), a reforming minister of Pius VI in the Papal States in the 1780's who had been made a cardinal for his services, organised an insurrectionary army against the French in January 1799, reoccupied Naples in May, and negotiated the surrender of besieged republicans on terms of safe conduct that were scandalously repudiated by

is, however, fully equalled by the servility of his creatures. The last speech in the Council of Five Hundred by Jacqueminot, on Christmas eve, could only have been ventured in a nation, whose riotous holidays were over, on the *black Monday* of its recommencing slavery. It has all the sacrilegious adulation of the age of Louis XIV. without its elegance and genius.[8] On the supposition that this despotism should maintain itself for a few years, it remains a deeply interesting question in what degree it is likely to increase or diminish the military energy, and consequent ambition of France. Our thoughts on this subject we mean to offer to our readers on some future day.[9]

ON PEACE. II

OVERTURES

2 January 1800, Thursday. *EOT* I 193–9, in SC's group of certain attributions.

THE report of a Messenger from France having arrived at Dover on Monday with propositions of Peace resembled so much the Stock-jobbing falsehoods repeatedly given to the public, that we were cautious of allowing it credit in our Paper of yesterday.[1] But we find, by a letter from Dover, that a Messenger from the French Government certainly did arrive, with a letter from Talleyrand, Minister of

---

Nelson. For an account of Ruffo that considers his "constructive efforts" see R. R. Palmer *The Age of the Democratic Revolution: The Struggle* (Princeton 1964) 387–9.

[8] Jean Ignace Jacqueminot (1758–1813). His speech of 24 Dec on the dissolution of the Council of Five Hundred (printed in English translation in this day's *M Post*) congratulates the legislators for having restored internal peace, "placed property on a solid foundation", disdained vain theories, and attached themselves, with their glorious new Constitution, to consecrated "principles" (a mockery for C to wince at); on having "perceived that an immense Republic cannot be governed like a little town of Attica"; on having recognised in Bonaparte one of the profoundest thinkers and most extraordinary geniuses of the age and having charged him to "close the abyss" of the Revolution to become greater than Washington in peace as already in war. "May he hasten to join to the titles of Conquerer of Italy, Legislator of Egypt, and Hero of Aboukir, the still more glorious title of *Pacificator of Europe*."

[9] See 2 Jan 1800, concluding paragraph, below.

[1] It was brazen of Stuart to let C put such words into his paper; in 1796, as his foes never forgot, Stuart had been convicted of forging a French newspaper and having it delivered "from Dover", to influence the price of stocks by a false report of preliminaries of peace between Austria and France. Lucyle Werkmeister finds evidence that he continued to engage in this and similar forms of "stock-jobbing".

Foreign Affairs at Paris,[2] to Lord Grenville. The Messenger was not suffered to proceed further than Dover, where he was detained in custody, and no person but his keeper allowed to come near him; but the chief Officer of the Customs came up express with the French despatches to Lord Grenville's Office, where he arrived on Tuesday forenoon. These despatches certainly contain overtures of Peace from France to the British Government. A request is made, we understand, to open a negotiation; Ministers have long been prepared to expect such a request, and now endeavour by every means to prove it would be impolitic to listen to it. The proposal is extremely embarrassing to them,[3] who wish to continue the war, with the grace of being desirous of Peace; and it is believed that a negotiation must be opened. We anticipate no favourable result.—We believe ourselves guilty of no rashness in thinking, that peace and the restoration of monarchy in France are wishes which do not exist separate in the minds of the English ministry. A peace concluded with the present Government of France would tend to confirm its power, would render the cause of monarchy more hopeless than ever, and be an acknowledgment on the part of our Ministers, that they retired from the main object of their hopes baffled and disappointed. The events too of the last campaign, contrasted with those of the former, cannot but be encouraging to men whose impetuosity in *wishing* forbids us to believe them capable of forming rational *expectations*. Nor is it to be forgotten, that Russia is now[a] reconciled with Austria, and is pouring down armies to the seat of war; and that Austria, who has certainly received propositions of peace from the French Government through the Spanish Ambassador, has as certainly rejected them. Never was a moment, in which our Ministers were less likely to wish a peace, and in which the people, who do, and ought to, wish it, are less authorised to hope or expect it. The possession of the whole of the North of Italy is too important to the House of Austria to be

[a] *EOT*: not

[2] Charles Maurice de Talleyrand-Périgord (1754–1838), free-thinking bp of Autun (1789–91), had been cordially received in London by Pitt and Grenville in early 1792 as proposer of an *entente cordiale* between France and England. He returned to England after the September massacres but was expelled when war began in Jan 1793 and spent thirty months in the United States. In 1796 he returned to France; the next year he became minister of foreign affairs; and in 1799 he brought about the alliance between Bonaparte and Sieyès that prepared the coup of Brumaire; whereupon he resumed the ministry of foreign affairs till 1807. Letters from him and General Bonaparte dated Christmas day invited peace; texts and translations given in *M Post* 7 Jan are reprinted in *EOT* I 205–12.

[3] For evidence see *The Times* 2 Jan, p 2 col 4.

voluntarily relinquished, and the circumstance of having reconquered it is too flattering an appendage to the possession.

Nor is it to be expected on the other hand that Buonaparte would consent to give up, without a struggle, all the scenes of his conquests, and so make confession that his most brilliant victories were of no permanent utility, but only blazed and crackled, and then ended in smoke and ashes.[4] The late language of the Chief Consul, and the vigorous military preparations on all sides, demonstrate that France now despairs of a continental peace for this campaign. The Consulate of course made offers to Austria before they applied to this country, since, were France wholly disengaged from a continental war, that circumstance might have operated, as a motive of peace, on England. But having failed in their proposals to Austria, they know the inveterate temper of our Cabinet sufficiently to be well aware that they will fail with England also. Propositions of peace, or proposals for negotiation, at this time, can only have for their object the popularity of the new Government. They enable Buonaparte at once to throw the odium of continuing the war on the Allies, while he secures to his own Government the character of moderation and justice, and fulfils the promises he has made, of being as forward in pacification, as he has been brilliant in warfare.

Juvat ora tueri
Mixta notis Belli, placidamque gerentia Pacem.[5]

Such are our reasons for believing that we have no prospects of Peace, without at least another campaign; and what are our prospects in the war? The Archduke Charles,[6] in his late Proclamation to the Austrian Circles, and indeed in all his Proclamations, has avoided all mention of the restoration of French Monarchy. The war is evidently by him considered as a war of territory. He states as reasons against Peace, that the present faction are probably not sincere in their professions, and if sincere in their professions, there is yet no ground for believing them secure in their power. But the last sentence of his proclamation, like the postscript of a woman's letter, lets out the real truth. He professes to wish a peace, which

[4] Cf 1 Jan, above, on "a victory" lacking "any permanent advantage".

[5] Statius *Silvae* 1.1.16. "'Tis a pleasure to behold that countenance whereon the marks of war are blended with the guise of tranquil peace." Tr J. H. Mozley *Statius* (LCL 2 vols 1928) I 7.

[6] Charles (Karl Ludwig) (1771–1847), Archduke of Austria, third son of Emperor Leopold II, was president of the Austrian Council of War. He had been successful against the French in 1796 and 1799 but had withdrawn from Switzerland on the arrival of the Russians under Korsakov in Sept.

cannot be had without another campaign—"*a Peace, that may recompense the multiplied sacrifices, by which we have for a long time since sought to procure it.*"[7] As a sufficient comment on these ominous words, we refer to the conferences at Seltz, and in short, to the whole conduct and palpable aim of the Austrian Court, through the whole of the war. The secession of Russia, and the ambiguous conduct of Prussia, may probably have induced the Emperor to make some indefinite concessions concerning the re-establishment of the old governments in Italy; but is the necessity of making a promise always followed by the disposition to keep it? Is it quite an unexampled thing with an ambitious and wily Court first to avail itself of services, and afterwards to evade the conditions? Austria, it is asserted, claims the former Venetian islands as dependencies on Venice, while Russia is bent on the re-establishment not only of the old Venetian Government,[8] but of the old governments and respective territories in all the other Italian states. Is it credible, that Austria should all at once become a convert to the honest enthusiasm of Paul the First?[9] Or that with opposite final views they should continue to co-operate cordially? Much has been said on the effect of past experience; but while ambition and vanity exist, the light of experience, like the lights placed in the stern of the vessel, illumine[s] only the track, that is already passed over.[10] Russia, it is asserted, is in future to act separately. In all probability she will endeavour to pierce into France through Switzerland. This will create a powerful diversion in favour of Austria, whatever may prove the ultimate fate of the invading army. What that fate is *likely* to prove, Austria perhaps sees more clearly than his more enthusiastic brother Emperor. One thing, however, is plain and palpable, that no two armies of different nations ever acted long together without such rivalries and jealousies, as more than overbalance the advantage in number gained by the junction; and that if to avoid these jealousies they act separately, it is made easy to the enemy even with inferior forces to destroy both. No rapidity of mutual communication can be expected from different armies of different nations, equal to that which the armies of a single nation, acting under one plan, will easily realise.

7 Text of address as given in *M Post* 30 Dec 1799.

8 Bonaparte had offered Austria the territories of the Venetian Republic in his Campo Formio settlement of 1797; he would add Venice to his "Kingdom of Italy" in 1806.

9 See below, 24 Feb 1800.

10 C repeats this image 25 Sept 1802, below, and in *Friend* No 7 (*CC*) I 179–80 (II 106).

Let us be permitted to press this too on the public attention. Is it not probable that the dangers with which the Republic shall be[a] menaced by the Allies, may influence[b] the French people in the acceptance of the new Constitution? Is it not possible, that even the lovers of liberty there may perceive an increased necessity, that all the powers of the Republic should act in concert, and that this would be most surely realized by admitting a military dictatorship? If this be the case, if national terror have suspended political apprehensions, if Buonaparte retain his popularity, and the people their enthusiasm, then it would follow that France will open the new campaign with advantages which she has never before possessed.

Stung[c] by a sense of injury from rejected peace, united by apprehensions of a threefold invasion, which will transfer the seat of war into the heart of the Republic; and acting under one Commander in Chief, who at the same time has at his own immediate disposal all the powers and all the resources both of the Government and of the nation; France becomes sufficiently formidable to render hostility with her for slight or avoidable differences as little prudent as it is humane: it may fairly be demanded of our Ministers, to what purpose do we continue the war? To reduce the Republic to the *status ante bellum*, would be scarcely admitted as a justifiable motive from us, who, by the war, have annihilated the whole naval and commercial power of the Republic; at least, it would come with an ill grace from us, since our late vast and important acquisitions in the East. And French principles, let them be as detestable as they may, have assuredly lost all their popular allurement, and, consequently, can neither be object of alarm, or reason for hostility.

ON PEACE. III

THE PUBLIC DESIRE

3 January 1800, Friday. *EOT* II 348–52, in SC's "probable" group (see III 1019); claimed in C's certain essay of 4 Jan; linked closely to that and others; contains C's kind of thinking on semantic association, on the death and resuscitation of extravagant principles, on the "panic of property".

NO answer to the letter from the French Government, soliciting a negotiation for peace, has yet been sent by the British Cabinet. Ministers are greatly embarrassed by this measure; if they refuse to treat, they know the resentment of the nation will be roused, and if

[a] *EOT*: is [b] *EOT*: may have influenced [c] *M Post*: Shewing [corrected in *EOT*]

they treat, the Allies may become suspicious of our intentions, and may cool in the cause. No further particulars have transpired relative to the French dispatches. They have excited a general sensation, and this in our opinion is a circumstance of more favourable omen than the dispatches themselves. We have been so long at war, and to deny its justice and necessity has been so industriously represented as Jacobinism, that it had become doubtful whether or no there might not be a large number who had *forgotten*, and some perhaps who were *afraid*, to put the question—When shall we have Peace? War and the Republic are terms which have been so constantly associated together, that while the latter existed, the former seemed taken for granted: as if the French Republic were aught but a mere *term*, and that too a term of most variable signification; a term which almost every year has borne a different meaning.

It has been uniformly our creed, that in the present age of the world all extravagant principles must be necessarily short-lived; and that we only prolong their life by refusing to let them die a natural death.[1] But even if there had existed such danger from French principles, as had rendered a dignified neutrality impossible or impolitic for this country, still, however, both wisdom and humanity call upon us to inquire, whether or no such danger has not ceased to exist. In the earlier stages of the Revolution, the French Legislators endeavoured to erect a Government on the foundation of *personal Rights*. This absurd and impracticable doctrine, the French Jacobins disseminated with that ardour which novelty and fanaticism never fail to impart. A panic of property was struck throughout England![2] Humanity and compassion were called in to awaken national hatred, and religion was made an accessary; till at last the fears of the one party became as extravagant as the hopes of the other.

Surely it is now time that these fears should cease. The principles which caused them have been long out of fashion even in name. Spite of the oaths of fidelity to them made by their pretended or real enthusiasts, they never were and never could be practised. The doctrines of liberty and equality, in their wild and dangerous extent, were long ago renounced by the Directory; and then most when France was most victorious,—a clear proof that their renunciation was effected by other causes than the war. The present faction have

[1] C's metaphor, developed 4 and 6 Jan, below.

[2] As C would say again 4 Jan and 19 Mar, and in *Friend* (*CC*) II 143 (I 218, 219). His earliest use of "panic of property" is in *Conciones:* see *Lects 1795* (*CC*) 30–1 and n 1.

constituted a government in direct opposition to these doctrines; a government more jealous of popular power than our own. They have, indeed, admitted the sovereignty of the people, as a title by courtesy.[3] But it is a mere title; and to adduce it against negotiation with them, were as childish and insolent, as it was in the French negotiators to adduce His Majesty's title of King of France as an objection to treating with Lord Malmesbury.[4]

We deem the present Constitution of France founded on the most tyrannous Oligarchy: the warmest advocate of the Minister[a] cannot see its monstrous defects more clearly than we have done, or express his opinions more decisively. But let us not be misunderstood. The nature of a Government, considered simply and in itself, is no argument either for or against the possibility of peace with it.[5] Let the Emperor of Russia be as wise, as righteous, as heroic a Monarch as our Minister has chosen to paint him, still, however, no Englishman but would shudder at the Russian form of Government, if it were introduced into England. Yet, who is mad enough to deem this an objection against our alliance with the Emperor of Russia? The French tolerate Atheism and Deism; the Emperor of China tolerates both, and Idolatry to boot—and yet we send flattering Embassies to him. We have made treaties with the Arch-pirate of Algiers, and with the Delai Lama of Thibet. And why? Because we have nothing to do with the wickedness or absurdity of a Government, except as far as they are dangerous to ourselves. What are the present principles of the French Government? Those of a military Oligarchy—equally abhorred by every party in this country, and concerning the propagation of which it were idiotry[b] to entertain any alarm.

It were a paradox too bold even for Ministerial sophistry, that Jacobinism in England is to be destroyed by making war on a Government which is itself exerting a tyranny to destroy it in France. The truth is, that whatever nomenclature the French Executive may adopt, France itself has fallen back into its antient character, of an

[a] *EOT*: monarchy [b] *EOT*: idiotcy

[3] See above, 20 Jan 1798 (n 9 on Norfolk's toast) and 26 Dec 1799, and below, 28 Jan 1800.

[4] Malmesbury headed peace negotiations with the Directory in 1796 and 1797 in Lille (see above, 4 Jan 1798 n 1). French demands in 1797 included a stipulation that George III must desist from the practice begun by Edward III of styling himself "King of France".

[5] This and the following passage are a reworking of *Conciones*: "It has been repeatedly said, that we could not honorably negociate...our Government...the Ally of...that most CHRISTIAN Arch-pirate, the Dey of Algiers". *Lects 1795* (*CC*) 54–5.

ambitious, intriguing military Power; and its ambition is to be guarded against by this country, equally under a Monarchy as a Republic. But ambition forms no reason against fair negotiations for peace, which, if once concluded, would be found the securest provision against it. *And is France the only ambitious Power on the Continent?*

We hope most earnestly that the public voice may become decisive, and make itself audible. The desire for peace is as wise as it is general. For what danger can follow from it? Our empire in the East is secured beyond almost the possibility of attack:—Jacobinism in England can scarcely be said to exist, otherwise than as an abusive epithet; and it is disowned in France, its birth-place and its nursery.[6] French principles have lost all their popular allurement; the insolence of French conquest has been repressed: and the French nation wish for peace so ardently, that even the promise of pacification seems almost to reconcile them to a dictatorship. Never was a moment when peace promised so much, or threatened so little—never, we may add, a moment, when war threatened so much, and made promises so valueless and improbable. Her factions suspended by national[a] danger, and her pride insulted by rejected proffers, France will have placed herself like an army under the first military genius of the modern world! The fear of a threatened invasion will have restored to him all his popularity! And the man, who has atchieved by his exploits the splendor of a hero in romance, wields at his will the whole force of a romantic people, and unites in his single government the dispatch and unity of a despotism, with the enthusiasm and resources of a Republic.[7]

CHRISTIAN ARGUMENTS

3 January 1800, Friday. New attribution, on the basis of style and theme.

At this season we have been celebrating the birth of the author of our religion; and it may not be unappropriate to bring to the recollection of our *religious politicians* the dying words of one of our greatest Kings:—"When Christ came into the world, PEACE was

[a] *M Post*: natural

[6] For the changes rung on this phrase and for its appearance in C's report of Pitt's speech of 17 Feb, see below, 18 Feb 1800 and n 8.

[7] See the second paragraph of C's report of the same speech.

proclaimed; when Christ went out of the world, PEACE was bequeathed! And he is a Christian in name only, who does not obey the proclamation, or endeavour to prove his claim to the legacy."[1] But this, we suppose, was meant only for a *spiritual* peace, quite compatible with the pillage and throat-cutting of the *outer man*!

Independent of the *vital Christians*, we trust that there are few so ignorant of the state of religious opinions on the continent of Europe, as to adduce the nature of the ecclesiastical arrangements in France as a serious *Christian* argument against peace with that country. If any such there be, they are scarce worthy to be informed, that the disbelief of revealed religion is unfortunately not more common among the people of education in France than it is in Germany, Spain, and Italy.

ON PEACE. IV[1]

4 January 1800, Saturday. *EOT* I 199–204, in SC's group of certain attributions.

THE CABINET

YESTERDAY a Cabinet Council, consisting of Mr. Pitt, Lords Grenville, Spencer, and Camden,[2] and Mr. Windham, sat in Downing-street, upon the two letters received from the French Government, the one from Buonaparte, addressed to the King, the other from Talleyrand, addressed to Lord Grenville; and we have no dread of being wrong when we assert, that their decision was against entering into, even a negotiation.[3]—The language of Ministers and their friends warrants this conclusion; and another excellent guide, the Funds, confirms it.[4] For we have often had occasion to notice, that somehow or other, important events which affect the

[1] Untraced.

[1] For a report on a "Theatrical Dispute" in this day's *M Post*, possibly by C, see App A, below.

[2] In Pitt's cabinet George John, 2nd Earl Spencer (1758–1834) was first lord of the Admiralty, and John Jeffreys Pratt, 2nd Earl (later 1st Marquess) of Camden (1759–1840) was minister without portfolio.

[3] The arrogant confidence of Grenville, based on the assumption that France was on the run, and of Archduke Charles, who assumed that more fighting would bring the Allies more spoils, led them into a basic miscalculation of the political and military situation that gave Europe another decade and a half of war. C's essays stress the underestimation of both the genius and the popularity of the First Consul.

[4] The proprietor of the *M Post* was keenly aware of the impact of news of war or peace on the market price of the government bonds known as the Consolidated Funds. Stuart had more than once been accused of tampering with such news in order to make a killing on the market.

funds find their way into the Stock Exchange; and accordingly stocks fell about one per cent. It may be recollected that some time ago we gave as the cause the funds rose, the prospect of a negotiation for peace;[5] a measure which Buonaparte was pledged to attempt. The hope has now disappeared, and the funds will probably decline still farther.

The delay in deciding upon the French dispatches arose partly from the necessity of taking the opinion of several Cabinet Ministers, who were in the country passing their holidays. Yesterday, however, the answer, written by Lord Grenville, and addressed to Buonaparte, was sent off by Mr. Stow, chief officer of the Customs at Dover, from whence it will be forwarded by the courier to Paris. Ministers, we believe, will soon publish a declaration of their sentiments and views in the further prosecution of the war, in which they will attempt to justify their present conduct.

The public will not be persuaded that because the French Government is an Usurpation, a Despotism, or a Tyranny, we therefore must prosecute the war. This was not the argument of Ministers themselves on former occasions. They contended that the war was justifiable to extinguish French principles and reduce French power; but they always disavowed any determination to persevere, merely to change the *form*[6] of the French Government. Their motives for rejecting overtures of peace, at this period, must therefore be an opinion that the principles of the present Government in France are dangerous to surrounding States, or that they have a certain prospect of reducing her power. In our paper of yesterday we endeavoured to prove that wild Jacobin principles having received a mortal blow by the last Revolution, can be no longer dangerous; and that prospects of conquest from France will prove delusive, the history of the war gives too much reason to dread. These, therefore, are unwise motives for continuing hostilities.

But we are told France is insincere in professing a desire of peace! If that were known to be the fact, Ministers would certainly treat with her, since they would again secure the support of the British people in the war, and expose the ambition of the enemy. We rather suspect that Ministers know France is *sincere*, and are apprehensive a negotiation would either entrap them into a peace, or shew, in a forcible manner, how desperately and unreasonably they are bent on the further prosecution of the war. No period was ever more

[5] *M Post* 31 Oct 1799 (not by C).

[6] Cf C's *Recantation* Ode, 16 Apr 1798.

favourable than the present for accommodation and adjustment. The last campaign has checked the views of France, and our reverses in Switzerland must have checked the views of the Allies also. Neither party has great cause of joy at the result. This temper of mind, neither elated nor depressed, is of all others the most favourable to negotiation. From the commencement of the war till now, France has been either insolent and flushed with victory, or thrown under the power of the Jacobins by defeats. Now for the first time her ambition has been checked; and Jacobinism, if not mortally wounded, yet requires all the aids of a war against France, to its resuscitation.[7]

JACOBINISM DEFINED

As events vary, so our Ministers vary their tone! Are we successful? The object of the war is to extirpate Jacobinism.—Are we beaten in all points? It then becomes necessary to check the progress of French ambition. It is melancholy that the war has produced, with rapid alternation, the two evils, for the prevention of which it is carried on and justified. We profess to wage the war against Jacobinism and ambition: and the moment France is threatened by our successes, Jacobinism revives and flourishes.

The war began with Austria and Prussia, May 1792, and on the 10th of Aug. following Royalty was overthrown, and the Brissotine Republicanism substituted. In February 1793, we joined the Allies; and the war was triumphant in every quarter. In the West the Chouans, who brought at once 80,000 men into the field; General Wurmser in the East;[8] the English on the South; and the Anglo-Austrians on the North. We took Toulon, Valenciennes and Condé. What was the effect? The Brissotine party, comparatively at least humane and enlightened,[9] was overturned by the faction of Robespierre, and the furies of Jacobinism were let loose on the devoted country. In May 1794, the Duke of York took Landrecy, and in imagination we were already the conquerors of France. Jacobinism still predominated, till in June the weathercock of success shifted. The French conquered Flanders, drove back Austria, and even foiled

[7] See the beginning of this idea, "On Peace" 3 Jan (above), and its extension, 6 Jan (below).

[8] Count Dagobert Sigmund von Wurmser (1724–97) had commanded one of the two Austrian armies of 1793–4 and had been at times found unco-operative by the British.

[9] C encouraged the comparison of his own political position to that of Brissot (a "sublime visionary": *Conciones: Lects 1795—CC*—35) and the Girondins; yet there are indications that at the fall of Robespierre C and RS felt not jubilation but shock as at the fall of a great leader whom they had admired. See Woodring 194–5.

the Duke of York; and in this flush of victory Robespierre and his party were annihilated. Then victories flowed in upon France in full tide; and the public opinions became more temperate, as the nation was less and less in danger from foreign enemies. The last constitution was framed; our ministerial papers, and then the Minister himself, spoke of the existing government in France as a power that might be treated with. We endeavoured to treat; France was insolent and vindictive; and the succeeding campaigns effected a reverse of fortune. The conquests of France in Italy were reconquered. Her armies ill organized and ill supported, and her frontiers threatened. What was the effect? The clubs were re-opened. Jacobinism was again brought into play, and became active and powerful in exact proportion to the degree of our success.

Hence it appears that the war against France as a Republic, produces in the French Republic ambition and insolence by its failure, and Jacobinism by its success; nor is this difficult of explanation. When a nation is in safety, men think of their private interests; individual property becomes the predominating principle, the Lord of the ascendant: and all politics and theories inconsistent with property and individual interest give way, and sink into a decline, which, unless unnaturally stimulated, would end in speedy dissolution.—But is the nation in danger? Every man is called into play; every man feels his interest as a *Citizen* predominating over his individual interests; the high, and the low, and the middle classes become all alike Politicians; the majority carry the day; and Jacobinism is the natural consequence. Let us not be deceived by words. Every state, in which all the inhabitants without distinction of property are roused to the exertion of a public spirit, is for the time a Jacobin State. France at present is only *preparing* to become so.—If the present Consulate can conclude a peace, the glory attached to it will, for a while, reconcile the people to an Oligarchy, which can only exist while it is popular; and as manufactures and commerce revive, the spirit of property will regain its ascendency, and the Government of France will be modified accordingly.

ON PEACE. V

6 January 1800, Monday. New attribution, related by many cross-references to C's known pieces; embodies a characteristic metaphor.

SINCERITY

THE Paris Papers to the 31st ult. have given us a list of the exiles permitted to re-enter the territories of the Republic. Their particular places of abode are specified, and each is to be placed under the superintendance of the Minister of Police in the Commune marked out for him. The choice of the Commune has been chiefly determined by its nearness to the families and business of the person appointed to reside in it. We have likewise copied from these journals an official list of the three hundred Legislators. Both these lists prove one point; that the new Government is using every possible means to make itself considered as the centre of union for all parties. Men of talents and character have been chosen, almost wholly without reference to their former opinions. This measure involves a most politic and judicious species of self-adulation; for it tells the people by facts, which carry with them no ordinary appearance both of fearlessness and humanity, that the necessity and propriety of the new order of things are so palpable, that no wise and honest man can refuse his assent to them. In the mean time the parties themselves, who have been thus chosen or recalled, will probably be prevented by personal delicacy and gratitude, from immediate hostility against the Constitution, while they really exert themselves in the cause of the Republic: nor is it indeed impossible that, menaced as France is at present, many sincere lovers of Freedom may perceive, in the usurpation of the modern Pisistratus,[1] such *temporary* advantages as reconcile them to a temporary submission. Other measures have been adopted, favourable to morals and civil Liberty. The free use of religious worship, and of the places dedicated to it on other days than the Decade, is permitted by a consular decree; and, instead of the oaths formerly exacted, a simple *promise* is required of fidelity to the Constitution. Of the French Armies nothing occurs particularly noticeable, except that the Army of Italy is reinforced by twenty

[1] Peisistratus (d 527 B.C.), tyrant of Athens who decreed marble temples, introduced dramatic contests, and commissioned scholars. The epithet suits C's current view of Napoleon's potentiality; he uses it again in *Courier* 29 Sept 1814 (see below). Except for this touch, the bulk of this paragraph, a summary of news from Paris, may have been supplied to C by Stuart or an assistant.

thousand men from Switzerland. General Moreau has arrived at the Army of the Rhine,[2] the right wing of which had entered into winter quarters.

No mention is made in these Journals of the letter sent by Buonaparte to His Majesty;—but those who have seen it, say that it is respectful and temperate. We continue[3] to give it as our decided opinion, that the French Government is *sincere* in its wishes for peace; and that Ministers believe as we do, and for this very reason avoid negotiation. We once stated[4] our conviction, that the French Government had no *hope*, that the English Cabinet would accede to pacific overtures, when Austria had rejected them. That conviction remains. However low we may estimate the integrity of Buonaparte and his faction, we think too well of their *discernment* to believe otherwise. But this in nowise impeaches the *sincerity* of their offers. To make offers without *expectation* that they *will* be accepted, does not constitute insincerity, provided a real *wish* exists that these offers *may* be accepted. Ministers were accused of criminal insincerity in the negotiations at Lisle, not because they had no *expectations* that their offers *would* be acceded to, but because it was believed they had no *wish* they *should* be successful.[5]—It is most assuredly not inconsistent with the strictest honour to make proposals, of which we really wish the acceptance, although our reason at the same time forces us to fear that what we wish will not take place. But where the wishes and the expectations coincide, and both are directed against the acceptance of our own proposals, this is indeed insincerity. With this Ministers were charged: with this we do not think Buonaparte chargeable.

TRUTH IS *OUR* POLICY

WE have been explicit, perhaps prolix, in our explanation. But he who is the creature of no party, who acts and feels for himself, unbiassed by any, *he* will be, of all others, most subject to malicious or ignorant charges of inconsistency.[6] While he criminates

2 Jean Victor Marie Moreau (1763–1813), victorious commander of the Rhine and Moselle armies in 1796, aided Bonaparte on 18 Brumaire.

3 See 4 Jan, above. *The Times* of 7 Jan independently supports the view that France is sincere, by conceding that Bonaparte's "insidiously manifested" disposition to negotiate means that he wants either a treaty to extricate France from present distress or, if it is rejected, a means to render continued war popular in France.

4 See 2 Jan, above.

5 This charge is hinted at in the essay of 6 Nov 1799 and alluded to 8 Jan 1800.

6 Cf C's response to an earlier charge of inconsistency: *Watchman* (*CC*) 196.

one Government, he is supposed to be tacitly praising its enemy: as if, of two balls, we could not call one black without implying whiteness in the other. We detest equally Jacobinism and usurpation in the French, and the principles of despotism preached by their opponents—we look with equal horror on those who murder a lawful Constitution, and those who, under pretence of medicine, administer poison to it. We deem it among the most fatal errors in some friends of freedom in England,[7] that they have thought it necessary to a consistent opposition to Ministers, that they should *slur over* the follies or wickedness of France. We think otherwise. TRUTH is *our* policy. We despise the absurdities and dread the fanaticism of France; believing, however, at the same time, that but for the war against France they would have died in their infancy. To the war carried on under the pretence of extirpating them, we attribute their unnatural longevity, and whole powers of propagation.[8] They are now at the last gasp: and without the reanimating aid of invasions and terror will die without hope of resurrection. It may be well and modest in the Journals that receive *mandates* from masters, to talk of opposition prints as having received instructions from their employers. We acknowledge no master; and have no other employer but the Public. To that employer we will remain faithful, careless concerning the calumnies and misrepresentations of the ill-meaning and the unmeaning, whoever they be, whether the hirelings or the opponents of the Minister.

In the service of the Public we persevere in putting to Ministers the deeply interesting question: Under what pretext do you persist in wasting the blood and treasures of your Country? Peace is evidently the wish, as it is undeniably the interest, of the New Government. The ambition of France, a just subject of apprehension, is checked: her principles, at which we were idly alarmed, are exploded. The continuation of the war with her will necessarily awaken either the one or the other. We deny, that a Peace concluded with the present Government would imply an admission on our side of its original legality. That all the despots in Europe are not equally *righteous*, is no reason why we should not be at peace with them all. We admit, that an honourable Treaty concluded with Buonaparte would tend to confirm his power, and that by this and his subsequent moderation

[7] See "Advice to the Friends of Freedom" 12 Dec 1799, above.

[8] This extends C's "Jacobinism... resuscitation" concept of 4 Jan (above); see also 8 Jan, below. Contrast his private wish for a return of the "Saviour of the East" (*CL* I 539).

it may continue, till the revival of commerce and manufactures in France calls into active power the spirit of property, and consequently brings with it a Government modified accordingly.[9] But we affirm, that war will not only confirm his power still more than peace, but that it will have a tendency to *justify* it; it will render moderation less necessary; and *should* his Government be overthrown, the analogy of all the past justifies us in affirming, that it will introduce some other usurpation equally violent, on principles infinitely more pernicious. Supposing for a moment, that Royalty could be restored—what reason have we for affirming its permanency? Will not the principles of Jacobinism remain? Can the faction of the Royalists boast more talent, more activity, more energy, than the Republicans? Will it not disturb the present state of property infinitely more than the usurpation of Buonaparte? And by the very act of disturbing property, will it not necessarily bring Jacobinism once more into play? And will not Royalty therefore, if restored, perish, like a bubble, by the very agitation that produced it?[10]

PAPER WAR. I

OVERTURES REJECTED

7 January 1800, Tuesday. *EOT* I 212–17, in SC's group of certain attributions; acknowledged by C in 1804 as "one on Lord Grenville's Politics—which I have never been able to think meanly of" (*CL* II 1075); recollected by Stuart (IX 487–8) as one of C's few memorable prose contributions and one of the few he wrote immediately on the occasion.

WE present our Readers with the correspondence between Buonaparte and the British Government.[1] The letter of the former does not contain "a mere renewal of general professions of pacific

[9] This repeats the closing sentence of 4 Jan (above).

[10] Cf: "[my] Dislike...was only for the moment, a bubble broken by the agitation that gave it Birth". *CL* II 1012 (14 Oct 1803). Royalty, perishable, is that "Monarchical part" viz "the Scum" in C's wine recipe (*CN* I 162 Gutch), comparable to the "feculence, which has boiled up on the surface of the revolutionary cauldron" to be "scummed off" (12 Dec 1799, above); a few days later C writes (13 Jan 1800, below) of the "bubbles of a fountain" as different and "not such as rise...on the muddy and stagnant pools of despotism".

[1] Authorised French and English versions of the letters of Talleyrand and General Bonaparte, of 25 Dec, appeared in the evening papers of 6 Jan and in this day's *M Post*, along with Lord Grenville's reply to Talleyrand dated 4 Jan—but no letter for the upstart Napoleon except an "Official Note" declaring the King's commitment to continued "exertions of just and defensive war". The texts are reprinted in *EOT* I 205–12.

dispositions."[2] It is the first direct overture which this country has received from France; in the affirmation that both Great Britain and France are already "powerful and strong beyond what their safety and independence require," it renounces all schemes of conquest; and in the admission that His Majesty "reigns over a free nation," it likewise renounces all *revolutionary* projects.

The concluding paragraph seems in the most respectful language to hint, that the consequence of continuing a war, which is professedly carried on for the preservation of "things as they are,"[3] may be the dislocation of all civilised nations. The whole letter is manly, and unsullied by the least inflammatory insinuation against the Government or the country. It were contemptible folly to suppose, that France conceived herself in nothing aggrieved by this country; but her Government gives the best possible pledge of its "sincere desire to contribute efficaciously to a general pacification," by a complete abstinence from the mention of all such supposed grievances.

The letter is now before our Readers; and it is scarcely possible, that the bitterest enemy of the French Government should accuse us of having represented its contents untruly. The official Note, in answer to this letter, begins with the *assertion*, that His Majesty's Ministers have given frequent proofs of their sincere desire for the re-establishment of general peace: and then, as if impatient even "of general professions of pacific dispositions," proceeds immediately to revive old grievances by the affirmation, that the war originated "in an unprovoked attack," which, whether true or false, is no reason for or against a negotiation at present, unless it be contended that a war begun unjustly by one party, must be continued *ad internecionem*,[4] by both parties. Having thus manifested its anti-pacific disposition[s] the Note goes on to assign in justification of them, that "the causes, which originally produced the war, have not ceased to operate." None either here or in France will affect not to understand what Ministers mean by these causes. Yet there is something insidious in their not being specifically stated. Had Ministers, instead of a general phrase, used the direct words "Ambition and Jacobinism," it was probably foreseen that the dullest reader would have objected that the new Government is manifestly built on the ruins of Jacobinism, and that both Jacobinism and Ambition in reference to this country are solemnly renounced in its overture.

[2] As charged in the seventh paragraph of Grenville's reply.

[3] Cf *MPL: Lects 1795* (*CC*) 7 and n 3; *Watchman* (*CC*) 145 n 3.

[4] "To the death".

These causes, however, are stated to have produced in Europe "a long and destructive warfare," and to the prevalence of the same system, it is said, "France justly ascribes all her present miseries." Whom do Ministers mean by France? The Royalists and Chouans? For surely the Republicans do not attribute all the miseries of their country simply to Republicanism? We can forgive a rhetorical figure, by which a small part is assumed for the whole; but we cannot avoid censuring severely this ungenerous mode of conveying into a country a proclamation against its Government, under pretence of an official answer to a pacific overture made by that Government. In a similar strain of invective, the ravages committed in Holland, the Netherlands, the Swiss Cantons, and Germany, are alluded to; and Italy is marked out by a particular sentence, as having "been made the scene of *unbounded* rapine and anarchy, though now rescued from its invaders." This low and peevish personality on the man, in answer to whose letter the Note was written, we might have expected from Ministers; but we did not expect that they would so palpably bring a bill of indictment against themselves for their negotiations at Lisle.[5]—These they themselves solicited: they *made* overtures to France, not *received* them; and yet at that time these very outrages not only existed, but had been newly perpetrated by the identical Government to whom they made those overtures, and while France gloried in her ambition, with Jacobinism scarcely suspended, certainly not subdued. Has Ministerial resentment put out the eyes of their prudence? And is this Note sent as a *payment in kind* for the insolence with which they were then repelled? The reference which follows to the intrigues with Tippoo Saib must be a wilful sophism. For Ministers are not so grossly ignorant as not to know, that our ejection from India was a darling scheme of the antient monarchy, and that the attempt to realise it by the Kings of France and Spain was only prevented by the Revolution: with the principles of which the late attempt, which ended in the fall of Tippoo, was wholly and absolutely unconnected.[6]

These charges and invectives lead to the heart-withering declara-

[5] See above, "On Peace" 3 Jan n 4.

[6] In 1784 the British had concluded peace with the sultan of Mysore, Tippoo Sahib (c 1751–99), son of Hyder Ali. In 1789 his ravaging of the territories of the raja of Travancore provoked a British invasion. Cornwallis's victory near Seringapatam in 1792 lost Tippoo half his dominions. In March 1799 the British renewed hostilities and Tippoo was killed during the storming of Seringapatam in May. Tippoo, planting trees of liberty and "instigated by the artifices, and deluded by the promises of the French, had entered into their ambitious and destructive projects in India", to quote the King's Speech of 24 Sept 1799.

tion, that open war is deemed by Ministers our only defence, as long as the present system in France shall continue; in other words, as long as France shall remain a Republic. This declaration is justified by an assertion, that "the most solemn treaties have only prepared the way for fresh aggressions." Has it then been proved, that Austria had no share in the guilt? Has Austria given no proofs of an ambition equally enormous? Has Austria yet done what the French Government now does—has she given any assurance of recantation?

The succeeding paragraphs declare this a war of principles, leaving the nature of those principles insidiously undefined; and then inform[a] the Chief Consul, that "the best and most natural pledge" that such offensive principles are permanently abolished, "would be the restoration of that line of Princes which for so many centuries maintained France in prosperity at home, and in consideration and respect abroad: Such an event would at once have removed, and will at any time remove, all obstacles in the way of negotiation or peace"![7] This is a repetition of the insult which we censured in the former part of the Note. Surely, with such power of communication with France as Ministers possess, there might have been found another vehicle for smuggling in a proclamation to the Royalists, than an official answer to the Chief Consul's overture. Besides, is it true, that the restoration of Royalty would be a pledge, that ambition and Jacobinism would be no more? Till the arguments have been answered, which we have in our late papers adduced to the contrary,[8] we shall continue to hold, that it will be no pledge. This paragraph is succeeded by an explanation, that "it is not to this mode exclusively that His Majesty limits the possibility of secure and solid pacification." But no syllable occurs which enables us to conceive, what other mode will be admitted. It can, indeed, be regarded only as a miserable loop-hole, through which Ministers mean to escape from the charge of inconsistency, in case Republican France, by her victories, should once again lay her enemies at her feet.—Then, when

[a] *M Post*: informs [corrected in *EOT*]

[7] The preceding paragraph reads: "Greatly, indeed, will His Majesty rejoice, whenever it shall appear that the danger to which his own dominions, and those of his allies, have been so long exposed, has really ceased; whenever he shall be satisfied that the necessity of resistance is at an end; that, after the experience of so many years of crimes and miseries, better principles have ultimately prevailed in France; and that all the gigantic projects of ambition, and all the restless schemes of destruction . . . have at length been finally relinquished:—But the conviction of such a change, however agreeable to His Majesty's wishes, can result only from experience, and from the evidence of facts."

[8] See 4 and 6 Jan, above.

she is insolent with prosperity; *then* she will be allowed, perhaps, to have atchieved *that other mode*, which renders negotiation possible. The whole concludes by proclaiming the continuance of "*defensive*" war against an enemy who petitions us for peace. This Official Note is disorderly in its arrangement, vague and indefinite in its expressions, and barbarous in its style; worthy of Ministers, but not worthy of their country.

APOLOGIA. I

ON THE LATE NEGOTIATION

8 January 1800, Wednesday; entitled "On the Late Negotiation". *EOT* I 218–27, in SC's group of certain attributions; confirmed by internal evidence.

NOTHING TO HOPE FROM WAR

IN our paper of yesterday we could only throw out some few remarks upon this important transaction; this day we resume the subject more at length, but even now not to the full extent of our wishes. In discussing it we are entitled to attention, since our former observations, (particularly in a long article "*On Peace*"), are now proved to have been prophetic.[1] We then endeavoured to shew that Mr. Pitt's administration was in its nature preclusive of peace.—We again repeat, upon the reasons then stated, that *an honourable and permanent peace never will be concluded by the present Ministry*.—We sincerely wish that this were no more than a bare *assertion*; but, unfortunately, all the facts, from the commencement of the war to the present hour, have combined to render it almost a *truism*. Ministers are entangled with promises; their character and pride are at stake; they are heated in the game; when they deem themselves prosperous, they offer insult; in adversity they receive it in return; and the first use which they make of their recovery from this adversity is to retaliate the retaliation. Alas! during this play of personal passions, tens of thousands are massacred, the interests of millions sacrificed, to whom "the very existence of such a war might have been unknown,"[2] had they known those things alone, in the events of which they were really interested!

[1] Article of 6 Nov 1799, not by C. See discussion at that date in App A, below. C is not quoting exactly; indeed, his words are closer to his own early statement (2 Jan 1798, above); C quite avoids the main theme of 6 Nov, advocacy of Fox as a minister of peace.

[2] Lord Grenville's Note of 4 Jan, paragraph 5.

The official Note of Lord Grenville contains precisely that which we had before stated it as likely to contain—recurrences, and criminations, and insult! only that it is still more, than we dared anticipate, calculated to strengthen while it irritates the new Government; to revive the hopes and re-animate the exertions of the Jacobins; and to inspire all parties of the Revolution with mingled contempt and horror towards Royalty. We did not dare anticipate that Ministers would display such ignorance, or such forgetfulness, of that proud nationality which is rooted in the hearts of all Frenchmen, as to proclaim to a mighty nation, that the restoration of an Emigrant "would confirm to it the unmolested enjoyment of *its antient territory*."[3] We have destroyed the whole colonial power of France; we have annihilated her commerce; we have ruined her navy; our own colonial, naval, and commercial power, we have more than doubled; Austria is feasting on spoils: and lo! we proclaim to France, as a lure and an encouragement to royalty, that the restoration of kingly power "would confirm to her the unmolested enjoyment of its *antient territory*." To the nation, which has secured to itself Belgium, and a great part of Germany, which still hovers upon Italy, which has driven the forces of two Emperors out of Switzerland, which has forced us *to ransom our army* out of Holland;—to this nation *we* offer as its reward for a restoration of Monarchy, that "it would confirm to it the unmolested enjoyment of its *antient territory*!" We abjure all speculation at present, concerning the good or evil, which might result to France, from the re-adoption of Monarchy, Nobility, and an established Priesthood; we look only to the immense aggrandisement of England and Austria, the rivals of France, and to the immense power and acquisitions of France, which counter-balance them. Contemplating the subject from this point of view singly, we should not hesitate to affirm, that the event implied in the confirmation to France, "of the unmolested enjoyment of its antient territory," would in its effects be nearly tantamount to dismemberment: that if this be the necessary consequence of Royalty, Louis XVIII. would purchase his throne at the price of his country. By the encouragement of the Chouans, Ministers had already associated with Royalism a conduct which we must not mention; and now what would they teach Frenchmen to associate with Royalty itself? There are moments of reverie, in which having long dwelt on such measures and such proclamations as these, we have regarded the dreams of

[3] Grenville's Note, the sentence immediately following that cited in 7 Jan (at n 7).

Barruel and Robison[4] with a transient faith; and have conceived it possible, that Illuminati and Jacobins may have crept into the Cabinets of Monarchs, in order to carry on the war against Jacobinism with deep-laid blunders and dexterous infelicity.

Bonaparte deserted the gallant army which his own ambition had led into Egypt; and, on his return into France, instead of the death which was due to him, he procured the unshared possession of the supreme power. Bonaparte is a fugitive and an usurper. These are our opinions; and, in a tranquil season, these would be the opinions of Frenchmen. It will remain to Ministers and their Allies to menace the Republic, till the love of liberty is suspended by the sense of national danger; to alarm and confuse the minds of its inhabitants, till they consider the very crimes of their usurper only as traces of an high and mysterious destiny; till in their distempered imaginations his flight from Egypt becomes a call from heaven for the saving of his country;[5] and his usurpation is believed to have suspended the forms, only to increase the energies, of freedom, even as the air acquires its explosive power by being condensed. If a fanatic veneration of their leader have metamorphosed the dark and hopeless Serfs of the North into warriors,[6] what may not a similar fanaticism produce on the susceptible and visionary mind of France?

Besides, is it absolutely certain that France will remain without an ally? Does there exist no great military power, who has an hereditary fear of Austria, and whose meanest subjects (since the wars of their hero King) draw in with their mothers' milk a feeling towards Russians, little favourable to the present contest?[7]

All fear of Jacobinism is removed from this power; the Revolution, which has established itself on its ruins, was probably concerted under his influence. What then justifies the supposition, that this power will stand by and behold a country reduced to an impotence, which at the same moment will render his own existence and that

[4] Widely influential textbooks of Anti-Jacobinism were the Abbé Augustin Barruel's *Memoirs, Illustrating the History of Jacobinism* (1797–8) and the Scottish Professor John Robison's *Proofs of a Conspiracy Against All the Religions and Governments of Europe* (Edinburgh 1797) interpreting the French Revolution and all that flowed from it as the work of organised conspirators. For Barruel and the reception of his work in England, see Bernard N. Schilling *Conservative England and the Case Against Voltaire* (1950) ch 13 and Bibliographical Notes.

[5] C had indulged just such "a piece of Blasphemy" in his letter of 15 Oct 1799. *CL* I 539.

[6] See below.

[7] The "great power" was Prussia, whose "hero King" had been Frederick the Great (1712–86) but whose ruler since 1797 had been the vacillating Frederick William III (1770–1840).

of his kingdom hazardous and improbable? Is it certain or likely that this power wishes the restoration of the Bourbon family in France? May he not have reason to fear, that personal gratitude to Russia and Austria for recent services might so far weaken in the minds of this family the influence of political duty, as that France, his natural Ally, should be perverted into an enemy; or at least be induced to remain neutral during his ruin? It is possible, that the conclusion of Bonaparte's letter meant more than meets the ear; and that he did not shelter himself under the licensed inaccuracy of a general sentiment, when he "ventured to say, the fate of *all* civilised nations is attached to the termination of a war which involves the whole world."

Let these conjectures be well-founded, or without foundation, there remains enough to fear, and nothing to hope, from the war. It has already transferred the whole trade of Europe into our hands, and it can do no more; if we conclude a peace, the surplus of our revenues may be applied successfully to the diminution of our national debt; commerce will not leave an accustomed channel all at once; nor is it possible for any nation suddenly to acquire the capital and confidence necessary to turn it from us; and ere any successful rival can arise to cut away from us one branch of trade, other branches may have shot out, and enabled us to bear the loss. WAR, we repeat, can do no more for us than it has already done: and the longer it is prolonged, the heavier will be the burthens which it will leave behind it; and if peace *should* operate to diminish our revenue, the less we shall be capable of sustaining that diminution. We may indeed make ourselves masters of new colonies; but this would only substitute the *en-bon-point* of dropsy for the muscular habit of health, if indeed it be not already substituted.

THIS IS THE MAN[8]

THE Ministers, however, have passed "sentence for open war." We protest solemnly against that sentence, *because we are Anti-Gallicans, and Anti-Jacobins*; because, if the war be unsuccessful, it will inflame anew "the gigantic projects of French ambition;"[9] and if it be successful, it will raise Jacobinism from its present state of suspended animation into new and frantic life.[10] All vulgar minds

[8] In the following paragraphs C's anonymity as a leader-writer is all but forgotten as he recapitulates his articles of 1, 2, 3, 4, and 6 Jan and defends himself as "the man" who, in writing them, has "produced no ordinary sensation" (see concluding sentences).

[9] Grenville's Note, again.

[10] This extends the resurrection idea of 4 and 6 Jan, above.

are indiscriminating. Accustomed to fight blindly under some Leader whom choice or chance has[a] given them, they take for granted, that the man who is the enemy of one faction, must needs be the partizan of its opponent. When we speak in due terms of aversion concerning French absurdities or enormities, a whisper is propagated that we are become the friends of the Minister. When we drop this subject, as exhausted or self-evident, and plead for peace, because these absurdities have lost the dangerous gloss of novelty, and have been disowned in their very birth-place; immediately the hirelings of Ministry join in a concert of abuse against us, as shifting our opinions at the breath of an employer.[11] We exhibited lately our detestation of Bonaparte as an usurper;[12] a few days afterwards we admitted him to be a great General.[13] And this, forsooth, is self-contradiction! We represented his Constitution as a Dictatorship, and that its pretensions to the name of a Representative System were fraud and mockery;[14] shortly after, on the question, What would be the internal powers of France in case of the continuance of war? we admitted the *military* resources of a popular and enlightened Dictatorship as immense and formidable.[15] And this too, forsooth, is self-contradiction! We have repeatedly pressed upon the attention of our readers the impracticability of all theories founded on *Personal Rights*; we have contended zealously, that the security and circulation of property, with political power proportioned to property, constitute a good Government, and bring with them all other blessings, which our imperfect nature can, or ought to expect.[16] We have stated it as a necessary event, that the Government of France will modify itself sooner or later into a Government of property, and the war against France, by calling too many individuals without property into political importance, is the true cause of the delay of this event.[17] Immediately after, an overture for negotiation is made by the new Government; and using and repeating these very arguments, we raise our voice and suffrage for peace!—And this too is self-contradiction!—We affirmed, that the wickedness and folly of any Govern-

[a] *M Post*, *EOT*: have

[11] "The two leading Papers [of Opposition] yesterday received their orders from their Employers: they totally changed their tone, and were just as eager that Ministers should acknowledge Buonaparte as Sovereign of France...". *Sun*, 2 Jan; with more of the same on 6 Jan concerning Opposition papers of 4 Jan.

[12] Esp 1 Jan, above.

[13] See "On Peace" 3 Jan, above.

[14] In C's series on the French Constitution.

[15] See 2 Jan, above.

[16] In 7 and 26 Dec 1799, above.

[17] See conclusion of 4 Jan, above.

ment, of Algiers or of Thibet, did not, simply as wickedness and folly, preclude negotiation, or constitute in us any right of interference;[18]—but that if the follies and crimes became really *dangerous* to ourselves, this *might* preclude negotiation, this *would* give us a right of interference by the great paramount law of self-defence. An hireling of Ministry accuses us before the public of the sentiment conveyed in the former part of the argument, and drops all mention of the conclusion; nay, has the shamelessness to answer the former part of our argument in his own person, with the very clause which we ourselves had annexed, or rather, indeed, the clause to which the former part of the argument was only introductory;—and he too charges us with self-contradiction! We have laboured to prove (and we believe successfully) that the Constitution established by Bonaparte, however much in speculation we may despise or abhor it, contains *nothing dangerous* to this country, should we make *peace* with France (that on the contrary it would make us contented with our own Constitution, by force of contrast); but that if we continued the war, a mighty Republic, subjected to a popular Dictator, full of enterprise, genius, and military experience, *did* contain circumstances full of peril—and, therefore, we raised again our voice and suffrage for PEACE!—and this too was self-contradiction![19]

We are sensible how wearisome and uninteresting to the public are the altercations and squabbles of Journalists. We have hitherto anxiously avoided them. We deviate from this line of conduct, not because we have felt pain from the calumnies or misrepresentations of corrupt or ignorant writers; not because we wished to sweep away dirty webs, which the insect will soon repair from his bag of poison, and weave afresh before the morning; but because it gives us a valuable opportunity of impressing the important truth, that to labour for peace at this present time is most eminently *their* duty and *their* interest, who most rootedly disapprove of revolutionary fanaticism. Ministers flatter the Jacobins most grossly, and pay them a false and wicked compliment, in commanding their writers to rail at the wish for immediate peace as Jacobinical. If there exist in this country such a mysterious being as an enlightened Jacobin, we affirm, and we have *proved*, that it would be his province and his interest to promote the continuance of the war. This truth we have endeavoured to exhibit to the public in every various light of which it is capable; and we congratulate ourselves with an honest pride, that we have produced no ordinary sensation. One proof we find in

[18] See 3 Jan, above.

[19] See 2 and 3 Jan, above.

the virulence with which we have been lately assailed by the Treasury Journals.[20] We must do these writers the justice to admit, that they are never irritated without cause. Imprudent party-speeches, conveyed in Gallican phraseology, or more imprudent palliations of French folly, suggested by the spirit of opposition to the Minister, these furnish to the aforesaid writers only subjects for amusing paragraphs, and self-complacent sneers. The viper basks at his ease, and varies his colours in the light. But when he swells, hisses, and vibrates his tongue, then be assured a more formidable enemy has approached—the enemy to whom this animal has the most instinctive antipathy! This is the man, who, attached, and avowing his attachment, to his country and its constitution, subjects himself to the title of Jacobin, rather than not oppose a Minister, whom he deems the true fosterer and dry-nurse of Jacobinism both here and in France.[21]

PREPARATIONS FOR WAR

10 January 1800, Friday. *EOT* I 227–30, in SC's group of certain attributions.

OUR Readers will find in our Paper of to-day some important additions to the Foreign intelligence which we yesterday communicated. Austria makes vigorous preparations for war, and is levying an Income Tax throughout her dominions; and we are assured, that Ministers have so won upon the condescending spirit of the Emperor, that he has actually consented to receive a loan of *three millions* from this highly obliged, and (we trust) grateful country.[1]—This, it is said, will be among the first measures submitted to Parliament.[2]—The plan of invasion is completed:—the French armies of the Rhine, the Danube, and Italy, are first to be completely routed; and Suwarrow, with an hundred thousand Russians, marches

[20] See the *Sun*, quoted above, n 11. Another kind of proof is this notice in the *M Post* of 8 Jan: "As many persons are daily disappointed of obtaining this Paper, in consequence of its increasing circulation, we acquaint the Public that at eleven o'clock, every fore-noon, the types are broken up. Before that hour, any number of papers may be obtained." Yet the paper claiming to be "by far the first in Circulation" was still the *Sun* (1 Jan 1800).

[21] For a documentary sequel to this essay, possibly compiled by C, see 11 Jan 1800 (App A, below).

[1] With a soaring deficit and despite forced loans the government of Francis II, the last emperor of the Holy Roman Empire (to become Francis I of Austria in 1805), required increasing subsidies; its paper money was pegged by decree to finance the current campaign.

[2] Pitt introduced the proposal gradually, moving an advance payment of half a million on 17 Feb, the occasion of the speech reported by C on 18 Feb (q.v.).

strait into Franche Comte, declaring himself Regent of France, by virtue of powers granted from Louis XVIII. The Archduke Charles takes possession of Alsace; Melas is to preface this, after more important conquests, by first over-running Dauphine and Provence;[3] and Great Britain is to lead the Chouans to Paris, though it is said, (we doubt the fact),[a] that the French Government concluded a treaty of peace with them on the 30th of December.[4] On the other hand a French Journal states, that the King of Prussia has declared to the Belligerent Powers, that if they do not accede to certain proposals of peace, he will join France. We give this, however, merely as the statement of a Journal, and without deciding on its truth or probability. If Prussia join France, what smaller Powers, who have hitherto remained neutral, may be annexed to either party, we can conjecture, but do not deem it either safe or proper to give such conjectures publicly.

We doubt the account of the Revolution at Naples, in which the Neapolitan and Russian troops were said to have been defeated, and the city seized by the Insurgents.[5]

BONAPARTE'S HARLEQUINADE

IF we understand the decree of the 13th Nivose, by which the embargo on neutral ships in the ports of the Republic is taken off without restriction, the letter of Bonaparte to the Hamburghers is honourable to his character. He reproaches them openly, and silently remits their punishment. His decree, which orders funeral honours to the Pope, considered in itself only, would appear amiable, and dictated by the spirit of that truly liberal philosophy, which regards as awful, and not to be irreverently approached, whatever possesses the reverential awe, and attaches to itself the feelings, of a large mass of our fellow-men.[6] But taken in context with the latter part of his Proclamation to the inhabitants of the Western departments,[7] it

[a] *EOT* supplies the parentheses

[3] The Austrian general Baron Michael von Melas (1729–1806) was ordered to drive the French from Italy and then link up with royalist insurrections in southern France that the British were to help provoke. In June at Marengo, Bonaparte would stumble upon Melas' army and win an armistice.

[4] On Hédouville's armistice with the Chouans, see nn on 1 Jan 1800.

[5] No rebellion occurred in Naples at this time.

[6] Pope Pius VI died a prisoner at Valence, France, on 29 Aug 1799. Is C consciously echoing Burke's admonition (in his *Reflections*) of awe toward the British Constitution?

[7] Bonaparte's proclamation of 25 Dec 1799 was very briefly charitable to the Chouans who would give up their arms. When the rebels did not sur-

becomes to the eye of a just observer no more than a handsome patch in the motley coat of a CHARLATAN—one trick more in the low Harlequinade of Usurpation!

Bonaparte, who so ambitiously prefixed the title of Member of the National Institute to Commander in Chief—Philosopher in Egypt—Mahometan in Syria, has now commenced preacher of the great mystery of Transubstantiation. "May the Ministers of the God of Peace return to those Temples that are again opened for them, and offer with their fellow-citizens that sacrifice (*i.e.* the consecrated wafer), which will expiate the crimes of war, and the blood which it has shed." This language, which in the mouth of the poor wretches who might believe it, would shock every enlightened Christian for its loathsome superstition, becomes blasphemy in the man who knows it to be superstition. A Papist and an Atheist are the only sects who dare use it without a sense of horror. Besides, whom does Bonaparte hope to deceive? Can he suppose the Chouans so ignorant as not to know his real opinions? Surely the metaphysician Sieyes is sufficiently acquainted with the eternal constitution of mind to have informed his friend (the acting partner in this new Government firm) that every, the meanest creature, feels himself insulted by an unsuccessful attempt to deceive him, and both hates and despises the man who attempted it.[8] But it is a common weakness with men in power, who have used dissimulation successfully, to form a passion for the use of it, dupes to the love of duping! A pride is flattered by these lies. He who fancies that he must be perpetually stooping down to the prejudices of his fellow creatures, is perpetually telling himself how much higher I am[a] than they;—but no real greatness can long co-exist with deceit.—The whole faculties of man must be exerted in order to noble energies; and he who is not in earnest, self-mutilated, self-paralysed, lives in but half his being.[9]

[a] *EOT*: he is

render, he suspended the constitution in the western *départements* and sent in armies with power of summary execution.

[8] C used this in *Friend* No 3 (*CC*) II 41 (I 39).

[9] C also used the three concluding sentences ibid: *CC* II 42 (I 41).

PAPER WAR. II

A METRICAL EPISTLE

10 January 1800, Friday. *EOT* I 231–7; *PW* (EHC) I 340–4; a prose draft of lines 70–2 is in the Gutch Notebook, *CN* I 253.

TO THE EDITOR OF THE MORNING POST

Mr. EDITOR,

AN unmetrical letter from Talleyrand to Lord Grenville has already appeared, and from an authority too high to be questioned:[1] otherwise I could adduce some arguments for the exclusive authenticity of the following metrical epistle. The very epithet which the wise antients used, "*aurea carmina*," might have been supposed likely to have determined the choice of the French Minister in favour of verse; and the rather, when we recollect that this phrase of "*golden verses*" is applied emphatically to the works of that philosopher, who imposed *silence* on all with whom he had to deal.[2] Besides, is it not somewhat improbable that Talleyrand should have preferred prose to rhyme, when the latter alone *has got the chink?*[3] Is it not likewise curious, that in our official answer, no notice whatever is taken of the Chief Consul, Bonaparte, as if there had been no such man[a] existing; notwithstanding that his existence is pretty generally admitted, nay, that some have been so rash as to believe, that he has created as great a sensation in the world as Lord Grenville, or even the Duke of Portland? But the Minister of Foreign Affairs, Talleyrand, *is* acknowledged, which, in our opinion, could not have happened, had he written only that insignificant prose-

[a] *PW* (EHC): person

[1] The covering "Letter from the Minister of Foreign Affairs in France" as officially translated 6 Jan and published in *M Post* 7 Jan 1800:

My Lord,

I despatch, by order of General Bonaparte, First Consul of the French Republic, a Messenger to London: he is the bearer of a letter from the First Consul of the Republic to His Majesty the King of England. I request you to give the necessary orders that he may be enabled to deliver it directly into your own hands. This step, in itself, announces the importance of its object.

Accept, my Lord, the assurance of my highest consideration.

(Signed) CH. MAU. TALLEYRAND

Paris, the 5th Nivose, 8th year of the French Republic (*Dec. 25, 1799.*)

Translations of the letter from Bonaparte and Grenville's reply and Note followed.

[2] The *Golden Verses*, metrical maxims of Neo-Pythagoreanism, were sometimes attributed to Pythagoras himself, whose disciples had to keep silent for five years.

[3] Talleyrand's belief in graft as the silent ingredient of all negotiation was notorious.

letter, which seems to precede Bonaparte's, as in old romances a dwarf always ran before to proclaim the advent or arrival of knight or giant.[4] That Talleyrand's character and practices more resemble those of some *regular* Governments than Bonaparte's I admit; but this of itself does not appear a satisfactory explanation. However, let the letter speak for itself. The second line is supererogative in syllables, whether from the oscitancy of the transcriber, or from the trepidation which might have overpowered the modest Frenchman, on finding himself in the act of writing to so *great* a man, I shall not dare to determine. A few Notes are added by

Your servant,
GNOME

P.S. As mottos are now fashionable, especially if taken from out of the way books, you may prefix, if you please, the following lines from Sidonius Apollinaris:

Saxa, et robora, corneasque fibras
Mollit dulciloquâ canorus arte![5]

Talleyrand, Minister of Foreign Affairs at Paris, to Lord Grenville, Secretary of State in Great Britain for Foreign Affairs, Auditor of the Exchequer, a Lord of Trade, an Elder Brother of Trinity House, &c.[a]

MY Lord! tho' your Lordship repel deviation
From forms long establish'd, yet with high consideration,
I plead for the honour to hope, that no blame
Will attach, should this letter *begin* with my name.
I dar'd not presume on your Lordship to bounce,
But thought it more *exquisite* first to *announce*!

My Lord! I've the honour to be Talleyrand,
And the letter's from *me*! you'll not draw back your hand
Nor yet take it up by the rim in dismay,
As boys pick up ha'pence on April fool-day.
I'm no Jacobin foul, or red-hot Cordelier,
That your Lordship's *un*gauntleted fingers need fear

[a] Text in *PW* (EHC) varies greatly in spelling, punctuation, capitalisation, italics, etc.

[4] Dwarf Talleyrand's "giant" is, of course, the diminutive Bonaparte. C uses the same image again 21 Jan, below.

[5] *Letters* 8.11.3, lines 20–1 of the poem "Phoebus to his well-beloved and own particular Thalia...". "By the tuneful utterance of his sweet-voiced art [he] charms rocks and oaks and hearts of horn." Sidonius *Poems and Letters* tr W. B. Anderson (LCL 2 vols 1936–65) II 461.

An infection, or burn! Believe me, 'tis true,
With a scorn, like another,[a] I look down on the crew,
That bawl and hold up to the mob's detestation
The most delicate wish for a *silent persuasion.*
A *form long establishe'd* these Terrorists call
Bribes, perjury, theft, and the devil and all!
And yet spite of all that the *Moralist prates,
'Tis the keystone and cement of *civiliz'd States.*
Those American †*Reps*! And i' faith, they were serious!
It shock'd us at Paris, like something mysterious,
That men, who've a Congress—But no more of't! I'm proud
To have stood so distinct from the Jacobin crowd.

My Lord! tho' the vulgar in wonder be lost at
My transfigurations, and name me *Apostate*,
Such a meaningless nickname, which never incens'd me,
Cannot prejudice you or your Cousin[7] against me:
I'm Ex-bishop. What then? Burke himself would agree,
That I left not the Church—'twas the Church that left me.[8]
My titles prelatic I lov'd and retain'd,
As long as what *I* meant by Prelate remain'd:
And tho' Mitres no longer will *pass* in our mart,
I'm *episcopal* still to the core of my heart.
No time from my name this my motto shall sever:
'Twill be "*Non sine pulvere palma*"‡ for ever!

* This sarcasm on the writings of Moralists is, in general, extremely just; but had Talleyrand continued long enough in England, he might have found an honourable exception in the second volume of Dr. Paley's Moral Philosophy; in which both Secret influence, and all the other *Established Forms*, are justified and placed in their true light.[6]

† A fashionable abbreviation in the higher circles for Republicans—Thus *Mob* was originally the Mobility.

‡ *Palma non sine pulvere*—In plain English, an itching palm, not without the yellow dust.[9]

[a] *EOT*: your own

6 On secret influence and William Paley's *Principles of Moral and Political Philosophy* see *Conciones: Lects 1795* (*CC*) 69 and n 5; see above, 20 Jan 1798 n 10.

7 Grenville's cousin is Pitt; both had recently used a scandalous amount of "secret influence" to purchase the votes for Irish Union; both had once favoured Parliamentary Reform.

8 Edmund Burke (1729–97) thus viewed his split with Fox and other fellow-Whigs who did not share his alarm about the French Revolution and would not join him in 1792 in support of Pitt and war with France.

9 Proverbial saying; cf Horace *Epistles* 1.1.51. Tr: "The [victor's] palm is not won without dust."

Your goodness, my Lord! I conceive as excessive,
Or I dar'd not present you a scroll so digressive;
And in truth with my pen thro' and thro' I should strike it;
But I hear that your Lordship's own style is just like it.
Dear my Lord, we are right: for what charms can be shew'd,
In a thing that goes straight like an old Roman road[?]
The tortoise crawls straight, the hare doubles about,
And the true line of beauty still winds in and out.[10]
It argues, my Lord! of fine thoughts such a brood in us,
To split and divide into heads multitudinous,
While charms that surprise (it can ne'er be deni'd us)
Sprout forth from each head, like the ears from King Midas.[11]
Were a genius of rank, like a commonplace dunce,
Compell'd to drive on to the main point at once,
What a plentiful vintage of initiations*
Would Noble Lords lose in your Lordship's orations.
My fancy transports me! As mute as a mouse,
And as fleet as a pigeon, I'm borne to the house,
Where all those, who *are* Lords, from father to son,
Discuss the affairs of all those, who are none.
I behold you, my Lord! of your feelings quite full,
'Fore the woolsack arise, like a sack full of wool!
You rise on each Anti-Grenvillian Member,
Short, thick, and blust'rous, like a day in November!†
Short in person, I mean: for the length of your speeches,
Fame herself, that most famous reporter, ne'er reaches.
Lo! Patience beholds you contemn her brief reign,
And Time, that all-panting toil'd after in vain,

* The word *Initiations* is borrowed from the new Constitution, and can only mean, in plain English, introductory matter. If the manuscript would bear us out, we should propose to read the line thus—"What a plentiful *Verbage*, what Initiations!" inasmuch as Vintage must necessarily refer to wine, really or figuratively; and we cannot guess what species Lord Grenville's eloquence may be supposed to resemble, unless, indeed, it be *Cowslip* wine. A slashing critic, to whom we read the manuscript, proposed to read, "What a plenty of Flowers—what Initiations!" and supposes it may allude indiscriminately to Poppy Flowers, or Flour of Brimstone. The most modest emendation, perhaps, would be this—For Vintage read Ventage.

† We cannot sufficiently admire the accuracy of this simile. For as Lord Grenville, though short, is certainly not the shortest man in the House, even so is it with the days in November.

10 An allusion to the sinuous Hogarthian "line of beauty".

11 Asses' ears sprouted from Midas. See Ovid *Metamorphoses* 11.146ff.

(Like the Beldam who rac'd for a smock with her grand-child),
Drops and cries—were such lungs e'er assign'd to a man-child?
Your strokes at her vitals pale truth has confess'd,
And zeal unresisted entempests your breast!*
Tho' some noble Lords may be wishing to sup,
Your merit self-conscious, my Lord! *keeps you up*,
Unextinguish'd and swoln, as a balloon of paper
Keeps aloft by the smoke of its own farthing taper.
Ye SIXTEENS† of Scotland,[15] your snuffs ye must trim;
Your Geminies, fix'd stars of England! grow dim,
And but for *a form long establish'd*, no doubt,
Twinkling faster and faster, ye all would *go out*.

Apropos, my dear Lord! a ridiculous blunder
Of some of our Journalists caus'd us some wonder:
It was said, that in aspect malignant and sinister,
In the Isle of Great Britain a great Foreign Minister
Turn'd as pale as a Journeyman Miller's frock coat is,
On observing a star that appeared in BOOTES!
When the whole truth was this (O those ignorant brutes!)
Your Lordship had made his appearance in boots.

* An evident Plagiarism of the Ex-Bishop's from Dr. Johnson.

Existence saw him spurn her bounded reign,
And panting Time toil'd after him in vain:
His pow'rful strokes presiding Truth confess'd,
And unresisting Passion storm'd the breast.[12]

† This line and the following are involved in an almost Lycophrontic tenebricosity.[13] On repeating them, however, to an *Illuminant*, whose confidence I possess, he informed me (and he ought to know, for he is a Tallow-chandler by trade) that certain candles go by the name of *sixteens*. This explains the whole, the Scotch Peers are destined to burn out—and so are candles! The English are perpetual, and are therefore styled Fixed Stars! The word *Geminies* is, we confess, still obscure to us; though we venture to suggest, that it may perhaps be a metaphor (daringly sublime) for the two eyes, which noble Lords do in general possess. It is certainly used by the poet, Fletcher, in this sense, in the 31st stanza of his *Purple Island*.

What! shall I then need seek a patron out,
Or beg a favour from a mistress' eyes,
To fence my song against the vulgar rout,
And shine upon me with her *geminies?*[14]

[12] *Prologue Spoken by Mr. Garrick at the Opening of the Theatre Royal, Drury-Lane, 1747* lines 5–8 (var): *B Poets* XI 843.

[13] Lycophron (b c 320 B.C.), author of *Cassandra*, proverbial for obscurity.

[14] Phineas Fletcher *The Purple Island* canto I st 31 (var): *B Poets* IV 385.

[15] The sixteen compounding Scottish peers, kept in the Grenvillean camp by control of patronage in the hands of Pitt's manager Henry Dundas, on whom see 22 Jan 1798 n 2, above.

You, my Lord, with your star, sat in boots, and the Spanish
Ambassador thereupon thought fit to vanish.
But, perhaps, dear my Lord, among other worse crimes,
The whole was no more than a lie of *The Times*.
It is monstrous, my Lord! in a civilis'd state,
That such Newspaper rogues should have license to prate.
Indeed, printing in general—but for the taxes,
Is in theory false and pernicious in praxis!
You and I, and your Cousin, and Abbe Sieyes,
And all the great Statesmen, that live in these days,
Are agreed, that no nation secure is from vi'lence,
Unless all, who must think, are maintain'd all in silence.[16]
This printing, my Lord—but 'tis useless to mention,
What we both of us think—'twas a cursed invention,
And Germany might have been honestly prouder,
Had she left it alone, and found out only powder.
My Lord! when I think of our labours and cares,
Who rule the department of foreign affairs,
And how with their libels these journalists bore us,
Tho' Rage I acknowledge than Scorn less decorous;
Yet their presses and types I could shiver in splinters,
Those Printers' black Devils! those Devils of Printers!
In case of a peace—but perhaps it were better
To proceed to the absolute point of my letter:
For the deep wounds of France, Bonaparte, my master,
Has found out a new sort of *basilicon* plaister.
But your time, my dear Lord! is your nation's best treasure,
I've intruded already too long on your leisure;
If so, I entreat you with penitent sorrow
To pause, and resume the remainder to-morrow.[17]

[16] The Newspaper Act of April 1799, putting proprietors and printers on record, and the continued suspension of Habeas Corpus, subjecting them to imprisonment without trial, gave the Government strong legal control. Unofficial control through the granting or withholding of subsidies had already severely circumscribed the independence of British journalism. In France most of the newspapers still were controlled by the royalists, many by Jacobins, but Bonaparte would shortly (17 Jan 1800) close sixty of the 76 existing papers. On 27 Feb 1799 the *Moniteur* had been constituted the official government organ.

[17] Note the Saturday announcement of a Second Part; it never appeared.

[11 January 1800, Saturday]

The Second Part of Talleyrand's Letter to Lord Grenville shall appear on Monday.[1]

FRANCE. II

13 January 1800, Monday. *EOT* II 353–6, in SC's group of probable attributions. C's authorship is unmistakable, partly from the links to his essay of 14 Jan but especially from the language and ideas: the quip about Sieyès' psychological talents, the application of the news of new artillery as a metaphor in the first sentence on Constant, the concluding contrast of bubbling fountain and stagnant pool. Further verification is in RS's letter of 16 Jan 1800 to C in which he comments on these paragraphs as "your paragraphs" (*S Letters*—Curry—I 214–15)—an assumption confirmed by C's reply of 25 Jan (*CL* I 563–4).

FEARFUL PREPARATIONS[1]

On Saturday night we received the Paris Journals to the 8th instant. The armies in all parts have gone into winter-quarters; consequently of them little new intelligence can be expected. The head-quarters of the army of Italy are removed from Sospello to Antibes in France. The ostensible reason of this movement is an epidemic distemper which rages at Nice; how far this is the real cause, and how far danger from the enemy co-operated, we know not. The French were in quiet possession of Genoa on the 28th ult. Moreau has taken the command in Switzerland, and is making new dispositions there. All is quiet down the Rhine; but vast and fearful preparations are making on both sides for the ensuing campaign. Attempts are made, at Vienna, to reconcile the Archduke and Suwarrow, with what probability of permanent success, a man may presume to decide on grounds of *human nature*, with less risk of disappointment, than Mr. Pitt in his speculations on *human nature* in Holland.[2] Without pretensions to Mr. Pitt's or Abbe Sieyes's *psychological*[3] talents, we dare believe, that such reconciliations are

[1] A second part of C's metrical epistle did not appear and was probably never written.

[1] A preceding news paragraph reports the rumour of French and Spanish readiness for an expedition to Ireland.

[2] In Parliament 26 Sept 1799 Pitt had argued from a "knowledge of human nature" that the Dutch would support a British expedition to deliver them from the French. After the failure of the expedition, Opposition never let him forget the remark. C never tired of using it sarcastically with political opponents.

[3] In writing of Shakespeare's pursuing the "psychological" method, in his Introduction to *EM*, C apologised "for the use of this *insolens verbum*. . .

necessarily hollow and short-lived; and this, as Mr. Pitt says, "*on grounds of human nature.*" The French Government has decreed a new organization of their artillery, by which they have gained so many battles. The war with the Chouans was renewed on the 5th, if indeed it was ever suspended. Report says, that the combined fleets, at Brest, will soon put to sea: The Admirals Bruix and Lacrosse have left Paris. Bournonville is on his way to Berlin, as Ambassador there. Carnot, it is said, has returned to Paris.[4]

THE NEW CONSTITUTION

NOT a word appears in the French Journals respecting the negotiation[a] with this country! They seem quite ignorant of it! But by far the most interesting feature in these papers is that presented by the discussions in the Tribunate. The Government claimed for itself the power of resuming its proposals *ad arbitrium*, and of returning them unaltered; and likewise the power of defining arbitrarily the time, within which the Tribunate should have completed its deliberation, which is no less than the power of rendering their deliberations at will nugatory and ridiculous. What if they proposed a law consisting of an hundred points, and allowed, as in the present instance, three days for deliberation? or one day?

These proposals, which occasioned these discussions, are important in themselves, as evincing in the new Government a spirit of encroachment on the shadowy privileges of its own creatures; but they are still more important, as displaying the indefiniteness arising out of the obscure brevity of the new Constitution; and as furnishing one fact more, for the absurdity of any *Constitution* whatever, in the French sense of the word. It is supposed paramount to the Legislature, and regulative of its proceedings; but the first law which a Legislature passes explanatory of its meaning supersedes it, as a constitution, and makes it thenceforward a common legislative act; and yet without such explanatory laws the question of what is constitutional would admit of no decision. If this new Constitution should continue (which we believe impossible), we venture to pro-

[a] *M Post, EOT*: negotiations

one of which our language stands in great need". Quoted in *Sh C* II 348.

[4] Pierre de Riel, Marquis de Beurnonville (1752–1821), was a general with royalist leanings. Lazare Nicolas Marguerite Carnot (1753–1823), a conservative but essentially anti-royalist general, had been one of the Directors urging peace in the Lille negotiations of 1797 and had been banished after 18 Fructidor; Bonaparte's appointing him Minister of War was diplomatically significant.

phesy, that, compared with it, the Apocalypse itself will have been barren in the production of controversies. What Sieyes meant, might be learnt perhaps; but the real question will ever be, what the people, when they acceded to it, supposed Sieyes to have meant? And this can never be decided.

As exhibiting an illustration of this truth, therefore, these proposals, and the discussions which followed, will excite, in the minds of men of reflection, no mean interest; but more important still is the opposition to the proposals—the manner of it—and the sensation which it appears to have created.

BENJAMIN CONSTANT

IN the foreground, and the principal figure in the foreground, is Benjamin Constant:[5] and all the artillery, in the uses of which *some regular Governments* are so dextrous, has been played off against him. We have given as specimens a quotation from Roederer, and a paragraph from the *Journal des Hommes Libres*.[6] The former attacks him with arguments applicable only against systematic oppositions, and takes no notice that these very arguments had been first adduced by Constant himself. (But this is a common trick among the agents of *more regular Governments.*)[7] The second heaps calumnies on the man and his connections; and boldly questions his Constitutional eligibility to the Tribunate, he being a Swiss by birth. This paragraph is extremely interesting as throwing considerable light on the state of parties and public opinion in France. The minority, in which Constant voted, appears respectable in number as well as talent; and his opinions on the subject of opposition are so judicious, and so far superior to any thing lately produced in French debates, that we deem it our duty to state them as fully as possible. Of Bonaparte,

[5] Henri Benjamin Constant de Rebecque (1767–1830), leader of a "moderate Republican" opposition, whose ideas cited here and in 14 Jan (below) are remarkably like C's own. In 1797 C had read James Losh's translation of Constant's "admirable pamphlet", *De la Force du gouvernement actuel de la France et de la nécessité de s'y rallier* (1796). *CL* I 308. A political and personal ally of Mme de Stäel, Constant had participated (with Talleyrand's assistance) in the coup of Fructidor; in 1802 he would be eliminated from the Tribunate.

[6] Postponed, actually, to the next day.

[7] Pierre Louis Roederer (1754–1835), editor of the *Journal de Paris* and the *Moniteur*, an associate of Talleyrand and a councillor of state appointed by Bonaparte, had been a Jacobin but in the interests of a firm and stable government supported the coup of 18 Brumaire. See sketch in Henry Redhead Yorke *France in Eighteen Hundred and Two* ed J. A. C. Sykes (1906) 216, 332–3.

he, and the other speakers who voted with him, speak with temperate admiration; but it is observable, that the whole Tribunate appear to have listened with impatience and disgust to the long, and adulatory panegyric passed on him by Riouffe[8] in his answer to, or rather personal attack on, the opponents of the proposals then discussed. It is cheering to observe, that scarcely any form, however defective, of deliberative and public assembly can be permitted without some efforts of free and manly thought being produced. Let them be as transient and void of immediate effect, as bubbles, yet still they prove the existence of a vital principle;[9] they are the bubbles of a fountain, not such as rise seldom and silent on the muddy and stagnant pools of despotism.[10]

[13 January 1800, Monday]

Many Advertisements and other favours, unavoidably omitted this day, shall appear to-morrow.

FRANCE. III

14 January 1800, Tuesday. *EOT* I 238–41, in SC's group of certain attributions; studded with C's language and ideas.

STATE OF PARTIES

THE account, which we gave yesterday, that the Brest fleet was ready for sailing, has been magnified into its being actually at sea. It is not probable that this would happen pending a negotiation;

[8] Of Honoré, Baron Riouffe (1764–1813), RS remarked: "Bonapartes reputation is in bad hands to be defended by such whelps as this man and Roederer." RS to C 16 Jan 1800: *S Letters* (Curry) I 214–15. RS recalled that Riouffe had written *Mémoires d'un détenu, pour servir à l'histoire de la tyrannie de Robespierre* (1795).

[9] C finds evidence of vitality in the fact that actual debates take place even in the mock legislature of the Tribunate. The modern historian agrees: "The composition of the legislative bodies rendered them unpopular from the first, and weakened them in their efforts to curb the despotic temper of the First Consul. But the persistent misconception that the constitution of the year VIII consecrated a dictatorship at the outset must be classed with other Bonapartist myths", says Geoffrey Bruun; it was the constitution of the year X (1802) that "signalized the establishment of Bonaparte's absolutism" (Bruun 17, 35).

[10] Cf 6 Jan 1800 (above); 12 Dec 1799 (above); *CN* I 162; Lect VI of the 1811–12 lectures (*Sh C* II 116); the bubbling up and overflowing of the scum of the French Revolution, in *Friend* (*CC*) I 410, and *CL* I 611.

and it is just only possible, that the result of this negotiation could have been (even by the Telegraph)[1] notified to the French Government time enough for such orders to have been issued to, and executed by, the fleet, so early as the date of the present report. And indeed, after sedulous inquiry, we have no reason to hesitate in pronouncing it a mere rumour, without foundation or plausibility.

We turn therefore to consider a more interesting subject—the state of the parties in France. The first and least numerous is, the Anarchical, or that of the absolute Equalizers, who, since the death of Baboeuf, have remained without any ostensible leader.—Among these new *fifth monarchy men*,[2] are to be found some men of crazy talent, the Sir Harry Vanes of France; but the mass is composed of the dregs of Paris, though it is believed that the restless activity of Baboeuf had spread these wild visions among the day-labourers in the provinces. Next to these are the absoluet Despotists; enthusiasts who fight at the command of priests in the full faith that they shall gain in the next world that paradise, which the Anarchists dream they can produce in this. The third party is that of the Parisian Royalists; the fine ladies and fine Gentlemen of the metropolis, and the bold free-thinkers who, when Royalty was the established form, were Republicans; and now that Republicanism is the legal Government, have become Royalists.

From these three parties nothing is to be hoped, and nothing feared. There follow to these the men who, believing that political liberty is not possible in a country so menaced by foreign and civil war, and so newly revolutionized as France, are advocates for a temporary Dictatorship, disguised from the grosser eye of the public as decorously as possible.[3] With these may be ranked the men who hold that liberty is at no time practicable, yet deeming that hereditary

[1] The cross-country semaphore system recently invented by Chappe.

[2] See *CN* I 254, *CL* I 517. In including François Noël (Caius Gracchus) Babeuf (1760–97) in the category of "absolute Equalizers" C "was making a common English error", observes Woodring (p 57), "for Revolutionists in France who wished absolute political equality opposed Babeuf and agrarian extremists who proposed to socialize private property. Coleridge essentially agreed with Babeuf on property but opposed instantaneous social, political, or landed equality." On Babeuf see also 28 Jan, below; also *Watchman* (*CC*) 289.

The "Equalizers" C cites from the time of the English Civil War are both less equalitarian and less democratic than the Levellers, whom he might have cited if writing less whimsically. The parliamentary republican Sir Harry Vane spoke from an aristocratic position; the Fifth Monarchists, of the last large revolutionary movement during the Protectorate, sought a new monarch in Christ but lacked a political ideology.

[3] This is C's ironic view: see 7 Dec 1799, opening paragraphs, above.

nobility and a dominating priesthood are evils necessarily attached to the restoration of the old family, but not necessarily inherent in monarchy simply considered, prefer from principle the Chief Consul Bonaparte to Louis XVIII. These two classes are the admirers of the new Constitution, and, together with that herd of flatterers and fanatics, which a romantic good fortune has secured to the Chief Consul, form the ardent supporters of it.—This party is called by their opponents the *Military Faction.*

The Jacobins, who wish to found[a] a Government on personal rights, independent of property; and the moderate Republicans, who deem that the highest possible quantity of civil and political liberty will exist in Governments, that take property for their chief basis; are the enemies, or at least the jealous *tolerators* of the new Government, and are styled the *civil faction.*[4] Among the most moderate of these, and perhaps the most distinguished for talent, is Benjamin Constant, who is at the head of the Opposition in the Tribunate. We shall hereafter give the introductory and philosophical part of his masterly speech on the first proposals of the Government.[5] His sentiments ask and merit the most serious attention.

BENJAMIN CONSTANT

It has been the opinion of wise and good men, that to act effectively, we must act in *parties*; that is, that men, who *really* agree with each other in certain *great* points, should keep up an *appearance* of agreeing in *all* points, and act and vote accordingly. If they deem of the men in power, that their fundamental principles are vicious, they conceive themselves justified in opposing systematically every particular measure of these men, though it should be good in itself, as becoming evil from its connection with their general system; and because by harassing they hope to distress and weaken the Government, of which they disapprove.

An opposition conducted on these principles, Benjamin Constant condemns and abjures;[6] 1. Because it tends to encourage the prin-

[a] *EOT*: form

[4] For C's idea of the right relation of power to property, see 8 Jan, above.

[5] The sum of Constant's speech had been given in *M Post* the day before.

[6] C annotated this passage on a clipping of the column, now in VCL: "Poor Benjamin! no such Ideas ever entered his Head: but *twas a good Vehicle.*" VCL MS F 1.9. The implied criticism of the English Opposition may have prompted this wry comment in the *M Chron* (17 Jan), i.e. in a paper that could conceive only in terms of party: "Some of the papers represent Benjamin Constant, who has appeared in the tribunate in opposition

ciples of self-delusion; disguises, while it flatters, the love of power; and introduces the jesuitical morality of practising real[a] evil for uncertain good.[7] 2. Because such practices must necessarily disturb and deceive the intellectual powers of the opposition party, and substitute that poor and heartless dexterity in argumentation, which belongs to hired advocates in Law-Courts, for the comprehensive views, and plain *straight forward*[8] reasoning of Legislators. 3. Because it really disappoints its own purposes, and enables a bad Government with much plausibility to throw odium on the general principles of the party, by detecting and exposing inconsistencies in the detail of its conduct. 4. (and of most importance) Because it diffuses among the people a spirit of indifference to the sentiments and reasons produced during legislative discussions, in consequence of their belief that the persons themselves who bring forward such arguments and feelings are but playing a part; and that it thus prevents a legislature from realizing its highest possible utility, that of being the great organ of National Instruction,[9] and (of course) intrinsic and permanent amelioration.

From these motives Constant pleads most emphatically for the perpetual exercise of individual judgment, and contends that by this means a bad Government will be most certainly demonstrated to be bad, and fall in consequence; while a good Government will derive strength and activity from it, as from a *ventilation* at once mild and perpetual. Ministers might at length be accustomed to see particular measures opposed without feeling any opposition to themselves; to oppose might be conceived of as only an attempt to enlighten; infallibility would be pretended to by neither party; and the Executive and Deliberative branches avoid the fatal and common evil, of committing mutual follies from mutual irritation. No opposition to a Government, and a systematic opposition, are founded on the same principles, and produce the same effects. They are both alike justified

[a] *EOT* omits

to the Government, as a man of great abilities, and likely to be the head of a party.—Benjamin Constant is known to many in this country [he had lived in England and known Erskine and Mackintosh], but no man ever supposed him qualified to head a party; he is forward and intriguing, and distinguished by an eccentricity more allied to insanity than to genius. He wished to make a gaudy speech, and this is the whole of his Opposition."

[7] On the "gigantic Error of making certain Evil the means of contingent Good", see *MPL* and *Conciones: Lects 1795* (*CC*) 6, 36.

[8] The italics suggest that C felt "straight forward" to be a neologism; no example this early is given in *OED*.

[9] Cf 7 Dec 1799 at n 12, above.

on the pretended necessity of sacrificing individual judgment to general harmony; they both teach mankind to consider discussion as implying discord; the former makes a legislature one army and subjects it to military law; the latter forms a separate and hostile body, but acts, in itself, on the same principles.

IRELAND. I

RIPENING PROJECT[1]

15 January 1800, Wednesday. *EOT* II 357–60; in SC's group of probable attributions; unmistakable from internal evidence: e.g. the link to the essay of 27 Jan; the profession of political "*weather-wisdom*"; the images of strait-waistcoating, the wen, the Burkean state-harpies, the magician torn by his own imps. The changes in *EOT* (see textual notes) mute the point that censorship still prevails.

IN our Paper of Monday, we mentioned, that the subject of the Union is to be left unnoticed in the Speech, with which the Lord Lieutenant will this day open the Irish Parliament;[2] and that this circumstance had been construed in many circles as presumptive evidence that the Question of an Union was suspended for the present, if not entirely dropped.—A Ministerial Paper of yesterday says—"It is, we believe, true, as stated in an Opposition paper of yesterday, that the speech of the Lord Lieutenant of Ireland, upon the opening of the Session to-morrow, will not mention any thing respecting the measure of a Union.—There are, no doubt, good reasons for this omission. We can assure the Public, however, that the measure is not the less ripe for being brought forward; and, if we are not misinformed, it will, soon after the meeting of the Irish Parliament, be introduced into the House of Commons there in the shape of a Message from the King."[3] Thus we find our intelligence confirmed, and accompanied by an assurance, the accuracy of which we see no reason to question. All, indeed, who from observation of parliamentary intrigues, have attained any degree of *weather-wisdom* as to changes in the political atmosphere, were prepared to interpret the Lord Lieutenant's silence as a sufficient indication that all the power and all the artifices of Ministerial influence were at work

1 For a criticism of this essay and C's reply, see 22 Jan, below.

2 The Lord Lieutenant or Viceroy of Ireland, from 1798 to 1801, was Charles Cornwallis, 1st Marquis Cornwallis (1738–1805), who had been a major-general in the American War, then governor-general of India, 1786–93. In 1801 he would be appointed to negotiate the Treaty of Amiens.

3 *Sun* 14 Jan 1800.

to *ripen* the project, which has some *crude* parts still, though it is certainly "not the less ripe," from its not being formally pre-announced by the Viceroy.[4]

On the general policy of this measure, we have never ventured an opinion: though the means which have been adopted to carry it into effect have received from us all the abhorrence which we could *express*![a] (For no *safe*[a] expressions[b] could convey all which we felt and still feel.)[5] The vindictive turbulence of a wild and barbarous race, brutalised by the oppression of centuries, was to be coerced; and no better expedient suggested itself, than to permit, or at best to connive at, a system of *retaliation*![6] To give an example of horrors, under the pretext that they were only following one; by the vices of a government, to occasion the vices of popular rage, and by retaliations, to inflame that rage into madness; to *iron* and *strait waistcoat* the whole country by military law,[7] and then gravely intreat the inhabitants to exercise their free will and unbiased judgments; these were the measures intended to smooth and prepare the way to a great national union, founded in assent, and cemented by affection! However wise and benignant the plan might have been in itself, it certainly becomes questionable, whether it may not be unsafe and impolitic

[a] *EOT* omits italics [b] *EOT*: expression

[4] The project of uniting Ireland with Britain under a single Parliament was, after all, mentioned in the address, and the vote on the address was 138 to 96. In February a bill for Union would be carried by 158 to 115; in April the English House of Commons would approve the measure by 236 to 30.

A sequel to the crushing of the Irish Rebellion of 1798 was the Act of Union, which first required the Irish Parliament to vote itself out of existence. The first attempt at such a vote, in Jan 1799, was defeated, but by Jan 1800 the borough owners and members had been won over by promises of peerages and £1½ million in patronage. Support of the Catholics was obtained on a tacit understanding that Pitt would assist the passage of a bill for their political Emancipation in the united Parliament—though Pitt knew he would be unable to overcome the King's resistance; in 1801, when cornered, he would resign (see below). In 1811 Catholic Emancipation would be talked of "as the engine to a repeal of the Union" (*Courier* 5 Aug 1811, below).

[5] Stuart's papers had averted attention from Ireland as long as possible. An adjunct of the military repression had been the rigorous censorship of English expressions of sympathy, and the punitive sentencing of three *Courier* proprietors in 1799 for a patently innocuous paragraph (borrowed from "respectable" papers that were not molested) can only be understood against the background of the *Courier*'s support of Irish independence. By the time Stuart emerged as an owner, the paper, with Street as editor, had learned to be as silent as the *M Post* on such subjects.

[6] Cf 8 Jan 1800, first par (above), on ministers' effort to "retaliate the retaliation".

[7] The image recurs 3 Dec 1801, below. See the "Strait Waistcoat" idea in *Cambridge University Magazine* and *RX* 458, cited above, 9 Jan 1798 n 5.

at present, in consequence of the agitation produced by the mad and sanguinary precurrences. This consideration has doubtless influenced many in their opposition to it; while others have found their national pride attacked, and stabbed in the vitals by the idea, that their country was to lose its individual being and character, and without heart or lungs of its own, to be fed, like a wen, by the circuitous circulation of a nobler body.[8] Yet still, when we contemplate the materials of which the Orange Confederacy is composed,[9] we experience some degree of surprise at the strength and obstinacy of their opposition. A virtuous *opposition* it cannot be! We know that faction too well. With them public depravity is not softened down even by the hopeful vice of hypocrisy:—general sympathy in corruption supersedes the necessity of a vizard. Jobbers, place-hunters, unconditional hirelings, whatever their immediate conduct may be, they will gain no credit from honest men for their motives. Desperate state-harpies, they are now opening against Ministers the ravenous mouths, that had been even now devouring ministerial bounties; and presume to fight for their country with talons impeded by their country's blood![10] *Timeo Danaos vel dona ferentes.*[11] These men recall to our mind the fable of the Magician, who having ordered his ministering imps to destroy the infernal abodes, was himself torn in pieces by them, and carried off in a whirlwind.[12]

The reason why the Union is to be preceded by no allusion from the Lord Lieutenant in his speech, is derived from the number of election writs which it will be necessary to issue after the meeting of

[8] For the wen see *CN* I 110 and n; 20 Jan 1798, above; 25 Sept 1802, below, and C's review of Clarkson in 1808: *IS* 371.

[9] The Orange Confederacy, a rich and powerful Protestant society formed in 1795 throughout Ireland but especially in Ulster, supplied armed bands against the rebels of 1798 and was now exerting pressure for Union. The opposition, potentially most Irishmen, was represented in the Irish Parliament partly by borough-owning magnates, rising noblemen, and landowners in financial difficulties, "dependent on the continued control of the Irish patronage machine for part of their prosperity and consequence". G. C. Bolton *The Passing of the Irish Act of Union* (Oxford 1966) 182–3. For C's later views of the Orangemen see "To Mr Justice Fletcher", 20 Sept–10 Dec 1814, below, esp Letter V (3 and 6 Dec); also "Orange Men", App B, 1814, below.

[10] Gillray had caricatured the English Opposition on 7 May 1799 as *Harpyes Defiling the Feast* (print No 3 of a series called *The New Pantheon*)—his three harpies being Tierney, Shuckburgh, and Jekyll.

[11] Virgil *Aeneid* 2.49 (var). "I fear Greeks, even when bringing gifts." Tr H. Rushton Fairclough (LCL 1916) I 297.

[12] For related magician passages see 21 Jan and 6 Feb 1800, below; for C's interest in RS's *Thalaba* and its sources, on the subject of magicians and counter-magicians, see Schneider 134, 136, 224.

Parliament. More than twenty seats will be vacant; and all in the government interest. Some of the former Members for these seats have died; others have gotten places, and must be re-elected; and some in honour have resigned, rather than obey the desires of their patrons.—The accession of the new Members will secure, it is supposed, a majority. But this plan the Anti-Unionists hope to defeat, by moving a question on the Union this day, in order that they may negative it before the Ministerial forces can be fully mustered. But Ministers have confident expectations that, even in the present state of their forces, they possess a small majority, which will be made decisive by the arrival of their new recruits, and re-elected friends. The Anti-Unionists are certainly numerous, and even more perhaps than their numbers justify, certain of success; but should Ministers render their cause once hopeless, by however small a majority, the *conversions* will be rapid, and the new converts as zealous, as if each were to be made Secretary of War, or Minister for Foreign Affairs.[13] Such we believe to be the plan of the campaign, which will this day commence. A question the most important that can occur in the annals of nations is to be decided; it will be lost or won by half a neck. But whether lost or won, depends not so much on the justice of the cause, as on the success of the previous intrigues among the jockies!

[17 January 1800, Friday]

Remarks on the Stile of Language used in Lord Grenville's Note to-morrow.[1]

PAPER WAR. III

TALLEYRAND'S REPLY[1]

21 January 1800, Tuesday. *EOT* I 242–7, in SC's group of certain attributions.

Dated 14 January, a second letter from Talleyrand to Lord Grenville was presented thus in the *M Post* of 21 January, along with C's editorial:

The last communication from France consists merely of a letter from Talleyrand to Lord Grenville. It is, we understand, of considerable length: it touches upon the origin of the war, the conduct of the different persons and parties which have governed France since the Revolution, the views of the

[13] The posts held by Windham and Grenville, targets for every sarcasm in the *M Post* at this time.

[1] See 22 Jan, below.

[1] For a paragraph of 16 Jan possibly Coleridgian, see App A, below.

Emigrants, the wishes expressed for the restoration of the Bourbon family, and in short upon all the points contained in Lord Grenville's Reply:—

"The French Minister begins by informing his Lordship that his Official Note has been laid before the Chief Consul, who has commanded him to acquaint our Government, that some parts of that Note appear to require that the French Government should explain, and should justify themselves on the points to which they allude. Alluding next to that part, which alleges that His Majesty has contended against an unprovoked attack, he asserts, that it was not France that began the War against England, but, on the contrary, the latter that committed the first aggression, and, in order to prove this assertion, he reverts to the arguments and facts contained in the Proclamations and Manifestoes published at different times by France. He proceeds then to confess, that some of the different Rulers who have governed France since the Revolution, have given *real* cause to its inhabitants for anger, and have afforded *just* motives for alarm and complaint to Foreign Powers; but the opposition which they have met from part of the French People, excited and supported by the Foreign Powers leagued with us in their designs of overturning the Liberty of the French, and of forcing on them their old form of Government, affords, he says, a justification of their conduct." He next alludes to that part of the Note, which expresses a wish for "the restoration of that line of Princes which for so many centuries maintained the French Nation in prosperity at home and in consideration and respect abroad;" and he "contends, in reply that France would have quite as much right to prescribe a Democratic Government, or a King of the House of Stuart, to England, as the latter has to attempt to compel France to receive a Monarchical Form of Government, or a King of the House of Bourbon."

After dilating upon, and arguing all the points, he concludes his letter by stating, that "none of the circumstances which relate to England, to France, and to the rest of Europe, appear to him to be an obstacle to immediate negotiations for Peace. He therefore presses our Ministers to accede to a conference, and proposes that it shall be held at Dunkirk, or any other place which may be deemed more convenient."

Such is the substance of the French Minister's second letter to Lord Grenville. It is not attempted to be denied that the style of it is respectful, and it will not, we believe, be contended that the tone of it is not moderate. The new Government were informed that His Majesty saw no reason for departing from the long established forms for transacting business with foreign states. The new Government defer to His Majesty, and adopt those forms. In this second letter the free people of England and their Ministers are not *insulted* with the words *Liberty, Equality, and the Sovereignty of the People*.[2]

What reply our Government will return to Talleyrand's letter we know not; that it has placed them in a very embarrassing situation we can readily believe. The Ministerialists tell us "that they will refute, and it will be easy for them so to do, the obsolete sophisms by which Talleyrand endeavours, but without the hopes of success, to throw upon our Government the odium of aggression in the war; that they will treat the other topics either with the attention or the silence which they deserve, and that they will refer, both with respect to what relates to the Princes of the House of Bourbon, and to what concerns the proposed Negotiations, to their first Note." By such an answer we are desired to believe, "Ministers will act in these circumstances with the dignity, the wisdom, and the caution which their situation requires!"

[2] C can hardly have written this paragraph, but he may have contributed to the editorial discussion behind it. Stuart had already announced (17 Jan) C's "Remarks on the Stile of Language..." and would shortly announce (22 Jan) his "Observations on 'The Sovereignty of the People'".

A COUNCIL of the Cabinet Ministers was yesterday held at Lord Grenville's Office, which continued near three hours: the result was laid before His Majesty at Buckingham-house; and we expect the French courier will be immediately sent back with no other answer than that which was given to the former communications.

The official letter from the French Minister of Foreign Affairs to Lord Grenville, which was brought on Saturday by the former Messenger, has not yet been *officially* published. From the outline given in the Ministerial Papers, it should appear to be a controversial answer to Mr. Windham's Note.[3] With respect to the origination of the war, it retorts the charge of aggression on the English Ministry, and supports it by reference to Proclamations, Manifestoes, and other public acts of our Government. In answer to the invectives against the former Rulers of France, and the inference that nothing better is to be expected from the present, Talleyrand acknowledges (we quote from a Ministerial Paper) "that some of the different Rulers who have governed France since the Revolution have given *real* cause to his inhabitants for anger, and have afforded *just* motives for alarm and complaint to foreign Powers; but the opposition which they have met from part of the French people, excited and supported by the foreign Powers, leagued with us in their designs of overturning the liberty of the French, and of forcing on them their old form of Government, affords a *justification* of their conduct."

How the inhabitants of a country can have *real* cause of anger,

[3] There were journalistic reasons for pretending that the author of the Grenville "Note" was Windham. That it was actually written by Lord Grenville himself was doubtless well known; we know it from the Dropmore MSS (and from the circumstantial assertion by Lord Holland *Memoirs of the Whig Party*—1852—I 155). But the *M Post* preferred to believe Windham the author. Thus the statement 16 Jan that "Twenty thousand copies in French, of Mr. Windham's *elegant* note, signed by Lord Grenville, in answer to Bonaparte's letter, have been printed and sent for distribution among the Chouans in France" looks like news but is probably all jest. In the same day's paper Windham's supposed authorship is "established" by an obvious hoax, a letter to the Editor signed "A Friend of Lord Grenville's" "Pall Mall, Jan. 13". Reversing the actual situation, this "Friend" protests at the *Post*'s "insinuation that the Note...was written by Lord Grenville" and insists that Ministers "are indeed anxious it should be known" that "it was the production of Mr. Windham alone". (A similar hoax on 17 Jan, in the same position on the page, is signed "Ben Bruiser" "At the Sign of the Cross Buttock" and begins, "The Members of the *Boxing Club* are much delighted with Lord Grenville's Answer to Bonaparte's Letter. We admit no *Brother Buffer*...". The implication is that all but bruisers would be ashamed to have written the Note.)

or[a] Foreign Powers *just* motives of complaint, against a Government, whose conduct is *justifiable*, we confess ourselves at a loss to explain. And unless Talleyrand's words have been reverberated to us by a sort of *Irish echo*, which has contrived to improve on the original, by a blunder of its own,[4] we "must proceed to confess," that Talleyrand and Mr. Windham are most happily matched!—Would to Heaven no other shot might pass than their paper-pellets, and no other wounds be inflicted than their's on logic and grammar![5] The letter concludes by contending that no causes exist of a nature to prevent the propriety of immediate negotiations for peace. "He therefore presses our Ministers to accede to a conference, and proposes that it shall be held at Dunkirk, or any other place which shall be deemed more convenient."

Our Ministers, it is stated, will make replication to this reply; but will refer to the first note with respect to the proposals for negotiation. As this note, therefore, is appointed *Atlas* for life, to bear on its shoulders the whole weight of Ministerial argument, we are compelled, however reluctantly, to pay it once more the compliment of a confutation. Ministers are tender perhaps of their *untouched* proofs, and humanely consider that no subsequent confutation can affect arguments already confuted. It were well for poor Humanity, if the same use could be made of the men that have been already "*killed off*;"[6] if the War Secretary could imitate the magician in the old romance, and march against the enemy an army of dead soldiers, "thrice slain," yet fighting still![7]

The French Government appears to us to have proposed to itself two objects in its letter; first, to convince the people of England, that their first proposals were not mere professions, held forth to obtain popularity for itself, and throw odium on its enemies, but proceeding from a serious and earnest desire of peace. And this object the letter has already answered, for the Ministerialists now waive all

[a] *M Post*: in [corrected in *EOT*]

[4] C liked the blundering illogicality of Irish bulls and considered it close to poeti chyperbole. Cf *CL* vi 1015 (to Calvert 13 Oct 1802); also *Watchman* (*CC*) 279n.

[5] See the "Advertisement" of 24 Jan signed "Taste. Grammar. Logic. Humanity" (App A, below). See C's later comment on paper bullets, 4 Nov 1802, below.

[6] Windham's famous remark in Parliament 2 Dec 1795; see *Parl Reg* XLIII 499; cf *Watchman* (*CC*) 61 and n 3.

[7] The story of the "everlasting battle" (an enchantress bringing the dead soldiers back to life), traditional in Northern literature, appears e.g. in Snorri's prose Edda. Cf also "And thrice He routed all his foes; and thrice He slew the slain." Dryden *Alexander's Feast* line 68.

their former suspicions of insincerity, and affirm that the Chief Consul is desirous of peace from feelings "of his own interest—it is his inability to support the war—it is then from conviction that war must overturn his power, and that peace may perhaps maintain it. It is not a peace of principle but of necessity." This is very natural language from the organs of the Ministers; for men almost uniformly attribute to others those motives which alone, they are conscious, would influence themselves. It proves however, undeniably, that this second application from France has removed all doubt of the Chief Consul's sincerity; and this we stated to have been the first object of the letter.

The second object seems to have been, officially to contradict the assertion contained in our note, that the present French Government, in *its official capacity*, had admitted all the preceding Governments to have been incapable of concluding, in the name of the nation, treaties of peace, and of maintaining the same. And this object too has been answered; for we find it already admitted, that in relation to Foreign Powers, the preceding Governments are justified by the present Rulers of France, and that "by this justification Bonaparte has put himself in a common cause with them." This was the second object. But the passage in our Note here answered is curious, and deserves a further comment.

"His Majesty cannot place his reliance on the mere renewal of general professions of pacific dispositions. Such professions have been repeatedly held out by all those who have successively directed the resources of France to the destruction of Europe; *and whom the present Rulers have declared to have been all from the beginning, and uniformly incapable of maintaining the relations of amity and peace.*" The latter clause of this period was doubtless considered by its author as a *home-stroke*. And were the subject of the official Note no more than a paper war between Mr. Windham and Bonaparte, we should admit it to be a dexterous controversial *thrust*—a missile from a dwarfish intellect, driven into the forehead of the Goliah of France.[8] But the Note lays claim to a higher character: it is an answer decisive of the lives of thousands, from England to France; nor can we remember one other instance, in which a foreign nation has built a national argument on the basis of a party assertion. The *argumentum ad hominem* is a figure of rhetoric, which may be admissible in the warmth of senatorial retort, and which is certainly very useful in pointing newspaper paragraphs; but it is most unworthy of a man

[8] Cf 10 Jan, above; but Bonaparte now appears a true giant.

writing or speaking in the person of his Sovereign. But it is with the War-Secretary, as with bad actors; he can represent no character but his own, and his own character is interesting only to himself, and formidable only to devoted Emigrants on Quiberon expeditions.[9] His mind is coarse and anarchical; and possessing the irritability without the inspiration of Genius, he forgets the solemnity of declaration in the pertness of debate; and carries with him the habits of a Disputing Club into the adyta of the Cabinet.

Our Ministers ought to have specified treaties made by one ruling party in France, and afterwards broken by the party that succeeded them, in order to give any weight to the argument deduced from "a fresh Revolution" in France. Revolution! a change of Ministry in England could be accompanied with no less convulsion, and would, we trust, in reality, though not in forms, be attended by a much greater change of measures. Had Bonaparte, instead of an intemperate personal sally against the *ci-devant* Directors, declared, as Chief Consul, that he would respect no treaty concluded by them in the name of their country, then, indeed, he would have furnished an argument not only against himself, but likewise against the nation which tolerated his Government. Besides, what security has any Government for the faithful observation of the treaties concluded with it, except its own strength, and the interest of the party treating? Was ever treaty kept after it had become the interest of the contracting party to break it?[10] In what cause but ill-faith in the observation of treaties have the whole series of modern wars originated? But we are, perhaps, uselessly employed in detecting absurdities so glaring. The Note was not meant for the Statesman, Bonaparte. The Chouans! the Chouans! They have warmer passions and less logic: and the Ministerial retainers at home, who are more fearful of silence, than ambitious of sense, wish only to have some words put in their mouths; with these they can answer all arguments with the promptness of parrots, and with as obstinate and *unadding* a fidelity. Mr. Windham may apply to Bonaparte the words of the famous Lulli to the Virgin Mary. This great Composer, as he entered a church, hearing some light music of his most unappropriately[a] set to a very solemn hymn, exclaimed, "Pardon me, holy Mother! but indeed it was not meant for you!"[11]

[a] *EOT*: inappropriately

9 Cf 24 Dec 1799, above.

10 On treaty-breaking see *Friend* No 22 (*CC*) II 307–8, in which C is concerned with the rupture of the Peace of Amiens and the seizure of the Danish fleet but goes on to discuss the problem in general.

11 Anecdote not traced.

PAPER WAR. IV

THE STILE OF LORD GRENVILLE'S NOTE[1]

22 January 1800, Wednesday. Reprinted in *Courier* of same date. *EOT* II 261–6, in SC's certain group but with uncertainty about the date ("Probably January 22, 26, or 27"), which means SC was using a signed clipping.

WE think *in* words, and reason *by* words.—The man who, while he is speaking or writing his native language, uses words inaccurately, and combines them inconsequentially, may be fairly presumed to be a lax and slovenly reasoner. False reasoning is perhaps never wholly harmless; but it becomes an enormous evil, when the reasoning, and the passions which accompany it, are to be followed by the sacrifice of tens of thousands. If this be a true statement, even a merely verbal criticism on an important State-paper merits the attention of the public; and believing that it is a true statement, we shall proceed to consider Lord Grenville's Note, relatively to the language and stile.

"Until it shall distinctly appear that those causes have ceased to operate, which originally produced the war, and by which it has since been protracted, and in more than one instance renewed." Here the simple and intelligible word "war" must have had a species of ministerial *duplicity* imparted to it: for how can one and the same thing be at once "protracted and renewed?" That which is protracted cannot have been finished; and that which has never been finished cannot possibly have been renewed. "The *same* system, to the prevalence of which France justly ascribes all her present miseries, is that which has *also* involved the rest of Europe in a long and destructive warfare, of a nature long since unknown *to* the practice of civilized nations." Here the connective word "also" should have followed the word "Europe."[2] As it at present stands, the sentence implies that France, miserable as she may be, has, however, not been involved in a warfare. The word "same" is absolutely expletive; and

[1] Announced with this spelling 17 Jan.

[2] Lamb, on recently renewed terms of intimacy, immediately wrote to C "acknowledging the obligations myself, and the readers in general of that luminous paper, the 'Morning Post,' are under to you for the very novel and exquisite manner in which you combined political with grammatical science, in your yesterday's dissertation on Mr. Wyndham's unhappy composition. It must have been the death-blow to that ministry. I expect Pitt and Grenville to resign. More especially the delicate and Cottrellian grace with which you officiated, with a ferula for a white wand, as gentleman usher to the word 'also,' which it seems did not know its place." *LL* I 168.

by appearing to refer the reader to some foregoing clause, it not only loads the sentence, but renders it obscure. The word "to" is absurdly used for the word "in." A thing may be unknown *to* practitioners, as humanity and sincerity may be unknown to the practitioners of State-craft, and foresight, science, and harmony may have been unknown to the planners and practitioners of Continental Expeditions; but even "cheese-parings and candle-ends"[3] cannot be known or unknown "*to*" a practice!!

"For the extension of this system." Christ *extended* the moral law of Moses; but the Apostles did not *extend*, they *propagated* the system of Christ. "Germany has been ravaged: Italy, *though* now rescued from its invaders, has been made the scene of unbounded rapine and anarchy." Is this a figure of speech? And is the whole put for a part? We have always understood, and even the Ministerial writers have not contradicted it, that *Naples* "*though*" rescued from its invaders, has been made the scene of unbounded rapine and anarchy.[4] But that Suwarrow, "*though*" he had rescued the North of Italy from its invaders, should have pillaged and anarchised it in so unbounded a manner—this we did not expect to hear asserted in a State Paper, written by the Ministers of his good and generous Ally! "It is to a determined resistance alone that is now due whatever remains in Europe of stability for property, for personal liberty, for social order, or for the free exercise of religion." This may be all excellently good *Grammar*, Mr. Windham! but it is most villainous *English*!

"Such professions have been repeatedly *held out* by all those who have *successively* directed the resources of France." Young children, who have been lately *held out* by their nurses, often talk as vulgarly. The latter part of the sentence should have been, "who successively have directed," not "who have successively directed."—Is not Mr. W. Metaphysician enough to perceive the difference?

"But the conviction of such a change, however agreeable to His Majesty's wishes, can result only from experience, and"—What is to follow this "and?" Experience we apprehend to mean "the evidence of facts." We will substitute this definition, and then observe what follows—"But the conviction of such a change can result only from

[3] See above, 22 Jan 1798 n 5.

[4] The "rescue" of Naples from the "Jacobins" of the Neapolitan Republic, in May 1799, had been notoriously—and C hopes exceptionally—savage. Cardinal Ruffo's "Christian and Royal Army" had pillaged without control, and, as Englishmen bitterly remembered, the safe-conduct granted by Ruffo to the besieged republicans had been repudiated by Nelson, who had had them hanged.

the evidence of facts, and" (what else?) "the evidence of facts!" Mr. Windham! your writings will die of a *plethora* of meaning.

"It would confirm to France the unmolested enjoyment of its antient territory; and it would give to all the other nations of Europe, in tranquillity and peace, that security which they are now compelled to seek by other means." Are tranquillity and peace then *means*?

Louis the 14th left no pernicious example of disturbing the security of nations; this was a mushroom of republican growth! But hush! our criticism must be *verbal*; else we could have smiled in observing, how curiously and expressly the sovereignty of the people is admitted and recognised in the following paragraph:[5] "or in whose hands she shall vest the authority,"&c. But we have given enough "by which to judge." 'Twere a wearisome and idle task to pluck *all* the nettles and stinking henbane out of a ditch where not a flower grows to be injured by them.

From a metaphysician we naturally expect a logical combination of sentences; from a scholar, accuracy in the use of words; from a Gentleman, ease and elegance of style. Mr. Windham is believed to be at once Gentleman, scholar, and metaphysician. Can it then be true, that Mr. Windham is the author of the Official Note? In almost every paragraph we meet with solecisms "unknown *to* the practice" of any classical writer. So endless are the repetitions and recurrences in this Note, that it seems almost to explain by analogy the curious difficulty how the same thing can be at once "protracted and renewed." Indeed so obscurely is it worded, that it appears little calculated to produce an "*extension*" of Ministerial power at home, or a *propagation* of their system abroad.

Through the whole of this note we may observe the clearest marks of labour strangely modified by two opposite principles, the consciousness of debility, and the self-complacent pride of office. The forms of connection are multiplied unnecessarily, and in the most obtrusive manner; but the connection itself is sufficiently slender for a Pindaric Ode. The same idea is repeated in a variety of phrases, than which no stronger proof can be given of dimness in the intellectual, and vanity in the moral, character. It is a mad beggar's dream of riches. We conclude with two quotations, one from Lord

[5] In his notebook C had written: "Sovereignty of the People *admitted*—a Paragraph—", a jotting that, as Kathleen Coburn observes, is "possibly an injunction from Stuart, or Coleridge's own reminder to himself, to write the essay [that] appeared on the 28th" (*CN* I 645 and n). This same day (22 Jan) the essay was announced as coming "To-morrow" (see below).

Rochester, the other from Geoffrey Chaucer; and leave the application of the first to our readers.

Nature's as lame in making a true fop,
As a philosopher: the very top
And dignity of folly we attain
By studious search and labour of the brain—
God never made a coxcomb worth a groat.

ROCHESTER[6]

"And if it be so, that we have yshewed in our lith English trewe conclusions, conne us the more thank, and praye God save the King that is Lord of this language, and all that him faith bereth, and obeieth everiche in his degree, the more and the lass."—CHAUCER'S ASTROLABIE.[7]

APOLOGIA. II

LETTER FROM "L. L." AND REPLY

22 January 1800, Wednesday. New attribution. The Reply is reprinted in Colmer 198–9; the evidence for its attribution to C is given in Colmer 182–3 and in the following notes. There is less evidence for the highly probable conjecture that the letter of "L. L." was written by C himself. Both Letter and Reply are accepted here.

TO THE EDITOR OF THE MORNING POST

SIR,

I AM a warm admirer, and an unfailing reader, of those excellent political speculations with which you occasionally favour the public, in your leading paragraphs. I look upon them as forming a periodical digest of wholesome information upon the most interesting and important of subjects; a course of familiar lectures on the science of politics, conveying instruction in the most agreeable, the most useful, and the most permanent manner; delivered in an order governed only by the occurrence and prominency of the objects and events which form their varying topics; and of inculcating their doctrines upon the attentive mind, with a forceful impression of their truth, not likely to be soon destroyed, associated as they are with reality, corroborated by fact, and calculated for *practice*.

6 John Wilmot, Earl of Rochester *A Letter from Artemisa in the Town to Cloe in the Country* lines 154–7, 159: *B Poets* VI 408.

7 Chaucer *The Conclusions of the Astrolabie: Works* ed John Urry (1721) 439, with elisions and "I" and "me" changed to "we" and "us".

After a short acquaintance with this part of your paper, I have regularly resorted to it, in the confidence of finding there, the crowding incidents of the present eventful drama performing on the stage of the world, the actions and opinions of the men who sustain the principal parts in it, and of those who guide, or are supposed to guide, them, together with the causes of those incidents, the motives and grounds of these actions and opinions, the results that may be expected from them, and the abstract principles by which they ought to be appreciated and judged, canvassed with singular acuteness, developed with sound judgment, with enlightened and liberal philosophy, and discussed in correct, classical, and elegant language. This confidence has not often been disappointed. Were I called upon to be particular, I think I should choose to name the series of strictures upon the new Constitution of France, upon the overtures of Peace to this Country, and the answer of Ministers, and "the Advice," inserted, I believe, some time before, "to the Friends of Freedom," as *recent* instances of the excellencies I have attempted to do justice to.[1]

With these sentiments I took up your paper of this day:[2] your animadversions upon the affairs of Ireland, to those who are acquainted with the subject, bespeak their own justness and propriety;—you know the subject *well.* But could you not, Mr. Editor, find terms more qualified at least, wherein to speak of the inhabitants of that devoted country? "A wild and barbarous people!"[3] Has then misery, such as their's! lost its last sad privilege, a claim to the commiseration even of words!—and shall the friends of freedom, too, abet and sanctify that interested and ungenerous calumny, which persecuting malignity, for the vilest purposes, has raised against its victims, and which pursues them even beyond the grave!

There are those who have injured too deeply ever to forgive, and who naturally wish to degrade below men those whom they are conscious they have treated worse than brutes. And may not minds not ignoble, but uninstructed—feelings not unworthy, but ungoverned, constitutionally warm as those of the Irish are, be goaded into excesses, terrible as those into which they have been driven, by such provocations as they have received? I have given you credit for knowledge of this subject, and I fearlessly appeal to that know-

[1] All these are C's contributions (as only C and Stuart would have known): the "Advice" of 12 Dec; the series of 7, 26, 27, 31 Dec; the strictures of 2 Jan (and perhaps 3 and 4 Jan).

[2] 15 Jan; see above.

[3] See above, 15 Jan, second paragraph.

ledge. The origination, at least, of these horrors, may, I think, be fairly described in the touching words of the poet of nature:

———Thy pleasure was my *dear* offence,
My punishment itself was all my *treason*,
And that I *suffered* was all the harm I *did*![4]

This letter, you will readily perceive, was not intended for publication, even if it could be thought worthy of it; it was designed for a better purpose, respectful admonition and temperate remonstrance, for which, or for any, it is at your service.

I have only to apologise for this address, of the length of which, when I began it, I had not an idea; but its subjects were fascinating; the well-earned praise of distinguished merit, in the successful discharge of a most important public duty, and the defence of slandered and unadvocated wretchedness. I am, Sir, your's, &c. a constant reader,

L. L.[5]

January 15.

NOTE BY THE EDITOR

In our paper of Wednesday we used the words "a wild and barbarous people, brutalised by the oppression of centuries," as descriptive of the lower classes of the Irish.—We find by the above spirited and well-written letter, which was not intended for insertion, but which our Readers will thank us for publishing, that this phrase has been misunderstood. The word "barbarous" was meant to be perfectly synonimous with "uncivilised;" and this defect of civilisation, with its accompanying evils, attributed as a crime to the successive administrations of that much injured country, and adduced as an apology for *their* conduct, "into whose souls the iron had entered."[6] *Apology!* We fear that this is a cold and inapplicable phrase. The extravagancies of one, whose eyes have been burnt out by his gaoler, demand a deep and indignant condolance, not apology. It is the doom awarded *against* a bad Government by the eternal wisdom, that even the horrors committed against it must be enumerated among its own crimes. What it does is not more its guilt than what it suffers; it is wounded by the rebounding of its own weapon. We

4 Shakespeare *Cymbeline* v v 400–2 (var).

5 "L. L." is not likely to have been Charles *Ll*oyd, at this date; it *might* be the Lambs, Charles and Mary, though the style seems too humourless. The manner and the *use* of the Letter, ironically "not for publication", suggest C as the most likely author.

6 Cf Prayer-book Psalter: Ps 105. 18.

peruse the accounts of the ferocious vindictiveness of savage tribes with terror, rather than moral disapprobation. They have been instructed by none, and none have had the power of instructing them. It is far otherwise with the ferocities which may have been perpetrated by the poor sufferers in Ireland. These have, indeed, excited our moral sense to a painful excess of feeling, not against that which they are, but against those who, causing them to be what they are, have cut them off from that great and enlightened character, of which, indeed, their very ferocities are at once the proof and the perversion.

> Each pore and nat'ral outlet shrivell'd up
> By ignorance and parching poverty,
> Their energies roll back upon their heart,
> And stagnate and corrupt!—[7]

The Irish national character we have ever contemplated with a melancholy pleasure, as a compound of strength and vivacity; an amalgama of the qualities of the two rival nations, England and France. Ireland itself is placed in the most enlightened part of the world, the sister of, perhaps, the most enlightened kingdom in it. It has had the same gracious line of Kings with ourselves. What indignation, then, must not every good mind feel against that parricidal faction, which has contrived, as it were, to mock a miracle of God, and make a *Goshen*[8] of darkness in a land surrounded by dawning or noon-day light! The opposition of such a faction to the measure of the Union, we cannot but consider as a species of presumptive argument in its favour, if there be no weightier arguments on the contrary side. But iniquitous as this faction has evinced itself to be, yet still their actions shall not prejudice our minds against their reasoning. TRUTH is of too divine and spiritual an essence to be susceptible of commixture with the foulness of its accidental vehicle. Light is light to us, though it be flung from the torch of a fury! If we could dissever from the ideas the ludicrous association, we would personify REASON as a ventriloquist; it is of inferior importance into what uncouth vessel she throws her voice, provided only that it is audible.[9]

[7] Lines 6–9 of C's *The Dungeon*, modified from the text in *LB* (1798). See *PW* (EHC) I 185.

[8] C rephrased this as "a land of darkness, a perfect *Anti-Goshen*" in *BL* ch 12 (1907) I 168.

[9] This too is revived in *BL* ch 9: "I regard truth as a divine ventriloquist: I care not from whose mouth the sounds are supposed to proceed, if only the words are audible and intelligible." *BL* (1907) I 105. The personification and image are a favourite Coleridgian complex. In 1795 Conscience is the ventriloquist (*Conciones: Lects 1795—CC—*31); in 1809 Reason

If it were *possible* (but we are convinced it is not) that Ireland could make and maintain itself an independent nation, uninfluenced by France, and retaining for England that feeling of compatriotism, which the use of the same language ought in nature to communicate—if this were possible, we should be ready to admit, that though the same blood flows in the extremities as in the heart, yet, that in the extremities it necessarily flows more languidly![10] But we appear to ourselves to see a necessity that Ireland should remain connected with this country; and this being taken as a postulate, we do not perceive how, in the present state of feeling and opinion among the majority in Ireland, such an independent legislature can be given to it, as will be able and inclined to take off the oppressive laws of exclusion from the people, without presenting cause of alarm to this country. If the Members from Ireland are to form a part only of an Imperial Legislature, the rights of suffrage, and every concomitant privilege, may then be safely conceded, and indefinitely extended. Still, however, we are not blind to the evils of a national minority; but here we seem to have only a choice of evils. These opinions we venture *in transitu*; and not without great self-distrust. *Adhuc sub lite est*.[11]

[22 January 1800, Wednesday]
Observations on "*The Sovereignty of the People*,"*—To-morrow*.[1]

PAPER WAR. V

23 January 1800, Thursday. *EOT* I 248–53, in SC's group of certain attributions; in confirmation note especially the concluding parable of child and drum.

A MESSAGE from the King yesterday communicated to the House of Commons the particulars of the two attempts in favour of a negotiation from the Chief Consul, and the answers of

---

(*Friend* No 9—*CC*—II 127); in 1811 Conscience again (*Courier* 26 Sept, below). Other variants occur in *Sh C* I 82; II 162, 245; *Misc C* 54, 90, 394, 411; *CL* IV 979.

10 This image appears to derive from the "circuitous circulation" of 15 Jan (second paragraph), above.

11 "It is still under trial"—i.e. the Union is still under debate and it is unsafe to have an opinion until the vote is in. For the phrase cf *Friend* (*CC*) I 55 (II 48).

1 See 28 Jan, below.

our Government. Monday next is the day appointed for taking them into consideration. The second letter from France with its inclosure, and the answer from Lord Grenville, we this day present to our readers.[1]

SECOND FRENCH LETTER

We stated in our Tuesday's Paper the two objects which appeared to us to have influenced the Chief Consul to this repetition of his proposals, and reply to our Ministers' objections, viz.—to remove all suspicion of his sincerity in the former proffer; and secondly, to repel the charge of incompetency in *any* French Government since the Revolution to preserve the relations of peace and amity, either as having existed in itself, or as having been acknowledged by *him* in his official capacity. These objects are of the first importance; in the means adopted to realise them, it became necessary to notice the assertion of our Government, that the war originated in an unprovoked attack from France, lest silence should be construed into assent, and this too be hereafter adduced, as "an express testimony (given at the time) of the Government of France itself." The French Note commences, therefore, by retorting the charges of aggression on England, and supports them by an enumeration of facts, particularly by that of the dismissal of the accredited Minister of France. It then alludes to the selfish and ambitious projects of the Powers leagued against her; projects which our Ministers themselves have never had the confidence to deny. Thus attacked, and thus menaced, "the Republic could not but extend universally her efforts of self-defence;" and if amid that unexampled career of victory, which rewarded the energy of her resistance, "the Depositaries of her Executive Authority did not always shew as much moderation, as the nation itself had shewn courage," let it be remembered, that "the fatal and persevering animosity with which the resources of England have been lavished to accomplish the ruin of France," leave them not wholly unjustified. "The circumstances of the internal situation of France were critical;" the immense revenues of Great Britain were still at the disposal of the same Ministers, who in the season of her distress had threatened her with extermination, and whom the terror of her successes, and the necessity of satisfying the people at home, had impelled to pacific conferences, not any real alteration in their feelings towards the French Republic, or any sincere recantation of their opinions. The French Executive had to choose between open and

[1] Given in full in the preceding columns of *M Post*.

concealed war, and in the then critical state of her internal circumstances, they deemed the former less formidable to the Republic than the latter.[2] Their desire of conquest was made reasonable by the annihilation of their commerce and navy, and justifiable on the system of a defensive war by anticipation; even as *we* now justify our late conquests in the Mysore.[3]

The Chief Consul's eagerness for a general peace (the power of Great Britain continuing in the present hands) evidences his convictions of "the strength and solidity" which the present constitutional system both contains in itself, and has secured to the interior of France, and his sagacity in acting unhesitatingly on the great political axiom, that the bad principles of an enemy present an obstacle to a peace, only while they remain dangerous. "But why, instead of attempting apologies for the war, on either side, should not attention be rather paid to the means of terminating it?" Why is the imprescriptible Right of the People to confer the Sovereign Power, under what "form and with what limitations they please," acknowledged and recognized, and yet an interference in the internal affairs of the Republic exercised by insidious invitations which tend palpably to excite and encourage internal commotions? By what species of argument can the English Ministry ward off the charge of gross inconsistency, in having petitioned for a negotiation from France in the moment of her triumphs, when the principles of her Leaders were less assimilated to those of other Governments, and refusing to accept the offer of negotiation now, when "the present and reciprocal situation of affairs promises a rapid progress to them?" "The Chief Consul proposes therefore to put an immediate end to hostilities by agreeing to a suspension of arms, and naming plenipotentiaries on each side, who should repair to Dunkirk, or any other town as advantageously situated for the quickness of the respective communications, and who should apply themselves without any delay to effect the re-establishment of a peace and good understanding between the French Republic and England."

Such is the substance of the letter—such is the *spirit* of the argument. We have arranged and elucidated the reasoning, but not altered it. This we have done, partly because the English translation is so inexpressibly barbarous, so utter a jargon, as to be only not unintelligible, and partly because we wished to exemplify the deter-

[2] This recapitulates C's analysis of the French attitude in his essay of 2 Jan 1798, above.

[3] The overthrow of Tippoo Sahib (see above, 7 Jan) justified by his association with the French.

mination which we have ever and uniformly professed, of preserving sacred the distinction between the personal crimes of Bonaparte, as an usurper, and his political sagacity and moderation, as the existing Chief Magistrate.

SECOND BRITISH REPLY

THE answer, which our Ministers have returned, is but a slovenly and ill executed *da capo* of their former note. The spirit and the style are such, that we conjecture it must have been composed originally by some emigrant Priest, and translated into a *resemblance* of English by Mr. Windham or Alderman Anderson.[4] The first sentence is as exquisite in language, as it is dauntless in assertion. "His Majesty cannot forbear expressing the concern with which he observes in that Note, that the unprovoked aggressions of France, the sole cause and origin of the war, are systematically defended by her present rulers under the same injurious pretences, by which they were originally attempted to be disguised." The Ministers must attribute to His Majesty a large stock of superfluous concern, if they suppose that he has any to lavish on so natural an occurrence, as that of a nation's refusal to acknowledge itself an unprovoked aggressor! That were an instance of candour of which we know no precedent in times past or present. Lord Grenville might, with reason, have repelled such an unexampled *deviation from the forms long established in the intercourse between civilised States!* We must now proceed.

"With respect to the object of the Note, His Majesty can only refer to the answer which he has already given. He has explained without reserve the obstacles which, in his judgment, preclude, at the present moment, all hope of advantage from negotiation; all the inducements, &c. the personal disposition, &c. the power of insuring the effect, &c. and the solidity of the system, &c. all these are points which can be known only from that test, to which His Majesty has already referred them: the result of experience, and the evidence of facts." Excellent!—In order to prove the pacific dispositions of a Government, and by way of giving a fair trial to the solidity of a system newly established, 100,000 Russians, twice as many Austrians,

[4] Sir John William Anderson (c 1736–1813), MP for London and Alderman of the City, is the "Court Alderman" of C's "Epigram. On Sir Rubicund Naso", *M Post* 7 Dec 1799 (see App D, below, and *PW*—EHC—II 958). On the Opposition's contempt for Anderson as sycophant and alarmist, see Woodring 232–3.

and a vast army of Englishmen, are to pierce into France in three different directions, and Suwarrow to be proclaimed Regent! And this is the test which Bonaparte's pacific dispositions, and the internal solidity of the new system are to undergo!—Even so the child will not remain satisfied with the sound of his drum without the test of experience, and the evidence of facts: and in consequence, he proceeds to bore a hole in the parchment!

[24 January 1800, Friday]

The Press of Irish and English Debates, Birth-day Intelligence, Foreign News, &c. &c. has prevented the opening of some New Plans this week....[1]

Observations on the late Negotiation—on the Sovereignty of the People—an elegant Poem by Mrs. Robinson, &c. &c. are all delayed till to-morrow by the same causes.[2]

PAPER WAR. VI[1]

25 January 1800, Saturday. *EOT* I 253–61; in SC's group of certain attributions, and one of C's most characteristic essays.

THE OVERTURES FOR PEACE

WE detected and exposed, in our paper of Thursday, the two leading absurdities of Lord Grenville's second note, viz. that of expecting from a great nation an acknowledgment that it had been an unprovoked aggressor, and that of continuing a tremendous war against a country which petitions for peace, as the means of arriving at facts to evidence such pacific dispositions; but the lateness of the hour, and the limits of our paper, prevented us from analysing this note with that minuteness which its importance, though not its merits, demanded. We shall now resume it; nor will our Readers yield us a reluctant attention. It is the popular faith that stars, on reaching the earth, are turned at once into shapeless and offensive jellies; but offensive and shapeless as it might appear to our earthly

[1] For Stuart's "New Plans", announced 27 Jan, see Introduction, above, I xciii n 1.

[2] The first appeared as promised, "The Sovereignty of the People" on 28 Jan. Mary ("Perdita") Robinson's *The Poor Singing Dame* appeared on 25 Jan and pleased C much "both" in metre and matter" (*CL* I 562–3).

[1] For a conjectural attribution of 24 Jan see App A, below; for an Epigram that day see App D, below.

senses, yet who would be weary of examining a star? It is sufficiently dignified by the place from whence it came down to us.[2]

"His Majesty cannot forbear expressing the concern, with which he observes that the unprovoked aggressions of France, the sole cause and origin of the war, are systematically defended by her present rulers, &c." If these professions of concern be any thing more than the common-place hypocrisy of a State declaration, they argue in the Ministry a gross and unthinking spirit. Were France justly criminated, yet that she should herself confess the justice of the crimination, so far from becoming an object of expectation, ought not even to be wished. To have been the sole and wilful cause of a war like the present, involves such enormous guilt,[3] that the latest posterity of that nation would be weighed down under the load, and suffer the punishment of *imputed* iniquity. We are not unconnected with the crimes of our ancestors. Let a few years elapse, and will there be a man who would not, spite of his reason, feel the shame of guilt, if it were truly objected to him, that his father had been a slave-merchant, or the planner of a Quiberon expedition? or that his forefather had served the British Ministers as scalp-commissary in America, and had aggrandised his family by the per centages which he had received for his purchases from the savages, purchasing scalps for tomahawks?[4] We are the creatures of sympathy and imagination; therefore the goodness of Providence has almost uniformly involved, in a wise obscurity, the real origination of so vast a horror as a war. Mutual accusations have proved only mutual guilt: the genuine documents have been destroyed, or, if preserved, have been jarring and contradictory; aggressions have referred to former aggressions; and causes and effects have been alternated; till the whole argument moves in a giddy circle, and history either leaves the controversy undecided, or is permitted to pronounce a mock-decision, only because the passions and feelings of men are no longer interested in its truth or falsehood.

These unprovoked aggressions, however (the opening of the Scheldt, &c.), were the sole cause and origin of the war! If this were indeed true, how grossly have not Mr. Pitt and Mr. Windham calumniated themselves in the whole series of their parliamentary declarations! In what ignorance must they not have kept the poor

[2] On star-jelly—algae that form gelatinous pellets on marshy ground—cf *CN* I 1703 and n.

[3] Guilt for one's nation, expanding to guilt for the woes of all mankind, is a recurrent theme for the author of *The Departing Year*, *Destiny of Nations*, *Religious Musings*—not to mention *The Ancient Mariner*.

[4] In *Conciones: Lects 1795* (*CC*) 56–9 C details the English responsibility for scalping.

Duke of Portland, who declared in the House of Lords that the cause of the war was the maintenance of the Christian Religion![5] Mr. Burke's pension seemed to imply the existence of no small confidentiality between him and the Government;[6] yet Mr. Burke declared, that the true cause of the war had never yet been officially stated to the people, and blamed Ministers for their reserve and timidity in this respect. If no miserable subterfuge be attempted, if the internal revolutionary regulations in France, religious and political, be not classed among her unprovoked aggressions; we commit this assertion undoubtingly to the common sense and common honesty of the people of England for trial and for judgment.

"His Majesty will not enter into a refutation of allegations now universally exploded, and (in so far as they respect His Majesty's conduct) not only in themselves utterly groundless, but contradicted both by the internal evidence of the transactions to which they relate, and also by the express testimony (given at the time) of the Government of France itself." *Universally* exploded! Does the present French Government explode them? Are there no exceptions among the myriads of enthusiastic Anti-Anglicans throughout France?—Have Mr. Burke's 80,000 incorrigible Jacobins exploded them?[7] Has Mr. Erskine, and all the numerous converts which his pamphlet made in the score or two of editions through which it passed,[8] exploded them? What facts have Ministers lately adduced of an evidence so overwhelming, as to produce this universality of assent to a question so involved and complicated? These allegations have

[5] 21 Jan 1794, quoted in *Watchman* No 1 (*CC*) 19. William Henry Cavendish Bentinck, 3rd Duke of Portland (1738–1809), the "convenient cipher" who served as head of the Fox–North ministry in 1783, was Pitt's secretary of state for the home department, 1794–1801.

[6] On Burke's pensions see *Watchman* Nos 1, 2 (*CC*) 36–7, 86–7.

[7] "Of these four hundred thousand political citizens, I look upon one fifth, or about eighty thousand, to be pure Jacobins; utterly incapable of amendment...". *Two Letters...on the Proposals for Peace with the Regicide Directory of France* Letter I (1796) 17. Burke's immediate object of attack was Lord Malmesbury's peace mission. See below. See also *CN* I 1258.

[8] Thomas Erskine (1750–1823), successful defender of Lord Gordon (1781), Stockdale, and Tooke (1794), would become lord chancellor in Grenville's ministry in 1806. His *View of the Causes and Consequences of the Present War with France* (1797) urged recognition of the Directory and argued that Pitt's insistence on remaining at war with France helped spread republican ideas throughout Europe. The pamphlet was in its 35th "edition" within two months of its first; it is the subject of a bibliographical discussion of the meaning of the term "edition" by William B. Todd, "Recurrent Printing" *Studies in Bibliography* XII (1959) 189–98.

been repeated and repeated, till those who are the most convinced of their truth have become weary of repeating them; and it has been the policy of Ministers to answer them by abusive epithets and a feigned contempt, as some have been said to have scared away a lion simply by staring him full in the face. But the phrases "ridiculous," "stale nonsense," "exploded absurdities," &c. are a defensive armour which has been so long used in controversial warfare, that it is now completely worn out, and is as ridiculous as the barber's bason on the head of Don Quixotte, which the fancy of that valorous Knight had transmuted into Mambrino's helmet.[9] As to the express testimony of the Government of France itself, it ought to have been distinctly and circumstantially stated. Was it an *official* testimony, or was it only a party speech, or perhaps a *report* of a party speech? One of these express testimonies, on which our former note founded its main argument, the testator himself has solemnly and officially contradicted.

A CAUTIOUS PARENTHESIS

ALLEGATIONS, in order to have been "universally exploded," must, we should suppose, be "not only in themselves utterly groundless," but be likewise "contradicted by internal evidence," if not by "express testimony." The allegations of the French, against the Coalition in general, are (it is asserted) universally exploded. What then can this "*and* (*in so far as they respect His Majesty's conduct*)" signify—this conjunction of *accession*, and this cautious parenthesis? Are they intended to convey the idea, that the assertions which follow do not apply to His Majesty's *Allies*, but only to His Majesty's own conduct? or that Ministers *doubt* whether they do or no? or at least dare not pretend to affirm them with *equal* certainty? This, or something like this, the parenthesis must mean, or it means nothing at all. And if this *be* the meaning, with what justice can the allegations against the Allies be said to be *universally* exploded, when, as it should appear by this parenthesis, the Ministers themselves do not presume wholly to explode them?

Let it not be too hastily thought, that we are captious and hypercritical. The contradiction, deducible from this parenthesis, *may* indeed have arisen merely from the want of logical precision in the

[9] *Don Quixote* pt I ch 21. Cf an entry in Lord Glenbervie's diary of 23 Oct 1801: "...Windham is thought an honest, ingenious man but a Don Quixote, and that he [Lord Guilford] never sees him without thinking he has a barber's basin on his head". *The Diaries of Sylvester Douglas* (*Lord Glenbervie*) ed Francis Bickley (2 vols 1928) I 266.

mind of the man who drew up the Note. But we appear to ourselves to have discovered a more important cause. We appear to ourselves to have detected, both in this and in the following paragraph, proofs of no mean presumptiveness, that the unanimity, which is assumed in the Senate, does not always exist in the Cabinet. The contradictions in certain religious articles, which even our most determined Theologians have found so difficult to reconcile, history explains at once; for history has preserved the fact, that the drawers up of these articles were themselves not of one mind, and that their disputes were finally settled, not by mutual conviction, but by mutual *compromise.*[10] Each threw in his opinions; and the whole was left at once to combine and to counteract, like the drugs in an old prescription.

We confess, that our late Official Notes exhibit to us this same complexion. Mr. Pitt, and the disciples of Mr. Burke, may differ essentially in politics, practical and theoretic, nor is it quite certain that "the King's friends" do not differ from them both. What *were* the *real*, and what *ought* to be the *ostensible*, causes of the war; under what character we ought to class the conduct of all the Allies in the former, and of Austria in the latter, campaigns; with what degree of strength England is entitled to press for the restoration of the old Monarchy, and with what degree of definiteness other possible conditions of peace ought to be stated; these are difficult questions, that have been prolific of dissentions among the junto in power! But finding discussion fruitless, and considering inconsistency as a less evil than inco-operation, they have at length agreed to mingle up all their notions as decorously as possible, in an *olla podrida* of mutual accomodation;[11] and these Official Notes have been the result. The restoration of Monarchy is demanded as the condition of peace with all Mr. Windham's *Chouannerie*; but somewhat has been conceded to the opinions and fears of Mr. Pitt, and "in explicit terms," the *possibility* is admitted, that other circumstances undescribed and indescribable may arise, which shall be capable of realizing the same good purpose.

[10] In 1553 forty-two Articles of Religion, to which those who take orders in the Church of England subscribe, were published; by 1571 disputes aired in Convocation had reduced them to the Thirty-Nine Articles. On the contemporary resistance to subscribing to the Articles, cf *PD: Lects 1795* (*CC*) 310 and n 3.

[11] For a metaphor of political accommodation as a ladder rather than a stew see 22 Mar 1802, below.

PARTIES IN THE CABINET

THIS admission answers two ends; it is a corps of reserve to cover some future retreat, and it is a concession to the feelings of those, who, it is whispered, on the late discussions in the Cabinet, have voted in the minority. The personal friends of a Great Personage, who think a government with the forms of freedom preferable to an avowed despotism, chiefly because these forms, by multiplying the modes of patronage, render power more intense; Mr. Pitt and his friends, who think that their own importance depends on the Constitution, containing *something* more than the forms of freedom; and Mr. Windham, &c. who are so panic-struck from Jacobinism and Atheism, that they do not *think* at all; these are heterogeneous elements, combined by reluctant affinities, easily decomposible by mere accidents, and indebted to a felicity of accident for their preservation from decomposition. They are indeed rather held in suspension, than combined; and, sooner or later, one or other of the compounds will necessarily be *precipitated*. Mean time, in consequence of their joint love to the people of France, they will heap taxes, even to exhaustion, on the people of England, in order to send into France almost half a million of men, commissioned to——do all, that is meant by the goodly phrase of a *vigorous defence*! Unfortunate France, alike unfortunate in thy pretended guardians, within and without! Hylax, a wolf-dog (said the admirable Lessing, from whom we translate the fable), was guarding a sheep. Caesar, who (like Hylax) both in hair, snout, and ears, resembled a wolf, rather than a sheep dog, flew with open mouth against him, exclaiming—"Wolf! what art thou doing with that sheep?"—"Wolf indeed! (cried Hylax) Impudent ruffian! *thou* art the wolf! away! or thou shalt soon find that I am placed here, as the sheep's defender!"

This answer of course enraged, not convinced, the wolf-dog, Caesar; he proceeded to take away the sheep from Hylax with force and fury; with no less force and fury, Hylax struggled to retain it; and the poor sheep (O such excellent defenders!) was torn in pieces between them![12]

[12] Cf No 11 of Lessing's *Second Book of Fables*, in any edition: "Das beschützte Lamm" (The Protected Lamb). (C had bought a copy of the *Fabeln* in Germany in 1798: *CN* I 340.) C has changed one of the dogs' names and somewhat expanded the text. Here is a literal translation:

"Hylax, of the family of wolf-hounds, was guarding a gentle sheep. Lykades, who in hair, snout and ears also resembled a wolf more than a dog, saw him and went at him. Wolf, he cried, what are you doing with this lamb?—

"Wolf yourself! Hylax replied.

GENERAL WASHINGTON. I

OBITUARY[1]

27 January 1800, Monday. Reprinted in *Courier* 16 Aug 1811 with new introductory paragraph. Reprinted Erdman (1957); Colmer 199–201. New attributoin; see Erdman (1957) for full details of evidence (discounting that drawn from doutbful essay of 21 Apr). SC lacked access to this day's *M Post*. The text of the *Courier* reprint, presumably corrected by C, is slightly improved in punctuation and capitalisation and has been followed here in most details.

THE officers and sailors of the American ships in the port of London, yesterday paid a just respect to the memory of their deceased friend General Washington, by attending at St. John's Church, Wapping, in naval mourning. We dare not record his death without attempting to pronounce his panegyric.[2] This mournful office is both our duty and our inclination; but we confess, that we feel our powers oppressed into sluggishness by the sense of its difficulty. To build up goodly phrases into rhetorical periods, and attach to the name of Washington all splendid generalities of praise, were indeed an easy task. But such vague declamation, at all times an unworthy offering to the memory of the departed, is peculiarly unappropriate to the sober and definite greatness of *his* character. Tranquil and firm he moved with one pace in one path, and neither vaulted or[a] tottered. He possessed from his earliest years that prophetic consciousness of his future being, which both makes and marks the few great men of the world, who combine a deep sense of internal power, with imaginations capable of bodying forth lofty undertakings. His feelings, constitutionally profound and vehement (and which, if uncounteracted by the majesty of his views, would

[a] *Courier*: nor

(Both dogs mistook each other.) Get out, or you will find out that I am its protector!

"But Lykades wants to take the lamb away from Hylax by force. Hylax wants to keep it by force, and the poor lamb—O, admirable guardians!—is torn apart in the process."

At this time C was "clogged by the life of Lessing" he intended to write. RS to Poole 30 Jan 1800: *S Letters* (Curry) I 220.

[1] For the editor's announcement of principles, on this day, and for a definition of C's relation to it, see Introduction, above, I xcii–xciii.

[2] Washington's death on 14 Dec 1799 had been rumoured in London 23 Jan and reluctantly accepted as fact, by the *M Post*, on Saturday the 25th. Other papers printed eulogies on the 24th and 25th, mostly drawn from the recently published *Travels Through the States of North America During the Years 1795, 1796, and 1797* by Isaac Weld. C also draws upon Weld (see Erdman 1957).

have been wild and ferocious), gave him a perpetual energy; while the necessity of counteracting and curbing these feelings gradually disciplined his soul to that austere self-command, which informed and moulded the whole man, his actions, his countenance, his every gesture. Thus, sympathising inwardly with man, as an ideal, not with men as companions, he perfected in himself that character which all are compelled to feel, though few are capable of analysing, the character of a commanding genius.[3] His successes, therefore,[a] great in themselves, and sublime in the effects which followed them, were still greater, still more sublime, from the means, by which they were attained. It may be affirmed, with truth, that if fortune and felicity of accident were to resume from his successes all which *they* had contributed, more would remain to him than perhaps to any man equally celebrated: his successes were but the outward and visible language of that which had pre-existed in his mind. But this character and these praises others have approached or attained, who, great in the detail of their conduct for the purposes of personal ambition, had subdued and fettered their feebler passions, only to become more entirely the slaves of a darker and more pernicious influence.

In Washington this principle and habit of self-subjugation never degenerated into a *mere* instrument; it possessed itself of his whole nature; he ripened his intellectual into moral greatness, intensely energetic yet perseveringly innocent, his hope, the happiness of mankind; and God, and his own conscience, his end! Hence among a people eminently querulous and already impregnated with the germs of discordant parties, he directed the executive power firmly and unostentatiously. He had no vain conceit of being himself all; and did those things only which he only could do. And finally, he retired, his Country half-reluctant, yet proud in the testimony which her Constitution and liberty received from his retirement. He became entirely[b] the husband and the master of his family: and the lines which Santeuil composed for the statue of the great Condé in the

[a] *Courier* omits [b] *Courier* omits

[3] In Weld's report (quoted in *M Post* 25 Jan: *Travels*—1799—p 60n) of the painter Gilbert Stuart's interpretation of Washington's countenance—as that of a man of native fierceness controlled by "judgment and great self-command"—C found his clue to the character of the President's unostentatious yet commanding genius. C's portrait of Washington (completed 25 Mar) both matches and supplies points of contrast to the portraits of Pitt (19 Mar) and Bonaparte (11, 13 Mar). Pitt lacks the qualities of "a commanding genius"; Bonaparte has them but attained the throne of a republic "by foul means".

Gardens of Chantilly were yet more applicable to the Father and Hero of the American Republic.

> Quem modo pallebant[a] fugitivis fluctibus amnes
> Terribilem bello, nunc docta per otia princeps
> *Pacis amans*, laetos dat in hortis ludere fontes.[b] [4]

Washington thought, felt, and acted in and for his age and Country; the same temperance presided over his opinions as his actions. He sympathised with the moral and religious feelings of the great mass of his fellow-citizens, and was that sincerely, which others assuming politically have betrayed hypocrisy, when they meant to have exhibited condescending greatness. He neither rushed before his age and Country, nor yet attempted to under-act himself; his actions, from the least to the greatest, he inspired with one high and sacred charm, by being always in earnest! Posterity will adjudge to him the title of GREAT with more sound and heart-felt suffrage, because he appeared no greater!

IRELAND. II

UNION WITH ENGLAND

27 January 1800. *EOT* I 266–7; in SC's group of certain attributions, though she did not know the date and must have worked from a clipping.

THE result of the Irish debates has confirmed our opinion of the ungroundedness of the hopes which the Anti-Unionists appeared to have entertained.[1] We know too well the materials of which that faction is composed, who form a large part of the Parliamentary Anti-Unionists. On the question itself, in all its bearings, we shall have frequent occasion to deliver our sentiments;[2] at present we shall only express our surprise and regret, that Sir Laurence Parsons should have rested so much of his argument on the merits of the

[a] *Courier*: paliebant [b] *Courier*: fonte

[4] Jean Baptiste de Santeuil in *Opera omnia* (3 vols Paris 1729) III 26 (var); this ed is closest of those examined. Tr: "That prince, terrible in war, before whom rivers once turned pale and fled, now, loving peace, in cultivated leisure, decrees joyful fountains to play in gardens."

[1] This is a tardy comment on the debate of 15 Jan, favouring Union by 138 to 96 (see above). The *M Post* reported the news 20 Jan; the ensuing debate in Dublin 18 Jan was reported 24 Jan.

[2] This would not prove true; it would still seem unsafe or at least indiscreet to discuss the question "in all its bearings".

Irish Parliament.[3] His very motion, as Lord Castlereagh justly observed, was in direct contradiction to his argument.[4] What must that assembly be, in which a question of such immense national importance can be lost or carried by a low manoeuvre? Twenty writs are issued. It is known that the persons returned will be creatures of Government; and we must therefore anticipate this intrigue by a trick of our own. Thus must the motion be construed: it admits of no other construction. "But" (says Sir Laurence) "if the subserviency of the Irish Parliament were a fair ground to call for its extinction, would not the argument be at least as strong against that of England? Let any man state to me an instance of base servility to the Minister by the Irish Senate, and I will pledge myself to find him one equally base and servile in the British Parliament." Let this be accurate or erroneous, it does not appear that the question of the Union is affected by it; for even on the hypothesis that both Parliaments were involved in one character, it would by no means follow that it is better and more *oeconomic* for the empire to have two vicious assemblies than one. An honest man, who should give his real opinions on certain subjects, would probably exhibit more *truth* than *prudence*; but were we to enter on the comparative merits of certain great assemblies, we should be inclined to decide in favour of one of them, not only from national partiality, but because, if, as Mr. Burke observed, "*vice* loses half its evil, by losing all its grossness,"[5] corruption may be more pernicious by being more palpable, even though it should not be more intense.—"*I keep up appearances, Sister!*"[6]

[3] Sir Lawrence Parsons (1758–1841; 2nd Earl of Rosse, 1807) had been dismissed his militia command in 1798 for "mistaken lenity". On 24 Jan 1799 his motion to expunge the paragraph on Union in the address had carried 109 to 104; the same motion had now (15 Jan) been defeated 138 to 96.

[4] Robert Stewart (1769–1822), later 2nd Marquess of Londonderry but since 1796 bearing the courtesy title of Viscount Castlereagh, had entered the Irish Parliament in 1790, the British in 1794. In 1797 he had become acting chief secretary in Ireland and had displayed impressive vigilance and severity in suppressing the Rebellion in 1798. With Cornwallis he had conducted a vigorous campaign for a pro-Union vote in the Irish Parliament in 1799, which would be resumed with success in the summer of 1800.

[5] This quotation from Burke *Reflections on the Revolution in France* (3rd ed 1790) 113 is oddly applied. Burke was lamenting the extinction of the chivalric honour "under which vice itself lost half its evil, by losing all its grossness".

[6] The famous advice to "keep up appearances" is found in Charles Churchill *Night* line 311.

PAPER WAR. VII

THE SOVEREIGNTY OF THE PEOPLE

28 January 1800, Tuesday; entitled "The Sovereignty of the People". *EOT* II 363–7; in SC's group of probable attributions, but confirmed by *CN* I 645 and the announcements of 22 and 24 Jan and by ample internal evidence: the qualities of the etymological and prosodic discussion; the concept of Babeuf and Windham as meeting extremes (see 14 Jan re Babeuf); the metaphor of the "grammatical subauditur".

It is said "that the first reply of our Government has put an end to the pretensions of the Chief Consul to write directly to our King; and the not less impudent one of addressing Monarchical and Legitimate Governments with the Revolutionary and insulting preface of *Liberty*, *Equality*, and the *Sovereignty of the People*."

To the former part of this curious sentence we make no objection. It suggested itself to us on the first perusal of the Chief Consul's Letter, how amusing it would seem to some future historian, while he contemplated retrospectively the Beings whose strong arm had given its projectile force to the political world; how *amusing* it would appear that BONAPARTE should have pretended to have written directly to OUR KING! To the former part of the sentence, therefore, we make no objection; but the subsequent words are not equally admissable.[1] "*Impudent!*" Wherein consists the impudence of using the forms prescribed by that constitution, in virtue of which he announced himself Chief Consul? Would it not have been impudence in *him* to have omitted them? Talleyrand and Lord Grenville are both Ministers of Foreign Affairs; the rank of both is equally incapable of being misunderstood; to Talleyrand's letter, therefore, there needed no explanatory superscription. But the title of Chief Consul is a new one; and surely, it was modest and conciliating in Bonaparte to preface a letter to our Sovereign Lord the King by an acknowledgment, that he did not address him as a personal equal, but as the Ambassador and subject of a higher power, viz. The collective Majesty of the French Nation.

[1] C treats the first part of "this curious sentence" ironically, the rest straightforwardly. The apparent inconsistency led Terrett (262–3) to conjecture that Stuart's blue pencil was responsible for the reiterated "we make no objection" in an effort to cancel out C's irony: but is not the reiterated clause the pivot of the irony? Terrett goes on to hazard the guess that Stuart's interference was the beginning of the end of C's editorial power on the *M Post*; but see discussion of Stuart's announcement of 27 Jan, Introduction, above, I xcii–xciii.

Let those, who are angry at the application of the word "Majesty" to a whole people, examine the meaning of the word *etymologically* and *historically*, and they will find that it was only *transferred* to a single person, and that it originally meant the power and dignity resident in the majority of the common weal. Our King is the lawful representative and *personification* of this power and dignity; which he superscribes *inclusively* in his own superscription.[2] But this highest honour Bonaparte did not presume to claim, and wrote therefore to the King of England, in the name, and as the *servant*, of the French Nation. But it was impudent, it seems, thus to address *monarchical* and *legitimate* forms of Government! Legitimate is too vague a word to be understood without a definition: the Jacobites were indefatigable in bandying it against the House of Brunswick, and those attached to the old Constitution of Poland have applied it against the two Emperors of Russia and Germany; a term so vague signifies nothing but the passion of the man that uses it. The epithet "Monarchical," however, needs no definition: and in a Poet Laureate's Ode, when the verse demanded a dissyllable, the word "Monarch" might pass unexplained, as well as undefined. But there is no *licentia prosaica*; and we would fain admonish the hirelings of Ministers, that however strongly their wishes tend that way, yet, thank Heaven, it is still our possession, as well as birth-right, that we have a KING, and no *Monarch*![3] The 24th and 25th statutes of Henry VIII. declare the Crown of England *Imperial*, and the Kings *Emperors*[a] of the realm; and after the Union, our Ministers (who are partial to precedents drawn from reigns *so favourable to liberty*)[4] will, it is said, renew the title. But even that detestable tyrant, Henry the Eighth, is no where stiled a *Monarch*, or his government monarchical. Our King is not the sole supreme power; but as Bracton observes (Lib. 2. c. 16), "*Rex habet superiorem Deum, item Legem, per quam factus est Rex; item Curiam suam*, viz. *Comites et Barones, quia Comites dicuntur quasi Socii Regis, et qui habet socium habet*

[a] *EOT*: King *Emperor*

[2] Cf *PD: Lects 1795* (*CC*) 295, *C&S* (*CC*) 20.

[3] C had himself used "Monarch" pejoratively—in *Joan of Arc*: "Rebels from God, and Monarchs o'er Mankind!", changed to "Tyrants o'er" in *Destiny of Nations* line 314; and in *France* line 30: *PW* (EHC) I 141, 245. But of course laureates were hired to praise.

[4] In connexion with the Two Bills, C had accused Grenville of favouring precedents from the reigns of Elizabeth and Charles II, which were measures giving such "security to the Monarchy" as to produce the great Rebellion. *PD: Lects 1795* (*CC*) 302–3.

Magistrum: et ideo si Rex fuerit sine fraeno, i.e. *Lege, debent ei fraenum ponere*."[5]

Therefore however hateful the word "liberty" may be to the creatures of a Minister who has *alarmed* a nation out of its best and dearest liberty, that of the press, yet still to our *kingly*, not *monarchical* Government, it is an address of brotherhood, not insult. Equality likewise, if it have any signification different from that equality which we possess (viz. the subjection of all to the same laws), ought to give us no greater offence than the phrase of "Federal Republic" in the American State-papers. For America, as well as France, had excluded an hereditary Nobility: and the word "Republic," in the modern sense of it, implies this exclusion. But what other equality, than that which results from such exclusion, has any French Government recognised? "The Sovereignty of the People"—this perhaps is the stumbling-stone of offence![6] This, however, is expressly recognised by the Ministers in their own Note. "His[a] Majesty makes no claim to prescribe to France what shall be the form of her Government, or in whose hands she shall vest the authority necessary for conducting the affairs of a great and powerful nation." What is meant by the word "France?" Assuredly no constituted power; for the acknowledgment of any such power, as existing in that country, is avoided through the whole Note with a studied accuracy, and a *pettifogger's* cunning. It must mean, therefore, the People of France; and in them it expressly affirms the *imprescriptible* right of conferring

[a] *EOT*: Though

[5] Henry de Bracton *De legibus et consuetudinibus Angliae* bk II ch 16 ed Sir Travers Twiss (1878; 1st ed 1569) I 268–9. The quotation is almost exact, but breaks off in the middle of a sentence—as it does in Milton's *Defensio pro populo Anglico* ch 8, evidently C's source; cf *A Complete Collection of the Historical, Political, and Miscellaneous Works* ed John Toland (3 vols Amsterdam 1698) III 62. "The King has his superior [in God]; the Law, by which he is made King, and his Court, to wit, the Earls and the Barons: Comites (Earls) are as much as to say, Companions; and he that has a Companion, has a Master; and therefore, if the King will be without a Bridle, that is, not govern by Law, they ought to bridle him". Tr Milton *Defence: Works* II 638.

[6] On the contemporary application of the concept, see the remarks of G. K. Fortescue in his ed of Thibaudeau (xi–xii): "From the day when, having disembarrassed himself of Sieyès, Bonaparte entered upon his usurped inheritance as the Heir of the Revolution, and still more after this inheritance was ratified by the vote of the 'Sovereign People,' he might say of himself with more truth than Louis XIV., 'L'État c'est moi.' The doctrine of the 'Sovereign People' was unquestionably the central principle of the Revolution, and to no person, assembly, or constitution since 1789 was given so fully, or by so large a vote, the mandate to govern in the name of the people, as to Napoleon Bonaparte, both as First Consul and as Emperor."

the Supreme Power. But a power must be possessed before it can be conferred; and in this by undeniable consequence is involved the Sovereignty of the People. These are not our doctrines, this is not our belief,[7] but we affirm that it is the sole meaning of which the words in the Note are susceptible. But so it is ever! Baboeuf and Mr. Windham are both in extremes; and extremes meet![8] Perhaps, one reason why Talleyrand omitted to superscribe his letter with the phrases in dispute, is to be found in this very passage. The titles were already allowed; to repeat them, therefore, became superfluous; they might be suppressed without being omitted, and exist virtually, like a grammatical subauditur,[9] or like an admitted postulate, in the implicit and cryptical syllogisms of the old logicians.

[28 January 1800, Tuesday]

In a few days we shall present very important Observations on the intercepted Correspondence.[1]

PARLIAMENT. II

VOLCANIC FERMENT

30 January 1800, Thursday. *EOT* II 361–3; among SC's probable attributions, confirmed by internal evidence of tone and rhythm and image—and by links to the certain attributions.

WE can fully sympathise with the public in their anxious expectation and curiosity concerning the motion (and consequent debate) on the Chief Consul's proposals. The disappointment of Monday was repeated yesterday, and the motion is once more deferred to Monday next; nor do we see any reasons, which authorise

[7] As for C's own belief, while his present bias is so far toward *Le Contrat social* (or so much like Milton's in the *Defence*) as to seem to make little distinction between "Sovereignty" and "Majesty", his doctrine (here expressed only in the quotation from Bracton) is already essentially that declared in a letter of 1831: "...tho' neither Whig nor Tory, I am enough of the latter, I trust, sincerely and habitually to fear God: and to honor the King, as ordained of God—i.e. as no Reflection or Derivative from the (pretended) Sovereignty of the *People*...". *CL* VI 863. In 1800 Bonaparte may not be an ordained king but is to be recognised as, effectually, "the *servant*" of his nation.

[8] A proverb C was fond of. See *Friend* (*CC*) I 110 and n 5.

[9] Something not expressed but understood; *OED* cites Beddoes *Hygeia*: "It will not pass like a *subauditur* in grammar."

[1] See 3 Feb, below.

us to promise ourselves, that our hopes on Monday next will not be compelled to submit to a further procrastination.[1] The causes assigned for these repeated delays have been various. Mr. Pitt is said to be indisposed, and as great a variety of disorders have been attributed to him, as a quack medicine professes to cure;—hoarseness, blue-devils, spasms in the stomach, &c.—others have stated the absence of Mr. Dundas as the cause, and there seems to be some reason for this opinion, as he is not expected in town till the end of the week. But we suspect (and have reason for our suspicion) that certain Parliamentary Intrigues are going forward, and not yet concluded; and that the country Gentlemen (and some others who have been stiled Independent Members) are dissatisfied with the vulgar arrogance with which the French Proposals have been rejected; and alarmed by the nature of the motives, which are circulated, as the real causes of the support of the Ministers in the continuance of the war, and which go to a complete sacrifice of the permanent and landed interest of the country to the moneyed and commercial interests.[2] This, however, is *made certain*, by the late Debates in the House of Lords, that many, who now vote with the Minister, vote with mistrust and hesitation; and even *if* no *facts* should openly appear in the House of Commons on the ensuing debate to the same import; yet let it be remembered, that many and *volcanic* revolutions may be fermenting under ground, while the *surface* remains undisturbed.[3]

The debate in the House of Lords, we cannot but consider as a confession of a complete defeat on the part of Ministers in point of argument,[4] otherwise it were scarcely conceivable, that even Lord

[1] Parliament convened 21 Jan, but the debate on the question of peace, set for the 27th, was put off several times. We can deduce from Stuart's announcement of 27 Jan (see Introduction, above, I xcii–xciii) that C had pledged himself to assist in reporting the great debate when it occurred; he did so 4 and 18 Feb (see below).

[2] Cf 1 Feb 1800 and n 7, below.

[3] Cf the "revolutionary cauldron" of 12 Dec 1799, also with surface scum above ferment. Images of volcanic and fermentative eruption are blended in the same way and with the same import as those of fire and sprouting grain in the "DEAR Buonaparte" letter (*CL* I 539): the effect of Bonaparte is again to ruin the prospects of English reaction.

[4] On 28 Jan Grenville moved an address to the throne "ushered in by an harangue of outrageous abuse and violence against the first consul" (William Belsham *History of Great Britain from...1688, to...1802*, XI—1805—315). The Earl of Liverpool had supported him with a commercial argument (see the next essay). Lords Bedford, Romney, and Carlisle variously opposed this argument and the violence of the Notes to France, but "the address was carried by the usual overwhelming majority". In the House of Commons 3 Feb Henry Dundas moved a similar address with a similar harangue, which precipitated an extensive and heated debate, partly reported by C for 4 Feb.

Grenville could lay the whole proof of the identity of the present French Government with that of the Jacobins, on their non-acknowledgment of the aggression, when, as we have before stated, no precedent exists in all history, antient or modern, of such an acknowledgment having been made; otherwise it were scarcely conceivable that even a Lord Grenville could have been childish enough to have enumerated all the crimes and follies of France, and have dropped all those of her enemies; as if all her enemies had been immaculate, or as if their crimes and follies had had no influence in producing or continuing those of the French Government:[5]—otherwise, we repeat, it were scarcely conceivable, that even Mr. Pitt's Vicegerent, in a House of Lords, could have the folly to state, that the stability of a treaty could depend on the life or character of Bonaparte, without proving that any treaty had been ever violated by a French Government, simply, because it had been concluded by its predecessors; or, that any treaty had ever been observed by *any* Government, longer than its own interests induced, and the strength of its rival compelled, the observation.[6]

PARLIAMENT. III

OUR COMMERCIAL POLITICIANS

1 February 1800, Saturday. *EOT* I 268–74; among SC's certain attributions, entitled "On the Late Debate" in *M Post*. Reprinted as an unsigned letter "To the Editor" in *Courier*, 1 Feb.

LORD GRENVILLE on Tuesday night stated, "That peace was an object, not only to be devoutly wished for, on the score of humanity, but that the interests of our commerce likewise were decidedly in favour of so desirable an event."[1] The Earl of Liverpool,[2] on the same evening, found his arguments so completely anticipated by Lord Grenville, and their opinions so perfectly *similar*, as to leave him little occasion to develope them in his own person: and almost immediately hereupon proceeded, in words of the following import: "Our commerce, since the war, has prospered beyond example. In

[5] Cf *Conciones*: "Admire, I pray you, the cautious Delicacy of our Government! that will profess itself the Ally of the Immaculate only...". *Lects 1795* (*CC*) 54.

[6] Cf 21 Jan (at n 8), above.

[1] See the preceding essay, n 4.

[2] Charles Jenkinson (1729–1808; Earl of Liverpool, 1796) had been leader of the "King's Friends" in the House of Commons in the 1760's; president of the board of trade since 1786, privy councillor since 1772.

fact, we may almost be said to have the whole commerce of the world in our hands. Our trade, manufactures, and agriculture, also flourish extremely. Ought we, then, to consent, by a premature peace, to open the ports of France, to let them share our commerce, and to enable the Republic to revive their manufactures and trade?"

We shall not insult the discernment of our readers by pointing out the perfect *similarity* in the opinions of the two Noble Lords, nor animadvert on the enlarged policy of pleading against a *premature* peace; an argument which either proves nothing at all, or proves the propriety of perpetual war with France, or a war to be terminated only by her utter destruction. Two rival tradesmen were engaged in the same line of business: the one of them, by a fortunate train of circumstances, had already *ruined* the other; and, not content with this, he perseveres in a plan to murder him and his family. And why? Simply, because if he do not, it is possible that the man and his family may once more set up against him?[3]

The Earl of Liverpool is distinguished by his enlarged policy; for, as Lord Grenville observed, "an enlarged policy is necessarily built on *humanity*." Still, however, this argument of Lord Liverpool's is the *only argument* which was adduced by Ministers during the whole of the debate; it is the chief, and, perhaps, only argument, which affects the minds of men out of Parliament; and as such it demands from us a fuller and more detailed examination.

That our commerce has been greatly increased since the war, and by the war, is as undoubted a fact, as that our manufactures and agriculture must have been, more or less, injured by it. The injury which our agriculture has sustained *may* be only *negative*. That is, the progression of improvement cannot have been equal to that which it must have been, had all the men now in our fleets and armies, who belonged to agriculture, been still employed in it. Whether some positive injury may not have been suffered likewise, is a question which we are not competent to answer. The injury sustained by our manufactures is both negative and positive. That they had not increased, our commerce having been so greatly increased, would have been a sufficient proof of the former; and that they have decreased, the whole county of Devonshire, the manufacturing towns of Norfolk, the multitude of untenanted houses in Manchester, and even Birmingham, and the immense multitude of recruits from Norwich,

[3] Lewis Patton calls attention to a similar illustration in *Watchman* (*CC*) 16–17 in a note by C on a speech of 15 Dec 1792 by Liverpool's son, Robert Banks Jenkinson.

Manchester, and Birmingham, yield an accumulation of evidence. These injuries (viz. the negative injury sustained by our agriculture, and the injuries, both negative and positive, inflicted on our trade and manufactures) have been occasioned wholly by the war; nor is there a shadow of reason to doubt that they would be wholly removed by the consequences of a peace.[4]

The questions, therefore, are, 1st. To what degree, if at all, will a peace decrease our commerce? And, 2d. To what degree may our commerce be decreased without real detriment to our national interests, or, at least, with no greater detriment than may be counterbalanced by the increased prosperity of our manufactures and agriculture? Now, first of all, it is certain, that it is opposite to the very nature of commerce for it to quit an accustomed channel suddenly, or otherwise than slowly. This, which is true at all times, will be eminently true in the present case, from the novelty and revolutionary nature of the French Government, and from the insecurity and want of credit arising from that, and from other sources. We should stand against France as one banker, who has stood firm in a general crash, against a repeated and fraudulent bankrupt. The very energies which France will make to restore her manufactures, &c. will, by the reviviscence of a commercial spirit, of itself greatly increase the demand for our manufactures, and for the raw articles, which she will be able at first to gain from us only. Thus, for a while, our commerce would probably continue to increase; and, ere France could aspire to any degree of rivalry, we are justified, by every analogy of the past, in expecting that new branches would shoot forth, which would compensate us for those that had been lopped off, and planted in the possessions of our rival. Thus the renewal of a vigorous trading and commercial spirit in France would, at first, be a benefit and stimulus, even to our commerce; but it would be still more importantly beneficial, both to us and to the quiet of all Europe, in a political light, by giving the death-blow to Jacobinism, by reviving all the wholesome and Anti-Revolutionary influences of property, and by that assimilation of the pursuits and feelings of the French nation to our own, which must infallibly end in assimilating the *spirit* of their Government to that of ours.

The restoration of the old Monarchy we scarcely think possible, and if possible, yet by no means desirable. (That so many of our commercial politicians in power think it so desirable for us, is indeed

[4] Cf C on war and commerce in *Conciones: Lects 1795* (*CC*) 59, 68.

an involuntary confession that it is not desirable for France;[5] and proves, that, spite of their contempt for French freedom, they *now* fear a peace with the Republic, not from apprehension of Jacobin principles, but from an anticipation of Republican energies).[6] Yet, though we profess ourselves no friends to the restoration of the Monarchy, and though we believe such restoration barely possible, yet we do not hesitate in affirming it as our opinion, that peace is a far more likely mean thereto than war. For war never has been, and never will be, able to bring about aught else but a stormy alternation of Jacobinism and Dictatorship; while peace, by reviving the spirit of permanent property, *might* incline men to the old Government, if only from that idea of security associated with all that is old, and therefore seemingly consecrated by experience. Add too, that a peace granted to France, on fair and honourable terms, would naturally incline her to a favourable leaning towards the Government which had granted it; but peace rejected insolently, and war with threats of a threefold invasion, and accompanied by mutual pledges between two Emperors, not to intermit it till they have forced a King on the country—what other effect can these circumstances produce, than to create or deepen the general hatred in France of Emperors and Kings, and all that relates to them?

But on the supposition that by a perpetual continuance of the war, or by a restoration of despotism, or by any other means, we could be and remain the monopolists of the commerce of Europe, is it quite ascertained, that it would be a real *national* advantage? Is it quite certain, that the condition and morals of the lower and more numerous classes would not be progressively deteriorated? Is it quite certain, that it would not give such a superiority to the moneyed interest of the country over the landed, as might be fatal to our Constitution?[7] Has not the hereditary possession of a landed estate been proved,

[5] The argument again of 2 Jan 1798, above.

[6] C recognises an important distinction between "Jacobin principles" and "Republican energies", the latter being not only possible (under Napoleon) but acceptable.

[7] When C approves of a republic based on property, he means agrarian property, the only "secure" kind. He considers landed property susceptible of democratic "diffusion", the hindrances being chiefly "Priesthood & the too great Patronage of Government" (letter to RS 25 Jan: *CL* I 564). C was currently (28 Dec, 25 Jan) urging upon RS the writing of a history of the Levelling Principle, to be worded cautiously so as not to alarm the Tories yet sufficiently Aesopian to illuminate youthful readers.

At the end of the war C would express, in the widely noticed *LS*, his concern at the "overbalance of the commercial spirit" and the confusion of the wealth of a nation with its welfare. *LS* (*CC*) 169–70.

by experience, to generate dispositions equally favourable to loyalty and established freedom? Has not the same experience proved that the moneyed men are far more malleable materials? that Ministers find more and more easy ways of obliging them, and that they are more willing to go with a Minister through evil and good? Our commerce has been, it is said, nearly trebled since the war; is the nation at large the happier? Have the schemes of internal navigation, and of rendering waste lands useful, proceeded with their former energy?[8] Or have not loans and other Ministerial job-work created injurious and perhaps vicious objects for moneyed speculations?—And what mean these Committees for the labouring poor? These numerous soup-establishments?[9] These charities so kindly and industriously set on foot through the whole kingdom? All these are highly honourable to the rich of this country! But are they equally honourable to the nation at large?—Is that a genuine prosperity, in which healthy labourers are commonly styled "the labouring *poor*," and industrious manufacturers obliged to be fed, like Roman clients, or Neapolitan Lazzaroni?[10] It was well said of revolutions,

> In principatu commutando civium
> Nil praeter domini nomen mutant pauperes.[11]

And other goodly names, besides that of Liberty, have had still *worse* effects.

Finally, commerce is the blessing and pride of this country. It is necessary, as a stimulus to the agriculture which sustains, and as the support of the navy which defends, us; but let us not forget that commerce is still no otherwise valuable than as the means to an end, and ought not itself to become the end, to which nobler and more inherent blessings are to be forced into subserviency.[12]

[8] For C's interest in the question see *PD: Lects 1795* (*CC*) 318 and *Watchman* No 6 (*CC*) 224–5.

[9] During the winter and spring of 1798–9 four Soup Houses in London served 1,232,254 meals or pints of soup—at half the "first cost" (*Times* 2 Jan 1800). The bad harvests of 1799 still further worsened the plight of the "labouring poor".

[10] Cf C's observation to Allsop (I 27) that to make the poor dependent on charity was to make them "more and more exchange the sentiments of Englishmen for the feelings of Lazzaroni". See Colmer 143. In *Watchman* No 3 (*CC*) 101 C objected to a "broth-machine" to feed the poor, that "if the poor were fed daily in this manner, they would rely less and less on their own industry, and sink at last into a class resembling the Neapolitan Lazaroni".

On the term "labouring poor" see *LS* (*CC*) 207 and n 1.

[11] Phaedrus 1.15.1–2. Tr: "By a change of leadership of the citizens the poor change nothing but the name of their master".

[12] C's economic distinctions comprise the central assumptions of the Parliamentary Reformers, including in

[1 February 1800, Saturday]

We again desire our readers to be prepared for some VERY IMPORTANT *observations on the intercepted Egyptian Correspondence, on Monday next.*

INTERCEPTED CORRESPONDENCE. I[1]

3 February 1800, Monday; *M Post* title (without "I"). *EOT* I 275–83, in SC's group of certain attributions (and see *EOT* III 1020); confirmed by strong internal evidence.

Sed unum hoc ego per hanc dignationis vestrae sinceram audientiam rogo, ut praesente Synodo, quae nunc de *pace* litigat, pauca me de EPISTOLIS EGYPTICIS dignemini audire.

—HILARIUS AD CONSTANTIUM[2]

THE authenticity of these letters hitherto has not been publicly disputed. Have they then received the suffrages of all men of sense, as authentic? And is this the cause, that they have remained

this period the Foxites and, shortly, the Burdettites, who see the political and economic health of England in a greater development of agriculture and industry than of mere commerce. Five years earlier he had had nothing good to say for commerce at all. See LRR VI: *Lects 1795* (*CC*) 223ff.

[1] These "very important Observations" were twice announced, 28 Jan and 1 Feb, but could have maximum effect published as they were on the morning of the great debate. The sensational work under review was a three-volume series of *Copies of Original Letters from the French Army in Egypt... Intercepted by the British Fleet in the Mediterranean*, the third volume of which had been published in the second week of January 1800 by the Grenvilles' bookseller, John Wright. These letters of Bonaparte and his associates concerning his departure from Egypt in the previous autumn were edited (by William Gifford and George Canning, of the *Anti-Jacobin*) in such a way as to "let Englishmen learn *from* [Bonaparte] *himself* what reliance is to be placed on his engagements: and let them then recollect that THIS IS THE MAN, who has recently required of *their* SOVEREIGN to trust implicitly to *his* individual sincerity...". (For Lord Grenville's responsibility for the publication, and Gifford's for the notes and Canning's for the preface, see *Dropmore MSS* VI 97, 98, 106 and *Lady Holland* II 42–4.)

Part the First had been published 27 Nov 1798 and *Part the Second* 8 Mar 1799, according to dated frontispieces. The variant main titles and part-titles of editions of *Copies of Original Letters* make accurate citation difficult and confusing.

[2] St Hilary *Opera* bk II ch 8 (altered): Migne *PL* X 569. Tr: "But I ask this one boon of you in this candid audience that you have deigned to grant me, that you will condescend, at the present Council, which is now adjudicating upon the *peace*, to hear a few words from me about the LETTERS FROM EGYPT."

C has been reading St Hilary of Poitiers, who, in a synod of bishops

unquestioned? Or is it agreed upon by all men of sense, that they are forgeries? And may not this circumstance (joined to *prudent* apprehensions respecting the Government under whose auspices the letters were published) have produced the silence? These are possible queries. We think, therefore, that we shall perform no unimportant service to the Public in general (but especially to the *believers*), if we subject the letters to some trial, and cross-questioning.[3]

Should our objections appear trifling, sophistical, and vexatious, we shall yet have given a proof, which, without us, would not have existed, that the authenticity of the letters is admitted from the want of reason and ability to evince the contrary, and not from the absence of courage or inclination to make the attempt. It is the high privilege of TRUTH,[a] to transmute objections into proofs; and with the stones, that had fallen short of her, to build up a wall, which not only insures her security, but prevents even all future *attack*. Promising ourselves therefore no unfavourable hearing, we proceed directly to offer some *doubts* (*Jovi Congregatori Nubium sacrae*)[4] respecting the three pamphlets, which are affirmed to be faithful and uninterpolated "copies of original letters from the French army in Egypt."—These pamphlets were published at different times, and the letters are said to have been intercepted at different periods; as therefore the

[a] *EOT*: truth

at Seleucia in A.D. 359, joined with Egyptian Athanasians to make a Homoiousian majority in a debate on creed. After the convocation Hilary went to Constantinople with a personal petition to Emperor Constantius, *Ad Constantium Augustum liber secundus*, from which C wrenches a passage (Ch 8) to suit his purpose. Hilary wrote of a synod debating on faith ("de fide"); C makes this an allusion to the debate on peace ("de *pace*"). Hilary wished to call the emperor's attention to "scripturis euangelicis"; C to call the public's attention to "EPISTOLIS EGYPTICIS", changing the singular petition to Constantius ("digneris audire") to a plural petition to readers ("dignemini audire"): "condescend to hear".

[3] It was generally known that the *Copies of Original Letters*, like the Grenville "Note", were a ministerial concoction; what C set out to demonstrate, perhaps with tongue in cheek, was that they were a ministerial *forgery*. A month later, 17 Mar, with equal solemnity, though briefly, the *M Post* in an essay evidently by C himself, would declare them not a ministerial but a French Republican hoax, which had taken in the Ministers themselves! Four years later, in an unpublished essay on Egypt, C would speak simply of "that inauspicious 'intercepted Correspondence,' and the eloquent and masterly Preface and Notes" as having "unfortunately spread and authorized" a misleading opinion of the economic insignificance of Egypt. BM Egerton MS 2800 f 121 (see below, App B, III 192).

[4] Tr: "sacred to Jove the gatherer of clouds". This may be C's own Latin translation of Homer's epithet for Zeus (*Iliad* 1.511, etc), "cloud-gathering".

authenticity of one part does not necessarily imply the authenticity of the other, we shall examine each part separately.

Any work, which claims to be held authentic, must have had witnesses, and competent witnesses; this is external evidence. Or it may be its own competent witness; this is called the internal evidence. Or its authenticity may be deduced from indirect testimony, such as the absence of all contradiction; or from the *absurdity* of supposing it to be a forgery, as in the case of the works of Virgil, Cicero, &c. which the Jesuit Hardouin contended to have been forged by Monks, in the dark ages.[5]

First, then, what is the external evidence of the first part of the Intercepted Correspondence? Who are the witnesses? are they competent witnesses? "It was intercepted at different periods by the Turkish and English ships of war."[6] So we are informed by an anonymous editor; and this is all the positive testimony which the public has received. Why were not the ships of war named? Why, in a work, the impression and importance of which have been the subject of so much Ministerial eloquence, were no affidavits given from the commanders of the vessels, both that they had intercepted certain letters, and that these were without interpolation the identical letters which they had intercepted? No single name has been given. We are told, that the letters speak for themselves; and that the originals lay[a] open for inspection.—Ridiculous! Who were to inspect them? What could we inspect? Letters. That they were originals or not originals, no inspection could prove but that of those acquainted with the hand-writing of the different correspondents. To have attempted at proofs, and to have brought forward *such* proofs as the result of the attempt, is a circumstance that justifies suspicion. But, it is said, their authenticity is proved from indirect testimony: they have not been contradicted in France. That they *will* not be contradicted, at least some of them, we have had no proof given us: and that they *have* not been contradicted proves nothing, until it be shewn by what means they *could* have been contradicted, even on the supposition that they were forged. Who was to contradict them? The persons to whom the letters were addressed? But the best answer to this is contained in the following extracts from the introduction to the second part—"We begin then with a bold assertion, it is, that with

[a] *EOT*: lie

[5] C is here in effect drawing upon his discussion of internal evidences of Christianity in LRR IV: *Lects 1795* (*CC*) 183ff. On Jean Hardouin see 183 n 1.

[6] *Copies of Original Letters* I (1798) i.

the exception of such packets as were on board the Généreux, and which might reach Paris by the way of Ancona, the Directory have not received a single original dispatch, nor the people of France a single original letter from the Army of the East, since the capture of Malta." "The uncontrollable dominion which we possess in the Mediterranean, and the annihilation of the French flag in that sea, have rendered what before was a matter of extreme difficulty, almost an impossibility. All the intercepted letters are full of complaints of the want of intelligence: none is received, and none is sent, unless to be taken before their eyes by our cruisers. Nay, so completely are the French in Egypt secluded from the world, that[a] we find them ignorant of the three events, which most concern them, the hostility of the Turks, the revolt of the Maltese, and the renewal of the war in Italy. Bonaparte himself is so sensible of the innumerable obstacles which oppose his communicating with France, that he has long since ceased to attempt it in the usual way. From the period of his defeat by Ibrahim Bey, he has ceased writing altogether, and has had recourse to the press." P[ages] 12, 13, of introduction to the second part.[7] How then were the persons in France to receive letters which might enable them to contradict the authenticity of the intercepted ones? How could they send to inquire? If Ministers wished the circumstance of these letters not having been contradicted in France, to have had any real weight with thinking men, the letters ought to have been deposited in Paris, not in London: and even then, it would remain a doubt whether a genuine letter had not been intercepted, and the hand-writing imitated.[8]

[a] *M Post*: that, events which [a printer's error]

[7] Ibid II (1799) xii–xiv (with omissions).

[8] Possibly the originals survive in some archive, but even without them there is no serious question but that the letters, given in French and in English translation, with a few facsimile bits in the second part, are in the main what they purport to be, letters written by French officers in Egypt intercepted by the Turkish and English fleets. The letters of Bonaparte have been duly accepted into the canon and are printed in the Official Correspondence (some had reached Paris in duplicate copies).

The French themselves granted the authenticity of the letters but found "un mot changé, une phrase intercallée, une incise ajoutée, un sens forcé", so that "le tableau se compose; et puis viennent les interprétations, les conférences de tel passage avec tel acte ou avec telle circonstance. On en tire les inductions qui plaisent, on fait une construction chimérique, on affirme des propositions controuvées, et puis c'est ainsi qu'on détrompe l'Europe, qu'on éclaire l'univers. Voilà...le véritable échafaudage de ce libelle." Thus E. T. Simon, for the Directory, which republished the first volume in the Year VII with Simon's counter-notes giving the English annotator insult for insult: *Correspondance de l'armée française en Égypte*...(Paris An VII [1799]) xxiv–xxv.

The last mode of proof, *ab extra*, still remains: the *argumentum ex absurdo*. They are authentic: for an absurdity is involved in the idea of their being otherwise. What absurdity? Was there no much-desired end to be answered from their forgery? Is the immaculate veracity of the persons concerned a self-evident truth? We appeal to any man possessed of calmness and common-sense! Let him read the introduction and notes to these letters (introduction and notes beyond all doubt authorised by the Ministers), and then let him declare, whether he can pronounce any *pious fraud*[9] too gross for men so fanatically distempered! For men, who, substituting their wishes for their knowledge, can describe the country of Egypt, as an accumulation of "nauseous and peculiar diseases, intolerable heats, pestilential winds, devouring myriads of venomous insects, and the stench and putrefaction of ten thousand stagnant pools;"[10] and yet afterwards allow it to be "a very fine country!"[11]

Some of our readers may recollect the pretended letter of Mons. de Barbaczy to the Archduke Charles, published in The Sun, Wednesday, Oct. 16, 1799. This was a manifest forgery, for the purpose of transferring to the Directory the horrible guilt of the assassination of the French Ambassadors;[12] and we have adduced it here, as an instance that *such forgeries have been, and for what they have been, and by whom they have been, either executed or patronized.*

If then fanaticism, as experience demonstrates, be at all times, and almost by an inevitable process, the parent of imposture, much more must it render the mind an easy *dupe* of imposture. Where is the impossibility that these letters had been forged by French Emigrants, or hired deserters, or traitors,—and purposely thrown in the way of capture? Were there no ends to be answered by the forgery? All correspondence with France having been cut off, was it not an excellent opportunity to represent Bonaparte as a *monster*, leagued with the Directory, to sacrifice 40,000 chosen men of France to a foreseen and miserable fate; and by this representation to make the people of France disgusted with all which had thrown glory and splendour on their Revolution, and consequently disgusted with the Revolution itself? To trace the possibility of this hypothesis step by step, would be no insurmountable difficulty, it might be accomplished with a

[9] In *Friend* (*CC*) I 37 (II 39), C expresses "an especial dislike to the expression, PIOUS FRAUDS".

[10] *Copies of Original Letters* I xix (var).

[11] Ibid III 142.

[12] Joseph Barbaczy was the commander of the troop of Austrian Hussars who waylaid and assassinated two of three French ambassadors to the Congress of Rastadt (see 24 Feb 1798 n 4, above) on 28 Apr 1799.

little ingenuity, but not without a large share of *fool-hardiness*. THE HABEAS CORPUS ACT IS SUSPENDED![13]

It appears to us, therefore, that the first part of the intercepted correspondence has deduced its authenticity from no species of external evidence. So far from having brought forward competent witnesses, it has brought forward no witnesses at all! So far from there being any absurdity in the assumption of the correspondence being a forgery, there are more hypotheses than one, which would render the mode of its being forged easily conceivable! And as to the indirect evidence arising from the authenticity not having been hitherto contradicted in France, we have shewn, that such contradiction was impossible; that those who appeal to this argument, have themselves given evidence to prove its impossibility; and that this appeal following an evidence so inconsistent, renders it probable, that the knowledge, that the authenticity *could not* be contradicted, was the encouragement to the forgery!

So much for the external evidence. But, perhaps, the internal evidence will make amends: "*penes me habeo fidem, exteriore non egeo*."[14] The letters speak *too plainly* for themselves, says the Editor: and we assent to his words, though not to his meaning, with an emphatic *Amen*! We must, however, defer our detailed investigation, and content ourselves for the present with a few cursory remarks. First then, we were struck with the very small number of allusions to particular persons, their fates and fortunes. The writers are reasoning and criticising on the expedition, praising the English, and heaping contempt and ridicule on their own exploits, when we should have expected them to have filled their letters with incidents of themselves, and their acquaintances. The No. 22 is in particular a great curiosity; and we shall conclude our remarks for the present, with paying it the tribute of our admiration. Speaking of the capture of Alexandria, in which he had been himself engaged, the writer informs his father and mother that "men, women, old, young, children at the breast, ALL are MASSACRED!"[15] Now the *truth* of this is far more than prob-

[13] It was the very real threat of jail without trial that compelled the press to censor itself. In 1803 C would welcome Addington's reinstatement of Habeas Corpus; see 20 Aug 1803 n 19, below.

[14] C is again quoting from St Hilary *Ad Constantium*, a few lines further on in Ch 8. Tr: "I have the faith within me, I need no external proof."

[15] *Copies of Original Letters* I 150. Other accounts indicate there were such deeds; the French, thinking the town theirs, found themselves fired upon from the houses and attacked. One cannot rule out, however, the possibility that the phrase "tous sont massacrés" may have been an editorial insertion such as Simon suspected here and there.

lematic (it contradicts not only the French, but the Turkish accounts); and that a French officer should thus speak of an affair in which he himself had acted, and in a letter to his father and mother—that a Frenchman should thus describe himself and his countrymen,—it is a mountain, and we have not faith enough to remove it! This same impartial and humane young officer indulges himself, p. 159, with a sneer on the abolition of the Slave Trade!!—The hand-writing and signature of this letter are undistinguishably similar to that of the preceding letter, which is signed *Boyer*. But some little incautious *contradictions* in the two letters had been discovered; and the ingenious editor found it convenient to suspect that these two letters could not have had the same author. But two men writing a hand undistinguishably similar in the same army—it is rather remarkable! But that these two men should be both called Boyer; nay, that is somewhat *too* remarkable! So the Editor left the difficulty unsolved. But since the publication of the two first parts it has been discovered, that there is an officer in the Egyptian army, named Royer; and doubtless, he it is to whom the second of these letters does by right belong! Royer and Boyer! Their hand-writing not to be distinguished from each other! Curious coincidence! Happy solution![16]

Our limits oblige us to defer our further remarks. But one circumstance in Bonaparte's Letter (p. 21. of the third part, the first edition), *must be* anticipated by us; and we shall conclude our strictures for the present, by pressing it on the attention of our Readers. Bonaparte is made to write these words: "Of all the chiefs which its inhabitants may rally under, there are none less to be apprehended by us than the Cheiks, who are all timorous, unacquainted with arms, and, *like all other Priests*, know how to inspire the people with fanaticism, without being fanatic themselves."[17] To this the Editor has annexed the following note—"Bonaparte's ignorance is inconceivable. He has been amusing himself for fifteen months with hunting out and destroying Arabs, Turks, and Copts: and yet he seems to know as little of their distinct policy as if he had never left home. Who ever heard before of Cheik Priests? A Cheik is an Arabian Chief, neither

[16] The allusion to the slave-trade (I 151, not 159) is hardly a sneer. For Boyer and Royer see I 147–8n, II ix n.

[17] An instance of what the *C Rev* XXV (May 1800) 449 complained of as significantly unfaithful translation. Here it served C's purpose to be inattentive to the French text (and to be ignorant of the fact that some sheiks were religious leaders). But "ne savent pas se battre" and "comme tous les prêtres", if translated "don't know how to fight" and "like a bunch of priests" or even "like all priests", would seem plausibly authentic expressions of Bonaparte's evaluation of the submissive Moslem officials.

timorous nor unacquainted with arms, as he has frequently found to his cost, &c." To all this we fully subscribe. A Cheik is an Arab Chief practised in arms from his youth, and no Priest, or connected with Priesthood. That Bonaparte, almost a year and a half in Egypt, employing himself with ambitious zeal, and all his well-known indefatigable sedulity, to make himself acquainted with the manners and policy of the country; that Bonaparte should be ignorant of this; that Bonaparte, near a year and a half in Egypt, and engaged in treaties with Cheiks; that he should make a blunder which no common reader of a book of travels ought to have made;—this is not only inconceivable, but morally impossible. READER! IN THE FOURTH EDITION OF THIS THIRD PART THE EDITOR HAS OMITTED HIS NOTE! *May he not have been made conscious, that he has betrayed his own friends!* and that in his exultation over the supposed ignorance of Bonaparte, he has excited the incredulity of his readers to a pitch that may lead to the detection of a very ignorant and very impudent forger?

PARLIAMENT. IV

PITT'S SPEECH OF 3 FEBRUARY[1]

4 February 1800, Tuesday. Not in *EOT* but identified through C's notes (*CN* I 651 and n), and by his claim in *CL* I 568 to have "reported that part of Pitt's which I have inclosed in crotchets" (in a marked copy, now lost), presumably the part his reporting notes cover. Reprinted in evening *Courier* of same date. In the

[1] Stuart's notice (27 Jan) of preparations for "copiousness and accuracy" of parliamentary reporting may mean only that he had lined up a team of four or five reporters; but among them C, his new mainstay, was to supervise the coverage, take his turn at the reporting, and supply afterwards an "Analysis or Skeleton of the Debate" (see 6 Feb). C had acquired a good deal of experience in 1796 in the scumming and clarifying of parliamentary harangues: see *Watchman* (*CC*) 56ff and 473 (Index: "parliamentary debates/speeches").

He went to the Commons 27 and 29 Jan for the debate that was put off till 3 Feb, when he "went at a quarter before 8" and "remained till 3" the next morning (*CL* I 568). The day and early evening were taken up by unreported business and the speeches of Dundas, Whitbread, Canning, and Erskine and perhaps others. One by one the reporters would have gone to the newspaper office to write out fair copy for the compositors and come back. Then Pitt spoke, for over two hours, and after the first hour or so C relieved the first reporter. He stayed to hear, but not report, Fox, and then at three, before the division and adjournment, C repaired to the office "& then sate writing, & correcting other men's writing till 8...". The Fox speech would have come in during that time, but I see no trace of C's attention to it, though his conclusion was: "I could make a better speech myself than any that I heard, excepting Pitt's & Fox's."

M Post the speech begins near the top of p 2 col 5; we pick it up in the middle of p 3 col 2, a passage corresponding to p 321 in Debrett's full-length (shorthand) report.[2]

C's notes taken while Pitt spoke are in Notebook 4, BM Add MS 47500 ff 49–42v, 18–13v, 41–37. Folios 49–45 are palimpsest. The transcription in *CN* I 651 differs considerably from mine given in footnotes here, and Kathleen Coburn and I differ in opinion as to what is actually legible; I therefore quote in this instance directly from the ms.

IF any one wished to contemplate the picture of French cruelty, he would ask, whether it was not the natural result of the French Revolution, and of those principles which had made as much misery in France as in the rest of the world? He alluded to the conduct of France towards America, which, he said, if any thing had been wanting, that completely changed the minds of those who had before entertained the least doubt; their conduct had been sordid in the highest degree, and formed a new instance of that spirit of Revolution, which was not confined to Europe alone. The only subject that remained to speak upon was, the expedition to Egypt; but first, he would advert[a][3] to the island of Malta, merely to shew there was no place too small to [b]elude the vigilance[c] of the all-searching eye of the French Revolution. The attack on Egypt, he observed, was made in the name of the French King, who had been murdered, and was pretended to be sanctioned by the Grand Seignior, whose dominions were invaded; that the assent of the Grand Seignior was withheld by the machinations of Russia; that they had abjured Christianity in favour of the Mussulman faith; and that their object was to attack the English possessions in the East Indies. At the very moment negotiations for peace were carrying on, they were accompanied by

[a] Unique in *M Post* [b–c] Unique in *M Post*

[2] On the first half of Pitt's speech, see 6 Feb. For an extensive and comparative account of C's parliamentary reporting, see Erdman (1960).

[3] "Unique in *M Post*" here designates salient words or passages not found in any other report of Pitt's speech (except, of course, in the verbatim reprint in *Courier* 4 Feb). For a full collation of all independent reports extant, see Erdman (1960). Pitt may have spoken 40,000 words on the occasion; the shorthand report (in Debrett, from a pamphlet published by John Wright) amounts to 25,000; the *M Post* has 5500; the *M Chron* 4200.

More than half of the 990 legible words in C's notes are confirmed as verbatim by the collation of other reports, and half the remainder are accounted for as simplifications. C's report stands out, both as capturing more of the memorable phrases of Pitt and as adorning his report with more of his own invention. Of the 28 salient words or phrases unique in C's account, among newspapers, 15 were probably C's creation, 10 are in C's notes as heard by him in some form, the other 3 are in Wright (as are 6 of the 10 in C's notes).

a revolutionary attack, according to the system of the French, by sending messengers of peace and freedom to the East, who were to recommend destruction to all Sovereigns except their good ally, Citizen Tippoo. They have been truly rewarded in their perfidy by having now [a]no other Sovereign on the throne of France, than a rank Citizen Tippoo.[b][4] The nature of the French system was nothing but an insatiable love of aggrandisement: that was its governing principle: it was the soul that animated it at its birth, and certainly would not desert it till its extinction: it had been invariably the same at every stage of the Revolution: it equally belonged to Brissot, Robespierre, Reubell, and Barras; but it belonged more than all to Bonaparte, in whom were united all their powers and all their crimes.—He described France, in her present situation, as bleeding at every pore,[5] and by her miseries, asking pardon of God and man for her enormities. With no means of enjoyment herself, she yet possessed gigantic powers to annoy and harrass her neighbours; the French Republic marched forth, the terror and dismay of the world, and made every nation the theatre of her crimes. But he trusted, while the people of this country could wield a sword, or procure the sinews of war, they would not cease to oppose them. He observed, that history would be inadequate to record such a black catalogue of crimes as characterized France at this time. He asked, whether it was possible the recent change of Government could have furnished any security against the common danger? Not one of the Republics which had been raised by France has continued long enough to deserve the character of stability. Against this revolutionary system what was the security offered? He could not better sum it up than in the words of the reporter (Boulay de la Meurthe)[6] when the new constitution was recommended to the French nation at the point of the bayonet.[7]—(He here read the extracts from the report.)

a–b Unique in *M Post*

[4] This witticism has no parallel in the other reports. They concur in quoting Pitt to the effect that Tippoo Sahib was a congenial ally for France, being "what Bonaparte was speedily to become at Paris, a Military Usurper". The *M Post* thus reverses the emphasis in calling Bonaparte a Tippoo; it may be supposed that if Pitt had done this, the other reports would hardly have reverted to the lamer remark. For details see Erdman (1960).

[5] See *Friend* (*CC*) I 109 and n 3. C probably had this reference to France (Europe) in mind; reference to a later domestic allusion by Fox is misleading.

[6] C's first reporting note (N 4 f 49) is almost illegible: "States [?it/in] not [. . .] at the [. . .] [?by] of private [?Mem. . ./Merits/Meurthe]." Antoine Boulay de la Meurthe (1761–1840), politician and writer who helped prepare the new constitution, was a member of the council of state.

[7] Pitt's point was that Boulay de la Meurthe's exposition of French in-

Such had been the evidence given by Bonaparte himself, against the competency of his predecessors, in whose service he had won those victories, which have procured him too easily the fame of unrivalled fortune! [a]Thank Heaven! that Fame was now eclipsed by the exploits of a General, superior to him in fortune as in talents; and the star of Bonaparte, "dims its ineffectual light,"[8] before the rising splendor of Suwarrow! Eclipsed in his military reputation, he has now commenced Statesman and Legislator; and has with a sudden violence and lucky temerity effected that change in the government of France, on the merits of which, and of his own character, he grounds the possibility of negotiation.[b][9]

But let us see what this change has been, let us pause and examine what is [a]its peculiar character, what is its probable stability, what are its promised fruits?[b] There has been a change indeed, but a change in the exterior forms rather than in [a]reality and principle.[b] The new Government has erected itself on the same contempt of public opinion as the former Governments. Like the former, it is a military despotism,[10] and differs chiefly in being more naked[c] and undisguised, its ensign of power is the sword, and not the sceptre.[11] But this despotism, which in the former Government had been shared among a few, is now concentered and united in one. [a]This one man invites us to negotiate for peace with him, and adduces his own character as an inducement.[b][12]

We will suppose for a moment, that this man were a stranger to us: that this man, who comprehends in his single person all the real power of France, Executive and Legislative; who is [a]the sole proposer of all laws to mock-legislators, of whom he was the sole creator;[b][13] who has all the civil and all the military forces at his immediate disposal, and all the officers of that great Empire, both civil and

[a–b] Unique in *M Post* [c] Unique in *M Post*

stability was not a private opinion but a public statement. Cf C's summary of 6 Feb: "Bonaparte...through... Boulay de Meurthe, 'tells us'...".

[8] Cf *Hamlet* I v 90.

[9] This entire paragraph, salient or otherwise, is unique in C's report; yet Pitt must have said something in praise of Suvorov, for Fox in his reply (Debrett x 347) quotes sarcastically a roughly similar passage.

[10] C's reporting note, N 4 f 48ᵛ: "in Now let us see what this change has been—its Quality—from its—[blank space] Change but not great—Contempt of in public opinion military Despotism".

[11] "Sword not Sceptre". C's note f 48ᵛ.

[12] "More than any Despot What in his character of promise?" C's note N 4 f 48.

[13] The concept of Bonaparte as sole creator of mock-legislators is not in C's notes or other reports; he may be its sole creator.

military, in his immediate patronage; that this man, invested with all the powers of all their Directors and Councils, all uncurtailed and unmodified, and this one man invested with them all; we will suppose for a moment, that this man were a stranger to us! [a]He invites us to negotiation,[14] and he offers his own character as the pledge; and he acts consistently in this offer.[b] For he is the sole governor of France, and on his character all depends. Before then we suspend our efforts; before we lay down those arms which have given us security, we may be allowed to ask, who this stranger is? But this man is no stranger to us: we know him; and what do we know of him? He tells us of his well-known pacific dispositions; and these proposals are, it seems, the second attempt on his part towards a general pacification.[15] Yet we find no proposals for a general peace; he adopts the same plan as his predecessors, and still aims at separate Treaties. He proposes to us to negotiate—we return [a]a cold answer,[b] and inform him that his proposals are not *likely to be* accepted by us, except in concert with all our Allies. Not discouraged, he makes his second application, and in this he endeavours to shift the ground of aggression; he defends the conduct of his predecessors, but still he makes no proposals for a general Peace. Yet we must per force give him credit for his pacific dispositions and undoubted good-will towards this country. These pacific dispositions and this good will, we may aptly illustrate by two anecdotes. [a]In the flush of victory,[b] when he had even now terminated the war with Austria, [a]he addressed his soldiers as the future[b] army of England, and [a]proclaimed to them, that yet more glorious laurels were reserved for them: they were to pluck them[b] on the banks of the Thames. At the same time he dispatched Monge and Berthier,[16] his friends and confidants, to the Directory;

a–b Unique in *M Post*

[14] This refrain seems to be C's own contribution (see the conclusions of the two preceding paragraphs); it pulls against the point Pitt seems alone to have emphasised: that Bonaparte "makes no proposals for a general Peace".

[15] "If he were a new name so invested &c—all this invested in one person—All as before uncurtailed only all in one unmodified before we lay down our security—We only ask who this stranger is—But we have heard of him and what do we know of him?—First we are told it is second attempt—but my [Honourable] has [stated] it—[in] I too". C's note N 4 ff 48–47v.

[16] Pitt refers to the proposed invasion of England in 1798. Bonaparte having been given command of the Army of England 26 Oct 1797, the embarkation was ordered for 28 Feb 1798. In a Cruikshank cartoon of 20 Feb 1798 (George vol VII, No 9172), *Intended Bonne Farte Raising a Southerly Wind*, Bonaparte, General Berthier, and Gaspard Monge, Comte de Péluse (1746–1818), are shown as in passage—the last as the first Frenchman ashore in England, because he had been

and these, in the person of their commander, addressed the Directory. "Citizens, we have humbled Austria: Britain remains. France and Britain are incompatible! [a]Now then for Britain!"[b][17] Such were his dispositions as a pacificator; what do we know of his fidelity to his country? The constitution of the third year he presented to his fellow citizens on the [a]point of the bayonet,[b] and took the oaths to it afterwards![18] On another occasion, in [a] speech to his soldiers, he exhorted them to swear fidelity to it by their banners [a]consecrated by victories,[b] and by the manes of the patriots who had died by their sides![19] Again on his return from Egypt, he renewed his oaths to this Constitution on the morning of that day, in which he destroyed it![20]

These are specimens of his fidelity to his adopted country; his fidelity to other powers, his fidelity as pacificator, remains to be exemplified. All the treaties which France has made since the Revolution have been all broken; and the name of Bonaparte is attached to far more of these treaties than the names of all the other Generals. His was the treaty with Sardinia; his the treaty with Genoa, which he followed by [a]merciless exactions;[b] his the treaty with Milan, which led the way to a contribution of 5,000,000 sterling;[21] and after this to a military execution; his was the treaty at Modena, to which State he first granted protection, then extorted a contribution, then insulted his new friends by the personal arrest of their Duke, and concluded by new plunders!—his too was the treaty with Rome;[22]

[a-b] Unique in *M Post*

minister of marine and reputed inventor of the giant raft supposed to spearhead the invasion. Berthier became Bonaparte's war secretary in 1800.

17 "No proposals for general Peace All for separate Treaties The former disposition illustrated by anecdotes recalled banks of the Thames—this not on mere authority Monge & Berthier Campo Formio War with Austria terminated—Britain & France now then for Britain". C's note N 4 f 47.

18 "What do know of him as a pacifi[cator] of his fidelity [first] to his country—1st day of the 3rd year presented the Con[stitution] by his army of Triumvi[rate]". C's note N 4 f 46v.

19 "Revolution which drove Lord M[almesbury] from Lisle procured by the adherence of the soldiers to him—His Speech to His Soldiers—Sworn on new Banners Patriots that have died——[?on]". C's note N 4 f 46.

20 "The morning before the Evening in which he destroyed this C[o]nst[itution]". C's note N 4 f 45v.

21 "In all the Treaties all broken Bonaparte's name with most—his Sardinia—in Lom[bardy] in [terms] of property [an]d Peace this on Milan from Milan[ese] Contribution of 5 Million [sterling]". C's note N 4 f 45v.

22 "military execution at Genoa [nevertheless] at Modena First protection promised then exaction—then personal arrest of the Duke—then new Plunders—at Rome—". C's note N 4 f 45.

a treaty accompanied and followed by every degrading act of fraud, perfidy, and inhumanity![23] His, finally, was the treaty with Venice, which he purported to have delivered from Austria, which he revolutionised, defrauded, ransacked, and then transferred it, as a thing of barter, to that very Austria from whom he had made it his boast to have delivered it.—These exploits and proofs of his fidelity as a pacificator were followed by his expedition to Egypt, of which expedition he was at once the planner, the executor, and the deserter;[24] and from which he has [a]skulked away, in order to play a new part,[b] to rest his pretentions to a negotiation on the merits of his own character, and to address the kings of Europe in the high tones of official equality. (Here some pointed quotations from the Intercepted Correspondence were introduced, relative to the treaty which Kleber was to enter into with the Grand Vizier, and as pointedly applied to the faith with which he would enter into negotiations with England.)[25] But it has been said that Bonaparte has an interest in *these* negotiations, which ensures his fidelity. What interest? Not in Peace; at least, not in the preservation of Peace. He has doubtless an interest in drawing England away from her allies, in palsying Russia, [a]in amusing all, if so he may recruit the revolutionary energies[b] of France; he has precisely that interest, which it is both our interest and [a]most awful duty[b] to oppose and prevent.[26] War is the only possible means of his permanence; his hold upon France is on the sword. He is connected neither with the soil of France nor the hearts of Frenchmen. A foreigner, a fugitive and a usurper, alike detested by the Republicans and the Royalists; he appeals to his fortune, that is, to his soldiers and his sword. He cannot afford to let his military fame die away; with no end but ambition, no passion but a criminal glory, he must [a]groan to regain[b] his laurels, which our gallant countrymen had [a]plucked from his brow,[b] before the walls of St. Acre; and probably a treaty is desirable to him, as furnishing an opportunity of landing an army in Ireland, and

a–b Unique in *M Post*

23 Here C is going at the rate of about 30 words to a whole page in Debrett.

24 "The proceeding to Venice to deliver them from Austria revolutionized purchased its all by—& all ransacked—then transferred to Austria—This followed by Egypt—the planner Executer, & Deserter—". C's note N 4 f 44^{v}.

25 "to speak on an Equality with the Kings of Europe—Quot. from Intercepted Letter. applied to England". C's note N 4 f 44.

26 "B's interest in Negotiation—not in Peace or its Preservation in drawing England away, in palsying Russia—recruit France—he has precisely that Interest which commands us to not to lend ourselves to it—". C's note N 4 ff 44–43^{v}.

there to keep the treaty with his wonted good faith, [a]at the head[b] of an army.[27]

I have ever understood, that of all Governments, a military despotism was in its nature the least stable. No Government can long stand that is not built on the public opinion. [a]The follies and enormities[b] of the French Revolution have fixed and made firm on this public opinion all the other Governments of Europe. [a]Men have been taught to feel blessings, and perceive advantages, by the fearful contrast.[b] The new constitution is stamped with every character of instability. What then is the inference I draw? In no case to treat with Bonaparte? By no means.[28] The concerns of nations, and above all, those of peace and war, are not to be reasoned upon by extremes. But where all presumption is against a man, we ought to wait for new evidence in his favour: where all the facts hitherto tend to suspicion or grievance, we are entitled, we are compelled, to demand the evidence of new facts, and not to relax in our exertions till they have been afforded to us. There are few facts, I acknowledge, that would be of sufficient importance to weigh against our former experience; but every thing depends on degree and comparison. If different maxims be assumed and acted upon in France; if the effects of the arms of the allies should delude our present well-grounded expectations; if the hopes of substituting the antient Government should become less; in short, if the risk decrease,[c][29] and the success diminish; then I promise for myself and my colleagues, that we shall not remain uninfluenced, and shall regulate our advice to our Sovereign accordingly.[30]

[a–b] Unique in *M Post* [c] Unique in *M Post*

27 "His Permanence—his Hold upon France is on the Sword—how connected with the Soil—Hearts of France —Stranger, Usurper, opposite to Republicans, Royalists—he appeals to his Fortune—i.e. Soldiers & Sword—Can he afford to let his military fame die away—Can he hope &c &c Aboukir & Smith Insurrection of Ireland". C's note N 4 ff 43v–42v.

28 "I have heard that military Despotism least stable—if any as—applied No Government can stand that does not opinion—Revolution has made all Govern. stand on opinion—French G. an exception—in May last past the greatest violence to opinion—Out of all others Bonaparte might If opinion be new it stamped with Instability. What then is the inference I draw—In no case treat with B. By no means!—". C's note N 4 ff 18–17.

29 The "increase" in the notebook was correct: "decrease" is a mistake.

30 "We have a right to Fact when all Presumption is against him—For Fact ~~suff~~ would be of power sufficient every thing depends on Degree & Comparison. If different maxims be assum'd—& his Interest appear differ. if the Effects of the Armies of the Allies, if the Hope of substitut[ing] less—if the risk increase, & success diminish—these for myself & colleagues have a due weight to regulate our advice to Sovereign—". C's notes N 4 ff 17–16.

It has been said, what hope can you entertain that Monarchy can be forced on the French nation? I never thought that it could be *forced* on France; I never wished it—I never hoped it! But I do hope, that by the efforts of the Combined Armies, the pressure of the military may be so far removed or lightened, as to allow the nation a vent for their real wishes. The experiment ought to be made, whether or no France really prefers to the antient line of Princes an anomalous Government, of which my Honourable Friend has justly observed, that it has all of monarchy, but its legitimacy, stability, and limitation.[31] The Western Provinces have decided, and I solemnly assure the House, wholly without the instigation of this country. I can venture to state, that the present warfare in those provinces is the spontaneous and violent effect of their own uncontroulable ardour in opposition to the wishes of this Country, who wishes to have husbanded and reserved their energies to a more certain opportunity. Yet, the condition of these Royalists forms, I admit, of itself, an objection to a negotiation.[32]

Here Mr. Pitt animadverted on the argument of Mr. Erskine against the possibility of the restoration of Monarchy from the existing state of property in France. This fear of the transfer of property did not prevent the Revolution, and by what process is it to prevent therefore a Counter-revolution? The Learned Gentleman had said, that his attachment to the Constitution of his country rose from the state of the 3 per Cents. in this country. He gave the Learned Gentleman credit for nobler motives, even though the 3 per Cents. should continue to rise as much as they had risen in the last three years, in consequence of the measures which the Learned Gentleman had uniformly opposed. In France, indeed, there was no parallel for these 3 per Cents. In France, they had performed an operation on

[31] George Canning, who had spoken just before Erskine and had made this point.

[32] "But there is nothing all goes to the counting combined arms every hope that the Contest will make us comparatively worse What is your Hope from Change? From Monarchy—against the Nation—I never thought it, I never hoped it, I never wished—but I did hope, that the people might be allowed to have a vent hole—that experiment we ought to make/ all of monarchy not legitimacy, stability and limitation—appeal to the Western Provinces—not by the instigation of this Country—I can venture to state that it is the spontaneous & violent effect in opposition to the wishes of this Country—their Condition alone an objection to Negociation—But what time is necessary?—This [?our/one] Circumstance/we are not to be discouraged too, nor persist in it too long—". C's notes N 4 ff 15^v–14. Here C ceased note-taking for a moment and wrote (f 14): "Stiff thin Cutting Pencil", and then he pencilled his contempt for Pitt's views: "That a man can talk of Bourbon who has Bonaparte!"

their national debt, which they named Republicanising: they struck off at once two-thirds of it, and of the remaining third they had forgotten to pay the interest. He had been informed that the stocks in France were 17 per Cent. and he confessed, that he felt a degree of jealousy at the account.[33] But on a further inquiry he discovered that it was 17 for the whole hundred—a depreciation of 83![34] "France is so exhausted, that nothing but the torture applied by revolutionary tyranny can [a]draw an effective revenue[b] from her;[35] and while that revolutionary tyranny exists, I see no possibility of such a peace, as would justify a liberal intercourse. Therefore, as a lover of peace, I [a]press forward[b] to a system which may secure[c] to us a real and solid peace![36]—As a lover of peace, I will not sacrifice the hopes of that solid peace to vain attempts at a peace which would be more dangerous than war. We treated before, because the old and established modes of finance in this country were no longer competent to struggle with the convulsive grasp of revolutionary revenue. It was necessary, therefore, that an appeal should be made to the people, and in order to this appeal, it was important that the people should receive an absolute proof of the necessity of the war. Were we then insincere?[37] No; in the then existing circumstances a peace, though dangerous, appeared less dangerous than a war carried on by the regular means. We therefore wished a peace, or a war the necessity of which had been rendered plain and palpable to the people at home.—If we had succeeded in the treaty, we should have chosen the

[a–b] Unique in *M Post* [c] Unique in *M Post*

[33] "Is it nothing whether a System shall be sanctified by the Transfer of Property? Answer to E[rskine]'s—That which did not prevent the Rev. from taking place—What is the value of Property now? Therefore cheaply repurchased. It is therefore superficial rallying & complaint in E's 3 per cents —If they should rise as much as in the 3 last years No parallel in France—they perform an op. on Debt, republicanized. 2/3 struck—17 per cent.—". C's notes N 4 ff 13[v], 41–40[v].

[34] Pitt's argument gets lost here. See Debrett x 341; and see Comte Mollien *Memoires d'un ministre du trésor public 1780–1815* (Paris 1898) I 218.

[35] Here C omits the further qualifications of France's formidability that were in his notes (N 4 f 40).

[36] "France is so exhausted that never any thing but the Torture to be applied by revolutionary means/ Suppose the House of Bourbon restor'd—enough to do to rekin[dle] exhausted F. cant be formidable—and rev. power with-[out] rev. Leader not form[idable]—against such a Confederacy With that rev. power/ I see no possibility of that Peace which justifies liberal interest & on that ground as Lover of Peace I look at that System which ensures solid Peace. As a Lover of Peace I will not sacrifice its peace". C's notes N 4 ff 40[v]–39[v].

[37] "We treated before because the vast means of France had exhausted our regular means—therefore appeal to the People—& Negotiations at Lisle as proof—/ Were we then insincere?" C's notes N 4 f 39.

least of two evils; and I did, therefore, think a negotiation preferable to a war conducted, as without the negotiation, it must have been conducted. Even if peace had been made it could not have been durable.[38] By what process of argument, then, can our negotiations at that time be adduced in favour of acceding to negotiations at present, now that all the former inducements have been removed, and all the former dangers remain? We are now more likely to gain by war than peace, and every month of war, by exhausting the resources of the Republic, draws us nearer to [a]that solid and durable peace!—that peace of safety, confidence, and friendship, which alone deserves the efforts of the wise, or the wishes of the good![b][39]

PARLIAMENT. V

ANALYSIS OR SKELETON OF THE DEBATE IN THE HOUSE OF COMMONS, MONDAY, FEBRUARY 3, 1800[1]

6 February 1800, Thursday; so entitled, except "Parliament. V". *EOT* I 285–92, among SC's certain attributions. This was a journalistic novelty, and C was evidently pleased to keep a signed clipping.

MINISTERIAL ARGUMENTS

France was the original and unprovoked aggressor in the war. This is evinced, 1. by the opening of the Scheldt; 2. by the decree which allowed the French armies to pursue their enemies into neutral countries; 3. by the decree of the 19th of November 1792,

ARGUMENTS OF THE OPPOSITION

It is on the whole more probable, that this country was the aggressor; and out of all doubt, that Austria and Prussia were. Concerts of different kinds had been entered into, not indeed to dismember France, but most certainly to interfere by means of

[a–b] Unique in *M Post*

[38] "I know nothing that would justify being [in]sincere—but on the principle of combination & comparison—danger of Peace against War. I did believe that a Neg. preferable to War to be conducted as without Neg. it must have been—I found that ~~what~~ even if Peace had been made, it could not have been durable." C's notes N 4 ff 38v–38.

[39] "Will this operate as motive to any men, now all the Inducements are gone—Every month by which we exhaust, draws us nearer—We are now more likely to gain by War than Peace—but we are at liberty to decide differently." C's notes N 4 ff 38–37. Observe that C supplies a much stronger conclusion than his notes warrant. Debrett (x 346) has a conclusion that is longer but as lame as that in C's notes, with no stress on peace at all.

[1] For C's verse epigram on 5 Feb see App D, below.

offering assistance to all nations against their Governments; and, lastly, by the decree of the 15th of December, authorising the Generals to impose a Republican Constitution on all countries, into which they should enter.—*Dundas, Canning,*[2] *and Mr. Pitt, at great length.*

great armies in her internal Government. Austria and Prussia declared themselves ready to attack France, and force the French people to restore their antient line of Kings, as soon as the other Princes shall agree to co-operate with them. The decree of the 19th of November was a wild and insane act against all nations, not against England in particular; and it was explained away by Chauvelin.[3] If this explanation was not satisfactory, we should have told him so, and demanded another; but we dismissed him, which dismissal, by the treaty of commerce, was a declaration of war. But what avail these recriminations? Our present concern is, not how we got into the war, but how we are to get out of it.—*Erskine and Fox.*[4]

England was not the aggressor. She sent away Chauvelin, it is true; but Chauvelin was the accredited Minister of Louis the Sixteenth, and of course his credentials fell away on the murder of that Monarch.—That England did not wish to interfere in the internal affairs of France is proved by a document sent

The document is an admirable paper, well composed, and of the truest principles. Pity that Ministers *acted* in direct contradiction to it; pity, that instead of being sent to our Minister at Petersburgh, to be heard of now for the first time, it had not been sent openly to Paris. The document proves nothing, or only proves

2 George Canning (1770–1827), one of the twelve commissioners for India since 1799; a confidant of Pitt, though not in the Cabinet. He had been under-secretary for foreign affairs, 1796–9, and a main contributor to the *Anti-Jacobin* in 1797–8.

3 François Bernard, Marquis de Chauvelin (1766–1832), London representative of the National Convention of France, was told by Grenville on 29 Nov 1792 that the Convention's decree of 19 Nov, offering fraternity and assistance to all peoples, would have to be revoked.

4 Fox, returning to Parliament in this crisis, had delivered a "long, animated and masterly speech" (*A Reg* 1800, History 98–9) insisting on the people's desire for peace.

from His Majesty's Ministers to our Minister at Petersburgh, implying the wish of Ministers to prevent all such interference, provided France would bind herself to refrain from all aggressions and conquests.—*Pitt.*

that the Ministers acted against their better knowledge.—Chauvelin received new credentials; our refusal to accept of them was in itself an act of aggression, a direct interference in the justice or injustice of the existing Government in France.—*Fox.*

The Republican Government of France from the commencement of the Revolution had been oppressive, perfidious, ambitious, breakers of treaties, &c. &c.

The crimes and follies of the French Republic are admitted; but it is contended, that they are no greater than those of the Partitioners of Poland; that all the acts and schemes of the Republic have been but imitations of the acts and schemes of the Bourbon family; that the Bourbons, unmenaced, unalarmed, unagitated by revolutionary enthusiasm, had been oppressive, perfidious, ambitious, and, above all, breakers of treaties. Yet who ever refused to conclude a treaty of peace with them?—*Whitbread*[5] *and Fox.*

France has been engaged in war with every established Government but two; and even these two had been obliged to withdraw their Ambassadors from Paris. She has been at war with Austria, the Empire, Prussia, Spain, Great Britain, Genoa, Modena, Sardinia, Venice, Rome, Naples, Tuscany, Russia, and the Porte. These are incontestable facts; and can they have been the effect of accident?

Every established government in Europe, but two, has been engaged in war with France. Can this be the effect of accident? No! of mutual folly; and, above all, of the intrigues of Ministers. What had France done to Russia?

[5] Samuel Whitbread (1758–1815), brewer, Foxite Whig, MP for Bedfordshire since 1790, a strong advocate of peace even in May 1803.

We cannot expect that France will keep any treaty. She has broken almost every treaty which she ever made.—*Dundas, Canning, Pitt.*

What government observes treaties longer than its interest induces, or its weakness compels it? France has observed her treaty with Prussia. Why so? Because it is her interest. Our security for her observation of treaties is as great as it ever was in the time of the French Monarchy, and even greater, because our commerce and navy are greater.—*Whitbread, Erskine, Fox.*

Bonaparte, on whose character and stability the security of the treaty must depend, is a sanguinary monster, a hypocrite, a Mahometan,[6] &c. &c. &c. Above all, his name is attached to almost all the treaties which France has made; and all which he made he has broken.—*Dundas, Canning, Pitt.*

Bonaparte!! Suwarrow!! We must not be too minute in examining the personal characters of men, lest our Allies and their Generals should come off still worse than our enemies. The expedition to Egypt, and the designs on India, originated in the old Monarchy; and Mr. Whitbread confuted the broad assertion, that Bonaparte had never observed any treaty which he made: it has never been pretended that the preliminaries of Leoben were broken,[7] or in the smallest degree infringed; the punishment of the Cisalpine Republic was the act of the Executive Directory; the armistice was not broken; and as to the treaty of Campo Formio, that

[6] In Cairo in 1798 Bonaparte made an "easy adaptation to the African mind and manners"; he permitted his orthodoxy to be "proclaimed from the minarets of every mosque", in return for an order of allegiance; how far he went "in his personal behaviour towards professing Mohammedanism it is hardly fair to judge from Parisian gossip and English caricatures". J. M. Thompson *Napoleon Bonaparte* (Oxford 1953) 119–20.

[7] A fairly generous treaty with Austria, which Bonaparte signed at Leoben 18 Apr 1797.

could not be broken by Bonaparte; for at the time of the breach of it, he was not in France, nor had been from almost the time of his having made it.[8] Besides, it is false, that the observation of any treaty which Bonaparte may conclude as First Consul depends on his stability. What treaty has been broken by any Government in France, because it was entered into by its predecessors? What Government has denied the legal power of its predecessors, or the bindingness of their agreements with foreign countries?—*Fox and Whitbread.*

Bonaparte himself, through his organ, Boulay de Meurthe, "tells us," that all the preceding Governments were incompetent to preserve the relations of peace and amity.

Now there exist no better reasons for his competency, than for that of his predecessors. Can we have better proof of the unfitness of a negotiation?

Bonaparte himself, as Chief Consul, tells us officially that the Governments of France were at all times competent. The report of Boulay de Meurthe was the report of a party-man in the struggle of party; and the French might, with equal justice, adduce against Ministers an indiscreet speech in the House of Commons as an act of Government.

Ministers negotiated at Lisle, because it was necessary to give the people a palpable proof of the unavoidableness of the war, in order to gain their concurrence to a new mode of finance. That[a] cause no longer exists; why then should we negotiate?—*Mr. Pitt.*

The repeated offer of the French proves, that war *is* avoidable. We have tenfold greater reason for negotiation now than for that at Lisle. Then the French were insolent with victory; now, neither party have much to boast of. And surely, the people will require as strong

[a] *M Post*: Their [corrected in *EOT*]

[8] On the treaty of Campo Formio see above, 24 Feb 1798 n 4.

reasons for the continuance, as they were justified in requiring for the commencement, of this new mode of finance.—*Mr. Fox.*

Even if we should make a peace, such is the state of principles in France, that it must be a narrow and jealous peace; a peace that will admit of no liberal or confidential intercourse. A peace would be as expensive as war. Suppose at the present moment a treaty of peace was to be signed, would you wish His Majesty to disband his troops, or dismantle his fleets? Prussia has at this instant a very large army in the field, for the purpose of protecting a line of demarcation; we have also a line of demarcation to protect. The same forces we have now on foot would be equally necessary in the midst of peace. We must be equally guarded at all points, both for the protection of possessions at home and abroad. We must be prepared with troops for the defence of our colonial possessions, and we must keep our fleets in pay for the same purposes.—*Dundas and Pitt.*

A peace would not be as expensive as war. We should be burthened with no subsidies, no Chouannerie, no continental expeditions.—Prussia has a very large army in the field; yet Prussia finds peace far less expensive than war! Besides, is there no other argument against war, but that of expense? Are the crimes, massacres, and miseries of mankind nothing?

We have strong hopes, that in the next campaign we may complete the successes of the last. Let Gentlemen consider what was the situation of Europe, and of Italy in particular, previous to the last campaign.—*Dundas and Canning.*

Let Gentlemen consider what was the situation of Europe, &c. previous to the last campaign. What has been may be again. The reverses of the French were owing, in great measure, to the misconduct and ignorance of the Directory. Military misconduct and ignorance will scarcely be attributed to Bonaparte. But jealousies and inherent differences of final end are attributable to us and our Allies; and the evil consequences which have accrued from them may accrue again. It is shocking to build the rejection of proposals for peace on a presumptuous confidence in victory.—*Whitbread and Erskine*.

We have now great hopes of restoring Monarchy, in consequence of the successes of our Allies, and the assistance we shall be enabled to lend the Chouans. The argument adduced by Mr. Erskine against the possibility of a counter-revolution, from the great transfers of property which it would occasion, is ungrounded; for how can that prevent a counter-revolution, which did not prevent the Revolution?—*Pitt*.

The successes of the Allies and Chouannerie have hitherto produced, and given energy to Jacobinism. France has appeared favourable to moderate principles at home exactly in proportion as she has been secure or victorious abroad. Mr. Erskine's argument[9] is irrefragable. Property is now more divided than it was before the Revolution: and if the transfers of property which followed in consequence of the Revolution had been foreseen or feared, the Revolution itself *could not* have taken place. Now they are foreseen, and a Counter-Revolution is, in consequence, in the highest degree improbable.—*Fox*.

The experiment is worth making. If we are beaten and frustrated, then we can make peace with Bonaparte.—*Pitt*.

It is not clear that the substitution of Louis XVIII. for Bonaparte is an experiment worth making. Let us remember too, that though *one* can make war, there must be *two* to make peace. If we should be beaten and frustrated, we shall wish very

[9] C as well as Erskine had been reiterating this argument.

naturally to make peace with Bonaparte; but is it quite so natural that Bonaparte will wish to make peace with us? What is this declaration of Ministers less than this—we will have no peace without Monarchy in France, except in consequence of our defeats—that is—we will have no Peace with the Republic, but a disgraceful peace!—*Fox*.

PARLIAMENT. VI

THE SENSATION CREATED BY FOX

6 February 1800, Thursday. *EOT* II 367–71; among SC's probable attributions, confirmed by strong internal evidence.

THE sensation created[a] in the public mind by the debate on Monday has been as great as the importance of the occasion, [b]and circumstances of novelty accompanying the occasion,[c] had led us to expect.[1] The result of that debate does not, we trust, consist in the state of the votes in that Assembly in which it was held. The public will review the arguments, and their suffrages are alone of ultimate importance.

They will perceive by the speech of the Minister, that war is to be continued with the French Republic, till we have overthrown it, or till it has baffled and disgraced us. An awful sentence! But by what arguments has it been supported? The French have broken treaties; we therefore can make no treaties with the French. But did not all our Allies, at the commencement of the war, enter into solemn treaties not to lay down arms but by mutual consent? And did they not all break this treaty? What is the whole history of modern Europe, but a succession of wars, originating in broken treaties? It is absurd to apply that against a treaty of peace with one country, which does not apply against even a treaty of alliance with all other countries; and yet, as Mr. Fox well observed, the moral character of our friends and fellow-labourers is assuredly of more importance to us than that of those whom we wish only not to be our enemies.

[a] *EOT*: excited [b–c] *EOT* omits

[1] The rumoured novelty was Fox's return from retirement.

Let any man mention any act of folly, treachery, or oppression in the French Republic, and we pledge ourselves to find a *fellow* to it in our own allies, or in the history of the line of Princes, upon the restoration of whom an honourable peace is now made to depend. To us the turn of the debate on Monday is matter of hope and exultation. The harangues of the Ministers were absolute confessions of weakness. Long and tedious details of French aggressions, which, if they had been as fair and accurate as they were false and partial, would still prove nothing; violent personalities on Bonaparte, and as violent panegyrics on the superior science, talents, and humanity of the conqueror of Warsaw and Ismael;[a][2] and the old delusive calculations about French resources, calculations always accompanied by prophecies, which prophecies have been always, even to a laughable degree, falsified: these formed the substance and contents of the Ministerial orations.

More than one half of Mr. Pitt's speech was consumed in the old re-repeated tale of the origin of the war. This can be nothing more than an appeal to passion. For let us suppose for a moment, that we and not the French were the aggressors, the unprovoked aggressors; that they were innocent, and we guilty—yet how would this affect the subject of peace? Is any man so contemptibly ignorant of the rules and first foundations of State morality, as to affirm that because our Ministers had entered into a war knavishly, that therefore the people were bound in honour or honesty to conclude a peace ruinously? The interest of nations, the true interest, is and ought to be the sole guide in national concerns; and all besides is puerile declamation, only serviceable as covering a defeat, and preventing the appearance of an absolute rout, such as would have been implied in silence. What two nations were ever at war, and did not obstinately charge the aggression, each on the other? Has not this been matter of course since the time that the introduction of the Christian Religion has made the Governors of mankind afraid to state conquest or glory as their motives? And to adduce this as a political reason against the propriety of concluding a peace, or even of entering on a negotiation! This, the truth or falsehood of which is absolutely indifferent to the great question! O shame! shame!—Are the principles of French Government dangerous, and such as are alluring enough to be susceptible of propagation? Yes! says Mr. Dundas!

[a] *EOT*: Ismail

[2] C never ceased deploring association with Suvorov, scourge of Warsaw and Ismail.

for though all the Rights of Election are removed, and though the Legislative and Executive [a]of France[b] is the farthest possible removed even from the forms of popular freedom, still the Municipalities remain the same as in the time of Robespierre! Had the Kings of Europe refused to treat with the Protectorate of England, which they were never mad enough to do; had the Kings of Europe refused to treat with *our* great usurper and regicide, Cromwell, they might, on Mr. Dundas's argument, have *refused* likewise to *treat* with the country after the Restoration. For though the Government and the Governors were all changed, still the country was a regicide Republic; for it had its old vestries, and the very same modes of electing its constables and churchwardens!

Mr. Pitt railed most bitterly at the character of Bonaparte, and charged all the treaties that were broken to him, upon no other ground, for the greater part, than that he was instrumental in making them! But the truth is, Mr. Pitt knows Bonaparte to be sincere, and, therefore, will not negotiate; because that negotiation would lead to a peace, which peace would baffle that idle hope of restoring the French Monarchy, which, spite of the document sent to Petersburgh,[3] is and has been the real object of Ministers, both in beginning and continuing the war. If Mr. Pitt believed Bonaparte really insincere, we venture to affirm, that he would have accepted his proposals; for according to his own confessions he must have known, that the result of them would have been to have united all parties, and to have facilitated his own schemes of extra-regular finance.—Mr. Pitt built up his periods, as usual, in all the stately order of rhetorical architecture; but they fell away at once before that true eloquence of common-sense and natural feeling which sanctifies, and renders human, the genius of Mr. Fox.[4] Like some good genius, he approached in indignation to the spell-built palace of the state-magician, and at the first touch of his wand, it sunk into a ruinous and sordid hovel, tumbling in upon the head of the wizard that had reared[c] it.[5]

[a–b] *EOT* omits [c] *EOT*: *reared*

[3] Pitt had now disclosed that in 1792 he had instructed the British Ambassador at St Petersburg to ask Russia to mediate a general peace. Fox: unfortunate that "this very commendable paper...was never communicated to the French; never acted upon, never known to the world until this day" (Debrett x 352).

[4] Here C reaches the zenith of his enthusiasm for the humanness of Fox, the sincerity of Bonaparte—and of his contempt for Pitt despite the stately order of his rhetorical architecture, some of which C himself had shored up. Cf *CL* I 568: "Pitt & Fox completely answered my pre-formed Ideas of them."

[5] Though a "stately" dome that does not melt away like Catherine's

[6 February 1800, Thursday]

Observations on the Intercepted Correspondence—To-morrow.

[7 February 1800, Friday]

The further Remarks on the intercepted Corrsepondence are excluded this day by the arrival of the Paris Journals.

[8 February 1800, Saturday]

Remarks on the Intercepted Correspondence shall positively appear on Monday.

[10 February 1800, Monday]

The press of temporary matter again excludes many favours.[1]

PARLIAMENT. VII

SHERIDAN'S SPEECH OF 10 FEBRUARY[1]

11 February 1800, Tuesday. Not in *EOT*; not directly alluded to in any letters; only discovered as C's when Kathleen Coburn transcribed Notebook 10 for *CN* I 652. Reprinted in evening *Courier* of same date.

C's notes taken while Sheridan spoke are in Notebook 10, BM Add Ms 47507 ff 2–11. The transcription given in footnotes below differs somewhat from that in *CN*.[2]

MR. Sheridan rose to reply.—"I shall trouble the House but for a very few minutes, and chiefly for the purpose of noticing two allusions which have been made to me, one from a Gentleman opposite to me, the other from my Honourable Friend here by my side (Mr. Taylor).[3] The latter, in that very facetious manner, which

ice palace, it is not, like the Khan's, worthy of rebuilding by the poetic genius. See Carl Woodring "Coleridge and the Khan" *Essays in Criticism* IX (1959) 361–8.

[1] For the continuation of the "Intercepted Correspondence" see 17 Feb, below.

[1] This was the first day of major debate after 3 Feb; C "attended...from 10 in the Morning to 4 o/clock the next morning" (*CL* I 569)—which must include three hours in the newspaper office, since the House adjourned at one. C's notes cover only Sheridan's brief concluding remarks, nor do any other reported speeches, including Sheridan's main speech moving for an inquiry into the failure of the Netherlands Expedition, reveal any Coleridgian flashes.

[2] No full report exists of this speech, but C's notes seem to have been verbatim, if selective. Nearly all the words in at least the first half of his notes appear also in *M Chron* (source for Debrett x 457–60 and the collected *Speeches of Sheridan*, 1842, III) and nearly all are used in *M Post*, where 1000 words represent an amplification of 336 words of notes, a tripling. The whole centre of the speech was omitted, probably from lack of space at the very end of the day's reports. For details see Erdman (1960).

[3] Michael Angelo Taylor (1757–1834) had assisted Sheridan in the impeachment of Warren Hastings. Once a Pittite, Taylor joined Fox after the establishment of the French Republic.

is peculiar to himself, has arraigned me of softening truth down into falsehood; or, that I may use his own words, of being *meally-mouthed*.[4] He believes himself to have caught me tripping in a lie of candour,[5] for which, he hopes, I shall atone in my reply. Meally-mouthedness, and inaccuracies from excess of candour, are faults which have seldom been laid to my charge. And still more grievously has my Hon. Friend mistaken me, in his statement that I had no desire of removing His Majesty's Ministers. Could any arguments of mine produce this effect, could I flatter myself that any powers vested in me [were] adequate to a purpose so devoutly to be wished, I should feel myself roused to exertion, even without the consolatory argument of the change of places.[6] I admitted, indeed, that I saw no use in holding forth to our allies the influence, which Ministers convicted of incapacity would still retain over the House and the people;[7] for I professed myself convinced, that their conviction would not produce their removal. My Hon. Friend is of a different opinion. He believes, that were the people persuaded that the failure of the expedition was attributable to Ministers, these Ministers would be instantly changed. I am to infer, therefore, from this opinion of my Hon. Friend, that the people have not yet found any similar fault; that they have not yet found in His Majesty's Ministers any rashness in planning, incapacity in executing, or pride and stubbornness in persevering. If this be indeed true, if they have been found delinquent in this one instance alone, surely to remove them for one error would be a little hard.[8] My Honourable Friend is in an unfortunate case. He does not agree with the Ministers, so he cannot go over to them; and if they were removed he does not agree with me, so I am afraid, I could not carry him over: he must of course stop half way, and I can conceive no possible place for him, except the

[4] "For a very few minutes—we have allusions one from opposite Gent honour[able] friend in a very facetious manner arraigned *Mealy* mouthed". C's reporting notes N 10 f 2.

[5] The *M Chron* makes it "a line of candour" and garbles the whole passage. "Softening truth down into falsehood" may be C's own wording, but it conveys the general sense. Reporters notoriously failed to capture Sheridan's darting mirth; C does better in this respect than any of the others.

[6] "tripping in a lie of candour atone for in reply mouthed[ness] that I no desire of Maj. Ministers could any arguments of Mine [blank space] Even without the consolatory argument." C's notes N 10 ff 2^{v}–3.

[7] "Saw no use in holding forth to allies the influence of Ministers.—" C's notes N 10 f 3.

[8] "I am to infer from my honourable friend that the People have yet found—if in one instance ~~only~~ surely, a little hard a loud laugh—". C's notes N 10 ff 3–3^{v}. Other reporters miss this sarcasm, but C has the laugh in his notes, even though he uses only a later one.

Speaker's Chair (*a loud and continued laugh*), which is already so admirably filled, that I can scarcely wish even my Hon. Friend to step into it.[9] The other personal dispute consisted in rather a singular species of attack, for not bringing on the motion in October. With all my vivacity, however, I could scarcely think of subjecting the failure to discussion, before the failure was known, and when it was known, Parliament was not sitting. The very first day that Parliament did meet, I gave notice of my intended motion.[10]

"And now let me re-affirm in a more solemn tone, that with regard to the Officers, and all concerned in the execution of the expedition, I hold them as free from *disgrace*,[11] in the proper sense of the word, as if they had returned exulting with victory. I attach disgrace to the planners of it.—An army may be defeated after an hard fought battle; a citadel may capitulate after having stood a long siege; and yet even by the suffrage of the enemy honour may attach to them.[12] Disgrace consists in leading others by boasts and false promises into perilous adventures; if these fail, the boasters must needs be disgraced more or less. If you enter a country, the inhabitants of which are living peaceably, if by proclamations you rouse them against their existing rulers, if, by the appearance of your army, you call them into actual service against their Government (which, thank Heaven! Ministers did not succeed in doing in Holland), and, after all, instead of being able to protect them, you are obliged to capitulate yourself—then you are disgraced—disgraced in the darkest sense, and a milder word were either irony or falsehood.[13]

[9] "I would not carry ~~I could~~ him over—stop half way—". C's note N 10 f 3v. This remark varies in the different reports. C's version makes the most political sense. Taylor had been expected to become Speaker in 1789, when the Whigs were to take office under the regency. Sheridan leaves little doubt that he thought Taylor unsuitable then and now. The current Speaker was Addington.

[10] "The other personal Dispute rather a singular species of attack for not bringing it in October—all my vivacity—before the failure known—Parliament not sitting—The very first day that Parliament did meet". C's notes N 10 ff 3v–4.

[11] Sheridan put all blame on the Ministers, but it may be in this connexion that C at about this date made himself a memorandum: "The pedantry of *Generals & Officers*—all party men—all *lie* in each party (their ignorance/ what did ignorant men ever do?) Examine this minutely". *CN* I 665, N 4.

[12] "With regard to Officers and all concerned free from disgrace no question attached it to the Planners—a defeat, a citadel standing a siege with honor—". C's notes N 10 f 4v.

[13] "disgrace consists in leading others by boasts & false promises—If this fails, more or less disgraced Enter a country inhabitants living thus peaceably—if—if—if—instead of being ~~obliged~~ to protect them obliged to capitulate yourself." C's notes N 10 ff 5–5v.

"North Holland was the most whimsical place[14] to attempt a landing at, as the French influence was the strongest there. But, suppose that it had not been so, suppose that a great number of wealthy farmers, of merchants, or of public characters, had been seduced by our appearance and boasts, still the result might have been, and probably would have been the same.—What must have been our feelings when, in addition to the shame of our own baffled vaunts, and humiliating capitulation, we had[a] continued to receive, by every mail, fresh accounts of executions, confiscations, and ruin of whole families?[15] We talk of *repeating* this![16] Do we dream the Dutch can be so duped?[17] We appeared in their country with a superior force; and not a single man was induced to forego his caution. And will our failure operate in our favour on a second attempt.[18] The Ministers are determined to refuse inquiry in this House; but there

[a] *M Post*: have

[14] "then North Holland the most whimsical place—". C's note N 10 f 5ᵛ; missed by other reporters.

[15] "But suppose that a great number of wealthy farmers had been seduced still the result would have been the same—What then the feelings—executions, of Family, confiscation/". C's notes N 10 ff 5ᵛ–6.

[16] Here about a third of the speech is omitted, comparing British invasion of Holland with a French invasion of Ireland. C's notes (a third of the whole, N 10 from f 6ᵛ to f 8ᵛ) are rather sketchy, but they match this third of the account in *M Chron* and should not have been difficult for C to transcribe:

"If in Ireland the French had landed/& it is a melancholy If with our selves if 4500 French in Ireland—would they not have been in disgraced Nation under French caused all the Hangings Torture Boasts not to [?Peace] will [?ignominious]—Much has been said on Diversion—3 objects—Dutch Fleet ([?any] not answered) no insurrection wishing success, yet that that mode of getting the Fleet [?more] Mutiny not systematic by a general manifestation of the will of Dutch But the Diversion how reconcilable with Rest[oration] of Prince of Orange—Russians no part of the Diversion as good as Swiss. to the British Force alone—Would the French have left Batavia naked?—If so, how done with Fr Tyranny they would have done no so such—not perhaps so great an army—Recollect the nature of the Country—to be kept back by an inferior—".

[17] "This not my principal objection—If—Join—but When—arm[am]ents Princes, civil order, Liberty—that you will persist/ then to have this in reserve it will do pretty well as a Diversion—and repeated—will the Dutch come forward again—". C's notes N 10 ff 8ᵛ–9.

[18] "There never was an opportunity in which so clearly proved that the Dutch not willing—a superior force—not a single man induced to forego their caution.—tho' not quite compelled—". N 10 ff 9ᵛ–10. Here another fifty words of notes are unused, ff 10–11: "another point—I approved, but added in proportion as great & momentous, &c, and as the failure fatal to Stadtholder—in that proportion be more cautious unquestionably [?necessary] of contradiction— There is another point—I heard express disapp[ointment] of Dutch Fleet— If we had stopped short, immortal power—my single Opinion/".

[are] other suffrages. The public, I am sure, will inquire; and this refusal of Ministers will be taken by the public as presumptive evidence against them."[19]

Mr. M. A. Taylor in explanation said, he had no desire to go over to the other side of the House; and that the Hon. Gentleman (Mr. Sheridan) wanted a place much more than himself.[20] The House then divided,

For Mr. Sheridan's motion—45 | Against it—216

Adjourned at ONE o'Clock this morning.

DIPLOMACY. I

WITHDRAWAL OF RUSSIA

12 February 1800, Wednesday. *EOT* II 371–3, in SC's group of probable attributions and in her ms list of "Conjectural"; made quite certain by internal evidence.

THE intelligence brought by the last Hamburgh Mail of the recall of the Russian troops, and of their secession from the war, in conjunction with Austria, is believed by the best informed persons, though Ministers affect to entertain a contrary opinion; and the advocates for the war, who had built so confidently on the power of past experience, in precluding discord and jealousies among the combined Powers, feel an approaching discomfiture of their hopes.[1] It is probable, that on the first open jarring between the two Imperial Courts, our Ministers sent over such proposals to both, as they deemed certain of producing a reconciliation; and in the interim, in virtue of that figure in poetry and rhetoric, by which the present tense is used for the future, they affirmed the wished-for reconciliation realized. But this will not have been the first time, that the impolite obstinacy of events has given the flat contradiction to those inspired historians, who, like our Ministers, venture to relate beforehand.

Past experience, to be effective, must have made the mind *dispassionate*; otherwise, it is but as the torch in the hand of a blind Cupid, which may guide others, but is useless to himself. But unfortunately, the past experience in the present case has been made up of the most rankling passions, the wounds of which may skin

[19] Cf the third sentence in C's leader of 6 Feb. C's note is "the Public, I am sure, will condemn" (N 10 f 11).

[20] C's final jotting reads: "Mr Taylor—with respect to any [?place] &c" (N 10 f 11).

[1] Russia and Austria were now openly at odds; the Tsar was ready to jettison his anti-Bonapartist general, Suvorov; Russian troops were being withdrawn from encampments in Bohemia and Austria.

over, but seldom heal up. It has been made up of jealous rivalry between ambitious Generals, and public attacks on the nicest feelings of soldierly honour.—These are real, efficient, lasting causes, the true and vital springs of human conduct; compared to which the speculations of a common interest will be ever found to be shadows in the distance, yea, almost abstractions!

Of the character of that righteous and magnanimous Emperor, Paul the First,[2] it behoves us to speak most cautiously. It is, however, generally understood, that his imagination teems and buzzes with activities of equivocal generation, and that he is ambitious to stand out in *alto relievo* on the walls of the Temple of Fame, as the heroic restorer of the feudal honours in Europe.[3] That he will therefore stand by and merely *look* in upon the important game between England, Austria, and France, we confess to be highly improbable. But suppose that the regress of his troops should once more be countermanded, will Austria think herself secure in future, after such specimens of political coquetry? And will Russia be prevented from perceiving that she is playing a game against herself in aiding the plans of Austria? And what lesson ought we to learn from this? Will the Anglo-Russians remain exempt from jealousies? Is there that similarity of manners and character between British and Russian officers, which we doubt not subsists in every respect between British and Russian statesmen? Let us recollect the calumnious attack of the Russian General on our brave countrymen and their[a] commanders in the Dutch expedition, and deduce the probable cordiality and harmony of future co-operation.[4] This too is past experience.

[a] *EOT* omits

[2] Pitt had praised Paul's "magnanimity", as Sheridan recalled sarcastically (10 Feb, Debrett x 431), and was not to be allowed to forget it. Russia was still claimed as a cordial ally of Britain; yet the Tsar had responded with none of Grenville's hauteur to Napoleon's Christmas letter to *him*. One reason for suppressing inquiry into the Netherlands expedition was the matter of alleged faulty co-ordination of the British and Russian forces, the Russians holding the British to blame for failures of supply and for joining an attack "two hours too late" (see below). See Dundas's reply to Sheridan, Debrett x 429–30.

[3] Paul was said to have drunk to the health of Consul Bonaparte and desired his portrait, as C may have known. Paul may be the dwarf C had in mind at the end of the Washington essay, with ambition to stand out in relief. C's picture of Paul here and in the sequel of 24 Feb makes a sort of ridiculous companion-piece to his portraits of Washington and Bonaparte.

[4] Sheridan (Debrett x 427): "Do you feel so little for the military fame of your country, as to suffer your brave soldiers to stand in the face of Europe branded with such a stigma? Do you esteem so little the reputation of the

THE ELECTOR OF BAVARIA[1]

17 February 1800, Monday. New attribution, on the evidence of style; a reiteration of C's contribution to Stuart's article of 15 Feb (see App A, below).

IT would be an injustice to the Elector of Bavaria, were we to place his character on the same footing with that of the Emperor of Germany.[2] The Elector is a man of mild and benevolent feelings; and it is for his attachment to men of literature and the arts; but above all for his inclination to correct old vices of Government, and ameliorate the condition of his subjects, that he has been called an *Illuminee*;[3] a character which we cannot better explain, than by saying it is the opposite of that admired by some of our vigorous statesmen, who think nothing but bayonets, halters, whips, and tortures, can tame the people; and that even reading and writing have a tendency towards Jacobinism.

---

gallant officers employed in Holland... as to allow the aspersions cast upon their renown in the libellous letter of General Hessen to remain uncontradicted?" He had just cited, from the Petersburg *Court Gazette* of 29 Oct 1799, Hessen's letter to the Tsar reporting that the English had turned victory into retreat by joining the attack "two hours too late" and by delays in supply.

[1] For an essay of 15 Feb of doubtful authorship see App A, below. On the same day the reports of Commons debates (one page), which C had attended at Stuart's insistence (according to *CL* I 572), probably owe something to C, but they are brief, routine digests: of a motion and query preliminary to the big debate on the King's message, coming on the 17th, and of a discussion of Whitbread's efforts to get his poor-law bill on the calendar.

[2] Maximilian IV Joseph (1756–1825), Elector of Bavaria 1799–1806, when Bonaparte made him King of Bavaria, was his most faithful German ally until the eve of the battle of Leipzig in 1813. He granted his subjects a liberal constitution in 1818.

[3] See 17 Jan 1798 (2), in App A, below.

INTERCEPTED CORRESPONDENCE. II

17 February 1800, Monday; entitled "A Second Essay on the Intercepted Correspondence". *EOT* II 374–81; in SC's group of doubtful attributions; but quite certain, both as a continuation of his 3 Feb essay and as distinctly Coleridgian in argument, allusions, style.

> Si licet, et falsi positis ambagibus oris,
> Vera loqui *sinitis*
> OVID[a1]

THE frequent allusions to the intercepted letters, and the evident stress laid on them by the Minister,[b] during the debate in the House of Commons on Monday se'nnight—is this a circumstance which should scare us from the farther investigation of the authenticity of these letters?[2] We have no wish to apply to the Minister the words which he applied to Bonaparte: "it remains with us to investigate whether we can place that confidence in his language, which is absolutely necessary, before we can venture to rely on him." No! we are willing to believe, that Ministers are incapable of a direct and wilful violation of the laws of truth. The affair of the bills falsely dated from Hamburgh was indeed an instance of gentle *equivocation*; but it were prudish to call a venial *finesse* of trade by the harsh name of forgery.[3] We believe Ministers incapable of a direct falsehood, but are they therefore incapable of being deceived? Do not their passions, and their wishes, render them open on all sides to delusion? But hitherto, however, with the exception of one instance, we have steered clear of the Ministers. The authority of Government is expressly given to the Third Part only of the Correspondence; and we have not yet emerged from the First Part.

The First Part we have shown to possess no species of testimony. What is its internal evidence? This point we shall examine, undeterred by the dread of *their* abuse, from whose praises alone we could apprehend any injury to our characters. We affirm again that sentiment with which we introduced this examination, that were we believers in the authenticity of these letters, and nowise sceptical, still we should deem such a scrutiny as the present, the best, the most

[a] *EOT* omits motto from Ovid [b] *EOT*: Ministers,

[1] *Metamorphoses* 10.19–20. "...if it is lawful and you permit me to lay aside all false and doubtful speech and tell the simple truth...". Tr F. J. Miller (LCL 1916) II 65. C italicises "you permit".

[2] See above, 3 Feb.

[3] C had condemned the Hamburg loan in blunter terms in *Watchman* No 2 (*CC*) 62–3.

effectual, and the most honest mode of evincing their authenticity. "True religion (says a great Christian Philosopher) is more indebted for the clearness of its evidence to its adversaries, than to its defenders."[4] Quintilian recommends as a duty of the first importance in a good advocate "in aliam ei personam transeundum est, *agendusque adversarius*, proponendum, quidquid omnino excogitari contra potest,[a] quidquid recipit in ejusmodi disceptatione natura. Optimus est in dicendo patronus incredulus."[5] Let us not then be blamed, if being sceptical, we attempt that as a *duty*, which it would have been for the *interest* of the cause to have done, had we been believers.

We shall therefore proceed fearlessly "interrogare quam *infestissime*, ac premere," if only on this account, that "dum omnia quaerimus, aliquando ad verum, ubi minime expectavimus, pervenimus."[6] And first, in the examination of the internal evidence of this correspondence, we are impelled to remark with the Editor that "one thing has struck us, in looking over these letters, as a singularity not easily to be accounted for. It is that, there should not be a single letter, no, not a single line, from any man in the ranks! How is this? Are they interdicted from writing, lest they should disclose too much"[7]—(We should suppose, that a fierce and mutinous army, who amused themselves, as we are told in the correspondence, with calling their officers as they passed them, "Jack Ketches of the French," would not be so easily interdicted from that, which their natural affections must sc impetuously have prompted. And what more could they disclose than the officers have done? Is it possible, that any man in the ranks could write more like a well-paid Anti-Jacobin, or reason more like an Emigrant, than the majority of the letter-writers have done?)—

[a] *EOT*: protest

[4] Not identified, but cf "That a religious conscience is necessary in any station, is confessed even by those who tell us that all religion was invented by cunning men, in order to keep the world in awe. For, if religion, by the confession of its adversaries, be necessary for the well-governing of mankind; then every wise man in power will be sure...to carry some appearance of it himself...". Jonathan Swift "On the Testimony of Conscience": *Works* (19 vols 1801) x 51–2. See 26 Sept 1811 and n 8, below.

[5] *Institutio oratoria* 12.8.10 (var), 12.8.11 (var). Tr: "...he must assume another character and *adopt the rôle of his opponent*, urging every conceivable objection that a discussion of the kind we are considering may permit. The advocate who is most successful in pleading his case is he who is the most incredulous." Tr adapted from H. E. Butler (LCL 4 vols 1920–2) IV 433.

[6] *Institutio oratoria* 12.8.10–11 (var), 12.8.11. Tr adapted from Butler: "...to conduct a *most hostile* cross-examination and to allow our client no peace...by enquiring into everything, we shall sometimes come upon the truth where we least expect it".

[7] *Copies of Original Letters* pt II Intro p i n (with an omission).

"Are they—but we can form no satisfactory conjecture on the subject."[8] We will endeavour to suggest one conjecture to the Editor's imagination. The names of a few officers might be easily gained, and their connections in France too might be known, by the Emigrants employed in the Mediterranean in manufacturing the "last dying words," and the "more last dying words," and the "more last dying words still," of the French Army in Egypt. But the names of the men in the ranks could not be so easily learnt, and (as the lists are in possession of the Government in France) to have *invented* names might have furnished occasion for unpleasant detections. We will content ourselves with letters from officers.

The three first letters are written immediately after the arrival at Alexandria; and contain the merest *generalities*. It appears to us little less than impossible, that men just arrived in Egypt, with imaginations in a state of great excitement, could have been so little impressed by particular images, or have given so few images of particular things. Nothing is painted, as an eye witness *fresh* from the scene would paint it; nothing described in the order of time, as it met the eye. On the contrary, where description is *attempted*, it gives us the idea of one who has heard a story, or read a book, and then repeats to a third person what he has heard or read, according as his memory suggests it, with *artificial* arrangements, and not with the natural ones of time and place. All is written exactly as an Emigrant would write for Jaubert and Louis Bonaparte,[9] not as they would themselves have written. This fact of mind has been most acutely applied by Sir Isaac Newton and Dr. Hartley, in proof of the authenticity of the Gospels.[10] St. Matthew, an eye-witness, narrates in the natural order; St. Luke, who compiled his Gospel from the accounts of others, arranges his narration more artificially. The fact, however, is far more striking, and even obtrusive in these letters, than in St. Luke's Gospel; and yet Jaubert and L. Bonaparte are intended to write as eye-witnesses!

[8] Ibid.

[9] *Copies* identifies Jaubert as "commissary to the fleet" and suggests the probability of his "perish[ing] in the explosion of the l'Orient" (see below). However, Pierre Amédée Emilien Probe Jaubert (1779–1849), a young Orientalist, went to Egypt as first secretary-interpreter of the general-in-chief (he later accompanied Sébastiani to the East), and may be the author of the letter. Louis Bonaparte (1778–1846), Napoleon's brother, his aide-de-camp in Egypt 1798–9, later King of Holland. In pt I the first letter is from Louis Bonaparte, the second and third letters from Jaubert.

[10] See Newton "Observations upon the Prophecies of Holy Writ..." pt I ch 11 in Newton *Opera* ed Samuel Horsley (5 vols 1779–85) V 388–9, and David Hartley *Observations on Man* (1791) II 103 (pt II ch II prop 23). Cf LRR IV: *Lects 1795* (*CC*) 185–90.

The third letter is indeed a curiosity; scarce a sentence in it but has a ministerial purpose. Jaubert is made to puff by implication the Knights of Malta, and to infer the miseries occasioned by the conquest in which he has been assistant. "Malta is without a supply of provisions, and with an immense population, which was wholly supported by the order."[11] In the next page (*i.e.* p. 32), he writes Anti-Jacobin squibs. "You will laugh outright, perhaps, you witlings of Paris, at the Mahometan Proclamation of the Commander in Chief. He is proof, however, against all your raillery; and the thing itself will certainly produce a most surprising effect. You recollect that produced by the magic cry of *Guerre aux Chateaux, Paix aux Cabanes!*"[12] Admirable! a Republican compares the first enthusiastic outcry of revolutionary fanatics to a Mahometan proclamation of "a cold-blooded philosophist."—The violent dragging together of these two ideas is precisely that which we might expect from an emigrant still smarting even to madness in consequence of that magic cry! Indeed the writer himself seems to be aware that he has transfused too much of his own feelings, and qualifies it with "as I have been rather too open in this letter, you will oblige me by throwing it into the fire as soon as you have read it."[13] Besides, Jaubert had "perished in the explosion of the l'Orient,"[14] and it is worthy of remark, that the greater number of those officers *selected for Correspondents*, are allowed to "have perished."

All is excellently well contrived, except that the contrivance is somewhat too palpable. The fifth letter commences the tale of miseries; the sixth rises in pathos; the 7th is from a very *cautious* Gentleman, and is intended to hint the suspicious tyranny with which all letters were examined by the agents of the General. It is rather unfortunate, that all the other letters, so profusely anti-gallican, seem in direct contradiction to this 7th letter. But it is not possible to heap every kind of vice on a man's character, without incurring some trifling contradictions; and these must be excused. The 9th proves Bonaparte's dishonesty; and General Damas (if he have not unfortunately perished) might be a candidate for the office of note-writer to the new budget of correspondence from Seringapatam! He writes like a veteran Treasury hireling, vide p. 79.[15] The 12th

[11] *Copies of Original Letters* I 31 (with an omission).

[12] Ibid I 31–2.

[13] Ibid I 36.

[14] Ibid I 36n.

[15] "I do all I can to preserve unity among the different parties; but all goes very ill. The troops are neither paid nor fed; and thou may'st easily guess what murmurs this occasions..." etc. Ibid I 79.

letter is, independent of its complaints and apprehensions, intended farther to evince that Bonaparte is an avaricious Monopolist! Mercy on the man! What a bundle of incompatible villanies have they strung together, and christened by his name! Frantic, cold-blooded, avaricious, visionary, &c. &c. &c.!!! The rest of the letters have, almost without exception, each its *purpose*; and the common purpose of all is to describe "an accumulation of misery and despair, the inveterate hostility of the Arabs, the treachery of the Egyptians, the destructive warfare of the Mamelukes, together with the nauseous and peculiar diseases of the country, the intolerable heats and pestilential winds, the devouring myriads of venomous insects, and the stench and putrefaction of ten thousand stagnant pools."[16] It may be answered that these letters have been selected from a multitude, as answering each its purpose. Supposing the *truth* of this account, yet what less does it amount to than a confession of *virtual* forgery? From a large mass of letters, to select those only that suit a purpose, and to omit all those which might thwart it, constitutes what the old casuists style a "lie by omission."

To the curious coincidence of two men, both of the same name, and both writing a hand indistinguishably similar: and to the *late* discovery, that their names are not the same, but that the one was Boyer, and the other Royer—to this curious coincidence, and ingenious discovery, we have already paid the tribute of our admiration in our first Essay. In that Essay, we likewise pressed on the attention of our Readers the superfluity of general reasonings, observable in the whole of these letters, and the paucity of particular incidents. To this it has been objected, that these incidents are probably among the omissions; and we reply to the objection, that this grand PANACEA for all possible cases of improbability is excellently well-contrived, save only that the contrivance is somewhat too palpable! We shall not weary our Readers with any detailed examinations of the second Part: because it stands in point of external testimony exactly on the same grounds with the First Part; and because all our remarks on internal evidence apply to both totidem verbis.[17] Indeed, this Second Part seems to have been published purely *for the benefit* of the Editor; and we congratulate the Minister on possessing a means of rewarding his creatures, so little burthensome to himself or the public. The Third Part is of higher importance, and stands on other grounds. The investigation of this shall appear on the first open day.[18]

16 Ibid I xix (Introduction).

17 "All in the same words".

18 See 17 Mar 1800, below.

PARLIAMENT. VIII

PITT'S SECURITY SPEECH OF 17 FEBRUARY[1]

18 February 1800, Tuesday. *EOT* II 293–306; authorship verified by C's notes in Notebook 10, *CN* I 653 (BM Add Ms 47507 ff 34–15), and by his claims, e.g. *CL* I 573. Reprinted in *Courier* of same date. C recovered a third more of Pitt's actual terms than did other reporters; he also made many more creative embellishments. Most of the vivid language not confirmed by his notes or by other reports (see the textual notes) may be credited to C rather than Pitt. The transcription of C's notes, given in footnotes below, differs somewhat from that in *CN* I 653.

BRITISH PARLIAMENT. HOUSE OF COMMONS

MR. Pitt.—The Hon. Gentleman[2] calls upon Ministers to state the object of the war in one sentence. I can state it in one word. It is security.[3] I can state it in one word, though it is not to be explained but in many. The object of the war is security; security against a danger, the greatest that ever threatened this country; the greatest that ever threatened mankind; a danger the more terrible, because it is unexampled and novel.—It is a danger which[4] has more than menaced the safety and independence of all nations; it is a danger which has attacked the property and peace of all individuals; a danger which Europe has strained all its sinews to repel; and which

[1] Working "till 5 o'clock" in the morning, C reported Pitt's speech "with notes so scanty" that he felt largely responsible for the eloquence of the report (*CL* I 573). Seventeen years later he prepared to print it at the head of a collection of his political essays. See App B, ms of Jul 1817 (C's first footnote), below.

Collation does not indicate that C's notes were more scanty than other reporters' but does bear out his claim to have made Pitt speak more eloquently than usual. This was partly a matter of better reporting. Of vivid or at least image-bearing words or phrases common to at least two reports (hence probably uttered by Pitt) C reported 25 as against 17 each in *M Chron* and *The Times* (fewer in others). It was partly a matter of greater invention. Of especially vivid phrases unique in a given report (hence probably the reporter's coinage) the *M Post* contains 43 as against 7 in *M Chron*, 10 in *The Times*, 11 in the *Morning Herald*. For details see Erdman (1960).

C's later anecdote of having fallen asleep and then "*volunteered* a speech for Mr. Pitt" (*C Life*—G—I 207–8) is belied by his notes and in part applies to his reporting of the speech of 3 Feb. The angry contradiction by Stuart (x 486–7) adds further garbling. Again for details see Erdman (1960).

SC, in *EOT* III 1009–19, reprints *The Times* report as if it were *the* speech, but it too is only a digest, and one both less accurate and less inventive than C's. No full-length report of the speech was made; the digest in Debrett derives from the *True Briton*.

[2] George Tierney. Pitt's remarks, made in response to questioning, were briefer and pithier than the set speech of 3 Feb.

[3] For C's parody of this declaration, see 3 Dec 1801, below.

[4] C's notes in N 10 f 34: "Security—against a danger the greatest that ever threaten'd that never threaten'd that it is a danger which".

no nation has repelled so successfully as the British; because no nation has acted so energetically, so sincerely, so uniformly on the broad basis of principle; because no other nation has perceived with equal clearness and decision the necessity, not only of combating the evil abroad, but of stifling it at home;[5] because no nation has breasted, with so firm a constancy, the tide of Jacobinical power;[6] because no nation has pierced with so stedfast an eye through the disguises of Jacobinical hypocrisy.[a]

But now, it seems, we are at once to remit our zeal and our suspicion; that Jacobinism, which alarmed us under the stumbling and drunken tyranny of Robespierre; that Jacobinism, which insulted and roused us under the short-sighted ambition of the five Directors;[7] that Jacobinism, to which we have sworn enmity through every shifting of every bloody scene, through all those abhorred mockeries which have profaned the name of liberty to all the varieties of usurpation; to this Jacobinism we are now to reconcile ourselves, because all its arts and all its energies are united under one person, the child and the champion of Jacobinism, who has been reared in its principles, who has fought its battles; who has systematised its ambition, at once the fiercest instrument of its fanaticism, and the gaudiest puppet of its folly!—[b][8]

[a] Words *not* unique, among six other independent reports in nine newspapers: Mr. Pitt.—The Hon. Gentleman . . . to state the object of the war in one sentence. I . . . state it in one word. It is security . . . in one word . . . it . . . The object of the war is security; security against a danger, the greatest that ever threatened . . . country . . . that . . . threatened . . . a danger. . . .—It is a danger which . . . menaced . . . all nations; it is a danger which has . . . Europe . . . which no nation . . . so successfully as . . . because no nation has . . . so energetic, so sincerely . . .uniformly . . . principle; because . . . other . . . perceived . . . the necessity . . . abroad, but . . . at home . . . Jacobin . . . disguises . . .

[b] Words not unique: . . . now . . . that Jacobinism, which . . . under . . . tyranny of Robespierre . . . Jacobinism . . . of the five Directors; . . . Jacobinism . . . shifting . . . scene . . . all . . . mockeries . . . name of liberty . . . all the . . . usurp . . . now . . . because all . . . all . . . are united under one person, the child and the champion of Jacobinism, who . . . been reared . . . principles . . .

[5] "no nation so successfully—because no nation so energetic—because none other perceived abroad—but here—". C's note N 10 f 33[v], continuing with the unused "that we are attractive [at will]".

[6] ". . . Coleridge reported Pitt to have said, England had 'breasted the tide of Jacobinism.' I recollect objecting that Pitt did not say so, but it passed as Coleridge wished" (Stuart x 478–9). Stuart had C's text and Debrett in front of him when he wrote this in 1838. C had nothing in his notes.

[7] C's notes read: "That which we did not dream of under tyr. Of Robes[pier]re 5 directors" (N 10 f 33). Most papers have simply "the jacobinism of Robespierre, of Barrerre, the Jacobinism of the Triumvirate, the jacobinism of the Five Directors"; *The Times* supplies a different set of epithets: "The dreadful system of Robespierre. . . the perfidy and devastations of the Triumvirate. . . the horrible policy . . . under the Five Directors".

[8] C's notes read: "shifting of that scene—mocking name of Liberty to that Usurpation because all Hope united under one person, the nursling & champion—& pars ipse sine of

The Hon. Gentleman has discovered, that the danger of French power and French principles is at an end, because they are concentred, and because to uniformity of design is added a unity of direction; he has discovered that all the objects of French ambition are relinquished, because France has sacrificed even the *appearances* of freedom to the best means of realizing them; in short, that now, for the first time, Jacobinism is not to be dreaded, because now, for the first time, it has superadded to itself the compactness of despotism.[9] But the Hon. Gentleman presses hard, and requires me to be definite and explicit. What, says he, do you mean by destroying the power of Jacobinism? Will you persevere in the war, until you have received evidence that it is extinct in this country, extinct in France, extinct in the mind of every man? No! I am not so shamefully ignorant of the laws that regulate the soul of man.[10] The mind once tainted with Jacobinism can never be wholly free from the taint; I know no means of purification; when it does not break out on the surface, it still lurks in the vitals; no antidote can approach the subtlety of the venom, no length of quarantine secure us against the obstinacy of the pestilence.[11] Those who are now telling us that all danger from

Jacobins—" (N 10 ff 33–32v). Pitt, in the cluster of words out of which most reporters selected "child and champion" (*M Chron*, *Oracle*, *True Briton*, *Packet*), also said "reared" and perhaps something like "reared and nursed". Since C's notes had "nursling & champion", Stuart only "with difficulty" (x 487) prevailed on him to adopt "child and champion". (SC, comparing only two papers, jumped to the false conclusion that her father had coined the phrase. *EOT* III 1010.) But C was primed to hear "nursling". In 1795 he had defined Mystery as "the Dry-nurse of that...Imp, Despotism" (*Conciones: Lects 1795—CC—*30). On 3 Jan 1800 (above) he called France the "birth-place and...nursery" where Jacobinism was now disowned; his next charge, 8 Jan (above), was that it had left its "birth-place" and that Pitt was now the "true fosterer and dry-nurse of Jacobinism". Here was Pitt using essentially the same epithets—on Bonaparte. (Two years later C would accept that application, writing "parricide child and champion" 2 Oct 1802, below). The further epithets in the present sentence may be considered C's own embroidery.

9 "The hon. now discovery that they are at an end. because concentered—because by the unity of Direction and design uniformity of Design [he thought] The best means is all then [?Despotism]". C's notes N 10 f 32.

10 By putting these words into Pitt's mouth C is again shooting at Pitt's professed "knowledge of human nature" that had proved so erroneous in Holland.

11 "What do you mean by destroying the power of fanaticism in—Extin-g[uish]ed in every man—No! The mind once tainted, can never wholly free itself from it. I know no means of purification—". C's notes N 10 ff 31v–31. Reports agree that Pitt spoke of a *mind* or *minds once tainted*. C alone pursued the diagnosis from mind to vitals and skin. Cf C's public Letter to Fox, 4 Nov 1802 (below), wishing Fox's speeches had been "the natural and certain cure...the antidotes to this delusion" of Jacobinism.

revolutionary principles is now[a] passed by, are yet endeavouring to call up again the very arguments, which they used at the commencement of the war, in the youth and rampancy of Jacobinism;[12] and repeat the same language, with which they then attempted to lull the nation into security, combined with the same arts of popular irritation. They are telling us, that Ministers disregard peace; that they are prodigal of blood; insensible to the miseries, and enemies to the liberties of mankind; that the extinction of Jacobinism is their pretext, but that personal ambition is their motive;[13] and that we have squandered 200 millions on an object, unattainable were it desirable, and were it not unattainable, yet still to be deprecated.[b14]

Sir, will men be governed by mere words without application? This country, Sir, will not. It knows that to this war it owes its prosperity, its constitution, whatever is fair or useful in public or domestic life, the majesty of her laws, the freedom of her worship, and the sacredness of our fire-sides. For these it has spent two hundred millions, for these it would spend two hundred millions more; and, should it be necessary, Sir, I doubt not that I[15] could find those two hundred millions, and still preserve her resources unimpaired. The only way to make it not necessary is to avail ourselves of the hearty co-operation of our allies, and to secure and invigorate that co-operation by the firmness and vigour of our own conduct.[c16]

[a] *EOT* omits

[b] Words not unique: The Hon. Gentleman...discovers that the danger...power and...principles ...at an end, because...concentred...because...uniformity of design is added a unity of direction...all...*appearances*...Jacobinism...now...But the Hon. Gentleman...What...do... mean...the war, till...is extinct...extinct in the mind of every...? No!...The mind once tainted with Jacobinism can never be wholly free from...I know no...purification...no...quarantine.... Those who...now tell...us that...danger...is now passed...are...endeavouring to call up... arguments, which they...at the commencement of the war...lull the...into security...arts.... They are telling us, that...disregard...that...are...blood...that we have...200 millions...

[c] Words not unique: Sir, will...be governed by mere words...application? This country, Sir, will not. It knows...its prosperity, its constitution,...laws...freedom...it has spent two hundred millions, for...would spend two hundred millions more; and...it...necessary...find...resources ...to avail ourselves of the...co-operation of our allies, and to secure...vigour...

[12] Is this an echo of the Miltonic "ramp" in line 54 of C's *Recantation* Ode?

[13] C's report is unique in giving Pitt this strong definition of Opposition charges; on the other hand it is also unique in giving Pitt a consciousness of "sincere and honest intentions".

[14] "Those who are now telling us, Jacobins—are now endeav. to call~~ing~~ up all those arguments that lulled us into security—they are telling us that d^{o}—200,000 millions". C's notes N 10 ff 31–30^{v}.

[15] The sense calls for "she" or "it", as in C's notes.

[16] "Sir, will men be governed by mere words without application—This Country will not. It knows—its prosperity—Constitution—2 or 200,000 million—spends & it can find/ the only way to make it not necessary to avail ⟨allies⟩ hearty ⟨coop⟩—& by your own Conduct—". C's notes N 10 ff 30^{v}–29^{v}.

The Hon. Gent. then comes back upon me, and presses me upon the supposed dissonance between our views and those of our allies. But surely there may allowably exist in the minds of different men different means of arriving at the same security. This difference may, without breaking the ties of effective union, exist even in this House; how much more then in different kingdoms? The Emperor of Russia may have announced the restoration of monarchy, as exclusively his object. This is not considered as the ultimate object by this country,[a] [17] but as the best means and most reliable pledge[b] of an higher object, viz. our own security, and that of Europe; but we do not confine ourselves to this, as the only possible means.—From this shade of difference we are required to infer the impossibility of cordial co-operation!—But here the Honourable Gentleman falls into a strange contradiction. He affirms the restoration of monarchy an unjust object of the war, and refuses expressly and repeatedly to vote a single farthing on such a ground; and yet the supposed secession of Russia from the allied powers, the secession of that Government, whose *exclusive* object is the restoration of monarchy, is adduced by him as another and equal ground for his refusal. Had the Emperor of Russia persevered in directing his utmost forces to the attainment of that object, to which Austria will not pledge herself, and which the Honourable Gentleman considers as an unjust object, then the Honourable Gentlemen would have been satisfied.[18] But I will not press too hard on the Honourable Gentleman, or lay an undue weight on an inadvertence. I will deal most fairly with him. If I did believe, which I do not, that Austria saw no advantages in the restoration of Monarchy, yet still I would avail myself of her efforts, without changing my own object. Should the security of Britain and of Europe result from the exertions of Austria, or be aided by her influence, I should think it my duty to advise His Majesty to lend the Emperor every financial assistance, however those exertions and that influence might spring from principles not in unison with our

[a] Words not unique: The Hon. Gent.... may... exist... different... different means... security. ... The Emperor of Russia may... the restoration of monarchy... his object... not... the ultimate object... this country...

[b] *M Post*: pledges [corrected in *EOT*]

17 "The H. then comes back upon me—There may be in the minds of diff. diff. means of Security—even in this House—The Em. of Russia may have announced rest[oration] of Monarchy tho not of this Country—". C's notes N 10 ff 29–28ᵛ.

18 "The H. falls into contradiction—Had the Emperor of R. What E. & A. not—then he would have been satisfied—". C's notes N 10 f 28ᵛ.

own. If the Hon. Gentleman will tell me, that the object of Austria is to regain the Netherlands, and to reconquer all she may have lost in Germany and Italy, so far from feeling this as a cause of distress, I feel it a ground of consolation, as giving us the strongest assurance of her sincerity, added to that right which we possess, of believing Austria sincere, from our experience that Austria, above all, must know the insecurity of peace with Jacobins.[a][19] This, Sir, would be a ground of consolation and confident hope; and though we should go farther than the Emperor of Germany, and stop short of Russia, still, however, we should all travel in the same road. Yet even were less justifiable objects to animate our ally, were ambition her inspiring motive, yet even on that ground I contend that her arms and victories would conduce to our security. If it tend to strip France of territory and influence, the aggrandisement of Austria is elevated by comparison into a blessing devoutly to be wished! The aggrandisement of Austria, founded on the ruins of Jacobinism, I contend, Sir, to be a truly British object. But, Sir, the Honourable Gentleman says, he thinks the war neither just nor necessary,[20] and calls upon me, without the qualifying reservations and circuitous distinctions of a special pleader; in short, without BUTS or IFS, to state the real object; and affirms, that in spite of these buts and ifs, the restoration of Monarchy in France is the real and *sole* object of Ministers, and that all else contained in the official notes are unmeaning words and distinctions fallacious, and perhaps meant to deceive. Is it, Sir, to be treated as a fallacious distinction, that the restoration of Monarchy is not my sole or ultimate object; that my ultimate object is security; that I think no pledge for that security so unequivocal as the restoration of Monarchy, and no means so natural and effectual? *but* if you can present any

[a] Words not unique: But ... the Honourable Gentleman ... ground ... Had the Emperor of Russia ... I ... deal ... fairly with him. If I ... believe, which I do not, that ... no ... restore ... yet ... I ... avail myself of ... without changing my own object ... the security ... exertions ... If the Hon. Gentleman will tell me, that the object of Austria is to regain the Netherlands ... to ... so far from ... I feel ... experience ... Austria ... must know ... security of peace ... Jacobins. ..."

19 "I will deal most fairly— If I did believe which I do not, that Aust. saw no advantages in Restor.—yet still I would avail myself of him without changing my own object—security of B[ritain] & Europe—I [2/3 of page torn away] think it my with that right of believing it sincere [page torn away] Mem. *their* experience with Austria above all must know the Insecurity of peace with Jacobins—". C's notes N 10 ff 28–26v.

20 "Yet even ambition—even on that ground it—to our security—if it tend to strip France of territorial aggrandisement, yet (Jacobinism) aggrand. of Aust. a true British Object— But, Sir—the H. says he has another motive because he thinks not just a necessary (Conversation across the Table)". C's notes N 10 ff 26v–25v.

other mode, that mode I will adopt. I am unwilling to accept an inadequate security; but the nature of the security which it may be our interest to demand, must depend on the relative and comparative dangers of continuing the war, or concluding a peace. And *if* the danger of the war should be greater than that of a peace, and *if* you can shew to me that there is no chance of diminishing Jacobinism by the war, and *if* you can evince that we are exhausting our means more than our enemies are exhausting theirs, then I am ready to conclude a peace without the restoration of Monarchy. These are the *ifs* and the *buts*, which I shall continue to introduce, not the insidious and confounding subtleties of special pleading, but the just and necessary distinctions of intelligible prudence; I am conscious of sincere and honest intentions in the use of them, and I desire to be tried by no other than God and my Country.—But are we not weakening ourselves?[21] Let any man calmly, and with the mind of an Englishman, look round on the state of our manufactures, our commerce, and[a] all that forms and feeds the sources of national wealth, and to that man I can confidently leave the following questions to be answered. From the negotiations at Lisle to the present moment has England or France weakened itself in the greater degree? Whether, at the end of this campaign, France is not more likely to suffer the feebleness ensuing an[b] exhausted finance than England?—If Jacobinism, enthroned in Bonaparte, *should* resist both the pressure of foreign attack and its own inherent tendencies to self-destruction, whether it must not derive such power of resistance from the use of such revolutionary and convulsive efforts, as involve, and almost imply a consequent state of feebleness? And whether, therefore, if any unexpected reverse of fortune should make it expedient or necessary for us to compromise with Jacobinism, it would not be better for us to compromise with it at the end of the campaign, than at present?[22]

[a] *EOT*: on   [b] *EOT*: on

[21] "Is it to be treated as a fallacious Distinction, not sole object—my object security—& I think nothing tends to that as Monarchy. But if you can present any other mode, that mode I will adopt/ I am unwilling to accept an inadequate but—& *if* if you can shew to me that there is no chance of diminishing Jacobinism—if you can shew to me that we are exhausting our means more than Enemy—these are the Ifs & the Buts/ not the special Pleading & I desire to be tried by no other than my Country/ But are we not weakening ourselves—". C's notes N 10 ff 25v–24.

[22] "from Lisle to now has Engl. or Fr. more weakened themselves—Whether in the End of the Campaign Fr. more likely—Whether if Jac. enthroned in Bonaparte—Whether therefore it would not better to compromise with Jacobinism, it would not be safer then than now—". C's notes N 10 ff 24–23.

And by parity of reasoning, whether it be not time (even on the supposition that Jacobinism is not to be routed, disarmed, and fettered); yet, that even on this supposition, the longer we defer a peace, the safer that peace will be![a]

Sir, we have been told that Jacobinism is extinct, or at least dying. We have been asked too, what we mean by Jacobinism? Sir, to employ arguments solely to the purposes of popular irritation is a branch to[b] Jacobinism. It is with pain, Sir, that I have heard arguments manifestly of this tendency, and having heard them, I hear with redoubled suspicion the assertions, that Jacobinism is extinct. By what softer name shall we characterise the attempts to connect the war by false facts and false reasoning with accidental scarcity?[23] By what softer name shall we characterise appeals to the people on a subject which touches their feelings, and precludes their reasoning? It is this, Sir, which makes me say, that those whose eyes are now open to the horrors and absurdities of Jacobinism, are nevertheless still influenced by their early partiality to it.[24] A somewhat of the *feeling* lurks behind, even when all the *principle* has been sincerely abjured.[25] If this be the case with mere spectators, who have but sympathised in the distance, and have caught disease only by *looking on*, how much more must this hold good of the actors? And with what increased caution and jealousy ought we not to listen to the affirmation, that Jacobinism is obsolete even in France? The Hon. Gent. next charges me with an unbeseeming haughtiness of tone, in deeming that the House had pledged itself to the present measure by

[a] Words not unique: ground I . . . that . . . The aggrandisement of Austria . . . Jacobin . . . be a true British object . . . the Honourable Gentleman says . . . thinks the war neither just nor necessary . . . calls upon me, without . . . special pleader . . . without BUTS or IFS . . . buts and ifs, the restoration of . . . *sole* . . . Is . . . be treated . . . the restoration of Monarchy . . . not my sole . . . object . . . object . . . security . . . pledge for . . . security . . . as . . . restoration of Monarchy . . . effectual, *but* if . . . any other mode . . . I will adopt . . . unwilling to . . . but . . . must . . . comparative dangers of continuing the war . . . peace. And *if* the danger of the war . . . peace . . . *if* . . . shew . . . me . . . no . . . diminishing Jacobinism by the war, and *if* . . . that we are exhausting our means more than . . . enemy . . . exhausting . . . a peace. . . . These are the *ifs* and the *buts*, which I . . . special pleading . . . I . . . to be tried by no other . . . God and my country.—But are we . . . weakening ourselves? . . . negotiations at Lisle . . . has England or France. . . . Whether, at the end of . . . campaign, France is not more likely to . . . exhausted . . . Jacobinism, enthroned in Bonaparte . . . whether . . . compromise with Jacobinism . . . at the end of the campaign, than at . . .

[b] *EOT*: of

23 For the way in which C connected the war and the scarcity, see his *M Post* review of Young's pamphlet, 27 Mar 1800, below.

24 In Nov 1802 C will use this argument upon Fox—and himself.

25 "To connect the war by false facts & false reasoning with accidental Scarcity because to appeal to the people on a subject which touches their feelings & precludes their reasons—it is this which makes me say, that those who are now open yet from early partiality—". C's notes N 10 ff 23–22.

their late vote for the continuance of the war. This is not accurate. I did not deem the House pledged: I only assigned reasons of *probability*, that having voted for the continuance of war, they would deem themselves inconsistent if they refused assent to those measures by which the objects of the war were most likely to be realised. My argument was, not that the House had pledged itself to this measure directly, but only as far as they must perceive it to be a means of bringing the war to that conclusion to which they have pledged themselves: for unless Gentlemen will tell me, that though they cannot prevent votes in favour of the war, they will yet endeavour to palsy the arm of the country in the conduct of it; and though they cannot stifle the vast majority of suffrages to the plan, they will yet endeavour to way-lay it in its execution; unless the Gentlemen will tell me so themselves, I will not impute it to them.[a][26]

(Here Mr. Pitt made a short reply to some observations of Mr. Bouverie in the early part of the debate,[27] and then proceeded.)

It was said of himself and friends (and often said) by a Gentleman who does not now commonly honour us with his presence here,[28] "We are the Minority who represent the opinions of the country." In my opinion a state of universal suffrage, formal or virtual, in which, nevertheless, the few represent the many, is a true picture of Jacobinism. But, however this may be, if smallness of number is to become a mark and pledge of genuine representation, that Gentleman's friends must acquire the representative character in a continual progression; for the party has been constantly decreasing in number, and both here and out of this House, they are at present fewer than

[a] Words not unique: Jacobinism...extinct...attempts to connect the war by false facts and false reasoning...scarcity...appeals to the people on a subject which touches...feeling...and precludes their reasoning? It is this...which...that...who...Jacobinism...partiality...*feeling*...spectators...the actors....The Hon. Gent....that the House...pledged...to the present measure...vote ...the continuance of the war....I did not...pledged: I only...voted for the continuance of war ...consistent...refused...argument...not...measure...pledged...Gentlemen...they cannot prevent votes...the war, they will...endeavour to palsy the arm of the country in the...cannot... unless the Gentlemen will tell me so themselves...I...not...

[26] "if not to these spectators, how much more Danger I did not deem them pledged—but assigned my reasons of probability—My argument to the majority was not that they had pledged themselves to this meas[ure]—but only a means—of bringing the war to the conclusion, to which they have pledged themselves—For unless Gent. tell me that tho' they cannot prevent votes, they will endeavor to palsy the arm of the country in the execution <I will not impute it to them—>". C's notes N 10 ff 22–21.

[27] "Now, Sir! however the G. it appears to form an Instance I did not hear from B[ouverie]—who said the most against the early part of the Debate—". C's notes N 10 f 20^{v}. Speaking in opposition had been William Henry Bouverie (1752–1806), M.P. for Salisbury since 1776.

[28] Charles Fox.

they ever were before. But they vote for peace, and the people wish for peace; and therefore they represent the opinions of the people. The people wish for peace—So do I! But for what peace? Not for a peace that is made to day and will be broken to-morrow! Not for a peace that is more insecure and hazardous than war. Why did I wish for peace at Lisle? Because war was then more hazardous than peace;[29] because it was necessary to give to the people a palpable proof of the necessity of the war, in order to their cordial concurrence with that system of finance, without which the war could not be successfully carried on;[30] because our allies were then but imperfectly lessoned by experience; and finally, because the state of parties then in France was less Jacobinical than at any time since that aera. But will it follow that I was then insincere in negotiating for peace, when peace was less insecure, and war more hazardous; because now with decreased advantages of peace, and increased means of war, I advise against a peace?[31] As to the other arguments, it is of less consequence to insist upon them, because the opposition implied in them holds not against this measure in particular, but against the general principle of carrying on the war with vigour. Much has been said of the defection of Russia, and every attempt made to deduce from this circumstance so misnamed causes of despair or diminished hope. It is true, that Russia has withdrawn herself from confident[a] co-operation with Austria, but she has not withdrawn herself from concert with this country. Has it never occurred, that France, compelled to make head against armies pressing on the whole of her frontiers, will[b] be weakened and distracted in her efforts, by a moveable maritime force?[32] What may be the ultimate extent of the Russian forces engaged in this diversion,

[a] The word was probably "Continental"

[b] *M Post*: will not [corrected in *EOT*]

29 "a few representing the many—this is Jacobinism—from that G. who is not often here—the minority who represent the opinions of the Country—if general abuse stamps representation they have been fewer here & extra than ever before—the people cry for peace—so I am? But what peace—broken tomorrow.—not, because peace insecure & hazardous as war—Why did I wish for Peace at Lisle—because War then more hazardous—". C's notes N 10 ff 20ᵛ–19.

30 Here only C's wording is unique; a similar assertion is reported by the *Oracle*.

31 "it then resulted from parties new in France less Jacobinical than any thing since—with increased danger of Peace with increased means of War—will it follow that then I was insincere?—". C's notes N 10 ff 19–18ᵛ.

32 "Then as other Argum. of less consequence because opposition not made to this measure but to the general principle of carrying on the war with Vigour—Defection of Russia—withdrawn itself from confident. Coop not from concert with this Country—has it never occurred that army of France to make head against armies—& internal will it not be distracted by moveable maritime force". C's notes N 10 ff 18–17.

we cannot be expected to know, cut off as we are from the Continent, by the season and the weather. If the Russians, acting in maritime diversion on the coast of France, and increased by our own forces, should draw the French forces from Switzerland and Italy, it [a]does not[b] follow that the Russians [c]may not[d] be greatly, and perhaps equally useful to the objects of the campaign, although they will cease to act on the Eastern side of France. I do not pretend to know precisely the number and state of the French armies, but reason only on[e] probabilities; and chiefly with the view of solving the Hon. Gentleman's difficulty, how the Russians can be useful, if not on the Continent.[33] It is unnecessary to occupy the time and attention of the House with a serious answer to objections, which it is indeed difficult to repeat with the same gravity with which they were originally stated. It was affirmed, gravely affirmed, that 12,000,000£ would be wanted for corn! I should be happy, if, in the present scarcity, corn could be procured from any, and all parts of the world, to one third of that amount. It will not be by such arguments as these, that the country will be induced to cease a war for security, in order to procure corn for subsistence. I do object, that there is unfairness both in these arguments in themselves, and in the spirit which produces them. The war is now reviled as unjust and unnecessary; and in order to prove it so, appeals are made to circumstances of accidental scarcity from the visitation of the seasons. The fallacy of these reasonings is equal to their mischief. It is not true that you could procure corn more easily if peace were to be made to-morrow. If this war be unjust, it ought to be stopped on its own account; but if it be indeed a war of principle and of necessity, it were useless and abject to relinquish it from terrors like these. As well might a fortress, sure of being put to the sword, surrender for want of provision. But that man, Sir, does not act wisely, if, feeling like a good citizen, he use these arguments which favour the enemy.[34] God forbid, that an opposition in opinion among

a–b *M Post*: does [corrected in *EOT*] c–d *M Post*: may [corrected in *EOT*]
e *M Post*: in [corrected in *EOT*]

33 "—What may be the ultimate extent of Russia's cut off from contin. by weather ministers can't be expected— If Russ. acting on maritime diversion—if our own force increased if greater than drawn from Switz. ?—& Italy—it does follow—I don't know positively the number of F. Army, but reason, on probabilities." C's notes N 10 ff 16–15ᵛ.

34 "12 Million needed for corn—this gravely stated—Not cease a war for security in order to procure Corn for own subsistence—I do object that unfairness—unjust & unnecessary—the fallacy is equal to mischief—it ~~does~~ is not true that you could procure corn more easily if Peace were made tomorrow—but to assume the War unjust, it ought to be stopped on its own account—but if Fortress sure of being put to the sword would not—

ourselves should make us forget the high and absolute duty of opposition to the enemies of our country. Sir, in the present times, it is more than ever the bounden duty of every wise and good man to use more than ordinary caution in abstaining from all arguments that appeal to passions not facts; above all, from arguments that tend to excite popular irritation on a subject and on an occasion, on which the people can with difficulty be reasoned with, but are irritated most easily.[35] To speak incautiously on such subjects, is an offence of no venial order; but deliberately and wilfully to connect the words, war and scarcity, were infamous, a treachery to our country, and in a peculiar degree cruel to those whom alone it can delude, the lower uneducated classes. I will not enlarge upon that subject, but retire with a firm conviction that no new facts have occurred which can have altered the opinion of this House on the necessity of the war, or the suitableness of similar measures to the present to the effectual carrying of it on, and that the opinion of the House will not be altered but by experience and the evidence of facts.[a][36]

a Words not unique: It was said of himself and friends...by a Gentleman who...not now...us with his presence here "...the Minority who represent the...of the country"...the few represent the many...of Jacobinism...small...fewer...they...the people...for peace....The people...for peace—So...I! But...what peace? Not for a peace...more insecure...than war....I wish for peace at Lisle? Because war was then more...than peace...the state of parties...in France... Jacobinical than...any...since....I was...insincere in...for peace, when peace...secure...the ...arguments...not against this measure...particular...the war...Russia...Russia has withdrawn herself from...co-operation with Austria...this country. Has it never occurred, that France...to make...armies pressing...frontiers...be weakened...by a moveable maritime force? What...extent...Russian forces...Continent...If the Russians...maritime diversion...increased...our own forces...Switzerland...Russians...objects...campaign...of France....the Hon. Gentleman's...the Continent...with...gravity...stated...that 12,000,000£ would be wanted for corn! I should be happy, if...could be procured...unfair...unjust and unnecessary ...scarcity....The fallacy of...reasonings is equal to...mischief. It is not true that you could procure corn more easily if peace were...made to-morrow. If...war...unjust, it...be stopped on its own account...if...a fortress...of being put to the sword, surrender....But that man, Sir, does not act wisely...like a good citizen...arguments...favour the enemy. God forbid...duty ...to connect the words, war and scarcity...cruel...I...not...this House...the necessity...the House...

Surrender for want of provisions ~~If he~~ That man does not act wisely if he act like a good Citizen, if he use those Arguments which favour the Enemy—". C's notes N 10 ff 15^{v}–14. The rest of the speech was reported—or improved—without benefit of notes.

35 C's own creed (see his letter of 10 Mar 1798 to his brother George: *CL* I 396–7); yet he may be attaching his own elaboration to something Pitt said—and no newspaper fully reported—about "misleading the public mind" (*True Briton*).

36 Only C puts into Pitt's mouth this abused phrase from the first Grenville Note. For Poole's complaint that C had decked out a wretched speech in "magick" language, and C's reply that it was "wretched Rant" but had "made a great noise here", see *Poole* II 6 and *CL* I 574–5. But see also *Poole* II 156–7 on Pitt as a "wonderful" orator.

DIPLOMACY. II

PITT AND AUSTRIA[1]

22 February 1800, Saturday. *EOT* II 306–10; in SC's group of certain attributions; also firm internal evidence.

IT has been the fate of our Minister, that he has almost uniformly stated some reason for the continuance of the war just on the eve of the event which flatly contradicted that reason. He was urging Parliament how rich in zeal Austria was, and how fit therefore it must be that a Loan should be granted to the Emperor, just at the time[2] that the Emperor himself was making peace; or (to use the phrase of a Noble Lord)[3] had turned Jacobin. He is now pursuing the same conduct, and repeating the same language; and now likewise, there is no mean probability, that the Emperor is carrying on secret negotiations. Even so late as the debate on the dispatches from France, the formidable and flourishing state of the Chouans was urged as a main argument for the rejection of the French proposals: and lo! the Chouans are pacified and disarmed, and their Chiefs destroyed or reconciled.[4] And still the Minister talks as fluently of a moveable maritime force,[5] as if an army of forty or fifty thousand Russians could remain hovering on the Western coasts of France, as easily as half a dozen fishers' skiffs!

Thus too, Austria and Bavaria are coupled together, joint objects of a weighty subsidy; while it is reported in the last Paris papers, with every appearance of probability, that Bavaria will not receive our subsidy, and is in reality perhaps more afraid of the ambition of Austria, than of the Jacobinism of the Chief Consul. This report, we cannot indeed trace to any source so authentic, as that we dare vouch for its accuracy; but we do think it entitled to a high degree of credit. It is well known that the Court of Bavaria is intimately

[1] For an article of 19 Feb perhaps inspired by C, see App A, below. On 21 Feb Longman and Rees advertised C's translation of three plays of Schiller forming "one connected Work", with "an annexed Essay on the Merits of Schiller, by the Translator". The first play, *Wallenstein's Camp*, and the Essay never appeared.

[2] In the winter of 1796–7 Pitt had been under fire for a secret subsidy to Austria (defended in his speech of 7 Dec 1796); Bonaparte had forced an armistice in Apr 1797.

[3] Possibly Lord Hawkesbury (see Debrett x 602, 610); possibly the Earl of Clare, quoted in the article of 19 Feb.

[4] On the Chouans, see 24 Feb, below.

[5] Here and in the next paragraphs C is taking up points emphasised in his report of Pitt's speech of 17 Feb.

connected with that of Russia; that in the weight of Russian influence, and in the presence of the Russian armies, she had expected and sought protection from the views of more than *one* powerful neighbour. "The aggrandisement of Austria, founded on the ruins of Jacobinism," may, or may not be, "a truly *British* object";[6] but most certainly it is not a *Bavarian* object. The Russians having seceded, how, except by an honest neutrality, can Bavaria have any security, that, in the events of the campaign, Austria may not yield her up to France, or France give her in compromise to Austria? But will a neutrality secure her? We answer, that neutrality will give her a common interest with Prussia, and the North of Germany, and of course entitle her to the same advantages of common defence. Besides, it is in the highest degree improbable that the causes, which have produced the effect of withdrawing the zealous Paul I. from co-operation with his politic brother Emperor, should be wholly foreign to the interests of the Elector.[7] But it may be objected, that no injury is done by our having shewn ourselves willing and able to support our allies; by our having evinced that, if the great cause of monarchy *is* given up, *they*, and not *we*, were in fault. But is it no injury to the honour of Parliament, that in a continued succession of instances, Parliament should appear to the people at home, and to all Europe, blind to events, which all but itself had anticipated and calculated upon? Is it no injury, at a time when it is above all things necessary for national quiet and content, that the Parliament should maintain even the minutiae of dignity and independence—at such a time is it no injury to us, that the Parliament should appear as the easy organ of Ministers, giving credit to no facts, but those which *Ministers* submit to them, seeing with *their* eyes, and hearing only with *their* ears, like a hollow statue in the oracular temples of the antients?

This is no ordinary time. Far be it from us to deduce arguments of irritation from the internal calamity which threatens us;[8] but we *do* affirm, that such a calamity does afford a powerful reason for the desirableness of a peace, were it only on this account, that, *however falsely*, the lower and uneducated classes *will* connect it with the war! Is the Minister "so shamefully ignorant of the laws that regulate the soul of man,"[9] as not to know that the most prominent circumstance which co-exists with any great calamity, will always and necessarily

6 Pitt 17 Feb, as reported by C.

7 See 17 Feb 1800 (1) n 2, above.

8 The scarcity of grain and butcher's meat, harbingers of famine; see Debrett x 607, 710, 656, 722.

9 Pitt 17 Feb, as reported by C.

be considered by the many, as the *cause* of that calamity? If *we* were required to state and *particularise* the object[a] of peace, we should blush to pretend to be able to *particularise*, and then to answer by a vague and *general* phrase. Yet if we *would* use a general phrase, we too would state it to be *security*. "Would a fortress (says the Minister), sure of being put to the sword, capitulate for want of provision?"[10] Is it possible (we reply) that any but children can be deluded with so puerile a sophism as that which is made up by connecting and confounding a metaphor and a reality?[11] The want of provision, Ministers themselves assure us, is an undoubted and threatening reality! but that we are sure of being put to the sword—this is too absurd even to admit of a *metaphorical* explanation.—Will a peace annihilate our population, our commerce, our insularity, our navies? We must conclude, that Ministers attribute to peace all those "contagious blastments,"[12] or their conduct and their reasons become alike unintelligible. But it is done! Ministers have dashed the budding olive-branch to the ground; and if by the natural magic of that very act it should, like the rod of Aaron, be turned into a serpent,[13] they will then snatch an apology from the effects of their own insolence. If, in the events of the campaign, France should be successful,[14] she will become ambitious; if she should be defeated and endangered, she will become jacobinical; and this ambition, and this jacobinism, the legitimate offspring of the continuance of the war, will have an imaginary *pre-existence* assigned them, and be confidently adduced by Ministers as justifications for their having rejected a peace![15]

[a] *M Post*: objects [corrected in *EOT*]

[10] Pitt 17 Feb, concluding paragraph.

[11] C's earliest explicit discussion of metaphor mistaken for reality seems to be *CN* II 2711 and 2724 (1805).

[12] Laertes in *Hamlet* I iii 42.

[13] Cf *CN* I 18, where the rod transformed is "Love—a myrtle wand".

[14] Parliament voted to send 20,000 men to support Austria in the Mediterranean; they would arrive only in time to hear of Marengo and a June armistice between Austria and France, in Italy, followed in July by an armistice in Germany.

[15] This argument was Fox's in the 3 Feb debate—and C's earlier and later.

DIPLOMACY. III

RUSSIA, AUSTRIA, FRANCE

24 February 1800, Monday. New attribution; SC had it twice in her "Conjectured" list (VCL MS 19 v. 1 f 12), noting the "*coquetry* of Paul's", which links it to his 12 Feb essay, but finally omitting it from *EOT* as "chiefly report". So it is; but the first, third, and concluding paragraphs are rich in Coleridgian texture; there are links also to 22 and 27 Feb and, on Paul, 2 Jan.

WHEN the intelligence first arrived of the secession of Russia from the continental war, we ventured to predict that Paul the First would retain his purpose of remaining inactive, only while the bustle and first heat of his quarrel with Austria kept him in activity. We regarded the secession as no other than an act of political coquetry, well knowing that his vanity was too deeply interested, and the dream of his being the deliverer of Europe too fondly fostered, to let him remain either neutral, or only a subaltern, in this war of religion and territory.—Nor did we forget, or omit duly to appreciate the influence and intriguing genius of the crowd of French Emigrants at Petersburgh.

Our predictions have been fully verified by the Paris Journals to the 20th, which we received yesterday. By these it appears,[1] that a courier from Petersburgh arrived at Vienna on the 1st instant, with orders for the Russian armies to go back to the Rhine, and other Russian troops from Lithuania are to march thither, so as to enable the Russians to open the campaign in great force. This intelligence is confirmed from all parts of Germany; and orders are even given at Memmingen and other places, to prepare quarters and provisions for the Russians. Suwarrow seems to have expected this counter-order, as he took Vienna on his way home. The conferences at Prague, at which Suwarrow, Lord Minto, and the Austrian General Bellegarde assisted, had for their object to explain the differences which had arisen between the Austrians and Russians, and to reconcile those nations. The representations of Suwarrow upon the result of those conferences seem to have induced the Emperor Paul to order his army back to the Rhine. A misunderstanding between the Russians and Austrians at Ancona is given as the cause of the disagreement between the two Courts; but we know others more important exist, such as the situation in which Suwarrow found himself in Switzerland, the ambitious views of Austria in Italy, and her refusal to pledge herself to fight for the restoration of the Bourbons.

[1] The following news digest may have been prepared by an assistant.

These causes cannot have been removed. The Emperor of Russia may have ordered his armies back to the Rhine, but we cannot believe, that the reconciliation is sincere, or if it be sincere, that it will be permanent. The selfish ambition of the House of Austria will ever make her an object of suspicion to her continental allies; and the vanity which has prompted the crazy hope of transmuting barbarians into chivalrous heroes[2] has undoubtedly rendered the other party jealous and querulous from feelings of rivalry. We cannot, therefore, entertain any sanguine hopes from such a coalition—a coalition which has been so often rent and torn, that the very substance of the texture must have been injured by the botchery with which it has been stitched together again—a coalition which not only has no common object, but of which the objects are in absolute contradiction to each other; of which therefore "the parties travel in one road"[3] only to jostle and distract. We are assured Austria and Russia never have been reconciled since the failure of Suwarrow in Switzerland; and it is to be expected that the Emperor Paul will again display views so enthusiastic, or a disposition so querulous, that his coquetry will embarrass the campaign.

It appears probable that the immediate cause of this change of conduct in the Russian Cabinet may have been a threat on the part of Austria to make peace with France, if she were left alone to oppose her. It is certain that Bonaparte made propositions of peace directly to the Austrian Minister Thugut,[4] without the mediation of Prussia; the *contre projet* of Austria is said to have been extravagantly unreasonable. And we shall pay and support Austria, to enable her to extort extravagant terms from France! Duroc,[5] Bonaparte's confidential Agent, has arrived at Strasburgh, apparently with some important communication to Austria. Whatever may be the final result of this precarious state of affairs, preparations are making on both sides to open the campaign. The Archduke is to be reinforced with ten thousand troops of the Empire, and the Elector of Bavaria is to provide 40,000 men. Moreau[6] is actively employed in organising

[2] Cf 8 Jan (above): "metamorphosed the dark and hopeless Serfs of the North into warriors", also 6 Aug (below): "Suwarrow and his Russians [and]...our Bond-street officers... transmute into the chaste, gentle, and sober knights of ancient chivalry...". For other transmutations see 3 Feb, 19 Mar 1800; 2 Oct and 4 Nov 1802.

[3] Pitt, as reported by C, speech of 17 Feb.

[4] Baron Franz Maria von Thugut (1736–1818), Austrian Foreign Minister since 1793.

[5] Géraud Christophe Michel Duroc (1772–1813), Bonaparte's chief aide-de-camp.

[6] For Moreau see 6 Jan 1800, above, n 2.

the French army of the Rhine, which, the Paris papers say, will be commanded by Bonaparte in person. A scarcity of provisions, and the inclemency of the season,[a] have compelled the Austrians to retire from the advanced posts in Piedmont. A scarcity, we might have said a famine, prevails in Genoa, Piedmont, and Switzerland, in all the countries from the Mediterranean to the Rhine at Basle; and it is added, that the Piedmontese, exasperated by the Austrian and Russian exactions, and indignant at finding their King not restored, are ready to receive the French with open arms.[7]

The Paris Journals give some important details of the further suppression of the Chouans. Those who have surrendered with a sincere intention of submitting to the Republican Government have been spared. Georges and other Chiefs are actually arrived in Paris.[8] But others, suspected of a design to make peace only that they might the better be able, at a future period, to make war, are treated in a different manner. Frotte offered some time ago to make peace, but it is said he refused to give up his arms, and he was suspected of being very insincere in his proposals, which were in consequence rejected. He has since been taken with his staff, and is to be tried by a military commission. His fate may be anticipated from the publication of his letter in *The Moniteur*, to shew his insincerity.[9] While pardon and oblivion are held out to those Chouans who sincerely surrender, instant death is threatened to all those taken with arms in their hands, or any ensigns of Royalty. An Agent of the Chouans is said to have been discovered in Paris, in whose possession an extensive correspondence has been found; among other articles, the instructions of the English Government, in which the Chouans are desired to make peace now, in order that at a future period they may burst out into war, when that war can be rendered effective by the co-operation of the English and Russians. Our readers will remember, that Mr. Pitt in his speech on the 3d of February affirmed, that this *premature* attempt of the Chouans was in opposition to the wishes and advice

[a] *M Post*: seasons,

[7] Piedmont had belonged to Charles Emmanuel IV, King of Sardinia; its return had been one of Pitt's desiderata in 1798 and would be so again in 1814–15.

[8] Georges Cadoudal (1771–1804), Breton leader of the Chouans, had an interview in Paris with Bonaparte but was suspected of plotting to murder him and fled to England (as he had often done). He would return in 1803, with British Government drafts to finance a rising in Paris, would be arrested following the exposure of Pichegru, and guillotined.

[9] Louis de Frotté (1755–1800), general of the royalist army, though assured of safe conduct, was tried 17 Feb and shot 18 Feb at Bonaparte's own order.

of the English Government. The instructions are therefore not improbably genuine; or if they be forgeries, and meant as the retort courteous[10] to the manufacturers of Intercepted Correspondences in England,[11] still they are to be regarded as signals of severe measures against the Western Insurgents.[12]

PARLIAMENT. IX

PITT'S NEW BUDGET

26 February 1800, Wednesday. *EOT* II 310–13, in SC's group of certain attributions; also firm internal evidence.

OUR Readers will have observed, that the Minister concluded his speech on Monday night, without the usual eloquent peroration, and was content to practise one species of his art magic; that namely of telling fortunes by the casting of figures.[1] We must consider, therefore, the budget of this year as a comet without its tail, but are by no means disposed, on this account, to regard it as the less ominous or alarming. The circumstance was, no doubt, intended to convey the idea, that *facts* declared the solidity of our financial system so perfectly that any subsequent declamation could only weaken their effect. "It will strike astonishment (say the friends of the Minister) into the bosoms of our enemies, that in the eighth year of the war the Government should have to impose taxes to no greater amount than the sum of 350,000*l*. The only fresh taxes are the new tax on Tea, and that on the articles of British Distillery."

How gladly should we join these gentlemen in their joy and exultation,[2] would they but instruct us how to acquire that same

[10] Shakespeare *As You Like It* v iv 76.

[11] See 3 and 17 Feb, above, and 17 Mar, below.

[12] SC transcribed an article of 25 Feb 1800, but noted: "D. Stuart most likely." VCL MS LT 84.

[1] Pitt consistently overestimated the yield of his proposed taxes. He had estimated the "triple assessment" would produce £7 million but under protest revised this to £4½ million: the actual yield was £3 million. In 1798 he counted the total income at £102 million and reckoned that a 10% tax would produce £10 million. The yield for the first year, 1799–1800, was about £5,800,000. His estimate now (24 Feb) was £7 million; it would yield again only a little over £5,800,000. See A. Farnsworth *Addington, Author of the Modern Income Tax* (1951) 12, 14, 19, 22.

[2] C takes his cue from the levity of Pitt's budget speech. Coming to the section headed "Taxes", which "used always to be contemplated with such dread", Pitt expected the public to "see the beneficial effect" of his new system; he "concluded by saying, that he needed not to add any thing to a statement so highly satisfactory" (Debrett x 699–700). One member's speech of criticism was met from the Treasury benches with astonishment

serviceable treacherousness of memory by which *they* have forgotten the continuation of the Income tax! What if a quack, newly arrived from America, on being questioned concerning the state of health in some particular part of that continent, should answer—"O! we are uncommonly well there, thank Heaven, and *my* grand infallible preventives! There's nothing new in the way of disease, except indeed a sort of cough attended by a slight attack on the spirits."—"*What! are you quite free from the Yellow Fever?*"—"Nay, nay; not from the Yellow Fever! But then *that's* nothing *new*, you know."

When the Collector knocks at the door, the industrious man will not find one pang less at his heart, or one penny more preserved in his purse, because the tax which he is to pay was *first* levied in 1799,[3] and only *continued* in the present year. The professional man, who is prevented by it from looking forward to leisure in his old age; the tradesman, whose profits are eaten up, and whose affairs are exposed to an injurious publicity by it;[4] the poor annuitant, who must give up for the shedding of blood, and the restoring of the Bourbons, that part of his pittance, which he would otherwise have laid aside for his children or widow; these will feel the Income Tax always new; every year some new circumstance, domestic sickness, or public scarcity, will cause it to be paid with new sensations, with new aversion. Why have we so few new burthens in this year? Because an attempt is to be made to perpetuate the Income Tax, that heaviest of all burthens; that Income Tax, which the Minister *smuggled* into a law, under the false cover, that it should be of short duration.

The breaking of a solemn pledge is made a subject of exultation, and the honey of praise extracted from the night-shade of perfidy. But it has been ever the conduct of the Minister to procure powers under colourable pretexts for a limited time, and afterwards to pass them into perpetual laws; or to answer the same purpose, by having them renewed at stated periods in the Medea cauldron of a confiding majority! Thus, in the Russian and Spanish armaments in the years

"that the honourable gentleman should attempt to repress the joyful sensations which every one must" feel. "Never had the nation greater cause for joy or a greater call for gratitude to the Minister who conducted its concerns" (x 707).

3 Voted for in Nov 1798 as less odious than the triple assessment that caused such protest in Dec 1797.

4 In actual fact, a weak point in Pitt's tax was an inability to enforce collection of anything like their share from the men of trade. Their 10% the first year should have been £4 million: they paid only £1,200,000. For the second year the unexposed tradesmen paid even less. (The general situation was considerably saved by the "Voluntary Contributions" allowed for in the act.) Farnsworth 19–22.

1790–91.[5] New taxes were raised, like a toll-gate at a subscription bridge, which were to pay the entire expenses of those armaments in a few years, and then to be discontinued; but these, too, are permanent. Thus, too, the suspension of the Habeas Corpus Act, which is to *cast its skin* annually, and undergo a mimic death only to insure itself a perpetual existence.

Alas! we follow the superstition of antient Rome, that once in a time of alarm believed a serpent to be Aesculapius![6]

The Minister tells us, that in the next year the Income Tax will become more productive; and that it may be so, he will probably pursue his old system of killing two birds with one stone, and make regulations that will at the same time increase the power and influence of the Administration. But he must remember, that what almost all will attempt to do, many will do successfully, and that he first gave the lesson of deceit. We should not therefore be surprised, if the tax should become yearly less, instead of more productive. But *while* it continues, in the name of common sense, let the creatures of Government be silent concerning the lightness of the fresh burthens! While it continues, the whole science of financial phlebotomy may safely lie idle! The Minister has no need to open new veins, he has already touched an artery.[7]

DIPLOMACY. IV

THE PATRIOT KING OF PRUSSIA

27 February 1800, Thursday. *EOT* II 381–3; in SC's group of probable attributions, confirmed by strong internal evidence. Reprinted in *Courier*, the same day, headed "The King of Prussia".

BY the last news from Paris, we are assured the Emperor of Germany[1] is indignant at the attempt of Prussia to mediate between him and France.—It is more than probable, both that

[5] The confiding daughters of Pelias cut up their father to be made young again in Medea's cauldron—while Medea fled. (In *CN* I 882 C summarises this fable, suggesting it be "Applied to revolutionary Incendiaries". In 1802 he suggests it to Sotheby for a tragedy: *CL* II 857–8.) The ironies are intricate. Although the "laws" of ministerial power are death to (suspension of) the Law, the confiding legislators who constitute the cauldron for Pitt's herbs may imagine they assist in a ritual of rejuvenation, such as *some* of Medea's concoctings were. Ovid *Metamorphoses* 7.251–349. On the Russian armament, see above, 24 Dec 1799.

[6] See Ovid *Metamorphoses* 15.628–744; and see C. Kerényi *Asklepios: Archetypal Image of the Physician's Existence* tr Ralph Manheim (1959) 3–17.

[7] For another metaphor linking taxation and the circulation of blood, see *Friend* No 10 (*CC*) II 159 (I 229).

[1] I.e. Francis II.

Bournonville took with him to Berlin definite propositions of peace, and that these propositions have met the approbation of the Prussian Court. If this should be confirmed, and if the propositions made by France, and delivered in by Prussia at Vienna, should be rejected; and if it should appear evident that this rejection originated in the ambition of the House of Austria; Prussia, by the joint necessities of honour and self-preservation, must become a party in the war.[2]

Beyond all doubt the young King will previously use all possible means of pacification. The ultimate success of these attempts is an object of our anxious hopes, but it lies far beyond the ken of our foresight. In the mean time it cannot be disguised that the Nobles in the less civilized parts of the Prussian dominions look with jealous eyes on their King's partiality to a system of Reformation; that his attempts to ameliorate the wretched situation of the oppressed peasantry have been crossed and thwarted by them; and that his determination to subject all ranks equally to a legal taxation has been received by them, as such schemes have been always received by privileged orders. "How (observed our great Milton) can such men not be corrupt, whose very cause is the bribe of their own pleading?"[3] The officers, however, who are all Nobles, the whole army, and the people, of course, throughout Prussia, are attached to the young King with an enthusiasm unexampled since the time of the Great Frederic, who, say the Prussians, is now for the first time no longer Frederic the *Unique*. The exquisite beauty, the simplicity, and pure domestic character of the Queen, render this attachment more intense, and throw around it the rich colouring of a chivalrous passion.[4] A fragment from one of Wieland's celebrated "*Dialogues between you and me*," has appeared in an Evening Paper. In these dialogues, published so early as March, 1798, Wieland had indicated the expediency of making Bonaparte Dictator in France.[5]—One of

[2] Napoleon's way of wooing young Frederick William III of Prussia, who had moved tentatively to liberalise the feudal rigour of the decaying system he inherited, was to invite him to mediate between France and Austria. The move would eventually involve Prussia in temptations to an alliance with France.

[3] Milton *Of Reformation Touching Church-Discipline in England* bk II: "...how can these Men not be corrupt...". Milton is writing of office-holders defending "their Bishopricks, Deaneries, Prebends, and Chanonies...". *Works* ed Toland (Amsterdam 1698) I 273.

[4] In Jun 1799 C himself had gone to Cassel to see the King and Queen Louise. *CN* I Notes p xxiv; cf *CL* I 577.

[5] Christoph Martin Wieland's "Dialogues between Four Eyes" is quoted in *The Times* of 22 Jan 1800 under the heading "Prediction respecting Bonaparte" and is interpreted as foretelling the overthrow of the 1795 Constitution and the choice of a Dictator with a foreign name. "Bonaparte then?...

our foreign Ministers accompanied the extract with a commentary, in which he expressed his belief, that this prophecy was not the result of conjectural sagacity, but that it had arisen out of communications with Sieyes, or some other of the new philosophers, and that it is another proof of the existence of the conspiracy developed in the books of the Abbe Barruel.[6] To have conjectured that the dead calm of real slavery should succeed to the tempests of a nominal freedom,[7] and that the mastership should fall to the man who had been crowned by victory and the sciences with a two-fold laurel, required, we should suppose, no peculiar illumination. If, however, these dialogues do indeed expound the Book of Fate, an unfulfilled prediction may be added to the one already verified; for in the same work a hint is thrown out, that the young King of Prussia is to confer a new Constitution moulded after the British on the whole North of Germany, and to merit by his docility in the school of existing circumstances, and by his mild equity, the peculiar praise of Marcus Aurelius. This, of course, would not be effected without a quarrel with Russia and the Emperor. In other respects he might make the attempt without much hazard. The events of the French revolution have so much strengthened monarchy, and depreciated plans for political liberty, that a patriot King would run much less risk of eventual despotism, than of seeing his charters returned, like those

---

Who else?" The publication in March 1798, four months after young Frederick's accession to the throne, was in the *Neuen Teutschen Merkur* I (1798) 259–88: "Gesprache unter vier Augen. ii. Ueber den neufränkischen Staatseid: 'Hass dem Königthum'." These "Dialogues" or "têtes-à-têtes" constitute vol XXXI (*Unter vier Augen*: 1799) of Wieland's *Sämmtliche Werke* (Leipzig 1794–1811).

[6] For Barruel see 8 Jan 1800, above, n 4. The repercussions are described in William Taylor *Historic Survey of German Poetry* (3 vols 1828–30) II 487–8: "in the second dialogue on the French oath of hatred to royalty, occurs the proposal, afterwards acted upon by the French, for investing Bonaparte with dictatorial power, as the most tried and efficient remedy for anarchy. This proposal, however natural and obvious a consequence of the known opinions and learning of Wieland, appeared, after its realization, like the inspired dictate of supernatural prescience....In order to destroy the merits of this guess, or counsel, the enemies of Wieland's sentiments attributed it to secret intelligence, conveyed through supposed confederacies of the illuminati. The vulgar (ambassadors belong sometimes to the vulgar) weakly credited this imputation: the curs of anti-jacobinism were hallooed throughout Europe upon the sage of Osmanstadt: he was reviled and insulted as the hired mouth-piece of Parisian conspirators."

[7] Cf the contrast between the "cadaverous tranquillity of despotism" and the "breezes and noisy gusts" of freedom, in *PD: Lects 1795* (*CC*) 289—a passage cited above in relation to 27 Dec 1799.

of Honorius by the Gauls, as likely to occasion an useless expence.[8] Desire has perished with Hope; and Hope has died of a dead palsy, occasioned by excess of stimulation!

[1 March 1800, Saturday]

A great variety of poetical and other favors shall be inserted next week.

[10 March 1800, Monday]

The admirable Remarks on Bonaparte came too late for this day. They shall positively appear to-morrow.

BONAPARTE. I

IN HIS RELATIONS TO FRANCE[1]

11 March 1800, Tuesday; except "I", *M Post* title. *EOT* II 313–19, in SC's group of certain attributions. The portrait of Bonaparte as "commanding genius" relates to that of Washington, 27 Jan and 25 Mar, and was to have been expanded to make a contrasting pair with Pitt, 19 Mar.

IT is too common to mistake for the causes of the late Revolution in France the accidents which determined the manner and moment of its explosion. The arrival of Bonaparte from Egypt, his ambition, his temerity, and his good luck, were indeed indispensable as occasions and subordinate agents; but would of themselves have been as powerless, and of as rapid extinction, as the sparks from a sky-rocket let off in a storm of rain.[2] The real causes of the usurpation must be sought for in the general state of the public feeling and

[8] The point to which C refers, in Gibbon III 280 (ch 31), is rather that the Gauls "seem to have declined this imaginary gift of a free constitution, as the last and most cruel insult of their oppressors". Honorius had proposed an assembly of the seven provinces of Gaul, A.D. 418.

[1] For an article of 4 Mar to which C may have made some contribution, see App A, below. During March C was attempting to pay up his promises to Stuart, while holding to his original resolve to leave London by April. Stuart, however, was hoping to draw him into a larger scheme, offering "half shares in the two Papers, the M.P. & Courier, if I would devote myself with him to them". See *CL* I 578–9, 582, 584–5. Whatever "half shares" meant, C talked of having turned down an almost certain "2000£ a year".

C's essays of 11, 13, 19, and 27 Mar constitute a partial settling of accounts—with his readers and editor, and with Pitt and Bonaparte—during which he makes further promises.

[2] A variant of C's favourite image from Burns, of snow falling upon a river. See *Friend* (*CC*) I 110 and n 4 (II 74); *BL* I 60.

opinion; in the necessity of giving concentration and permanence to the Executive Government; and in the increasing conviction that it had become good policy to exchange the forms of political freedom for the realities of civil security, in order to make a real political freedom possible at some future period. The reasons for preferring a new power under a new title to the restoration of Monarchy were many and irrefragable.

First, the attempt could be realised without any approximation to that most dreadful of all revolutions, a revolution of property; a fact, the knowledge, and deep feeling of which, attach all the new rich men to the Chief Consulate. Now in all great cities in all countries, much more therefore in a revolutionary country, the possessors of wealth newly acquired will be more powerful than men of hereditary wealth, because they are more pliant, because they are more active, and because, in consequence of having experienced a greater variety of scene and circumstance, they have, collectively, more talent and information. Add to this,[3] that in France, the men of hereditary wealth are of very various creeds respecting the restoration of Monarchy; but the new rich men *can* have but one creed on that subject, and of that one creed they are not only unwavering believers, but likewise zealous apostles.

Secondly, a Chief Consulate admitted a choice of person; a circumstance of incalculable significance in the present affairs of France. It is, we confess, a grievous error to calculate on the virtue and wisdom of any nation; but still we cannot, with Ministers, expect such excess of folly in the French, as to believe (however as Englishmen we may wish it), that (menaced as France now is by the boundless ambition of Austria, and stripped of her navy, her commerce, and her colonies, by the monopolising marine of England), the majority of the French nation will consent to entrust the supreme power to a weak man, the puppet of Priests and irritated Nobles, and bound by an unnatural weight of obligation to the natural enemies of his country. In conniving at the usurpation of Bonaparte, they have seated on the throne of the Republic a man of various talent, of commanding genius, of splendid exploit, from whose policy the peaceful adherents of the old religion anticipate toleration; from whose real opinions and habits the men of letters and philosophy are assured of patronage; in whose professional attachment and individual associations the military, and the men of military talent, look confidently for the exertions of a comrade and a brother; and,

[3] In 1802 C will neglect this argument.

finally, in whose uninterrupted felicity the multitude find an object of supersitition and enthusiasm. The Patriots of France, who mourn that their country is too unregenerate to be capable at present of genuine Republicanism, are not however ignorant or insensible of the immense difference between the rank and prosperity of Great Britain under Cromwell, and its degradation, weakness, and national depravity, under that[a] brotheller, that ——[b] of Sidney and Russell, its restored Monarch.[4]

Thirdly, a Chief Consulate was the only conceivable means of uniting the parties in France, or at least of suspending their struggles. Even if we should concede (what appears to us an absurdity), that the majority in that kingdom are as decidedly in favour of Louis XVIII. as in the first years of our Revolution the majority in this kingdom were in favour of the Pretender; still, however, the restoration of the Monarch would leave the minority irreconcileable. It would leave no possibility, it would permit no hope, of the realization of their projects at some more distant period. But the Chief Consulate is a much more malleable thing. It pretends to no sacredness; it is no Nile, made mysterious by the undiscoverableness of its fountain-head;[5] it exists, because it is suitable to existing circumstances; and when circumstances render it unnecessary, it is destructible without a convulsion. The Republicans, the Jacobins, and even the *patriotic* Royalists, can still hope, can still contemplate the usurpation, as only the transient means of a permanent end. How well this delusion is adapted to human nature, how quietly a suspension and re-suspension of our freedom is submitted to, where a *formal* repeal would be resisted with life and property, we in this country are now suffering under the proof.[6] It is well known, that a considerable part of the submission to William the Third was owing to the hopes, which the Jacobites conceived from his successor.[7] In all innovations in human

[a] *EOT*: the [b] murderer

[4] In 1683 the Whig opposition to Charles II was liquidated by the trial and beheading of eminent republican leaders, including Algernon Sidney (1622–83) and William, Lord Russell (1639–83). If C had directly named Charles their "murderer" he and Stuart would have been open to a charge of libel on the monarchy. See *Friend* (*CC*) I 79 and n 1. Note the shift of blame to "those, who misled an English Jury to the murder of Algernon Sidney" in *Friend* I 92 (II 67) in, appropriately, a chapter on libel.

[5] The mysterious source of the Nile, somewhere in Abyssinia, had great symbolic fascination for C and WW.

[6] Alluding to recent re-enactment of suspension of the Habeas Corpus Act. See above, 26 Feb.

[7] C implies that the House of Brunswick, even before the Act of Settlement, was understood to be the line of succession.

affairs, that change bids fairest to be permanent, which permits to the discontented a hope of further change; still more so, when, as in the present case, it may be made appear even as the means of that further change.

These seem to us the causes, which placed Bonaparte in the Chief Consulate. Of his own share in that event we have repeatedly declared our abhorrence; but it is required of us by truth and common justice to admit, that since then, his interests, and those of his country and of Europe, have run completely parallel. The first and chief article of the test required of those whom Bonaparte employs in the service of the Republic, is, not that they shall have such or such opinions, but that they shall assent to the necessity of suspending the operation of such and such opinions, wherein they run counter to the existing circumstances. By this toleration he has collected around his immediate interests all the talent of France; and as man is a placable being; as abstract notions give way to surrounding realities; as assumed opinions soon become real ones; and the *suspension* of a tenet is a fainting-fit, that precedes its death; it is probable, that by this toleration he may really reconcile those whom he has brought together, and convert this armistice of factions into a permanent peace. Meantime, it is undeniable, that already his commanding genius has introduced a new tone of morality into France, and that it is now fashionable to assume the rigid and simple character of the Great Consul.[8] Vice cannot now perpetrate its orgies under a gauze cover, as during the Monarchy; or in the open air, as during the dynasty of the Jacobins. It must now shut the door, and draw the curtains. This may be hypocrisy; but let it be remembered, that however execrable hypocrisy may be in the individual, yet in a nation at large it is a symptom of convalescence. Perhaps even in individuals, in every reform from vice there is a middle, a transient, and half-conscious state of hypocrisy. Now for the first time since the Revolution, neither the savage sansculotterie of the Jacobins, nor the intensely selfish frivolity, so fashionable during the weak Government of the Directory, is tolerated—but a composed and serious manner is demanded from men, even as a test of good breeding, in the present awful pressure of France upon all the world, and of all the world upon France. In his individual character and conduct, the

[8] "Since the elevation of Bonaparte, who is remarkably taciturn, gravity is come into fashion, and what you would call a good *horse laugh* is deemed to be quite vulgar. The women dress more decorously." Letter from Paris, quoted in *M Post* 27 Feb. The sensuality of the French had been one of C's grounds for Recantation in 1798.

Chief Consul has hitherto[9] supported the part of a man ambitious of greatness: too intensely pre-occupied to be otherwise than austere in morals; too confident in his predestined fortune to be suspicious or cruel; too ambitious of a new greatness for the ordinary ambition of conquest or despotism. He has opened the prisons and the churches; he has recalled the zealots, if only they were lovers of their country; and the priests, if only they were quietists; and both by consular edict, and private example, has endeavoured to persuade his fellow-citizens not to yield themselves up to their dissensions as politicians, till they had first submitted themselves to the kindly operation of their common sympathies, as men. In his[a] usurpation, Bonaparte stabbed his honesty in the vitals; it has perished—we admit, that it has perished—but the mausoleum, where it lies interred, is among the wonders of the world.

BONAPARTE. II

IN HIS RELATIONS TO ENGLAND[1]

13 March 1800, Thursday; except "II", *M Post* title. *EOT* II 384–8; in SC's group of probable attributions; linked by title to the certain essay of 11 Mar; certified also by details of style: the Minister animated by the spirit of an angry woman;

[a] *M Post, EOT*: this [a misprint]

[9] Deutsch (pp xv–xx) cautions against judging Napoleon "too much as a fixed and definite personality". It is especially fallacious "to interpret the views and intentions of Bonaparte, First Consul, by the actions and expressions of the Napoleon of the Grand Empire". At first he accepted and pursued the traditional French policy of securing a "natural" eastern frontier; "only after the overwhelming triumph of 1805 did [Napoleonic policy] turn into a system of unlimited aggression". Peace *was* achieved in 1802; renewal of war "was not merely the result of Napoleon's personal policy....During the brief period of general peace the First Consul was usually considered an influence for moderation and stability in France and even in Europe. Not only was he looked upon as the sole individual strong enough to curb the Revolution, but it was not forgotten that he had used his great personal triumphs (the splendid victories of the years IV and V, the 18th brumaire, and Marengo) to attempt to bring about peace. Even so antagonistic a spirit as Friedrich Gentz was for a time sympathetically inclined toward the young Consulate. Writing a month after the coup d'état, he declared with relative optimism: 'For the first time since the Republic came into existence, the desire for peace promises to be more than a trick of war or a cloak for extortion.' (*Historisches Journal für 1799*, II, 477)."

[1] C, while working up studies of Bonaparte and Pitt, now discontinued writing leading paragraphs, though he was willing to help with them. He may at least have suggested points for the days' leaders of 12, 14, 15, 17 Mar; after that his traces cease until mid-April. See *CL* I 581, to Stuart, undated but fitting early March: "I will send

the incomprehensible policy and grammatical syntax of the Grenville Note; the artful parallel to British arguments in the hypothetical French ones (second paragraph); the ironic twist in the concluding sentence.

AMONG the first public acts of Bonaparte, as Chief Consul, were his pacific overtures to Great Britain. He had assumed a new office, had advertised himself in a new character, and imposed a new Constitution. In all this he had gratified the ruling propensity of the French Nation, to whom a certain degree of novelty, by whatever means it is procured, appears to have become a necessary stimulus. Not to have evinced himself ambitious of peace would have been inconsistent, and have betrayed as opprobrious a slovenliness, as that of the scene-shifter who left a camp standing in front, after he had changed the side-wings to a temple of Janus.[2] His conduct, therefore, was equally the dictate of individual interest, and enlarged political wisdom. For pacific overtures, whether they were successful or unsuccessful, would have a necessary tendency to unite the real lovers of their country. If they were welcomed on the part of the enemy, and led to a final pacification of the two countries, the greatness and reality of the blessing (a blessing too bestowed so undeniably by *his* zeal and moderation) could not fail to give a permanent popularity to his Government. If they were repelled, after every honourable pledge of their sincerity had been afforded, a national unanimity in the vigorous prosecution of the war was to be expected, both from a sentiment of the indignity sustained by the repulse, and from the demonstrated unavoidableness of the evil. Add to this, such repulse on the part of Great Britain could only be occasioned by the avowed determination of her Minister to restore Monarchy and the hereditary Noblesse in France, and would therefore remove from the character of the Chief Consul all suspicions of a concealed attachment to Feudalism.

It might, indeed, have been urged by the advocates for the war in France, that the avowed hatred of the English Minister to the existence of a French Republic rendered a peace with England insecure and dangerous; and that in the present unsettled state of French parties, it was better that the revenues of Great Britain should

---

you by Lamb this Evening three or four paragraphs of 7 or 8 lines each". This may refer to matter for one leader—or to several nuclei. (It could refer to Coleridgian or Lambian squibs; but none appear in the *M Post* of March or April.) For the leader of 12 Mar see App A, below.

[2] Perhaps an allusion to a contemporary production of, for example, *Coriolanus*. On the temple of Janus see also 22 Mar 1802 and n 5.

be expended in expeditions to Quiberon, Holland, and the West Indies, than in the corruption of Frenchmen, and those counter-revolutionary intrigues, to which a nominal peace would but facilitate the means, instead of removing the propensity. On these grounds the same reasoners had justified the policy, though not the insolence, of the Directory in their negotiations at Lisle. The Chief Consul could not but be aware of that portion of truth which was conveyed in these representations; but considering that the former Governors of France had given real cause of offence to Great Britain, by national denunciations equally intemperate with those of the English Minister, he waived the objection. He pleaded for mutual forgiveness and reciprocal amnesty—or if these blessings could not be realized, he was at least assured of evincing that the fault was now confined to the enemy. Accordingly, he commenced his proposals for peace by an absolute renunciation of Jacobinism, admitting His Majesty to be the lawful Sovereign of a free and happy nation; and then proceeded to disavow all projects of aggrandisement by conquest, affirming that both countries were already more powerful than their own true interests made requisite.

These respectful and even complimentary proposals were rejected in an answer, the policy and grammatical syntax of which were equally incomprehensible. Our Minister seems to have been animated by the spirit of an angry woman, who shuts the door with a fling against a rival, but first however eases her temper by a fit of scolding. Bonaparte was too great a man to be made angry by such anger. That respect, which the dignity of the British nation demanded, was not to be withheld in consequence of the vulgar heat and insolence of the Cabinet at St. James's. In proof of that respect, and of his sincerity in his former proposals, he made a second overture with a scrupulous observance of all accustomed diplomatic forms—forms, arbitrary indeed, and of little importance; but which, from that very circumstance, it is even more puerile to object to, than to insist upon. He was again repelled, and in the same tone; and a public declaration made, that the Restoration of Monarchy in France was the only possible condition, or, (which differs in reality but in words) the sole *definable* condition of peace.

The after language of Ministers in Parliament, and of the Ministerial slave-gang out of Parliament, our posterity will probably be preserved from knowing by its intense stupidity. But the Chief Consul has never forgot *his* character, or suffered his Ministers to forget theirs. No single inflammatory, no one resentful expression, has been uttered, or authorised by the French Government; they have been either employed in removing false prejudices against the English Ministry, as in the case of the French prisoners in England, or have been wholly silent. Conciliatory language may lead to peace, but abuse and recrimination can be of no service to the conduct of war.

It was a real and important concession to the merits and intentions of Bonaparte, that the Government, which were making the restoration of the old feudal system in France their sole and ultimate object, had considered *him* as the greatest obstacle to the accomplishment of that object; that his usurpation they had passed slightly over, but of his attachment to liberty and progressive amelioration they had proclaimed an overflowing conviction by their charges of Jacobinism; and that they had closed their high, though involuntary panegyric, on his genius and humanity, by pronouncing him a complete contrast to that redoubtable conqueror of Warsaw and Ismail, Prince Field-Marshal Suwarrow.[3] We sincerely wish, for the sake of our country, and of mankind, that these praises may be confirmed by the event; but we must wait, ere *we* can give our full assent to them.

BONAPARTE. III

THE HOPE FOR PEACE

15 March 1800, Saturday. *EOT* II 388–91; in SC's group of probable attributions; she noted the "Midas" figure as characteristic (VCL MS 19 v. 1 f 12[v]), and there are other slight but telling marks of C's style.

YESTERDAY we again received French Papers, and up to the 12th inst. The spring of the year approaching, in which nature begins to re-produce, and man re-commences the work of destruction, each successive communication, however undecisive the facts communicated may be, cannot but rise in interest. It is, therefore, a pleasing superstition, not wholly unworthy of a momentary indulgence in a generous mind, to regard the late unwonted rapidity of intercourse as an happy omen. These Papers convey to us two facts that *confirm* our remarks of yesterday, rather than afford materials for any new observations.[1] Bonaparte has addressed the people of

[3] See 4 Feb (Pitt's speech of 3 Feb) and n 9, above.

[1] In the *M Post* of 14 Mar three columns of new Proclamations by Napoleon are accompanied by renewed predictions of peace: "By the language of Bonaparte...it is plain he expects peace; he expects and wishes it, and it is not probable that he will be deceived." In the present essay C says the same thing more subtly. At the end of the month, one thing that prevented his

France on the wisdom and duty of preparing for war, by personal enthusiasm and financial sacrifices; and uses as motives of inducement, not the ordinary appeals to terror or indignation, but the more sublime and humane excitement of hope. In consequence of the official communications, a deputation waited on the Chief Consul, to convey the wishes and approbation of the Tribunate. Bonaparte replied, that all was to be anticipated from the dispositions of France, should she be compelled into a war; *that however all probabilities of peace had not vanished*, and *that the Consuls still entertained the hope of concluding it speedily, without fresh sacrifices on the part of the French*. The Consuls here allude, no doubt, to certain propositions of peace sent to the Rhine from Paris, and from thence conveyed to Vienna by the Austrian General Stippchuts.[a] To these no answer has been yet received, but a favourable one is expected.

The temper of the French nation seems to be precisely that which was predicted, as the natural consequence of an earnest and repeated wish for a general peace having been rejected untried, and with repeated contumelies. They appear to have become that which involves only a verbal contradiction, enthusiastic Moderates. We see not, what one interest any Continental Power can have in continuing the war. It were idle to suppose, that our allies contemplate our monopolizing commerce with our feelings, or even without some alloy of feelings diametrically opposite. Austria has, indeed, ambitious projects to realise; and it is therefore necessary that France should place her vast strength in the attitudes that may most convincingly display it; while she still confines herself to terms, the refusal of which cannot but connect the North of Europe still more closely with her interests. Russia, her only remaining continental enemy, is too suspicious of Austria, too remote from any sympathy in her general principles, and probably too much engaged in nearer anxieties, to be relied upon by the Emperor as an effective Ally.

The Emperor can now treat on high and honourable conditions: the events of a campaign cannot *add much* to the advantages which he may now gain without it; and it may *detract* all: it may give France new Allies, and facilitate new Revolutions, more formidable than the

[a] *EOT*: Stippohuts [elsewhere "Stippochintz"]

writing a final essay "of Bonaparte" was the fact that Bonaparte marched off to war, Austria having proved as stubborn as Grenville.

In her "Conjectured" list SC considered "March 14—Bon. expects peace" (VCL MS 19 v. 1 f 12), but she did not include it in *EOT*. The progression by flat assertion is Stuartian.

French, because conducted on principles less distant from the habits and opinions of the great mass of mankind. We think, therefore, that Austria will finally consent to peace; for though ambitious, she is not mad! But this country, whose navy, whose colonies, whose commerce have been almost doubled by the war, what is to be hoped from this country? We will hope this—we will hope of the good sense, which has distinguished Englishmen, that they will have learnt that commerce and commercial prosperity is an accompaniment and an accessary of a real and national prosperity, but by no means the essence and self-sufficient constituent of it.[2] We will hope, that they will not justify the sneer of those who have compared us to Midas, whose touch turned every thing to gold, and who wanted bread in the midst of it.[3] It is, however, proper, that we should state to our readers, that the accounts from Germany and France tend to the idea of the approaching recommencement of the war. Both the French and Austrian armies are preparing to meet. But when we reflect that these accounts are for the most part created by military movements, which the simple uncertainty of a peace would alone produce and render politic, we are inclined to consider the declarations of the Chief Consul, and the palpable interests of the contending powers, as more than balancing the evidence.

INTERCEPTED CORRESPONDENCE. III

17 March 1800, Monday. *EOT* II 391–4; in SC's group of probable attributions; linked closely with C's preceding and subsequent essays on the subject, though it is "chiefly report" (SC in VCL MS 19 v. 1 f 12v).

PREPARATIONS continue to be made for two Expeditions, which, according to report, have very different objects. One, it is said, is destined for the Mediterranean, and another for Holland or the Western coasts of France; and the preparations for both carried on at the same time cover each other, confounding and perplexing those who attempt to discover, by particular circumstances, the point of attack. The first Expedition is to be commanded by General Sir Charles Stuart, aided by the gallant General Moore, scarcely recovered from his wounds, by Generals Simcoe, St. Clair, &c. General Stuart has commanded in Minorca and other hot climates; General Moore served in Corsica, the West Indies, &c, and the

[2] On C's view of commerce, see 1 Feb 1800 and n 12, above.

[3] See the Midas reference in 10 Jan (2) at n 11, above.

character of the whole of the Staff supports the probability that the Mediterranean is to be the scene of the enterprise. We naturally ask, what is its object in the Mediterranean? Some say Genoa, which must be attacked from the sea; but we have ships enough near that city, and there are Austrian and Italian troops in the neighbourhood sufficient for such an enterprise. Malta may be *an* object in such an expedition, but it cannot be *the* object, especially since the Emperor of Russia has claimed it. Corsica, Cadiz, Toulon; if it were necessary, we could give reasons to shew none of these are the object; nor can any wise object be pointed out in the Mediterranean, except Egypt.

That this is the point of attack has appeared a reasonable conjecture for some time, but we have refrained from being the first of the public journals to mention it; not that we see any danger in its being noticed, since it is publicly spoken of, and believed in well-informed circles, and the French Government is unable to send to Egypt any assistance. Our Cabinet, we believe, begin to suspect that the *intercepted correspondence* was a *hoax* of the French Republicans, to prevent England from sending troops against them in Egypt, by persuading us the French were perishing of all the plagues possible to be imagined. We know, that a year ago, the advice of military men to Government was, not to send troops against the French in Egypt, but to hem them in there and suffer them to perish by disease, the sword, and famine. This advice would have been wise, if the intercepted correspondence had told truth; but we suspect it is found to be false, fabricated for the purpose of deluding us, and filled with the grossest abuse of Bonaparte to disguise and make palatable the poison.[1]

If it be true that the French have deluded us with a false opinion of their weakness in Egypt while they really were in full possession of the country; if it be true that their chief and only dread was the English, to keep whom away they fabricated the correspondence; and if they are now, with an appearance of success, negotiating a peace with the Porte, which will leave them in tranquil and permanent possession of Egypt; then an expedition against the French in that country becomes not merely a diversion of war, but a just and necessary undertaking. Were the French left in possession of Egypt, they might in time expel us from our Eastern possessions, and

[1] C has abandoned his earlier demonstration of ministerial forgery of the letters for this more fruitful hypothesis that ministers were themselves dupes of forgery.

annihilate our India commerce.[2] With Malta and Egypt, France might almost monopolise the commerce of the East. The wisdom, the necessity, the indispensable necessity, of depriving the French of the means of striking so fatal a blow to the power of England, are unquestionable.

Orders have been issued to the Officers on leave in Great Britain and Ireland, from regiments at Gibraltar and Minorca, immediately to take their passage for these garrisons, in a ship which is appointed to convey them. It is probable that the expedition will chiefly consist of English troops, seasoned to the climate, taken from Portugal, Gibraltar, Minorca and Sicily, and that they will be replaced by the regiments now sending from England, among which are two battalions of the 4th foot, two of the 5th, three of the 9th, two of the 17th, one of the 31st, two of the 35th, two of the 40th, two of the 52d, making sixteen battalions, provided the health of the 31st regiment, which we lament to learn has been and continues sickly, should be sufficiently re-established. It is said that Egypt cannot be General Stuart's object, as the troops he takes with him have been completed from the English Militia, who engaged not to serve out of Europe; but if these troops only replace others in Portugal, Gibraltar, Minorca, and Sicily, the engagement with them will not be broken. We confess ourselves not possessed of the slightest information as to the object of the expedition. Our remarks are only such as any thinking man might make upon this general and very interesting topic of conversation.

[17 March 1800, Monday]
PITT and BONAPARTE to-morrow.

[18 March 1800, Tuesday]
The admirable article on Mr. PITT and BONAPARTE, to-morrow.

---

[2] C is moving away from unqualified approval of peace with Bonaparte toward the more imperialistic position of his "Observations on Egypt" of 1804 (BM Egerton MS 2800 ff 118–26; see App B, *Courier* 1804, below). See Colmer 83–4, 168. The 1804 view is that the British should regard Egypt not merely as a door to India but as a colony of potentially "permanent possession".

PITT AND BONAPARTE
PITT

19 March 1800, Wednesday; *M Post* title. *EOT* II 319–29, in SC's certain group; boasted of by C as written "without previous meditation" in one evening (*CL* I 581). Reprinted in the same day's *Courier* under heading "A Pair of Portraits".

PLUTARCH, in his comparative biography of Rome and Greece, has generally chosen for each pair of Lives the two contemporaries who most nearly resembled[a] each other. His work would perhaps have been more interesting, if he had adopted the contrary arrangement, and selected those rather, who had attained to the possession of similar influence, or similar fame, by means, actions, and talents the most dissimilar.[1] For power is the sole object of philosophical attention in man, as in inanimate nature; and in the one equally as in the other, we understand it more intimately, the more diverse the circumstances are with which we have observed it co-exist. In our days the two persons, who appear to have influenced the interests and actions of men the most deeply and the most diffusively, are beyond doubt the Chief Consul of France, and the Prime Minister of Great Britain: and in these two are presented to us similar situations, with the greatest dissimilitude of characters.

William Pitt was the younger son of Lord Chatham;[2] a fact of no ordinary importance in the solution of his character, of no mean significance in the heraldry of morals and intellect. His father's rank, fame, political connections, and parental ambition were his mould:— he was cast, rather than grew. A palpable election, a conscious predestination controlled the free agency, and transfigured the individuality of his mind; and that, which he *might have been*, was compelled into that, which he *was to be*. From his early childhood it was his father's custom to make him stand up on a chair, and declaim before a large company; by which exercise, practised so frequently, and continued for so many years, he acquired a premature and unnatural dexterity in the combination of words, which must of necessity have diverted his attention from present objects, obscured his impressions, and deadened his genuine feelings. Not the *thing* on which he was speaking, but the praises to be gained by the speech,

[a] *EOT*: resemble

[1] As C did in his parallel lives of Erasmus and Voltaire, Luther and Rousseau, in *Friend* (*CC*) I 130ff (II 111ff).

[2] William Pitt, Earl of Chatham (1708–78), the Great Commoner.

were present to his intuition; hence he associated all the operations of his faculties with words, and his pleasures with the surprise excited by them.

But an inconceivably large portion of human knowledge and human power is involved in the science and management of *words*; and an education of words, though it destroys genius, will often create, and always foster, talent.[3] The young Pitt was conspicuous far beyond his fellows, both at school and at college. He was always full grown: he had neither the promise nor the awkwardness of a growing intellect. Vanity, early satiated, formed and elevated itself into a love of power; and in losing this colloquial vanity, he lost one of the prime links that connect the individual with the species, too early for the affections, though not too early for the understanding. At college he was a severe student; his mind was founded and elemented in words and generalities, and these too formed all the super-structure. That revelry and that debauchery, which are so often fatal to the powers of intellect, would probably have been serviceable to him; they would have given him a closer communion with realities, they would have induced a greater presentness to present objects. But Mr. Pitt's conduct was correct, unimpressibly correct. His after-discipline in the special pleader's office, and at the bar, carried on the scheme of his education with unbroken uniformity. His first political connections were with the Reformers; but those who accuse him of sympathising or coalescing with their intemperate or visionary plans, misunderstand his character, and are ignorant of the historical facts. Imaginary situations in an imaginary state of things rise up in minds that possess a power and facility in combining images.—Mr. Pitt's ambition was conversant with old situations in the old state of things, which furnish nothing to the imagination, though much to the wishes. In his endeavours to realise his father's plan of reform, he was probably as sincere as a being, who had derived so little knowledge from actual impressions, could be. But his sincerity had no living root of affection; while it was propped up by his love of praise and immediate power, so long it stood erect and no longer. He became a Member of the Parliament—supported the popular opinions, and in a few years, by the influence of the popular party was placed in that high and awful rank in which he now is. The fortunes of his

[3] C, having thought long and deeply with WW about the growth of creative minds, makes inspired political use of the distinction between genius and talent. A note on the subject (*CN* I 669; cf 669n) occurs in Notebook 10, near C's reports of Pitt's speeches. For a critique of the political application of the genius–talent opposition see Colmer 62–7.

country, we had almost said, the fates of the world, were placed in his wardship—we sink in prostration before the inscrutable dispensations of Providence, when we reflect in whose wardship the fates of the world were placed!

The influencer of his country and of his species was a young man, the creature of another's predetermination, sheltered and weather-fended from all the elements of experience; a young man, whose feet had never wandered; whose very eye had never turned to the right or to the left; whose whole track had been as curveless as the motion of a fascinated reptile! It was a young man, whose heart was solitary, because he had existed always amid objects of futurity, and whose imagination too was unpopulous, because those objects of hope, to which his habitual wishes had transferred, and as it were *projected*, his existence, were all familiar and long-established objects!—A plant sown and reared in a hot-house, for whom the very air, that surrounded him, had been regulated by the thermometer of previous purpose; to whom the light of nature had penetrated only through glasses and covers; who had had the sun without the breeze; whom no storm had shaken; on whom no rain had pattered; on whom the dews of Heaven had not fallen![4]—A being, who had had no feelings connected with man or nature, no spontaneous impulses, no unbiassed and desultory studies, no genuine science, nothing that constitutes individuality in intellect, nothing that teaches brotherhood in affection! Such was the man—such, and so denaturalised the spirit, on whose wisdom and philanthropy the lives and living enjoyments of so many millions of human beings were made unavoidably dependent. From this time a real enlargement of mind became almost impossible. Pre-occupations, intrigue, the undue passion and anxiety, with which all facts must be surveyed; the crowd and confusion of those facts, none of them seen, but all communicated, and by that very circumstance, and by the necessity of perpetually classifying them, transmuted into words and generalities; pride; flattery; irritation; artificial power; these, and circumstances resembling these, necessarily render the heights of office barren heights, which command indeed a vast and extensive prospect, but attract so many clouds and vapours, that most often all prospect is precluded. Still, however, Mr. Pitt's situation, however inauspicious for his real being, was favourable to his fame. He heaped period on

[4] As WW would say of Bonaparte (in a sonnet in *M Post* 16 Sept 1802), "what food | Fed his first hopes? what knowledge could *he* gain?" For the psychological assumptions involved see Erdman (1956).

period; persuaded himself and the nation, that extemporaneous arrangement of sentences was eloquence; and that eloquence implied wisdom.[5] His father's struggles for freedom, and his own attempts, gave him an almost unexampled popularity; and his office necessarily associated with his name all the great events, that happened during his Administration. There were not however wanting men, who saw through this delusion: and refusing to attribute the industry, integrity, and enterprising spirit of our merchants, the agricultural improvements of our land-holders, the great inventions of our manufacturers, or the valour and skilfulness of our sailors to the merits of a Minister, they have continued to decide on his character from those acts and those merits, which belong to him, and to him alone. Judging him by this standard, they have been able to discover in him no one proof or symptom of a commanding genius.[6] They have discovered him never controlling, never creating, events, but always yielding to them with rapid change, and sheltering himself from inconsistency by perpetual indefiniteness. In the Russian war, they saw him abandoning meanly what he had planned weakly, and threatened insolently.[7] In the debates on the Regency, they detected the laxity of his constitutional principles, and received proofs that his eloquence consisted not in the ready application of a general system to particular questions, but in the facility of arguing for or against any question by specious generalities, without reference to any system.[8] In these

[5] C draws somewhat on Dr Thomas Beddoes *Essay on the Public Merits of Mr. Pitt* (1796), as quoted in *The Watchman* No 9; e.g.: "Fluency of elocution however does not appear to be more closely connected with wisdom than facility or elegance of composition." *Watchman* (*CC*) 312.

[6] The contrast with Bonaparte and Washington is meant to be damning. In 1811 C would find another such genius as these in Wellington (*Courier* 22 May 1811). But in *BL* (ch 2) he would distinguish between the peace-time destiny of the "commanding genius" as architect-gardener and his destructiveness "in times of tumult". *BL* (1907) I 20–1. And by 1816 he would express loathing for the whole breed (in App C of *SM*). In a late notebook (No 44, cited in Beer 268, 342) Moses is called "a Man of Commanding Genius". Woodring (pp 199–200) notes that the "commanding genius" of C's prose had "a dramatic senior, the 'commanding spirit,' inspired by the Titanic heroes of Schiller" and appearing in C's *Osorio* and *Piccolomini*. Woodring adds: "In *Zapolya*, after Napoleon had cast a lurid glow over both spirit and station, one evil character recommends another even more evil on Schiller's now-soured principle: 'Let the commanding spirit Possess the station of command!'"

[7] On the Russian crisis of 1791 see 24 Dec 1799 n 4, above.

[8] C pictures Pitt at the threshold of 1788, regarded with hope and suspicion, e.g. during the famous debate of 10 Dec 1788, when the Opposition thought that Pitt's goal was a Regency Council with himself at the head, thus usurping the rights of the Crown.

debates, he combined what is most dangerous in democracy, with all that is most degrading in the old superstitions of Monarchy, and taught an inherency of the office in the person, in order to make the office itself a nullity, and the Premiership, with its accompanying majority, the sole and permanent power of the State. And now came the French Revolution. This was a new event; the old routine of reasoning, the common trade of politics, were to become obsolete. He appeared wholly unprepared for it. Half favouring, half condemning, ignorant of what he favoured, and why he condemned, he neither displayed the honest enthusiasm and fixed principle of Mr. Fox, nor the intimate acquaintance with the general nature of man, and the consequent *prescience* of Mr. Burke.

After the declaration of war, long did he continue in the common cant of office, in declamation about the Scheldt, and Holland, and all the vulgar causes of common contests! and when at last[a] the immense genius of his new supporter had beat him out of these *words*, (words, signifying *places* and *dead objects*, and signifying nothing more) he adopted other words in their places, other generalities—Atheism and Jacobinism—phrases, which he learnt from Mr. Burke, but without learning the philosophical definitions and involved consequences, with which that great man accompanied those words. Since the death of Mr. Burke, the forms and the sentiments, and the tone of the French, have undergone many and important changes: how indeed is it possible, that it should be otherwise, while man is the creature of experience! But still Mr. Pitt proceeds in an endless repetition of the same *general phrases*. This is his element; deprive him of general and abstract phrases, and you reduce him to silence. But you cannot deprive him of them. Press him to specify an *individual* fact[b] of advantage to be derived from a war—and he answers, SECURITY! Call upon him to particularise a crime, and he exclaims—JACOBINISM! Abstractions defined by abstractions! Generalities defined by generalities! As a Minister of Finance, he is still, as ever, the man of words, and abstractions! Figures, custom-house reports, imports and exports, commerce and revenue—all flourishing, all splendid! Never was such a prosperous country, as England, under his administration! Let it be objected, that the agriculture of the country is, by the overbalance of commerce, and by various and complex causes, in such a state, that the country hangs as a pensioner for bread on its neighbours, and a bad season uniformly threatens us with famine—this (it is replied) is owing to our PROSPERITY—all *prosperous* nations

[a] *M Post*: least [corrected in *EOT*] [b] *EOT*: *fact*

are in great distress for food!—Still PROSPERITY, still GENERAL PHRASES, unenforced by one *single image*, one *single fact* of real national amelioration, of any one comfort enjoyed, where it was not before enjoyed, of any one class of society becoming healthier, or wiser, or happier. These are *things*, these are realities;[9] and these Mr. Pitt has neither the imagination to body forth, or the sensibility to feel for. Once indeed, in an evil hour, intriguing for popularity, he suffered himself to be persuaded to evince a talent, for the Real, the Individual: and he brought in his POOR BILL!![10] When we hear the Minister's talents for finance so loudly trumpeted, we turn involuntarily to his POOR BILL—to that acknowledged abortion—that unanswerable evidence of his ignorance respecting all the fundamental relations and actions of property, and of the social union!

As his reasonings, even so is his eloquence. One character pervades his whole being. Words on words, finely arranged, and so dexterously consequent, that the whole bears the semblance of argument, and still keeps awake a sense of surprise—but when all is done, nothing rememberable has been said; no one philosophical remark, no one image, not even a pointed aphorism. Not a sentence of Mr. Pitt's has ever been quoted, or formed the favourite phrase of the day—a thing unexampled in any man of equal reputation.[11] But while he speaks, the effect varies according to the character of his auditor. The man of no talent is swallowed up in surprise: and when the speech is ended, he remembers his feelings, but nothing distinct of

[9] "No person I can believe—no thing I can disbelieve", C jotted in his notebook, at Lamb's four days later. *CN* I 711.

[10] On 22 Dec 1796 Pitt asked leave to bring in his Bill, full of blanks to be filled up by a committee after circulation in the country; on 28 Feb 1797 "while strangers were excluded from the Gallery, there occurred what the *Parliamentary Register* calls 'a conversation upon the farther consideration of the report of the Poor's Bill,' in which nobody but Pitt defended the Bill, and Sheridan and Jolliffe attacked it. With this its Parliamentary history ends." J. L. Hammond and Barbara Hammond *The Village Labourer* (1919) 149. "It was in truth a huge patchwork, on which the ideas of living and dead reformers were thrown together without order or plan." Ibid 151. Bentham's criticism is the most famous, but the Hammonds believe the Bill was killed by the flood of hostile petitions from dismayed magistrates and ratepayers.

[11] Beddoes (*Essay* p 60) had raised this question: "Has a single sentiment that circulates in conversation darted from his lips?" C reopens it, feeling himself to be the author of most of the quoted phrases of Pitt's recent speeches. Beddoes also, in his next sentence, had given the clue ("Has he on any occasion manifested that talent, by which truth is brought before an audience distinctly embodied, and brightly illuminated?") for C's analysis of Pitt's lack (and of Washington's possession) of the "imagination to body forth" realities.

that which produced them—(how opposite an effect to that of nature and genius, from whose works the idea still remains, when the feeling is passed away—remains to connect itself with other[a] feelings, and combine with new impressions!) The mere man of talent hears him with admiration—the mere man of genius with contempt—the philosopher neither admires nor contemns, but listens to him with a deep and solemn interest, tracing in the effects of his eloquence the power of words and phrases, and that peculiar constitution of human affairs in their present state, which so eminently favours this power.[12]

Such appears to us to be the Prime Minister of Great Britain, whether we consider him as a statesman, or as an orator. The same character betrays itself in his private life, the same coldness to realities, [b]to images of realities;[c] and to all whose excellence relates to reality. He has patronised no science, he has raised no man of genius from obscurity, he counts no one prime work of God among his friends. From the same source he has no attachment to female society, no fondness for children, no perceptions of beauty in natural scenery; but he is fond of convivial indulgences, of that stimulation, which, keeping up the glow of self-importance and the sense of internal power, gives feelings without the mediation of ideas.[13]

These are the elements of his mind; the accidents of his fortune, the circumstances that enabled such a mind to acquire and retain such a power, would form a subject of a philosophical history, and that too of no scanty size. We can scarcely furnish the chapter of contents to a work, which would comprise subjects so important and delicate, as the causes of the diffusion and intensity of secret influence; the machinery and state-intrigue of marriages;[14] the overbalance of the commercial interest; the panic of property struck by the late Revolution; the short-sightedness of the careful; the carelessness of the far-sighted; and all those many and various events which have given to a decorous profession of religion, and a seemliness of private morals, such an unwonted weight in the attainment and preservation

[a] *EOT*: the other [b–c] *EOT* omits

[12] Cf *Friend* No 7 (*CC*) II 106.

[13] For a sober assessment of Pitt's drinking, which "helped kill him in the end", see John Ehrman *The Younger Pitt* (New York 1969) 585ff.

[14] The tale of the Prime Minister's efforts to cope with the public consequences of the marriage of the Prince of Wales secretly to Mrs Fitzherbert on 15 Dec 1785 (not mentioned in Pitt's 1787 financial settlement of the Prince's affairs) and then the Prince's state marriage to Caroline of Brunswick 8 Apr 1795 would require indeed a "delicate" investigation.

of public power. We are unable to determine whether it be more consolatory or humiliating to human nature,[15] that so many complexities of event, situation, character, age, and country, should be necessary in order to the production of a Mr. PITT.[16]

(*To-morrow of Bonaparte.*)[17]

[15] For Pitt on "human nature" see above, 13 Jan and 11, 18 Feb 1800.

[16] According to C, "Since the Time of Junius no single Essay ever made more noise in a newspaper than this" (to George Coleridge 2 Oct 1803: *CL* II 1007). Hazlitt acknowledged this "masterly and unanswerable essay" as the source (along with "the conversation of the author") of most of his own remarks on Pitt's speeches, in *Free Thoughts on Public Affairs* (1806). The same note, in Hazlitt's *Political Essays* (1819), continues: "See also Dr. Beddoes's Letter on the public merits of Mr. Pitt..." (Hazlitt 393, with reprint of C's essay, 394–400).

[17] For earlier announcements and later repetitions of this promise see above, I xcv–xcvi, clii, clviii, n 1. The *Courier* this day (19 Mar) reprinted C's essay, headed' 'A Pair of Portraits. Pitt and Bonaparte...To-morrow of Bonaparte)", and repeated the announcement 29 Mar. But after waiting in vain five months the *Courier* editor, T. G. Street, wrote and printed his own "Bonaparte" on 10 Sept. On 7 Oct, still promising Stuart that "Bonaparte shall not loiter", C asked "to see Mr Street's Character" (*CL* I 629). Stuart evidently complied, for in the SC papers there is a leaf from this *Courier* inscribed in the margin: "Essay on Buonaparte. | September 10 | N.B. Not by S. T. C. | but by Mr Street | S. T. C." It is marked in one place with approval and in two with disapproval, if I interpret plus and minus signs aright. VCL MS E F15.4.

Years later C would claim that he had actually written the promised Bonaparte essay but had been driven into an "obstinate refusal to publish it" by Bonaparte's eagerness to read it! See ms Note of c Jul 1817, App B, below. The earliest version of this claim is in C's letter of 2 Oct 1803 to his brother George (*CL* II 1007), written when Bonaparte's invasion of England was momently expected. Here C boasts of the "noise" his Character of Pitt produced and says that "...in somewhat more than a month after the appearance of 'PITT,' *Otto* [Louis-Guillaume Otto, representative of the Consulate in London from Jan 1800 to Nov 1802] sent privately to Stuart, & inquired when the character of Bonaparte would appear—" and, again, through "a confidential friend", told Stuart that "the question was asked at the instance of Bonaparte himself, who had been extremely impressed with the Character of Pitt, & very anxious to see his own—which, no doubt he expected, would be a pure eulogy.—Stuart immediately came to me...". It is easy to credit Bonaparte's curiosity. We know that he had all English newspaper items "which had any reference to France" translated and brought to him regularly (see Henry Redhead Yorke *France in 1802*—1804—121). And occasional items in the *M Post* reveal the editor's direct acquaintance with Otto. Yet C does not seem to have heard about the Napoleonic inquiry at the time, nor could its effect upon him have been as he described it in 1803 or later.

The anecdote of 1803 must be mistaken about the date—or the fact—of Stuart's communicating the inquiry in a conversation. Some time is required ("somewhat more than a month", as C himself says) for Napoleon to have discovered a delay in the appearance of C's eulogy and to have inquired through Otto. But C left London within sixteen days of the publication of the "Pitt", not to return until Nov 1801. Nor would C, in 1800, have responded as he claims in 1803: "Stuart immediately came to me, & was in very high spirits...I turned sad, & answered..." that a dictator "so childishly solicitous for the *panegyric* of a Newspaper Scribbler" would "prove a Tyrant, & the deadliest enemy of the Liberty of the Press"; "Stuart has often talked of publishing this conversation of mine as an instance of political prophecy". *CL* II 1007.

Seven years later, preparing the anecdote for publication (in his notes of 1810, *C Life*—H—512–13), C changed this "conversation" to a correspondence: "...I wrote a prophetic Letter to Mr Stuart, who had considered this anxiety of the First Consul's as a proof of his regard for the Press—I deduced from it, that he would become its bitterest enemy". A main point of the tale in either version is that Napoleon's interest caused C to *refuse* "to publish" his Character, or to refuse to write it ("I did not do it" is ambiguous in the 1803 version): in either version there is supposed to reside an explanation for the non-appearance of a "Bonaparte" in 1800.

The "correspondence" version is more plausible; yet what in fact do we find C saying in his letters of 1800? To Samuel Purkis, 27 Mar, he does "not despair of making Bonaparte as good as *Pitt*..." (*CL* I 583). C's first extant letter to Stuart after leaving town promises: "On Thursday I will set to, & will not leave off, on my word & honor, till I have done a second part of Pitt, & Buonaparte" (I 603, 15 Jul). No refusal, no word of Otto. In the next two letters to Stuart, c 28 and c 30 Sept (*CL* I 626, cf 627) C is still blithely promising "without fail a second Part of Pitt, & Bonaparte —better late than never". Still no Otto, no refusal, six months after the "Pitt". To rescue C's story we must suppose that, although Bonaparte's inquiry may have reached Stuart a month or so after the "Pitt", it did not reach C for about twenty months.

From a letter by C, 7 Oct 1800, in answer to a letter from Stuart, now lost, it can be made out that Stuart had just told C he had reason to believe Bonaparte would be interested in his writing, but had excused himself from giving that reason. By this date peace was in the air, and Stuart seems to have suggested that C make a trip to Germany and France, dangling the bait of interviews with Schiller and Bonaparte. C's answer was that he would rather stay home, that he might like to be known to Schiller (whose Wallenstein plays he had just translated) but would "not stir 20 yards" to make his acquaintance, that he "would doubtless stir many a score miles" to "*see* Bonaparte" but had no ambition to attain "his praise or admiration or notice...". *CL* I 628–9. C in the same letter promised that "Bonaparte shall not loiter", making no connexion in his mind between the promised Character and the proposed interview, though we may suppose there was a connexion in Stuart's. Plainly Stuart had not told any tale of Bonaparte's personal interest in the pair of Characters. He appears to have written hypothetically or subjunctively: Believe me, Bonaparte will be personally interested in what you write.

If the inquiry through Otto had actually occurred, Stuart must have been hinting at it, but too vaguely to be understood. Also *if* Stuart felt he must wait to tell his tale in personal confidence, then we can understand its never reaching C by mail. This leaves us free to believe that the prophetic conversation of the anecdote actually took place—but not until C returned to London late in Nov 1801, when we may suppose Stuart to have explained his hints. C's first mention of Bonaparte to Stuart in this period, in 19 Jan 1802: "What a pitiful Note that of Bonaparte's to the Legislature.—Damn the fellow!—" (*CL* II 781) will

[21 March 1800, Friday]

The CHARACTER OF *BONAPARTE, and many valuable favours, are omitted for want of room.*

GENERAL WASHINGTON. II

HIS WILL[1]

25 March 1800, Tuesday; entitled "General Washington". New attribution; evidence detailed in Erdman (1957), and see 27 Jan, above. Reprinted in *Courier* 25 March, "General Washington"; reprinted Colmer 201–3.[2]

WE would fain believe that the whole of General Washington's Will[3] has been perused by no man without some portion of that calm and pleasurable elevation which uniformly leaves us better and wiser beings. It would have been deeply interesting, considered

---

come in aptly as expressing his attitude *after* the disillusioning story. By this time, however, C's view of Napoleon had so greatly changed since March 1800 that there can have been little *prophetic* interest, whatever personal excitement there was, in the conversation with Stuart about the inquiry. The anecdote loses entirely its value as an explanation of C's resistance to the writing of a Character of Bonaparte in 1800—though it may explain a probable refusal in 1802 if Stuart reopened the question.

In Sept 1802 Stuart told C that his essays comparing France to Rome were being translated for Peltier's anti-Napoleonic French-language journal (see Stuart to C 29 Sept 1802, App B, below). Peltier does not appear to have carried out the intention, but C must thenceforth have supposed that he was reaching a French audience including Bonaparte.

By Oct 1803 C had become a violent anti-Bonapartist and had written essays in 1802 that it pleased him to believe had "extravagantly irritated the First Consul". *CL* II 1007. It did not take much stretching to extend this to a belief that his *not* writing the "Bonaparte" had been the first irritant. For his conservative brother's benefit his not having "done" the Bonaparte could now be explained as a fine instance of his having done the right thing when he appeared to procrastinate—and of his having had the right view of Napoleon long before the newspaper he wrote for had shown any outward signs of it.

(The despatches of Otto, in the Archives des affaires étrangères: Correspondance politique, vols 593ff, at the Quai D'Orsay, are silent on the matter.)

[1] For a brief related paragraph, 21 Mar, of doubtful authorship, see App A, below.

[2] This essay seems to have been immediately popular. In the United States it turned up in such odd corners as the New York *Lady's Magazine and Musical Repository* II (Jul–Dec 1801) 25–9, curtailed of its last two sentences and signed "A." (Anonymous?), and the Philadelphia *Juvenile Magazine, or Miscellaneous Repository of Useful Information* IV (1803), 13–21, entire and unsigned.

[3] Filling several columns on 21 and 24 Mar.

only as the last deliberate act of a life so beneficial to the human race; but independently of this sublime association, it is in itself an affecting and most instructive composition. Like all the former manifestations of his character, it gives proof that a true and solid greatness may exist, and make itself felt, without any admixture of wildness, without any obtrusive appeals to the imagination: it gives proof, consolatory and inspiriting proof, how many virtues, too often deemed incompatible with each other, a thinking and upright mind may unite in itself. It were scarcely too much to affirm of this Will, that all the main elements of public and private morals, of civil and domestic wisdom, are conveyed in it either directly or by implication. It is, indeed, no less than an abstract of his opinions and feelings, as a PATRIOT, FRIEND, and RELATION; and all arising naturally and unostentatiously out of the final disposal of a fortune not more honourably earned than beneficently employed. Appertaining to his character, as the American PATRIOT, more exclusively than the other pages of his Will, is the plan and endowment of a CENTRAL UNIVERSITY. The motives which impelled the General to this bequest, he has stated with such beauty and precision, as scarcely leave any thing for the philosopher or the eulogist to add. We can only subjoin to the advantages so ably enumerated, that such an institution must be eminently serviceable to America, as having a direct tendency to soften and liberalise the too great commercial spirit of that country,[4] in as far as it will connect the pleasures and ambition of its wealthier citizens, in the most impressible period of life, with objects abstract and unworldly; and that while by friendships and literary emulations it may remove local jealousies, it will tend to decorate the American

[4] It distressed his friend John Thelwall, and probably C himself, to think that America, the ideal country for utopian plans of retirement, was developing such "avidity for commercial aggrandisement" as to make one "tremble at the consequences...upon posterity". *M Mag* VIII (Sept 1799) 618, excerpts from a diary written by Thelwall on his way to visit C in 1797.

Washington's declaration was: that as "it has always been a source of serious regret with me to see the youth of these United States sent to foreign countries for the purpose of education...contracting too frequently, not only habits of dissipation and extravagance, but principles unfriendly to Republican government, and to the true and genuine liberties of mankind"; hence he wished "an UNIVERSITY, in a central part of the United States, to which the youths of fortune and talents, from all parts thereof, might be sent for the completion of their education, in all the branches of polite literature, in arts and sciences, in acquiring knowledge in the principles of politics and good government, and...by associating with each other, and forming friendships in juvenile years, be enabled to free themselves, in a proper degree, from those local prejudices, and habitual jealousies, which...are...pregnant with mischievous consequences to this country".

character with an ornament hitherto wanting in it, viz. genuine local attachments,[5] unconnected with pecuniary interests.

Of a mixed nature, partly belonging to the patriot, and partly to the master of a family, is the humane, earnest, and solemn wish concerning the emancipation of the slaves on his estate. It explains, with infinite delicacy and manly sensibility, the true cause of his not having emancipated them in his life time; and should operate as a caution against those petty libellers, who interpret the whole of a character by a part, instead of interpreting a part by the whole. We feel ourselves at a loss which most to admire in this interesting paragraph, the deep and weighty feeling of the general principle of universal liberty; or the wise veneration of those fixed laws in society, without which that universal liberty must for ever remain impossible, and which, therefore, must be obeyed even in those cases, where they *suspend* the action of that general principle; or, lastly, the affectionate attention to the particular feelings of the slaves themselves, with the ample provision for the aged and infirm.[6] Washington was no "architect of ruin!"[7]

In the bequests to his friends, the composition evidences the peculiar delicacy and correctness of his mind. The high value which he attached to his old friend, Dr. Franklin's legacy of the gold-headed cane, by bequeathing it, and it alone, to his brother, Charles Washington; the spy-glasses, left, with the modest parenthesis, "because they will be useful to them where they live;" yet not without stamping the value on those precious relicts, as having been useful to himself in the deliverance of his country; the wisdom of remitting the box to Lord Buchan, with the gentle implication of the impracticability and impropriety of performing the conditions, with which the box had

[5] On "local attachments" see e.g. *Courier* 27 Sept 1811 ("The Scotsman"), below.

[6] Washington's need for "infinite delicacy" in the matter of the emancipation of the slaves on his estate is clearly indicated in the details of his testament: "Upon the decease of wife, it is my will and desire that all the slaves which I hold in *my own right* shall receive their freedom. To emancipate them during her life would, though earnestly wished by me, be attended with such insuperable difficulties, on account of their intermixture by marriages with the dower negroes [i.e. those constituting his wife's dowry], as to exite the most painful sensations"; but the dowry Negroes were, as reported 21 Mar, freed by Martha Washington at the time of publication of the will.

[7] Cf Burke's speech on the army estimates 9 Feb 1790: "The French had shown themselves the ablest architects of ruin that had hitherto existed in the world. In that very short space of time they had completely pulled down to the ground their monarch, their church, their nobility, their law, their revenue, their army, their navy, their commerce, their arts, and their manufactures."

been originally accompanied; that reverence for the primary designation of a gift, implied in the words "agreeably to the original design of the Goldsmiths' Company of Edinburgh," and which words were besides necessary, in order to prevent the interpretation, that he had remitted it from inability to find any man in his own country equally deserving of it with the Earl;[8] the bequest of the bible, and of the swords, the first without annotation, the last with the solemnity of a christian hero; all and each of these we have dwelt upon, as evidences of a mind strong and healthful, yet with a fineness and rapidity of the associating power, seldom found even in those who derive sensibility from nervous disease. The gratitude, the deep and immortal gratitude, displayed in the declaration of the motives of his bequest to his nephew, Bushrod Washington, is of a still higher class of excellence; and the virtue is individualised, and has a new interest given it, by his attention to the very letter of an old promise, no longer in force. The accuracy with which the estates are marked out will aid the distant posterity of the present Americans, in their reverential pilgrimages to the seat of their great PATER PATRIAE. The attachment which he has shewn to all his relations; the provisions he has made for them all; and the attention to honourable causes of local preferment in these provisions; are circumstances highly noticeable. Highly noticeable too is the disjunction of this family attachment from that desire of the aggrandisement of some one branch of the family, so commonly adherent to it. He has weakened by evidence the best and almost the only argument for primogeniture, *in new countries*.[9] One fact strikes us particularly in the perusal of this Will.—Of all Washington's numerous relations, not one appears as a placeman or beneficiary of the government—not one appears to have received any thing from their kinsman as President and Influencer of the United States, yet all have evidences of the zeal and affection of the President, as their kinsman. *It is not so every where.*

[8] A box "made of the oak that sheltered the great Sir William Wallace, after the battle of Falkirk", had been given to Washington as a comparably patriotic warrior, with a request that it pass on his decease to the one of his countrymen who seemed to merit it best. Deeming it "not for me to say" whether it would be easy "to select THE MAN", Washington conceived it best to recommit the box to the Earl of Buchan's "own cabinet", where the original donors had wished it to be.

[9] I take the "evidence" to be Washington's amicable and equable parcelling of his estate among his and his wife's relations in such a way that they could be expected to constitute a harmonious community, holding on to their fairly equal and contiguous plots of land without jealous passions. For C's view of the relation between property and suffrage, see 7 Dec 1799, above.

There is something in the arrangement of the will, beyond any example, which we recollect, instructive and judicious. He commences with a positive or perfect duty, the payment of duties; then goes immediately to the most respectful and affectionate attention to his wife, which becomes more intellectual, more moral, from the circumstances, which he after notices, of his having remained without issue; he proceeds to his concerns as master of his family, and provides for the emancipation of his slaves; and having finished his most immediate and *most* sacred offices, viz. the domestic duties, he rises, *then*, and *not till then*, into the PATRIOT;[10] and founds a central University.[11] After his own family comes his country, and then his relations by consanguinity not of his own family—after these his friends; and all those whom fellowship in arms, or old acquaintance had endeared to him; and last of all, he proceeds to the circumstantial disposal of his estate. Throughout the whole, there reigns a *humanness*[12] of feeling, a complete union of himself with the mass of his fellow-citizens, so as even to avoid references to any public characters in that country; and above all, an ardent wish for improvement, combined with reverential observance, and affectionate awe for present and existing customs and feelings. But Washington was too great a man to court singularity. The dwarf, that steps aside from the crowd, and walks by himself, may gain the whole crowd to turn and stare at him—Washington could attract their admiration, while he moved on with them, and in the midst of them.

[10] "The paternal and filial duties discipline the Heart and prepare it for the love of all Mankind." *Conciones: Lects 1795* (*CC*) 46.

[11] The project was to have been financed by fifty shares in the Potomac River Development Company and perhaps given "a fostering hand" by the General Government. But unfortunately the General Government withheld its hand, being, in the matter of federal aid to federal education, somewhat behind the crowd rather than with them or in the midst of them. And the *idea* or image of reality temporarily embodied in the Potomac Development Company, although it was a favourite image of Washington's and a very fertile one when realised in the Erie canal, departed from the body of the Potomac Company in 1828, leaving the stock worthless and the University unendowed. So there was no direct flow into outward and visible realisation either of instruction in reading and writing for the bound Negroes or of education in polite literature for the youth of fortune and talents.

[12] The word "*humanness*" appears to be italicised as a conscious coinage. *OED* cites: 1727 Nathan Bailey; 1802 Coleridge, in a letter; 1871 H. B. Forman. C uses it thus in a paragraph on Fox in the *Courier* of 15 Sept 1806: "...there was said to be more of *humanness*, if we may coin a word, about him—" (than about Pitt). The parallel of Fox and Washington is instructive.

REVIEW

OF A PAMPHLET BY ARTHUR YOUNG, ESQ. F.R.S. AND SECRETARY TO THE BOARD OF AGRICULTURE, ENTITLED, "THE QUESTION OF SCARCITY PLAINLY STATED, &C."

27 March 1800, Thursday; *M Post* title. *EOT* II 395–403; assigned by SC "chiefly from the style, and because the subject is one which he appears to have been interested in and to have dwelt upon" (III 1020); confirmed by C's letter to Purkis claiming "a Review of a curious Pamphlet connected with" the "Pitt" (*CL* I 583) (for the connexion see Stuart's notice this day.)

THE Public are well acquainted with Arthur Young.[1] Formerly agasp for reform, he now raves against all reformation, as dogs contract the hydrophobia from excessive thirst.[2] We impeach him not of insincerity: a proneness to charge either church or state-prophets with the guilt of conscious imposture we hold an unequivocal symptom of a vulgar and unreflecting mind. Arthur Young sympathised with his country in a sentiment of horror[a] against the excesses of the French Revolution: he was aware that some portion of this horror[a] would [b]attach to[c] all those who, like himself, had blown the trump of gratulation on the first approach of that Revolution; and he hastened to avow his recantation in a work almost *lyrically* unconnected, and set to a more boisterous music than would have suited any species of the Lyric, except the *Palinodia*.[3]

> Quid amplius vis? O mare! O terra! ardeo,
> Quantum non[d] atro delibutus Hercules
> Nessi Cruore——
> Quae finis? aut quod me manet *stipendium?*
> HOR. Epod. 17[4]

[a] *M Post*: honour [corrected in *EOT*] [b–c] *EOT*: attack [d] *EOT*: neque

[1] Novelist, social economist, experimental farmer, Arthur Young (1741–1820) had begun publishing *Annals of Agriculture* in 1784; in 1787 he had made extensive *Travels in France* (published 1792); in 1793 he had been appointed secretary to the new Board of Agriculture.

[2] C develops the idea 21 Oct 1802: "celebrated Anti-Jacobins...infected with some of the worst symptoms of the madness against which they are raving". In the review Young is politely credited with sincerity, but see the contemporaneous notebook entry: "Apology for Treasury Scribes—Dog yelping—not against Socrates—but for its master". *CN* I 667. C had been able, in *Watchman* No 1, to quote Young's *Travels* against interested defenders of "all the old governments of Europe". *Watchman* (*CC*) 11.

[3] It is curious that Young's recantation, which had taken the form of a prose pamphlet, *The Example of France a Warning to Britain*, is described by C in terms that seem fitter for his own *Recantation*, *An Ode*, which he sometimes called his Palinode.

[4] Horace *Epodes* 17.30–2 (var), 36. "What more dost thou desire? O sea! O earth! I burn as neither Hercules,

The Minister accepted and rewarded his conversion, and thereby secured its permanence.[5] Opinions, that are the tenure by which a man holds the comforts and luxuries of a good fortune, are commonly very sincere opinions; though it were as absurd to attribute any moral worth to such sincerity, as to believe that there is any *religious* merit in the *unusual* strictness with which the poor of this kingdom observe the present Lent.[6] Self-interest is a chilling principle; but is of excellent use to Ministers in the condensation and phialling of any hot vapour that suits their purposes, and which might otherwise have passed off "*tenues commixtus in auras.*"[7] But though we consider Arthur Young at present as little less than a "*Gentleman in the confidence of Government*," to use the courteous phrase of a Learned Judge,[8] yet still he is a man of undoubted information, and, in his particular and most important province, entitled on all occasions to the most respectful attention. We procured his present pamphlet, therefore, with eagerness. "The Question of Scarcity plainly stated, and Remedies considered,"[9] and this too by Arthur Young, excited in us not only curiosity, but a deep and serious interest. We had ever considered the subject as intimately connected with all the main evils, and nominal properties of the nation. We can scarcely describe the sensation which we experienced in reading the first sentence of the ADVERTISEMENT prefixed to the pamphlet. "The Author of these papers has but one motive in printing, which is that of convincing the people that the evil they suffer at present is to be attributed only to the unfavourable seasons." We however suspended our feelings, and proceeded to the pamphlet itself, which we do not hesitate to

---

steeped in the black blood of Nessus. ...What end or *penalty* awaits me?" Tr (slightly adapted) C. E. Bennett *Horace. The Odes and Epodes* (LCL 1914) 411.

[5] Young had applied for a government pension in 1797 through Windham (*Windham Papers* II 63), but perhaps C refers to his secretaryship to the Board with a salary of £600 and other alleged emoluments.

[6] Cf C's "Essay on Fasts" *Watchman* No 2 (*CC*) 54–5.

[7] "Mingled with thin air". Cf Virgil *Georgics* 4.500.

[8] Sir James Eyre, during one of the state trials of 1794, when a witness admitted he was a spy for Dundas, instructed the jury that "a Gentleman in the confidence of Government" was as good a witness as anyone else and that the government had to employ such gentlemen for its protection. Cf C's Lecture on the Two Bills: *Lects 1795* (*CC*) 264 and n 2.

[9] The title continues: "with observations on permanent measures to keep wheat at a more regular price". London, 2 shillings. Preface dated 14 Mar 1800. Lamb refers to "Arthur Young's Treatise on Corn" as among things wisely left behind when C left town: "better suited [to] the flippancy of London discussion than the dignity of Keswick thinking". *LL* I 198.

recommend as the most masterly confutation of this first sentence, that we could have hoped or almost wished for. He has proved indeed (what we never doubted), that the attacks on millers and monopolists are unfounded, inflammatory, and impolitic; that there exists a *real* and alarming scarcity; and that the unfavourable season has produced it. But is this "*the* evil, which the people suffer at present?" Is it not an evil, a gigantic evil, that in a country in which unfavourable seasons are so often to be expected, an unfavourable season should produce a real and alarming scarcity? and is this evil "to be attributed only to unfavourable seasons?" The pamphlet itself furnishes us with the best and completest answer to these questions.

The work is introduced by some very just observations on the errors arising from the "fear of aggravating the evil by sounding alarm, from the generalising of individual experiences, and from confining the inquiries on the subject to the *proportion* of the crop, and not paying a sufficient attention to the *price*."[10]—"It should seem (observes Mr. Young) as if men would be pretty well satisfied, provided they could prove the deficiency to amount only to a fourth or a fifth, forgetting that the people are suffering a very heavy distress, whatever that proportion may turn out, of what account to them your fine speculations in arithmetic, while they pay five pounds a quarter?" He proceeds to state the average crop of the kingdom, which he concludes to be near 24 bushels an acre, and certainly not[11] to have *increased* in quantity for the last 12 years (p. 83), and then under the head of POPULATION, gives it as his opinion, and as having been proved by the indefatigable researches of Sir John Call,[a] that within the years 1787 and 1797, the people have increased *one third*.[12] We have not facts enough before us to determine on the probability or improbability of this assertion. If true, it is a most alarming truth; and whether true or false, it is worth our while to observe that it occurs in the 17th page of a pamphlet written for the sole purpose of proving, that the evil is owing entirely to an unfavourable season!!

Mr. Young shews next, by a mass of authorities, the existence and degree of the deficiency of the last crop, and gives extracts, arranged in tables, from the answers to his circular letters, with the names of the correspondents—with the most noticeable miscellaneous circum-

[a] *EOT*: Cull

10 Not a direct quotation but a paraphrase of pp 5–7; the next passage is verbatim from p 7.

11 Expressed on p 83 as hypothesis, not certainty.

12 Sir John Call, 1st Bt (1732–1801), MP for Callington (from 1784), had been commissioned to report on the management of Crown lands.

stances furnished by each correspondent. The *result* is melancholy, no less indeed, than (to quote the words in p. 29), that "famine stares us in the face."[13] Next follow observations on the *consumption of wheat*, and on the STOCK IN HAND LAST HARVEST. This last subject is treated with great acuteness and accumulation of just reasonings and interesting facts. The observations on the small effect of speculations and monopolies are excellent; one paragraph is too *curious* not to be quoted. "But suppose corn in autumn and winter is cheaper than it ought to be, from little and poor farmers carrying too much to market, the consumption of the people will be in some measure proportioned to the price, *and they will be eating more than the crop allows*. Now, I ask, whether it is not, in such a case, much to be desired, that jobbers, or millers, or monopolisers, should take advantage of the price, and lay in great stocks?"[14] We do not dispute the conclusion; but what a confession is implied of the misery of the people at large; that bread must be kept from them, as gingerbread and sweetmeats from children, lest they should *over-eat* themselves. In the villages in the north of Germany *white* bread, in various forms, is put up to sale at the fairs, as a dainty;[15] but we never understood before, that bread itself was so *tempting* a viand in our own country. On the contrary, we should have supposed, that if bread were cheap, the only result would be, that the people, who are now but half-fed, would then have their belly-full, and that those who have now enough would employ the spare money in adding to their meals the rarities of beef and mutton. If the people eat more bread than comes to their share, in the cheap months, it is an undeniable consequence that at other times they have not bread enough to eat.

The next head is entitled *quantities calculated*—from which we shall quote the following sentences without further annotation, than that it is true of an enlightened country in consequence of an unfavourable season; and yet that country is puffed up with the self-conceit of its *prosperity!* "If the rich feed the poor, *which is very much the case at present*, the *price* is no longer bounded by the faculties of the poor, for the wealth of the whole kingdom comes into competition for food: as long as such demand continues, *price*[a] may rise.

[a] *EOT*: *prices*

13 Out of context; but Young's actual conclusion is bad enough, that the deficiency of wheat is more than a third (p 41).

14 P 53.

15 A leaf out of C's recent German experience: "White bread is so uncommon, that at a *fair* in a little Village, instead of Sweetmeats & Gingerbread, as in England, there were in trays... Rolls & *Twists* of *White* Bread". To Mrs C 10 Mar 1799: *CL* I 473.

And this has been the case for the last five months.—*Had the poor in many of the counties been left without this support and assistance of the rich, they must have perished for want of food, till numbers had lessened to the proportion of the supply.*"[16]

The last, and of course the most important article is, the REMEDIES.—These[a] are, 1. the encouragement of potatoes by a premium (with a justification of premiums, in answer to the disciples of Adam Smith). 2.[b] The prohibition of oats for the feed of horses kept for pleasure: which, he affirms would of itself have prevented the evil. These[a] are immediate *remedies.* As *alternatives*, and as necessary to prevent a relapse, he recommends, and very ably comments on, the following means:—1. Ascertain the prices of corn. 2. A general inclosure. 3. Give land to the cottagers. 4. Parochial assistance in food to be in rice, soup, and potatoes. 5. Number the people. 6. Register the acres of wheat and rye sown. And afterwards we find a proposal for something like a public granary of rice "by inducing the East India Company so to provide themselves as to render an Act feasible, which should direct, that as soon as wheat shall rise, on the average of the kingdom, to[b] 4*l.* per quarter, and so long as it remains at or above that price, the Company should sell rice in hundred weights, to all persons demanding it, at 25*s.* per hundred weight, or any other price which shall on an average of years be adequate."[17]

We shall conclude with three short quotations, briefly remarking on each. The first is in page 83.—"Had the people and acres been numbered in 1788, and again in 1798, and the one found to increase nothing, but the other one-third, who would[c] be surprised at scarcity?" And this is said by the man, [d]and all the former grand and national measures are proposed by the man,[e] whose sole motive for printing is to shew, that all *the evil* we are suffering (not the immediate high price, but all THE EVIL) is to be attributed entirely to an unfavourable season!!—The second is from page 69.—"The farming bailiff I sent to the Duke of Liancourt ten years ago, is now in London, having left France but a fortnight, and has given me many accounts of French husbandry, one circumstance of which deserves notice—*that every scrap of waste and neglected land is converted into little possessions by the poor, and cultivated most assiduously; much*

[a] *EOT*: There [b] *EOT* omits [c] *EOT*: could [Young reads "would"]
[d–e] *EOT* omits

[16] P 62; C supplies all italics except *price.*

[17] Pp 80–1.

by means of potatoes."[18]—We recommend to Mr. Arthur Young to annex this quotation from his own work as a motto to the next edition of his—"*The example of France a warning to Britain!*"—We have, alas! too often mistaken newspaper anecdotes of rogues in Paris for the annals of the French nation since the revolution; and in our rage against a phantom of Jacobinism, have shamefully neglected to calculate the blessings from the destruction of Feudalism. The vine[a] of liberty shall not be blasphemed by us, because the Noahs of the revolutionary deluge, who first planted it, were made drunk by its untried fruits.[19]

The third and last quotation is on an awful subject, we take it from page 85—"*It is the hand of the Almighty which has afflicted the nation!*"[20] As men and Christians, how can we suppress the indignant feelings which this sentence excited in our inmost soul? By the author's own confession immense tracts of land are lying waste; the evil which we are suffering might have been wholly prevented by suspending the use of oats for our pleasure-horses; the money which our expeditions to Quiberon and Holland cost us would have purchased rice enough to have kept the cheek of every cottager's child fat and rosy, and have made the deficiency of our crops an unfelt evil; and yet we are gravely assured, that it is the hand of the ALMIGHTY which afflicts[b] us; and among other reasons for *infidelity* and *atheism.* The hirelings of Ministers, and the supporters of a sanguinary war, under the blasphemous plea of a war for the religion of Jesus;—*these* are not infidels, not atheists—only the *occasion* of infidelity, the *causes* of atheism.—The hand of the Almighty afflicts us!—Thou ETERNAL GOODNESS!—far rather art thou by gentle and fatherly premonitions drawing us back from the brink of that abyss, to which an evil spirit has been luring us; and a placeman dares draw off our eyes from our own follies and those of our rulers, and proclaims to a suffering nation, that it is thy hand alone which has afflicted them![21]

[a] *EOT*: voice [b] *EOT*: affects

[18] C's italics.

[19] Cf 31 Dec 1799: "Buonaparte, the Deucalion of this new inundation"; and 6 Aug 1800, below.

[20] C's italics and exclamation point. In his interpretation of this passage C is not quite fair to Young, whose argument was that God chastises us for pride, for neglecting the education of the lower classes, for failing to provide for the poor. "The wisdom of legislation, the means of policy, ought all to be exerted with vigour and activity, but still in a full reliance on the blessing of the Almighty to give them effect, and a firm persuasion that without it, all will prove but vain and nugatory." C ignores their similarity of outlook.

[21] To read Young's pamphlet alongside C's review is to discover much political as well as economic agree-

[27 March 1800, Thursday]
Of PITT and BONAPARTE To-morrow. The Admirers of this Article should read the Review of Mr. Young*'s Pamphlet, in our Paper This Day, to prepare them for To-morrow.*

[28 March 1800, Friday]
Bonaparte—Sappho—Parisian Fashions, to-morrow.

PARLIAMENT. X

THE ADULTERY BILL AND THE RIGHTS OF WOMEN

16 April 1800, Wednesday. New attribution, on grounds of style and C's note to himself of c Feb 1800 (*CN* I 650): "Mem.... An Essay on the Adultery Bill".

A few years ago, several books were published in defence of the Rights of Women. In general, those works were too absurd to require any answer;—but with more reason might a book on that subject be written when women are run down with severity by the new Divorce Bill, now before the House of Lords.[1]—All good men abhor the crime of adultery, and good women too abhor it; but is it equal justice to make the whole weight of punishment fall upon the weaker sex?[2] Is not every guilty woman punished throughout life in her reception by society? But what punishment is inflicted upon the man beyond that which the courts of common law, or his own conscience, may inflict? Why is the man, the superior being, the protector of the other sex; why is he to escape when he uses his great endowments for wicked purposes, and betrays his trust? We shall not

ment. Young did argue for immediate palliatives such as the Stale Bread Bill, but his larger aim was to lead the administration (as its friend) away from Adam Smith and toward a policy of active support of agriculture. The great point of disagreement was the link to war, which Young evaded, whereas C implied that a Whig ministry would cease chasing the "phantom of Jacobinism", make peace with the French Republic, and learn from her some agrarian lessons.

[1] Lord Auckland introduced the bill, one of the most extensively debated of the session, in the House of Lords 2 Apr; it passed a second reading, 4 Apr, 30 to 11. On 16 Apr Auckland withdrew the bill as defective but offered in its place a new one; that passed its third reading, 23 May, by 77 to 69. Introduced into the House of Commons 26 May, it was defeated 10 Jun.

[2] Auckland's first bill would prohibit persons on account of whose adultery a divorce was obtained from intermarrying: "the adulterer should not marry the adulteress". The Duke of Clarence led the opposition. Auckland's revised bill stressed *punishment* for adultery.

object to further punishment for the crime, even in the persons of women; but before we consent, a very severe punishment, indeed, must be decreed against the male seducer.[3]

THE WAR NOT A CRUSADE[1]

6 August 1800, Wednesday. *EOT* II 409–12; attributed by SC on the grounds that it "may have been sent from Keswick. It has considerable resemblance to my Father's early manner, and is unlike the ordinary run of *The Morning Post* articles, furnished by other hands" (III 1019–20). Evidence of style conclusive, e.g. "enthusiasm and imagination, mutually feeding each other"; "alchemy of our expeditions"; "marriageable arms". Reprinted in *Courier* 6 Aug 1800 as "The Crusades".

THE comparison which Mr. Fox, in his celebrated Letter to the Electors of Westminster makes between the war of the Crusades, and the present war, has been very much misunderstood, and a paper of Friday repeats the error.[2]

It has been too fashionable among those who call and believe themselves the friends of Liberty, to name *the present war a crusade.* In so doing they appear to us to be paying the present war (contrary to their own intentions) a very high, and, in our opinion, a very undeserved compliment. A new religion had fanaticised whole nations. Men bred up in the habits of a wild and roaming freedom, had been brought together by its influence, and taught to unite the energies of a savage life with all the harmony and calculable coincidencies[a] of a machine. But this religion was deadly to morals, to science, to civil freedom: no society could be progressive under its influence. It was favourable to superstition, cunning, and sensual

[a] *EOT*: coincidences

[3] For examples of C's frequently expressed objections to double standards and the subordination of women, cf *IS* (1951) 303–11.

[1] Between 16 Apr and 6 Aug C probably contributed no prose to the *M Post*; for a doubtful attribution 21 Apr see App A, below. He probably encouraged Stuart's reprinting *The Mad Mother*, from *Lyrical Ballads* (see notices of 2 Apr and 21 Jun in App D, below). He sent in "from Bristol" (*CL* I 603–4) WW's *The Farmer of Tilsbury Vale* (see 21 Jul in App D, below).

[2] Fox, at the climax of his *Letter... to the Electors of Westminster* (1793, p 40), deduced that those who sought through war to produce a counter-revolution in France were seeking "no other than the conquest of France", and he apostrophised the comparatively moderate crusaders of old: "The conquest of France!!!—O! calumniated crusaders, how rational and moderate were your objects!"

I can find this reference in none of the likely papers "of Friday" (1 Aug, 25 Jul, 18 Jul); perhaps it occurred weeks earlier.

indulgence; but it bore no fruit, it yielded no marriageable arms to the vine, it sheltered no healing plant. The soil was grassless where it grew; the fox made its nest at the root, and the owl screamed in its branches.—Such was the religion of Mahomet. The situation of the countries subject to our righteous ally, the Grand Seignior,[3] forms[a] the best commentary on the Koran. Yet the first disciples of this religion had conquered Asia, had made formidable acquisitions in Europe, and even mastered Spain; they made it a prime article of their creed, that they were commissioned by Heaven to force their religion on all nations by the sword. Our ancestors were at length roused to resistance. Such was the commencement of the Crusade. Never was a war, in the best sense of the word, so holy: it is, perhaps, the only war in history in which defence by anticipation was no trick of Statesmen, but the demand of nations, the impulse of a general inspiration.—If, therefore, the present war be unnecessary in its origin, unprovoked in its primary movements, let us call it any thing: ONLY NOT A CRUSADE.

The Crusades were as favourable in their effects, as they were honourable in their causes. Then first did Europe feel and become conscious of the blessing of a common religion, and of civil institutions, differing only as the branches of one family, "*qualis decet esse sororum*."[4] The warriors brought back from the holy land imaginations highly excited, minds enlarged by the contemplation of a scenery, and of customs so new to them, and manners polished beyond the experience of former ages. A new aera commenced in the world; a new sun rose on our social habits, on the tone of Governments, and on the nature of our literature. The Monkish Legend, and obsolete miracle gave way to Knights, and Giants, and Genii; and enthusiasm and imagination, mutually feeding each other, were brought to act on the side of gentleness and public justice. Unless therefore it shall be admitted, that Suwarrow and his Russians have returned home poets and gentlemen; or that our Bond-street officers have been transmuted, by the alchemy of our expeditions, into the chaste, gentle, and sober knights of ancient chivalry; let us call the present war any thing: ONLY NOT A CRUSADE.

These crusades were likewise the parents of all the freedom which

[a] *EOT*: form

[3] The Ottoman Empire ruled by Selim III (1789–1807) included among its subject nationalities Albanians, Arabs, Bulgars, Copts, Rumans, Serbs.

[4] Ovid *Metamorphoses* 2.14 (var). Tr: "Such as is meet among sisters".

now exists in Europe. The pecuniary distresses of the Monarchs and Nobles compelled them to part with many and various privileges; the anarchy, which prevailed during their absence, procured to the lower classes many others. Commerce was diverted from the Venetian and Genoese monopolisers; and there began to arise in all countries, but more especially in England, that greatest blessing and ornament of human nature, an important and respectable middle class.[5] The Monarch became more an office,[a] and less a person; the Nobility were [seen] gradually to draw nearer to the class of the people; and long before the first dawn of religious reformation, the poetic genius imported from the East[b] had prepared the way for it, by continued and successful satires on the absurdities and crimes of the Priesthood. Unless therefore it be admitted that the *direct* object of the present war is to lay the foundations of a greater freedom than we before enjoyed; unless it be admitted, that it has tended to prevent commerce from being a monopoly of one nation; unless it be granted, that it, viz. this present war, spite of the Assessed and Income Taxes, is peculiarly favourable to the increase and permanence of a middle class; that it militates against all attachment to Kings as persons, and Nobles as *privileged* classes; and to the Roman Catholic superstitions, as absurdities; unless all this be conceded by the Friends of Freedom, let them call the present war any thing: ONLY NOT A CRUSADE.[6]

A WHOLESOME EDUCATION

11 September 1800, Thursday. New attribution, on the evidence of style, e.g. the "grand hinge" and the "cobweb penalties".

THE great Lord Bacon, speaking of the laws for curbing immorality, and checking the torrent of a general corruption of manners, says, "The chief concern ought not to be so much employed in restraining corruption by laws, or in punishing offenders, as in

[a] *EOT*: officer [b] *EOT*: last

[5] On a middle class as "the foster-nurse of general humanity", see *Friend* (*CC*) I 231 (II 161).

[6] The publication in *M Post* 9 Aug of a long "Narrative of the Infancy and Youth of Robert Burns, the Poet" from Currie's ed of Burns *Works* was probably due to C, who was with Currie in July and recommended the work to Poole; see *CL* II 607. For a paragraph on the "Law of Nations in Time of War", probably C's, see App A, 28 Aug, below.

regulating and watching over the education of youth."[1]—The lassitude of morals, and the growing and confirmed inattention to religion perceivable in youth, even just emerged from the University and other seminaries, plainly evince that this grand hinge, upon which much of the good of society depends, has been neglected.—Thus, a wholesome education under a manly discipline would supersede the cobweb penalties which catch the small, and let go the great offenders.[2]

[20 September 1800, Saturday]

The Eulogy on General Washington appeared in this Paper some months ago.[1]

[2 October 1800, Thursday]

In our Paper of to-morrow will be presented, No. 1, of a series of excellent Letters, inquiring into the truth of the opinion that Farmers are monopolists. We can assure our readers they will receive much pleasure and instruction in the perusal of them.

MONOPOLISTS AND FARMERS[1]

AN INQUIRY INTO THE TRUTH OF THE POPULAR OPINION CONCERNING THESE CLASSES OF MEN

NO. I. OF MONOPOLISTS

3 October 1800, Friday; *M Post* title. *EOT* II 413–21; see III 1021. Reprinted in *Courier* of same date. Based on a letter from Poole (*Poole* II 11), as indicated in

[1] This seems to be C's summary of ideas expressed in other words in Bacon *Of the Advancement of Learning* bk I: *Works* (4 vols 1740) II 421, 438, 441, 446. He was reading the *Advancement* in Oct 1800; see *CN* I 826 and n.

[2] Bacon *Apophthegms* No 291: "One of the seven was wont to say; that *laws were like cobwebs; where the small flies were caught, and the great brake through*." *Works* III 291.

[1] Probably a reference to C's eulogy of 27 Jan and 25 Mar (above), though the inquiry from a correspondent *may* have concerned the verse *Eulogy on the Death of Gen. George Washington*, by Edmund Everard, in the *M Post* 11 Aug.

[1] This "series of excellent Letters" (ed announcement 2 Oct), though inspired and largely written by Thomas Poole, is opened and concluded by essays primarily C's own. SC printed them as a unit in *EOT*, but though some Coleridgian touches will be noted in Letters II–IV it seems proper in the present edition to relegate these to the Appendix of collaborative work.

The Letters were evidently planned while C was in Bristol in June. In July Poole wrote two, which reached C in Keswick in Aug (*CL* I 618). By 28 Sept C had sent to Stuart Letters I and II (his own introduction and Poole's first essay), and he promised "five more...two on the War as respecting

footnotes, but described by C as "*chiefly* of my own Writing" (*CL* I 634). SC evidently reprinted from a tattered clipping (see textual notes).

AN Evening Paper,[2] which distinguishes itself by its regular pretensions to impartiality, has in these last months played a part so cruel in itself, so destructive of social peace, and so treacherous to the cause of freedom, that the writer of the ensuing inquiry feels himself authorized to denounce its conduct to the public, in that way in which alone the conduct of a Newspaper ought to be denounced, viz.[a] by an attempt to evince the falsehood and malignant nature of its opinions. For six weeks previous to the appearance of riots and disturbances[b] in the kingdom,[3] scarcely a day passed but some one paragraph at least appeared in the paper alluded to, affirming,

[a] *EOT*: that is, [b] *EOT*: troubles

Agriculture [Letter III in two parts], one on the Raising of Rents in consequence of high Prices of Provisions [Letter IV]", and two that never materialised—on the bread riots and on "the countenance which Government have given to the calumnies, &c of foolish people..." (*CL* I 626). Ultimately he did send a brief postscript, touching on these two subjects, which for convenience we designate Letter V (14 Oct). Poole, it should be noted, took some of his material from Adam Smith *Wealth of Nations* bk IV ch 5, "Digression Concerning the Corn Trade and Corn Laws".

[2] The *Star*, evening associate of the *M Chron*; for its retort see 14 Oct, below.

[3] The grain harvest of 1799 had been deficient by a third or more; in 1800 the price of wheat, normally about 6 shillings per bushel, reached 11/10 in Jan, 13/11 in April, and 16/10 in July. On 4 Jul an "eminent cornfactor" was tried and found guilty of speculative purchase and resale (forestalling and regrating), and Lord Kenyon, the chief justice, praised the jury as public benefactors; market demonstrations, some of them riotous, swept the land; wheat dropped 4 shillings in August. There were further riots in September. For an investigation and excellent analysis of the interacting and diverging moralities of paternalists such as Lord Kenyon and of the active populace, brought into play in time of scarcity, see E. P. Thompson "The Moral Economy of the English Crowd in the Eighteenth Century" *Past & Present* No 50 (Feb 1971) 76–136.

Like most consumers, C "knew" there were crafty monopolists who throve on scarcity. In *Watchman* No 9 (*CC*) 331 he had published evidence of an agreement among them. Even after reading Poole's first essays he could seriously ask whether there had been "*any* Scarcity" (*CL* I 618). But Poole, himself a farmer as well as a tanner and an organiser of benevolent associations, replied that the fact of scarcity was ridiculously "obvious", and C made up Letter I out of the points of obviousness that Poole enumerated. (*Poole* II 11–13). Nevertheless, in 1815 at the time of the Corn Bill, C would revert to his awareness that "the Landowners & the great Farmers" were masters of the land in their ability to set the price and quantity "of the Poor Man's cold dry Dinner" (*CL* IV 555). It was easy to get caught in the current debate as to whether prices reflected actual scarcity or a conspiracy of monopolists instead of asking whether the masters of the land took an unfair advantage of their command of a prime necessity.

or purporting, that no real scarcity had ever existed in this country; and that all the sufferings of our distressed fellow subjects were attributable solely to the factors that had accumulated, or the farmers that withheld, the grain. If these paragraphs had contained any thing but assertions and idle stories; had there been in any of them even a visible *endeavour* only to substantiate this opinion, by any species of proof, either by collection of facts, or by general calculations, that Newspaper would never have been pointed out by the present attack. The author knows too well the complexity of all questions relative to political economy, to convert the blunders, or sophisms, in any attempt to solve such questions, into moral delinquency. We shall now attempt to shew the groundlessness of the opinion, and the subserviency of a paper which has adopted such modes of propagating that opinion, to ministerial projects of war, and novel ways of taxation. The questions, therefore, of which the present inquirer proposes to attempt the solutions,[a] are, first, Is such a monopoly as could *create* a scarcity, possible? secondly, Does it exist? If we should be enabled[b] to answer these questions in the negative, we may then ask, does the scarcity rest with the farmer? and is he the proper object of public obloquy? This first essay will be confined to the two former questions.

First, then, is such a monopoly possible? This may well be doubted. It would beseem those who assert the possibility, to ascertain the existence of warehouses and granaries, belonging to the corn trade, capable of containing such a quantity of grain. It appears, on the *surface* of the question at least, that grain is an article too bulky, too widely diffused, and too valuable, ever to be monopolised, even[c] by the large capitals[d] allowed to exist in this country.[4] The nature of the article [e]makes it in the highest[f] degree improbable, independently of any particular[g] evidences. We admit, however, that what appears[h] very unlikely may nevertheless be [i]true. Truth[j] and probability do not always go hand in hand.—But then the burthen of the proof lies with those who assert the reality of a thing so improbable, and not with those who assert the falsehood of it. Now, not a shadow of evidence has been adduced, not a single calculation entered into, to prove that subtracting the capitals employed in our enormous commerce, manufactories, and agriculture, there would

[a] *EOT*: solution, [b] *EOT*: called [c] *EOT* omits [d] *EOT*: capitalists
[e–f] *EOT*: renders this in a high [g] *EOT*: other [h] *EOT*: is [i–j] true: that fact

[4] C is now drawing on Poole almost verbatim, except that Poole does not say "ever" and adds "without the thing itself being actually scarce"—a point C deals with later on.

remain (in the single[a] corn trade) enough to buy up the grain of the whole island, to such a degree as to convert plenty into scarcity. We are authorised, therefore, in answering, that such a monopoly is not possible.[5]

But let us admit for a moment, that a capital does exist in the corn trade, sufficient to buy up this quantity, and granaries sufficient to contain it, yet would such a monopoly be the interest of the corn-factors? High rents and heavy taxes have contributed, with the healthful variety of their occupations, to make our farmers an eminently shrewd and watchful race of men. The efforts to buy up corn will be almost immediately noticed by them; the markets will rise; those who are obliged to sell, will sell at an advanced price; and most of the large farmers do not want capital sufficient to enable them to keep the corn themselves, in order that they may themselves receive the advantages of the still[b] further increase in the price.[6] From the number and the different dispositions of the farmers, it is morally impossible that their grain can be bought up at once, or even rapidly; before one tenth part of the desired quantity has been procured, the farmers will have taken the alarm; the rich farmers will stand aloof; the monopolists become competitors with the immediate consumers to purchase up what the small farmers bring to market: of course the prices rapidly advance, and the monopolist must at length purchase the corn but little cheaper than he can expect to sell it at. However, we will suppose him and his brethren to have drawn it, at whatever price, into their granaries, and to have withheld it long enough to produce all the effects of a real scarcity. During all this time their stock and capital are lying idle. At length, they bring it to market: some time or other they must bring it to market. For, surely, no one will attribute to them the prophetic powers of Joseph in Egypt, that they should foresee seven years of famine, or revenues sufficient to convert for seven years together, preceding the seven years of famine, plenty into a scarcity, little less than famine. They must bring it to market some time or other; and they must bring it *all* to market: for they have bought it at too dear a rate to make any partial destruction of the article, like that of nutmegs among the Dutch, a possible specu-

[a] *EOT*: simple [b] *EOT* omits

[5] This paragraph and the next were reprinted in the *Courier* 19 Sept 1811, with slight changes. See below.

[6] Poole: "Moreover, most of the large farmers have their senses about them and do not want capital, and if they see a probability of corn being dearer, they keep it themselves to receive the advantage of increased price."

lation.[7] Now is it not self-evident[a] that if there be no *real* scarcity in the country, the very act of bringing it back to the markets must very rapidly, or perhaps immediately, produce such a sudden fall in the prices, as must be ruinous to the authors of the artificial scarcity?—However gradually they may bring it in, their time is limited; and if there be no real scarcity, in whatever way they bring it in, the effect must ultimately be the same. The longer they delay it, the greater their loss must be; for the high prices of corn will of course occasion an increased production of that article. It appears, therefore, little less than madness to suppose, that it can ever be the interest or wish of any number of men to monopolise the grain of a country, unless they were seriously convinced that there existed a real and alarming scarcity of that article.[8] If these convictions are well founded, then the men falsely called monopolists, who employ large capitals in buying up corn when it is cheapest, may be fairly reckoned among the most useful and praise-worthy members of society.[9] Their interest preserves them constantly on the watch; their extensive connections and correspondences[b] ensure them the best and earliest information; their consequent measures give the alarm to the farmers, to withhold their corn in expectation of higher prices; and from what is thus bought up, and thus withheld, the scarcity is not so much anticipated, as it is diffused over a larger surface of time, and thereby[c] rendered more tolerable. Suppose two ships, each[d] bound on an equally long voyage, both equally without any means of revictualling; suppose the relative quantity of their provisions exactly the same, and that quantity diminished by the same accidents in the same proportion; and suppose that the officers in one ship compel their crew to short allowances six weeks before the other ship, which of the two crews, think you, would suffer the least from famine? which would arrive in harbour in the[e] best plight? What the officers are in the ship, the men called monopolists are in a kingdom.[10] Nay, they are far more; for they not only necessitate an early economy, but they sharpen the wits of men[f] to the discovery of substitutes,[11] and by exciting a

[a] *EOT*: (evident) [b] *EOT*: correspondence [c] *EOT*: therefore [d] *M Post*: both [e] *EOT* omits [f] *EOT*: the men

7 This example of nutmegs and the Dutch is taken from Smith *Wealth* bk IV ch 5.

8 Poole: "without the thing itself being actually scarce".

9 Cf Smith bk IV ch 5.

10 The example of the two ships is from Smith ibid. It was given, as from Smith, in an *M Post* leader of 15 Sept.

11 To this a letter signed "Cincinnatus" (dated 6 Oct, in *M Post* and *Courier* 25 Oct) retorted: "...but they sharpen their *appetites* also; and if praise be due to them for this, then

spirit of rivalship against themselves by the circumstance of their profits, they divert large capitals into the importation line, with the accompanying influence, activity, and talents of the capitalists, which would otherwise be employed in importing wines, perhaps, or logwood,[12] or some other worthless or pernicious superfluity. By these means they actually increase the quantity of provisions in the kingdom, while they diminish the consumption.

But [a]admitting, it will[b] be said, that no number of men [c]would buy up corn unless they believed[d] that there was or would be a scarcity in that article, yet, as men are apt to believe what they wish, so these men may become the dupes of their own avarice, and produce the scarcity by over-rating it. We answer, that the *possibility of creating* a scarcity, in such an article as corn, remains unproved: secondly, that it is more likely, that in some years they may appear to have over-rated the scarcity by the diminished consumption, which they themselves had been a[e] principal means of occasioning; and lastly, [f]who are[g] they who accuse them of ignorance or [h]blunder?—not[i] the farmers,—not their fellow corn-factors.[j] All who have the best means of estimating the quantity of grain in the country are silent. The secretary of the Agricultural Society, with laudable[k] industry, procured and published[13] the opinions of the most respectable

[a-b] *EOT*: perhaps it may [c-d] *EOT*: could buy corn, knowing
[e] *EOT*: the [f-g] *EOT*: that [h-i] *EOT*: blundering are [j] *EOT*: corn-dealers
[k] *EOT*: great

housebreakers may be equally well entitled useful and praiseworthy members of society, because they sharpen the wits of men to the discovery of stronger fastenings to prevent their devastations".

[12] An example from C's Lecture on the Slave Trade: *Lects 1795* (*CC*) 236 and *Watchman* No 4 (*CC*) 132.

[13] Arthur Young, secretary of the Board of Agriculture, published its first two volumes of *Communications* in 1797 and 1800, here cited, and his reports and correspondence for this period fill vols XXXV and XXXVI of his serial *Annals of Agriculture*. C had reviewed Young's *The Question of Scarcity* belligerently 27 Mar (see above), but in their basic assumptions and deductions Young, Poole, and C agree. All minimise the effects of speculation and stress the natural scarcity. Young inspires confidence with his analyses and surveys, and one is inclined to dismiss "the monopolist" as a vulgar phantom. Yet how politically *convenient* to conclude that the actions of the hungry populace were misconceived. If one reads on into the winter in Young's *Annals*, one suddenly comes upon the sage in panic, confronted by a continuing rise in prices (Jan, Feb 1801) that "mocks equally the conclusions of reason and the deductions of calculation" and brings Young to his knees before "Something unknown, unseen" that "operates as if to convince us that we are children in inquiries...that our ignorance seems to darken as our experience advances". For Young finds the "present rates" "utterly unaccountable" except on the supposition—which he *cannot* accept—of a

and independent land-holders,[a] throughout the kingdom, and of the best [b]informed men[c] in every district; and these were nearly[d] unanimous in the opinion, that there existed [e]a real and[f] alarming scarcity.

Whether the corn has been kept back by farmers, [g]or corn-factors,[h] longer than the exigencies of the time required, is a question[14] which is satisfactorily answered by the present price of the article, after so plentiful[i] a harvest.[15] If there were, really, so large a [j]quantity of old wheat[k] in the country, as is rashly affirmed, [l]after a crop[m] so dreadfully unprosperous as [n]last year,[o] what will there not be this time next year,[p] after a harvest of such unexampled prosperity? Does it not stand to reason, that the possessors would crowd with it to the markets before the new wheat is threshed out? Besides, does any one see old stacks of corn in farmers' yards now? There used to be one or more in every respectable farmer's yard,—but now, if there exist an instance of it, the possessor is pointed out, and stories invented of his having attracted the fury of a mob, in order that he *may* attract that fury. In short, the exertions of the corn-trade, the custom-house reports of the importations of corn, and the suffrages of independent and well-informed men, collected throughout the whole kingdom by a national institution, are the[q] evidences for the existence of scarcity; and what are the evidences adduced on the other side? We hear of one man having so many quarters of corn, and another having so many quarters of corn—and ought it not to be so? In a community so numerous as this, in an article of the first necessity, can, or ought things to be so balanced, as that the last quarter of old wheat shall be consumed on the day when the new wheat[r] comes into the market? Supposing that the wheat harvest had been a month later, as it well might have been, and as before the setting-in of the dry weather, there was every reason to believe it would be, where then would have been the superfluous quantity of

[a] *EOT*: landlords   [b–c] *EOT*: yeomen,   [d] *EOT* omits   [e–f] *EOT*: an
[g–h] *EOT*: and factors   [i] *EOT*: bad   [j–k] *EOT*: stock   [l–m] *EOT* omits
[n–o] *EOT*: was the season   [p] *EOT*: year (Oct.)   [q] *EOT* omits   [r] *M Post, EOT*: quarter

group of monopolists with "the power of withholding from the market or feeding it just in that proportion which will keep prices to the pitch required" (*Annals* XXXVI 482–4).

[14] This clause and most of this paragraph beginning "does any one see old stacks" derive from Poole's letter (*Poole* II 12).

[15] The harvest was early and at first promising, but by Oct it was known that a second year of worse than average yield would have to be mitigated by greater importation. SC in the light of later information emended "plentiful" to "bad".

old corn?—or, supposing that in addition to this, we had had wet weather during the wheat harvest, so that the wheat would not have been in a state to be ground for two or three months to come—where then would have been the overplus so bitterly complained of? and what if, in further addition, we had had no monopolists to alarm our farmers, to excite early importation, early economy, and providence in substitutes—should we not have been starved?

If the author of this essay were asked—Would you then be a *monopolist*, as it is called, in the corn-trade? he would answer, No! he would *wish* to be of no employment, in which his own welfare was connected with the misery of his fellow-beings, even though that employment ultimately lessened their misery.[16] But he reverences the profession, and pities the individuals. But what are the motives and characters of the individuals to the utility of their profession? There may be, and probably are, hard-hearted corn-factors!—some perhaps may become hard-hearted by being corn-factors; but this is no more than is true of surgeons, of all useful men, the most unequivocally useful!

This essay is already prolonged beyond the usual limits of a newspaper. The importance of the subject must be an apology. In the next number[17] we shall consider the nature of that obloquy, under which our farmers labour: as far as they have speculated in the purchases of other men's corn, they are included in the considerations of this essay; in our next therefore we consider them as farmers, as possessors of that corn which they themselves have produced.[18]

[16] Cf C's preference for simple farming, "unpartaking of the evil thing", expressed at the close of the *Ode on the Departing Year*: *PW* (EHC) I 168.

[17] For Letters II–IV see App A, 4, 6, 9 Oct 1800, below.

[18] Street, who edited the *Courier* for Stuart, reprinted this first Letter (3 Oct) with some misgivings ("...we certainly by no means agree with the writer of it in many of the points he has urged"). On 7 Oct he published a letter "To the Editor of The Courier" signed "Alpha" suggesting that the author's "'reverence for the profession, and pity for individuals,' [had] made him say more than was prudent" and had "certainly made the *motive* of his zeal appear questionable". Alpha discovered the writer to be "perfectly ignorant of the manner in which most of the corn-markets in England are conducted" and proceeded to explain. "The farmers have a very different opinion of the unwieldy bulk of grain. They (even the most opulent) feel little difficulty in bringing the produce of their farms to market in their *coat-pockets*. When the corn-factor makes his purchase, he will often stipulate for the corn to remain on the farmer's premises for a fortnight, three weeks, or longer, and often till *that* corn is re-sold at another market. Thus warehouse room is provided by the original seller, the expence of carriage is borne by the *second* purchaser, and the corn-factor not only succeeds in putting a large profit in his pockets, but prepares the markets for the future depredations of himself and

[6 October 1800, Monday]

It must not be concluded, because this Paper is open to impartial discussion on the subject, that we take a part in favour of Forestallers. The present series of Essays on the Scarcity of Provisions will be concluded on Wednesday, when we shall give place to Letters of a very different description.[1]

others. The *bulk* of grain is therefore no preventative against monopoly. If grain is *widely* diffused, so also are the *speculations* of the monopolist—*they are not confined to Mark-lane.*"

("Cincinnatus" makes a further comment on this point, in *M Post* 25 Oct: "The capital of the country is such, that two or three monied individuals joining together can speculate upon the production of a whole county; and such a quantity, though small in proportion to the remainder, will affect the whole. But the farmers, you say, will take the alarm at the efforts to buy up corn, and those who are rich will [not] stand aloof. I grant it. The rich farmers..are, many of them, monopolists themselves.")

"When I wrote a letter upon scarcity", C recalled twenty-one years later (*BE* II 220), "it was generally said that it was the production of an immense cornfactor, and a letter was addressed to me under that persuasion, beginning 'Crafty Monopolist.'" No letter exactly so addressed has been found, but C perhaps was thinking of "Alpha", who calls him in capital letters "DEFENDER OF MONOPOLISTS", or of "Cincinnatus", who more gently calls him "a most excellent advocate in behalf of the monopolisers and farmers". Allan Macleod, editor of the *Albion* (the remaining radical newspaper after the *Courier*'s transformation by Street in 1799), at once guessed—or found out—the author of Letter I and threatened to make "strict but impartial digests" of his other "writings, *religious*, *moral*, and *political*". (*Albion* 3 Oct; Macleod quotes twenty lines and pretends, hoaxingly, to find an "aukward slovenly style".)

It should be observed that Stuart had already begun a counter-series of letters by "W" investigating in sober detail the "extravagant increase of Jobbing, which gives to the Corn Market more the appearance of a stock exchange, than one for the sale of the absolute necessaries of life". The third and fourth "W" Letters (10, 14 Oct) get beyond the dilemma of scarcity-yes-or-no and provide a more searching contribution to the discussion. Street chose to print all the "W" letters but only half the C series, Letters I and II before the "Alpha" criticism, but only Letter IV after it. Street was not committed to C as Stuart was; he also had a more delicate reputation to maintain, that of the *Courier*, which had been the most radical Opposition paper and must still have had a readership sensitive to "betrayal".

[1] See App A, 9 Oct 1800, below.

MONOPOLISTS AND FARMERS

LETTER V
TO THE EDITOR OF THE MORNING POST, BY THE AUTHOR OF THE INQUIRY INTO THE TRUTH, &C. &C.[1]

14 October 1800, Tuesday; entitled "Letter To the Editor. . .&c.". *EOT* II 451–6; see III 1021: ". . .certainly my Father's, since the writer speaks of himself as living 300 miles from London; which applied to him and not to Mr. Poole". The title and first paragraph identify the series; the style narrows the authorship to C.

SIR,

LIVING at a distance of three hundred miles from London, I did not receive your paper of Monday, October 6, till a late hour this evening. In this paper you announce a series of letters of a very different description from those which I have addressed to you on monopolists and farmers.[2] I shall of course wait for them, not without impatience. If they convince me, I shall be forward to acknowledge that conviction; if my old creed remains unshaken, I shall again claim a place in a paper, so open to impartial discussion,[3] for the support of that creed. In the mean time I beg to offer a few miscellaneous remarks and queries.

I have now before me an evening paper of Saturday, September 6. In one column of this paper we are told, "That the only mad dogs of this season are the monopolists.—The hue and cry against them is pretty general." In another column of the same paper I read, "The present riots in different parts of the country prove what erroneous notions the mob entertain of the means of rendering provisions cheap. In order to lower the price of bread, we find them, in more than one instance, destroying the flour and burning the mills."[4]

[1] For the tally of C's verse contributions from 13 and 14 Oct 1800 to 26 Sept 1801, see App D, below.

[2] See editorial notice of 6 Oct and n 1 to Letter III (App A, 6 Oct, below). From the present paragraph and the date of 8 Oct it would seem that Stuart's notice of intent to end the series reached Keswick in time to discourage C from sending more than this final rebuttal, whatever else he may have had in hand.

[3] Cf editorial notice of 6 Oct, above.

[4] C is quoting the *Star* of 6 Sept practically verbatim. His initial attack in Letter I had drawn vehement, if somewhat incoherent, protests from the *Star*, to which Stuart had in turn replied heavily. Allan Macleod's sarcastic summary of this battle, in the *Albion* of 25 Oct, is headed "The Star Attacks The Post!!", and it deplores the efforts of "the poor decrepid lady . . .to break a lance with that mere jilt", called earlier "the young trull of 'Change Alley" (3 Oct). Stuart, having begun his career with stock-jobbing forgeries, was now suspected of forging political opinions for the corn-factors.

The *Star* "hath alledged that her little cousin in the Strand hath pros-

Now, Sir, I am one of those who greatly reverence the *feelings* of a multitude, though I have not the same respect for the *opinions* that excite them. A multitude may, and too often do, take up false opinions; but, these admitted for truths, they rarely, indeed, act *inconsequentially*. If monopolists, farmers, and millers, are in reality the guilty causes of the present scarcity, it would be a difficult task to detect any error in the *deductions* of our mobs, who wished to counterpoise the passion of avarice by the passion of terror. Avarice can do great things—we know, though, perhaps, our posterity will scarcely believe it, that avarice can make a man an African slave-merchant; but then where does he reside? Among those whom he has made miserable? No! among his accomplices, or at least among those who are enjoying the luxuries which he procures, without having their bodily sympathies disturbed by the miseries which he creates. But avarice, in its most diseased excess, would never impel him to live among the fathers, brothers, husbands, and wives, of the men, women, and children, whom he was in the habit of carrying into slavery, among those who had detected his guilt, and possessed all the *physical* power of the country to punish it. Now, say our rioters, such and such are the fellows that starve us, in order to make money out of our hunger. We will prove to them that they are *found out*. Is it credible, that a man would long continue in an occupation which exposed him night and day to the operation of opinions like these?—opinions, which, if just, cannot be transient. I deduce, therefore, that if monopoly be the real cause of our scarcity, our mobs have acted imprudently and wickedly, but not absurdly nor *inconsequentially*. What is the real operation of these too successful attempts to raise the popular indignation against particular classes?—

tituted herself for *money*, and...that this money was paid for some jobs that were undertaken to show that monopoly and forestalling are the only true means of supplying a country regularly and cheap with corn and flour, and consequently the people with bread. Hence the *Star* contends that the *Post* has received money for inserting attempted vindications of those who are suspected to be the principal causes of the supposed scarcity, and actual dearness of provisions, at present in this country." Macleod agrees that the *Post* would do nothing except for money but finds it also suspicious that the letters in question "are almost reprinted; so copious are the extracts the *Star* has made from them". Perhaps "the *Star* has been alike guilty as the *Post* of a trifling coquetry with the forestallers".

Stuart may have taken personal revenge on Macleod, for the *Albion* was the Banquo's ghost of the old *Courier*; by the end of November Macleod was writing his editorials from "The State Side of Newgate" and claiming that the machinations of Stuart and Mackintosh had got him there (see *Albion* 10 Dec).

Are the Ministry wholly unfavourable to these attempts? Is it impossible that they themselves are well aware that the causes of national scarcity lie deep, deep in the very heart of what is called our national prosperity; that years of dearth are likely to have almost regular recurrences; and that popular rage against corn-traders would greatly facilitate the attempt to place the corn-trade, and even the agriculture of the country, under Ministerial controul? This, at least, is, I believe, certain, that the present withholding of corn does in great part depend on His Majesty's Ministers. When, by the assertion of Ministers in Parliament, the existence of scarcity to an alarming degree was a fact no longer to be doubted; promises were undoubtedly made to corn-merchants to encourage them to the most fearless speculations, as to any quantity which they could import. Vast quantities of corn are at this moment withheld,[5] because the corn-merchants are left in a state of uncertainty, whether Ministers mean to keep their promises. But on this subject I shall obtain your permission to speak a few words, when I have seen the letters in which the popular cry against the corn-traders is to be substantiated.

In the first letter of your correspondent W. in your paper of Tuesday, Sept. 30,[6] it is *assumed* as a fact, that the farmers *grew*, and the traders *bought up* the corn (which they now sell at an advance of 40*s*. a quarter) at its usual price. That the traders *could not* buy up the corn at its usual price, and that the farmers *would not* be such idiots as to sell it, I trust I have amply proved in the first number of my inquiry. But it is *assumed* as a *fact* in this letter, that there was no real scarcity. This, Sir, should not have been *assumed*; it should have been *proved*. It is the corner-stone of the whole question. Deduction, Sir, is an easy business. The ground-work of *facts* is the important, useful, and difficult part of a reasoner's trade. What if I were to assume as a fact, that your correspondent writes on a subject of which he is ignorant. The *deduction*, that his letter is not worth the reading, would be legitimate and inevitable; but the whole of my argument would be as contemptible in reason, as it would be deficient in common politeness. The march of the question is this:

[5] With this concession C's rebuttal turns to a retreat.

[6] See above, nn on 3 Oct, and below, App A, 6 Oct. By now C has also seen W's second letter, 1 Oct; readers will have seen the third, 10 Oct, and will find the fourth in adjacent columns 14 Oct. The moral imperative of the Coleridge–Poole position was that to make clear the reality of the scarcity was to decrease the pressures that made prices high. "W" now argued the reverse: that it was the prevalence of the *idea* of a real scarcity that enabled the speculators to raise prices to a height that only famine should have produced.

1. Has there been a scarcity, and to what degree? 2. To what degree beyond the natural exertions of the corn-trader have the traders been extra-regularly stimulated by the promises and exhortation of the Government and Legislature of their country? And were the Government right or wrong in their interference? 3. Suppose the whole quantity of the grain in the kingdom to be measured and known, what would be the residue, if a whole month's national consumption were subtracted? This in common justice ought to be done, for the harvest has been a month earlier than it *might* have been: and where the food of ten millions is in question, it would be madness not to provide for the worst. 4. What is the strict definition of a forestaller in the article of corn? Wherein is he distinguishable from the fair trader? and what have forestallers, in the strict and legal sense of the word, been able to accomplish?

These questions demand an answer—an answer of facts, not assumptions. I have often heard unthinking people exclaim, in observing differences of price in different parts of the country, What has become of Adam Smith's *level?* I, God knows, am no friend to those hard-hearted comparisons of human actions with the laws of inanimate nature.[7] Water will come to a level without pain or pleasure, and provisions and money will come to a level likewise; but, O God! what scenes of anguish must take place while they are coming to a *level!* But still the sneer against Adam Smith, as to the simple fact, is absurd. The tide in the rivers Trent and Parrot flows in in a *head.*[8] Now if a spectator should exclaim to a writer on fluids, What has become of your *level* now? Would he not answer, *stay* and see!

I remain, Sir, your's, &c.

———[9]

Wednesday night, Oct. 8, 1800

[7] In his *Wealth of Nations* Smith described market prices of every commodity as "continually gravitating, if one may say so, towards the natural price" (bk I ch 7). The example of waters reaching "a level" above and below open flood-gates, with a comparison to the price of gold and silver coming "to a level", is in bk IV ch 5. E. P. Thompson (article cited above, p 89) cites *An Inquiry* by J. Arbuthnot (1773): "Let corn flow like water, and it will find its level."

[8] In *Courier* 30 May 1811 C would again say: "*Things* may find their level; but the *minds* and bodies of men do not." See also *LS* (*CC*) 205–7. On the Trent and Parret/Parrot see *CL* I 217; *CN* I 296; *M Post* 12 Oct 1802; *CL* IV 830n.

[9] C and Poole did not carry on the discussion, though C requested "one more Essay, of considerable length, detailing the effect & operations of paper currency on the price of the articles of Life" (*CL* I 634), and Poole a month later supplied some ideas on paper as the "great cause of the rise of the price of everything" (*Poole* II 17–19). Poole left the monopoly

question high and dry, ignoring C's intimation that they needed more data, such as might be found in Frederick Eden's *The State of the Poor*, and not otherwise responding to C's appeal for a final triumphant Essay supporting "the Stress of the Battle, and the Hope of the Victory".

In the *Post* and *Courier* the debate wound on, "A. B." on 23 Oct supporting the Poole–Coleridge position with extracts from a treatise on the grain shortages of 1767 and 1768; "Cincinnatus" on 25 Oct attacking, as we have seen; "S. X." on 4 Nov and an anonymous contributor on the 7th blaming the real scarcity on the war and on Pitt's system of finance.

Stuart in retrospect (Stuart x 26) emphasised the great boost in circulation attained by his assistant George Lane's extensive reporting of "the corn riots in 1800"; indeed the *M Post* in weeks preceding the Letters had been filled with riot accounts, quoted denunciations of monopolists, and inflammatory rumours of rotting hoards of flour, published with little editorial concern for consequences.

Except for a few verses, C's next contribution to the *M Post* is the *Ode to Addington* of 27 May 1801, his next substantial one a series beginning 27 Nov. But for indications of some assistance to Stuart in late 1800 see App A, 21, 23 Oct 1800.

1801

27 May–18 December

AN ODE TO ADDINGTON

27 May 1801, Friday. New attribution, on the evidence of verse and prose styles and the density of characteristic allusions, with numerous parallels in *The Friend* and C's notebooks and elsewhere. Included here as at least half prose—and all political, not to say journalistic.

TO THE EDITOR OF THE MORNING POST

THE following Ode was sent to Mr. A--d--n,[1] at a very critical moment indeed, when he was extremely agitated, and tremblingly hesitated, whether he should or should not resign the Chair.

The Author now enjoys the conscious satisfaction of having determined him, by these lyrical and persuasive strains, to obey the commands of his most gracious Sovereign, and gratify the wishes of a loyal, devoted people, by his acceptance of the Seals, with a modest and becoming reluctance.

Mr. A. in conjunction with his noble rival and colleague, Lord H--ksb--y, has revived Messrs. P--t's and D--d--s' glorious Administration; and we may now expect, with confidence, a continuance of the same invaluable and extensive blessings, which have endeared the names of those two illustrious statesmen, and embalmed their memory in the hearts of all true Britons and Anti-Jacobins.[2]

I am, Sir, Your's, &c.

1 The blanks fill easily as: A*dding*t*o*n, Ha*wk*e*sbury*, and P*itt*'s and D*und*a*s*'. Henry Addington (1757–1844; 1st Viscount Sidmouth 1805), an intimate of Pitt and Speaker of the House since 1789, became Chancellor of the Exchequer on Pitt's resignation in Feb 1801. For Hawkesbury, see note below. C pretends to have sent Addington this *Ode* of advice before his resignation of the speakership to become prime minister—and, in effect, to have "determined him" to do so.

Though fanciful—the *Ode* can hardly have been written before early May, when the Egyptian victories it alludes to were first known in England—this claim or admission on C's part is of some interest. Since Oct 1800, despite proddings by Stuart, C had contributed nothing to the *M Post* except a few verses (see App D, below), and his "France-&-England-Curiosity" (*CL* I 630) had seemed in abeyance. His first response to news of Pitt's resignation was the private comment: "Change of Ministry interests *me* not—I turn at times half reluctantly from Leibnitz or Kant even to read a smoking new newspaper..." (to Poole, 13 Feb 1801: *CL* II 676). Pitt's fall, ostensibly over the Catholic question, was reputedly to cover his not wanting to have anything to do with the peace negotiations.

2 Here the cynicism offsets the preceding claim. Addington brought "his noble rival" into the cabinet;

AN EXPOSTULATORY AND PANEGYRICAL ODE,

Addressed to the R. H. H. A–D––G––N

Quem virum, aut heroa, lyra vel acri
Tibia sumis celebrare Clio!
Quem deum! cujus recinet jocosa.
NOMEN IMAGO—Hor. car. 12. l. 1[3]

AH! why resign yon splendid chair,
Where you preside with solemn air,
Of *Ayes* and *Noes* Recorder?
Your wig in flaxen tresses twines,
And flowing gown with lustre shines;
To keep the House in order.

Hatsel's wise laws with winning art,[4]
You gravely state, and touch the heart
By your pathetic chat:
What can escape your sage (1) *owl* eyes?
'Mid Fox's speech the mandate flies—
"Bar! Bar! take off your hat!"[6]

(1) "The owl bends both his eyes on the object which he observes, and has thence acquired the name of the Bird of Wisdom." Darwin on Female Education.[5]

Dundas resigned with Pitt; yet anti-Jacobinism persists. Lords Portland, Westmorland, and Chatham (Pitt's brother) were retained in Addington's cabinet; the additions, besides Hawkesbury, were Lords Eldon, Hobart, St. Vincent, Hardwicke, and, in June, Pelham—a ministry weak in everything but lords (Barnes 390). Resigning with Pitt and Dundas were Grenville, Loughborough, Cornwallis, and Windham. Grenville and Windham would soon act as a New Opposition, joined by Canning and Malmesbury.

[3] Horace *Odes* 1.12.1 (The Praises of Augustus). Tr: "What man, what hero dost thou take to herald on the lyre or clear-toned flute, O Clio? What god? Whose name shall the playful echo [iocosa imago] make resound...?" Tr C. E. Bennett (LCL 1947) 35. C's punctuation seems to make the *name* an *echo*—i.e. Addington's name a shadow of Augustus' (Pitt's).

[4] John Hatsell (1743–1820), authority on parliamentary procedure, had retired as chief clerk of the House of Commons in 1797.

[5] Erasmus Darwin *A Plan for the Conduct of Female Education in Boarding Schools* (1797) 99 (var, with an omission), in a chapter on "Squinting". Darwin and owls were both of interest to C.

[6] Addington is perhaps enforcing a Hatsell ruling, that a member take off his hat when he passes the bar of the House of Commons, beyond which non-members were not allowed. It is also at the bar that a person stands while the Speaker of the House delivers a reprimand or an admonition.

4. *Sketch of the Interior of St Stephens, as it Now Stands.*
Print by James Gillray (1 Mar 1802)

Addington, in the House of Commons, comes forward with his "Treaty of Peace with ye Democratick Powers" (i.e. the definitive Treaty of Amiens). Behind him, the four prominent MPs are, from bottom to top, Hawkesbury, Nichol (with cane), Tierney (not caricatured), and Wilberforce. Engulfed in his official wig sits Abbot, newly elected Speaker. Coleridge's "Ode" of 27 May 1801 introduces the new Chancellor; the articles of 23 Feb and 22 Mar 1802 define his administration

Yet, faith, you have no other choice;
Cheer'd by your KING and Country's voice,
O'erleap the shackling pale:
With Hawk–s–––ry's (2) spirit and his fire,
Who with short steps pursues his sire,
To catch him by the tail. (3)

BRITANNIA asks his trenchant blade
To smite the Dane and haughty Swede,
Rous'd by mad Paul's intriguing.
Jenky, to arms; new grind your lance,
To Paris march, and conquer France
By burning Copenhagen![9]

Tho' Paul and Frederick combine,
BRITANNIA, trench'd in her own brine,
Laughs at their brandish'd spears;
From Christian states with scorn she flies,
To hire congenial cheap allies
At Tunis and Algiers[10] (4).

(2) Mr. P––t's panegyric on those two accomplished Statesmen, Lord Liv–rp––l and Lord H––ks––ry, was the most brilliant part of his speech on Mr. Grey's motion.[7]

(3) Sequiturque patrem haud passibus aequis. Virgil.[8]

(4) A treaty, offensive and defensive, highly honourable to Great Britain, and the Republic of Algiers, is, I hear, now negotiating between the Dey's Ambassador, and Lord Hawkesbury, by which the whole maritime force of that great naval state is to be at our absolute disposal. Religion, morality, and social order, are the basis of the treaty. The proceedings and decrees of our Admiralty Courts in

[7] The two Hawkesburys were Charles Jenkinson (1729–1808), Lord Hawkesbury until he became Earl of Liverpool in 1796; now ailing but lingering on in Addington's cabinet with two offices (though never attending); and his son, Robert Banks Jenkinson, Lord Hawkesbury and (1808) 2nd Earl of Liverpool (1770–1828), entering Addington's cabinet as Foreign Secretary. "Jenky" the son had made an impressive speech against Grey's motion for Parliamentary Reform in 1793.

[8] Virgil *Aeneid* 2.724 (var). "And follows his father with steps that match not his." Tr Fairclough (LCL 1916) I 343. C's subsequent footnotes have been renumbered, this and the following note having been printed "(3)".

[9] One of the first acts of Addington and his Foreign Secretary was the sending of a naval squadron to Copenhagen to spike the Second Armed Neutrality, in late March.

[10] Cf C's similarly sarcastic praise of "the cautious Delicacy of our Government! that will profess itself the ally of the Immaculate only—of the MERCIFUL Catharine, the HONEST King of Prussia, and that most CHRISTIAN Arch-pirate, the Dey of Algiers!" *Conciones: Lects 1795 (CC)* 54–5. Paul had replaced Catherine, and Frederick William III had succeeded his father, Frederick William II, as King of Prussia.

"Rule, BRITANNIA! rule the waves!"[12]
Blacken your sugar isles with slaves,
  Speak mercy, preach devotion;
On foaming billows rear your throne,
Sea without ports, is all your own,
  You rule a shoreless ocean.[13]

And art thou gone, St. Malta's Paul?
As mad a Knight as Israel's Saul,
  Touch'd by celestial ire:
In Death's strait waistcoat bound at last,[14]
Deaf—till the trumpet's final blast,
  Tho' P---s sound his lyre.[15]

In France, tho' Jacobins are dead,
Their vengeful ghosts you wisely dread,

---

the West Indies are now translating for the instruction of the Algerine Tribunals, as a new Code of Laws is to be formed by the Barbary States on similar principles; any thing in Sir W. Scott's bill to the contrary notwithstanding.[11]

[11] In other words, the Barbary pirates were to be guided by rules now proposed to be reformed by the Bill for the Better Regulation of Prize Courts in the West Indies introduced by Sir William Scott, Lord Stowell (1745–1836), judge of the consistory court of London (1788–1821) and of the high court of Admiralty (1798–1828), MP for Oxford (from Mar 1801). The bill had its first reading in the Commons 19 May.

[12] Words from the naval patriotic song in the masque *Alfred* (1740) by James Thomson (with music by Thomas Augustine Arne).

[13] The epithet "shoreless Ocean" is in C's *Reflections on Having Left a Place of Retirement* line 37: *PW* (EHC) I 107.

[14] Tsar Paul I had been assassinated on 24 Mar. Bonaparte, about to surrender Malta to the British, had given it to Paul, who had been made Grand Master by the Knights of St John who had fled to Russia; and Grenville had promised either to return Malta to the Knights or to assign it to Paul. But Britain kept Malta.

C's jests about Paul's insanity—"Touch'd", "strait waistcoat" etc—were not off the mark. "As his [Paul's] wrath at Bonaparte's seizure of Malta largely accounts for Russia's participation in the Second Coalition, so, too, his childish joy at receiving the island as a present from Bonaparte when it was certain to surrender to the British goes far to explain Paul's swing round from friendship to hostility in the summer of 1800." *The Cambridge History of British Foreign Policy* I (Cambridge 1922) 299.

[15] Charles Small Pybus (1733–1810), MP for Dover, a lord of the Treasury under Pitt, published a poem in heroic couplets, in folio, *The Sovereign* (1800), addressed to Paul. In Jul 1802 C thought of writing an essay on Pye, the poet laureate, "& his Dative Case Plural, Pybus" (*CL* II 829). "Pye and Parvum [Small] Pybus" became a catch-phrase for poetasters.

Shrouded in Tallien's (5) cloak;
So, by the brain's mechanic pow'r,
The ideot counted ev'ry hour,
When the town clock (6) was broke.

But *here*, the knaves combine and swear,
We've Irish evidence from C--re;[18]
Altho' they fawn like spaniels;[19]
But see our guardian angels sit,
Expound Ezekiel's text (7) with P–tt,[21]
And treason find in Daniel's (8).

(5) M. Tallien's dangerous designs, and assassinating plots, were providentially discovered; and he was ordered away at a minute's warning. He had been elected a member at Brooks's; visited Mr. Fox at St. Anne's-hill; went with him and Mr. Sheridan to Drury-Lane; and was magnificently entertained every day by the Members of Opposition.[16]

(6) See Addison's paper in the Spectator, No. 417, where this curious fact is referred to in Dr. Platt's History of Staffordshire.[17]

(7) "And thou pretend, wicked prince, O Israel, whose day is come, when iniquity shall have an end."[20]

Thus saith the Lord, "Remove the diadem, and take off the crown: this shall not be the same: exalt him that is low, and abase him that is high."

"I will overturn, overturn, overturn it: and it shall be no more, until he come whose right it is, and I will give it him." Ezekiel xxi. 25, 26, 27.

These were favourite High Church Jacobite texts, on the Accession of George the First; and are now treasonably adopted on similar principles by the Jacobins.

(8) "Then shall stand up in his estate a raiser of taxes, in the glory of the kingdom: but within a few days he shall be destroyed, neither in anger, nor in battle."

"And in his estate shall stand up a vile person, to whom they shall not give

[16] Tallien, a hero in C's *The Fall of Robespierre*, had been captured on his way from Egypt to Paris in 1799 and was well received by the Whigs. He would return to France in 1802, at the Peace, but C here appears to be inventing a story of his being ordered away. From the fact that Tallien had been in the first instance a journalist, the parallel to C's later account of his own being warned away from Rome, at Napoleon's approach, is understandable.

[17] The use of this bit from Addison (*Spectator* No 447, not 417; cf *Friend* No 7—*CC*—II 98: "...as an Ideot would tell the Clock at noon—one, one, one, etc", also *CN* I 1242 and III 3961) is evidence for C's authorship. The point here is the idiocy of continuing to count Jacobins, though Jacobinism is dead in France. "Dr. Platt" is Robert Plot *The Natural History of Staffordshire*.

[18] John Fitzgibbon, Earl of Clare (1749–1802), lord chancellor of Ireland, a rabid anti-Roman Catholic, responsible for the coercive policy in Ireland; responsible more than any other man for the passing of the Act of Union; hated by the Irish. He wrote a tract in favour of Union in 1799: *No Union! But Unite and Fall!* "By Paddy Whack, in a loving letter to his dear mother, Sheelah, of Dame Street, Dublin".

[19] C hated lap-dogs; cf *Rufa: PW* (EHC) II 960.

[20] A garbling of Ezekiel 21.25: "And thou, profane wicked prince of Israel...".

[21] To "expound Ezekiel's text" *with* Pitt might be to apply the prophetic

They tell what traitors think or say,
Whether they (9) nod, give toasts, or pray,
  Or, in their cups are merry;
And vote Horne Tooke a Consul's chair,
Or, to reform the Church with care,
  The See of Canter-*ber*ry.[25]

the honour of the kingdom; but he shall come in peaceably, and obtain the kingdom by flatteries."[22]

This prophecy has been applied most traitorously and wickedly, by the Jacobin prints, to our two great luminaries of State, the Burleigh and Walsingham of England. Sir J. Scott, the present Chancellor, is the only enlightened expounder of prophecies. He foretold the fate of the East India Bill, from the Revelations; and the condemnation of Horne Tooke and Hardy, from the celebrated Act of Edward III.[23] His brother, Sir William, if we may venture to judge from his profound and mysterious elucidatory comments on ordination and marriage, may be joined in this sacred office.[24]

(9) "Insurrections among the manufacturers of different parts of Lancashire. This was to be done by associating as many as possible under the sanction of an oath, which, with an account of the *secret sign* which accompanied it, has been transmitted from various quarters to Government, and laid before your Committee." Committee of Secrecy, Report, page 13.

overturning to Addington; yet the prose note points attention to the recent overturning of Pitt. As for Daniel 11.20–1, quoted in C's n 8, the raiser of taxes is of course Pitt, who has been destroyed "neither in anger, nor in battle"; so the "vile person" obtaining the kingdom "by flatteries" must be Addington. These are "the Burleigh and Walsingham" of modern England—loosely similar to Queen Elizabeth's two councillors, William Cecil, Baron Burghley (1521–98) and Sir Francis Walsingham (c 1530–90).

22 See n 21, above.

23 Sir John Scott, 1st Earl of Eldon (1751–1838), lord chancellor since 14 Apr, had made his maiden speech against the East India Bill of Fox and North; at the bill's 3rd reading the same year, 8 Dec 1783, he had read verses from Revelation comparing the beast having seven heads with the seven commissioners of Fox's bill and making other applications to the bill as evil. In 1794 he had been responsible, as attorney general, for the State Trials of Tooke and Hardy; they were acquitted, but he probably did predict their conviction. On the 1351 Act of Edward III defining high treason, see *Watchman* (*CC*) 387 n 4.

24 During the third reading of the Clergymen's Eligibility Bill on 19 May Sir William Scott "maintained the indelibility of the clerical character, which he conceived to be very distinct from the possession of a benefice....A Clergyman could no more resign his clerical character, than a Nobleman could divest himself of his nobility; that holy orders, though not strictly a sacrament, were in the nature of marriage, which, though not strictly a sacrament, either partook so far of it as to be indissoluble, without the interference of the Legislature, under particular circumstances; and that, by the constitutional law of the country, the House of Commons was a lay assembly, of which a man vested with a clerical character could not be a member". *M Post* 20 May.

25 "They" (the "knaves" of the stanza above) are the Committee of Secrecy from whose *Second Report... to the House of Commons*, presented 15 May 1801, C quotes in his notes. They

See sixty thousand canting Tykes,
With text-scrawl'd daggers, holy pikes,
  Headed by old Methus'lem,[26]
For Brothers's Millenium roar,[27]
And join a *half* and *million* corps,
  To fight for new Jerus'lem (10).

Lest Jacobins the Crown assail,
No *Habeas Corpus*, and no bail,
  Give martial law—INSTEAD (11);[28]
While trade, and wealth, from taxes spring,
And well-fed peasants gaily sing,
  Rebellion roars for bread.

Sydney, no more your treaty boast,
The French are caught on Egypt's coast,

(10) "Jerusalem. A Society appears to have been formed in part of Yorkshire, under the title of New Jerusalemites, whose leaders have inspired them with a belief of the pretended prophecies of Brothers, and who look under his guidance for the speedy commencement of the Millen[n]ium." Second Report of the Committee of Secrecy, page 14.

(11) "They (*i.e.* the traitors) were not insensible of the proceedings of Parliament on the subject of the Martial Law Bill in Ireland, which they were apprehensive might be applied to the suppression of their enterprises here." Nothing can save this country but a similar bill; and I hope it will be the concluding auspicious act of this first session of the Imperial Parliament.

"Copies of Lord Cornwallis's and Mr. Pitt's letters, and Justicative Manifesto, addressed to the Roman Catholics of Ireland (exhorting them to keep the peace, and persevere in their allegiance), were made out for the inspection of the Committee of Secrecy, and presented by the Chancellor of the Exchequer to the House of Commons."

---

report what "traitors" say in their meetings: nodding with "secret sign" or voting for Horne Tooke. In 1796 the Westminster radicals had supported Tooke for Parliament; in 1800, taking his seat 15 Feb 1801, Tooke had been brought in for the rotten borough of Old Sarum by Lord Camelford as a gesture of defiance. The poem implies that alarmists see the support of Tooke as equivalent to an effort to make him an English Bonaparte—or a reforming Archbishop of Canterbury: a bill to exclude him, as a person in holy orders, from sitting in the House of Commons had been introduced 6 May. There is a pun on his right-hand supporter, Col Barry, I believe. And a pun on *bar*ring: see n 6, above.

[26] Old Methusalem is Major John Cartwright (1740–1824), perennial advocate of Parliamentary Reform.

[27] For C's sympathy for Richard Brothers (1757–1824) see *CL* I 156 and *Watchman* No 2 (*CC*) 53.

[28] Although the new Ministry began by a release of political prisoners detained under suspension of Habeas Corpus (4 Mar 1801), the Secrecy report was made the excuse for renewal of its suspension and for outlawing Seditious Meetings. See 3 Dec 1801 n 23, below.

Horse, camels, foot, and gunners;[29]
So thieves are *nab'd* (a dang'rous corps),
If they break in, we lock the door,
Then send for Bow-street Runners.

Ceylon a show'r of nutmegs flings,
O'er Britain shakes her *all-spice* wings,
And winnows, cloves, and mace;[30]
Let Belgium (12) Austria's sceptre own,
Peace yield Nassau Batavia's throne,
And crown the Bourbon race.

Lo! pious Kings, with joyful eyes,
See the Bastile with lustre rise,
While Nuns and Friars kiss;
The Church waves high her holy hand,
Tithes, Titles, Corvées, sow the land
With future crops of bliss.

Minto will smooth the Consul's frown,
By Corsic's (13) abdicated crown;

(12) The restoration of the Netherlands, and the re-establishment of the Stadtholder, must be the *sine quâ non* of Lord Malmsbury's second Negotiation for a Peace.[31] The island of St. Domingo, which has already cost us twenty millions, and forty or fifty thousand lives, may be ceded (when conquered), as some sort of equivalent to the House of Bourbon; if the atheistical Republicans still refuse to acknowledge Louis XVIII.

(13) It must flatter the pride and vain ambition of the usurping Corsican, to have the same diadem bestowed on him by Lord Minto, which was accepted by his Lordship, for his British Majesty; and the Coronation Oath taken by the Royal Representative of the Monarch, and the Oath of Allegiance administered to the Representatives of the Corsican nation.

[29] Sir William Sidney Smith (1764–1840), as a commodore, had negotiated a treaty 24 Jan 1800 with Bonaparte's Gen Kléber—which Admiral Keith was instructed not to ratify. In Mar 1801 a British expeditionary force under Abercromby had landed in Egypt; by late March the French had been decisively beaten—as London heard in May. See n 34, below.

[30] Retention of Ceylon, formerly a Dutch colony, now a British prize of war, seems to induce in the poet such extravagant visions that he proceeds to conjure up, as obtainable by Addington and Hawkesbury, a fully Bourbon peace: Belgium given to Austria, the Netherlands to the Stadtholder, the Bastile rebuilt, and all the pre-Revolutionary bliss of "Tithes, Titles, Corvées" returned to France.

[31] The irony of supposing such a peace to be gained from "Lord Malmsbury's second Negotiation" is, first, that his first negotiation (1796–7) was a complete failure, and second, that Malmesbury was now out of office and actively opposing peace as "an unwise and weak measure" at this time. Farrer 109.

And make him blithe and hearty;[32]
We'll vote him of the Brunswick line,
H----s---y[33] will breach his right divine,
And hail King Bonaparte!

Who check'd the Gaul's Egyptian flight? (14)
D--nd-s renown'd for *second sight*,
To war's great science bred;[34]
Hence British valour wins the coast,
Where their lov'd Chief, the soldier's boast,
Conquer'd like Wolfe and bled.[35]

O Add-ng--n, thy sterling praise,
Stamp'd by Paul's bard in golden lays,
Shall future ages view;
See how thy honey'd rhet'ric drops,
And for a *recipe* of hops,
No Willis equal you.[36]

At Britain's Bank let traitors rail,
Her paper treasures ne'er can fail,
Valu'd as gold by law;
Tho' Sparta's coin from iron rose,
What mint can e'er exhaust old cloaths,
Or mines of rags and straw?[37]

(14) This unanswerable and triumphant reason may be assigned for not permitting the French to evacuate Egypt, namely, the opportunity it has given the British troops to display an intrepidity, spirit, and discipline, which has never been excelled. Our wise and prescient War Minister, therefore, acted with his usual sagacity, by providing for this glorious event.

[32] Sir Gilbert Elliot, 1st Earl of Minto (1751–1814), now British ambassador at Vienna but seeking to resign, had been British governor of Corsica in 1794–6. The proposal is to flatter Bonaparte into accepting the crown of Corsica as his sole regality.

[33] H*awkesbury*.

[34] Dundas as Pitt's secretary for war was responsible for the instructions to Lord Keith in Egypt rejecting the terms of the Treaty of El Arish of 24 Jan 1800 arranged by Smith and Kléber. At that time the British preferred to have the French troops stay in Egypt rather than be returned to Continental battlefields. Kléber refused to yield them as prisoners, and the war was renewed, with a French victory over the Turks that led to complete restoration of French power in Egypt. By the following October Dundas was persuading a reluctant King George to authorise the expedition that reached Egypt in Mar 1801.

[35] Sir Ralph Abercromby (1734–1801), who commanded the Mediterranean troops, died from a fatal shot in the victorious battle near Alexandria 21 Mar.

[36] During the King's illness in 1801, when Dr Willis despaired because the King was unable to sleep, Addington suggested a pillow of hops. The King slept and improved immediately.

[37] On the suspension of cash payments in 1797, see C's essays on the Bullion Controversy in 1811, below.

While you enjoy unhop'd-for bliss,
Give P–tt the fond fraternal kiss,
  As earnest of the steerage;
The coronation oath deface,
And promise him your pow'r and place,
  For pension, and a peerage.[38]

From you the humble Bishops pray,
To light the church, one sacred ray,
  Clouded by Popery's vapours;
They preach in no mysterious tone,
That Ministers betray the throne,
  Who spread seditious papers.

Courage, great Sir, the chair resign,
Your oily eloquence will shine,
  And lull the storms of state;
Quit melting scenes of nuptial life—
For frowns, hard words, and bitter strife,
  In many a sharp debate.

So Regulus,[39] by Horace (15) sung,
Though babes and wife around him clung,
  Display'd the Roman still;
At Carthage cask'd, 'midst pointed nails,
Such rage in Jacobins prevails,
  They roll'd him down the hill.

(15) Fertur pudicae conjugis osculum,
Parvosque natos ut capitis minor,
Ab se removisse et virilem,
Torvus humi posuisse vultum.
Hor. Car. 5. Lib. 3.[40]

[38] On the allegation that Pitt had an arrangement with Addington to step down, see 27 Nov and n 10, below.

[39] Addington is being advised to leave the comforts of domesticity and enter the strife of parliamentary debate as a brave Roman. Marcus Atilius Regulus, to whom he is compared, was a Roman consul and general who had been captured by the Carthaginian foe in 255 B.C. and five years later sent to Rome on parole to negotiate for peace or an exchange of prisoners. Instead he had urged the senate to reject both proposals, though this meant his being torn from his family once more and returned to torture in Carthage. C identifies the Carthaginians as "Jacobins", i.e. French. Thus the implied advice to Addington is *not* to negotiate peace with France but to resist the doves in Parliament, painful as the personal consequences may be.

[40] Horace *Odes* 3.5.41–4. "'Tis said he put away his chaste wife's kisses, and his little children, as one bereft of civil rights, and sternly bent his manly gaze upon the ground...". Tr Bennett

PARLIAMENT. XI

THE CLERGY EXCLUSION BILL

23 June 1801, Tuesday. New attribution, as inferentially sent to Stuart in C's letter of 16 May and clipped off for use when the Report of the Committee on the Clergymen's Non-residence Bill reached Parliament, as it did 23 June. The remnant of C's letter ends: "In the question respecting the Disfranchisement of the Clergy it appeared to me...[Remainder of manuscript missing.]" *CL* II 730.

A CORRESPONDENT observes,[1] on the Clergy Exclusion Bill,[2] that whatever unfortunate circumstances may attend the property of the clergy in tythes, it *is* property as sacred as any other, and yet there is no doubt that sooner or later it will become the object of legislative discussion; and who are their *representatives*?—the representatives of their *property*?—the Bishops. Is it then a clear point, that the Bishops sit in Parliament in any other way than as Peers by tenure?—in virtue of their baronies, and temporalities holden of the King?—I believe it has ever been the Constitutional and *Whig* opinion at least, that they do not. If so, *they* no more *represent* the Clergy, than the other Barons represent the land-holding commonalty.—Add to this, that the House of Lords is composed of men whose property is chiefly landed—on whom, therefore, tithes press hardest.—Therefore the Bishops, who, no doubt, would defend the rights of their brethren (though their own property does not depend much on tithes), would yet have to plead to Judges, deeply interested, in passing sentence against them.—In the House of Commons are many men of very small property—many whose property is monied and personal—many officers, civil and military—of course, the House of Commons is the proper place for Clergymen to have their property *capable*, at least, of representation.

(LCL) 197. In *CN* III 3690 C compares a hypochondrist's body to "a Regulus's Tub, with nails driven thro' its Hoops", referring to the popular story, as in this last stanza, that the Carthaginians put Regulus to death by enclosing him in a cask with nails pointing inwards and rolling him downhill.

1 Note editor's acknowledgement of source.

2 See 27 May 1801 nn 23, 24, above.

CABINET. I

COMBINABLE ELEMENTS[1]

27 November 1801, Friday. *EOT* II 456–64, ascribed by SC "on internal evidence alone" (III 1021). This is very strong (see notes) and is now complemented by ms evidence of C's authorship of the concluding essays in the series, 23 Feb and 22 Mar 1802.

As we expected, Sir Francis Burdett's[2] motion was postponed last night till after the Christmas holidays, and perhaps it will never now be made. This is obviously produced by the negotiations on foot between the parties, between Ministers and the Members of the old Opposition.[3] It was yesterday reported that Mr. Addington has waited on Mr. Fox; that the former is to be created a Peer, and to hold a high station in the Cabinet;[4] that the latter is to be one of the Secretaries of State, Mr. Grey another, Lord Hawkesbury the third, and Mr. Tierney Chancellor of the Exchequer.[5] We only mention this to shew what are the rumours. We believe no direct overtures or engagements have been made; but it is certain that negotiations are on foot, and that under all circumstances the present

[1] The announcement on 3 Oct "that the PRELIMINARIES OF PEACE are SIGNED between FRANCE and BRITAIN!" soon brought C to London again (15 Nov) and to the *M Post*. A leader of 23 Nov on "Burdett's Motion" seems Stuart's, but its penultimate sentence—"We have several facts to produce in a few days, which shew that the Members of the present Cabinet are as eager in their scramble for cheese-parings and candle-ends, that they employ undue influence as openly, and attend as little to economy as their predecessors"—is in effect an announcement of this series ("Cabinet I–IV") and a forecast of the climactic essay of 22 Mar 1802. (For Windham's "cheese-parings and candle-ends" see *M Post* 22 Jan 1798 and n 5.)

[2] Sir Francis Burdett (1770–1844), a friend and disciple of Horne Tooke, was brought into Parliament in 1796 by his father-in-law, Thomas Coutts, the banker. Though early an admirer of Fox, Sir Francis was "never a Whig, but in part a Tory, in part a Radical". M. W. Patterson *Sir Francis Burdett and His Times* (2 vols 1931) I 53.

[3] Burdett's motion for an inquiry into the conduct of the late Ministers, announced on 13 Nov but postponed on 26 Nov by his friend Sheridan "till the Definitive Treaty should be signed and interchanged", was meant to open to criticism the whole conduct of the war. It would have brought out differences among the politicians at a time when some were seeking to bury theirs.

[4] On Addington's replacing Pitt as Prime Minister, and on the makeup of his cabinet, see 27 May, above. He would resign in Apr 1804 but be created Viscount Sidmouth in Jan 1805 to assure Pitt the support of the "King's Friends".

[5] The rumour that Tierney was willing to take office under Addington would almost defeat him in 1802; that June he would become Addington's treasurer of the navy and a privy councillor, but would quarrel with Addington in 1804.

Ministers must either renew the War, or fly to the Members of the old Opposition for support. Should they adopt the last course, as report asserts they will,[6] the country will be highly benefited by their conduct, as, we are persuaded, the Opposition will only give their support, on condition, that Ministers shall act upon the genuine principles of the Constitution.

So important an event, as the termination of a war, has, we believe, never taken place in this country since the Revolution, without effecting a derangement in the existing state of parties. One of the many reasons of this may be found in our insular situation, and the preponderance of our naval power, which exempt us from those sudden impulses, both of ambition and of[a] terror, that have at times electrified our great continental rival, uniting all parties, as it were, by fusion. Inaccessible to all direct hostility, England has, in every war, had a party of more or less strength, who have been able to adduce plausible grounds fcr doubting or disbelieving the justice and necessity of it. These, by their continued and eloquent opposition in both Houses of Parliament, have driven or surprised the servants of the Crown into declarations so decisive, and language so irritating and intemperate, as have made it oftentimes difficult for them to terminate the war at all; and impossible to do it, or to justify it when done, without inconsistence with their former language, and a *tacit* retraction at least of their former principles. Hence a peace has been always concluded in one or other of these two ways: either the Opposition have displaced the Ministry and made the peace; or else the more violent part of the Ministry have resigned, and left both the glory and the ignominy of the pacification to those of their party, who had been somewhat less dogmatic in their principles, or at least less intemperate in the language, in which they had publicly avowed them. Now unfortunately it so happens, that the most moderate men are seldom the men of splendid talent in either

[a] *EOT* omits

6 "It is reported, that Mr. Pitt and Mr. Addington begin to disagree on the system of politics to be pursued by the Government, Mr. Pitt advising the Grenville, the Alarmist system, and Mr. Addington inclining to the popular side. Mr. Canning urges Mr. Pitt to throw off all connection with the present Ministers, and it is thought his support of them will last no longer than the conclusion of the Definitive Treaty—Ministers then must fly to the old Opposition; and, it is probable, a Government upon sound constitutional principles may be formed." *M Post* 25 Nov. Indomitable Foxite (and Stuartian?) dreams of support from the Prince of Wales are expressed in the next sentence: "In promoting this work, we understand no one interests himself more than a Great Personage."

party. They are permitted to form a Ministry, in order that a Peace may be made; and then the very Peace which they have concluded, (or at least some scheme of measures necessarily resulting from that change), is made the pretext for the attempt to displace them. At all events it never fails to raise up a new and powerful opposition, transfiguring[7] friends into enemies, and enemies into friends. This is the natural course of things; and it is well for our Constitution that it is so.

All wars must increase the patronage and influence of the Executive Power; and most of our wars since the Revolution having been wars of *Principles*, and connected with domestic disturbances, they have facilitated the passing of laws abhorrent from the spirit of our Constitution, and unfavourable to the liberty of the subject. This evil scarcely admits of a complete cure; but the natural palliative and check is the breaking up of parties, in consequence of which the obnoxious laws are repealed, or suffered to expire, and many of the most lucrative and desirable Places in the gift of the Crown are possessed by the leaders of the new Opposition, as the *spoils* of their Ministry,[a] or the prices of their resignation.

The application of these general remarks to the existing state of politics is abundantly obvious.—But indeed an action much less powerful than that of Peace with the French Republic, would have been sufficient to have dissolved our parties into the present chaos. The Opposition, wearied out by the repetition of ineffectual efforts, and almost disorganised by the measure of the secession,[8] could[b] scarcely be called a party. It was at least two parties, when its whole number, as one, was perhaps too small to effect those common purposes, which render an opposition a part of our constitution. At the same time the party of Government was composed of materials still more heterogeneous, and whether taken, as the Cabinet exclusively, or as including the whole of the adherents of Ministry, contained in itself all the principles of approaching dissolution, personal jealousies, difference of dispositions, difference of prior connections, difference as to the final object of their measures, difference as to the means of effecting it; to all which we must of necessity add the different relations, in which different Members of the Administration stood, to the feelings and opinions of the Sovereign

[a] *EOT*: Ministers [b] *EOT*: would

[7] Cf C's frequent use of "transmuting" in the same sense.

[8] The secession of Grey and Fox from 1797 to 1800; see 24 Dec 1799, above.

and his Family. It required little quickness to hear the creakings of a machine so disordered,[9] and little sagacity to draw the proper conclusions[a] from them. The question of The Catholic Emancipation was in part a cause, and in part an honourable pretext, of the resignation of Mr. Pitt, who had the address, or the good luck, or both, of taking out of the Ministry with him precisely those very men whose weight in the Cabinet he had found the most oppressive, and whom he could[b] either stand in union with or in opposition to, as after circumstances might render convenient; and, on the other hand, to leave in power those men whom he might, in some future time, once more head as their leader, with less fears of indocility, and whom, if this project should fall to the ground, he could oppose with more assured hopes of rapidly displacing them.—Alas! that circumstances should so often, so unexpectedly, unravel the fineliest-spun webs[c] of state policy, and that the men, who do not find in honesty the best policy, should so seldom possess the genius that can command circumstances![10] Selfish views are ever the progeny of minds low and uncomprehensive.[d] And the cunning of selfishness, therefore, is but a sort of ingenious ignorance, a poison that contains within itself its own antidote. If these last observations can be justly deemed inapplicable to Mr. Pitt, we are confident that they are inapplicable only as *premature*, and not as *false*. But of Mr. Pitt hereafter; we return to the general state of parties in the kingdom. We ventured to call it a chaos; and if our ears have not been

——— peal'd
With noises loud and ruinous,———[11]

we must attribute this in part to the decencies of recent friendship, and in part to the anxiousness of uncertainty that naturally impresses silence, and the slowness and gradual approaches with which public characters venture to announce any glaring change[e] of party or inconsistence of principle. Into what forms this chaos is destined finally to be organised it would be rash to assert positively; but those assuredly are likely to form the best conjectures on this subject who have the most accurately enumerated the *elements* of the parties,

[a] *EOT*: conclusion [b] *EOT*: would [c] *EOT*: threads [d] *EOT*: incomprehensive [e] *EOT*: charge

9 The development of this image in 3 Dec (q.v.) reveals the machinery to be clockwork.

10 Pitt, lacking "commanding genius" (19 Mar 1800), had failed to foresee that his creature Addington would not readily step aside; he had not followed honest policy when promising the Irish Catholics a concession he knew the King would not grant.

11 Milton *Paradise Lost* II 920–1.

and most attentively watched their affinities with each other, either directly, or by means of an intermedium.

These *elements* we may perhaps name in the following order: First, all those who belong to every Minister, as Minister. Secondly, a small number of inoffensive, and, in many points of view, respectable men, who dislike any thing that sounds or looks violent; who have no other criterion of truth, than the appearance of moderation; who listen to an argument from one side, and say, "*that is very true!*" and to the answer on the other side, and say, "*that is very true likewise!*" and who, sometimes voting on one side and sometimes on the other, give more frequent proofs of their independence than of their wisdom. Third, all those who are attached to the war by motives of private and personal interest, and who do not foresee for themselves any adequate compensation in the peace-establishment of the country. Fourth, the enthusiastic Anti-gallicans, men who fear the power and ambition of France more than its principles (which they could not but see would die a natural death), and who joined the outcry against the principles of the Revolution only as a means of exciting resistance to its power. Fifth, the enthusiastic Anti-jacobins, who may be subdivided into three classes, accordingly as they have been ague-stricken either by the panic of *property*,[12] the panic of *feudal subordination*, or the panic of religion and morals.[13] The fourth and fifth classes are of course so intimately blended, that it is difficult to know in many men whether they most fear the ambition or the principles of the Great Nation; yet we are inclined to believe that we are not deceived in stating Lord Hawkesbury, Mr. Windham, and Mr. Wilberforce,[14] as the leaders of the three subdivisions of the Anti-Jacobins, though, no doubt, they are almost equally zealous as Anti-Gallicans.—Sixth, those of the former Opposition, who, seeing nothing to blame in the recent *actions* of the present Ministry, are willing to *waive* any nice inquiry into the *principles*, on which they act, and who, by their conciliatory speeches, and other good offices, are seeking a cordial for that "sickness of the heart, which cometh from hope long delayed".[15] In blunter

[12] A tell-tale Coleridgian phrase: see 3 Jan 1800 ("On Peace") n 2, above; also e.g. *Courier* 26 Sept 1811, below.

[13] Terrett (p 313) observes that C will drop mention of the last two panics when his politics grow theocratic.

[14] William Wilberforce (1759–1833), close friend of Pitt since the 1780's, member for Yorkshire since 1784; parliamentary leader of the campaign against the slave-trade; one of the "Clapham Sect" of Evangelicals who began the monthly *Christian Observer* in Jan 1801.

[15] Proverbs 13.12 (var).

language, those of the late Opposition who were not of such rank or importance in their party, as to make it beneath their characters or their expectations, to accept of subordinate honours and emoluments under the new Ministry. Seventh, the great bodies and powerful individuals concerned with our colonies, in the East and West Indies, who, it is to be apprehended, will regret the Peace in exact proportion to the rapidity with which France extends her commercial prosperity and colonial power, and who will, of course, be more or less friendly to the pacificators,[a] according to the degree of their alarm. Lastly, we must place each in a class by himself, Lord Grenville, Mr. Pitt, Mr. Fox, and the present Chancellor of the Exchequer; the probable views of each of whom we may endeavour to develope on an early day, at the same time that we shall then hazard a conjecture as to the *compounds* into which these elements must soon combine.[16] We shall only observe, that the new Ministry wish to connect themselves with the *High Party* by their *principles*, and with the *Opposition* by their *actions*; and we cannot therefore but regret, that Sir Francis Burdett's motion has been so *mysteriously* postponed; for it was certainly well adapted to produce an effect which all honest men must desire, namely, to perplex the movements of *certain men* on both sides, and either to convict them of inconsistency, or force them to *retraction. Ne videlicet sub nomine Pacis publicae servitutis sit nutrimentum et causa; et quae fuerunt vitia, mores tacite fiant.*[17]

[28 November 1801, Saturday]

The beautiful Poem "TRANQUILLITY" *shall appear on Monday—we particularly desire the attention of our Readers to it.*

The Conclusion of the Article "ON THE STATE OF PARTIES," *shall appear on Monday also.*

[30 November 1801, Monday]

Many favours are this day excluded by the French News.

[1 December 1801, Tuesday]

The Article "On the State of Parties," which the length of the Parliamentary Intelligence this day excludes, shall positively appear to-morrow. The Public will find it deeply interesting.

The beautiful Poem "TRANQUILLITY," *is only delayed by the same reason.*

[a] *EOT*: pacification

16 This Coleridgian chemical imagery begins on p 272, above. C was seeing Humphry Davy in London at this time.

17 Untraced. Tr: "Lest, that is to say, under the pretext of national concord it should be the sustenance and cause of public slavery, and what were crimes silently become customs".

An interesting article, on the Report that Mr. Grey is to succeed Lord Hobart, as Secretary of State, is intended for Thursday. It will disclose some important facts.[1]

[2 December 1801, Wednesday]

The press of temporary matter still delays the appearance of the important article on the State of Parties, to which we again beg the particular attention of every Friend of Liberty and Supporter of the conduct of the Old Opposition. It shall appear to-morrow. As all persons interested in the State of Parties will be desirous of a copy, we beg they will take notice, that no papers can be published after Half-past Ten o'clock.[2]

CABINET. II

THE REPORTED CHANGES[1]

3 December 1801, Thursday; entitled "The Reported Changes". *EOT* II 464–77; attributed by SC "on internal evidence alone" (III 1021); an organic part of the series including 23 Feb and 22 Mar 1802, for which there is now ms evidence. This article all but filled p. 3.

MEN who possess (or who imagine that they possess) a few secret anecdotes of men in power, as a part of their own private collection, are generally disposed to consider all causes deduced from the state of society at large, as idle dreams or unmeaning generalities. But such men mistake accidents for principles.[2] Even when the stories, to which they give credit, are facts, and have had an actual influence, still these facts must have derived their power of being powerful from the tone of public opinion, and the aggregate of national circumstances. They are sometimes *occasions*, but scarcely ever *causes*; they may sometimes determine the particular moment, on which an event shall take place, but they rarely, indeed, give birth to the event itself. When these private intrigues are most powerful, they are no more than the minor springs of the machine, and most often they are merely the indexes and minute hands.[3] We

[1] The notice betrays Stuart's ignorance of the fact that the article "On the State of Parties" was (or would become) the article on the report about Grey—in short, the second instalment of the series begun 27 Nov. *Tranquillity* appeared on 4 Dec.

[2] The type had to be distributed for printing the evening *Courier*.

[1] See Stuart's announcements of 28 Nov and 1 and 2 Dec; for C's verse contributions see App D.

[2] Cf C's emphasis on "the necessity of *bottoming* on fixed Principles, that so we may not be the unstable Patriots of Passion or Accident". *MPL* and *Conciones: Lects 1795* (*CC*) 5, 33.

[3] This is the machine whose "creakings" are heard in 27 Nov; note its rapid degeneration to mere weathervane.

hear abundance of these secret anecdotes, and when there exists no moral or prudential reason for the contrary, it is our duty and business to amuse the public with them; but we never wish to affix to them an importance which they do not possess, or pass them off for anything more than they really are. In short, we look at the weather-cock to be informed *which* way the wind blows—not to discover *how* it happened to blow that way.[4]

We have been induced to hazard these general remarks in consequence of sundry rumours relative to a coalition between the New Ministry and certain Members of the Old Opposition. Whether any *formal negotiations* are on foot, or any *direct overtures* have been made, we do not know. We remember too many cases in point, not to be convinced that such rumours *may* have their foundation in truth, notwithstanding the most positive assertions to the contrary in the subservient prints of the two parties. Indeed, the *form* only has been denied in the present instance; the substance has been admitted. It has been admitted, that Mr. Addington has given conciliatory explanations respecting his plans of administration. And this is itself the opening of a treaty. For it is not to be supposed, that any direct overture will be made till, by means of these friendly intermediators, who have been employed by the one party to sound the dispositions of the other, so much is *understood* on both sides, as renders the direct overture a matter of form—the mere seal and subscription of the bond, which had been previously drawn up by mutual agreement. From what we know, and from what we have heard, we are inclined to fear, that it is probable, that a *virtual* coalition is taking place between the present Ministry, and a part, at least, of the old Opposition. It may, perhaps, commence (as the Duke of Portland's, &c. with Mr. Pitt)[5] by a mere support of certain given measures; but neither human nature, nor the particular constitution of our Parliament, permits the continuance of this half friendship; and we have little doubt, therefore, that it will end in a complete partnership. Some circumstances have come to our knowledge which gave an *appearance of plausibility* to the rumour, that direct proposals had been made to one highly respectable member of the Opposition.[6] But this is no more than a rumour; and, even if this, and reports like this, should be connected with the real state of the case, we attribute

[4] This paragraph was rewritten for *Friend* No 7 (*CC*) II 107, and *SM* (*CC*) 14, with application to the French Revolution.

[5] Stuart argued, 23 Nov, that Pitt had played just such a game in the last months of 1792.

[6] I.e. to Tierney; cf 27 Nov and n 5.

but a subordinate importance to them. However the whispering advertisers of state secrets may smile at our ignorance, we shall continue to believe, that personal intrigues can, in the present state of mankind, be only the proximate causes of the formation of any party; the ultimate and true cause must be sought for in public opinion and national circumstances.[7] We believe, that the temper of the public mind at present is favourable to the formation of such a party; but, we likewise believe, that this present temper cannot be permanent, and that the party, if it be formed, will be both transitory and inglorious. Any change gives a temporary pleasure to the mass of the people; moderate and quiet men are glad to see even the appearance of union and moderation; and, of the men of more active minds, almost all have something to be ashamed of;—they have either *hoped* like enthusiasts, or *feared* like fanatics; and, conscious of more or less inconsistency in their own political opinions, they are less eager or precise in their demands of consistency in others. Such, we believe to be the tone of the *public* feelings at present; and such, no doubt, must, in a certain degree, be the feelings of many of the members of the Opposition, connected, perhaps, with the prospect of a nearer approach to the objects of an ambition, which is, in itself, the reverse of immoral or dishonourable.[8]

The national circumstances, which have in part created this tone of feeling and opinion, are equally favourable to the formation of the party. If, on the one hand, Jacobinism is everywhere discredited; on the other hand, the better and wiser part, even of the friends of Government, begin to acknowledge, that it never existed in this kingdom in such strength, as at all to justify the alarm which it excited, or the measures of alarm to which it gave birth. And though, on the other hand, the dread of the power of France has greatly increased, and with great reason; yet none of the opponents of the Peace have been able distinctly to point out, in what way the prolongation of the War would tend to lessen that power.[9] That the

[7] This was also rewritten for *Friend* No 7 (*CC*) II 107: "I have known Men who, with most significant nods...a sort of State Secret...".

[8] For C's own kindling and quenching of "a spark of ambition...even if it should end in my being Minister of state..." see his letter to Poole 5 Oct (*CL* II 766, cf 1112).

[9] In view of C's later claim, in 1802 and 1803, to have disapproved of the Peace of Amiens from the beginning, it is instructive to see that in 1801 his private view (see *CL* II 771) and his public, in these essays, coincided with Fox's—and with Stuart's. "If there was danger from French arms", said the *M Post* on 20 Oct, developing Fox's argument that the war had not been defensive on England's part and had in effect aggrandised France, "that danger never existed to so alarming a

dominion of the Chief Consul would have been more insecure in War, than it is likely to be in Peace, has been asserted; but no shadow of proof advanced for the opinion. To have prolonged hostilities, in the hope that by the excitement of internal disturbances, we might *cut off* the Chief Consul, would assuredly not have damped the zeal or boldness of his enterprises against this country during the war; or inclined him to moderation in the terms of a future peace. And again, to prolong a war, in the hope of a counter-revolution, and to avow, that we desire a counter-revolution, because we dread the might and prosperity of the Great Nation, if Bonaparte remain the Chief Magistrate, is a strange scheme of inducing the Great Nation to desire a counter-revolution, and to prefer a Bourbon, because he is to cut down the prosperity of his country to the Procrustes bed of its rival's wishes, to a Bonaparte, who has made that country the object of our terror and jealousy. The Peace, which has been concluded, may be a bitter pill to our pride; but though we may exclaim, bad is the best, yet still, the best must be taken.[10] Ashamed, therefore, of its late alarms at Jacobinism, and with a half-ludicrous conviction, that deceived by the animal's noise, it had mistaken a bull-frog for a bull; compelled too by common sense, to prefer a peace of anxiety to a war without hope or object; the nation is just in that temper of mind, which will dispose it to acquiesce in, and languidly support for a while, the Ministry which is now forming: a Ministry, made up of the *middle-sized* talents of all parties; and, like the peace, which it will definitively conclude, the best that can at present be had; *and bad is the best!*[11]

On the side of the Ministry, all circumstances favour the desire

---

degree, as at the very moment in which we have concluded Peace." A year later C would have it that he wanted Fox to say in Oct 1801 "that a peace had been concluded at the very first period, at which a war had become indisputably just and necessary". The words are similar: the arguments are at opposite poles.

Still later, in *BL* ch 10, C would describe the Peace of Amiens as having realised "a national unanimity unexampled in our history" and imply that the unanimity was in support of war against Jacobinism. *BL* (1907) I 123. At the time, he was looking for developments that would mean national unity for a prolonged peace.

[10] In the Nov 1801 debates on the Peace Preliminaries and in the May 1802 on the Treaty, critics attacked the many unreciprocated concessions restoring great colonial territories to France, Holland, and Spain; the evacuating of Malta and Egypt; the "abandonment" of the Prince of Orange, the King of Sardinia, and Portugal.

[11] Here and above C is quoting Fletcher et al *The Bloody Brother* IV ii: "Bad's the best of us".

of such a coalition. To have concluded a Peace, after so dreadful a War, a Peace with the French Republic, must of necessity have been the ruling and marked event of *any* administration, however vigorous and splendid it were; much more then of an administration so naked of *first-rate* talent (at least, of the *reputation* of first-rate talent), as the present. The Peace, and the conditions of the Peace, Mr. Addington, and his compeers, must defend and abide by. This is the great measure, which makes their ministry important to their contemporaries, and which consigns their names to history. They, who support the Administration in this measure, are, for a time, at least, its natural friends, however different the principles on which they justify their support of the measure, may be from the motives which impelled the Ministry to adopt it. Still, however, this diversity of motive and principle, if it were often and loudly avowed, would necessarily introduce a dissention among the supporters of the Peace, which would weaken the measure, both in the public mind, and in the minds of those *independent* Members of Parliament, who combine but loosely with *any* party, and can scarcely be expected, therefore, to remain firm to a party, divided in itself. Now, whatever weakens the party, which supports the Peace, will give strength to the opponents of it. The avowal, therefore of this dissentience, must, if possible, be prevented; and this can be done in no other way, but, by uniting all the great efficient Members of the Old Opposition *in* the Ministry, conciliating their silence by gratifying their ambition. They, mean time, find in the moderation, with which Ministers are disposed to *act*, a motive for a general *amnesty* as to principles, and prior conduct.

It is rumoured (and we believe[a] the rumour), that Mr. Pitt has receded from the New Ministry, and that he is daily receding further. This, it is said, gives both the *motive* to Mr. Addington to negotiate with the Opposition, and a prospect of success to the negotiation. For never can we deem so meanly of the honour or prudence of *any* part of the Old Opposition, as to suspect for a moment that they would go over to the Addington Party, without insisting on a complete separation from Mr. Pitt as a *sine quâ non* of their union. It would indeed crush them for ever in the opinions of Englishmen, if they gave their influence for the purpose of raising the Ex-Minister once more into that power from which their great leader, who, more than any other individual, possesses the affection and confidence of the great *mass* of the people, is excluded by those prejudices *in a*

[a] *M Post* correction the following day: would fain believe

certain quarter[12] (we purposely use a word tame and palliative, when we say only *prejudices*), which the Ex-Minister had both fostered and deepened. If, then, this separation from Mr. Pitt's interests should take place, and if Mr. Fox consent to remain in secession, the road seems smooth and easy. It *seems* smooth, but it is treacherous and insecure, and, as it appears to us, leads by labyrinthine windings to the very den of the monster, from which we all wish to escape.[13]

We are told, indeed, that Mr. Addington promises to suffer the obnoxious laws to expire, and to conduct the Government in the spirit of the Constitution;[14] and we are told that, if he is faithful to his promise, there is no room for opposition. No room for opposition!—As well might you whisper in the ear of a man whose nose had been pulled—"Why do you remain angry?—Your adversary is ready to shake hands with you *under the table*." A public insult demands a public explanation. Many of the most obnoxious measures of the present Ministry, both as Ministers and as supporters of the late Administration, were execrable, not so much for the immediate evil which they occasioned, as for the precedent which they tended to create. Such in particular were the repeated suspensions of the Habeas Corpus Act. Like the tooth of the viper, it inflicted but a trifling wound, but it dropped in a deadly poison.[15] The *proper* antidote of the venom would be a direct vote of the next Parliament stamping the obnoxious measures as unnecessary and unconstitutional.—It was in this way that the liberty of election was secured (in the affair of Mr. Wilkes), and the personal safety of Englishmen bulwarked against the tyranny of general warrants.[16] The friends of freedom at that period did not think it sufficient that the Ministers suffered the persecution to intermit, and Mr. Wilkes to resume his seat in the House of Commons—and then asked, "What room is there now for opposition?" The resignation of Sylla did not remove the *precedent* of his dictatorship, and Caesar knew how to avail himself of it.[17] Let

[12] George III was adamant against the admission of Fox, essentially because his goal was to reduce the power of the Crown. Perhaps George could have been forced to accept Catholic Emancipation, for he was ultimately forced to accept Fox. But Pitt was not the commander to force him.

[13] Cf C's use of the labyrinth image in *Conciones: Lects 1795* (*CC*) 45.

[14] See 22 Mar 1802, below.

[15] Cf the same venom image 6 Oct 1800 at n 3, App A, below.

[16] Elected and expelled from Parliament four times in 1769, John Wilkes (1727–97) on re-election in 1774 was tacitly admitted. But he continued to move that the record of his expulsions be expunged "as being subversive of the Rights of the whole body of Electors of this Kingdom" until the motion finally passed 3 May 1782 by a majority of 68.

[17] Cf *Conciones: Lects 1795* (*CC*) 62.

it be remembered, that they who permit a precedent help to make it: and every place they afterwards accept will be rightly regarded as the purchase-money of the desertion of the liberties of their country.

We are told that it is idle "to discuss what men are likely to do when great leading differences among them have ceased;"[18] in other words, idle to anticipate the places which the members of the old Opposition may accept, when they and the present Ministry have honourably become friends. But can they coalesce with honour, unless Mr. Addington and Lord Hawkesbury publicly disavow the principles of the war, and by branding them with an open retractation, prevent them from becoming *precedents*? Is there any probability that they would do it, if they could; or that they could do it, even if they wished it, and retain their situations as servants of the Crown? It is now, perhaps, believed by them that the government of France, an iron and military Despotism, holds out no inducements to the desire of change; and this being the case, they are willing to intermit those laws which they had passed, when the politics of France wore, or were deemed[a] to wear, a more seducing form. Now that the raving madness of Jacobinism hath sunk into the melancholy madness of despotism, they consent to unlace the strait-waistcoat, in which they themselves had confined the nation, *lest* it should go mad.[19] But are we quite sure that the volcanic force of the Revolution has wholly spent itself?[20] And what? If the Chief Consul should disclose certain traits of character, which Mr. Windham would be more disposed to believe than Mr. Addington, what pledge have the Opposition received, that we shall not once again be plunged into a war *of principles*?[21] The precedent is recorded, unerased, unrepented of. It is well known that the seditious dramatic libel, which was used as a pretext for subjecting the London stage to the controul of a licenser, was written for that very purpose by a creature of the then Administration.[22] These[b] have been common tricks of state policy in all

[a] *EOT*: doomed [b] *EOT*: There

18 Untraced; evidently referring to supporters of Addington.

19 See 15 Jan 1800, above, for the "strait waistcoat" image.

20 Cf the volcanic images of 27 Dec 1799, 30 Jan 1800, and 6 Jan 1803.

21 By 25 Sept 1802 (q.v.) C will be ready to view the principles of the French with sufficient alarm to propose that the English, "in war, whenever it becomes inevitable...will be, as ever, their controlling and thwarting genius; in peace their monitor, and outward conscience".

22 In 1737 an anonymous farce *The Golden Rump* (never performed) was sold for £1000 to Walpole, who cited its scurrility as pretext for the Licensing Act of 1737. "It was hinted at the time that Walpole himself had caused it to be written by one of his hacks...." F. Homes Dudden *Henry Fielding* (2

governments. Now, what if the faction of the Alarmists should send some of their spies to *enact* sedition in a garret, or to tempt some half-witted, half-starved journeymen[a] to commit the crime in good earnest; what pledge is the new Ministry disposed to give, that they will not once again constitute a Committee of ——,[23] with a careful exclusion of every man who has ever dissented from them; and, on the report of *such* a Committee, once again suspend the Habeas Corpus Act? They have a PRECEDENT in their favour, and they may, any month in the year, safely aver that they do it now on still stronger ground than they had in the last suspension. If, then, the creatures of *any* faction ask us, what is the object of the hostility which we wish to see waged by the friends of freedom against the new Ministry, we, too, can compress our answer into one word—SECURITY![24]

Admitting that there existed any shadow of reason[b] to induce us to waive all consideration of the conduct of Mr. Addington and his compeers, as the adherents of the late Ministry, and arraying them on their entrance into official situations in all the spotlessness of a new creation, there have been two acts of their own administration which have *out-heroded*[c] all the measures even of their immediate predecessors. The first is the re-suspension of the Habeas Corpus Act on the report of a Committee, from which they had excluded every Member of the Opposition, and assigning, as a reason, that the Members of the Opposition could not with safety be entrusted

[a] *EOT*: journeyman [b] *EOT*: reasons [c] *EOT*: *out-heralded*

vols Oxford 1952) I 208. For C on the licensing act, see *PD: Lects 1795* (*CC*) 296–7 and n 7.

23 Committee of Secrecy. The dash is a sarcastic precaution. On Addington's swift capitulation to "secret" evidence culled from printed material, see next paragraph. His ministry began with liberation of political prisoners (in Cold Bath Fields and other gaols), then "professed to have acquired speedy proof of the necessity for renewing Habeas Corpus Suspension ...and adding a fresh Seditious Meetings Bill....The justificatory material, put before Committees of Secrecy in both Lords and Commons [27 Apr, 15 May], must have been the work of the most unscrupulous informers, and, even so, the Committees can hardly be acquitted of the charge of eagerly swallowing the most improbable 'information' provided it was sufficiently alarmist." The Commons report "professed to tell the story of treasonable organisation in London, the provinces and Ireland and even at its most restrained is a lurid example of what 'seditious' tavern-talk, 'reported' by police-spies and interpreted by alarmists, has a habit of becoming". Maccoby 146–7.

Parliament had first been induced to suspend the Habeas Corpus Act on the basis of the report (presented without evidence) of the Committee of Secrecy, which examined the papers of the various reform societies seized in May 1794 when Tooke, Thelwall, Hardy, and others were arrested.

24 Mocking Pitt's speech of 17 Feb 1800.

with any knowledge, which it was necessary for the safety and welfare of the country to keep secret. Surely, if ever the wrongs of individuals could become sacred, and exempted from all duties of forgiveness, by being intimately blended with the wrongs of the country, it was in this instance. Ambition has a strange power, if it can cause this "*leading* difference" to die by voluntary oblivion—if it can cause this insult to the country, in the person of the individuals, to be done away, without having been retracted as formally as it was offered. The second act is the Bill of Indemnity, which established *espionage* by law, purchasing calumnies by impunity, interposing the ominous shadow of a particular act between the injured man, and the law of the land, and eclipsing its blessed light, that assassins might escape in the unnatural darkness.[25] When the authors of acts, like these, seem inclined to shake hands with freedom, we dread the poisoned gloves of Italy. With these men, we are assured, it is scarcely possible, that the great patriots, who have almost identified their names with those of peace and liberty, can ever yield even a semblance of union. We trust, therefore, that the rumours, which have excited our alarm,[a] will *end* in nothing; though we dare not affirm, that they *originated* in nothing. We respect the persons, and the rank, we revere the talents,[b] and, above all, the services of Opposition. We remember with grateful admiration the patient endurance, and the intrepid courage, with which they defended the Laws and Constitution of their country, and the rights of all mankind, in "evil days" and among "evil tongues."[26] In the trying hour, when liberty was, as it were, fixed on the cross of shame and public abhorrence, amid the earthquake, that rent, and the darkness, that covered, the whole earth; they persisted to acknowledge, and proclaim, the divinity of its mission;[27] and we cannot, we will not believe, that such men will, on

[a] *M Post*: alarms, [b] *EOT*: talent

25 After passing the Sedition Bill 28 Apr 1801, a Bill of Indemnity was introduced to indemnify all persons concerned in securing, imprisoning, and detaining individuals under the suspension of Habeas Corpus since Feb 1793. Opponents argued that it was calculated to screen misconduct, but it passed; on 12 Jun a similar bill was passed for Ireland, extending the wording to cover all acts done for preservation of the public peace.

Lucyle Werkmeister calls attention to *Friend* No 10: "I have said that to withstand the arguments of the lawless, the Anti-Jacobins proposed to suspend the Law, and by the interposition of a particular Statute to eclipse the blessed Light of the universal Sun, that Spies and Informers might tyrannize and escape in the ominous darkness." *Friend* (*CC*) II 142–3. C repeats this in *BL* ch 10 (1907) I 142n.

26 Milton *Paradise Lost* VII 26.

27 C refers to the political "hour" in Nov–Dec 1795 when Pitt introduced his Two Bills against "Treasonable Practices" and "Seditious Meetings"

the very eve of that resurrection, which they themselves had foretold, associate their fair names with those of that priestly and pharisaic faction, whose fanatical outcries occasioned the *Barabbas* war to be let loose upon us.[28] In the depth of [a]our alarm[b] we seek for reasons to evince the groundlessness of it; and we hope, and struggle to believe, that it *is* groundless. But we have felt it our duty to state these alarms, ignorant how far the Members of the Opposition may sympathise with that tone of public feeling and opinion, which we have described as existing, but which, we are confident, will be transitory; ignorant too, how far they might be seduced by the best feelings to transfer that facility of forgiveness and reconciliation which is so natural to generous minds, from the events of private life, where it is most amiable, to public men and public events, where it would be error and apostacy.[29] We know, that between the support of the measures, and the support of the men, the interspace is sloping and slippery—and as every good and wise man, in the ensnaring business of public life, must needs have the humility to fear for himself, so no good and wise man can be offended with others that fear for him. Besides, we have the strongest reasons for declaring our opinion on events which it would be dotage not to look forward to as *possible*, however great the improbability may be. For if the alarm should pass away, like a vapour, the principles, which we have declared, will ably plead our forgiveness with the great advocates of those principles; and if, alas! the alarm should be substantiated, we shall perhaps have done prudently in thus declaring our opinions of the event previously to its accomplishment. For after *such* an event it may be problematical how far we should dare to do so—at least the *subservient* Paper (that tail of the weathercock of the French revolution) has informed the public, that it is an axiom in politics, that no new Government can tolerate the Liberty of the Press.*

* *The Morning Chronicle* of Saturday last contained an Article more hostile to free Government than any which the Anti-Jacobin writers have produced. It was an apology for all the acts of the despotism of Bonaparte—among other

[a–b] *EOT*: alarms

to silence criticism of monarchy and to stop public meetings. See Lecture on the Two Bills and *PD: Lects 1795* (*CC*) 257–318 and *Watchman* No 1 (*CC*) 13–14.

[28] These are the rôles assigned in C's 1794 sonnet on Pitt as Iscariot. Liberty suffered from the alarm against sedition just as Christ suffered from the alarm against Barabbas. Terrett (p 316) observes that the climax of this essay is only to be compared to similar passages in the *Conciones*.

[29] The allusion is to the Fox–North coalition at the end of the American war.

To-morrow, if possible, this subject will be continued, and the argument concluded, in an Article, on the Report that Mr. Grey is to succeed Lord Hobart, as Secretary of State.[31] *In this article will be disclosed important facts.*[32]

[4 December 1801, Friday]

In the article of yesterday on the Reported Changes, which we shall conclude to-morrow, towards the bottom of the second column, for "It is rumoured, and we believe the rumour, that Mr. Pitt has receded," read "and we would fain believe the rumour."

[5 December 1801, Saturday]

The press of temporary matter, this day, excludes the conclusion of the Article on the State of Parties.

[9 December 1801, Wednesday]

The press of Parliamentary Intelligence, and the necessity of obliging our Advertising Friends, have delayed the conclusion of the Article on the State of Parties; but we have no doubt of presenting it to the Public to-morrow.

[10 December 1801, Thursday]

The Press of temporary Matter still delays the appearance of the Article on the State of Parties; but as the House of Commons yesterday adjourned till to-morrow, it shall then positively appear.

---

things, justifying his suppression of the Liberty of the Press! This from a Newspaper pretending to defend the cause of freedom!!—No *new* Government, it was said, can allow the freedom of the Press. Did the writer never hear of the United States of America?[30]

30 From this interpretation one would hardly guess the tone of the *M Chron* article of 28 Nov, "Parties in France". The French are said to have suffered so cruelly by the Revolution that to prevent its renewal they now prefer "a strong, vigilant, concentered Government". "If the people of France, after so terrible a Revolution, are to crown it with liberty, it is fit that they should hear in their Assemblies the language of Freedom....Discussion must serve to enlighten them....It may be considered as an axiom in politics, that no new Government can endure free inquiry. It is only in Governments that feel themselves strongly bottomed where men are allowed to think as they please, and to publish what they think." The point is considerably elaborated.

31 Robert Hobart (1760–1816; Lord Hobart, 1793; 4th Earl of Buckinghamshire, 1804) had been appointed secretary of state for the colonial and war department in March.

32 SC says, "This article did not appear" (*EOT* II 477). But see 11 Dec, below.

CABINET. III

THE REPORTED CHANGES[1]

11 December 1801, Friday; entitled "The Reported Changes". Not located by SC, but an unmistakable part of C's series, with close links to 3 Dec 1801 and 22 Mar 1802 and much characteristic metaphor.

We affirmed that the Members of the Old Opposition could not honourably coalesce with the present Ministry, without having previously compelled them to such retractions as it were idle to suppose the present Ministry inclined to make; and that if they did coalesce without compelling any retraction, they would return by a maze to the den of the monster, from which they wished to escape.[2] We are confident that we have fully evinced the truth of the former part of the assertion; the latter remains to be proved, or, at least, made probable. To prove this, let us suppose for a moment that the Opposition join Mr. Addington, and suffer the obnoxious laws and measures of this and the late Ministry to pass into precedents. Hereby they cannot but strip themselves of all that influence which is derived from the affections of the people, and the independent friends of our laws and constitution. They give up their great freehold estate in the public opinion, and become tenants at will under the favour of the Court. At the same time, by uniting themselves with Ministers, without extorting any censure of the war, they bring themselves forward, and *volunteer* the ill-fame in which the inglorious, perhaps dangerous, conditions of the peace will probably involve the authors of it. At present the Opposition may say, with truth, "Our support of the peace was wise and necessary; and that it was so, is the bitterest satire on the commencers and conductors of the war, who rejected, with insult, the enemy's proposal, in the hour of her danger and humiliation, and chose the moment of her fullest triumph to make the same proposal themselves." But when they shall have united themselves in the Ministry, and have shared the *good things* of the State with their old opponents, this plea will have become too indecent, if not to be made, yet certainly to be listened to. They will have the cry of all parties against them.

In the mean time, it is not to be supposed but that they will

[1] For announcements of this continuation of the evidently popular "Article on the State of Parties" see 4, 5, 9, 10 Dec, above. On 4 Dec appeared C's *Tranquillity, an Ode* (see App D, below), also with impressive advance announcement; a sort of counterweight to the Article.

[2] Recapitulation of 3 Dec, above.

endeavour to re-establish themselves in the affections of the public by some avowed efforts in favour of a free and liberal Government; it is not to be believed but that the feelings of personal honour, as well as of an old attachment, will incline them to make a struggle to unite Mr. Fox with them in the Ministry; and should the pacification and the conditions of it become universally unpopular, no doubt they will attempt to throw off the odium, by bidding the shame of the peace rest on the authors of the war.—All these are sure cards in the hands of the faction of the Alarmists, and the friends of the Court. Their attempts at popularity, and the measures tending to it, will offend and alarm the inner Cabinet; their attachment to Mr. Fox will certainly tend to reconcile the King to Mr. Pitt, by compelling him to a *comparison of dislikes*; and the attempt to *shift* the ignominy of the peace to the proper shoulders, cannot fail to create dissentions, and open hostilities in the Ministry itself.—Nor is it improbable that the Opposition Members may be at variance among themselves, in consequence of these personal jealousies and heart-burnings, which the division of honours and places seldom fails to create in the formation of every new Ministry. Thus, then, divided in itself, suspected by the Sovereign, and unpopular with the people, this heterogeneous Ministry will yield but a feeble resistance to a party strong in its own members, united by hope and a deeply-rankling hatred of all free measures, openly* favoured by the Court, and probably supported by a great part of the commercial and colonial interests of the country.[4] We fear that there can be little doubt of the

* One may generally penetrate the self-estimation of a Party, and its real hopes, by the reeds it leans upon, or the twigs at which it catches. The reception which Mr. Windham met with from his Royal Master at the last levee, is the momentary consolation of the Opposers of Government, and the enemies to the peace. His Majesty certainly shewed the most marked condescension for this great Statesman, whom he detained a-part, in secret and apparently in very serious conference for a full half hour, during which, from the frequent obeisances and general manners of Mr. Windham, it was conjectured that he was making acknowledgements for some expressions of approbation, or other testimony of the King's confidence and good will, and at least a favourable interpretation of his late conduct in Parliament.—(*Times*).[3]

[3] "Though the King does not like Wyndham as a man of business", wrote Lord Hawkesbury on 9 Aug 1801 after a day of sailing with the King, "I can perceive he is in great personal favour." Aspinall *Correspondence of George III* III 592n. Hawkesbury attributed this to Windham's agreeable conversation and "particularly respectful" manners to the royal family, but his view of the peace must also have pleased King George. In Commons 29 Oct and 4 Nov he said that "Ministers had signed the death warrant of their country" and lamented that "we are a conquered people".

[4] "English merchantmen crowded French ports, only to find the prohi-

ultimate success of this party, and, if they succeed, no doubt at all, that they will return to power with all the strength of a complete victory, and with a strong opinion of the public in favour of their consistency, while their old opponents, ejected and hopeless, are disliked by one party for their former professions of free principles, regarded by another party as apostates from those principles, and disowned by all parties but that which their personal influence may create.

Indeed, we have little doubt that the really powerful and effective part of the present Ministry are connected heart and hand with the party of Lord Grenville and Mr. Windham, and that they stretch out their arms to their old opponents to *strangle*, and not to *embrace*.[5] Nay, we suspect that they wish to dupe the Opposition into this disgraceful coalition before the dissolution of Parliament, and that the first session of the new Parliament will be the death-bed of this short-lived Ministry. We are induced to this suspicion by no vague speculations, but by positive facts, which appear to us to admit of no other interpretation. First, it is well known that Mr. Addington keeps aloof from all election concerns; and that the interest of the Crown will not be exerted in favour of the men of moderate principles. It is, indeed, pretty well understood that the Ex-Ministers will manage the next election, nearly as if they were still in office. Secondly, the man whom they have singled out as the first to be brought over, and the particular office which has been pitched upon for him, are equally suspicious. The confidential paper of Government,[6] on Saturday se'n-night, said, "Lord Hobart, it is reported, goes out to India, to succeed Marquis Wellesley as Governor General. His successor, as Secretary of State, has been mentioned to be one of those who have heretofore been distinguished on the Opposition bench of the House of Commons." Another paper

---

bitive penalties strictly enforced.... Addington...sincerely anxious for the success of his pacific policy, strongly hinted the necessity of [a commercial treaty] to M. Otto in London. But Bonaparte, listening only to the interested cries of French manufacturers, refused adequate concessions; and the commercial class in England soon began to feel that peace with France had assumed a form of hostility more dangerous to their interests than war, which had given them almost a monopoly of the maritime trade of Europe." Walter FitzPatrick in *Dropmore MSS* VII xvi–xvii.

[5] "Has Mr. Pitt stopped the negociation with Mr. Grey?...there are symptoms that lead me to imagine that Mr. Addington will go through this session as he has begun it, and will save himself from opposition by coquetting with them." Buckingham to his brother Lord Grenville, 20 Dec. *Dropmore MSS* VII 71.

[6] The *True Briton*; see below.

affirmed that the Member of Opposition is Mr. Grey. This report was circulated before it appeared in the papers; in stating it, therefore, we are in no danger of being accused as the authors of it.

It is an obvious piece of policy in the Ministers to gain over a man of high honour, constant integrity, and great personal weight; a man deeply rooted in the esteem of his country. All this, and more than this, they found in Mr. Grey;[7] and they have pitched upon, perhaps, almost the only office, the acceptance of which would bring in its train such deserved odium, as even his high character could not bear up against; and with this design they must assuredly have selected it, if it be true, that the place destined for Mr. Grey is the same which is now held by Lord Hobart. (Nay, if* it be false, we shall almost believe that the creatures of the late and present Ministers have purposely circulated the story, as well knowing that the very report would leave a scar behind it.) For that office exists in contradiction to Mr. Burke's Bill,[9] and to that system of economy in Government, which Mr. Grey, in concert with all the Old Opposition, uniformly and strenuously recommended. When a third Secretary of State was created in the person of Mr. Dundas, Opposition complained of it as a direct violation of a Bill adopted by Parliament in an awful crisis, and with circumstances of more than usual solemnity. The Ministers overruled the objection, on the ground of the absolute necessity of the office; and whether it were or were not *necessary*, yet it cannot be denied that during the war it was an important and active employment. But Peace is concluded, and the office continues. Another pretence, of course, must be found for its continuance, and

* One of the Daily Papers[8] promises a very interesting Dissertation on the Report of Mr. Grey's becoming Secretary of State in the room of Lord Hobart. In the first place, the report was never in existence among any well-informed persons; and it is not paying any great compliment to the Hon. Gentleman to appoint him to an office which there is reason to suppose will be abolished at the Peace. A dissertation on such a subject must be very interesting.—(*Times*).

Though *The Times* of yesterday contradicts the report which we stated long ago, that Mr. Grey and Mr. Tierney were likely to hold official situations, the report is not the less prevalent, even amongst the best informed in the higher circles, and the contradiction in question is only another proof of the ignorance of the Paper alluded to.—(*True Briton*.)

[7] Grey carried the banner of Parliamentary Reform for the Opposition, though he had urged the secession; he retained his high character but also his general inactivity.

[8] *M Post*—see announcements of 1 and 3 Dec, above; see C's next footnote.

[9] Burke in 1780 had brought forward a bill for the suppression of useless places and other measures of "Public Oeconomy", which passed in much diminished form in 1782.

Lord Hobart is called *the Secretary of State for the Colonies.** The business of the Colonies has hitherto been transacted (even during the busy and anxious years of the war) by the Secretary of State for the Home Department, the office now filled by Lord Pelham,[11] and no other true reasons can be given for this alteration; than that the pure, the patriotic Mr. Addington feels the convenience of extensive patronage as forcibly as any of his predecessors, and takes as shameless measures to effect it. Between thirty and forty thousand pounds per annum of the public money are expended to keep up, or rather to create, an unnecessary establishment; and the first unfavourable impression on the mind of the people, which in these cases is deemed the chief evil, this is to be transferred to Mr. Grey; and thus a twofold end effected—an extension of patronage will be secured, which Ministers want much; and the character of a powerful and popular patriot tarnished, which, if we mistake not, they want still more. We flatter ourselves that we have proved that no Member of the Opposition can unite with the present Ministers, their principles remaining unretracted, without a desertion of his own; but to deliver up these principles into the hands of a faction for a price, and that price an illegal, or at best an unconstitutional office——

> Who would not scoff, if such a man there be?
> Who but must weep, if Atticus is he?[12]

Were we for a moment even to drop all considerations of public virtue and public interest, and consider it merely as an every day bargain between trading statesmen, we should still blush to see a man, whom it has become a habit with us to honour, wear a boot,

* The very day on which *The Times* sneered at this Paper for promising this article (imagining, as every honest man would imagine, that Lord Hobart's office would be abolished at the peace); it inserted the following paragraph, which for the *first time* publicly noticed Lord Hobart's *new title*. The paragraph manifestly came from authority:—"We have authority to state, that it was on the presentation of Lord Hobart, as Secretary of State for the department of War AND COLONIES, and not of Sir James Turner, as erroneously reported in the papers of yesterday, that Mr. Mackenzie, the Gentleman who first penetrated through Canada to the Frozen and Pacific Oceans, had the honour of presenting to His Majesty, at the Levee on Wednesday, the Book he is about to publish on that interesting subject."[10]

[10] Sir Alexander Mackenzie (c 1755–1820) published in London in 1801 his *Voyages from Montreal, on the River St. Laurence, Through the Continent of North America, to the Frozen and Pacific Oceans; in the Years 1789 and 1793*. He was knighted 10 Feb 1802.

[11] Thomas Pelham (1756–1826; Lord Pelham, 1801; 2nd Earl of Chichester, 1805), a friend of Fox and Windham, who joined Pitt during the Whig schism of 1794.

[12] Pope *Epistle to Dr Arbuthnot* lines 213–14 (var); see *B Poets* VIII 119.

which even Lord Hobart finds too small for him, and is to seek elsewhere the patronage, and consequent means of providing for his friends and family, which have, it seems, been all *forestalled* at Whitehall.[13] And most true it is, that the Duke of Portland, before he resigned, had "*picked the bone clean.*" Nothing seems to have escaped his penetrating glances. A very lucrative sinecure place in Jamaica, now held by Mr. Wyndham, and given to him in reversion by the late Lord Egremont, his father, when Secretary of State,[14] the Duke of Portland has secured, by reversion, to his grandson, an infant scarcely a year old. Another sinecure, held by Lord Ducie, Marshal of Barbados,[15] the Duke of Portland has secured in reversion for an *Eleve* of his, a Mr. Carter, possessed of 3000*l.* per annum, independent fortune. What other sinecures and reversions the Duke has secured for his family and supporters, we are not as yet particularly acquainted; but we have good reason to believe, that his Noble successors, the Lords Pelham and Hobart, looked blank on each other, when they found that his Grace had not only left the stream of patronage low, but had actually turned the *course* of it into his own grounds.

But, it may be objected, it is with Mr. Addington, and not with the Duke of Portland, that Mr. Grey is solicited to coalesce, with Mr. Addington,

———————Whose pure soul is
A pattern to all Ministers living with him,
And all that shall succeed.[16]

And is Mr. Addington then really this disinterested man, whose actions disarm all suspicion, and *leave no room for opposition*? No sooner is he seated at the helm,[17] than (with that Lynx-eyed perception[18] of the before unsuspected virtues and talents of their own relations, which new Ministers are always blest with by virtue of their office) he discovers, that his wife's sister's husband, Mr. Adams, is very fit for a Lord of the Treasury: and a Lord of the Treasury he makes him! With an eye no less microscopically powerful he detects

13 An apt pun at a time of popular alarm against forestallers of grain.

14 Percy Charles Wyndham (1757–1833), secretary and clerk of the courts of Barbados; his father, Sir Charles Wyndham, 2nd Earl of Egremont (1710–63).

15 Francis Reynolds–Moreton, 3rd Baron Ducie of Tortworth (1739–1808).

16 Parody of Shakespeare *Henry VIII* v v 23–4, 26. On Addington's "barefaced self-patronage" see the comment a year later in *CN* I 1289 (and see note).

17 Observe the development of this ship-of-state metaphor in the essays of Feb and Mar 1802.

18 Cf "the lynx-eyed Watching for Opportunities" in *Friend* No 10 (*CC*) II 139.

in Mr. Bragg, his sister's husband, a similar fitness for Treasurer of the Navy (a place worth 4000*l*. a year), and a Privy Counsellor: and of course, it stands with reason, that his brother, Hely Addington, that his own brother *must be* the fittest man in the kingdom to be Secretary of the Treasury.[19] This latter instance is an additional proof, that humility and true prudence are inherent in the very blood of the Addingtons. Hely, once a Lord of the Treasury, sate at the board as the Secretary's master; but he descends from dignity to wealth, from their Lordships' definite salaries to a Secretary's numberless perquisites. Mr. Hely Addington is a true Bat! In the gentle owl-light of preferment, when it was neither light nor dark with the family, he soared aloft, as a bird; but now that the family greatness has risen, like the morning sun, he resigns the privilege of wings, becomes a true snug mouse, and feeds upon the *cheese-parings* and *candle-ends*.[20] *Proh pudor*![21] And these are the men with whom Mr. Grey is to be joined in office! What is even the Duke of Portland's conduct compared with this? He only predestined the honours and rewards of the State to an infant, who, for aught we know to the contrary, may turn out hereafter to be as prudent, gentle, and temperate a Statesman as Mr. Wyndham, the present possessor of the office, to whom his father, Lord Egremont, had in the same way secured it in reversion! to an infant, who may even turn out as *wise* a Statesman as his own grandpapa, and, in the event of a scarcity, write as *wise* letters to the Lord Lieutenant of the county of Oxford![22] But Messrs. Bragg,

[19] Addington had just made Charles Bragge (afterwards Bragge-Bathurst, c 1754–1831) treasurer of the navy. John Hiley Addington (1759–1818) had been a junior lord of the treasury since Dec 1800 under Pitt, an appointment renewed by Addington Jul 1802. James Adams had just been made junior lord of admiralty. Finding places for these relatives of Addington would be a major concern when Pitt, again in office in 1804, would attempt to bring Addington into his cabinet. Barnes 451, 459–60.

Canning's lines on the brothers were:

When his speeches hobble vilely,
What "hear him's!" burst from
Brother Hiley;
When his faltering periods lag,
Hark to the cheers of Brother
Bragge!

Quoted in *Lord Granville Leveson Gower: Private Correspondence* ed Castalia, Countess Granville (2 vols 1916) II 2n.

[20] See 22 Jan 1798 and n 5, above.

[21] Tr: "For shame!", a catch-phrase of antiquity.

[22] In an "Official Letter from the Duke of Portland to the Lord-Lieutenant of the County of Oxford" dated 29 Sept 1800 and given to the newspapers, Portland urged the Lord-Lieutenant to combat in the community and in his own mind the pernicious belief "that the late scarcity was artificial". See *A Reg* for 1800 (1801) 2141–3. The Duke's *wisdom* (which C now sadly doubted) lay in the pious certainty that "the prosperity of this country...under Providence" would resume its perfection of wealth and power as soon as "the markets should

Adams, and Hely Addington—alas! alas! they are full-grown realities, and it would be a violation of all Christian faith, hope, and charity, not to presume somewhat better of the infant. Old Dr. Bentley[23] was accustomed to pass by all the Seniors, &c. of his College unnoticed; but always and most respectfully touched his cap to the *Freshmen.* "The young ones (said the Doctor) *may* come to something; but the others, I *know* what they are."

We would fain believe it impossible that a man like Mr. Grey (no trading Statesman,[24] no mere man of business, but one who has ever addressed his country in the high and commanding tone of genuine English principles) that such a man should coalesce with a Party, whose principles and whose measures he has repeatedly and loudly affirmed to be the assailers of the Constitution of his country, and the Liberties of all mankind, who have retracted no one of these principles, and who, in the very outset and maiden blush of their Ministry, betray all the rapacity and selfishness, not to say corruption, of their predecessors! He will not, we are assured, join himself in any Ministry, from which Mr. Pitt is not excluded; the only result of which will be, that Mr. Pitt will, of course, return, a somewhat humbler man, to the Alarmists and Friends of the Court, who will gladly receive him as their *General* in the political campaign, if he only will yield a more direct obedience to the decisions of the *inner War Council.* Thus with a Leader, who has certainly the opinion of the monied men in his favour, as a Financier, and with sure friends and agents in the Ministry itself, the Alarmists wait securely for the moment, when the ambition, or bad faith, or prosperity of the enemy shall have spread dissatisfaction among the people, or any attempt at measures in consistency with their former professions on the part of the proselytes to the new Ministry shall have disgusted or alarmed the Court: the word is given; Lord Hawkesbury and Mr. Addington resign, and fall back into their former ranks, or ascend into dignified inaction, the remaining Ministers are displaced, and all things return to their former position, except the character and strength of the Opposition. They, alas! are gone forever. It was thought convenient to make a Peace; the least important and least ostensible part of the

be free and open" with no restraint on the sale or withholding of commodities.

23 A Cambridge anecdote, of Richard Bentley, the classical scholar, who died in 1742. See *CN* I 311–14 and nn.

24 The term implies venality, as "trading Justices" does in *Lects 1795* (*CC*) 267 (and see n 3). Cf *Courier* 24 Feb 1804 (at n 6), below.

Old Faction are brought forward on the front of the stage to conclude it; and the character of it is to be shared by the Opposition. They have full confidence that this peace will not be permanent, at all events that it will become unpopular; and they have made the feint of yielding to the Opposition, that they may throw them off their guard, and out of their ranks, while they, making a circular movement, fall upon them in the rear, in the moment of their greatest disorder.

No man can wish to play into his enemy's hands; and when he believes his enemy to be the enemy of his country, no good man ought to wish it. And it is on this ground chiefly that we wish to rest our argument; and this, we would fain believe, will be the most powerful with the patriot, whose name we have thought it our duty to bring forward.——In revolutionary governments, (and, in a less degree, in governments purely despotic) measures must be judged of by their immediate consequences, for they create no precedents. It is far otherwise with us. With us the stability of our laws and constitution is every thing. We derive one inestimable advantage from this, namely, that our politics and our morals are built on the same foundations: it is the EXAMPLE, the PRECEDENT, which constitutes the importance, and determines the character of public measures, equally as of private actions.[25] It requires nothing but a good heart to perceive how favourably this must act on the dispositions and understandings of a free nation, which habitually interests itself in the proceedings of its government; how it tends to make us what by foreigners we are believed, and, we hope deservedly believed to be, at once a calculating and an honest people. The Ministers, who made light work with the Habeas Corpus act, the Bill of Rights, and the laws which forbid the sending of money out of the kingdom without the consent of Parliament, have both attacked the morals of the nation, and weakened the foundations of our internal peace. By innovating on those laws, which were made to protect the subject against the government, they prepare the way for innovations in those laws, which make the government sacred in the eyes of the subject. On these high grounds the Opposition have appeared to us to act, on all important occasions, through the whole of the war—at least, in all the questions relating immediately to *English* politics. They form, not only their justification, but their well-merited panegyric, if they complete the

[25] In eight years C would have changed his mind. Cf *Friend* No 24: "...the influence of *example*...is of considerable importance in the moral calculations of an Individual; but of little, if any, in those of a Nation". *CC* II 327.

work they have begun;—but their sentence of condemnation, and the bitterest satire on them, if they themselves unravel *in the dark* the web, which they had half-woven in the day-light.[26] For now is the time that must decide whether the acts of the late and the present Ministry are to be recorded as precedents, or as warnings:—whether those who have hitherto shewn themselves the skilful and honest physicians of the state, shall degenerate into quacks, administering the "poppy and mandragora"[27] of oblivion and unnatural reconciliation, at the moment, when the knife and the cautery alone can prevent the foam of a mad faction from being taken up into the blood, and carried into the very heart of the Constitution. The Opposition must either continue to criminate the Ministers as a pernicious faction, or plead guilty to the charge, which these Ministers have so repeatedly urged against them, that they are themselves one. If, unhappily, they satisfy themselves with bargaining for the permanent exclusion of one or two obnoxious individuals, and without further advantages, consider stepping into their places, as gaining a victory, it will be a victory in which

> Heu! retulit praedas, non palmam, victor ab hoste.[28]

That the present Ministry are desirous that this reconciliation should take place, we cannot doubt: for they will gain a support, which they stand in need of. But, we doubt, still less, if possible, that the faction of the Alarmists; that the Earl of Liverpool, Mr. Windham, and Lord Grenville, look on to such an event, with at least equal pleasure. For the support, which the Opposition will afford to the present Ministers, will, from various causes, be both transitory and incomplete; but the *tarnish* on their characters will be complete and permanent—and, any after Opposition which the party may wish to institute, will be regarded by the people, as little more than the snarling at a bone between dogs, who had just before been hunting in couples.—"*Fellows of mere outside and bark.*"[29]

26 Like Penelope; cf Homer *Odyssey* 2.104, 105, etc.

27 *Othello* III iii 331.

28 Untraced. Tr: "Alas! the conqueror brought back booty from the foe, not the palm of victory."

29 Untraced; the pun suggests that C himself may be the author. Cf *CN* III 4342 and n.

1802

23 February–31 December

[15 February 1802, Monday]

To-morrow, or the first open day, we will present some interesting observations on the late reported changes, and on Mr. Addington's Administration.

[22 February 1802, Monday]

Observations on the late reported changes, to-morrow.

CABINET. IV

THE REPORTED CHANGES[1]

23 February 1802, Tuesday. New attribution. Internal evidence confirmed by ms in C's hand (see App B, below). Part of the series, as announced by Stuart, though used this day as the leading paragraph and hence without title.

It is now known, that the negotiation between the present Ministers, and certain Members of the Opposition, is at an end. Mr. Fox's speech at the Whig Club gave it the finishing blow.[2] We doubt not that this great statesman declared all that he himself actually knew; but the public would be greatly deluded, if they should infer from

[1] For verse contributions by C in Dec and by WW (perhaps directly) in Feb, see App D, below.

[2] Both Fox and Sheridan (see next note) made public response to the warnings of the *M Post* and others. Fox at a Whig Club meeting in the London Tavern 9 Feb said "he highly rejoiced in the peace...he did not rejoice in the unfortunate situation.... With respect to the internal state of this country, he had heard many reports of the salutary measures that were to be pursued by the new men in power; that the principles of the late Ministry were to be abandoned; the obnoxious bills were to be repealed; that retrenchments in our public establishments were to be made; that a system of conciliation with regard to Ireland was to be pursued; that the people were to have a fair share of liberty and power; for, he must observe that power is the necessary foundation of liberty....He had heard of all this, but, he was sorry to observe, that he had not seen one step taken towards any one of these objects. ... He could not suppose any Members of the Club were inclined to waver in principle, and adopt a new course...he could assert that the great and eminent persons to whom the Club looked up, are firm, and he would as soon believe himself false to the principles he had professed as believe they would change. ...He would only assert with confidence ... that in the House of Peers the Dukes of Norfolk and Bedford, in the House of Commons, Mr. Sheridan and Mr. Grey—were as attached as ever to the principles...". *M Post* 10 Feb 1802.

that speech that no negotiation ever had been on foot. It is an undeniable fact, that certain gentlemen of high character, the known friends of the Members, whose names were given in almost all the public prints, did speak openly of a Coalition, as a probable event. It is undeniable, that efforts were made to form such a coalition, and much activity and stratagem used by more than one or two men of distinguished talents and high reputation on either side. From a knowledge of these proceedings, and still more from what we observed of the general tone of public feeling, we thought it our duty (now two months ago) to warn the Opposition of the snare laid for them by the new circumstances of the times.[3] Men are never so strongly tempted to abandon consistency of principle, as when the opposite expectations, which opposite principles had led the two hostile parties to form, are both equally disappointed. To this state of general feeling, this seeming crash and break-up of all parties, was added the incautious gratitude of certain of the Opposition to Mr. Addington, as a peace-maker; and a further bond of union seemed to be formed by the new opposition of Lord Grenville, and the high Anti-Jacobins. It was a pardonable mistake to think him their friend, whom they perceived to have a common enemy.

We rejoice that no evil (at least no serious or irremediable evil) has arisen from the peril in which the friends of the country were placed. But we were justified by facts as well as by probable reasons, in the warning which we gave. Nay, we may even appeal to the late speeches, both of Mr. Sheridan[4] and of Mr. Fox, for the truth of our assertion, that there were grounds for *fearing a schism* in that body of men, which by its great talents and consequent influence on popular opinion, if not by the number of its votes, has often restrained the Ministers from acts of oppression; and though it could not prevent powers from being incautiously delegated to them, has yet compelled them to be cautious in the exercise of those powers—a body of men, who strove to save the country from a ruinous war, in the first place, and who would have afterwards procured for it an

[3] A clear reference to C's essays of 3 and 11 Dec 1801.

[4] It is generous of C to pass over the Sheridan speech in silence (Whig Club 19 Jan, *M Post* 20 Jan). The speech indicated "a desire on his part of shaming his friends out of an arrangement" (as Thomas Grenville observed, *Dropmore MSS* VII 76), but it infuriated Grey ("I do not think Sheridan can have the excuse of being drunk for what he said"), though Fox tried to assure Grey that Sheridan's slur on "Friends of the People for a time" who "desert the popular cause" was aimed at Tierney (see above and Fox *Correspondence* III 354). The effect was a further alienation of Sheridan (and Tierney) from the chiefs of their own party (Trevelyan p 127).

honourable peace, if its advice had been taken while Britain was capable of making an impression on the enemy.[5] However, the negotiation, of whatever kind it may have been, and in whatever causes it may have originated, is now at an end. Mr. Fox's speech informs us indeed, that none of the *leaders* of Opposition ever listened to the overtures which the Ministers were making: while, on the other hand, the friends of Ministers assert, that the negotiation broke off on Mr. Addington's part. There is one way of reconciling the apparent contradictions in these assertions; and this way is probably the truth. We may suppose, that overtures were made by Ministers to one or more Gentlemen of high honour and character, and that such terms were insisted upon by them as the conditions of their acceptance, as would have rendered the coalition strictly honourable on their part, though it would have called for such retractations from the present Ministers as they neither would make if they were able to do, nor could make, if they were willing, retaining their official situations.

That the parties never could coalesce with honour every man of common sense foresaw: or if there were any one of the persons immediately concerned who did not perceive it, this is only a new proof how much the wishes may sophisticate the understanding. The state of parties remains at present the same as at the resignation of Mr. Pitt.[6] The party of Mr. Windham and Lord Grenville opposing the peace with consistent principle, the old Opposition supporting it with consistent principle, and the Ministers persevering in it in contradiction to all their former principles, and without reference to any new distinct principle. Simply they needed it, as the means of their power.

Nothing was more easy than to make such a peace. A general compliance with the enemy's demands formed the whole of the recipe. But it was necessary to their popularity, nay, even to their existence as a distinct party, that they should obtain a peace from the enemy; and they may be almost said to have taken out a patent for their ministry from the First Consul. How long this state of parties will continue will depend in a great measure on the plans of Bonaparte—on how long he may find it wise to abstain from measures which this country cannot look to and remain quiet. Whenever his forbearance ceases, the most probable event is, that Mr. Pitt will once again be called to the head of affairs, and new disputes will re-unite

[5] Cf C's ms draft of this paragraph, App B, below.

[6] A transcript by SC from this sentence to end of article is in VCL (MS LT 84).

his party (we can scarcely look on Mr. Addington in any other light), and that of the high Anti-Jacobins. But grant that happier omens may soon arise!

It is, however, of no small consequence that the public should thoroughly understand the character of the present Minister, lest false expectations should confer on him a false popularity, and prolong the Premiership of a man who might, no doubt, guide the vessel of the state in the regular trade-wind of a long established peace, but who has surely neither the talents, nor the experience, nor the decision of character requisite for a steersman in a sea, where a calm is only the uncertain pause of the tempest.[7] We propose, therefore, to-morrow,[8] to analyse both the character and the proceedings of the Minister; and to his encomiasts, who may imagine that we detract from his merits, we wish to recommend the speech of the Roman Philosopher, concerning his pupil—*Melius de Nerone sentio quam tu: cantare enim tu illum dignum putas, ego autem tacere.*[9]

[24 February 1802, Wednesday]

The Character of Mr. Addington's Administration is delayed by the press of temporary matter till To-morrow.

[25 February 1802, Thursday]

The Article on Mr. Addington's Administration to-morrow.

[27 February 1802, Saturday]

While Mr. Addington labours under domestic calamities, we shall delay inserting the Article we have prepared respecting his Administration. This may look like affectation, and nothing is more probable than that if Mr. Addington were more happily situated, he would

[7] Canning may have been influenced by these essays (see also 22 Mar) when he coined a slogan for the New Opposition, "The Pilot that Weathered the Storm", in a song for a dinner on 28 May inaugurating a "Pitt Club" (see John Colmer "Coleridge on Addington's Administration" *MLR* LIV—1959—69–72). C may not have liked what he was predicting, war and Pitt; but those who did were quite happy with this image. Yet the application was scarcely new. Paine in *Rights of Man* pt 2 (1792) called Pitt the pilot at the helm. And cf C's image of Robespierre, "that dreadful pilot", in *Conciones: Lects 1795* (*CC*) 74.

[8] This was delayed until 22 Mar; see that day, n 1.

[9] C is imperfectly recalling the speech, not of "the Roman Philosopher concerning his pupil" (i.e. Seneca on Nero), but of the Greek Apollonius of Tyana on a visit to Rome. This is a Latin translation, source untraced, of Philostratus *Life of Apollonius* 4.44. Tr: "I think better of Nero than you do: for you think he is fitted to sing, I to hold his tongue."

neither see nor hear of the article; but we apprehend it might look like harshness and want of feeling on our part to lay it before the Public at present.

[13 March 1802, Saturday]

On Monday or Tuesday we shall give our promised character of Mr. Addington's Administration.

[20 March 1802, Saturday]

The character of Mr. Addington's Administration we intend for Monday.

MR. ADDINGTON'S ADMINISTRATION[1]

22 March 1802, Monday; *M Post* title. New attribution, from internal and external evidence; see Erdman (1959 a) 105–9 and Colmer *MLR* LIV (1959) 69–72. C's ms notes, on the back of the ms fragment of his essay of 23 Feb, are cited in the editorial footnotes below and given in full in App B, below.

C's jottings are chiefly metaphoric images; when he writes in essay form, he transmutes these either by redirecting the original metaphor or by leaving it behind for another suggested by the original one. I take this evidence that C's basic ingredients are metaphors as justification of my method of testing his style chiefly in its metaphoric nodes.[2]

WE easily forget, or forgive, or perhaps overlook, the faults and errors of men of small talent.[3] The existence of such faults does not alarm our fears, and the detection of them does not gratify our

[1] See the announcements of this capstone to the "Reported Changes" series, 24, 25, 27 Feb, 13, 20 Mar, above. C had evidently written the article before the end of Feb (he left London a few days before 7 Mar); Stuart was ready to print it when news came that Addington's eldest daughter had a "very alarming" case of putrid fever; Stuart promised (27 Feb) to "delay inserting the Article" while the minister labored "under domestic calamities", and he ran bulletins on Miss Addington's health through 4 Mar, when she was reported "somewhat better". Stuart then held off, however, to let the dust settle after the political explosion explained in n 19. Since the main theme of C's essay was Addington's mediocrity, this afforded a choice illustration; C was out of reach, and it must have been Stuart who inserted the allusion to Addington's "contest with Mr. Robson" as a decisive "test of Mr. Addington's abilities". For two weeks the *M Post* was filled with the affair, C's "character" being saved for peroration.

[2] SC did see the essay and make extensive notes and a transcript; she even meant to cite it in her preface in support of her belief "that the view of the Add administration taken in that paper [*M Post*] was substantially my fathers, & that the material of argu[ments] spun out of the paper from time to time afterwards [after he largely ceased contributing in 1800, as she supposed] was all pulled out of what was around his distaff at the beginning" (VCL S MS F 10.3, omitting deletions); but she had no ms evidence, and she had a theory that C had not contributed between 3 Dec 1801 and Sept 1802; so she left it out of *EOT*. At the end of her transcript, the first part of which is misdated 1801, she noted: "Probably by Sir J. Mackintosh". VCL MS LT 84.

[3] C's notes for this essay (see App B, below) begin with a phrase from Tacitus, from which this sentence takes

envy. It is on this ground (for we would not willingly have recourse to the supposition of any assumed and *convenient* blindness) that we must explain a circumstance which surprises us not a little, namely, that the Administration of Mr. Addington has been pronounced hitherto unobjectionable by men who nevertheless declare aloud their hostility to the measures of his predecessors.[4] What language Mr. Addington may have held in private, what hopes he may have encouraged, what plans he may have disclosed, we know not—neither do we pretend to determine whether he has disclosed the same views to Mr. Pitt and Mr. Tierney, or whether, previously to his closing the brazen Temple of *Janus*, he has thought fit to pay his devotions to the two-faced God.[5] However this may be, yet private conversations must be made to weigh more than either experience or theory will justify, if they can counterbalance the whole of the Minister's public and parliamentary acts. His Administration has been proclaimed unobjectionable by men, who yet can find no words too harsh for the measures of Mr. Pitt and the faction of the Grenvilles. Now, one of the very first acts of his Administration was the Bill of Indemnity,[6] by which he openly identified himself with his predecessors, in all the measures which had most provoked the hostility of the friends of freedom, and made it public, that he dissented from them in that point only to which the friends of freedom were naturally the most inclined to yield their assent. But, was this the only objectionable measure?—Objectionable, in the strongest sense of the phrase, it surely was; and we challenge the admirers of our history to point to any measure of Government since the Revolution, by which the spirit of our Constitution and Laws has been equally violated, or the common moral feelings more grievously insulted.—The Court Party are not so easily satisfied, it seems, as some of the old supporters of free principles appeared *inclined* to be.

---

its departure: "Rather free from faults than possessing virtues" (tr of C's Latin notes).

4 Cf C on Charles II and the political value of his "weakness", 12 Oct 1802, below. Lord Holland observed, years later, that Addington's "very mediocrity recommended him to those (and they are not a few) who dread and dislike all superiority of talent". Barnes p 390.

5 The bronze doors in the Forum were open in time of war and closed in time of peace; Addington had closed them. The image of two-faced Janus, here representing duplicity, was often used by C for its retrospective–prospective characteristic; cf *Friend* (*CC*) II 278 and, below, *Courier* 31 Aug 1811, last textual note.

6 Cf 3 Dec 1801, at n 25, above.

The Court Party seem to have taken for their maxim the words of the jay—

> There is a difference in fact
> 'Twixt a promise and an act.[7]

They demanded *acts* from the Minister, and what they demanded he willingly gave. When Mr. Addington came into power, it was necessary that the war should be supported. For such support he could look only to his predecessors in office, the Grenvilles, and the high Anti-jacobins. He seemed to have courted these by the attempt to exceed in violence all that had been most obnoxious in their administration. He continued the martial law in Ireland under circumstances more severe; he suspended the Habeas Corpus Act in England, as if from no other motive, than to shew the people of England what a trifle he deemed the suspension of the Habeas Corpus Act to be; and while he made a solemn apotheosis[8] of all the crimes and blunders of his predecessors by the Bill of Indemnity,[9] he stigmatised even with a wantonness of insult the members of the Opposition, by excluding them all from the Committee of Secrecy, as unfit to be entrusted with the welfare of their country. The former Ministers, even in the very heat and tumult of the contest, had always allowed on such Committees one or two members of Opposition, and some independent members of parliament; Mr. Addington, who had just before passed all the illegal acts of the former Ministers, into law and precedent, afforded himself a new precedent, by composing a committee appointed to examine into the real state of Treason and Sedition in these kingdoms, entirely of placemen and fanatical partizans. These were the steps of the *accommodation ladder*,[10] all, no doubt, pre-adjusted, before Mr. Addington was suffered to climb up into office by means of it. But when he gained the height, it was clear that he could retain it only by making a peace with France. We must, therefore, suppose, that those of the

[7] Source untraced.

[8] C had jotted: "Pessima res est errorum apotheosis"—Nothing is so mischievous as the apotheosis of error: a rather different use of the idea.

[9] See n 6, above. The indemnity granted by the bill would protect ministers from lawsuits resulting from their prosecution, over many years, of persons accused of sedition or treason.

[10] C is continuing the nautical imagery of 23 Feb 1802, last paragraph, defining Addington as pilot. C's note is simply "accomodation-ladder" (a light staircase occasionally fixed on the gangway of the admiral's or fleet commander's ship, to facilitate embarkation and disembarkation); but the term appears also in *CN* I 655, in an entry dated c 27 Feb 1800 by K. Coburn. If that date is correct, C kept the term two years, at the time using instead "an *olla podrida* of mutual accomodation" (*M Post* 25 Jan 1800).

old Opposition, who have been able to see nothing objectionable hitherto in Mr. Addington's administration, date that administration from this event; or that their gratitude to the Minister, as a Pacificator, has been so intense and intoxicating, as to have made them not only forgive, but even forget, all his preceding measures.[11] Mr. Addington, on his part, now assailed by a division of his former friends, and blest by the same spirit of forgiving and forgetting, stretches out his arms to the Opposition,[12] and makes dazzling overtures to men, whom a few months before he had stigmatised by a public act that, interpreted in its utmost, would go nigh to throw a suspicion on the first and fairest characters of the country, as the favourers of revolution.[13] Their intellect, their talents, their experience, were all undoubted*. And what then, but unsound principle, could be adduced, to stamp such men as unfit to be entrusted with the suppression of Treason! But now the preliminaries of peace are signed—a peace, with which every one, but the Grenvilles and Burkites, were delighted, with the *terms* of which every one, but the Ministers themselves, were disgusted or humbled!

This peace was signed and must be supported. His old political connections, the Grenvilles, were its bitter enemies. To the Opposition Mr. Addington was necessarily obliged to look for aid. Something more however than the mere signing of preliminaries was necessary to unite in support of his general Administration, men to whose principles it had been hitherto in every other respect hostile. The unconstitutional measures and personal insults of last spring had raised a wall of separation between them and the new Minister, which he could not overleap. To effect an union, he was obliged to

* See the Report, page 474.[14]

[11] These remarks and indeed the tenor of the whole essay put a severe strain on our acceptance of C's claim in *BL* ch 10: "From the commencement of the Addington administration to the present day, whatever I have written in THE MORNING POST... has been in defence or furtherance of the measures of Government." *BL* (1907) I 144–5. In their curious way perhaps these essays of early 1802 *were* in furtherance of the measures—but certainly at the expense of the men, and only *if* the measures should become genuinely those of the Old Opposition (which is not C's later meaning).

[12] Cf 11 Dec 1801 (at n 5), above: "... stretch out their arms to their old opponents to *strangle*, and not to *embrace*".

[13] C refers to the stigma implied by Addington's exclusion of all Opposition members from the committee investigating sedition. See above.

[14] The passage C has in mind has not been traced; the page reference must be an error.

shew a disposition to undermine, and, like Pyramus, to breathe his amorous wishes through it.[15] Accordingly insinuations were made, and half promises held out, of the adoption of a system consonant with the feelings and principles of Opposition. He was to suffer the Habeas Corpus Suspension, the Treason and Sedition Acts, to expire.—The Government of Ireland was to be tempered with mildness and moderation. Our establishments were to be reduced—all selfish jobbing was to be discountenanced—and a rigid economy to be observed in the public expenditure. As Mr. Addington ran before the wishes of the Grenvilles to obtain their support during the war, so now he promised to run before the wishes of the Opposition after the Peace. He had no principle but a love of power, no feeling but a sense of weakness. Conscious debility always endeavours to supply the want of strength by address and cunning. Mr. Addington was all things unto all men, in hopes that all men would be of one mind and temper to him.—Great plausibility and affected candour were called in to his aid, and he contrived to be at the same time on good terms with Mr. Pitt and Mr. Tierney, while he was adored by the English Jacobins.—These appearances were flattering, but they were delusive. Events have deadened the spirit of all parties, but the calm of disappointment must not be mistaken for the calm of content.[16] Whenever the Definitive Treaty shall be signed, parties will form, and if Mr. Addington does not provide against that period, he will find the appearances which led him to suppose he was supported by both sides, denoted that he was supported by neither. Had he pursued a true system of conciliation, he would not in any instance have gone the full length of either the one side or the other; but by outrunning the unconstitutional career of the Grenvilles in so many instances, he has rendered it impossible for him to shew any countenance to the Opposition without exciting the disgust of the one party and the suspicion of both. It is not, by alternately vibrating between Jacobins and Royalists, that Bonaparte conciliates the affections of these parties in France, but by accommodating himself to both to a certain extent. This is acting on a solid foundation, and with a view to a permanent effect. The system of Mr. Addington is the very reverse. It is a temporising, fugacious policy, that loses

15 The story of Pyramus and Thisbe and their communicating through a chink in the wall is told in Ovid *Metamorphoses* 4.55ff, Chaucer's *Legend of Good Women: 2. The Legend of Thisbe of Babylon*, and in burlesque fashion in *A Midsummer Night's Dream* III i, to name the three main sources.

16 Cf C's *Tranquillity*, in *M Post*, 4 Dec 1801.

all its power and effect the moment it comes to be exposed.[17] It is a system of dissimulation, and as it has been already seen through, it must have consequently excited suspicions in both parties, however prudent they may have found it to conceal their sentiments. To some of the Members of Opposition he may hold out that he enters into their views, but dare not, by an immediate and practical avowal of them, break with Mr. Pitt, lest he should be left in a minority. To Mr. Pitt, he may hold out that he only sooths the Opposition, with a view to public quiet, while he considers himself a mere *locum tenens*, until favourable circumstances shall arise for his return to power. These plausible pretexts, and the daily hope of the Definitive Treaty, will secure his Administration from the attack of either party pending the Negotiation. As events shall afterwards arise, he may expect to fall in with the one side or the other; and while he may congratulate himself on the certainty, under any change, of a peerage and a pension, with the office of Speaker of the House of Lords, he may cherish the hidden hope that changes will be difficult and that the mutual jealousy of contending parties will enable him to preserve his power. If he can retain the premiership, his success is complete. If he cannot, he still succeeds in the degree, as he will retire with profit, and the reputation, which want of enemies leaves to the feeble and the inoffensive in power. It is more easy to discover the chance upon which he calculates with a view to personal interest, than to reconcile his proceedings with any fixed principles of national policy, or any solid system of Government.

We have already hinted our opinion of the abilities of Mr. Addington. They are beneath mediocrity. Long used to a situation of parade and specious appearance, a daily witness of the homage rendered to eloquence,[18] he seems to have considered them as the only essential qualifications. In the two former, habit has come successfully in aid of nature. No Minister need be more pompous and shewy. In his cultivation of eloquence, he has not been equally fortunate. An imposing manner, and some facility in applying common place observations, constitute the extent of his oratorical attainments. In his style of speaking; nay, in his very tone and manner, as well as in his conduct, he labours to imitate Mr. Pitt. He sets out with an air of openness and candour; but he makes so

[17] The thought is in a different image in C's notes: "One of these plants that thrive best in the shade".

[18] Again C departs from his first image: "Praise like musk &c"; cf *CN* I 223: "A dunghill at a distance sometimes smells like musk . . .".

many reservations, so many conditions in his progress, that his proposition, which was at first laid down as positive and precise, becomes at the end equivocal and indefinite. There is a difference, however, between him and his model in this particular. Mr. Pitt puzzles his audience by his ingenuity, Mr. Addington by his confusion. The one renders himself unintelligible by his sophistry; the other is not understood, because that which is not clearly conceived, can never be clearly and definitely expressed. He never displays dexterity in debate, expansion or vigour of mind, a strong discriminating power, originality of thought, or richness of fancy. His intellect is too short-sighted to see beyond the point immediately before him, and hence, in a case of complexity, it is mere chance if one part of his argument does not contradict the other. He is easily thrown into confusion, and he betrays a total want of ability to rally. He cannot repair an error, or cover a retreat. Whenever he is defeated, his defeat is most decisive.

There is scarcely a public occasion in which his powers have been brought into action, that does not furnish proof of these remarks. Two must be particularly in remembrance. One last Spring, when he gave up Mr. Abbot on the Irish Martial Law Bill.[19] The other, his late contest with Mr. Robson,[20] on the subject of the bill for 19*l.* 10. protested at the Sick and Hurt Office, exposed still more the small wares of which his mind is composed.[21] The ignorance which

[19] There had been a slight flare-up when Addington refrained, on his "own personal opinion", from supporting his cabinet's motion, presented by Charles Abbot, then MP for Helston and chief secretary for Ireland. See *M Post* 28 May, 10 Jun 1801. Abbot (1757–1829; 1st Baron Colchester, 1817) had recently (11 Feb 1802) been elected speaker.

[20] On 4 Mar 1802 an independent MP, Richard B. Robson of Okehampton, a gadfly whom a more adroit statesman than Addington might have ignored, announced as evidence of the government's insolvency that "a fact had come within his knowledge, of a bill accepted by Government having been dishonoured", a bill for £19.10, protested at the Sick and Hurt Office. There was a "general exclamation of Hear! hear!" and Addington reacted as if to a bombshell, with further wrangling ineptitudes on 9 Mar. "Mr. Addington, we must presume, never heard of the *stoppage* of the *bank*, or the *national debt*", twitted the *M Post* on the 8th. For a time the *M Post* gave so much space to the hecklings of the plaindealing Mr Robson and his ally Mr Tyrwhitt Jones, some called it "Robson's and Jones's Gazette". *M Post* 3 Feb 1803.

For the whole petty performance see Debrett XVII 124–9, 149–70. Hazlitt cites the episode in the Preface to his *Political Essays* (1819) xix.

[21] This passage (to the end of the paragraph) cannot have been written before 10 Mar or by C. The only non-Coleridgian turns of phrase in the essay occur in this passage: "wares of which his mind is *composed*"; "disclosed his state of *intellects*"; "convicted of one error . . . he denied some other fact"; and perhaps "to blink

he betrayed of the practice of the public offices was no impeachment of his understanding, though highly disreputable to him as a minister. But the manner in which he took up the subject disclosed his state of intellects. He inferred national insolvency (and contended for it) from a practice which has ever existed without injury to the public credit. No sooner was he convicted of one error than he denied some other fact, till at last, beaten from every position, he was obliged to blink the question in moving the order of the day on Mr. Robson's motion, giving that Gentleman a complete triumph over him. This affair in itself is a matter of no importance; but as a test of Mr. Addington's abilities, it is decisive. In the city there is but one opinion.

The country is deeply interested in understanding the character and views of its chief Ministers at this moment. Whether in war or peace, we shall have to struggle with a rival nation, at present the most powerful in Europe, guided by the greatest genius in the world, who is as restless, ambitious, and artful, as he is superior in ability. We shall have to struggle also with numerous financial and commercial embarrassments.[22] This is, perhaps, the most critical aera in our history, and it will require the most skilful talents to carry us through it. That Mr. Addington is equal to the task, standing as he does, without system or principles to guide his conduct, embracing to day what he rejected yesterday, confounded by the least difficulty, a Tory one hour, a Whig the next, changing with every new breeze; that he is fit to guide the helm no man of sense will believe.[23] No Statesman can rely upon him, and happy is it for England that the defenders of our constitutional liberties have not joined his administration. Paradoxical as it may seem, happy is it also for England, that his talents are of such a very inferior class. Had he less vanity, he would have been more reserved, and have studiously avoided those prominent situations which have so frequently exposed the extent of his powers. Had he possessed a little judgment, he would not have so frequently committed himself on points in which victory

---

the question in moving" instead of "by moving". (The *idea* of a mind as a warehouse *containing* ideas, is C's, usually applied to Mackintosh; I take this as a bad imitation. That it got into general circulation is evident from Farington II 178, entry for 23 Dec 1803.) Of her transcript of the section from I 308 ("We have already hinted...") to 310 ("...theree is but one opinion") SC noted: "& this shews the paper to be not STC's". VCL MS LT 84.

22 C's note reads: "It is said that improsperous Taxes &c of Pitt".

23 "Staggering with inconstancy" seems to be C's note for this sentence. This too is a nauticl image: see *Alice du Clos* lines 54–9:a*PW* (EHC) I 471.

was nothing, and defeat was fatal to his fame. Had he been a dextrous debater, he might have preserved himself, even with all his deficiencies, safe and untouched in the sort of warfare in which he has been hitherto engaged, and against the sort of assailants whom he has had hitherto to encounter.

Thus we should be now upon a dangerous sea with the double disadvantage of a bad pilot, and that pilot possessed of our utmost confidence. With an implicit reliance upon his skill, we should perhaps know nothing of our danger until our ruin became inevitable. Thanks to the vanity, the precipitancy, and indiscretion of Mr. Addington, we have not these complicated disadvantages to encounter. After the decisive proofs which he has given of his weakness, proofs on which the meanest capacity can decide; the public neither has, or can have, confidence in his talents. They must, therefore, look to themselves; and, whatever may be its danger, whenever the vigilance of a nation is thus aroused, it will always find the means to work its own salvation.

[20 September 1802, Monday]

To-morrow a Comparison of the Roman Republic under the Caesars, with the French Republic under Bonaparte, to which we call particular attention.[1]

COMPARISON

OF THE PRESENT STATE OF FRANCE WITH THAT OF ROME UNDER JULIUS AND AUGUSTUS CAESAR.[1] I

21 September 1802, Tuesday; except "I", *M Post* title. *EOT* II 478–88, in SC's group of certain attributions, presumably based on signed clippings; authorship

[1] Two earlier notices, which apparently led to nothing, may have been wrong guesses by Stuart as to what C was preparing: "To-morrow we hope to be able to present some important facts respecting the late misunderstanding with France" (14 Sept); "The article to which we alluded... to-morrow" (15 Sept).

[1] Announced 20 Sept (and possibly, in vaguer wording, 14 and 15 Sept). C had already resumed verse contributions; see 6, 11, 16, 17 Sept (App D, below). Stuart, in a letter begun the day before, wrote: "You'll see in this Days Paper your Article on France & Rome.—I wish much for the other part." He received C's second instalment by 25 Sept, printing half of it that day and half the 29th. By then he had received the third instalment, which he printed 2 Oct. See letters of Stuart to C 20–3 and 29 Sept 1802, App B, below.

confirmed by Stuart's letters cf 20–3 and 29 Sept, App B, below. C reprinted extracts in *Friend* (1818) I 145–8 (cf *Friend—CC—*I 89–90).

As human nature is the same in all ages, similar events will of course take place under similar circumstances; but sometimes names will run parallel, and produce the appearance of a similarity, which does not really exist. Indeed, it is generally observable that the instances in which the names run the most parallel, are not those that will best stand the tests of inspection and analysis. An examination, however, should always be instituted. We discover something well worth the trouble employed, if we do no more than detect a common source of fallacy, more especially when there is reason to suspect that this coincidence of names has been adopted by design, and for political purposes. The least attentive observer of the political world cannot but have noticed the solicitude of the French Government to represent their country as a new Roman Republic.[2] France has its Consuls, its Tribunes, its Senate, its Proconsular Provinces, its dependent Free States and Allies, its obedient Kings. In a recent instance it has attempted to force its language upon Europe, as a general language of state, as the successor and substitute of the language of the former masters of mankind. In the same spirit the First Consul, in his late address to Mr. Fox, divides the whole world into two nations, the European and the Oriental,[3] even as under Augustus the world was considered as consisting of

[2] April news of the "wretched Business" of "the French Concordat" (see *CL* II 803) was followed in mid-May by news of Bonaparte's election as first consul for ten years and his having initiated a decree to seek election for life. On 21 May WW began his sonnet "I griev'd for Bonaparte". At about this time C made the ironic (or ambivalent) notebook entry: "A *Throne* the Δος που στω of Archimedes—Poet Bonaparte—". *CN* I 1166. He was soon formulating "the germinating question behind" the essays comparing France and Rome (and Greece). See *CN* I 1191, 1195, and nn. The idea that Addington was too small for the obelisk upon which the situation now elevated him, jotted near the "*Throne*" entry (*CN* I 1170), does not emerge in recognisable form in the *M Post*.

[3] On 15 Sept Napoleon addressed Fox to the effect "That there were in the world but two nations, the one of the East, the other of the West. The English, French, Germans, Italians, &c. under the same civil code, having the same manners . . . are all members of the same family, and the men who wish to light up again the flame of war among them, wish for civil war." The *M Chron* emphasised the pacific aspect of this remark; the *M Post* derided this aspect as "the fraternal hug . . . borrowed from Anacharsis Cloots" and stressed Bonaparte's wish to reduce Europe to one nation under France; it did Fox the honour of assuming he "must have sneered inwardly" and proposed suitably ironic remarks he might have made but for "too much politeness" (10, 18 Sept).

two parts, the Roman Empire and the Barbarians. In the same spirit, too, the finest parts of Europe have been pillaged in order to convert Paris into a new Rome, a metropolis of the civilized world, of this one great European nation; and the books, statues, and pictures of Italy have undergone the same fate from the French conquerors, which those of Greece formerly experienced under the Italian.[a]* As far as the ambition and ambitious designs of the two empires are concerned, we must confess the resemblance is strict and real, the analogy in all its parts exact.

If we inquire, to what period of the Roman history the present history of France assimilates itself, the answer may prove unpleasant

* Even in the circumstance of *imitation*, the parallel holds good. For if the French are imitating the Romans, it is equally as certain that the Romans imitated the Greeks; and that Caesar, Pompey, and their predecessors, acted on the plans of Philip and Alexander. To make one great nation of the civilised part of mankind, with one common language, and to use them as the engine of subjugating and civilising the barbarous nations, were the sanctifying pretexts of the Greek and Roman conquests. The very language of Bonaparte and Anacharsis Cloots[4] is borrowed from Pliny. Sparsa congregare Imperia, ritusque mollire, et tot populorum discordes ferasque linguas sermonis commercio contrahere ad colloquia, et humanitatem homini dare, breviterque una cunctarum gentium in toto orbe patria fieri. *Plin. Nat. Hist. lib. 3. cap. 5.*[5] If the Romans placed their deceased Emperors among the Gods, the flatterers of Bonaparte have not hesitated, even in his life time, to style him THE PROVIDENCE of Europe;[6] if it was said of the Roman Perpetual General First Consuls, that they were elected, not by the people, but by the active influence of the Gods (numine deorum electi), for the establishment of unity and civilisation among jarring nations, Bonaparte speaks of himself as a divine envoy for the same great purposes, as *called* by him from whom all things emanate.[7]

[a] *EOT*: Italians

[4] Jean Baptiste du Val-de-Grâce, Baron de Cloots (1755–94), "orator of the human race" who headed the thirty-six foreigners in 1790 joining in the Declaration of the Rights of Man and Citizen (whereupon he changed his title from Baron to Anacharsis). In 1792 he voted the King's death in the name of the human race; in 1794 he was guillotined as an Hébertist.

[5] Pliny the Elder *Naturalis historia* 3.5.39 (C has changed Pliny's subjunctives to infinitives). "[A land... chosen by the providence of the gods to make heaven itself more glorious,] to unite scattered empires, to make manners gentle, to draw together in converse by community of language the jarring and uncouth tongues of so many nations, to give mankind civilisation, and in a word to become throughout the world the single fatherland of all the races". Tr H. Rackham (LCL 10 vols 1937–63) II 31–3. C is perhaps following up a reference to Gibbon *Decline and Fall* ch 2 (I 45 and n), in which Gibbon cites "Pliny *Hist. Nat.* iii. 5" as a note to his passage on the language of the provinces.

[6] See *Courier* 19 Apr 1811 and n 16, below.

[7] C is adapting the Pliny passage just quoted; the bracketed Latin words describe the land of Italy as "chosen by the providence of the gods"; C makes it the consuls.

to the new Roman Republic; but it is not the less true. If it resemble any period at all, it must be that when Rome ceased to be a Republic, and the Government was organized into a masked and military despotism (a despotism with a frightful half-mask on its face), when the sovereign power was repeatedly and ostentatiously affirmed to reside in the people, but the right of exercising it suspended for ever, when the popular elections were transferred to a trembling Senate, and all the powers of Consul, Tribune, and Generalissimo, centered in one person. Here indeed the points of apparent resemblance are sufficiently obvious. And surely it cannot be indifferent either to Europe or to France itself, whether there be *any* real resemblance; and if that cannot be denied nor softened down, whether it be a total or only a partial resemblance, whether they are to produce the same effects, to possess the same duration. No! It cannot be indifferent either to Englishmen or Frenchmen, whether the new Caesar * be likely to transmit his power to other Tiberiuses, Caligulas, Claudiuses, Neros, Vitelliuses, and Domitians, till such time as Providence shall have peopled and disciplined the [g]limitless desarts[h]

* It would be too great a digression to inquire, at present, which of the three first Caesars we mean, when, in imitation of his late addressers,[a] we style Bonaparte the new Caesar. His character comprises in it many of the good, and some of the bad, traits of all the three. If in courage, splendour of military fame, and[b] military success and conduct, and the love of science, he recall Julius to our memory; if he remind us of Augustus in his close application to public business, and his encouragement of the liberal arts, and great public works, we must at the same time admit, that he has likewise the imperious, irritable, and ostentatious mind of the former with the constitutional coldness and politic craft of the latter. But if reserve, if darkness, if the employment of spies and informers, if dread and hatred of all political discussions, if vindictive hatred of all bold political writings, if an indifference to all religions, except as instruments of state policy, with a certain strange and dark superstition respecting Fate, a blind confidence in his Destinies—if these be any parts of the Chief Consul's character, they would force upon us, even against our own will, the name and history of Tiberius.—Vide Suetonius, lib. 3. Tib. Caesar, passim. Non modo morosus, sed praetrepidus quoque, si qua famosa de se scripta[c], imo, versiculi, facti—animadversum est[d] in auctores, &c. scriptaque abolita—Nemini delatorum fides abrogatur.[e] Circa Deos et[f] Religiones negligentior, *persuasionisque plenus, cuncta Fato agi.*[8]

[a] *EOT*: addresses [b] *EOT*: in [c] *EOT*: ac suis carmina [d] *EOT*: est statim [e] *EOT*: abrogata. [f] *EOT*: ac [g–h] *EOT*: limited deserts

[8] Suetonius *Lives of the Caesars* III: *Tiberius*—rearranged passages (var) from §§ 63, 28, 59, 61, 69, in that order. "[He was] not only irritable but also extremely frightened; if anything libellous was composed about him, even trifling verses, the writers were at once put to death, &c., and their works destroyed—The word of no informer was doubted—[He was] somewhat negligent of the gods and of religious matters, *and firmly convinced that everything was in the hands of Fate*". Tr adapted from J. C. Rolfe (LCL 2 vols 1914) I 383, 335, 377, 379, 391.

of Russia and Asiatic Tartary, and a new deluge from the north sweep away slaves and dwarfs,[9] and put men and freemen in their places.

First, then, it cannot be denied that some resemblance does really exist. The prodigious influx of new wealth from the Asiatic conquests unsettled the balance of property in Rome, and of course the very foundations of the Roman Constitution. The same revolution was produced in France by the commercial spirit, and[a] consequent prosperity, political importance, and increased size and population of cities. In both Empires the spread of arts, sciences, eloquence, and free thinking, had been accompanied by luxury, of the most criminal kinds, corruption of domestic morals, venality, and[b] an inordinate overgrowth of social vanity, and a general contempt of the religious creeds and establishments of their ancestors. Both in France [c]and Rome[d] the metaphysics and ethics of Epicurus had become the fashionable philosophy among the wealthy and powerful; a philosophy which regards man as a mere machine, a sort of living automaton, which teaches that pleasure is the sole good, and a prudent calculation of enjoyment the only virtue.[10] In both States the people had been agitated by the wildest and most unprincipled demagogues, and projects of Agrarian Laws set afloat, to raise the people against the natural aristocracy[11] of the state, and consequently to throw them into the arms of a military despot. In both countries proscriptions, and tumults, and the most shameless venality had made the very name of liberty odious, and the vices of the leaders of all parties had introduced into the minds even of good men a despair of the Republic, and a disposition to submit to the sober despotism

[a] *EOT*: and the [b] *EOT* omits [c–d] *M Post* lacks [supplied from *EOT*]

[9] A snigger at Napoleon's smallness; cf the contrast of Washington to this "dwarf", 25 Mar 1800, above. C's passage seems reminiscent of Gibbon ch 2, which opens with a reference to "the sovereign of the Russian deserts [who] commands a larger portion of the globe [than ancient Rome]" (I 34)—cf C's "limitless desarts of Russia"—and ends (I 71): "...and the Roman world was indeed peopled by a race of pygmies; when the fierce giants of the north broke in, and mended the puny breed. They restored a manly spirit of freedom...".

[10] Cf Gibbon ch 2 (I 66) on Epicurus. C makes a distinction between Epicurus and his followers in LRR: *Lects 1795* (*CC*) 157. On Epicurus and Epicureanism see also *P Lects* Lect VI (1949) 212–18.

[11] For a recent and very different view of the aristocracy, see what crossed C's mind while attending a chemistry lecture on 6 Feb 1802: "If all aristocrats here, how easily Davy might poison them all—". *CN* I 1098 f 31.

of any individual, rather than the mad tyranny of a multitude. The distant conquests in Gaul and the Asiatic provinces had effected that in Rome, which the long and desperate war with all Europe had more rapidly brought about in France; the affections and duties of the soldiery were gradually weaned from the laws and free legislatures of their country, and transferred to their Generals. This is the common and natural course of political contests: they begin in *principles*, and end in *men*.

In France all these events followed each other more rapidly than in Rome; but the events themselves are the same. The admission of all the Italian States to the citizenship of Rome, and[a] the right of voting in the Campus Martius, was the same both in its own nature and in its consequences with that right of universal suffrage, which was passed into a fundamental law of the French Constitution by the Brissotines. Thus[b] all the elements of a military despotism were thrown together.—The soldiery in the course of so wild a war would necessarily grow into the knowledge and feeling of their own power; and a promiscuous mob in the mean time were called forth to overawe, oppress, and render contemptible the Legislature, and by all possible follies and excesses to afford the soldiery a pretext for the exercise of that power. Happily for France, Dumouriez antedated his plans, and happily both for France and for himself, Moreau appears to possess neither the impulses nor the talents requisite for political intrigue;[12] or the armies of the Rhine with those of the Interior, and those of Italy and Egypt, might play over again the parts of the Gallic and Asiatic Legions under Pompey and Julius, and France boast a new Pharsalia as an accompaniment of her new Caesar. The pressure of foreign enemies, from which Rome was altogether exempt, has been, in this respect at least, as fortunate for France, as it has proved luckless to England and Austria: its Republic has been changed into an empire without a civil war among its own generals. It has, however, been changed by the same steps as the

[a] *EOT*: and to [b] *EOT*: For thus

[12] Charles François Dumouriez (1739–1823), intriguing general of the French armies in 1792–3, whose goal had been to restore power to the King —or to seize it for himself in Napoleonic fashion—had attempted in 1793 to turn his troops against Paris and been compelled to flee to Austria. (By Aug 1803 and perhaps earlier he was secretly advising the British.) Moreau (see 6 Jan 1800) was a cautious and apparently stolid general in the campaigns of 1800–1, but in Feb 1804 in Paris he would be discovered in a British-supported conspiracy to "remove" the First Consul and lead a royalist uprising. Pragmatically, neither of these generals possessed "the talents requisite".

Roman Republic was, and under the same titles and phrases: only, as before, differing in the degrees of rapidity with which the same processes have been accomplished. The reigns of the three first Caesars have been crowded into the three first years of the reign of Bonaparte. He began by imitating the decency and decorous ambition of Augustus, who caused himself to be elected the First Magistrate of the Republic for ten years only, and at the expiration of that time[a] was re-elected. A shew of free-voting was at the same time allowed to the people. But Bonaparte soon found the bold and contemptuous impetuosity of Julius Caesar more accordant with his natural inclinations, and probably more flattering to his vanity, as well as more agreeable to his pride. In exact imitation of Julius Caesar he assumed the perpetual consulship with the imperatorial power, and the prefix of General, and appointed two Consuls in subordination to him. *Binos Consules substituit sibi* (*Suet Lib. I. Jul. Caesar*),[13] and he assumed it in nearly the same forms. The votes of the soldiers were taken, as of the army, and Bonaparte is fully entitled to proclaim his election[b] in the very words of the old Roman Emperors, "Delectu Militum, et authoritate patrum,"—by the choice of the soldiery and the assent of the senate.[14] Nor would it be difficult to discover in the biographies of Julius Caesar, striking*[c]

* Imitators succeed better in copying the vices than the excellences of their archetypes. Where shall we find in the First Consul of France a counterpart to the generous and dreadless clemency of Caesar?[d] Acerbe loquentibus satis habuit pro concione denunciare, ne perseverarent, Aulique Caecinae criminosissimo libro, et Pitholai carminibus maledicentissimis laceratam existimationem suam civili animo tulit.[15]

It deserves translation, for our English readers. "If any spoke bitterly against him, he held it sufficient to complain of it publicly, to prevent them from persevering in the use of such language. His character had been mangled in a most libellous work of Aulus Caecina, and he had been grossly lampooned in some verses by Pitholaus; but he bore both with the temper of a good citizen."

For this part of the First Consul's character, if common report speaks the truth,[16] we must seek a parallel in the dispositions of the third Caesar, who

[a] *EOT*: period [b] *M Post*: elections [corrected in *EOT*]
[c] *EOT* places C's footnote below, after "Bonaparte" (p 319 n *b*) [d] *EOT*: the first Caesar?

[13] Suetonius 1.76. "He substituted two consuls for himself." Tr Rolfe I 101. C misunderstands the Latin; Caesar in fact resigned the consulship in this year.

[14] Gibbon (ch 3) says: "The emperor was elected by *the authority of the senate* and *the consent of the soldiers*" (I 89), citing Tacitus 13.4 in a footnote. If C had looked up Tacitus he would have found: "de auctoritate patrum et consensu militum", but he appears simply to have composed his own Latin version and then translated it.

[15] Suetonius *Lives* I: *Julius Caesar* 75.5. C's tr follows.

[16] C does not write as though he knew his own ox had yet been gored; it is odd, if C at this time knew (as he

parallels to the fierce and intemperate speeches with which his imitator has threatened all who attempted to make a shadow of opposition to his measures.

The result of the whole is plainly this: that at present the French Constitution is precisely the same with that of the Roman empire under the Caesars;[17] and that this revolution has been brought about by similar causes. In both all effective power and patronage are in the hands of the General of the State, who has the privilege of recommending and finally appointing his own successor. In both the soldiers are to be kept, if possible, in decent awe, by the image of a civil Government, while all the powers of that Government, not included in those of the *Imperator et Consul Perpetuus*, are palsied by the dread of the soldiery.

If then there be no counterpoise of dissimilar circumstances, the prospect is gloomy indeed. The commencement of the public slavery in Rome was in the most splendid aera of human genius. Any unusually flourishing period of the arts and sciences in any country, is, even to this day, called the Augustan age of that country. The Roman poets, the Roman historians, the Roman orators, rivalled

---

dreaded the pen of a paragraph writer, [a]who hinted[b] aught against his morals and measures, with as great anxiety, and with as vindictive feelings, as if it had been the dagger of an assassin lifted up against his life. From the third Caesar, too, he adopted the abrogation of all popular elections.

[a-b] *EOT*: hinting

---

claimed in 1803 to have known almost "immediately") that Bonaparte had inquired about his own paragraphs in 1800, for C to allude here so impersonally to "common report". See 19 Mar 1800 n 17, above.

[17] The present essays constitute a sequel to the series of 1799–1800 on the French Constitution and use some of the same language and ideas; indeed, C's constitutional views show only a slight change: it is their context, including C's evaluation of Bonaparte, that now differs. For a striking statement of C's new view of Bonaparte and of his own earlier essays, see his note on Godwin's statement, in *Thoughts Occasioned by the Perusal of Dr. Parr's Spital Sermon* (1801) 6–7, that "the future Government of France will be popular, and her people free": "!!—Let not these!! be deemed the Sneer of after-wit—but see the Morning Post, then the sturdy adherent of Liberty, from the very day Buonaparte entered the Seat of Legislature to the promulgation of his constitution. In those essays it was demonstrated that the reign of pure despotism, (the worst of all pure despotism, military despotism) had commenced—& that all the preceding victories of Humanity ('all the great points embraced by the revolution' &c) remained only to be transmuted into the most direful means or facilitations of a bloody Ambition, a limitless Tyranny.—" *CM* (ms).

those of Greece; in military tactics, in machinery, in all the conveniences of private life, they[a] greatly surpassed the Greeks. With few exceptions, all the Emperors, even the worst of them, were, like Bonaparte,[b] the liberal encouragers of all great public works, and of every species of public merit not connected with the assertion of political freedom.

——O Juvenes, circumspicit et agitat vos,
Materiamque sibi Ducis indulgentia quaerit.[18]

It is even so, at this present moment, in France. Yet both in France and in Rome, we have learned, that the most abject dispositions[c] to slavery rapidly trod on the heels of the most outrageous fanaticism for an almost anarchical liberty.[19] *Ruere in servitium patres et populum.*[20] Peace and the coadunation of all the civilised provinces of the earth, were the grand and plausible pretexts of Roman despotism; the degeneracy of the human species itself, in all the nations so blended, was the melancholy effect.[d] To-morrow,[21] therefore, we shall endeavour to detect all those points and circumstances of dissimilarity, which, though they cannot impeach the rectitude of the parallel, for the present, may yet render it probable, that as the same Constitution of Government has been built up in France with incomparably greater rapidity, so it may have an incomparably shorter duration. We are not conscious of any feelings of bitterness towards the First Consul; or, if any, only that venial prejudice, which naturally results from the having hoped proudly of any individual, and the having been miserably disappointed.[22] But we will not voluntarily cease to think freely and speak openly. We owe grateful hearts, and uplifted hands of thanksgiving to the Divine Providence, that there is yet one European country (and that country our own) in which the actions of public men may be boldly

[a] *EOT*: the Romans [b] *EOT* attaches C's footnote here (see above) [c] *EOT*: disposition
[d] *M Post*: effects [corrected in *EOT*]

[18] Juvenal *Satires* 7.20–1 (var as in Gibbon ch 2, I 70n). "O young men! your Prince is looking around and goading you on, seeking productions worth his favour". Adapted from G. G. Ramsay (LCL 1918) 139.

[19] Woodring (p 217) notes that here C "traced with severity a curve that he fancifully decorated and prettified in *Zapolya*" (in celebration of Napoleon's overthrow).

[20] Tacitus *Annals* 1.7 (var). Tr: "Senators and people were rushing into slavery". Apparently not in Gibbon; used by C again in the *Courier* 29 Jun 1811 (see below).

[21] Four days later, on Saturday.

[22] Cf WW's confession of vain grief for Bonaparte; the date of intense Napoleonic sympathies is not indicated, but a safe conjecture would be 1799.

analysed, and the result publicly stated. And let the Chief Consul, who professes in all things to follow his FATE, learn to submit to it, if he finds that it is still his FATE to struggle with the spirit of English freedom, and the virtues which are the offspring of that spirit! If he finds, that the GENIUS of GREAT BRITAIN, which blew up his Aegyptian navy into the air, and blighted his Syrian laurels,[23] still follows him with a calm and dreadful eye; and in peace, equally as in war, still watches for that liberty, in which alone the Genius of our Isle lives, and moves, and has his being;[24] and which being lost, all our commercial and naval greatness would instantly languish, like a flower, the root of which had been silently eat away by a worm; and without which, in any country, the public festivals, and pompous merriments of a nation, present no other spectacle to the eye of Reason, than a mob of Maniacs dancing in their fetters.[25]

(*To be continued To-morrow.*)[26]

[23] Referring to Nelson's destruction of the French fleet in Aboukir Bay, Aug 1798, and the halting of Bonaparte's Syrian campaign at Acre in Apr 1799.

[24] Cf Acts 17.28.

[25] C in this paragraph has changed greatly from the lone watchman of the *Ode on the Departing Year* who warned his "mother Isle" that her ruin would come from her having offended the "Spirit of the Earth". Now identifying himself with the Genius of that Isle, he can see that the Isle and the Spirit are one; the "commercial prosperity" that seemed in 1799 a "pig cutting its own throat" (*The Devil's Walk*) has become "our commercial and naval greatness" and a flower of the tree of liberty.

[26] Continued 25 Sept. In the intervening days precedence was given to "Garnerin's Balloon and Parachute", the cord of which was held by Mrs Sheridan, and a "Diving Machine" at Ranelagh. But Stuart, though reserving C's articles "for such days as I stand in need of matter" (letter of 29 Sept), gave the series great prominence. He expected C to perceive, from "the way I insert it", that he admired the first essay "Extremely" (letter of 20–3 Sept). By Thursday he could report that it had been "much admired by" James Mackintosh, Jean Peltier, editor of the French royalist journal, *L'Ambigu*, clandestinely printed in London (see 25 Sept, n 7, below), and "many others you dont know". Indeed, by 29 Sept Stuart could report that "Peltier is translating it for his Journal". Cf Stuart to C 20–3 and 29 Sept 1802, App B, below. (For a cynical comment on Jean Gabriel Peltier—1770–1825—a year later cf *CN* I 1423.) No translation of or reference to C's series has been found.

COMPARISON
OF THE PRESENT STATE OF FRANCE WITH THAT OF ROME UNDER JULIUS AND AUGUSTUS CAESAR. II[1]

(*Continued from our Paper of Tuesday last*)

25 September 1802, Saturday; except "II", *M Post* title. *EOT* II 489–99, with revisions that may have been made by C on the clippings presumably used by SC: see textual notes.

DOES there exist any real resemblance between the present Empire and Government of France, under Bonaparte, and the Empire and Government of Rome, under the three first Caesars? This is the question, which we proposed to the attention of our Readers, in our Tuesday's paper; and (if we do not grossly deceive ourselves) we fully proved, that it must be answered in the affirmative. We are confident, that no Englishman will be weak enough to ask us, whether we have not forgotten the Cantonal Assemblies, the Electoral Colleges, the Tribunate, and the Legislature, of France. [a]All these will do no more than recal, perhaps, to the minds of some of our Readers, the old trick, which exercises the ingenuity, and excites the surprise, of *very young* children, when they first learn the rudiments of arithmetic. Take any number you like! (*there is the freedom of election*) add 12 to it! (*That* MUST *be done*) then double the whole. Thus doubled, halve it: then double it again: then halve it again: *then subtract your original number*, and there remains 12!! In all the movements of the present French Constitution, the trick is equally palpable, and vastly more tedious.[b][2] It is capable of demonstration, that the First Consul might as well nominate the Legislature and Tribunate in the first instance. We know of no end, that can be answered by the labyrinthine and improgressive steps of his tiresome figure-dance, but simply this: Frenchmen may be *idle*, but will never be *indolent*—wherein, Heaven be praised! they are the very antithesis of Englishmen, who think it wiser to do *nothing*, than *Nothings*,[3] and might possibly endure, for a little while, to be *slaves*, but never, never to be *puppets!* Notwithstanding, therefore, the whole Senatus Consultum of August the 4th, with all its TEN

[a–b] *EOT* prints as footnote to the word "France"

[1] For verses on 23 and 24 Sept signed ΕΣΤΗΣΕ see App D, below.

[2] Cf *CN* I 1.

[3] Cf *CN* I 1087: "better to do nothing than nothings—".

TITLES,[4] we persevere* in affirming, that in no essential point does the present Government and Constitution of France differ from that of Rome, under Julius, Augustus, and Tiberius. The effective offices of the

* We have made no mere *assertions*: we have adduced the instances and the proofs. If we be accurate, it would be worthy the magnanimity of the imitator of Alexander and Julius Caesar to suppress the anger, which an inconvenient truth is apt to excite. If we be deceived, let his official Journalists detect and expose our errors or blunders, in the spirit of freemen. It is easy to forgive accusations that are altogether unfounded. Many Englishmen were made merry, but none angry, by the article in the *Moniteur* of the 9th [8th] of August; because none of us have been led by it ever to suspect that Mr. Pitt and his colleagues "excited the massacres of September," or "encouraged the fabricator of the infernal machine:"[5] and because a vast majority of us are obstinate enough not to believe, though the First Consul himself assures us of it, "that the French Government is now more *stable* than the English." The First Consul himself believes it, of course, for he asserts it. But yet, if we may judge by the irritation and alarm which a few squibs in a foreign newspaper have awakened in our new Caesar, his faith resembles that of the ambitious beings mentioned in Scripture—he "*believes and trembles*;"[6] or perhaps it is a sort of ague faith, in which the hot fit is regularly followed by a cold one. One thing seriously astonishes us; how, after the infamous article in the *Moniteur* of the 9th of August, and the abusive libels that followed it in all the other French Papers, the complaint against the English Papers could have been received by our Ministry with common patience.[7]

[4] The rewriting of the Constitution of the Year VIII began with the introduction by Portalis (see below) in Nov 1801 of titles of a new Civil Code, which the Legislature rejected. On 4 Aug 1802 the Senatus Consultum that proclaimed Bonaparte First Consul for life also adopted ten titles (laws) that altered the Constitution in the direction of making the citizens spectators for life. A kind of monarchy or nobility (with a Legion of Honour) was established. The First Consul could name colleagues, choose his successor, and appoint forty members of the Senate and prescribe the subjects on which they could deliberate. The people could vote only for members of Electoral Colleges, who retained office for life and presented the Senate with lists of candidates; from these the Senate elected the Legislature and the Tribunate and its own members (except for the appointed forty).

[5] See n 7, below.

[6] Cf James 2.19: "...the devils also believe, and tremble".

[7] Despite the definitive signing of the treaty of Amiens, 27 Mar, belligerent abuse had continued between the London and Paris newspapers, with occasional protests by the French government and protestations of helplessness on the part of Ministers (though most of the violent papers, such as the *émigré* Peltier's *L'Ambigu, or Atrocious and Amusing Varieties*, had government support). The *Moniteur* of 8 Aug (not "9th") complained of "perpetual invectives against France" in a paper "under the Ministerial interest", *The Times*, and accused the English of sheltering intriguing *émigré* bishops, condemned murderers, rapists, and arsonists, and decorating Georges Cadoudal "as a recompense for the infernal machine", a mine that, on 24 Dec 1800, had missed Bonaparte but killed thirty Paris citizens. London papers responded on the 13th; one government paper, the *True Briton*, actually moderated its tone (Addington having privately told the editor that a recent paragraph was "abominable"), but others responded like sharks to blood. Stuart defended the "truth and independence" of *The Times* (with

state are in the same manner concentered to one person:[8] his power is built up upon the same foundations, his ambition directed to the same objects, and *attempted* to be justified by the same pretexts.

We proceed, therefore, to examine the second question. If, then, the resemblance between the *Government* of France at present, and that of Rome under the Caesars, be both real and strict, is there *any* resemblance between the *circumstances* of the two Empires? (the circumstances, we mean, both external and internal). And if this cannot be denied, are there not likewise some important circumstances of dissimilarity, that must act as a counterpoise to the partial

---

finger to nose, for he had just called it a paper "which can whisper the whole Ministry" [5 Aug]). On the 14th William Cobbett, in his new *Political Register*, undercut the pieties of Stuart and argued that the *True Briton* and *The Times* were all too subservient to their ministerial paymasters, cowed by "the impudence and insolence of the upstart Corsican . . .". (C took up the latter epithet, and SC thought him its coiner.)

The next step was police action in Paris. On the 25th the *M Post* discovered "that the French Government had...given orders to seize all the English newspapers received in the coffee-houses" precisely on the day that the newspapers of 13 Aug reached Paris, "so that it is highly probable that these very remarks" of the *M Post* and other "English journalists" "might have been the occasion even of this strong step . . .". It would be easy for a faithful reader of the *M Post* to suppose that his editor's goad was drawing blood from the French monster, just as it would later be easy for C to suppose (see below) that the really effective lances hurled were *his*.

For Cobbett's account of the chastening of the *True Briton*, see *Cobbett's Political Works* ed John M. and James P. Cobbett (1835) I 262–9, and George Pellew *Life of Sidmouth* (1847) II 157. Cobbett's story (I 263n) of Otto's applying in Feb 1801 to the English government to quell *him* for "his satires on the great conqueror" sounds suspiciously like C's later account of Otto's application to Stuart (see 19 Mar 1800 n 16, above). It may have suggested some elements of C's anecdote—or on the other hand it may be taken as evidence that Bonaparte and Otto did indeed meddle in the affairs of London papers.

In 1814, when C was lecturing in Bristol on Milton, he gave his audiences to understand (in the words of *Felix Farley's Bristol Journal* for 16 Apr 1814) "...that it was Mr. Coleridge, who wrote those essays and leading paragraphs in the *Morning Post* during the treacherous Peace of Amiens, which procured for all the English Newspapers, except the *Morning Chronicle*, the honour of exclusion from France; and which, as Mr. Fox asserted, produced the war with France, that war which has liberated Europe and human nature. Since that time Mr. Coleridge has not ceased to fight the same good fight; and as he informed us in his Lectures, in consequence, when he was on the Continent, his life was hunted for by the blood-thirsty tyrant, an order for his arrest was sent by express to Rome, and he escaped only by the providential favour of a noble Italian". See also App B, below (ms of Jul 1817), and *BL* (1847) I 340–1.

On the story of C's "escape" from Rome, see 9 Nov 1802 n 12, below.

[8] C is now using the arguments of Pitt's speech of 17 Feb 1800.

resemblance? And which forebode to the military despotism of France a duration as brief, as its rise has been rapid?

That *some* circumstances of resemblance exist in the manners, morals, and revolutionary events of the Roman and French people, we conceive ourselves to have proved satisfactorily, at the same time that we substantiated the *entire* resemblance of the two Governments. Yes, *some* circumstances of likeness assuredly there are, and these not minute, not unalarming, but of a nature that calls upon all Europe, and, above all, on Great Britain, to be always watchful, always on the guard. We must be jealous of the progress of their truly slavish language among us; we must be detectors and detesters of their mock philosophy, of their false and boastful pretensions in science and literature, equally as in politics.[9] In war, whenever it becomes inevitable,[10] we will be, as ever, their controlling and thwarting genius; in peace their monitor, and outward conscience. All this our national fear, equally with our national pride, demands of us. Having stated this, we turn to the more pleasant task of pointing out those circumstances of dissimilarity between the French and Roman Empires, which, though they cannot and must not take aught from that degree of alarm, which is necessary to watchfulness, yet present sufficient of hope to preserve us from dejection.[11]

First, then, it is some little at least in favour of mankind, that there has pre-existed a state of things similar to the present state of France. We have the example, and warning experience of Rome, familiar to us from our school-days; and we would fain hope, that facts do not accumulate altogether to no purpose—that experience will not be always like the lights in the stern of the vessel, illumining the tract only which we have already passed over;[12] that the human race will not always, like poor moths, fly headlong into a flame, that is already choked and bedimmed with the wings and half-burnt limbs of their predecessors. However, as we may always

9 Here emerges the most striking change in C's views. Even as recently as in the Addington essay of 22 Mar he remained an English "Jacobin" in the sense that he was still a "Friend of Freedom" rejecting the slippery path of accommodation to anti-Jacobinism; now he views French Jacobinism with alarm.

10 In these words C is doing just what, in 3 Dec 1801, he had feared Windham might do.

11 C's *Dejection* ode, written in April, would shortly appear in the *M Post*, 14 Oct.

12 C is reusing the metaphors of his 1799–1800 essays. The "figure-dance" above comes from 27 Dec 1799, above, to be repeated in *Friend* No 6 (1809) (*CC*) II 85 and *LR* I 249; the stern lights from 2 Jan 1800, above, to be used again in *Friend* No 7 (1809) (*CC*) II 106; cf *TT* 18 Dec 1831.

calculate with more safety on the folly than on the wisdom of nations, we lay no stress on this; but we consider the second point of unlikeness as really important. France has not the same justification which Rome had, either for her ambition, with regard to surrounding nations, or for the despotism of her internal government. And as all national justification must rest mainly on the existing state of mankind, what cannot be justified cannot be permanent. Rome was really an enlightener and civiliser of the world. The free Greeks had done something, and not much, by their colonies—[a](we may, indeed,[b] consider Rome itself as a Grecian colony). Alexander and the enslaved Greeks, like Bonaparte and his enslaved Savans, boasted much, and planned much, and did almost nothing.[13]—But Rome did really spread civilisation, sciences, and the humanising comforts of social life, over amazing tracts of country, and was the cause of the facility with which that religion was propagated over Europe, Africa, and Asia, to which we ourselves owe all we enjoy, in the purity of our domestic manners, and all we dare hope for in the ultimate improvement of the species. France has no claim of this nature. In the neighbouring nations of Sweden, Denmark, Holland, Germany, Switzerland, and Great Britain, it finds a race of men more moral, and better informed, than its own people (we speak of the mass of each nation); and, in proportion to the population of the different countries, at least an equal number of eminently enlightened individuals. To the South, Italy is somewhat, perhaps, but not greatly, inferior to France. Spain and Portugal are, indeed, wofully inferior; but it is a well-known fact, that it has been the constant policy and effort of Republican France, to prevent civilisation and liberty from spreading among those two unhappy kingdoms. Were they free, and well informed, they would soon present that bulwark against the ambition of France on the South, which Germany would *now* offer on the North, if only she were as united, as she is brave and enlightened. To all the grand purposes of civilisation and science, Europe, and European America, are already one people, beyond the most boastful dream of Roman pride. What would mankind gain, by turning this brotherhood in science and manners, into a political amalgamation? We should exchange national wars for civil wars. We should sink into barbarism from slavery,[c] into discord from barbarism; and thus, sacrifice our close union, as men, to an appearance of alliance, as citizens. Neither has France the same

[a–b] *EOT*: (unless, indeed, we [c] *M Post*: slaves [corrected in *EOT*]

[13] See *CN* I 1191 for an association between Alexander and Aristotle's *Politics*.

excuse with Rome for the despotism of her Government. In those feudal institutions, which her shallow mock-statesmen have now made the objects of an hostile oath, she had links of social subordination, a happy intertexture[14] of the interests and property of the state, which was in vain to be sought for in the original Constitution of Rome, in which every rich proprietor was regarded as an illegal oppressor; and that Agrarian Law was necessary for Rome, as a Republic, which would have destroyed it, as a society. And though, before the usurpation of the Caesars, the City of Rome, and the free inhabitants of the Italian States, enjoyed a sort of tumultuary liberty, yet the Empire at large was miserably oppressed; every blood-stained and rapacious Pro-Consul could be brought to trial only before his accomplices; and, it is an undoubted fact, that the Emperors, while they enslaved the city, alleviated the slavery of the provinces. But these circumstances are wholly foreign to France, considered as a mighty nation composed of Frenchmen. Her *true* Empire exists in herself; it is, indeed, one and indivisible, because it is composed of men, who have the same manners, the same language; and is not like the Roman Empire, a gorgeous robe of patch-work.—The provinces were the very body and limbs of the Roman Empire, but they are only the *wens* and diseases of the French. Rome *could* not continue free, because she *consisted* of incongruous parts; the liberty of the people was sacrificed to the life of the Empire. France *is* not free, because she has wilfully *incrusted* herself with an heterogeneous compound; in all the petty States, which she has bound to[a] herself, she has bound chains and fetters *around* herself. The soldiers, that enslaved Rome, were the natural and necessary parents of the Roman Empire; in France their power was originally *created* by the mad fear and rage of Great Britain, and her allies, at the commencement of the French Republic, and they are *continued* by the mad ambition of France itself, and at this moment rendered necessary only by reluctant and useless dependencies, by justly alarmed neighbours, and by the deep domestic discontents, of which the military despotism is itself the chief cause. Rome, in short, was *precipitated* by vice and corruptions into the slavery, [b]which suited[c] the nature of her empire; France, by the same vices and corruptions, into a slavery, which (as we shall shew hereafter) will under-

[a] *EOT*: *to*   [b–c] *EOT*: which, suited to

[14] Here C appears to lament not only Napoleon but the French Revolution; but below he will pull out the plum of Representative Government, free of equalitarian notions or universal suffrage.

mine her false power, and thereby bring her within the possibility of freedom.

To these considerations we must add the modern improvement in the science of politics, by the discovery of *Government by popular representation*; the great rule and law of which is, that it shall recede from universal suffrage, as the state of property in the nation to be represented recedes from the subdivisions of Agrarian equality.[15] It must appear strange to us, that so simple and natural an idea did not suggest itself to the antients; that it was never conceived, for instance, by the Antonini, who assuredly were not deficient in fervent desires for the liberty of Rome. But, perhaps, it is less strange than that neither Greece nor Rome discovered the art of printing,[16] the general idea of which is so simple, that Cicero stumbled upon it in a mere metaphorical illustration.[17] The difficulty is, indeed, much more readily solved in the one instance than in the other. For all the republics of Greece were *cities*, and at first not very large cities. Of course there was no[a] apparent necessity for representation: they would be as little likely to fall upon, or to approve, the idea, as the inhabitants of Westminster to approve the plan of choosing electoral colleges, instead of themselves choosing their own members by their own votes. What the cities of Greece always were, Rome was for a long time. Happy it would have been for her, if the plan of representation had been suggested and adopted, at the time of the admission of the Italian States to the right of suffrage; but who could have persuaded the citizens of Rome to have abandoned their own old custom and right of exercising the supreme power in their own persons; and for the Italian States to have sent representatives, while every Roman citizen voted in person, would have been infinitely more ridiculous and disproportionate than the number of

[a] *EOT*: an

[15] Cf 7 Dec 1799, above, in which there is still a trace of "aspheterism" in the proviso that property should *circulate*.

[16] C knew an economic reason: "the multitude of Slaves, & the circumstance that the manuscript Trade was in the Hands of the wealthiest Nobles". To RS 12 Mar 1803, *CL* II 936.

[17] Cicero *De natura deorum* 2.37.93. ". . . if a countless number of copies of the one-and-twenty letters of the alphabet, made of gold or what you will, were thrown together into some receptacle and then shaken out on the ground, it would be possible that they should produce the *Annals* of Ennius, all ready for the reader". Tr Rackham (LCL) 213. C's associating this passage with the invention of printing is probably owing directly or indirectly to an essay on the subject by John Toland in *A Collection of Several Pieces* (2 vols 1726, reissued as *The Miscellaneous Works* 2 vols 1747) quoting Cicero in I 298. C was arguing on the subject with RS the following year: see *CL* II 935–6.

Scotch Peers in our British House of Lords. Under the Empire, when the popular Assemblies ceased altogether, this objection of course no longer existed; but now the other Provinces of the Empire were more nearly on an equality, both in rights and pretensions with the Italian States. They of course would have claimed the privilege of sending Members to their Imperial Parliament; and it is highly probable, that a Parliament elected fairly from all the Provinces of the Roman Empire would have exhibited too jarring an assemblage of manners and interests, for the dignity or safety of the Empire. It is said, that this is felt in a slight degree, even in the American Congress at present, where all the difference is effected by the different climate and consequent modification of manners and opinions. None of these difficulties exist in France.[a] Imperfect as our representation is, we still have become a great and flourishing people under its auspicious influence. In America, where the nature of the property permits, and, indeed, commands a much more extensive right of suffrage, than any wise man would wish in England or France,[18] the result is equally in favour of a Representative Legislature. The Americans are neither very amiable nor very enlightened, as a people; yet what Government on earth has presented such continued proofs of wisdom, moderation, and love of Peace? Nothing can be conceived more violent than the contentions of the Candidates, nothing more [b]calm, dignified, and incurable,[c] than the conduct of the same men, as Legislators and Magistrates.[19] France therefore cannot justify her despotism by the same necessity as Rome could; and if this be true, Frenchmen will, and do, feel it to be truth; and the despotism, which cannot be justified—cannot be permanent.[20] (*To be continued.*)

[28 September 1802, Tuesday]

The continuation of the Comparison between the French and Roman Republics To-morrow certainly.

---

[a] *EOT* adds (possibly from a ms addition by C): The system has been tried in her presence, and its excellence proved before her own eyes.

[b–c] *EOT*: calm and dignified

[18] Cf 7 Dec 1799 and 25 Mar 1800, above.

[19] Cf *Watchman* No 6 (*CC*) 212.

[20] See above, par 4, sentence 5.

COMPARISON
OF THE PRESENT STATE OF FRANCE WITH THAT OF ROME UNDER JULIUS AND AUGUSTUS CAESAR. II (CONTINUED)[1]

29 September 1802, Wednesday; except "II (CONTINUED)", *M Post* title, with editorial note that "The following should have appeared in our paper of Saturday, as the conclusion of the second part of this Essay." *EOT* II 499–505, where the *M Post* instructions are silently followed, making this a part of the second essay, even without a paragraph indention.

SOME[a] *shew* of justification [b]for the present despotism of France[c] is, and will be, derived from the miseries and vices of the revolution. But the sophistry is too palpable not to be detected by every man, as soon as his feelings, passions, and individual sufferings, permit his reason to have fair play. The principle of disregarding property, both in the candidates and the electors, and the wild attempt to erect a government on the hypothetical *rights* of man, as a creature of nature, instead of his real and existing privileges, as a creature of society, were errors so egregious, that men will as little suspect or relinquish the system of a representative government, in consequence of these French experiments, as they would reject the present efforts in chemistry, in consequence of the mad schemes of the old alchemists. Besides, what wise man will make any deductions to the discredit of liberty, from the first extravagances of unfettered slaves? Even a common stage-coachman will not object to the amendment of a bad road, although he well knows, that *no* road can be so bad, as a road *a mending*? It is the fate and nature of revolutions, that the people at first are more than *angels* in their notions of rights and liberties; and less than men in the enjoyment and practice of them. It is equally natural, that the consequent failures should induce disgust; and that arguments should be deduced from the first outrages of a transient hope, to *justify* the despotism, which has its best foundation in an equally transient despondency. A sick stomach, and a throbbing head, are as little favourable to just conceptions, as the gay madness of the midnight carousal. This is the morning after a debauch.—As we would not rely on the promises of France, in her drunken mood, so neither shall we calculate on her passiveness and languor, now that she is *getting*

[a] *EOT*: It is true, that some [b–c] *EOT* omits

[1] For a song and an epigram 27 Sept see App D, below.

sober. We must wait till she *is* sober. We shall then see, that as the despotism and ambition of the French Government have no plea of necessity or advantage, derived from the circumstances of Europe at large, and consequently cannot be *justified*; even so, and for even the same reasons, it cannot be permanent.

For, in truth, the same reasons, that make the constitution and ambitious schemes of France less just and necessary than those of imperial Rome, make it likewise insecure. The very newspaper, which our reader has now in his hand, and which, in a few hours hence, he may probably rumple up for "vile uses," is so powerful an agent, as to constitute an essential difference between the probable duration of a despot's reign in the present age, and that which it often was in the time of Imperial Rome. If Bonaparte were told that Julius Caesar magnanimously contemned the libels written against his person and measures, we should not be surprised, if Bonaparte should answer—"He did well! But a manuscript libel was not a printed newspaper." When God sent Christianity into the world, he made men capable of freedom; when he permitted the discovery of printing, he gave men the means of acquiring and perpetuating it. The press is the only "*infernal machine*"[2] which is truly formidable to a modern despot.[3] And only the enemies to the freedom of their country, either fear or have cause to [a]fear it.[b] At this moment, the illumination of all Europe, and the European world, is acting upon each part of it. The rapid inter-communication of thoughts and discoveries, the amiable social vanity, that is the result of this free intellectual commerce; and the awe, in which each government stands, of the opinions of its nation, and in which each nation stands, of the opinions of its neighbours; these are the most effectual guards and warrants of mutual freedom: these will make all actual despotism short-lived; and will convert (and, in some measure, have already converted) formal despotisms into virtual free states. Prussia and Denmark are existing instances. It cannot therefore be, that France will long endure to be the pity and scorn of Great Britain! At present, she is dazzled, perhaps, almost to blindness, by her conquests and military achievements; but [c]infinite pains are now taking, by her rulers[d] to restore her eye-sight. A spy or two, in every restorateur and coffee-house, with soldiers parading in every street, lane, and alley, who come up,[e] and listen, if any three friends stand

[a–b] *EOT*: fear. [c–d] *EOT*: her rulers are taking infinite pains [e] *EOT*: advance

[2] See 25 Sept n 7, above.

[3] Here Stuart altered C's "Tyrant" to "Despot". Stuart to C 29 Sept 1802, App B, below.

talking together; and "*the best, greatest, and wisest nation of Europe*"[4] compelled to be silent, while the army, and the creatures of the generals, declare, in the name, and as the act, of this "*best, greatest, and wisest nation*," that they are not fit to be trusted with the choice of a bailiff, or the perusal of a newspaper; and that they totter upon the very summit of their integrity and political discernment, when they have humbly *recommended* a constable to the choice of the great I BY ITSELF I,[5] the AUTOCRATOR of France, and of all her six or seven "*free and independent*" Republics!—These are wrongs and insults which, it cannot be hoped, that even Frenchmen will endure—unless by compulsion. For it is not with *them*, as with the old Romans, who feared no Censors, and no proud Pitiers in Gaul, then semi-barbarous, and Asia always a slave. The finger of enlightened Europe points at *their* fetters; and their old rivals, the English, utter the words—"The FRENCH REPUBLIC," as a spell, as a love-philtre, that enamours them of their own constitution, of their own dear island; that is at once a majestic kingdom, and a free commonwealth. Formerly, when we spoke of Frenchmen, we used the words, slavery and wooden shoes; now we say, LIBERTY and EQUALITY—and we mean the same things, and mingle no whit less pity with our thoughts, and infinitely more contempt.

Let us add to all this, as a fact least of all to be omitted in this statement of difference, that on the death of Augustus, all the power, and all the exercises of power, were wholly taken from the popular assemblies. The *people* of Rome, as distinguished from the individuals, existed only as an audience in a play-house, or as a *spectatorate*[6] in an amphi-theatre. But France is not a city like Rome: it is a vast populous territory, and all its cities, and all its towns, feel an equal interest in the movements of government, and have been accustomed to exert almost an equal political activity with Paris. Even Portalis, who has supplanted Sieyes in his own manufactory,[7] and whom

[4] Source untraced, but cf a report from Paris of a speech (15 Aug) by Councillor of State Muraire before Napoleon: "You have said, if I might so address myself before all Europe assembled in this place, *the best of people shall be the happiest, as they are the most worthy of being so*...". Reported in *M Chron* 20 Aug 1802.

[5] Cf the "burlesque on the Fichtean Egoismus" in *BL* ch 9: "I, I, I! I itself I!" etc. *BL* (1907) I 101n–2. Cf also *Courier* 21 Sept 1811 (below), "I myself I", reworked in *Friend* (*CC*) I 26.

[6] Not in *OED*.

[7] Jean Étienne Marie Portalis (1745–1807), a member of the Council of Ancients 1795–7, had helped Napoleon prepare the Code Civile and the Concordat and had been made state counsellor and head of ecclesiastical affairs. For his collaboration with Bonaparte in emasculating the legislative branch, see Thibaudeau 36–44.

the Dey[a] could have no objection to as constitution-maker for the free Republic of Algiers, even Portalis has not ventured to sentence the whole population of France to absolute inactivity. So far are Frenchmen from being condemned to do nothing, that they are called forth to do a great deal—though, it must be confessed, nothing to any purpose. But to call forth large numbers of men to make fools of themselves, is a dangerous experiment; and it will require all the watchfulness of a *faithful* soldiery, and a large importation of fresh* Mamelukes, to persuade the whole people of France thus to keep their own fingers dancing to and fro before their own eyes, in order that they may not *see*, though they must *know*, that their pockets are in the act of being picked of those charters and privileges, for which many of them had bled, and all of them suffered—charters bequeathed to them in the field of battle, as the testament and dying legacy of more than a million of their best fellow-countrymen. The Cantonal Assemblies, the Electoral Colleges, the Tribunate, the Legislature, do not affect the *existence* of a pure Caesarean despotism in France; this we asserted, and this we re-assert; but we did not affirm, nor did we mean to imply, that they may not[b] affect the *duration* of that despotism. Consequently, these are to be counted among the important *circumstances* of difference between the Roman

* It is well known, that Negroes are beyond measure fascinated with splendid vestments and ornaments of dress. It is worthy, therefore, of being hinted to the First Consul and his Counsellors of State, whether the late soldiers of Toussaint might not be drafted to France, presented with rich regimentals, &c.; and whether in due time they might not be so far won over, as that a Consular Guard might be formed from them, more to be relied on than native Frenchmen.[8] The Mamelukes no doubt were an excellent thought; but how are they to be recruited? The Mamelukes too, it is well known, are addicted to certain detestable vices, which are by no means frequent among the Negroes; but whether, in the present state of the morals of France, this would plead for or against the Negroes, is a difficult question, which we do not pretend to decide. We offer the above hint with great humility, and fully conscious that the whole merit of the original idea belongs to the First Consul in his formation of the Egyptian guard.

[a] *EOT*: Dey himself [b] *EOT* adds "not", omitted in *M Post*

[8] Pierre Dominique Toussaint L'Ouverture (1743–1803), when a slave, had been made superintendent of a plantation but joined a Negro insurrection in 1791; when the French ratified a declaration of freedom he joined them and was named commander-in-chief of the French armies of Santo Domingo in 1796; when he had recruited a powerful force of blacks and conquered the whole country, he renounced the authority of France and declared himself the Bonaparte of Santo Domingo. Forced to surrender to a French army in Apr 1802, he was arrested in an interview with Gen Brunet 10 Jun 1802 and transported to France. (He died in Fort de Joux [Doubs] on 27 Apr 1803.) Slavery had been reinstituted in the French colonies. C may have meant to imply several ironies in his advice.

Empire under the Caesars, and the French under Bonaparte. Other, and equally important, ones are to be found in the personal character of the First Consul, and in the character of the different factions. But we have already transgressed the limits of a newspaper disquisition; and though they are of a nature to be more generally interesting, as being more personal, than the points hitherto adduced, yet we must turn them over to a third and last Essay, which will appear in To-morrow's Paper.[9]

[1 October 1802, Friday]

The third and last part of the Comparison between the French and Roman Republics, to-morrow certainly.

COMPARISON
OF THE PRESENT STATE OF FRANCE WITH THAT OF ROME UNDER JULIUS AND AUGUSTUS CAESAR. III[1]

2 October 1802, Saturday; except "III", *M Post* title. *EOT* II 505–14, with extensive revision, presumably authorial—i.e. deriving from clippings revised by C. See textual footnotes. Cf headnote 25 Sept 1802, above.

WE have heard, with equal sorrow and surprise, that an eminent public character, and one hitherto an assertor of English liberty, has expressed a disapprobation of the late boldness of the London newspapers.[2] Nay, he has intimated *his fears*, that it may be necessary *for peace* to conciliate the good will of Bonaparte, by imposing some additional restrictions on the freedom of political disquisition. We venture to have *our* fears too; our fears, that from the day, on which these fears of *his* were realised, another prophecy would date the *dawn* of its fulfilment: we mean that prophecy of the First Consul, in the *Moniteur* of the 9th [8th] of August, that the French Government will last longer than the English. Or rather, it will be idle to ask, which of the two Governments will last the longer, when they have both become one.

9 Continued 2 Oct.

1 For two "Original Epigrams" signed ΕΣΤΗΣΕ 2 Oct see App D, below.

2 Charles Fox, a "great statesman" not long since (23 Feb), is now attacked, like the hapless sage in C's *Tale* of the Mad Ox, for warning against the dangers of a hue and cry.

A zealous Bishop has taught us, that the subjects of Great Britain have nothing to do with the laws[a] but to obey them.[3] This Gentleman, it seems, has his fears, that it may be necessary to refine on this truly episcopal maxim, and to inform us by Act of Parliament, that we have nothing to do with the edicts[b] of the First Consul, but to *obey* them.[c] Has not the Chief Consul, by his Minister Talleyrand, presented the constitution of France to the Diet, stating it as his reason for so doing, that the tranquillity of all Europe is interested in the establishment of the Consular power? He, himself, informs us officially, that the present constitution of France greatly and nearly concerns us; and shall we not then have leave to examine it? or does he mean, some time or other, to *give* it "to the Department of the Thames;" and therefore expects that, according to the vulgar proverb, we shall not *look the gift in the mouth!* We, for our part, have no fears but such as arise from dispositions much nearer home, than those of Bonaparte; nor should we be *surprised* at the event, though we by no means *expect* it, if this parricidal child and champion of Jacobinism[4] should be disarmed of his terrors, even before it can be proposed in an English Legislature, that we should throw ourselves prostrate before them.

We believe, that this new Roman Empire will be of short duration: and we have made this highly probable, by shewing at large, that while its government, and its ambitious pretensions, are almost an exact copy of Imperial Rome,[d] in a great majority of the[e] circumstances,[f] external and [g]internal, it is[h] wholly unlike those of Rome, and the Roman world. This dissimilarity we are now to carry on by the induction of new facts. The insolence of Julius Caesar cost him his life; but this insolence and contemptuous tyranny was exerted wholly towards the Senate, whom the people regarded as their worst enemies, and since the murder of the Gracchi, and the suppression of the question of the Licinian law, as cruel and illegal tyrants. To the people of Rome Julius Caesar was respectful, liberal, almost adulatory. He was assassinated in the senate; but he was,[i] and he remained, the darling of the people. The dark[j] cruelties of Tiberius

[a] *EOT*: laws of their own country [b] *EOT*: *edicts* [c] *EOT*: *them.*
[d] *EOT*: Rome, it is on the other hand, [e] *EOT*: its [f] *EOT*: *circumstances,*
[g–h] *EOT*: internal, [i] *EOT*: had been [j] *EOT* omits

[3] Samual Horsley, then bp of Rochester, on 11 Nov 1795—quoted in C's *PD: Lects 1795* (*CC*) 285; see ibid n 2.

[4] The Pittian epithet of 1800, applied ironically; the parricidal aspect is developed in the next paragraph, in which Bonaparte in his anti-Jacobinism is contrasted with Caesar.

were endured in gratitude to Augustus, and in the hope of better days, of a second Augustus; and the mad tyranny of Caligula and Nero were directed almost wholly against the senate, and were regarded by the people not without complacency. These maniacs, in their worse excesses, provided for the real wants of Rome, as well as for the most splendid pleasures of its inhabitants; and though the materials for the history of those times are both scanty, and from very suspicious sources, yet enough remains to make it highly probable that the executions of the patricians were often regarded by the Romans, as an expiation for the atrocious murder of the Gracchi; and the confiscations of their prodigious and illegal property (which was in the main squandered by Caligula and Nero, on public shews, edifices, and largesses) appeared as so many extra-regular acts of the old Licinian law. If there stood no order of men, and no possibility of any order, between Bonaparte and the people of France, except the old nobility and farmers-general; and if the old nobility were the nominal magistracy of the state, there would be then some resemblance between the present state of France, and that of Imperial Rome; and Bonaparte, like the Caesars, might remain a despot, and transmit the despotism to posterity, as the protector of the people, as "*the child and champion of Jacobinism.*" We have so long connected the names of Brutus and Cassius with the word, Liberty, that we have forgotten that, by the Roman populace, they were considered as the leaders of the senatorian aristocracy—Caesar was the child and champion of Jacobinism. But Bonaparte is to the Jacobins what the senate was to the popular faction at Rome, and to the aristocracy of France, what Caesar was to the senate.[5]

If from Julius Caesar we turn to Augustus, we shall find the commencement of his power, and that of Bonaparte, so far similar, as that in both instances, all men, and especially all peaceable men, were wearied out by the horrors of civil discord, and prepared to acquiesce in any government, that put a period to them. But, dreadful as the revolutionary scenes in France may have been, they are trifling compared with those under Marius and Sylla, and afterwards under the triumvirate. Yet Augustus saw no reason to place such confidence in[a] this terror and despondency of men's minds, as to exempt himself from the necessity of the utmost caution, slowness, and decency. The total extinction of popular liberty was not, as at present in France,

[a] *M Post*: on [corrected in *EOT*]

[5] C has now prepared the ground for an essay defining Jacobinism. See 21 Oct, below.

effected at a blow. The popular elections were continued; and Augustus repeatedly, for himself and for his friends, acted the part of the most humble and unwearied candidate. He affected no pomp in his person, or palace, beyond that of other wealthy senators.[a] He received and returned visits, as a common senator. Spies were rigorously discouraged; and the utmost freedom, both in writing and speaking, was practised without danger. He was regarded with veneration, both by the people and the senate, not as the man who governed them by the soldiery—which is the light in which Bonaparte must be considered—but as the only man in the state, who had both the power and the inclination to retain the soldiery within the controul of the laws. Augustus reigned fifty-seven years, during [b]the latter[c] forty-seven of which, his character was truly that of the father of his [d]country; and all[e] this time there was no apparent change in the[f] constitution of the [g]Republic—all the old names, all the old offices, were retained;[h] and there can be no doubt, but that a vast majority of the Roman people thought their country a free Republic, and believed that it could only remain free under the protection and divinity of a Caesar. Thus more than a generation of men were born and died under the wise and well concealed despotism; and, at the accession of Tiberius, there were probably few Romans alive, who could have remembered any other times than those of Augustus.

It is tedious to be always drawing out formal parallels, or opposites; and, in this instance, it is wholly unnecessary. Soldiers in every street, spies under every window, political questions answered only by a look of terror and distrust, and a blank silence in every public company on all subjects of public interest—this is a picture of Rome under Tiberius. Does it bear any resemblance to the present state of Paris? If so, is there any man so unread in the human mind as not to know, that if the Roman Imperial Government had commenced with a Tiberius, it would have been strangled in its birth (though no doubt[i] it would again have arisen, from the absolute necessity of circumstances). In France the necessity does not exist; and yet in the very commencement of their despotism they are permitted to see what the Romans saw only after a lapse of forty-seven Augustan years. The memory of Augustus threw a glory over Tiberius, as that of Louis the XIVth over his weak and wicked successor; and if this had not been the case, yet the evils must have been endured, for who could suggest a remedy? There was no feasible novelty to look for-

[a] *EOT*: patricians. [b–c] *EOT*: at least [d–e] *EOT*: country. All [f] *EOT*: the nominal [g–h] *EOT*: state; [i] *EOT*: doubt in some after time

ward to: and as both Augustus and Tiberius left everything [a]*in name*[b] what it had always been, there was no mass of old [c]names, which[d] had been violently suppressed, and to which the people could revert by a direct counter-revolution. But what Augustus was to all the Roman Empire, in the first years of the reign of Tiberius, that Louis the XVIth is at this moment to a large part of France, and[e] the fondly cherished hope of a republic[f] to a majority of the remaining part.—Fear, hope, and memory, are the three great agents, both in the binding of a people to a Government, and in the rousing[g] them to a revolution. All three worked together in favour of Tiberius; but it should appear, that the First Consul must rely chiefly upon the first. His power is an isthmus of Darien, beat upon by the two oceans of Royalism and Republicanism: of Royalism, aided by a powerful superstition; of Republicanism, aided by the detestation of that superstition.

But while the army remain attached to the First Consul, all else, it may be thought, is of little importance. We have had a recent proof, that when an army vote under arms, the people have no other response left, than an Amen. This is undoubtedly true; the present existence of Bonaparte's power evinces its truth. But, on the other hand, it must be remembered, that the affections of the soldiery must be in great measure moulded by those of the officers;[h] and how long will Bonaparte retain these, [i]daily affecting[j] more and more[k] retiredness of manner, with a kingly demeanour, and[l] daily giving proofs of his partiality to the soldiers of the Italian and Egyptian armies, to the real or imagined neglect of the army of the Rhine, the real saviours of the Republic? Add to this, that an immense standing army, which cannot now be fed on the spoils of the countries which it had over-run, implies an immense expenditure; and financial difficulties are serious difficulties, indeed, in a country at peace, and no longer revolutionary, though they were most idly and perniciously calculated upon by our clerk-like Minister during the war.[6] But in the military affairs of France, there lies a great and important difference between the circumstances of its Perpetual Consulate, and the same authority under the Imperial title in Rome—a difference which we might with propriety have stated in a former part of this disquisition, but purposely deferred it from its immediate bearing on

[a–b] *EOT*: nominally [c–d] *EOT*: names to return to—nothing that [e] *EOT*: and that [f] *EOT*: republic is [g] *EOT*: rousing of [h] *EOT*: offices; [i–j] *EOT*: he, who daily affects [k] *EOT*: more a [l] *EOT*: and who is

6 A reference to Pitt as inept financier.

the personal concerns of the present First Consul. Rome had conquered her whole empire under the Republic: the Emperors, with the single exception of Trajan, contented themselves with maintaining what had been won, and this they accomplished with so little difficulty, that their few and distant wars can scarcely be deemed an interruption of the tranquillity of the Roman empire. Except in peace, the despotism and[a] the empire could not co-exist; as soon as the Northern nations became sufficiently disciplined, and had learnt the policy of combination to carry on regular wars, the Roman empire fell asunder. But,[b] surely, while there exist four such powers in Europe as Russia, Prussia, Austria, and Great Britain, even the grossest flatterers of the great Pacificator will not predict to France a perpetual peace. But if any long and serious war should take place, either the despotism must depress military merit, or fall a sacrifice to military rivals.[c] Valour and warlike genius are qualities safe only in an Emperor, in[d] a military despotism. If military merit were depressed, want of success would be the inevitable result, and the contempt of the soldiery, and the national alarm[e] deriving courage from the same contempt, would soon dash down both the despotism and the despot. If military merit were encouraged, civil wars would arise; army against army; till the common feelings of human nature would resort either to an hereditary monarch, or to a quick rotation of the supreme magistracy. Even if France were to continue at peace with all her neighbours, yet, the longer the continuance of the peace, the less would the influence and authority of the military become. Men of talents, men of spirit, men of virtue, would all relinquish a profession, in which there was no other employment than that of spies and executioners to their fellow-countrymen.

Summing together all these points of difference, we have no hesitation in predicting, that it is impossible that France can ever realise her ambitious dream of universal Sovereignty. Her present power, her present form of Government, so closely resemble those of Rome, that all the Powers of Europe, that remain unsubjugated, are called upon to suspicion, watchfulness, and prompt and firm courage: but the *circumstances* of the two Empires are so widely different, that there results the strongest hope that, with the exertion of these qualities, we are safe. There is much to alarm us, nothing to terrify.[7] Happy will it be for Europe, if her governors shall at last

[a] *M Post*: of [corrected in *EOT*] [b] *EOT*: Now, [c] *EOT*: rivalship. [d] *EOT*: under
[e] *M Post*: claim [corrected in *EOT*]

[7] This theme is developed in 6 Jan 1803, below.

perceive, that the more free a nation is, the less she will be disposed to conquest; that the absurd principles of demagogues are mere effects, and not causes, and will, at all times, die a natural death; but that, if opposed by violence, they may become indeed pernicious; not by their own proper action, but by the facility which they afford to the levying of armies, whose political fanaticism is soon transmuted[a] into [b]military passion.[c] A noisy republic is crushed;[d] and an iron-handed empire rises out of [e]its ruins.[f][8]

AFFAIRS OF FRANCE. I[1]

5 October 1802, Tuesday; except "I", *MPost* title. *EOT* II 515–21; certain attribution, often referred to by C.

The precipitant of this essay and its sequel was the following unsigned letter from Paris. Dated 18 Sept, it was published in the *M Post* 25 Sept with the comment that "if the letter . . . be accurate, very important events are on the eve of taking place in France". Since it was not, and they were not, we must seek the materials of C's essay first of all in this Parisian speculation:

"The leaders in the Government of France are already alarmed for the safety of the new political fabric which they have, with so much curious labour, and with such high promises, reared. In a late meeting of the Consular Privy Council, the present state of public opinion, and its disposition towards the existing Government, were the subjects of a long and serious deliberation. It was alleged, that neither the Jacobins nor the Royalists were now, separately, formidable; but a new party had, it was said, arisen, which presented to both those a common point of union. The personal enemies of the First Consul, and of those whom his administration chiefly employs and favours, those whose ambition the changes of the revolution have provoked and inflamed, without adequately gratifying it; the proprietors of lands newly purchased, who dread that the present government may have views inconsistent with their security in their possessions; Jacobins, who think that if new convulsions could be anyhow excited, the Sansculottes and the good old cause might once more triumph; and the Royalists, who fancy that to the restoration of Royalty, nothing more is wanted but Bonaparte's fall; are all

[a] *M Post*: transmitted [corrected in *EOT*] [b–c] *EOT*: a passion for military glory.
[d] *EOT*: interred; [e–f] *EOT*: the grave, its ghost, and its avenger.

[8] For Lamb's reaction to this series, beginning "I certainly recognize that your comparisons are acute and witty; but what has this to do with truth?", see *LL* I 320 (9 Oct). C himself, in *BL* ch 10, affirmed that the diagnosis of French Caesarism had been so prophetic that in 1816 "intelligent men" might think the essays contemporary. *BL* (1907) I 147. Colmer (69) considers the series as showing "how valuable a tool historical analogy might become . . .".

Stuart's delight in C's new vein was boundless: "I hope I shall never go to Newgate, but if I am destined to go there I pray it may be for such things as have lately appeared in the M Post ag[ains]t Bonaparte.—Apropos—a Gent. at attorney Generals table said there had been much true old English Spirit in the M. Post of late and he admired it greatly.—These are almost *your own* words." Stuart to C 29 Sept, App B, below.

[1] C's *Dejection: An Ode* appeared in the *M Post* of 4 Oct (see App D, below).

supposed to join in a many-headed party, whose machinations extend over all France, and which, if its growth and efforts were overlooked, might quickly menace the Consular Throne. It was agreed by all who were present at the discussion, that the public mind is, throughout France, not at all in a state most auspicious to the duration of the present government; and that the people think much more of the burthen of taxation imposed upon them, than of the splendid schemes which the First Consul is so zealous to advance. To crush the growing party, to put to silence the murmurs of discontent, no other course appeared to be left but one, in which all seemed entirely to agree, namely, that of a new and extensive deportation, including every person on whom suspicion could fall, as being an agitator in new intrigues. A committee was, therefore, nominated, consisting of Messrs. Laplace and Perregaux, with Generals Kellerman and Le Febvre, to digest a new plan of colonisation, such as may afford a fair pretence to send all who are obnoxious to Bonaparte, to wander among the wilds of Louisiana, or to perish under the torrid heats of Cayenne."

IN our comparison of the military despotisms of Rome and France, which, we have reason to hope, excited some degree of interest, we spoke of the two powerful factions in France, equally hostile to the existing Consular Government, the Royalists, and the Republicans. We could find nothing correspondent or equivalent to them in the history of imperial Rome, and we placed them, therefore, among the other *circumstances* of dissimilarity in the two despotisms, which combined to render it probable that the French will be as transient as that of Rome was durable. Our subject neither required, nor even permitted us, to do more. At the same time, we were fully sensible that the existence of these two parties (for perhaps we were not justified in styling them *factions*) involved more than one question of no easy solution. It was presumed, at the commencement of the Consulate, that Bonaparte would cautiously and solicitously adopt such measures as might win over both parties to an acquiescence in his government—the Jacobins, by the hope that it was to be for a time only, a dictatorship that would yearly relax and soften, and at length die away into a free Republic—the Royalists, by the apparent restoration of their old institutions under new names. To satisfy the Jacobins, there was but one alteration necessary in the constitution, as it first appeared;[2] namely, that the candidates chosen by the process of a three-fold decimation of the electors, should be again presented to the primary assemblies, and the final selection made by them, instead of the Senate or Consulate. This would certainly be the most unobjectionable form which a system of universal suffrage can assume, and would very greatly lessen the danger of an unwise or factious choice, while it left entire to the

[2] Noted in 31 Dec 1799, above.

nation the full exercise of its inherent sovereignty. To satisfy the Royalists was not, indeed, so easy; but still, by the remission of the persecution against them, by the recall of the priests, and of the majority of their emigrant relations, and by the re-establishment of the Catholic religion, it was presumed that they might at least be *pacified*; and that time would gradually undermine their prejudices, and national vanity over-power their personal attachment to a family, which had been long the pensioners of the natural enemy of their country.

At the commencement of the Consulate, these were the speculations of many friends of freedom, both here and in France; but they formed no part of *our* hopes or expectations; we stated them, indeed, as speculations, but at the same time expressly warned our readers not to anticipate any system favourable to rational liberty from a young man, who had formed his habits, feelings, and political creed, at the head of an army, and amid the career of dazzling victories. The result has fully verified our predictions.[3] Every succeeding month, from the first promulgation of the new constitution, has afforded some new outrage against the Republicans; and though immense sacrifices have been in reality made to the Royalists, yet every sacrifice has been so palpably a gratification of the Consul's own ambition and lust of power, that it *served*, but not *conciliated*, the party; nay, by bringing them so much nearer the object of their wishes, it rekindled a hope that was dying away, and with that hope gave them new courage and new activity. Nor was this all. These sacrifices have supplied them with new arguments in favour of Royalism; of no value, indeed, with the Jacobins, but of irresistible weight with those who, without being the creatures and hirelings of the present government, seemed willing to be its favourers. "You wish," say the Royalists, "for peace and domestic security; and to these you have offered up all your splendid visions of political liberty, all your civic rights, all your popular privileges. For these you have offered them all up; yet these you have not gained. You have paid down the purchase money, but you have not received the

[3] Is C further claiming to have said in 1799–1800 in the *M Post* what we know WW recently said in "I griev'd for Bonaparte" about the inauspicious formative influences upon the young hero's mind? C *had* given such an account (19 Mar 1800) of a young leader whose habits had been badly formed in elevation from the ranks in a dazzling career—but the young man had been Pitt, not Bonaparte. In Dec 1799 and Jan 1800 C had in fact defined the future of Bonaparte as different from and more auspicious than that of his Constitution. (C seems further to be claiming that he himself had never grieved for Bonaparte.)

purchase.—How can *you* feel a security, which the government itself does not feel? How can *you* hope for peace, and a settled order of things, which the government itself proclaims not to exist, by a garrison in every street, and an Egyptian plague of spies and informers in every Theatre, in every Coffee-house? Are not the seats billeted out, monthly, to your very Legislators, lest any half dozen of them should frame a conspiracy in whispers? Would not even an English newspaper, if found in your house, sentence you to a Bastile more certainly now, than a paper of high treason would have done under Louis the XVIth? You have sacrificed everything to a mere promise of peace and security; with what shadow of reason can you refuse to sacrifice a few names for the real possession? Put only King for Consul, and the rightful Heir of the throne for a Corsican; and, in the place of six thousand new military Nobles, one twelfth of the number from the most ancient families of France; and then we may indeed have not only peace and security, but a calm conscience and a reconciled God! Have you given your consent to the total abolition of real Republicanism? Then why disgrace the nation with the vile *nickname* of it? Have we killed the chimaera; and must we still wear it in our national arms? Surely, the three lilies were a handsome emblazonment." Such, we may easily conceive, will be the language of many an artful Royalist: and we sincerely wish, that Portalis or Roederer would furnish us with the answer.[4] We could indeed frame a very sufficient answer to many parts of the plea; but we do not see, with what consistency it could be uttered by an adherent of the Consulate. We are greatly deceived, if Bonaparte have not played an unwise game, and alienated his old friends, without winning over a single enemy.

This accession to the strength and proselyting spirit of royalism in France, we should have stated in our former disquisition, as fully as we have now done, but that it would have proved rather the in-

[4] There is satire (as well as evasion) in C's proposal to turn the questions of the "artful Royalist" over to these two. Portalis, a constitutionalist, and Roederer, a Jacobin who "*undulated* (serpenté) through the contests and parties of the time" (Thibaudeau 172n, quoting Mallet du Pan), had recently as members of Bonaparte's Council, taken great pains to justify the Concordat—and so ought to be able to explain or answer *anything*.

Roederer, nominally proprietor of the *Moniteur*, had sent out circulars in May and June to sound out sentiment for the Consulate for Life, but his own support stipulated that Bonaparte must re-establish complete liberty of the press. Bonaparte removed him from the Council by making him a Senator. Thibaudeau 235, 241–2, 305. See also Gustav von Schlabrendorf *Bonaparte and the French People Under His Consulate* (New York 1804) 68, 85.

security of the present despot, than the probable transiency of the despotism itself, and its accompanying scheme of Empire. For, as we before observed, the existence of the two parties involves more than one question. First, it is commonly believed, that the First Consul calculates on the mutual counter-action of the Jacobins and the Royalists. They are, indeed, it has been said, both equally hostile to him; but, possessing the same strength, and being in direct opposition, they must necessarily destroy each other's forces. Now is it true that the two parties are thus evenly balanced? and if they be, is not this notion of exact counter-action, a mere phantom in politics? a childish application of mechanics to a subject, in which even as metaphors, the phrases have scarcely any intelligible sense? Secondly, presuming to know nothing accurately of the comparative numbers of the two parties, may we not be able to offer some rational conjectures concerning the ultimate result of their contest, from our knowledge of the present circumstances of France and Europe, from the influence of property, commerce, and the desire of civil security? Thirdly, supposing the Royalists to be finally successful, and to introduce the Bourbons without terms, what change would this restoration effect or not effect, in the despotism and spirit of empire in France?—In other words, what are the advantages to Europe, and especially to this country, on which Mr. Windham, and other eager Bourbonists, calculate so confidently, as certain results of the re-introduction of the old monarchy in France? Lastly, is there any point of junction possible between the royalists and republicans?

We were led into these questions by the private letter from Paris, which we published in our paper some days ago.[5] We then said, and we repeat it, that we never place much confidence on private letters from Paris; and assuredly from its own merits[a] we should be little inclined to deviate from our habitual scepticism in favour of this letter. Such familiarity with the discussions in the Consular Privy Council, savours strongly of that bold spirit of conjecture, natural to Frenchmen, and which among every people is a necessary consequence of strangling the Liberty of the Press. We hear much of *groundless paragraphs*; and much idle abuse lavished upon them. But a paragraph may be easily traced to the paper in which it first appeared; and the paper that deals largely in such ware, will soon

[a] *EOT*: merit

[5] Letter of 18 Sept in *M Post* of 25 Sept, quoted in the headnote, above.

receive a broad hint from the Public to be more careful, by the diminished sale; to which add the facility of legal inquiry. But who is to hunt down a groundless whisper? or prosecute a coffee-house politician's lie? The letter states the existence of a many-headed party, each pursuing purely and nakedly its own old principles;—and yet as having a common point of union? Is this possible? Is it not very like nonsense? The letter concludes, with stating the nomination of a Committee, of La Place, Perregaux, Kellerman, and Le Febvre, to digest a plan of colonising Louisiana, by a violent deportation of all the malcontents out of France.[6] It is difficult to mention so extravagant a report with a serious countenance. Yet the very extravagance and incongruity of the contents of this letter, give it a sober interest, if it be taken in its proper point of view. Assuming that this letter conveys the substance of real conversations at Paris, it will mark to an attentive mind the troubled and gloomy expectation of men's minds in political circles; and it is probable, that there is some ground for the various reports, strangely as it may have been modified by the different reporters. No thinking man believes, that France will remain long in precisely its present presageful calmness: and we seem to be authorised in believing, that even an attempt made to solve the important question,[a] stated above, will not wholly fail of interesting our readers. We propose to do this to-morrow.[7] *Interea, tenuitatis nostrae memores nihil pertinaciter affirmemus; sed in re futurâ, et suo modo prodigiosâ, qui optime conjicit, optimus et vates et philosophus esto.*[8]

[a] *EOT*: questions

[6] Louisiana had recently passed from Spain to France, to the consternation and opposition of the United States. As for the rumour, there *had* been a deportation, by an act of 4 Jan 1801, of 130 prominent Jacobins following the attack on Bonaparte's life in Dec 1800, mentioned by C in 25 Sept 1802, above. That deportation had been to French Guiana and the Seychelles; the present letter mentions Guiana as well as Louisiana.

[7] For the continuation see 9 Oct, below. Of the four questions now raised, the first (Are Royalists and Jacobins evenly balanced?) is largely rhetorical but is expatiated in the sequel of 9 Oct; the second and third (Will the Royalists win and if so what will be the consequences?) are restated as the second and first questions of that sequel and dealt with, partially, in the essay of 12 Oct; and the fourth (Is junction possible between Royalists and Republicans?) will be again put off, though "Once a Jacobin" (21 Oct) is an essay that must have been suggested by it. Stuart's announcement of 6 Oct (see below) indicates that he is not clear what form C's next contribution will take.

[8] Untraced. Tr: "Meanwhile, mindful of our human weakness, let us make no firm pronouncement: but in the case of an event that still lies in the future and is portentous in a way peculiar to itself, let him who makes the best guess be accounted the best prophet and

[6 October 1802, Wednesday]

In To-morrow's Paper, we propose giving an Article of great interest, on the present state of France.[1]

MR. PITT'S RETURN TO OFFICE[1]

8 October 1802, Friday; *M Post* title. New attribution. The external evidence is fairly compelling, though its force may not be at once apparent; it lies in the Stuartian notices—on Wed announcing C's article on France and, at the end of this article, reannouncing it. (Cf the Mar 1800 announcement of C's review of Young.) The two essays are on different subjects; Stuart's announcements suggest they are by the same author. The internal evidence is not spectacular but firm enough to clinch the attribution. The essay is of a piece with C's other contributions on English parties, and the style and vehicles of the metaphors are Coleridgian: Pitt looking "as over children"; his "slight inward jealousy": "it is only under wings that they can fly"; "he walks himself alone"; he is forced to make way "for some of his clerks"; a sense of danger must exist "before any gigantic steps in finance"; Fox is "enamoured of the study of botany", Pitt "of drilling and dibbling". And note especially the two concluding paragraphs.

THIS subject gives rise to much conversation, or rather speculation, at present, and the reports upon it are as various as those respecting the duel in *The School for Scandal*.[2] Some insist that a coolness exists between Mr. Pitt and Mr. Addington; others, that they have actually quarrelled, and do not speak. The King, it is said, has consented that Mr. Pitt shall come into the Cabinet, provided he be not the Prime Minister who shall transact business personally with him. Again, it is rumoured Mr. Addington affects to wish Mr. Pitt would return, while he himself creates those obstacles which he pretends he cannot remove. To all these reports we pay no attention.

Nothing is more certain than that Mr. Pitt's particular friends, Mr. Dundas, Mr. Canning, Mr. Rose, Mr. Long,[3] &c. are disgusted

philosopher." C had written the Latin sentence in his notebook in March: *CN* I 1146.

C is obviously aware that there are distorting omissions and shifts of emphasis in his new representation of what constituted "our" view of the French Constitution and of Bonaparte in 1799–1800.

1 See 9 Oct, below.

1 For verses 7 Oct see App D, below.

2 Sheridan *The School for Scandal* v ii.

3 Charles Long (1761–1838; Baron Farnborough 1826), MP from 1789, joint secretary to the Treasury 1791–1801; a personal friend of Pitt and Addington who would mediate between them in 1803 and return to the Treasury under Pitt in 1804.

with Mr. Addington, and his Administration, in the highest degree; and that Mr. Addington's circle of personal friends and dependants dread and hate the personal friends of Mr. Pitt. Mr. Addington himself would, perhaps, act without Mr. Pitt's support, if he were able, and set the Pitt party at defiance; but he is not strong enough: Mr. Pitt, we believe, cares little about Mr. Addington's views or proceedings, or about the views or proceedings of his own friends, or of the friends of Mr. Addington. He knows his own power, his own superiority, and looks over all their heads as over children, at objects of real magnitude and deep interest. It is probable, that he may be occasionally worked upon, and irritated, against Mr. Addington, by the representations of the friends about him. He may, in moments of forgetfulness, entertain a slight inward jealousy even of the present Premier. The greatest men are sometimes jealous of the most contemptible efforts to rival them. We have heard, that Mrs. Jordan has been uneasy at the applause bestowed on Miss Biggs and Miss Mellon![4] Watching such momentary emotions in Mr. Pitt, his friends may have persuaded themselves, that a rupture with Mr. Addington was certain. They wish Mr. Pitt to come forward, as it is only under his wings that they can fly. They look only at him; he looks not at them; he walks himself alone,[5] and probably puts no one in possession of his thoughts or his views. He knows the Cabinet is at present filled by men, who must yield to his first attack. He keeps his late situation open, as securely, as if he had put in a deputy;[6] but the following reasons, probably, prevent his return, allowing it to be immediately in his power.

It is universally admitted, indeed woeful and daily experience confirms the opinion, that there is great danger, on account of Bonaparte's ambitious conduct, the present peace will not last long. Bonaparte complains of the hostile conduct even of Mr. Addington, who is as submissive to him as decency and the laws of

[4] The Drury Lane actress Dorothea Jordan (1762–1816), who played Imogen in Lewis's *Adelmorn the Outlaw* in May 1801 was now being assigned comic parts. But Harriot Mellon (*c* 1777–1837), an understudy of Miss Jordan in 1795–6, was found to have a "figure...surpass[ing] that of Mrs. Jordan" when she took over a "breeches part" from the latter in 1800; yet as an actress she "came in the second line, being eclipsed by Mrs. Jordan". Joseph Knight in *DNB*. Miss Biggs did not attain a reputation that has survived.

[5] Pitt, now in the ranks of the great, is between Napoleon, who "walks by himself", and Washington, who walks "in the midst": see 27 Jan and 25 Mar 1800, above.

[6] Cf the style of C's remark 23 Feb that Addington had taken out a patent from Bonaparte.

his country will allow. If Mr. Pitt were in office, with what appearance of truth would not Bonaparte inveigh against the perfidious measures of the English Government? The hatred in Mr. Pitt's mind towards Bonaparte can as little be doubted, as Bonaparte's hatred of the equality of power with France, which the English nation maintains. If Mr. Pitt were Premier, every accusation which the Chief Consul might throw out against the good faith of England would be believed. We should be told that Pitt was at work in all the Cabinets of Europe, stirring up a new coalition against France; that he was plotting against the life of Bonaparte; that he encouraged the British press to calumniate "the Envoy of God," &c. Whenever Bonaparte attempted some ambitious, unjust step, he would liberally throw out accusations against the English Government, in order to deprive it of credit or authority in opposing him. All his charges would be believed, if Mr. Pitt were at the head of the Cabinet. Every one would ask, "how could we expect peace would be maintained by Mr. Pitt?" And if a new war broke out, Mr. Pitt would be blamed as the author of it, though it were purely and wholly the effect of Bonaparte's ambition. Such a war Mr. Pitt could not conduct with vigour. He would be viewed as the author of the calamity, not as the champion of our rights, our privileges, and independence. A war cannot be carried on with energy, unless the People are persuaded the conductor of it is a sincere friend of Peace. Mr. Pitt would, therefore, find himself crippled and disabled at the outset of a war, begun during his administration; he would be obliged to submit to Bonaparte, or to proceed with defeat after defeat or to resign with disgrace, making way for some of his clerks, who would yield up all to the Chief Consul, and make such a *safe* and *honourable* peace as Mr. Addington has concluded.

On the contrary, Mr. Pitt, by remaining out of office, has the chance of two things: the renewal of war; or the continuance of peace. If Bonaparte provokes another war, of which there is too much probability, then Mr. Pitt will come forward into activity, and the country will demand that he should be Minister. As he rejoiced in the failure of the negotiations at Lisle, some years after they terminated, because they convinced the country of the truth of his predictions, that peace with France could not be had on safe and honourable conditions; so now might he rejoice in seeing his other predictions fulfilled, that no peace with France could be maintained; that peace, with a Jacobin government, with the child and champion of Jacobinism, is impossible; and that nothing is left for the existence of Britain, but to fight against France till those principles are destroyed; that is, till the Bourbon Family is restored, and France obliged to return to her antient limits. Mr. Fox has said, he liked the peace the better, because the terms were bad, as they were a just punishment of the authors of the war.[7] Mr. Pitt may hereafter also boast that he liked the peace the better, because the terms were bad, as they intoxicated France with pride and insolence, while they filled England with indignation, and inspired a spirit of revenge. The disgrace and insecurity of the terms, he may say, brought on speedily, while our resources were unimpaired, and before those of the enemy were established and secured, a contest which, sooner or later, must have been fought for our national existence. He may rejoice in the bad terms of Mr. Addington's peace, as he rejoiced in the humiliating conditions which he offered[8] at Lisle. He boasted that the failure of the negotiations at Lisle enabled him to establish his solid system of finance (the Income Tax); and, in the event of another war arising in the manner we have described, it is probable that, feeling himself strong in popularity, the country prostrate before him, anxious only for self-preservation, he would take some great and astonishing measures with regard to the Funds, and then boast of the present Addington peace as one of the happiest events, one of the most successful expedients, since it enabled him to retrieve the finances of the country. A strong sense of danger must exist before any gigantic steps in finance can be attempted.—Another war, under the circumstances we have described, would create this feeling to the deepest extent, and Bonaparte, it is too probable, will furnish the occasion.

On the other hand, should the peace continue, and should the two countries sink into real tranquillity, then Mr. Pitt, if he wishes to return to office, will only find himself in the situation, in which

[7] Fox had said at the Shakespeare Tavern, as quoted by *M Post* 12 Oct 1801, "It may be said, the peace is glorious to France, and to the First Consul, who governs the Republic. It certainly is, but is it unfair to say it ought to be so? Ought not a country which has struggled . . . against a powerful confederacy formed against its liberties and independence . . . come out of such a contest covered with glory and splendour? (*Loud applause.*) *We have made peace, without gaining the objects of the war. We certainly have, and I like the peace the better on that account.*—(The whole room rung with plaudits.)" Shortly afterward Fox conceded to Grey that his speech had been indiscreet and that "The triumph of the French Government over the English does in fact afford me a degree of pleasure which it is very difficult to disguise". Fox *Corres* III 347–8.

[8] Probably a slip for "he was offered"; it was generally considered that the stiff terms of the Directory caused the breakdown of negotiations in 1797 at Lille.

he at present stands. He may then boast, as many now absurdly boast, that we obtained by the war all the objects we had in view, that the war saved us from a revolution, and that to him the country is indebted as its Saviour. On these grounds he may put forth his pretensions to the office of Premier, when the peace shall promise to be permanent, and all the late War Party will support him. If place be his object, he may then resort to those very steps which he could now pursue for obtaining it; and, with this additional advantage, perhaps, that the King's dislike may be worn off.

We have not so despicable an opinion of Mr. Pitt, as to suppose he would desire place for the sake of its emoluments, or the silly vanity of being Prime Minister. He has favourite projects in view, like other ambitious men; he is animated into political life, only as they hold out prospects of success. At present he is disgusted with all public affairs, because he has been thwarted in his favourite plans of restoring the antient order of things in France, and reducing her within due bounds. The success of that plan is necessary to his character as a statesman; and are we to believe that a man of so much ambition as Mr. Pitt, does not hope to see the time arrive, when he will yet have the chances of success in his favour; when he will yet triumph and exult as the Deliverer of Europe, of civilised society? And are we to suppose Mr. Pitt will throw away this great chance, by which alone his character can be retrieved, his pride flattered, and his fame established, for the grovelling gratification of merely being in office, a defeated, and a disgraced Minister? No. We have a high opinion of Mr. Pitt's spirit. He will either be Minister pursuing the objects of his heart, or he will not be Minister at all. There is no chance of success in such a pursuit at present, and therefore he is disgusted with politics, he cannot bear to speak of them. Just so it was with Mr. Fox. He retired five years ago, because he saw no chance of attaining the favourite objects of his pursuits. He was disgusted with politics, and could not bear to speak of them. He became enamoured of the study of botany, and would converse about nothing but shrubs, or flowers; Mr. Pitt has taken a farm, and will soon know nothing but of drilling and dibbling. However the advocates of the war may boast of having attained its objects, as they absurdly do, nothing refutes their assertions more than Mr. Pitt's conduct. He, the prime conductor of the war, and of course the best judge of its design, has retired with the disgust of disappointment, the despondency of despair; while his antagonist Bonaparte, who really is victorious, pushes on step by step up the ladder of his ambition, emboldened by the confidence success inspires, flushed with the ardour of triumph.

From all this, we infer, without pretending to any particular knowledge on the subject, that there is no chance of Mr. Pitt's returning to office speedily, or, of even taking an active part in Parliament. He is, and will be, as much a seceder, as Mr. Fox, though not so formally avowed. Mr. Addington will thank us, for thus proving, that he may hold the reins of Government some time longer, if the peace lasts, and he will endeavour that it shall. He need not therefore despair of placing and pensioning his uncles and aunts, brothers-in-law, cousins, and children. He may still be enabled, when he retires from office, to lay his hand upon his heart, and conscientiously declare, he has fulfilled his duties as a—*husband* and a *father*.[9]

[8 October 1802, Friday]
The important Essay on the Affairs of France to-morrow.

AFFAIRS OF FRANCE. II[1]

9 October 1802, Saturday; except "II", *M Post* title. *EOT* II 522–31, a certain attribution, with revisions that are probably authorial but may possibly have been supplied by SC.

One of our correspondents in England, has received a letter from Paris, which we regret that we are not permitted to publish. It was incomparably more interesting, than private French letters commonly are, not for the novelty of its information, but from its having been written by a gentleman, who has had an opportunity of forming intimacies at Paris in the highest circles, and whose uncredulous, watchful, and profound understanding, stamps a kind of authenticity on the reports, which he considers as worthy of particular notice. His letter authorises us to repeat a conjecture,

[9] Cf *CN* I 1289 (Dec 1802): "What is Addington's nomination of his own Son to the Clerkship of the Pells—is it not taking 5000£ a year, as a Bribe?" Yet this paragraph, beneath the sarcasm, begins to support C's claim in *BL* ch 10 that he had written in defence of government from the time of Addington's administration. *BL* (1907) I 144–5. Cf C on *himself* as husband and father: *Friend* No 2 (*CC*) II 22n–3.

[1] C contributed an Epitaph this day; see App D, below.

which we lately hazarded, as now something more than a mere conjecture,[2] namely, that Bonaparte both is, and has good reason to be, more alarmed by the rapid spread of Royalism in France, at this present time, than in any preceding period of the revolution.

The present is an age, in which a man may be as easily politic over much, as righteous over much. We more than suspect, that this has been the case with the First Consul. The republicans and philosophers were his natural friends; but they would not endure a despot; and, besides, they are decidedly the minority in France. He applied himself, therefore, to trick the royalists, and the priests; and we think it not at all improbable, that they will have tricked him. It was not without reason, that so many of the republican generals were disgusted and alarmed by the late consecration of banners, &c.[3] They saw clearly, that in the minds of the soldiery, the attachment to liberty was grounded on a contempt for their old superstitions. The common people are no nice discriminators: opinions and attachments enter their minds *in companies*, and make their *exit* in the same manner.[a] The army had fought both against the [b]throne and the altar:[c] and, if it behoves them to repent of the one, they will not be slow in making atonement for the other. Or, if they remain faithful, they must be kept steady by such privileges and largesses, as will rouse the people of France by the sense of direct personal insecurity, and by the intolerable weight of taxes. Our only apprehension is, that the government may have recourse to the old preventive against domestic disturbances, and plunge the country once again into a foreign war.

We believe (and we now refer to the questions which we have stated in our paper),[4] that there are five Royalists to one Jacobin in France at present; and that there are nearly an equal number of *active* and *zealous* Royalists, as of *active* and *zealous* Jacobins. We can conceive no other[d] way, in which they can counteract each other's forces, unless it be by the fears, which the Jacobins entertain,

[a] *EOT*: way. [b–c] *EOT*: altar and the throne:
[d] *EOT* omits, but C means "other than war"

2 The conjecture of 5 Oct, based on the published "Private Letter" of 25 Sept. Possibly the new letter was from the same source, its publication rendered superfluous by C's essay. Might the source have been Peltier? Cf 21 Sept 1802 n 26, above.

3 That is, following the Concordat, published 17 Apr 1802 and celebrated on Easter day, establishing a *modus vivendi* between the Papacy and the Republic of France; the ceremony of coronation of Napoleon as Emperor would be held on 2 Dec. For C's earlier satire on consecrated banners, see *The Devil's Walk*; see also Pitt's speech as reported 4 Feb 1800, above.

4 That is, the questions of 5 Oct.

from a knowledge of the spread of Royalism. While the *name* of the republic continues, and the sovereignty of the people is taught by the government itself, as the basis of all rightful government, there remains a *hope* to the republicans. A more favourable moment may arrive; and the liberty of the press, and a genuine representative system, may be established by a single act of the legislature.—But if the Bourbons be once restored, they can never be re-ejected without a civil war. These considerations *may*, perhaps, preserve the republicans in a gloomy passiveness. Indignation may clutch the dagger of Brutus with convulsive grasp; but the fear of more lasting evils keeps it still sheathed.[5] A famous ex-bishop, now in England,[6] whom we may with justice class among the purest patriots of the revolution; a man, who dared avow his zeal for christianity under Robespierre, and his love of popular freedom under Bonaparte, said lately, as we have been informed—"the republicans in France endure the despotism, not as men, but as fathers. They hope, that their children will be free." As far as this can be deemed a counterpoise, so far the two parties may be said to counteract each other.

We are fully conscious that this is a very inadequate answer to the important questions concerning the strength of the two parties, and their mutual relations. But we wait for further information from France. We wish to present facts to our readers, not vague reasonings founded on sandy conjectures. To the three latter questions, we trust, we shall do somewhat more justice. 1st, What are the advantages to France, and to Great Britain, which may be expected from the re-establishment of the old Monarchy? 2dly, What are the circumstances, which do at this time especially favour the restoration of the Bourbons? 3dly, Is there any possible point of union between the Republicans and the Royalists?[7]

[5] The comparison reveals the survival of C's own Jacobinism, for by C's definition Brutus was not a Jacobin but a republican who was a Roman patrician (see 21 Oct 1802, below, and cf C's defence of Brutus in *Friend* No 23—*CC*—II 319). But more significant is the new alignment with such extreme anti-Gallicans as Cobbett and Peltier, whose current toying with the image of assassination was becoming an international scandal. C writes after (and knows about, if he has not read) Peltier's more rabid comparison of Rome and France and expression of a wish for Bonaparte's assassination (in the 1st and 3rd numbers of *L'Ambigu*, on sale in London 16 and 26 Aug)—subject of the libel case, tried 21 Feb 1803, in which Mackintosh defended Peltier. C's *private* jesting about Bonaparte and the guillotine in 1800 was a different sort of thing.

[6] A tongue-in-cheek quotation of Talleyrand; according to the *Moniteur* of 8 Aug, the "atrocious Bishop of Arras" was now in London (quoted in *M Post* 13 Aug 1802).

[7] As now put, the first and second questions will engender the essay on

In the first question we suppose an extreme case, namely, the re-establishment of the old Monarchy, without modification, or limitations. We must, therefore, in fair reasoning, suppose another extreme case, to compare it with: namely, the permanence of the present despotism. On this supposition, the advantages to France would be great indeed!

The First Consuls of France swear to prevent, as far as in them lies, the return of all feudal institutions. Lucien Bonaparte,[8] in the Tribunate, debating on the establishment of a Legion of Honour, treated hereditary honours as too absurd to be even disputed against in a Republic: and the First Consul is said to have expressed his surprise, that any man should be weak or wicked enough to propose, that the Supreme Magistracy should be hereditary in his family. These may be very orthodox politics in France; but it has been the habit of our mind to think with great respect of feudal institutions in general, and with an especial admiration of this particular part of it, hereditary succession. We regard it, as forming of itself a limitation of monarchical power: and, if we dared wish an abridgment of the power of the Crown in our own country in any instance (and the vote of the House of Commons on Mr. Burke's motion, surely authorises us to wish it),[9] it would be in this—that the creation of new Peers should be controuled by certain definite limitations. The influence which the late Minister derived from increasing the Peerage nearly one-third, is notorious, and has been often the subject of constitutional complaint.[10] What would it be, if every Peerage

the Bourbons, first announced on 12 Oct. The third will be left unanswered, but the implication is that the Jacobin who is a potential Brutus may make common cause with fellow patricians. By the same token C no longer quotes an imaginary "artful Royalist" but puts the Royalist arguments in his own language: the advantages of family pride and hereditary nobility. Soon C will be using the epithet "upstart Corsican" (4 Nov) and finding it a defect in Bonaparte that he lacks noble birth (9 Nov).

[8] Lucien Bonaparte (1775–1840), often at odds with his older brother, as a more sincere democrat; yet he had assisted in the coup of 18 Brumaire.

[9] On Burke's motions for economic reform, in 1780, see Maccoby pp 300–4.

[10] "In all, there were 119 creations and promotions in the peerage of Great Britain or of the United Kingdom during Pitt's periods as Minister, and of these 5 dated from his second Ministry of 1804–6. Of the 119, 89 were creations—87 in the first long Ministry—and there were no fewer than 45 creations and promotions between December 1783 and the general election in the summer of 1790. When one considers that there were 212 temporal peers at the end of 1783, one can see the size and pace of the activity that was so much condemned. For it was the magnitude and regularity of the process that caused the grumbles, and, in the end, alarm." Ehrman *The Younger Pitt* 624–5. Ehrman gives in detail both the social and the political import of the complaints.

returned to the Crown at the death of its possessor?—and not only this, but likewise the revenues attached to the Peerage? What if the Crown itself were at the disposal of the King?—Where should we look for any bulwark of our freedom? All those great and illustrious names, who, whether they oppose, or support, the Ministry, do in both cases equally influence and check its measures, would then perhaps be the servile, and daring[a] creatures, because the ambitious candidates, of the Crown. If the provision which the Crown can at present make for the younger branches of noble families, have gained the Ministry too many adherents in both Houses, what would be the result, if even the very existence of the whole family, as noble, depended on the will of the executive Government? If, in short, instead of our Percies, Russels, and Howards, we had a legion of Mandarins, without any of those antient internal regulations which controul the election of the Mandarins in China? The patronage of the Crown in Great Britain is enormous; but it [b]is, in part, only[c] nominally concentered to one person. No Ministry can exist without possessing the absolute disposal of the largest portion of it, unchecked by the Sovereign: and every great parliamentary landholder considers himself as entitled to make a certain number of claims upon the Ministry, in proportion to his consequence in the Legislature and in the country. That there are great inequalities in this[d] power, in consequence of the very disproportionate number of boroughs in the different counties, we know and regret. Yet the rule holds good, notwithstanding the exceptions.

Now, though this check on the power of the Crown arises in a great measure in this country from the power of our Parliaments, yet, we must not forget, that the power of the Parliaments did, itself, originally spring from the power of the great feudal families: and the same check, though not in the same degree, did exist in France before the Revolution; and to a certain degree exists at this time in Spain, dependent as it is on France; and, in Austria, it is nearly as great as in England. In France, at present, the military are the sole claimants on the patronage of the Government; men, who have no stake in their country, no honourable family pride, no natural influence. The only men, who dare ask, as those, that have a *right* to be gratified, are the men, to whom the Despot may venture to propose any baseness, any conspiracy against the rights and properties of the people, as the condition of the bargain. An hereditary Monarchy, with an hereditary Nobility, is, *ipso facto*, a limited

[a] Error for "darling"? [b–c] *EOT*: is only [d] *EOT*: the

Monarchy; and, whatever advantages a limited Monarchy possesses over a military despotism, those advantages France would gain, by substituting the Bourbons for the Corsican.

Add to this, that the majority of Frenchmen are decidedly[a] Royalists. Now it is scarcely possible to conceive a greater or more important difference than that of a majority, with the Government in its favour, and a majority, with a Government in direct hostility to it. For, in the first place, the Consular Government knows the strength of the Royalists better than the Royalists themselves know it; and becomes fierce, suspicious, and prone to violent measures, from the perpetual goading of its own terrors. But, let the Government become that of the majority, and every man then avows his opinion loudly; those, who were timid, or indifferent, become bold and zealous; their numbers are counted and known; the fact is ascertained, that they *are* the majority; and the Jacobins are not only disheartened, but even baffled by their own creed, of which it is a fundamental article, that the will of the majority is binding on the *actions* of the minority. The majority, thus conscious of their own superior strength and numbers, would communicate a sense of security to the Government; and such a Government can shew itself magnanimous with very little self-denial, and still less danger. Nay, this shew of magnanimity would be a necessary measure of policy in one instance, and that the most important. The restored Monarch would necessarily place his greatest confidence in the avowed affections of the people, while the object of his greatest fears would be the soldiery and their officers. To disband the army was the first step of the reign of Charles the Second; and, tyrant as he was, he tyrannised by Lawyers and Priests, and not by soldiers. In consequence, he entered into no wars, but those into which the Parliament absolutely compelled him.

And here, we presume, we are to find the advantages of the re-establishment of the old Monarchy in France in relation to Austria and Great Britain. Peace would be of necessity the first and fundamental policy of the Monarch, for many years. First, because a victorious General under Louis XVIII. would be no longer necessarily in the same devotion to his Sovereign as the same person must have been under Louis XIV.; but both himself and his army would justly become objects of suspicion. Secondly, because it would be idle to anticipate, under a regular and Monarchical Government, the same career of splendid victories which had accompanied the [b]enthusiasm and[c] gigantic efforts, and extra-natural resources of a

[a] *EOT*: decidedly, though passively, [b-c] *EOT*: enthusiasm,

revolutionary republic; and it would be therefore a most pernicious policy to hazard the comparison with[a] a people, whose very life and being are involved in national vanity. The same ambition and vain gloriousness, which drove Louis XIV. to perpetual wars, would impel his restored successor to perpetual peace; at least, it would have this tendency. And lastly, the complication of financial difficulties, and the difficulties attendant on the re-induction of the exiles into their properties and titles, would of themselves form enough of employment, and more than enough of anxiety.

Other causes might be stated, arising out of the depression of the Catholic interest in Germany; and the influence, which the fashionable zeal for religion—(for no doubt this would become *fashionable*, in the most emphatic sense of the word, after the restoration in France, and from the same causes that made debauchery and open contempt of religion fashionable, after the restoration in England); the influence which this new religious zeal would have in moderating the national ambition, and in prompting the pious son of the church to give back to Austria what the Republicans and Protestants had robbed from her. We would willingly add to all these the influence of gratitude to this country, for her unexampled hospitality; but this would be a compliment to priests, Romish priests, French priests, which we could not pay with sincerity. For of all men, priests are the least grateful, of all priests the Catholic, and of all Catholic priests the French. If it be asked, why? we answer briefly, [b]in consequence of an early abstraction from the humanising influence of being an ordinary man among ordinary men,[11] which is common to all priests; in consequence of the total banishment from the conjugal and parental affections which are peculiar to the Romish superstition; and in[c] consequence of the excessive vanity which belongs to them, as Frenchmen, and which is more incompatible with gratitude, than any other vice or weakness whatsoever. Any gratitude to this country for her efforts in the war, we do not even speak of. Mr. Pitt, in the first campaign, took care that we should have no claim of this kind. For our own purposes we waged war; and, for our own purposes, made peace.

[a] *EOT*: among

[b–c] *EOT*: 1. That to be and to appear an ordinary man among ordinary men is the firmest security for our best virtues, and that priests are less grateful than other men in consequence of that early removal, which is, more or less, common to all priests, into a permanent corps, with its appropriate and peculiar dresses, manners, and interests. 2. In consequence of the total banishment from the conjugal and parental affections which is peculiar to the Romish superstition. 3. In

[11] See C's essays of 1800 on Washington (above), whose greatness and humanness grew from the "union of himself with the mass of his fellow-citizens".

We have thus stated the advantages which would accrue both to France and to her neighbours from the restoration of the old Monarchy, without terms or limitations. We should strangely forget our best principles, if we overlooked, or omitted to mention, that great disadvantages would accompany them, both to France and Great Britain. But we shall introduce them more naturally in the solution of the two very interesting questions, which still remain. And in this solution, which we shall attempt to-morrow,[12] we flatter ourselves, that we shall place the present state of France in a light, in which it has not been generally seen in this country.

ROMANTIC MARRIAGE. I[1]

11 October 1802, Monday; except "I", *M Post* title. *EOT* II 585–7; attribution certain. De Q and Stuart attest that C wrote this first Buttermere report; internal evidence links to the same author those of 22 Oct, 5 and 20 Nov, and 31 Dec. See also *EOT* III 1022. Reprinted exactly in *Courier* of same day; also reprinted in *M Chron* of 12 Oct and *London Chronicle* of 9–12 Oct with cautionary note.

ON the 2d instant a Gentleman, calling himself Alexander Augustus Hope, Member for Linlithgowshire, and brother to the Earl of Hopetown,[a] was married at the church of Lorten,[b] near Keswick, to a young woman, celebrated by the tourists under the name of *The Beauty of Buttermere*. To beauty, however, in the strict sense of the word, she has small pretensions, for she is rather gap-toothed, and somewhat pock-fretten. But her face is very expressive, and the expression extremely interesting, and her figure and movements are graceful to a miracle. She ought indeed to have been called the Grace of Buttermere, rather than the Beauty.—She is the daughter of an old couple, named Robinson, who keep a poor little pot-house at the foot of the small lake of Buttermere, with the sign of the Char, and has been all her life the attendant and waiter, for they have no servant. She is now about thirty, and has long attracted the notice of every visitor[2] by her exquisite elegance, and the becoming manner in which she is used to fillet her beautiful long hair; likewise

[a] *EOT*: Hopetoun [b] *EOT*: Lorton [in court record *M Post* 14 Dec "Laughton"]

[12] See 12 Oct, below.

[1] For verses this day see App D, below.

[2] On Sunday, 1 Aug, C, alone, "drank Tea at the little Inn" (*CN* I 1395, *CL* II 835, 846) and evidently observed this "sensible, and observant woman", from her complexion to her handwriting. This first description of Mary Robinson, emphasising her grace and carriage and purity, set the tone for subsequent descriptions of her, including WW's in *Prelude* VII (1805) 316–59.

by the uncommonly fine Italian hand-writing in which the little bill was[a] drawn out. Added to this, she has ever maintained an irreproachable character, is a good daughter, and[b] a modest, sensible, and observant woman. That such a woman should find a husband in a man of rank and fortune, so very far above her sphere of life, is not very extraordinary; but there are other circumstances which add much to the interest of the story.

Above two months ago, Mr. Hope went to Buttermere upon a fishing expedition, in his own carriage, but without any servants, and took up his abode at the house[c] kept by the father of the beauty of Buttermere, in the neighbourhood of which he was called the Honourable Charles Hope, Member for Dumfries. Here he paid his addresses to a lady of youth, beauty, and good fortune, and obtained her consent. The wedding clothes were bought, and the day fixed for their marriage,[3] when he feigned a pretence for absence, and married the beauty of Buttermere. The mistake in the name, the want of an establishment suited to his rank, and the circumstance of his attaching himself to a young lady of fortune, had excited much suspicion, and many began to consider him an impostor. His marriage, however, with[d] a poor girl without money, family, or expectations, has weakened the suspicions entertained to his disadvantage, but the interest which the good people of Keswick take in the welfare of the beauty of Buttermere, has not yet suffered them to entirely subside, and they await with anxiety the moment when they shall receive decisive proofs that the bridegroom is the real person whom he describes himself to be. The circumstances of his marriage are sufficient to satisfy us that he is no impostor; and, therefore, we may venture to congratulate the beauty of Buttermere upon her good fortune. The Hon. Alexander Hope, the member for Linlithgowshire, is a Colonel in the army, a Lieutenant-Colonel of the 14th regiment of foot, brother to the Earl of Hopetoun, and Lieutenant Governour of Edinburgh Castle.[4]

[a] *EOT*: is [b] *EOT*: and is [c] *EOT*: home [d] *EOT*: to

[3] Contradicted in later accounts (see 31 Dec, below).

[4] Other papers picked up this story, despite or perhaps because of the misgivings aroused—the *M Chron* (12 Oct) because it "has much the appearance of a romance, and is strongly calculated to excite suspicion". Woodfall's *London Chronicle* for 9–12 Oct reprinted it from *M Chron* under date of 11 Oct.

On 14 Oct the *M Post* (and the *Courier*) printed the following letter, dated "Chatham, Oct. 12":

To the Editor

Sir—Having seen in your paper of yesterday, an account of a romantic marriage, supposed to be celebrated

[11 October 1802, Monday]
The Article on the probability of the restoration of the Bourbon Family, shall appear to-morrow.

ON THE CIRCUMSTANCES, THAT APPEAR ESPECIALLY TO FAVOUR THE RETURN OF THE BOURBONS AT THIS PRESENT TIME[1]

12 October 1802, Tuesday; *M Post* title. *EOT* II 532–42; certain attribution, often claimed by C. Not a revised text, the one addition in *EOT* being a necessary one.

IT was scarcely more than a month before his restoration, when Charles the Second appeared to all Europe as much an exile from the hope, as from the possession, of his Throne. He had neither

by the Hon. Col. Alexander Hope, with a young woman of inferior rank in life, at the church of Lorten, near Keswick, on the 2d inst. and at the conclusion of the account, you impress your readers with the idea of the authenticity of the marriage. I think it right to acquaint you that Col. Alex. Hope, the gentleman alluded to, has been abroad the whole summer, and by very late accounts was at Vienna; I must desire, therefore, you will contradict the said marriage in your next paper, and assert, that the person who called himself Col. Alexander Hope, must be an impostor. Yours, &c.

CHARLES HOPE.

The editor noted: "That the person married was the person he represented himself to be, we cannot affirm; but that the marriage took place under the circumstances we have stated, is certain."

A few days later there was another letter from Charles Hope (*M Post* 19 Oct):

SIR,

The person who has been travelling this summer in Ireland, the South of Scotland, and Cumberland, under the name of *The Hon. Alexander Augustus Hope*, and who, in that character, married a woman at Buttermere, is a notorious swindler and impostor.—Col. Alexander Hope has been in Germany for six months past. I am, Sir, yours, &c.

Edinburgh, Oct. 14 C. HOPE.

The *M Chron* on the same day scooped Stuart with a report that "Mr. Hardinge, the Welch Judge, passing through Keswick on a tour, has detected the impostor . . .". But by the 21st (see notice) C had sent in a tale of "the particulars of the novel of real life", which Stuart printed 22 Oct (see below).

[1] A sequel to 9 Oct, in which the comparison to the restoration of Charles II was touched upon. Colmer (69) contrasts this analogy with that of the Comparison of France to Rome as failing "to carry any conviction at all"; Roberta Brinkley (*C 17th C* 4) considers it "one of the most brilliant examples" of historical analogy.

army, nor treasure, no organized faction in England, no influence in the Continental Courts: he was countenanced by no foreign Power, and Cardinal Mazarine, the then master-spirit of Europe, was intriguing against him. His fortunes were at their lowest ebb; and they returned, as the tide does in our rivers, Trent and Parrot, not by any gradual growth,[a] but *in a head*, and like a wall of waters.[2] Had England then sunk in the rank of nations during her commonwealth? And were the inhabitants recalled to loyalty by national pride? Or had her commerce failed? Or was her naval strength giving way? Least of all things. Never had England stood crowned with equal glory; never had she spoken in so commanding a voice to the surrounding Powers! Lord Clarendon, and other contemporary writers, can find no other terms for this sudden restoration, than that it was *miraculous*, and effected by an immediate influence of the Deity. This was the natural language of gratitude and exultation at the time; but now it would be childish.

The inferences,[b] which thinking men have since drawn from this event, are these:—That to conduct with splendour the foreign concerns of a revolutionary nation is an easy task, but to settle its domestic troubles, exceeds the strength of the most gigantic genius; and that though a nation may be intoxicated for a while by their glory abroad, yet they will inevitably, sooner or later, be sobered by the sense of insecurity and oppression at home. The Republic of England was splendid and powerful; and the Pretender to the Throne a weak, and friendless exile. But the people of England were sick at heart with hope long delayed; it was natural for those, who had been disappointed of liberty, to compound for quiet. "For *liberty* they had fought, but they still found themselves *slaves*; and, weary of their military yoke, were easily induced to submit once more to that of the old Monarchy, as the lesser evil." (*Vide Ralph's Review of the Reigns of Charles II. and James II. p. 2*).[3]

These inferences we receive, as the fair solution of the apparent miracle, yet not without some addition and some correction. It ought not to be overlooked, that the revolution itself, its rapid change of constitutions,[c] and its quick successions of political

[a] *EOT*: increase [b] *EOT*: inference [c] *EOT*: constitution

[2] On the waters of the Trent and Parrot, see 14 Oct 1800, above.

[3] James Ralph (c 1705–62), the introductory part of *The History of England during the Reigns of K. William, Q. Anne, and K. George I. with an Introductory Review of the Reigns of the Royal Brothers, Charles and James* (2 vols 1744–6) I 2 (var). Ralph reads "to that of Monarchy, as the *least Evil*".

contrivances, had distempered the people with a craving for novelty, while new Constitutions, and new ordinances, became themselves stale and unattractive; and that the only novelty, which remained, of sufficient excitement to ease this craving, was the restoration of their banished Sovereign; and the more extraordinary the circumstances of this restoration, the more likely therefore was it to be effected. This addition is not only important in itself, but it is likewise eminently pertinent to our present purpose, for who among our leaders has not already detected the application? And the correction, which we propose, is on the same ground still more interesting. All the reasoners on this great event have spoken of the weakness and desertion of Charles the Second as circumstances which of themselves were unfriendly to the restoration, though they were more than counterpoised by the national discontents, contempt of transitory constitutions, and dread and hatred of the military despotism. Now we, on the contrary, feel a deep conviction, that this very weakness,[4] this very desertion of the Monarch, was a *cause* of his restoration equally powerful with any of those last enumerated; that it was a great *co-cause*, and necessary condition of his return. For, in the first place, it flattered both the national pride and the national morality; it was an act of its own free choice, a true election, a measure not of compulsion or foreign influence, but of conscience and genuine conviction; secondly, it did from the same reasons present nothing opposite to good policy and the welfare of the nation.

If Charles came back wholly unassisted by the power of the Continental Courts, he came back of course unintangled in their interests, with no obligations incurred that were likely to set the *gratitude* of the Throne at variance with the honour and prosperity of the nation; and, lastly, infatuated as the parliament appeared by its loyalty, yet the whole proceedings of all the parliaments of his whole reign make it amount almost to demonstration, that if Charles the Second had been powerfully backed by the armies and resources of France, Spain, or the Empire, he never would have been received without *terms*; that the discussion of *terms* would have rekindled the disposition to political controversy; that a spirit of Republican enthusiasm, which only slumbered, would have been re-awakened in the army; and that, instead of Charles the Second on the throne, England would have seen General Monk on the scaffold. These are no mere speculations; they are facts of

[4] Cf C on Addington's weakness, 22 Mar 1802, above.

history.[5] Hale, afterwards chief justice, moved in the new parliament, that a committee should be appointed to digest such propositions of terms, as might be sent over to the king. This motion was seconded; but immediately and successfully opposed by Monk, who swore solemnly, that though all was now quiet beyond expectation, he nevertheless could not answer for the army, if any delay whatsoever was put to the sending for the King: and as a sufficient answer to the general expediency of sending over terms, he uttered the following memorable sentences, which appeared so full of unanswerable good sense, that they were followed by a *shout* of assent over the whole House. "I cannot answer for the peace of the army, if there be any delay; and the blood and mischief, that will follow, will be on the heads of those who cause that delay, however plausible the pretext. —But in this instance, there is not even a plausible pretext. What *need* is there of *sending* over propositions to the King? May you not as well prepare them, and offer them to him, when he shall have come over? HE HAS NEITHER ARMY NOR TREASURE[a] to bring with him, wherewith either to frighten or corrupt you."

If it were unsafe or imprudent to compare these facts in open and direct terms with the present circumstances of the Bourbons, the resemblance is so close and striking, that we might confidently leave the inference to be drawn by our readers themselves. But it will be more pleasant to our readers to find their own thoughts in our words; and we have, besides, other facts and circumstances, *peculiar*

[a] *EOT* does not retain emphasis

[5] From here to the end of the paragraph C is paraphrasing Bishop Gilbert Burnet, as quoted in Ralph *History* I 6n. It is interesting to see how C reconstructed Monk's indirectly quoted speech from this portion of Burnet's report:

"He [Monk] told the House, that there was yet, beyond all Mens Hope, an universal Quiet all over the Nation; but there were many Incendiaries still on the Watch, trying where they could first raise the Flame. He said, he had such copious Informations sent him of these Things, that it was not fit they should be generally known: He could not answer for the Peace, either of the Nation or of the Army, if any Delay was put to the sending for the King: What need was there of sending Propositions to him? Might they not as well prepare them and offer them to him, when he should come over? He was to bring neither Army nor Treasure with him, either to fright them or to corrupt them. So he moved, that they would immediately send Commissioners to bring over the King: And said, that he must lay the Blame of all the Blood or Mischief that might follow on the Heads of those, who should still insist on any Motion that might delay the present Settlement of the Nation. This was eccho'd with such a Shout over the House, that the Motion was no more insisted on."

C ignores the concluding remark of Burnet: "To the King's coming in without Conditions, may be well imputed all the Errors of his Reign."

to France, which it belongs to our present purpose to place in their proper light; and lastly, although we are no adherents or partisans of the present ministry, yet we do believe that both ministers themselves, and the great officers[a] in the service of government, possess too much of the principles and temper of our constitution to regard, with an evil eye, any truly dispassionate, respectful, and unfactious reasoning, that has been conceived in the spirit, and expressed with the decency, of an Englishman and a gentleman. Whether the restoration of the Royal Family of France be the object of our hopes, or of our fears, whether it be an event which we implore or deprecate, we shall, in the present disquisition, give our readers no opportunity of concluding or even conjecturing:[6] for we shall confine ourselves to *facts*, and to the deductions that flow immediately from those facts. *Sedulo curavimus humanas res et actiones humanas non ridere, non lugere, neque detestari; sed* intelligere! (Spino. Tract. Pol.)[b][7]

When the Duke of Brunswick sent abroad his notorious proclamation, we can assuredly not condemn the French, for acting on the belief of the old adage—

Regnabit sanguine multo,
Ad regnum quisquis venit ab exilio.[8]

When Austria and England, the natural enemies of France, made the restoration of the Bourbons so far a[c] necessary condition of peace, as that Lord Grenville (though he did not in direct terms state it as the necessary condition, yet) stated it as the only means, the English Court were able to suggest, we can assuredly not wonder, if the French had serious doubts respecting the good policy of an event, which appeared to be so ardently wished for by those, who could not be suspected of very ardently wishing for the glory or prosperity

[a] *EOT*: offices [b] *EOT*: I. § iv.) [c] *M Post*: as a [corrected in *EOT*]

[6] C does not, however, anywhere discuss the other side of the question, i.e. the *disadvantages* in a restoration of the Bourbons; the implied conclusion of 21 Oct ("Once a Jacobin") is that all former Jacobins, English as well as French, are capable of combining to effect the Bourbons' restoration.

[7] Spinoza *Tractatus politicus* I iv: *Opera posthuma* (1677) 268 (var). Tr: "[*We*] *have carefully endeavoured not to deride, or deplore, or detest human* [*affairs and*] *actions, but* to understand them!" Tr William MacCall (1854) 14 (C's words in brackets).

[8] Suetonius *Lives of the Caesars* III: *Tiberius* 59.2 (var). Tr: "He ever shall reign with great bloodshed | Whoso made himself king, coming from banishment home." Tr adapted from Rolfe (LCL) I 377.

On Brunswick's manifesto of Jul 1792, threatening on the part of the kings of Austria and Prussia to exterminate Paris unless King Louis were at once restored, see *Prelude* X 9–13, also *Conciones: Lects 1795* (*CC*) 72.

of France.[9] We ventured at the time to state the impolicy of Lord Grenville's letter, and that the French would interpret it into these words:—"The Bourbons are to receive their throne at the expence of their country." Indeed, it was generally understood, that a peace, which should take place on the restoration of the Royal Family, was to be accompanied by a complete return of all Europe to its *status quo*.

Now, though neither Belgium, nor the Italian conquests, may prove ultimately of any true advantage to France, yet it was irrational to imagine, that it would be other than a mighty motive with that ambitious and military nation against the recal of the Bourbons, if it were accompanied by the loss of these acquisitions. Neither, indeed, was it altogether *fair* to propose a nominal *status quo* for France, when Great Britain had utterly ruined both the navy and commerce of France, had doubled her own trade and naval force, and almost doubled her empire in India. It was foreseen from the beginning of the contest, that it was contrary to every principle of human nature that a great, warlike, and vain nation should receive a family which was to be forced upon them by the arms of their enemies and rivals. A King might be a necessary medicine for France; but a full-grown nation will not endure to be *drenched*. We have ever been of opinion that the alliance of James with the Court of France, and the notorious, and in plain truth, *treasonable* attachment of the House of Stuart to that Court, were among the principal causes of the final victory of the Revolutionists over the Jacobites. And, it is no small confirmation of this opinion, and a fact, strikingly to our present purpose, that the time in which the Pretender was the nearest to his object, and the Jacobites the most powerful and numerous, was, in the latter end of the reign of Queen Anne, when the victories and conquests of the Duke of Marlborough and the Allies had reduced France almost to an object of pity: when the state of France resembled the present state of Austria. In short, the Bourbons now are free from all obligations, from all entanglement of English and Austrian interests;[a] we will not add, that the illustrious persons themselves consider themselves as injured and abandoned, and that their feelings are much more those of resentment, than partiality, or a sense of obligation; but we may surely say, without

[a] *EOT*: interest;

[9] An echo of C's arguments of 1798 and 1800. The next passage paraphrases 8 Jan 1800: "Louis XVIII. would purchase his throne at the price of his country".

offence, or danger of contradiction, that the French and the Royalists of France consider them in this light. No doubt, the argument is not lost among them. All former objections to the recal of the Monarch have ceased; we may have our King, and a Government of Laws and Religion, and yet not give up a hair's breadth of our present territory, and yet not lose a grain of sand from the weight of our present influence.

So far the affairs of France and the Bourbons are as nearly alike, as two distant events well can be, to the affairs of England and Charles II. But the state of property in Great Britain had undergone, during the civil wars, and subsequent commonwealth and usurpation, a change perfectly trifling, compared with that, which it has undergone in France during the revolution. And this, it must be admitted, is a difficulty of almost gigantic size; and the attempt, which Mr. Pitt, in answer to Mr. Erskine, made to obviate or weaken it, was utterly unsuccessful; and the futility of the attempt was unanswerably evinced by Mr. Fox, in his reply to that speech.[10] The difficulty still exists, but not in its former magnitude. First, it has been the policy of the Chief Consul to prevent the sub-division of landed property, for he has learnt that small independent properties are a nursery of freemen, and his policy has been aided, and carried into full effect, by the enormous fortunes, which a swarm of Generals, and Commissaries, and Diplomatists, have acquired, and which they have been encouraged to realise in land, and indeed, called on to do so, as a test of their attachment to their country. What the First Consul does from policy, the weak and abandoned Directory permitted from necessity or corruption. The result of the whole is briefly this, that the property, which must, and ought to be, restored on the re-establishment [a]of the Bourbons,[b] lies, for the greater part, in large masses, and in comparatively few hands; and that the proprietors likewise are for the greater part men stained with such crimes as would make it unsafe for them to remain in France on the restoration of Royalty, independently of the Government, and belong to that faction, which is equally unpopular with the Jacobins as with the Royalists. In those instances, in which the alienated property has been greatly subdivided, the small land-holders have been, and still are, so heavily taxed, and so constantly alarmed concerning the intentions of the Consulate towards them, that there is reason to believe, that

a–b Supplied from *EOT*—a curious omission

10 C refers to the debate of 3 Feb 1800 (q.v., above, 6 Feb 1800).

they would many of them rather be the farmers than the proprietors, if the government guaranteed to them a long lease, at a moderate rent, as the price of a voluntary surrender of their precarious rights, as freeholders.[11] Add to this, as mainly diminishing the difficulty, the number of emigrants, who have lately forfeited all claim on the exertions of the Royal Family of France by the court, which they have paid to Bonaparte. Those, who have consulted their own interests, neglecting those of the emigrant Sovereign, must have expected, that the Sovereign and his family would consult their own interest in the same manner. In short, no emigrant has any positive claim on the Bourbons, but those who have neither attempted to gain the forgiveness of the Consular Government, nor accepted it when offered. The difficulty, therefore, exists still; but it has diminished, and it is daily diminishing. The property of the church, and the whole of ecclesiastical affairs, have been so far settled by Bonaparte, that (unless the Bourbons are more bigoted in religion, and far less attached to the Monarchy, than we can believe them to be) the very authority of the Pope, and the necessity of preserving the consistency of the Papal proceedings in the eyes of the people, may be well pleaded by them, for a general adherence to the concordat, as far as it regards the Catholics. The concordat is indeed, one of the countless proceedings of the First Consul, which has smoothed the way for the triumphal entry of the Bourbons. The same measure has, indeed, called forth the Protestants into open day, and given them the knowledge of their own numbers and importance; but it has proportionally alarmed the Catholics, and effectually aided the general cause of Royalism. It is now time that we should state the difficulties on the supposition of the complete re-establishment[12] of the antient regime; and, whether, or no, the knots can be untied; and, if not, whether they may not be cut, by a plan that should embrace the grand principles of all honest men of all parties.

[11] WW would have been less casual about the fate of rural estatesmen.

[12] Of the Concordat C would say that it "first occasioned me to think accurately & with consecutive Logic on the force & meaning of the word *Established* Church...". To George Coleridge 3 Jun 1802: *CL* II 803. The Concordat did not establish a single church in France, but it set forth the terms of state control of and relation to the Catholic church. See also *CL* II 806.

[15 October 1802, Friday]

A very able Article on "Once a Jacobin, always a Jacobin," is intended for to-morrow.

[19 October 1802, Tuesday]

The very excellent Article of "Once a Jacobin, always a Jacobin," is intended for to-morrow.

ONCE A JACOBIN ALWAYS A JACOBIN[1]

21 October 1802, Thursday; *M Post* title. *EOT* II 542–52; reprinted, in part, with changes, in *Friend* Nos 10–11 (*CC*) II 144–6.

THIS charitable adage was at one time fashionable in the ministerial circles; and Mr. Pitt himself, in one of his most powerful speeches, gave it every advantage, that is derivable from stately diction.[2] What he thus condescended to decorate, it were well, if he had attempted to prove. But no! he found it a blank assertion, and a blank assertion he suffered it to remain. What *is* a Jacobin? Perhaps the best answer to this question would be, that it is a term of abuse, the convenient watch-word of a faction. Of course, it has either no meaning, or a very vague one: for definite terms are unmanageable things, and the passions of men do not readily gather round them. Party rage, and fanatical aversion, have their birth place, and natural abode, in floating and obscure generalities, and seldom or never burst forth, except from clouds and vapours. Thunder and lightning from a clear blue sky has been deemed a miracle in all ages. But though we should find it difficult to determine, what a Jacobin *is*, we may however easily conjecture, what the different sects of Anti-Jacobins have meant by the word.

1 Preceded, 14 Oct, by a revised version of the Recantation ode of 1798—*France. An Ode*—and a long excerpt from *Fears in Solitude* (see App D, below). The political message of all this publication is that the *M Post* is recanting from Bonaparte to Bourbon, from peace to preparation for war, and almost (C will spell it out in Nov) from Fox to Pitt—and is doing so in high style.

In Sept Bonaparte had attempted to resolve a struggle within the new "Helvetian Republic" between constitutionalists and federalists by demanding a government "friendly to France" and marching 30,000 men to the border. Hence the "peculiar... interest" (editor's note) in C's ode.

2 Pitt, as reported by C (18 Feb 1800), had said, "The mind once tainted with Jacobinism can never be wholly free from the taint"—and C had given the speech in statelier or more vivid diction than the other reporters. The present passage is full of suppressed amusement for C; he knows who gave the speech "every advantage" and who "condescended to decorate" it.

The base and venal creatures, and the blind and furious bigots, of the late Ministry, comprehended under that word all, who from whatever cause opposed the late war, and the late Ministry, and whom they hate for this opposition with such mortal hatred, as is usual with bigots alarmed, and detected culprits. "*Once a Jacobin, always a Jacobin,*" signifies no more in the minds of these men, than "*such a one is a man, whom I shall never cease to hate.*" With other men, honest and less violent Anti-Jacobins, the word implies a man, whose affections have been warmly and deeply interested in the cause of general freedom, who has hoped all good and honourable things both *of*, and *for*, mankind. In this sense of the word, Jacobin, the adage would affirm, that no man can ever become altogether an apostate to Liberty, who has at any time been sincerely and fervently attached to it. His hopes will burn like the Greek fire, hard to be extinguished, and easily rekindling.[3] Even when he despairs of the cause, he will yet *wish*, that it had been successful. And even when private interests have warped his public character, his convictions will remain, and his wishes often rise up in rebellion against his outward actions and public avowals. Thus interpreted, the assertion, "*Once a Jacobin, always a Jacobin,*" is so favourable a representation of human nature, that we are willing, too willing perhaps, to admit it even without proof.

There is yet a third class of Anti-jacobins, and of this class we profess ourselves to be, who use the word, *Jacobin*, as they use the word, *Whig*, and both words only for want of better; who confess, that Jacobin is too often a word of vague abuse, but believe, that there are certain definite ideas, hitherto not expressed in any single word, which may be attached to this word; and who in consequence uniformly use the word, Jacobin, with certain definite ideas attached to it, those ideas, and no other. A Jacobin, in *our* sense of the term, is one who believes, and is disposed to act on the belief, that all, or the greater part of, the happiness or misery, virtue or vice, of mankind, depends on forms of government; who admits no form of government as either good or rightful, which does not flow directly and formally from the persons governed; who—[a]considering life, health, moral and intellectual improvement, and liberty both of person and conscience, as blessings which governments are bound as far as possible to increase and secure to every inhabitant, whether he has or has not any fixed property, and moreover as blessings of

[a] Dash here and below supplied from *EOT*

[3] See *CL* I 539.

infinitely greater value to each individual, than the preservation of property can be to any individual—does consequently and consistently hold, that every inhabitant, who has attained the age of reason, has a natural and inalienable right to an *equal* share of power in the choice of the governors. In other words, the [a]Jacobin affirms that[b] no legislature can be rightful or good, which did not proceed from universal suffrage. In the power, and under the controul, of a legislature so chosen, he places all and every thing, with the exception of the natural rights of man, and the means appointed for the preservation and exercise of these rights, by a direct vote of the nation itself—that is to say, by a CONSTITUTION. Finally, the Jacobin deems it both justifiable and expedient to effect these requisite changes in faulty governments, by absolute revolutions, and considers no violences as properly rebellious or criminal, which are the *means* of giving to a nation the power of declaring and enforcing its sovereign will.

In brief, therefore, a Jacobin's Creed is this: 1. A government is the organ, by which form and publicity are given to the sovereign will of the people; and by which that will is enforced and exercised. 2. A government is likewise the instrument and means of purifying and regulating the national will by its public discussions, and by direct institutions for the comforts and instruction of the people. 3. Every native of a country has an equal right to that quantity of property, which is necessary for the sustenance of his life, and health. 4. All property beyond this, not being itself a right, can confer no right. Superior wisdom, with superior virtue, would indeed confer a right of superior power; but who is to decide on the possession? Not the person himself, who makes the claim: and if the people, then the right is given, and not inherent. Votes, therefore, *cannot* be *weighed* in this way, and they *must not* be weighed in any other [c]way, and nothing[d] remains possible, but that they must be *numbered.* No form of electing representatives is rightful, but that of universal suffrage. Every individual has a *right* to elect, and a capability of being elected. 5. The legislature has an absolute power over all other property, but that of article 3: unless the people shall have declared otherwise in the constitution. 6. All governments not constituted on these principles are unjust Governments. 7. The people have a right to overturn them, in whatever way it is possible; and any means necessary to this end become, *ipso facto*, right means.

[a–b] *M Post*: Jacobins affirms
EOT: Jacobins affirm that
[c–d] *EOT*: way. Nothing therefore

8. It is the right and duty of each individual, living under that Government, as far as in him lies, to impel and enable the people to exercise these rights.

The man who subscribes to *all* these articles is a complete Jacobin; to many, but not to all of them, a Semi-Jacobin, and the man who subscribes to any one article (excepting the second, which the Jacobin professes only in common with every other political sect not directly an advocate of despotism), may be fairly said to have a *shade* of Jacobinism in his character. If we are not greatly deceived we could point out more than one or two celebrated Anti-Jacobins, who are not slightly infected with some of the worst symptoms of the madness against which they are raving; and one or two acts of parliament which are justifiable only upon Jacobin principles. These are the ideas which we attach to the word Jacobin; and no other single word expresses them. Not Republican; Milton was a pure Republican, and yet his notions of government were highly aristocratic; Brutus was a Republican, but he perished in consequence of having killed the Jacobin, Caesar. Neither does Demagogue express that which we have detailed; nor yet Democrat. The former word implies simply a mode of conduct, and has no reference to principles; and the latter does of *necessity* convey no more than that a man prefers in any country a form of government, without monarchy or aristocracy, which in any country he *may* do, and yet be no Jacobin, and which in some countries he can do without any impeachment of good sense or honesty; for instance, in the purely pastoral and agricultural districts of Switzerland, where there is no other property but that of land and cattle, and that property very nearly equalised.[4] Whoever builds a Government on personal and natural rights, is so far a Jacobin. Whoever builds on social rights, that is, hereditary rank, property, and long prescription, is an Anti-Jacobin, even though he should nevertheless be a Republican, or even a Democrat.

If we have been prolix, let the importance of the subject induce our readers to consider it as a venial fault. Concerning a term, which nine-tenths of the nation have been in the habit of using, either as a name of glory, or a name of reproach and abhorrence, it is not only our advantage but even our duty to have clear, correct, and definite conceptions.[5] In the sense of the word, Jacobin, which we have here

[4] Property equalised: see n 10, below.

[5] On the importance of distinct conceptions see e.g. C to WW 30 May 1815 (*CL* IV 575). See also Erdman (1956) LX 497 and n, and below, II 459 (at n 25).

detailed (and, we dare be confident, that no other sense can be given which belongs exclusively to this word), the truth of the adage, "ONCE A JACOBIN, AND ALWAYS A JACOBIN," ought to be proved, before it can be used otherwise than wickedly and uncharitably. To prove its falsehood is rendered difficult by this circumstance alone, that there is no pretence, no shadow of an argument in support of its truth—no pretended facts, which we might invalidate—no train of reasoning, of which we might detect the sophistry. It is a blank assertion, the truth of which would be strange, inexplicable, monstrous; a fact standing by itself, without companion or analogy. An *assertion* therefore of its utter falsehood would be a complete overthrow of the *assertion* of its truth; and the only confutation, which it merits. It is an assertion that is consistent and pardonable only in the mouth of a thorough Jacobin, who held his principles to be of such undeniable, obvious, and eternal truth, that a man who had once understood could abandon them, no more than he could abandon the elements of geometry; and indeed we must admit, that the whole faction of Re-alarmists, from whose manufactory this precious adage proceeded, have both talked and acted precisely as if they believed in their hearts that Jacobinism presented arguments which were not answerable except by the sword, and charms, and an appearance of happiness, which were not to be withstood except by turning away our eyes from them.

Whence, but from these convictions, acting *unconsciously*, perhaps, did certain speeches proceed;[6] speeches containing such sentiments concerning the press and the public journals, as beseemed only the private conclave of an Inquisition, where every inquisitor was an Atheist, and yet bent to suppress Atheism? Whence that notable sentiment from the same orator, that those, who could be made *dumb*, ought to be so; and where this could not be, that the others were to be made *deaf*?[7]

From what other source that alarm concerning peace, because we should flock to Paris, and all come back *Jacobins*?[8] In the name of all that is sacred, of all that is great and honourable, in the name of Briton, unless this alarmist and his faction believe the truth

[6] C is referring to Windham's speeches on atheism etc at the beginning of the war, 1793–4.

[7] Windham on 7 Apr 1796: reported in *Watchman* No 7 (*CC*) 259.

[8] Windham's speech of 4 Nov 1801 on the Preliminaries of the Peace is extremely alarmist about the "contagion" of French principles and French *morals* that will infect England "in the soft hour of Peace". Debrett XVI 512–13 (the whole speech apparently printed from ms).

of Jacobinism, although from self-interest they oppose it, what do they imagine we have done with our common sense and common feelings? Is Jacobinism an absurdity—and have we no reason to detect it with?[9] Is it productive of all misery, and all horrors! and have we no natural humanity to make us turn away with indignation and loathing from it? Uproar and confusion, personal insecurity, insecurity of property, the tyranny of mobs, or the domination of a soldiery; private houses changed to brothels, the very ceremony of marriage itself only an initiation to harlotry, while marriage itself is degraded to mere concubinage—these, Mr. W[indham] and his friends, have said, and truly said, are the effects of Jacobinism! An insufferable licentiousness in their houses, and abroad an insufferable despotism! These are the effects of Jacobinism; and these, the whole English nation was to be clapped under hatches, lest they should see and fall in love with! "Once a Jacobin, always a Jacobin!"

And why? Is it because the creed which we have stated, is dazzling at first sight to the young, the innocent, the disinterested, and to those who, judging of men in general, from their own uncorrupted hearts, judge erroneously, and expect unwisely? Is it because it deceives the mind in its purest and most flexible period? Is it because it is an error that every day's experience aids to detect? an error against which all history is full of warning examples? Or, is it because the experiment has been tried before our eyes, and the error made palpable?

From what source are we to derive this strange phaenomenon, that the young, and the inexperienced, who, we know by regular experience, are deceived in their religious antipathies, and grow wiser; in their friendships, and grow wiser; in their modes of pleasure, and grow wiser; should, if once deceived in a question of abstract politics, cling to the error for ever and ever! though, in addition to the natural growth of judgment and information with increase of years, they live in the age, in which the tenets had been unfortunately acted upon, and the consequences, deformities, at which every good man's heart sickens, and head turns giddy? We were never at any period of our life converts to the system of French politics. As far back as our memory reaches, it was an axiom in politics with us, that in every country in which property prevailed, property must be

[9] From this sentence to the end of the penultimate paragraph quoted (var) in *Friend* Nos 10–11 (*CC*) II 144–6, "Mr. W[indham] and his friends" becoming "the wiser Advocates of Aristocracy".

the grand basis of the government; and that that [a]government was the best, in which the power was the most exactly proportioned to the property.[b][10] Yet we do not feel the less shocked by those who would turn an error in speculative politics into a sort of sin against the Holy Ghost, which in some miraculous and inexplicable manner shuts out not only mercy but even repentance!—and who now, that religious bigotry is dying away, would substitute in its place dogmas of *election* and *reprobation* in politics.

We were led to these considerations by the questions which we stated, and attempted in part to answer, in our last—and to which we shall again return, on the first open day[11]—namely, what are the circumstances that more especially favour the restoration of the Bourbons at this present time? What are the difficulties? And is there any possible point of junction between the Royalists and Jacobins? —The last of the three questions recalled to our memory the sentence, which we have been examining; and which we therefore examined, because we were unwilling that any of our readers should stumble at the threshold.[12]

[21 October 1802, Thursday]
Particulars of the romantic Marriage at Buttermere to-morrow.

[a-b] *EOT* prints in italics

[10] When reprinting this passage in *The Friend* C explained that he had not been a democrat but a Pantisocrat. By omitting to mention that he had once opposed private property, he keeps an appearance of changelessness in his definition. In pastoral Switzerland the equalitarian ideal may obtain (see above, at n 4); but the present passage implies that in the country where great inequalities of property exist (England) political representation should follow the same pattern. C would now have agreed with the landed Whig Reformers that "representation of the soil" was necessary to offset the increasing power of commercial interests. On the transitional phase in the Parliamentary Reform movement, see Erdman *PMLA* LVI (1941) 1071.

[11] No further essays on the subject appear.

[12] "I was particularly pleased with 'Once a Jacobin'", wrote Lamb (*LL* I 325–6); "though the argument is obvious enough, the style was less swelling than your things sometimes are, and it was plausible *ad populum*." That this was ironic praise is indicated by Lamb's next "hasty suggestion", which both implies objection to C's recent "comparison" essays and pretends to ignore C's now low opinion of Bonaparte: "a Parallel of Bonaparte with Cromwell, particularly as to the contrast in their deeds affecting *foreign* states". "Cromwell's interference for the Albigenses, B's against the Swiss", Lamb goes on: "Then Religion would come in; and Milton and you could rant about our countrymen of that period."

ROMANTIC MARRIAGE. II

22 October 1802, Friday; except "II", *M Post* title. *EOT* II 588–91; reprinted in *Courier* and *London Chronicle*, without comment.

Keswick, Oct. 15

THE following are the particulars of the novel of real life,[1] the scene of which has unfortunately been laid among our Mountains. The pretended Alexander Augustus Hope had not only paid his addresses to the young lady mentioned in your[2] first account, and actually fixed the wedding day, but had likewise made two others of Keswick (one the daughter of the fisherman who used to be his companion in his fishing expeditions) believe him under an engagement of marriage to them. Including his unfortunate wife, he had paid serious addresses to four women at the same time, one of rank and fortune, and three of humble life.

On the morning of his first departure from Keswick for Scotland, and of his marriage at Lorton Church, he transmitted to the gentleman, under whose protection the young lady at present is, a draft for 30*l.* on Mr. Crump, of Liverpool,[3] requesting him to pay some small debts in Keswick, and return him the balance. This the Gentleman immediately did, and sent him besides ten guineas, lest the pretended *honourable* should find himself short of cash. When the news came to Keswick (on the Saturday noon, Oct. 2) of his marriage, and suspicions were of course instantly awakened, the draft was sent to Liverpool for acceptance: and it *was* accepted. In a few days the Gentleman received a letter (from Dumfries, we believe, and *franked*, of course) informing him of the marriage. In this letter, the pretended HONOURABLE stated his purpose of returning within the time, which he had promised on his departure. And accordingly, he did return to Buttermere, in a coach and four, at the beginning of this week.

At this time, Mr. Judge Harding, who happened to be here, hearing that Colonel Hope was at Buttermere, and so romantically married (an old acquaintance of the Judge's, as it seems), sent over his servant, with a letter, requesting to see the Colonel. The servant

1 "Novel of real life" was a favoured subtitle in novels of the period; in his reviews C himself expresses a preference for "real life" in novels: see Erdman (1959b) 520 n 44.

2 The Keswick correspondent avoids identification with the gulled author of the 11 Oct report; yet later (20 Nov) he will claim them all.

3 On John Gregory Crump (d 1844) see below, 20 Nov n 5.

was introduced, and on seeing the man, instantly said, "Here is some mistake—this is not Colonel Hope."—The impostor took the letter, and replied, "'Tis not for me; it is for my brother Charles;" but sent word, that he should come to Keswick. And on Wednesday morning he came in his coach, but without his wife. He was, of course, interrogated by the Judge, who told him that he was not the person whose name he had assumed. He certainly[a] denied that he had assumed it; he had said that his name was Hope, but not that he was the Hon. Member for Linlithgow, or Dumfries. He was contradicted by the aforementioned Gentleman, who not only gave evidence that he had always spoken of himself as Lord Hopetown's brother, but that he had *franked* his letters as such. The respectable and intelligent Post-master of Keswick gave evidence to the same point. He was committed to our constable, while the examination was going forward.

He made light of the business; drew for another 20*l.* on Liverpool, which was cashed for him by the landlord of the Queen's Head, and sent to the Gentleman the ten guineas which he had borrowed. To amuse himself, he chose to make a little sailing expedition on the Lake, which the constable did not think himself authorised to prevent. Accordingly, he went with his old friend, the fisherman: and all remained waiting for his return. Evening and the darkness came on: he did not return: but was guided by the fisherman through the Gorge of Borrodale, and probably escaped over the Sta[k]e, a fearful Alpine pass, over Glaramara, into Langdale. No intelligence has since been received of him. The landlord retains the coach in pledge for his 20*l.* and has discovered the very alarming circumstance, that all his plate and linen were in the coach. From which it is concluded, that he meant to desert his poor wife, and that he has deserted her. I cannot express the sincere concern, which every inhabitant of the country takes in the misfortune of poor Mary, of Buttermere. I knew her well; and I can truly say, that she would have been an ornament to any rank of life. She was intelligent, and well-informed, and uniformly maintained her dignity, as a woman, by never forgetting, or suffering others to forget, that she was the Maid of the Inn, the *attendant* of those who stopped at the ale-house, and not the *familiar*. I never knew any one think otherwise than well and highly of her, who had demeaned themselves consistently with their own rank and character. I am convinced, that when the whole of the courtship is made known, she will rise in the opinion of the good

[a] *EOT*: confidently

and the sensible, instead of sinking. It seems, that there are some circumstances attending her birth and true parentage, which would account for her striking superiority in mind, and manners, in a way extremely flattering to the prejudices of rank and birth. It is amusing to hear at Keswick the extravagant encomiums on the impostor's manners and address.

Those who have been duped, find it pleasant to imagine all this; and the one or two whose suspicions were awakened from the first, as naturally imagine, that they saw the very contrary. Buttermere is nine miles from Keswick, by the horse-road; fourteen by the carriage-road.

[1 November 1802, Monday]

ΕΣΤΗΣΕ's Letter to Mr. Fox to-morrow, if possible.

[2 November 1802, Tuesday]

ΕΣΤΗΣΕ's Letter to Mr. Fox, shall, if possible, appear to-morrow. As it will occupy a great part of the Paper, we must devote a particular day to its insertion.

[3 November 1802, Wednesday]

The Foreign and Law Intelligence this day necessarily exclude ΕΣΤΗΣΕ's Letter to Mr. Fox; but, as those impediments cannot occur To-morrow, it shall then appear positively.

LETTER I. TO MR. FOX[1]

4 November 1802, Thursday; entitled "To Mr. Fox". *EOT* II 552–71; the text was not corrected by C, who often spoke of his Letters to Fox but apparently lost his copies of them. See *CL* III 543, IV 715.

SIR,

"A Letter to Mr. Fox," when not a personal lampoon, has usually been little more than a convenient form and title, for some political effusion, which has been thus dedicated to you *ex*

[1] C in Sept, seeing the *M Post* indulging in sarcasm about Fox's visit to France (see n 26, below), proposed to write some Letters to the Whig leader, and Stuart on 29 Sept (cf letter to C, App B, below) egged him on: "Pray write the Letters to Fox—*and pray* abuse those Coxcombs who pay adoration going to Bonaparte—Erskine Mackintosh &c". C must have sent the first Letter by mid-October, if we are to credit his later assertion that Stuart "kept them [the Letters] 3 weeks —afraid to publish them—" (*CL* II 912). Yet C was still "writing the Letters to Mr Fox—Eleven in the morning" on 20 Oct (*CN* I 1252), ten days before the first announcement,

officio as the nominal Leader of the Opposition. I hope, Sir, to have at least this one advantage over your former public correspondents, that while I address you exclusively on subjects of national interest, I shall yet scrupulously confine myself to actions and speeches, which are your's, and your's only. In common with the majority of our countrymen, and, I would fain believe, with all whose minds have not been distorted by political alarm,[a] or sicklied by religious cant, I have felt you, Sir, to be a genuine Englishman. We know that the original web of your character is English, notwithstanding some foreign fancy-patterns, which you may have incautiously suffered to be *worked* upon it. I have attributed to you, in an eminent degree, a *healthy* understanding, with *healthy* affections—if I may dare address so bold a Latinism to you, Sir![2] from the influence of whose future writings I hope and expect, that a pure and native English will once again become the taste and fashion of English writers.[3] Your honours and your occupations, as the Statesman, and as the leader of a party, have never overstepped and stifled your plain sense, and plain feelings, as a human being. Nature appears to me to have distinguished you from other men, not so much by rare and splendid faculties, as by an unusual portion of the good, which, in a lesser quantity, belongs to all men. For these reasons my admiration of your character has been without wonder, and, in consequence, accompanied with a proportionably greater confidence. My attachment too has been fervent and sincere, but not blind, not that of a partisan. By the clearness with which I have seemed to myself to detect your errors, and by the pain and sense of reluctance, with which this detection has been uniformly attended, I have given evidence to my

[a] *EOT*: alarms,

1 Nov. Stuart may have been somewhat taken aback by the intemperance of C's attack; yet C's position was a logical complement of the condemnation of Bonaparte unleashed in the "Comparison" essays, to the delight of Stuart *and* Mackintosh.

Ignorant of this chronology, and unaware that C was in Keswick, not London, a recent biographer of Fox commenting on Fox's speech of 3 Nov 1801 (but misdating it 1802) quotes C as having "rushed into print" with his attack, "enraged to find his political leader lauding Napoleon". Christopher Hobhouse *Fox* (1947) 236.

2 C's italics call attention to a "Latinism" of allusion: "mens sana in corpore sano"; he is raising a sly doubt as to Fox's present sanity.

3 Fox did not live to complete his great work, but *A History of the Early Part of the Reign of James the Second* was published posthumously in 1808. C in 1810 found it "grievously" disappointing, the work of "a well-thinking amiable man" but not of "the Philosopher, the high-minded & comprehensive Historian...". *CL* III 272.

own mind, that my zeal has been in the light of knowledge. The most important, as well as the most recent, of these supposed errors will form the subject of the present letter. As an Englishman, I have a right to notice it: for in your public conduct all your countrymen have more than a life-interest. As a lover of unsophisticated English liberty, I have a motive to exercise the right. Yet, with how much greater, with how much purer a pleasure could I turn to your enemies, if the occasion permitted it, and recount the instances of your wisdom and integrity![4]

The French Revolution makes it difficult to call up any impassioned attention to the political disputes which preceded it. It has to a wonderful degree diminished the impression even of those, which have been contemporary with it. What a tumultuous interest would not the Irish Union have excited in this country, if it had been attempted fourteen years earlier! The languid interest which it did excite (languid, compared with the importance and magnitude of the event), is a fact, not unworthy the notice of the philosophical historian. I shall confine my letter to that part of your political conduct, Sir! which has an immediate bearing on the French Revolution.

You welcomed this stupendous event, Sir! with the spirit of an Englishman; with a spirit, which even in its excess was truly English. If you shall ultimately appear to have erred, posterity will add more to your heart on this account, than it will detract from your sagacity. To have hoped too boldly of our common nature, is a fault, which all good men have an interest in forgiving.[5] As far as the final verdict on this part of your character lies with the good, you will be tried, Sir! by a jury of accomplices. I still flatter myself, that, the main source of your common error will have been this—you suffered yourself to forget, that the Revolutionists were Frenchmen. You were, however, Sir! assuredly on the further side of an allowable enthusiasm, when you pronounced the first Constitution of France, "a stupendous monument of human wisdom and human happiness."[6]

[4] "Coleridge has indited a violent philippic against Mr. Fox . . . a compound of expressions of humility, gentleman-ushering-in most arrogant charges. It will do Mr. Fox no real injury among those that know him." Lamb, *LL* I 331–2 (with misprint "gentlemen-").

[5] C used this sentence in *Friend* No 10 (*CC*) II 144.

[6] This also reappears in the same *Friend* (*CC*) II 144. It is oddly used as a preface to C's reprinting "Once a Jacobin" in *The Friend*. Fox on 15 Apr 1791 had called the French Constitution "the most stupendous and glorious edifice of liberty. . . in any time or country". See *Friend* (*CC*) I 220 n 1.

The wish must have been indeed "the father to the thought,"[7] when you imagined, Sir! that a constitution could receive its final and faultless shape at one cast; that the passions of a newly emancipated people, and that people the French, should run at once into the mould, like melted ores, and harden in a few hours into perfection.[8]

The first gust of Jacobinism was sufficient to overthrow this stupendous monument. It was overthrown, the Sovereign murdered, and all Europe seemed moving under arms. For your counsels and exertions at the commencement of this ominous war, and during the whole of its continuance, you have a just claim on the gratitude and admiration of your country. Your efforts were proportioned to the awfulness of the occasion, and the melancholy event has demonstrated, that a portion of the gift of prophecy still rests upon the wise and good. We must be compelled to add, that you yourself appear to have been in part the cause of the frustration of your own counsels. History—nay, even the daily experience of our common law-courts teaches us, that, in contests of all kinds, it is by no means necessary, that one party should be in the right. More frequently, both are in the wrong. It had been well for your fame, and well, perhaps, for your country, if you, Sir, had acted on this principle. But no! The English Ministry were to be attacked at every movement, and criminated in every measure: and so far, it must be admitted, their own blunders, their own lust of innovation, did but too amply justify you. But this did not appear sufficient, or, perhaps, practicable, to you, unless the French were as regularly defended. Where their conduct was too palpably, too outrageously, bad to admit of direct defence, a palliation was attempted; and you manifested at least a wish to defend. I do not mean to assert, that there were no parts in your numerous orations, which, if extracted, would not appear to contradict this statement—but I do assert, Sir, that such was the general spirit of your speeches, and the fact is notorious, that this was the general impression which they left on the minds of your countrymen. Your language, your sentiments, were felt as Gallican.—If your harangues in the House of Commons, and at the Whig Club, were to be published under any one title, *Vindiciae Gallicae*,[9] is that which, to the feelings of a large majority of Englishmen, would best designate their general contents. Your defences,

[7] *II Henry IV* IV v 91.

[8] Cf C's earlier images of casting: 12 Dec 1799, 19 Mar 1800, above.

[9] A side-swipe at Mackintosh, who would have wished to forget that he had welcomed the French Revolution in 1791 with a reply to Burke under this title.

your palliations, your phraseology, would have been plainly impolitic and offensive, had they been just and precise; and being too often incorrect or overstrained, they were injurious to yourself, and to the glorious cause which you were pleading, to the cause of peace, of freedom, and of the independence of nations in their domestic concerns. Others, both in Parliament and out of it, took their tone from you. The Paper which is devoted to your party, and which acts in the strictest conformity to its wishes, became, to all intents and purposes, the standing counsel for the French Government.[10] The prejudices and the good sense of the country were alike disgusted, and pious and sober men every where alarmed.

Similar praise is due to you, Sir! for your long and manly resistance to the violences which were offered by the late Ministers to our laws and constitution[11]—similar praise, and I fear, with similar deductions. I am not disposed to charge you with countenancing the Corresponding Society.[12] But, did you, or your friends, discountenance them? Did you, or your friends, speak publicly and uniformly with due abhorrence of their principles or proceedings? Did no kind of political courtship pass between these English Revolutionists, and the Friends of Reform? It was the policy, let me say rather, it was a trick of the associated Jacobins, or patrons of revolution and universal suffrage, in this country, to represent themselves, from the very infancy of their society, as already numerous and formidable. To be thought numerous, they knew, was one way of becoming so. I speak advisedly, and from personal knowledge of the fact. At [a]the time,[b] when their fifties would not have puzzled a New Zealander's arithmetic, when a savage might have counted them on his fingers, without any occasion for repeating the process, it was only in their more modest moods, when their travelling agents represented themselves as below a hundred thousand. I believe, that this advice was early given them by a man, whose talents and attainments ought to

[a-b] *EOT*: a time

[10] The *M Chron*, here tendentiously described.

[11] C is referring to Fox's opposition to the Two Acts and the suspension of Habeas Corpus.

[12] C may know that he is steering close to the sort of wild charges made in Burke's "Fifty-four Articles of Impeachment against the Right Hon. C. J. Fox" in *A Letter . . . to . . . the Duke of Portland* (1797). He is even improving on Burke, for Burke only charged Fox with countenancing societies with which he was closely associated, the Friends of the People and the Friends of Liberty of the Press (items 2 and 14). But presumably Fox in 1795 should have warned C against Thelwall and the London Corresponding Society—and certainly against Fox himself.

have inspired a nobler ambition, than that of becoming the leader and tool-master of a London Corresponding Society.[13] But these men were outwitted, by means of their own contrivances. The Ministers, and the Agents of the Ministry, echoed and re-echoed the lie: what Secret Committees were eager to hear, and predetermined to believe, spies and informers gained a foundation for relating, *Confitentem habemus reum*.[14] The conspirators themselves admit their numbers, and the extent of the conspiracy. The Ministers wanted a pretext for striking a universal panic of property.[15] This vulgar artifice furnished them both with the pretext and the means. The alarm spread; and the nation, then infatuated with loyalty, consented to be clapped under hatches in compliment to the audacious lie of a faction, which was in truth as contemptible in numbers and in weight, as it was abominable in morals and in principle.

Of these facts, Sir! you might have easily gained both the information and the proof. Had your eloquence been directed to the enforcement of them, I dare not affirm, that you would have been more successful; but I am sure, that you would have better deserved success. But alas! the general tendency of your speeches, was to invalidate the charges of Ministry against the tenets and designs of the English Jacobins, when you should have joined hand and heart with the majority in the admission and the abhorrence both of one and the other. You should have pledged yourself, Sir! to public activity in all legal constitutional modes of suppressing both the men and their measures, if the ordinary constables of the night should indeed be found inadequate to the task. You should have declared, and even to satiety repeated the declaration, that you and your friends were both Anti-gallicans and Anti-jacobins. You should have made your country feel, that you were indeed so. If there were any honest men in this country infected with jacobinical opinions (and some there were and chiefly from this cause, that they heard the

[13] Thelwall and Dyer were the travelling agents known to C; Horne Tooke was the "tool-master". In 1832 (*TT* 1 May) C further distorted this evident distortion by changing the unmentionable Corresponding Society to "the Friends of the People" and producing the curious charge that *Fox* "absolutely exaggerated their numbers" and even their "sinister intentions"—and this after "Mr. Stewart, of the Courier", who was "very knowing" in the politics of the day, had warned Fox of the club's "gross lies and impostures". In reply to this Stuart (IX 579, X 24) indignantly protested that he "never spoke to Fox but once" and that to "communicate to him some agreeable information".

[14] A proverbial saying, but perhaps first in Cicero *Pro Ligario* 2. Tr: "We have a prisoner who admits his guilt." On Secret Committees see 3 Dec 1801 n 23.

[15] On C's frequent use of this phrase see above, 3 Jan 1800 (1) n 2.

notorious enemies of all freedom the loudest in the yell against Jacobinism),[16] your speeches, Sir, would have been their natural and certain cure. It would have been policy and humanity to have made them the antidotes to this delusion. With what irresistible strength of argument might you not then have contended, that the Jacobins in this country possessed neither number nor influence; that in England they had never been truly formidable, or if at any time, only during the Jacobinical career of Mr. Pitt's partisans at the close of the American war; and then for these two plain reasons, because the country was unsuccessful and degraded, and because Jacobinism was as yet a mere theory. Let a free country be, or be supposed to be, in danger; and Jacobinism is the necessary consequence. All men promiscuously, not according to rank or property, but by the superiority of popular talents, and the impulse of superior restlessness, will take an active part in politics. And this is itself Jacobinism, a political disease, which, in certain periods of national danger and by a transient operation, may, like other diseases, be even salutary, and sanative. You might have shewn, that even in France the operation of Jacobinism would necessarily be transient. Incompatible with property, and even with personal security, its own absurdities ensured it a speedy and natural death, if only we would abandon it to its own destiny. By attempting violently, and by a war, to precipitate its dissolution, we should unnaturally lengthen out its existence, if our arms were victorious; and if we were defeated, we should transmute this transient fanaticism for visionary liberty into a military enthusiasm, and, alarmed by an ephemeral frenzy, play into the hands of a never-dying ambition. My language may appear presumptuous, the language of a man ridiculously forgetful of his measureless inferiority to the person, to whom he presumes to dictate. But no, Sir! they are the dictates of mere common sense. That your own prudence did not dictate them to your own mind, is matter of regret indeed, but not altogether of surprise. The plainest rules of the game are those which are the most frequently forgotten by the most skilful adepts, when heated with the play. The great Statesman and Roman Orator bewailing his own blunders, adds—a child, who had quietly overlooked the game, might have set me right.[17] The utmost extent of my presumption is to be that child in relation to Mr. Fox.

[16] One of the "infected" men had been C, of course; and if Fox had *then* been loud against Jacobinism, C would have considered him among the "enemies of all freedom".

[17] Untraced. Cicero, in exile, certainly bewailed his blunders, but not in these words.

Not contented with mere omissions, not contented with not being the confuter and antagonist of Jacobinism, you publicly adopted its most offensive phraseology, and declared yourself at the Whig Club an adherent to the doctrine of the *Rights of Man*.[18] It is possible, Sir, that a very innocent meaning may be attached to these words, laxly used. If we allow a little laxity in terms, to what form of words may not an innocent meaning be attached? But when you avowed your conviction, that all men had political rights, as by an act of courage, and with the avowed consciousness that you were acknowledging an offensive doctrine, you must be understood, of course, to imply that doctrine which had given the offence. Else why avow with so much form and emphasis a tenet which the most infuriate bigots of Monarchy had never controverted? I venture, Sir, to affirm, and if it shall hereafter appear necessary, am prepared to prove, that between the acknowledged truth, that in all countries both Governments and subjects have duties—duties both to themselves and each other;—that between this truism and the Jacobinical doctrine of the universal inalienable right of all the inhabitants of every country to the exercise of their inherent sovereignty, there is no intermediate step, no middle meaning. But you, Sir, had publicly, and in Parliament opposed the doctrine of universal suffrage.[19] It is true—you did so, Sir! What will this prove? No more, I fear, than that you have acted inconsistently; or that you uttered words without any previous analysis of their import; or that you juggled with the understandings of the populace, and gratified their feelings by the use of popular words, while in your own mind you had annihilated their obvious sense, and reduced them to a mere truism. Whichever were the case, you spoke unwisely, Sir, and imprudently. Those whom alone a great Statesman would wish to conciliate are proud of their rights, indeed, but of rights created by the laws, and modified by property. These men, Sir, would regard the orator who would persuade them to substitute the rights of man for their rights, as Englishmen, in the same light as they would regard a mad metaphysician, who should counsel them to burn the writings of

[18] C probably refers to Fox's toast, repeating Norfolk's, "Our sovereign, the people", at a Whig Club dinner in May 1798, which resulted in his dismissal from the Privy Council.

[19] In Parliament 26 May 1797, supporting Grey's motion for moderate electoral reform. Universal (male) suffrage was identified with the radical London Corresponding Society. Fox liked Grey's proposal of suffrage for all who paid the parish tax of "scot and lot" (a tax paid according to means) because it rested on an ancient common-law right.

their estates, and rest their claims on the demonstrations of Puffendorf or Wolfius.[a][20]

But the time arrived, Sir, when all your errors might have been retrieved in one hour, and the memory of them have dissolved away in one general sentiment of regard and admiration. PEACE was concluded with the FRENCH REPUBLIC; and both the spirit and the letter of your predictions received the seal of a complete and final fulfilment. It is natural, Sir, to anticipate the language and conduct of a favourite Statesman on the eve of some great occasion—some occasion fitted and prepared by his guardian genius to call forth the best energies of his understanding and his affections. I looked forward to the debate on the Peace with an anxious pleasure. I described you to my imagination, as enforcing, with all your own dignified impetuosity, and with a tenfold weight of argument, the grand *principles* of your former counsels; yet cautiously abstaining from all allusion to the counsels themselves, and by a generous silence provoking the whole nation to make them the objects of their deepest regret, the topic of their hourly talk, the conversation at the table, [b]the buz[c] in the market place![21] I described you, as evincing that a peace had been concluded at the very first period, at which a war had become indisputably just and necessary.[22] I seemed almost to hear you congratulating the Alarmists and the crusading Christians on the restoration of religion, and an intense Monarchy in France,

[a] *EOT*: Wolfins [b–c] *EOT*: and the buzz

[20] Samuel, Freiherr von Pufendorf (1632–94), German jurist, writer on jurisprudence, opponent of Leibniz. Christian, Freiherr von Wolff (1679–1754); see *CN* I 902–5 but also III 3256n. C links Pufendorf and Wolff in much the same way, dealing with rights of nations, in *Friend* No 24 (*CC*) II 322n (I 291n).

[21] It is instructive to look back to see what in 7 Oct 1801 the *M Post* (if not C) *had* expected to hear Fox say, in the debate on the Peace: "Mr. Fox, we now hear, will attend Parliament . . . he, it is said, welcomes Peace as we, and the great bulk of the nation do, and supposes Ministers made it on the best terms they could obtain; but comparing those terms with their lofty pretensions during the war, he will no doubt stigmatise the conditions of the Peace, and hold up to public censure the men who seduced the country to support a contest for views which could not be fulfilled—".

[22] "It is with Jacobinism as with the French Empire, we made peace just at the very time, that war *first* became just & necessary." Thus wrote C in the margin of a copy of Godwin's *Thoughts Occasioned by the Perusal of Dr. Parr's Spital Sermon* (1801), quoted in Colmer (68). C read the pamphlet in Aug 1801; Colmer presumes that he "added the comment . . . during the course of the year": very well, if we take the year to run through Aug 1802—for he may only have evolved this formula that autumn. Woodring (p 76) dates the marginalia "during or just after the Peace of 1802". See also 21 Sept 1802 n 17, above.

and then, with an indignation too restless to endure the clothing of irony, pourtraying the dreadful ambition, and undisguised lust of dominion, before which we had thrown ourselves prostrate. I imagined you, with all your fervid, and searching logic, exposing the hollowness of our boasted acquisitions, and bringing into the close view of the terrified peace-makers, the enormous and compacted empire of the enemy. Yet, nevertheless, you would give your vote for the PEACE.—Even if it continue for a year only, if only for six months, there will be a time in which the true and just motives of war may be extricated from that cant of hypocrisy, and those ravings of delusion, which in the year 1793 had impelled the Ministry to rush into hostilities, like madmen, and afterwards conduct them, like men besotted. There will be a time at least for a general forgiveness to pass between all parties. Our mutual errors must needs bring on a mutual amnesty. And if we are compelled to wage war anew, as alas! who can doubt but sooner or later, we shall be compelled, we shall wage it with one advantage, of almost incalculable importance, with definite, intelligible, unvarying, and universally admitted motives, and objects.

In the same spirit, Sir! did I venture to anticipate your consolations to the friends of liberty, that if France had now for the first time united all sects and all parties in one sentiment of abhorrence and terror, she had now for the first time also lost all the semblances of a Republic, and had yielded herself up to an unbridled despotism, without condition, or prospect. In the same spirit too, giving you credit, Sir! for language, illustration, and arrangement, far, far beyond the scope of my imagination to shadow out, I still seemed assured, that I had anticipated the meaning and general purport of your peroration. I conceived that it could be no other than a generous exhortation to the Ministers and the Parliament, to shew both by public declarations and by measures answerable to these declarations, that the government was no longer jealous of the country, that they abjured all further insult of a loyal people by suspensions of the habeas-corpus act, or inquisitorial treason and sedition bills, that they looked for vigorous and enthusiastic support against the common enemy, chiefly from the spirit of freedom and of free inquiry, confident that the few wretches who dared utter or publish the loose principles and mock-philosophy of these vile mock-republicans, would find their fittest and adequate punishment in the contempt and abhorrence of their readers.

I believed, Sir! and still do believe, that selfish ambition can no longer retain a place in your hopes or wishes, that you have long felt, how possible it is to be a great man without place or office. I imagined, therefore, that you would have concluded with freely offering to ministers your vote and your counsels to preserve the peace, while it was possible; and when war was rendered inevitable, a still higher energy in support of that war, and a concentration of your intellect and experience to spread your own patriotic enthusiasm among the people, and to direct that enthusiasm to the wisest purposes. All this, and more than all this, I expected from you, Sir! Your country expected it. And how, Sir! did you meet these expectations? Did you utter one word of alarm at the atrocious ambition of the First Consul? One sentiment of pity or indignation at the iron despotism, under which this upstart Corsican[23] had reduced forty millions of your fellow creatures? Not a syllable! Not a breathing! You *exulted*, Sir, that the war had *ended* as it *ought* to end, gloriously for France, ignominiously for Great Britain!![24] For the spirit of a man and a patriot, you abandoned yourself to the low and womanish temper, which finds in a triumphant, "*Did I not tell you so, now?*" a pleasure that overpowered and sunk into oblivion all the dangers and all the disgrace of a whole nation, and that nation your country! I am at a loss to determine, Sir, which was the greater, the inconsistency or the folly of this speech, the impolicy or the unfeelingness. It was inconsistent, because you had hitherto uniformly contended, that you and your party had spoken the sense of the nation; that the guilt and misconduct rested upon the ministers, their adherents, and their creatures; that every artifice had been used to inflame and delude the public mind, yet that the success had been only transient and partial—that the Ministry, well aware of this, had in every sense shunned examination—that they alone were guilty, and in the better days of the House of Commons would assuredly have met with the

[23] C has by now absorbed more than the phrase "upstart Corsican" from Cobbett (who advised the *M Post* to call Bonaparte that, as early as 14 Aug). A cynical observer of the London press might attribute much of the new bellicosity of the *M Post* to the goading from the radical right. Cobbett's scolding of the *M Post*, in the "upstart" passage of 14 Aug, for treating Bonaparte with respect, was followed by C's series of invidious comparisons with the worst Caesars. Now the *M Post* in abandoning Fox abandons its disapproval of "the late war" and a future one—a few weeks after Cobbett's *Register* of 9 Oct (II 438–9) had rebuked at length "The Morning Post (of the 7th instant)", which, "while it justly reprobates the proclamation of Bonaparté, seems unaware, that this glaring instance of the restless and encroaching disposition of Republican France, affords a new and irresistible proof, of *the necessity of the late war to prevent the overthrow of the English Government*".

[24] See 8 Oct 1802 n 7, above.

punishment due to such misdemeanours joined with such incapacity. With what shadow of consistency, Sir, could you then exult in the calamity and prostration of a people, on whose guiltlessness you had grounded, and on which alone you could ground the guilt and punishableness of the Ministers? Nor was it less foolish than inconsistent. You must have known, Sir, that a peace which had exchanged liberty for empire, that conquests and successes which had transformed the victors into crouching slaves, with no freedom but to be vicious; no voice but to utter brothelry and blasphemy, could not in the eye of reason be glorious, or matter of a wise man's congratulation. Frenchmen hold it glorious, it is true; and you, Sir, when you pronounced it glorious for France, only proved to your mourning and indignant country, that you thought and felt as a Frenchman! It was unfeeling, Sir! for your country was dejected, and smarting with her wounds; you should have poured oil into them, not corrosives. Lastly, it was impolitic. Such sentiments must tend to alienate from you the affections of your countrymen, of all who love their country. And though I have long held in suspicion those political saints, who deal in no other good deeds than those of supererogation, yet I must doubt whether your sentiments will win for you the suffrages even of our new philosophers, our philanthropists, our citizens of the world. I conceive that even these turn away with disgust from the Land of Promise, from this glorified country, in which the government is all powerful by military violence, but weak and sluggish with the laws, even those of its own making; this regenerated country, in which the public advocates of civil freedom are the most obnoxious criminals, and the criminals not punished, but *kidnapped*.[25]

Having thus, Sir, publicly expatriated yourself, nothing remained for you, but by some outward act and ceremony to naturalize yourself in your new country. You went to France.—Your ostensible, and, I believe, true motive, was honourable, and at any less inauspicious time would have been adequate. A man must be little versed, indeed, in literary research, who does not understand that no man can examine manuscripts for another, in reference to historical enquiries.[26]

[25] C is writing of Napoleon's opponents who were shipped to Guiana. See above, 5 Oct 1802 n 6.

[26] We see that the praise of Fox's "future writings", in the first paragraph, was disingenuous; but C did not invent his disapproval of an Englishman's going to Paris to see Bonaparte. "Had I been you, I would have... returned by Paris—& not gone to Paris first", he told Tom Poole, who in May had joined the "crowd of eager Englishmen . . . pressing forward with their Letters of Recommendation" to the French capital (*CL* II 799). C wanted to go, but to the *south*. WW in August chose not to go beyond Calais (where he had come on urgent

The subject of your history (I speak from the general report) is worthy of your intellect, and appropriate to the efforts of your political life.—If you live to complete your plan, I hope and believe, Sir, that your work will instruct and animate your countrymen, when your errors will have an interest attached to them, chiefly in consequence of your literary fame. It has been said, and I think, without extravagance, that the History of Thucydides was cheaply purchased by the long Peloponnesian war, which was its subject. Painful as it will be to me to return from this digression, I cannot deny myself the pleasure of uttering this one heart-felt wish:—may your name be dear in future ages, as the Thucydides of Great Britain! We are proud, perhaps boastful, of the names of Robertson, Hume, and Gibbon: yet I dare avow my conviction, that the true honours of an English historian lie untouched before you. For the annals of our own country this is now especially true. I know few books that have more deeply and extensively injured the principles of Englishmen, whether moral, religious, or political, than that History of England which alone stands in any high reputation.[27] You best know it, Sir, to be a perfidious Romance, not a history; the apologist for priestcraft, while it undermines[a] the first principles even of natural religion; extravagantly sceptical concerning the laws, where they have been wantonly broken by tyrants, and then only decisive and

[a] *EOT*: undermined

personal business) with the "creatures" posting forward "to bend the knee ... before the new-born Majesty". Poole had called on Tom Paine; gone with Kemble to gatherings of English, American, and French literati at Maria Williams's salon; become intimate with Fox's factotum and Talleyrand's secretary; and reported to C that Fox, lodging near the "great national library", had come chiefly "to examine the archives and libraries which contain any documents relative to the history he is writing" (*Poole* II 89–90). And inevitably Poole had gone to Bonaparte's levée, being introduced by Mackintosh of all people.

Fox was in France from 29 Jul to 17 Nov; the *M Post* had been forward in criticising the Whig leader for presenting "himself in the way of a compliment before such a man as Bonaparte" (8 Sept); and C's Letters, alarming to Stuart though they *may* have seemed in their temerity (see above, n 1), are but fungi springing from the dark hints of Stuart's own paragraphs: "Mr. Fox must have sneered inwardly when Bonaparte addressed him with the common-place cant of the Revolution" (10 Sept); "Mr. Fox has too much politeness, or he might have made a most happy ironical answer to the Chief Consul's trite bombast" (18 Sept), and so on.

[27] In *SM* (1816) C attacks Hume's *History of England* for its "cool systematic attempt to steal away every feeling of reverence for every great name...". *SM* (*CC*) 22. For C's similar comment on Hume (c 1825) in Pepys *Memoirs* (2 vols 1825) II i 108, cf *Misc C* 284.

embittered by the breach when the offence has become necessary, and the offenders have been patriots; often false in the statement, and still more frequently attaining the purposes of falsehood by the omission of facts; in reasoning a model of the mock-profound, and in stile, Irish, Scottish, Gallican—any thing but English. Yet in very truth, to write the history of that period, which you have chosen, without pain and weariness of spirit, it would be necessary to possess, like Mr. Hume, the head and heart of an atheist. For you will be compelled, Sir, to draw into light, in an almost uninterrupted series, actions disgraceful to our country and to human nature.

You must exhibit vices struggling with vices, the best ends frustrated by the worst means, dishonoured by the basest agents; lawless and godless tyrants, with the whole regiment of lawyers for their body guard, and the united priesthood of the kingdom for their advanced centinels; and, more humiliating than this, you will be forced to shew the persecuted athirst for the power to persecute, and the partisans of freedom stained so indelibly with treachery, perjury, corruption, and hypocrisy, as to yield a semblance of justification, even to the oppressions, against which they were struggling. In fine, Sir! you will crowd together, as into one vast picture, Daemoniacs and Lepers, with no Pool of Bethesda in the fore ground, and with no other Saviour than that great educer of good out of evil, whom with a master's licence you might paint with a countenance of angry sorrow looking down on the group from the clouds of Heaven. This great history-piece you must teach us to hang up in the temple of national humility. But you will yourself restore us to our self-estimation, as Englishmen, by the courage with which you will adhere to the cause of liberty, and of course to the natural worthiness of the human heart; and by the sagacity, with which you will detect, and the truly British eloquence, with which you will heap shame on those sophists, who have developed the vices of individuals, in order to enfeeble the virtues of the species, who have exhibited the depravity of a singularly corrupted age, as the means, not of deterring us from their vices, but of alienating our understanding from the best impulses of our own best affections.

Here, Sir! I would fain close my address to you. But so I should abandon the chief purpose, which induced me to this act of apparent presumption. It is something, however, even to pause, from the painful task of cross examining the conduct of Mr. Fox. Many men, Sir, think you worthy to hear praise. I think the same, and I think still more: I believe you worthy of hearing the truth; and though this appear as rhetorical common place, and is suspicious from the antithetical form of its expression, yet it has a meaning for a good man; and if you should condescend to read this public remonstrance,[28] you will feel, that with a zeal, which your habitual encomiasts have neither head or heart to apprehend, I am, Sir,

Your Friend and Well-wisher,

ΕΣΤΗΣΕ

THE FRAUDULENT MARRIAGE

5 November 1802, Friday; *M Post* title. *EOT* II 591–2; continuity and the Keswick address link it sufficiently with the rest of the series by C. Reprinted in *Courier* of same day.

Keswick, Oct. 30

THE pretended Colonel Hope, in his rapid flight, left behind him a costly dressing-box, which was opened last week by a warrant from a Magistrate. It was completely furnished with elegant silver toilet trinkets; and there were two letters found in it, one from Ballynahinch,[a] in Ireland, and directed to Colonel Hope, from which it appeared that he was concerned in some gang or other in that unhappy country. There was likewise a cash-book, in which a memorandum was made of 1200*l.* and odd, having been invested by him in the bank of Dimsdale and Co. in the month of March last. Nothing appeared leading to a discovery of his real name. But to day poor Mary of Buttermere, examining the box more narrowly, found that the box[b] had a double bottom; and in the interspace were a number of letters addressed to him *from his wife and children*, under the name of Headfield. This atrocious villain is therefore a bigamist, as well as guilty of felony for attaching the name of a Member of Parliament to a letter for the purpose of a fraud. Some of your correspondents will inform us, perhaps, whether a marriage under a false name, be a legitimate marriage. The wretch had endeavoured to

[a] *EOT*: Ballanahinck [b] *EOT*: it

[28] C was grieved (for he had "a sort of affection for the man") when he discovered "that Fox had not read my two Letters; but had heard of them, & that they were mine—& had expressed himself more wounded by the circumstance than any thing that had happened since Burke's Business". To RS 23 Jun 1803: *CL* II 954. Fox may be supposed to have heard soon of C's Letters. His speech of 8 Dec (Debrett I 276–8) may refer obliquely to them; they *may* have been in his mind 23 Nov when he named the *M Post* among bellicose newspapers. (Gossip of C's authorship was widespread by 19 Nov—see Farington II 64.)

persuade the girl and her mother, and nominal father, to sell their estate, and to go all together with him into Scotland; which they refused to do, chiefly from the prudent fears of the old man. It is greatly to be hoped that the wretch will be apprehended—a more detestable action was surely never perpetrated. Poor Mary is the object of universal concern.[1]

[5 November 1802, Friday]

The Second Letter of ΕΣΤΗΣΕ to Mr. Fox is intended for to-morrow's Paper.

[6 November 1802, Saturday]

ΕΣΤΗΣΕ's Second Letter to Mr. Fox on Monday.

[8 November 1802, Monday]

The arrival of Foreign Intelligence again delays ΕΣΤΗΣΕ's second Letter to Mr. Fox; but we make no doubt of being able to give it a place to-morrow.

LETTER II. TO MR. FOX

9 November 1802, Tuesday; *M Post* title. *EOT* II 572–82, text partly garbled.

SIR,

UNPUBLISHED Letters and Memoirs in manuscript have hitherto furnished better materials for the sceptic, than for the historian. The writers who have dealt the most largely and ostentatiously in

[1] This concludes the documents in the case heretofore reprinted as C's; but journalistic interest now soared, with the discovery of fraud and bigamy, and C soon came to Stuart's assistance. On 6 Nov the *Courier* printed almost a column on "The Keswick Imposter" (an elaboration upon the previous material, probably by Street and not used in the *M Post*); on the 8th both papers repeated the heading "Fraudulent Marriage" over a long "Police Notice" describing the wanted and now "Notorious Impostor, Swindler, and Felon". (SC printed this in *EOT* III 1023–4 and, missing the designation of it as from the police, struggled with the possibility that C wrote it. She concluded that it seemed "too incorrect to have been from [his] pen"; C quotes and borrows from it in his article of 20 Nov.) C arrived in London 8 Nov, planning to stay 3 or 4 days and "see no body but Stuart & John Wordsworth" (*CL* II 880); on 11 Nov the *M Post* announced "A detailed Account" to come. It was not published until 20 Nov and 31 Dec, perhaps partly because of its length, partly because further developments in the case supplied current matter and C's full Account could be left for "historical" publication later. But C must have written it before he left town, for a bout of travelling and visiting with Tom Wedgwood.

these wares, and whose histories have boasted the thickest appendix of original papers, do not stand in the highest credit among us for good sense, or historical credibility. I admit, however, without reserve or scruple, that the examination of the MS. formed a sufficient reason for your journey to Paris; if for a thing so innocent any other reason were requisite than that of general curiosity. But what has the examination of[a] MS. to do with the Levees of Bonaparte, or the dinners of Talleyrand? Dissatisfied with the apologies which your friends have made, I have sought for a better motive in the resemblance of the present state of Paris with that of England after the subversion of our Commonwealth. For with this aera, I have been led to believe, that your history is to date its commencement. The pernicious influence of revolutions upon morals is a fact, which will have therefore become profoundly interesting to you. A general interest it will indeed have excited in every thoughtful mind; but it has become your business, Sir! to understand it in detail. That certain fruits are poisonous, it behoves us all to know. The medical writer must seek to know, what parts the poison specifically affects, whether the blood, the nerves, or the stomach. He must particularise the various appearances which the diseased organs exhibit, and the symptomatic actions of the whole body, both those of sympathy with the part, and those of resistance to the venom. This, Sir! I admit, you could but imperfectly learn from books or records. As we anticipate the future only by the analogies of the past, so can we truly and vividly apprehend the past, only by a close observation of whatever is apparently analogous to it in the present. With such changes and deductions, as with the severest impartiality you must needs make in favour of your native country, your residence in the metropolis of France will have enabled you to paint from the life the court, and the factions under our second Charles and James. Thus, Sir! your history, like the prophecies of holy writ, will have a double sense, and a twofold value.

After the failure of mad projects in Government, and the usual transformation of popular tyranny into a despotism, our ancestors saw in England, what you have been viewing in France, a truly frightful licentiousness in private life, and among public men the most profligate venality, the most abject prostration. For the fullest survey of domestic depravity any selected or commanding point of view was altogether unnecessary. You might have seen as much as was useful for your purposes, and more than your moral feelings

[a] *EOT*: of the

could well endure, and yet have remained at Paris, an unnoticed individual. In the time of a great plague we may examine patients in abundance without the trouble of procuring an admission to the public hospitals. But to understand the complexion and habit of servile and rapacious statesmen, to people and invigorate your imagination with pictures, from the life, of an upstart despot, and his crouching creatures, required more than common opportunities. You thought the knowledge not too dearly purchased by becoming the temporary courtier of Bonaparte, and the visitor and intimate of Talleyrand. You look forward for absolution from the gratitude of posterity.

This, Sir, is the apology for your conduct, with which I attempted to satisfy my own mind. But I fear, that neither you, nor your friends, nor the public, will admit it either as the truth, or as fit to be the truth. You would condemn a man's religious morals as unwarrantably lax, who should be guilty of idolatry in order to make a drawing of the *idol.* It is utterly repugnant to the plainness and generous honesty of your nature to receive with every appearance of esteem and gratitude all possible favours and attentions from base men, merely that you might be able more livelily to display the colour and quality of their baseness. I must look elsewhere for more justifiable motives. Was it the attestation of the American Ambassadors in favour of Citizen Talleyrand's integrity,[1] which induced you, Sir! to honour him with your acquaintance? The purity of his domestic morals was it? or his consistency in his religious and sacerdotal character? Was it the First Consul's exploit at Jaffa, which has entitled him to the respect of the friend of humanity?[2] or was it the re-establishment of the Slave Trade, and his truly Corsican faith to the Blacks in St. Domingo, which have recommended him by any bond of sympathy to the great FRIEND and ADVOCATE of the unhappy AFRICANS?[3] Was it his message to the Legislature, his purgation of the Tribunate, his terror and hatred of free discussion by the Press, his contempt of popular elections and Representative Governments, his jealousy of trials by Juries, his system of espionage, the articles respecting the

[1] A reference to the famous XYZ affair of Oct 1797, when Talleyrand refused to receive the new American minister, Charles Cotesworth Pinckney. The other "American Ambassadors" of C's text were John Marshall and Elbridge Gerry. Talleyrand almost drove the United States into an alliance with Britain as a result.

[2] The charge of Napoleon's supposed massacre of 3800 men at Jaffa, 4 Mar 1799, gained credence on the publication, at about the time of this article, of Sir Robert Wilson's *History of the British Expedition to Egypt*.

[3] On the reinstitution of slavery in French colonies see above, 29 Sept 1802 n 8.

Police in his Milanese Code,[4] his deportation (or what in plain English, we should call *the kidnapping*) of untried patriots, or his incarceration of Toussaint less from political motives than from personal envy to a hero, in difficulty and splendour of exploit, and in true dignity of character, infinitely his superior?

Was it any, or all of these things which have recommended him to the MAN OF THE PEOPLE? Or was it his ambition, his interference in the Governments of Holland and Switzerland, and his desperate attacks on the independence of Germany, which have pleaded his cause with the English STATESMAN? Was it the wish to consolidate his usurped power by giving him consequence in the eyes of a vain and light people? Or was it merely humanity—a desire to alleviate the pangs of the indignant French patriots, by giving them an example of voluntary homage in an English patriot. A free will offering of prostration from the leader of the English Opposition?

I take shame to myself for addressing Mr. Fox in a strain of irony. It is indeed the natural language of indignation; and that indignation, Sir, is itself both the effect and a proof of the attachment and reverence with which I had hitherto contemplated you.[5] But I recall myself to a calmer mood; I will attempt in plain and direct argument to convince you, Sir, that the reason which has been assigned for your conduct in this instance, and which, I fully believe, was the sole cause of that conduct, is not a sufficient reason; that it ought not to have influenced, that it does not justify you.

You had received the most distinguished honours and attentions in France: it was expected by the First Consul that you should solicit a personal interview with him; and you could not endure to inflict pain, or to act with rudeness. According to the customs of courtesy between man and man you could not help doing as you did. This is the sum of the apology, for that your conduct needed an apology, your warmest friends have admitted. Now Sir, the honours which you received on your arrival in France, and during the various stages of your journey to Paris, were either by the command of the First Consul, or not. If not, you owed the return to the spirit of freedom that still lingers in that unhappy country; and the proper return would have been to have shewn your contempt and abhorrence of the

4 C evidently refers to the establishment of a commission of censorship to safeguard the constitution of the new Italian Republic, which replaced the Cisalpine Republic early in 1802.

5 C had included some reverence for Fox in his ambivalent feelings toward him; he would later deny the fact.

man who had gained his victories by the enthusiasm which the spirit of freedom alone inspired, and then abused the glory and power, which those victories conferred on his name, to extinguish that spirit, to subvert that freedom. But, if these honours were ordered by the First Consul, you were assuredly, Sir, blameable in making your purposes so notorious, and in thereby exposing yourself to the difficulty and the dilemma.[6] If you would have felt it painful to have refused the attendance at Bonaparte's levee, you ought to have considered that pain as a fit expiation of the fault and imprudence which alone could have occasioned the refusal to be painful. You complied with the customs of courtesy between man and man, but this was not an affair between man and man. I trust that you would feel yourself humiliated if you believed that Bonaparte had any sincere esteem or attachment for you.

Such attachment for you could only have arisen from his belief that you had been the enemy of your country, and the patron of his ambition. It was a mere trick of policy—a low attempt to persuade Frenchmen that their despot was attached to the cause of liberty by the honours ostentatiously paid by him to its most celebrated advocate; and to win from your homage, an apparent proof, that the most undoubted zealots for the rights and freedom of mankind, regarded him with sentiments of confidence and attachment. We all know the artifices, which impostors use to procure themselves to be noticed in public by some man of rank and character, the importance, which they attach to such notice, and the uses, they afterwards make of it. Would you, Sir! think it any justification to an English Nobleman, who should walk arm in arm with a swindler at Margate, or Brighton, knowing him to be so—would you think it a justification if the Nobleman should say, that the man had behaved with laborious attention and civility, and, that it would be uncourteous not to notice him; and, that it would wound and mortify the poor man, if he refused to do it? And, what, Sir! is that man, who has availed himself of his military fame, bought for him by the soldiers of liberty with rivers of blood—who has availed himself of his own professions of

[6] C. Hobhouse (*Fox* 238–9) gives the anecdote a Coleridgian slant: "But it was not in Fox's nature to refuse: so they met. Napoleon loaded Fox with compliments, and Fox was embarrassed: then he fired off some elaborate historical platitudes, and Fox's attention wandered. It was a very boring interview: but a week later they dined and talked foreign politics in serious. Napoleon criticised Windham, as well he might, and accused him of a plot against his life. 'Premier Consul,' said Fox, 'ôtez-vous cela de votre tête.' Napoleon was not used to such rebukes . . .".

republican enthusiasm—to institute a military despotism? We will not call him a swindler, Sir! The vocabulary of crimes is too rich in appropriate terms, to lead us into the temptation. But, if you believe of Bonaparte, what ninety-nine in every hundred of your countrymen think themselves justified in believing of him, you must admit the analogy to be strict, whatever becomes of the term. And, if, Sir! you believe otherwise, and have solid reasons for your belief, you will bring home news indeed from the Continent; and you owe it, Sir! to Peace, Truth, and Charity, to publish the news as widely and as speedily as possible.[7]

In examining the reason assigned as the justification of any action, the weight, we may attribute to it, must depend on the presence or absence, on the importance or insignificance, of the reasons in the opposite scale. The reason, or apology, which I am now examining, would scarcely produce a shew of inequality, were there nothing to weigh against it. How will it fly up, and strike against the beam, when we put in the counter-weights! I have examined the reason, why you paid, and repeated, your act of homage to the First Consul. I will now enumerate the reasons why you ought not to have done it.

Your absence from the Court of your own Sovereign is the misfortune of your country, but no dishonour to yourself. But to repay yourself for the privation by the honours with which you were received, at[a] the levee of the man, who a few weeks before had been the public enemy both of your Sovereign and the country—to appear in the first rank of favour at the Court of the mock Republic of France, when you could not, or would not appear at the Palace of the King of Great Britain—O, Sir! I seem to feel, that this was not delicate, not worthy of Mr. Fox.[8] To compare small things with great,

[a] *EOT* omits

[7] C leaves the same opening in his letter to RS in Jan 1803: "Have you heard any thing from France, which inclines you to think favorably of Bonaparte, of the French Government, or of Fox's apparent Adulation?" *CL* II 912.

[8] The closest parallel to C's political behaviour in these letters is Burke's attack on Lord Malmesbury's embassy to France in 1796 in *Two Letters . . . on the Proposals for Peace with the Regicide Directory of France*. Burke had lamented Malmesbury's cooling his heels in "the ante-chamber of Regicide" as a mortifying spectacle and had questioned whether visitors to the "degrading" court of France could ever again be "loyal and faithful subjects" of the King of England. Page 31 of Burke's pamphlet, as quoted in a review possibly by C in *C Rev* XVIII (Oct 1796) 201–2. The reviewer makes the application to Malmesbury. In any event Burke's *Peace with the Regicide Directory* was much in C's mind in 1802: it is the *ground* of his "Once a Jacobin" essay, and C makes a jotted reference to it in late Oct in *CN* I 1258.

it was in the spirit of Coriolanus, not Camillus; at all events you should have waited till the Ambassador from France had appeared before your Sovereign, or some of the Generals, or Frenchmen of rank and importance had paid their homage to the representative of the Majesty of our country. Political contests, and personal injuries, may pardonably make a patriot sore and indignant, while he remains at home, may pardonably inspire a certain portion of personal dislike: but, in a foreign land, I have always felt, and always understood, that party animosities cease to have existence in the breast of an Englishman. He no longer knows the names of Whig or Tory. His King becomes an abstraction in his mind, around which his best feelings gather. It is the particular man no longer: it is the Majesty of his Country. What Mr. Fox could not receive in England, he ought to have been too proud a patriot to have condescended to receive in France.

Secondly, Sir! let me revert to the offensive terms (be they right or wrong, that they were *offensive* to the country is a notorious fact), permit me, Sir! to revert, however reluctantly, to the effusive words, in which you exulted in the conclusion of the peace, because it was glorious for France, and disgraceful to Great Britain. Had this speech met with nothing in your after conduct answerable to it, though it cannot be excused, it might have been pardoned. A man who speaks with warmth and rapidity, will often express ideas in the very moment of their conception, and will have conceived them in consequence of mere verbal associations. In the minds of wise and good men these *Tirades* pass for that which they are—a precipitancy of the organs of speech during a momentary lapse of the understanding. Even in this instance your friends might have had the courage, Sir! to interpret your words, as simply signifying, that Mr. Fox had forgotten himself. But you went to France, Sir! and submitted to receive such honours from the recent arch-enemy of your country, as perhaps it did not beseem any *subject* to receive in his individual capacity. In the eyes of the world, Sir! you appeared to receive your reward, your hire.

Whatever charitable faith I may keep alive in my own heart, I confess, Sir! that I have not the courage to maintain against your antagonists, that your intended journey to France was not present to your mind at the moment in which you uttered those words. In England they excited indignation, in France alone they made you popular.

You hastened to the scene of your popularity, even as an actor after a perilous rant turns round on his heel from the persons of the drama, and facing the galleries, receives the thunder of applause from that quarter, at whose hearts and understandings the speech had been exclusively levelled. Conscious, Sir! of the incompatibility of such a motive with your real character, you may despise these *appearances*. But, Sir! in a public man, a contempt of appearances is want of good sense, want of an appropriate virtue. To a certain extent even our inward feelings have less of *reality* than our appearances: for they belong less to the external world, and act less upon our fellow creatures. If this be the case with all men, much more then with you. You have lost the right, Sir! to act as a common individual. It is, perhaps, one of the defects of your character, that in your habitual feelings you are not sufficiently aware of your own importance, and of the duties which it imposes upon you.

Sir, it is affirmed, and has remained uncontradicted, that your private intercourse with the First Consul has not been confined to a single interview: and it is, I suppose, not to be doubted that you have *more than once* attended at his public levee.—This fact, if fact it be, annuls altogether the apology deduced from "the laws of courtesy between man and man." Your name and your authority have drawn over to Paris, and to the Consular levees, a cluster of your Parliamentary friends. At least it has embodied them: it has given the form and semblance of a band[a] to a number of Gentlemen, who might otherwise have appeared as scattered individuals. This too is only an *appearance*, Sir! but it is an offensive, an unworthy appearance. It looks, Sir! as if you, and your friends, had felt the want of Court-favour as a heavy deprivation: as if rather than not receive the caresses of a Government, you would condescend to accept them from apostacy and usurpation, from the Ex-bishop of Autun, and the grateful Eleve of the Director Barras. The group of Englishmen who have appeared in their different insignia to do honour to Bonaparte, before any one Frenchman of rank had appeared at the Court of St. James's, and who have contributed their best efforts to confirm the despot in his pernicious, yet plausible faith, that he has humbled the pride of Britain, and decided at length the point of precedence between the rival countries—this group of degenerate Englishmen (though indeed to the honour of that name the greater number have been Scotchmen and Irishmen),[9] this group, Sir! will derive no

[a] *EOT*: bond

[9] Absurd—but perhaps a dig at Erskine and Arthur O'Connor, who had an awkward encounter in Paris. For the eighty MPs and 150 Peers and

authority or sanction from your example; but each component of it will shoot forth his portion of dark rays (the *tenebricosi Radii* of Paracelsus)[10] to cover you with a baseness not your own. Your country will, I trust, never forget their names. A Monarch's favour ought to bring with it new places, and new titles. By what better appellation can the whole party be known, than that of Bonaparte's COURTIERS? And you, Sir! you will no longer remain bald of place or title.—You will be his LORD CHAMBERLAIN for Foreign Affairs! My mind involuntarily reverts to questions which have already been examined even to satiety. But at this moment the reasons assigned for your conduct appear idler to me than the talk of a dream. Good-Heaven, Sir! what Circean cup transformed *you* into the leader of such a pack? And made *you* first in this vile chace? Was it, Sir![a] because he was master in the manufactory, in which *you* were head-journeyman, or foreign agent—the manufactory of this gloomy and ominous WAR PEACE? Or rather was it because this Caesar in all things, but genius, noble birth, and fearless clemency, had dared take the votes of his soldiery, as an army? Was it, Sir! on this putrid trail of old despotism that you opened out? Or was it, Sir! because some of your fellow-courtiers had procured themselves to be presented at St. James's, purposely and solely to enable them to appear at the levees of Bonaparte? And were you pleased, Sir! to see your Sovereign degraded thus into a mere Gentleman-usher to this low-born Corsican?

[a] Rest of paragraph garbled in *EOT*, with brackets indicating a tattered clipping; SC's guesses at mending often make matters worse:

M Post	*EOT*
Sir!	[that]
in which	*omits*
agent—	[agent in]
and ominous	[this menacing]
it because this Caesar	it, [that one who aped] Caesar
noble birth	nobleness
votes of his	[command of the]
this putrid	the—
Or was it, Sir!	[or was it]
fellow-courtiers had	[fellow-country men]
to appear	[to attend]
thus	*omits*
low-born Corsican	[upstart] Corsican

hundreds of others of "Napoleon's British Visitors" in 1802, see lists and a chapter of details in J. G. Alger *Napoleon's British Visitors and Captives 1801–1815* (Westminster 1904) 12–125, 316–18.

[10] The dark stars are described in Paracelsus *Opera omnia* (3 vols 1658) II 299. Cf *CN* I 1000I and n, 1674 and n. But the phrases "tenebricosi radii" and "astra tenebricosa" have not been found in Paracelsus or in Henry More or Sennertus.

You have long been a seceder, though not very[a] strictly or uniformly, from your duties as a member of the legislature. It has been a measure, concerning the propriety and good policy of which your warmest friends have been divided. (It required indeed all the warmth of friendship to entertain a doubt on so palpable a point.) Very lately you re-affirmed your intention of persevering in this secession. If you shall hereafter attend your duty in parliament, your character will therefore not stand clear of the charges of lightness and inconsistency. —But attend, Sir! you must. Secession now will be infamy. You have long been styled our Demosthenes. But hereafter, if you withdraw yourself from the public counsels of your country, you will be the Demosthenes of every caricature shop.—O! far worse than that—in the serious belief of all Englishmen, the Demosthenes *with the sore throat!* DEMOSTHENES, MUFFLED and MUTE! He could not take any part in the debate concerning the GREAT KING; for the Great King, the enemy of Athens, had become the friend and patron of the Athenian orator and statesman.[11]

With a true and fervent wish, that your return to England may clear away all these clouds that have gathered round your good name, even though your full and most honourable acquittal should bring an odium on myself for the present bold (but Heaven be my witness! most unfactious) address to you.

I remain, Sir!
Your humble[b] well-wisher,[12]
ΕΣΤΗΣΕ

[a] *EOT*: Sir! [b] *EOT* omits

[11] C uses a similar remark in connexion with the other side of the political picture in *An Answer to "A Letter to...Fox"*: "Sagacious men and *knowing* in their profession... remember that Demosthenes, a state-physician, when he wished to finger a large fee from Harpalus, yet was expected by his former connections to speak out according 'to the well-known tendency of his political opinions' found a *sore-throat* very serviceable ...". *Lects 1795 (CC)* 326. C's comparison is tantamount to accusing Fox of taking bribes from Napoleon.

[12] Omission of "humble" in SC's text may be owing to the condition of the clipping (though the word is not at the edge of a column)—or to family pride. Many in the family must have held the view expressed by John Wordsworth in a letter to DW of 7 Nov: "The M.P. on account of C. you may be assured I constantly look after. Yesterday his letter to Mr. Fox appeared. . . . I think no man who in a publick *manner* makes an address to another ought to shew any marks of humiliation—Independence is the order of the day, and a very good order too." (Text kindly supplied by Mary Moorman.)

A common reaction to the Letters was to assume C's venality. It was at once rumoured in Whig circles that "the *Morning Post*, and *Morning Chronicle* too," were in the pay of the Grenvilles. (See Thomas Creevey to

Dr Currie, 8 Nov 1802, in *The Creevey Papers*—New York 2 vols 1903—I 4.) Later it was assumed, in the same circles, that for his "scurrilous letters against Mr. Fox" C afterward "accepted, by way of recompense . . . a Commissaryship at Malta" (*Lady Holland* II 237–8). "How amusing", wrote William Taylor to RS in 1805, "that the author of 'Fire, Famine and Slaughter' should be a commissary fattening under War and Pitt!" (Robberds II 99; see also *CL* II 1105). For his actual mode of obtaining a place at Malta, see *CL* II 1087; but note that, a bit too late, Sheridan did offer (through Stuart) to introduce C to a presumably grateful Addington (*CL* II 1112, 1114).

Another, related assumption was that Stuart's intimate associate, the apostate and placeman James Mackintosh, had connived in the writing and publication of the Letters. Hearing in 1807 that Fox had been persuaded of this, Mackintosh fumed: "It is false. I had no communication, direct or indirect, with Coleridge, at any time, on these letters, or for a year (I think) before, on any subject. [But a ms note by Mackintosh on a copy of Kant's *Anthropologie*—Sotheby SC 17 Apr 1972—reads: "Given to me by Coleridge I think at the Lakes in 1801".] Coleridge is well known to have (capriciously enough) disliked me. He is also known to be a man not well disposed to receive suggestions, or materials, from any one. I had no controul over the editor of the paper, which could have prevented the publication of letters, in which I was myself, by very clear implication, abused." *Memoirs of the Life of . . . Mackintosh* ed R. J. Mackintosh (2 vols 1835) I 326. From Stuart's letters of Sept 1802 to C (App B, below) we know that Stuart expected C to abuse Mackintosh in the Letters to Fox, hardly to collaborate with him; yet that Mackintosh had been one of the admirers of the "Comparison" essays.

The legend on the other side is an almost equally false construction. Said C in *BL* ch 10: "I am not indeed silly enough to take as any thing more than a violent hyperbole of party debate, Mr. Fox's assertion that the *late* war . . . *was a war produced by the* MORNING POST; or I should be proud to have the words inscribed on my tomb." *BL* (1907) I 145. (See Hazlitt *Napoleon* II 375. See also *Courier* 21 Dec 1809 n 8, below.) To trace this hyperbolic account to its source proves easy. We may note that it is not Fox but C who equates the *M Post* with himself, and we will find that in 1802 it was not Fox but the *M Post* that took a general reference as an exclusive one to itself. On 23 Nov, first day of debate in the new Parliament, Fox asserted that "the cry for war" was "not the real cry of the people of England; it is their supposed cry, which the coalition of a certain number of newspapers ascribes to them"; and he declared it "dreadful indeed...if a country was to be driven into a state of war, because publishers of newspapers, for the purpose of selling their papers, or to raise the merit of their journals, state causes of mutual aggravation between two countries which have no existence" (Debrett I 74). On the second day of debate Fox became more concrete. As an example of "irritation" from the French newspapers he alluded to "an English paper printed at Paris", the *Argus*, and as an example of English newspapers that had been the opposite of "conciliatory" he alluded to Cobbett's *Political Register*, in which "To the shame of the country, I have heard that a paragraph has been inserted... declaring that Englishmen ought to fight Bonaparte with fleets and armies, but that Frenchmen ought to fight him with something more than the pen. Is not this, I ask, an instigation to the assassination of that person?" Fox did not, apparently, mention either paper by name, but later on, when he was deploring the war of newspapers yet expressing gratitude that it was not a war of armies, he summed up: "Let the Moniteur and the Morning

Post, the Times, and the Argus, go on in their hostile language, it is easier to be endured than a war of bayonets." (I quote partly from *M Post* but the last sentence from Cobbett, confirmed by the *Moniteur*. Oddly, the *M Post* in Dec quotes a fuller text of the first part of the speech.)

Fox ought to have named the *Register*, but perhaps he forgot the name; he was making a generalisation, not an indictment. But the *M Post* narrowed the reference, quoting Fox as saying: "let paper contend with paper, let the *Moniteur* fight it out with *The Morning Post*; but let not the two countries be involved in the quarrel". Worse still, the *M Post* insisted editorially that even when Fox spoke of "a coalition of some newspapers" he really "alluded to this Paper; indeed the allusion applied to no other" (3 Dec). (Stuart may have meant that while "coalition" might suggest the combination of his *M Post* and evening *Courier* the fact was that none of C's political essays of 1802 had been reprinted in the *Courier*.) Thus Stuart's boast to subscribers; though meanwhile, without naming Cobbett or his weekly, he had asserted for the record that the "paragraph said to have stimulated to the assassination of the Chief Consul" had not appeared "in any daily newspaper" (*M Post* 27 Nov).

It was almost inevitable that C should believe that Fox was alluding exclusively to the *M Post* and his essays when, in the final debate on a declaration of war, 24 May 1803, Fox reiterated his criticism of the "violent abuse" in the journals of "both sides" as having been "such as not only to have a tendency to create, but actually to have created, in France as well as in England, that degree of soreness and irritation, which, in his opinion, had had so large a share in accelerating the present crisis" (Debrett III—1804—394–5). These words are, of course, a reporter's précis and probably inexact. C may have received a more colourful text or one closer to his own recollected version. The other side of the coin, impressive when he had polished it for *BL* ch 10, was that C's series of comparisons with the Caesars *must* have irritated Napoleon—for in 1806 when C visited Rome had he not been "warned, *directly*, by . . . [not Napoleon but] the minister of the Prussian court at Rome" to flee "the tyrant's vindictive appetite"? *BL* (1907) I 145–6. For an obviously inspired account in the *Bristol Journal* of 16 Apr 1814, anticipatory of *BL*, see *Sh C* II 257. For C's various accounts of this affair, see the note in *BL* (1907) I 262–3. For EHC's assertion there quoted, and for other positive assertions of Napoleon's interest in the *M Post*, De Q's account in *Literary Reminiscences* (1851) I 207 seems partly responsible. Extant correspondence of C's contains no inkling, except indications that C was thinking up multifarious explanations for the meagre amount of "papers & effects" he would be returning home with. See *CL* II 1169, 1175, etc. Nevertheless, C was quite evidently warned, whether or not that Napoleon was aware of him particularly, that (after Austiterlz, 2 Dec 1805), Bonaparte was ordering an army to march to the "protection" of the Papal States and to drive the Russians and English out of Naples. Three days after the signing of peace between France and Austria on 29 Dec 1805, C "heard from Mr Jackson [probably the British diplomat Thomas Jackson] of the arrival of the French at Rome, to be expected on the 5th" and considered whether "To stay or not to stay—" (*CN* II 2785 and n). And he may next have been warned that Napoleon, responding with "vindictive appetite" to Pope Pius's demands for an increase of temporal power, had written on 11 Feb 1806 to his own archbishop in Rome, his uncle Fesch, "instructing him to insist on the expulsion of all English, Russians, Swedes, or Sardinians at the court of Rome" (J. M. Thompson *Napoleon Bonaparte* 260). For by 15 Feb C had departed thirty miles from Rome to his friend Washington Allston's house in

[11 November 1802, Thursday]
A detailed Account of The Keswick Impostor To-morrow.

THE KESWICK IMPOSTOR. I

A NARRATIVE OF WHAT IS AT PRESENT KNOWN AT KESWICK, OF THE KESWICK IMPOSTOR[1]

20 November 1802, Saturday; except the first "The" and "I", *M Post* title. New attribution, confirmed by Stuart's recollection[2] and by the fact that the author, in the first person singular, takes credit for "the former accounts, with which I first introduced our hero". Reprinted in *Courier* of same day.

On the 19th or 20th of July a Gentleman arrived at the Queen's Head Inn, in the town of Keswick, in his own carriage, but with no servant, and assumed the name of the Honourable Colonel Alex.

Olevano Romano (*CN* II 2794, so dated; cf 2796, 2802; for further sources of the story see 2785n). C did not finally leave Rome until 18 May (*CN* II 2848).

In Jul 1806 WW learned, from Stoddart, that C "when last heard of i.e. in April last...was at Rome Stoddart believed under a borrowed name, finding it necessary from the official situation he had been in, and other circumstances..." (WW to Scott 4 Jul 1806: *WL—M* rev—I 52). Fesch's men could be expected to know that C had been a British official in Malta; C's "other circumstances" could well be his own suspicion that Napoleon might remember his journalism. One reason for that suspicion could be Stuart's having told C in Sept 1802 that his "Comparison" essays attacking Bonaparte were being translated into French for Peltier's gadfly *L'Ambigu*. Stuart to C 29 Sept 1802, App B, below.

But to return to what Stuart may have read into—or what Fox may have meant by—Fox's allusion to "a coalition of some newspapers": either or both of these gentlemen may have been aware that C's Letters to Fox, and many subsequent paragraphs from the *M Post*, had been reprinted in the *Political Register* to reinforce Cobbett's own more vituperative abuse of Fox—and of Bonaparte. In "Conduct of Mr. C. J. Fox" *Weekly Political Register* Supplement to Vol II (Jul–Dec 1802) 1420–9, 1429–35, 1436–55, the two Letters (the second misdated "Nov. 7") are reprinted with paragraphs from the *M Post* of 27, 30 Nov and 2, 13 Dec, with some comment. Cobbett could not endure the conciliatory parts of the Letters: "They contain some excellent remarks; but we cannot insert them without observing, that we dissent from almost every word, that the writer has uttered IN FAVOUR of Mr. Fox, in whose life, moral or political, we have never discovered any one act worthy of praise."

[1] Announced 11 Nov and evidently written before then (see 5 Nov n 1, above).

[2] Stuart in 1838 remembered this article, but confused it with the first

Augustus Hope, the brother of the Earl of Hopetoun, and Member for Linlithgow. He appeared to be from 43 to 45 years old, his height five feet nine (or ten) inches. He had a full face, bright dark blue eyes, thick eye-brows, strong but rather light beard, good complexion, with some colour; thick, but not very prominent nose, a smiling countenance, fine teeth, a scar on one of his jaw-bones, near the chin; very long thick light hair, which he wore in a club.[3] There was a small lock or patch of grey hair on the right temple; but that which added much to the peculiarity of his countenance, and to the power of his large bright eyes, was the blackness of his eye-brows and eye-lashes, contrasted with his complexion, and the light colour of his hair. This effect might possibly have been produced by artificial means; but if it was indeed done for the purposes of disguise, it was trouble thrown away: there were too many other peculiarities of look and limb, which it was not in his power to hide or alter. He was a stout man, square shouldered, full breast and chest, rather corpulent and stout limbed, but very active, and he had somewhat of a spring in his gait, with apparently a little *hitch* in bringing up one leg. This was occasioned (as it should seem) by an old wound. The two middle fingers on his left hand are stiff, from an old wound, and he has a trick of frequently

---

(11 Oct) and supposed there had been only one. In his anger at the time, Stuart was intent on showing that C had "not materially contribute[d] to the success" of the *M Post*, his axiom being: "How could any man living at Keswick do so?" (Stuart x 126, IX 490). The case of the Keswick marriage was a very poor case in point, but evidently Stuart's memory had been jogged by De Q's "reminiscences" in *Tait's Magazine* (in 1834) mentioning a newspaper article of C's that "unintentionally furnished the original clew for unmasking the base impostor". This was a reference to the first "Romantic Marriage" story (11 Oct). What Stuart could recall was a long account that "filled upwards of three columns in black letter, (that is, technically, not leaded,)...in the back page". This is a precise technical description of the 20 Nov article, but Stuart supposed De Q and he were recalling the same article: "Coleridge was easily moved to resist oppression. It was he who brought the affair of the Beauty of Buttermere into notice. He sent me a long account of it, on which, it being rather a private domestic story, I placed no value...on a hungry day I placed it in the back page, as mere stuffing." Stuart had almost forgotten that C had stayed with the case when the private domestic story (11 Oct) became a public and sensational story of oppression and a mainstay of "domestic intelligence".

[3] C is drawing on the Police Notice (see *EOT* III 1023), as he admits at the end of the paragraph. The second sentence begins: "Height, about five feet ten inches, aged about forty-four, full face, bright eyes, thick eye-brows, strong but light beard, good complexion with some colour, thick but not very prominent nose, smiling countenance, fine teeth, a scar on one of his cheeks near the chin; very long, thick, light hair, with a great deal of it grey, done up in a club ...". C differs as to the grey hair.

5. *John Hatfield. The Famous Seducer &c. &c.*
Anonymous print (5 Jan 1803) from R. S. Kirby's *Wonderful and Scientific Museum* I (1803) facing 309

putting them strait, and *smoothing them up*, as it were, with his right hand. A quick ear would immediately suspect the Irish brogue in his speech; but it was not broad or obtrusive.[4] Part of this description we have adopted from the advertisements, but we know it to be more than commonly accurate and appropriate. Such was the person, and first appearance of the man.

After a few days spent at Keswick, he made an excursion to Buttermere, returned on the third day to Keswick, and from thence went immediately to Grasmere, and took up his lodging at the small Public-house, which is close behind the Church yard. Here he stayed three weeks, and formed an acquaintance with two gentlemen then sojourning in this simple and lovely vale; one of whom, a Mr. Crump, of Liverpool, has long threatened, alas! to build a fine house there.[5] Both these gentlemen, and especially the latter, he contrived to attach to himself by no every day feelings of esteem and admiration. This was indeed nothing wonderful. The attentions of a man of high rank, and antient nobility, must needs be flattering to persons of an inferior situation in society: and, in addition to this, our impostor possesses the face, look, and manners, of unusual sensibility, is attentive in the extreme, full of compliments, and skilful and discriminating in the choice and adaptation of them to the character of the person, with

[4] The Notice continues: "stout, square shouldered, full breast and chest, rather corpulent and stout limbed, but very active, and has rather a spring in his gait, with apparently a little hitch in bringing up one leg; the two middle fingers of his left hand are stiff from an old wound, and he has a custom of frequently putting them straight with his right: has something of the Irish brogue in his speech . . .".

[5] De Q has been suspected (see 22 Oct n 3) of moonshine in his account ("Literary Reminiscences" *Tait's Magazine* 1834) of a reconciliation, ten years later, between C and a certain Liverpool merchant, obviously this John Gregory Crump, who had been "meditating a house in the Vale of Grasmere" when offended by C's reporting. "Liverpoliensis" had "connected himself a good deal with Hatfield during his Keswick masquerade", says De Q, "and was said even to have carried his regard to that villain so far as to have christened one of his own children by the names of 'Augustus Hope.' With these and other circumstances, expressing the extent of the infatuation amongst the swindler's dupes, Coleridge made the public merry."

The bare mention of Mr Crump in 22 Oct hardly exposed him to ridicule; but with recovery of the 20 Nov and 31 Dec account we now see ample cause for public merriment and Crumpian wrath: *a* Mr Crump, easily fascinated, *a* Mr Crump who "has long threatened, alas! to build a fine house" in Grasmere (the house being deplored also by WW—see *WL—E* rev—534—who, however, became Allan Bank's first tenant when it was built). Before "ten years" had passed, C was referring to "My friend, Mr Crump. . .": *CL* III 219 (Aug 1809). We can see also that some of De Q's details, such as the naming of a Crump child, were falsely fathered upon C.

whom he is conversing. He has an astonishing flow of words, and his language, to the generality of men, would appear as choice and elegant, as it was undoubtedly fluent and copious. Add to this, that his conversation is of that sort, which is the most generally delightful: inexhaustible in anecdotes, he knows every thing of every body, and more particularly (as his assumed name and family rendered natural) of all persons distinguished by splendor of situation, birth, or military exploit.[6] In addition to this, his looks, gestures, and language, expressed on all occasions an enthusiastic sensibility to the pains and pleasures of all living things. It was common in persons, who spoke of him, to exclaim, "What an *entertaining* man he is! What prodigious *information* he possesses!" Expressions of admiration, which were generally followed by the phrase—"and then he is *so* good!" Few, I suppose, will be surprised, that a man marked out by such manners, and such accomplishments, was able to fascinate a Mr. Crump, of Liverpool: such a man, and a brother of the Earl of Hopetoun to boot!

Of the fashionable travellers, who pass through Grasmere in the summer months, I have observed no small number *asleep*. A much greater number are *reading* descriptions of the place, or lost in admiration of the landscape in aqua-tinta. Still, however, I hope, and trust, that a majority will remain of those, who have kept their eyes open, and their hearts awake. They must have been very unfortunate, if they have not had occasion to observe, that the beauties of this enchanting vale are not exclusively those of inanimate nature. There is a larger proportion of fine forms, or pleasing countenances (and not seldom both at once), among the women and children of this vale, than I have ever noticed elsewhere, in an equal number of inhabitants. As the property too throughout almost the whole mountainous district is very much subdivided,[7] the maid servants, who are often the daughters, and almost always the near relations, of the small proprietors (provincially called, *Estatesmen*), possess a sense of self-respect, a something of honest family pride, which renders them, both in manners and morals, greatly superior to the same class of women in the midland and southern counties. The public advertisements will have informed the reader, that our pre-

[6] Cf the Police Notice: "fluent and elegant in his language, great command of words, frequently puts his hand to his heart, very fond of compliments, and generally addressing himself to persons most distinguished by rank or situation, attentive in the extreme to females, and likely to insinuate himself where there are young ladies . . .".

[7] In this version of the Wordsworthian analysis of the society of Estatesmen, C emphasises the virtues of equality of property.

MARY of BUTTERMERE.

6. *Mary of Buttermere. Sketch'd from Life, July, 1800.*
Print by James Gillray (15 Nov 1802)
See articles of 11 and 22 Oct, 5 and 20 Nov, and 31 Dec 1802

tended Colonel Hope was "attentive in the extreme to females in general," and "frequently put his hand to his heart."[8] It would have been strange, if he had left Grasmere without an exercise of his amatory talents, and that he exercised them without success speaks much in favour of the young women of the vale. He made eager and repeated attempts to debauch one beautiful girl there; but was baffled continually by the watchful care of her worthy mistress.

After a stay of three weeks he turned to Keswick, where he remained a day or two, amusing himself with fishing expeditions, and chiefly in company with one Burkitt, a fisherman, and maker of fishing tackle. From Keswick he went again to Buttermere, which henceforth became his head-quarters, though not without occasional rides to Keswick. For, as far as I can learn, it was about this time that he made a promise of marriage to Burkitt's daughter; and, if I am not grossly misinformed, something very like a promise of marriage to one of the maid servants at the Queen's Head. These, however, were mere amusements, a wise precaution, perhaps, on the part of this *active* gentleman, that he might not take leave of any place disturbed by the novelty of a peaceful conscience; and lest his villainy should find a time to cool in.—For he was now pursuing nobler prey, at his quarters, at the Char—the small public house at the foot of the little lake of Buttermere. In the former accounts, with which I first introduced our hero to the attention in your paper,[a] I have already described "the beauty of Buttermere:" and I have nothing to add to that description, and nothing to detract from it. In my second communication, I ventured to affirm, that when the particulars of her late unhappy connection were made known, her former character for modesty, virtue, and good sense, would only receive confirmation, that poor Mary would rise, not sink, in the opinion of all wise and good men. The circumstances, which I am now to detail, will fully verify my assertion; but, I must previously remark, that I cannot state the dates with perfect precision; I heard, indeed, both the month, and the days of the month, and from the best authority; but have now forgotten them.[9] The facts, however, happened precisely as I shall state them.

[a] Error for "of your readers"?

[8] See n 4, above.

[9] In evidence of C's authorship of this essay, cf his similar remarks in connexion with biography, in his life of Ball, *Friend* No. 21: "I recollect many particulars indeed, but not the dates, with such distinctness as would enable me to state them (as it would be necessary to do if I stated them at all) in the order of time". *Friend* (*CC*) II 288 (I 539).

Our adventurer's second arrival at Buttermere was some time in the last ten days of August. He attempted without delay, and by every artifice of looks and language, to conciliate the affections of the young woman; and, in the first days of September, if not before, he offered to make her his wife, if she would go off with him, and be married in Scotland. She gave a positive refusal, assigning, as her reasons, the short period of his acquaintance with her, which rendered it impossible that his attachment should have been founded on any rational esteem for her; and the utter disproportionateness of the match. Her natural good sense informed her, that strange events are seldom happy events.

About this time he contrived to commence an acquaintance with an Irish Gentleman, a Member of the late Irish Parliament, who has been resident for some months at Keswick, with his wife, and part of his family. With this Gentleman, and under his immediate protection, there was likewise a young lady of family and fortune, and of great personal attractions.[10] This gentleman, in an excursion with his party to Buttermere, had, at the request of the landlord[11] of the Queen's Head Inn, permitted his servant to convey a small package of wine to the gentleman staying at the Char public-house. In a cottage, in which there is only one small sitting-room, persons of pleasant manners, who happen to come at the same time, as naturally form a slight acquaintance as in the cabin of a packet. One of the means which the adventurer used to introduce himself to this respectable family, was the following:—Understanding that the gentleman had been a military man, he took out an Army List from his pocket, and pointed to his assumed name—the Hon. Alex. Aug. Hope, Lieut. Col. of the 14th regiment of foot. I have thought it no waste of time to mention these minute circumstances. They may possibly be useful in the detection of some other rogue, for the progress of the present will, I trust, be too short lived to render them serviceable in *his* particular instance.

From this time our adventurer played a double game. It seems to have been a maxim with him to leave as few white interspaces as possible in the crowded map of his villainy.[12] His visits to Keswick

[10] These are named in accounts as Colonel Nathaniel Montgomery Moore and Miss D—, a young lady of fortune. In November C corresponded with Col Moore and sent, through his wife, his "Best respects to Colonel Moore—& his Lady & Miss D'arcy". *CL* II 889.

[11] George Wood.

[12] A characteristic metaphor, based on a word C was fond of using: cartographically ("the Hills . . . with less than half a mile interspace": *CN* I 1475), celestially ("one interspace of blue Sky": *CL* III 542), and metaphorically ("between . . . measures, and . . . men, the interspace is sloping": *M Post* 3 Dec 1801, above; "admira-

became frequent, and his suit to the young lady assiduous and fervent. Still, however, both at Keswick and Buttermere, he was somewhat shy of appearing in public. He was sure to be engaged in a fishing expedition, on the day on which any company was expected at the public-house at Buttermere; and he never attended the church at Keswick but once. The former circumstance could not excite any reasonable suspicion; it is assuredly not necessary to be an impostor in order to avoid, as carefully as possible, a crowd of strange faces in a small public-house: the latter circumstance appeared more extraordinary, as great and continued pretensions to religion, and to religious exercises, formed an outstanding part of his character. He himself once assigned some reason for it, which I have forgotten. I remember only that it was very impudent, and very foolish; but the people of Keswick, those few at least who had noticed the circumstance, candidly attributed this neglect to his being of a Scottish family and education. A week or two after Mary Robinson's first refusal to go off with him to Scotland, he renewed his entreaties, and gave her a written promise of marriage, which she returned to him, persevering in her former opinion, and determined at all events to do nothing which she could not do openly, and in the face of all among whom she was born and had lived. This, in a woman of her situation, must surely be considered as a great proof of virtue and uncommon good sense, if we reflect that she had no doubt of his being the man he pretended to be. How, indeed, could she, knowing him to be received into the intimacy of persons of undoubted rank, respectability, and consequent knowledge of the world? And it is probable that he would have desisted from this pursuit, if he could have induced the young lady before-mentioned to have consented to a private marriage.

To be continued.[13]

---

tion fills up the interspace": *AR*—1913—165); see also *CL* I 469; *Zapolya* II iv i 319 (*PW*—EHC—II 948).

[13] At the end of November Hatfield was captured in Wales; in December he was brought to London and during the month was given four public examinations at Bow Street; Stuart on the 18th announced that "poor Mary of Buttermere is with child"; an earlier wife travelled two days and a night to spend Christmas with the bigamist in Tothill Fields Bridewell. The second instalment of C's long narrative was held back while Stuart's shorthand men brought paragraph after paragraph from Bow Street.

THE KESWICK IMPOSTOR. II
(Continued from a former Paper)

31 December 1802, Friday; except "II", *M Post* title. New attribution. Not in *EOT*, yet listed in SC's notebook; omitted perhaps by mistake or perhaps from failure to locate the first half. The back reference asserts single authorship of all the reports we have collected as C's. Reprinted in *Courier*, without the "Continued" line.

In our Paper of November 20, we published half of an account of the arrival of Hatfield at the Lakes of Cumberland, and his proceedings there. The following is the other half. The first part left off with an account of his having offered marriage to a young Lady of rank and fortune, at Keswick; whose friends making the necessary enquiries, he then offered his hand to Mary Robinson, of Buttermere. —The narrative proceeds:—

IN the first account, which appeared in this paper, Oct. 11, were these words, "He paid his addresses to a Lady of youth, beauty, and good fortune, and obtained her consent. The wedding clothes were bought, and *the day fixed for their marriage, &c.*" Of this every circumstance is true, but the last.—This, however, is a very important one; and being false, it is fit and necessary that it should be contradicted, in justice both to the young Lady, and to the respectable character under whose protection she resides.[1] The day was not fixed; previously to its being fixed, she had persisted in insisting that the pretended Colonel Hope should introduce the subject formally to her friend. He was hourly expected to do so, and the Gentleman was prepared to have required, that "Colonel Hope's enthusiasm should not seduce him into an impropriety. They were strangers to each other. He must beg that Colonel Hope would write to certain Noblemen and Gentlemen both in Ireland and England, whose names and addresses he would furnish him with, and obtain from them every necessary information respecting himself and the young Lady under his protection. As some days would elapse before the answers could be received, he proposed to employ that time in a trip to Lord Hopetoun's seat," &c. &c. This I know, from the best possible authority, to have been the Gentleman's intentions; and our adventurer knew it likewise; and this knowledge determined and precipitated his public marriage with Mary of Buttermere. Ex-

[1] Miss D'arcy and Col Moore.

perience teaches us, that even among old family friends, the forms and etiquette appropriate to their rank in society cannot be neglected without danger; but among sudden acquaintances and fresh friends they are of absolute necessity, and none but fools or sharpers affect to despise them. Miss D'Arcy[a] will, I am well assured, reflect with grateful heart on those forms, the adherence to which plucked her back from the brink of an abyss of misery; and her friends, and the public, will give her credit for the good sense and virtue which determined her to adhere to them.

Our adventurer, well aware that perseverance in this pursuit would inevitably lead to his detection, applied himself wholly to gain possession of Mary Robinson's person. He made the most assiduous enquiries among the neighbours into every circumstance relating to her and to her family; and declared his resolution to marry her publicly at her parish church by a licence. Mary told him, that she was not ignorant that he had paid his addresses to Miss D'Arcy, a match every way more proportionate. This he treated as a mere venial artifice, to excite her jealousy—in part, perhaps, an effect of despair, in consequence of Mary's repeated refusal. The conclusion is already well known. The pretended Colonel Hope, in company with the Clergyman, procured a licence on the 1st of October, and they were publicly married in the church of Lorton, on Saturday, October 2. Is there on earth that prude or that bigot, who can blame poor Mary? She had given her lover the best reasons to esteem her, and had earned a rational love by innocence and wise conduct. Nor can it be doubted, that the man had really and deeply engaged her affections. He seems to have fascinated every one in all ranks of society; and if Mary had remained an exception, it would have detracted more from her sensibility, than it would have added to her prudence.

On the Friday our adventurer wrote to Mr. Moore,[b] informing him that he was under the necessity of being absent for ten days on a journey into Scotland, and sent him a draft for 30*l*. drawn on Mr. Crump, of Liverpool, desiring him to cash it, and pay some small debts in Keswick with it, and send him over the balance, as he feared he might be short of cash on the road. This Mr. Moore immediately did, and sent him ten guineas in addition to the balance.—On the Saturday, Wood, the landlord of the Queen's Head, returned from Lorton with the positive intelligence that Colonel Hope had married

[a] Name blank in *M Post* here and below
[b] Name usually blank in *M Post*, except for one "M——"

the Beauty of Buttermere. As it was clear that, whoever he was, he had acted unworthily and dishonourably, Mr. Moore's suspicions were, of course, awakened. He instantly remitted the draft to Mr. Crump, who immediately *accepted* it; and at least ninety-nine in a hundred of the people of Keswick were fully persuaded that he was a true man, and no cheat.

Mr. Moore, however, immediately on this wrote to the Earl of Hopetoun. Before the answer arrived, the pretended honourable returned with his wife to Buttermere. He went only as far as Longtown. He had bought Mary no clothes, pretending that on his arrival at the first large town they might be all procured in a few hours. A pair of gloves was the only present he made her. At Longtown he received two letters—seemed much troubled that some friends whom he expected had not arrived there;—stayed three days, and then told his wife that he would again go back to Buttermere. From this time she was seized with fears and suspicions. They returned however, and their return was made known at Keswick. A Mr. Harding, a Welsh Judge, and a very singular gentleman,[2] passing through Keswick, heard of this adventurer, sent his servant over to Buttermere, with a note to the supposed Colonel Hope, who observed, that it was a mistake, and that the note was for a brother of his. However, he sent for four horses, and came over to Keswick, drew another draft on Mr. Crump for twenty pounds, which the landlord of the Queen's Head (O the *wise* landlord) had the courage to cash.—Of this sum he immediately sent the ten guineas to Mr. Moore, who came and introduced him to the judge, as his old friend Colonel Hope. Our adventurer made a blank denial that he had ever assumed the name—and one who had been his frequent companion, his intimate, at Buttermere, gave evidence to the same purport. If I conceal this man's name, and his subsequent conduct, let him be thankful; he owes it in part to the respect which I bear his profession.[3] But if his power of working misery approached as nearly as his baseness does to that of the wretch, whose promises he had the wickedness and stupidity to be bribed by, my pity would not have justified me in thus hiding his

[2] George Hardinge (1743–1816), the "very singular gentleman", was senior justice of Brecon, Wales—a Cambridge scholar (Trinity College), who had married an heiress (who would outlive him), whose adopted son was a captain in the royal navy, who was an author of biographical notes and a non-returner of borrowed books—and was immortalised as the waggish Welsh judge of *Don Juan* 13.88.

[3] According to the trial account, this was H. Newton, attorney at Chester, employed in recovering an estate for Hatfield in the County of Kent. C's "respect" for lawyers is sarcastic.

name, and the particulars of his conduct, from the public, and his established superior: as it is, I leave him to the well merited contempt of his neighbours.

In spite, however, of the stammering lie of this worthy associate, the evidence against him was decisive; a warrant was given by Sir Frederick Vane,[4] on the clear proof of his having forged, and received several franks, as the Member of Linlithgow, and he was committed to the care of the constable.—The constable, as may be well supposed, was but little used to business of this kind; our adventurer affected to make light of the affair, laughed, threatened, &c. &c. and ordered a dinner at the Queen's Head, at three o'clock. In the mean time he should amuse himself on the Lake, which the constable unsuspiciously permitted. He went out in a boat, accompanied by his old friend, the fishing-tackler; and a little before three o'clock, a considerable number of inhabitants assembled at the foot of the lake, waiting anxiously for his return, and by far the greater part disposed to lead him back in triumph.[5] "If he was not this great man, they were sure that he would prove to be some other great man;" but the dusk came on; neither the great man nor his guide appeared. Burkitt, as I believe I have before informed you, had led him through the Gorge of Borrodale, up through Rossthwaite, and so across the Stake, the fearful Alpine pass, which leads over Glaramara into Langdale, and left him at Langdale Chapel—a tremendous journey in the dark![6] but his neck was probably predestined to a less romantic fate. It will hardly be believed, how obstinately almost all classes at Keswick were infatuated in his favour, and how indignantly they spoke of the Gentleman who had taken such prudent and prompt measures to bring the impostor to detection. The truth is, the good people of the Vales had as little heard, and possessed as little a notion, of the existence

4 Sir Frederick Vane-Fletcher (afterwards Fletcher-Vane), Bt (1760–1832), sheriff of Cumberland and MP for Winchelsea (1792–4, 1806–7) and Carlisle (1796–1802). To live "near the Sir Frederic Vane's great Library" had been one of the attractions of the district urged upon C by WW. *CL* I 490–1.

5 Except for the remarks upon Crump, most of C's ridicule of his neighbours is general.

6 "Coleridge [in the 22 Oct story] thinks that Hatfield made his way over 'the Stake, a fearful Alpine Pass, over Glaramara into Langdale.' But I think it far more likely he was piloted across Sty Head down to Wastdale, for he was seen on October 25 at Ravenglass", remarks Edward Abbott Parry in "John Hatfield, the Impostor" *Vagabonds All* (New York 1926) 65–82. The further detail about Langdale Chapel sounds convincing, however, though it might be only a bit of creative verisimilitude. Parry saw (and drew upon) this later account too, though he did not know it as C's.

of this sort of wickedness as of the abominations of Tiberius at Capreae.[7]

"What motive could he have to marry poor Mary? Would a shaper[a] marry a poor girl without fortune or connections? If he had married the Irish young Lady, there would be something to say for it;" &c. It was no doubt delightful to the people of the Vales, that so great a man, that a man so generous, so condescending, so affable, so *very* good, should have married one of their own class, and that too a young woman who had been so long their pride, and so much and so deservedly beloved by them. Their reasonings in the impostor's favour were, to be sure, very insufficient to counteract the evidence against him; yet of themselves they were not unplausible. It is a common blunder with those who know more of the world than the inhabitants of the secluded vales among the mountains can be supposed to know, to admit of no other passion, as the motive of crimes, except the love of money or of power. Our adventurer, in his rapid flight from Keswick, left behind him in his carriage a handsome dressing-box. After the lapse of some days an order was procured from a neighbouring Magistrate; the dressing-box was opened and searched. It contained a pair of very elegant pistols, and a complete assortment of toilet trinkets, all silver. The whole value of the box could not be less than 80*l.* There were discovered only one letter, a cash book, and the list of several cities in Italy, with a couple of names attached to each. From the cash-book nothing could be learned but that he had vested divers considerable sums (some stated to be on his own account), in the house of Baron Dimsdale, and Co. But from the letter, aided by the list of towns, a marvellous story was extracted. The letter was said to be from an Irish banditti, urging this Col. Hope to escape with all possible speed, informing him that a price had been set upon his head, and stating the writer's eagerness to assist him, but that his wounds confined him to his bed. It was concluded, therefore, that this pretended Colonel Hope was a great leader in the Irish rebellion; and the only doubt that remained was, whether the names of the Italian towns in the list were meant for Italian towns at which different agents from the United Irishmen were residents, or whether they were only marks of conspiracy;

[a] Error for "sharper"?

[7] For additional evidence of C's authorship of this article, see *CN* III 4240, in which C writes: "'The abominations of Tiberius at Capreae'. —These were the words, I dictated. My Amanuensis wrote them down exactly thus—'The burning Nations of Tibby Harris and Cap. Ray.'"

names by convention for different towns and cities in Ireland.—This list I never saw; but the letter was given to me to read. More to my amusement than astonishment, I discovered it to be neither more or less than a grateful letter from a poor exciseman at Glenarm, who had escaped with his life from an overset boat, and to whom our adventurer had performed some acts of kindness, and made (according to his custom) many splendid promises. The writer appears to be a simple, honest, pious Scotchman, and an exceedingly loyal subject. That such a story should have been deducted from such a letter, and that too by four or five intelligent men, proves no more, than that they thoroughly expected to find something very wonderful; and what people thoroughly expect they are very apt to create.[8] I venture to guess that blunders, as gross as this, have been made from the same cause, by other secret committees of higher functions,[9] and on subjects of infinitely greater importance. For some days nothing else was discovered but a bill for 100*l.* drawn on a Devonshire bank, which he had left behind him with Mary's father and mother; and with which they were to have paid off a mortgage on their little property.

I have already, I believe, mentioned, among the other villainous schemes of this merciless wretch, that he had attempted to persuade the old people to sell their little estate, to place the money in his hands, and to go with him into Scotland. This bill proved to be an old bill that had been long paid, and (as it will after appear) on his own bank.

We heard nothing more concerning the impostor till the 27th or 28th of October, when Mary Robinson discovered, at the bottom of a trunk, which had been left at Buttermere, a large mass of letters and papers. These she delivered to Mr Moore, who, with his wife and the young lady under their protection, have behaved to poor Mary with a kindness, tenderness, and respect, which does infinite honour to their hearts and understandings. This mass of papers was afterwards put into my hands, and never surely did an equal number of letters disclose a thicker swarm of villainies perpetrated by one of the worst, and of miseries inflicted on some of the best, of human beings.

The more interesting part of the story remains to be told. But my letter is already, I fear, almost too long for insertion; and what remains, deserves to be told in a higher tone, and with more excited feelings.[10]

[8] Cf *Dejection* st 4. Yet one of the data for the deduction would have been the fact that a much-publicised outlaw who had been in hiding since the battle of Ballynahinch (13 Jun 1798) in the Irish Rebellion, as a leading United Irishman, was a weaver's son named James Hope (see *DNB*).

[9] See 3 Dec 1801 and n 23, above.

[10] On 3 Jan 1803 the *M Post* announced that the dapper seducer, whose dress was influencing Bond

[*continuation of notes to p.* 415.]

Street loungers, was to be tried at Carlisle for the capital offence of forging franks. C saw to it that he and his friends were in Carlisle at the assizes of Aug 1803, for the last day of Hatfield's trial and one last interview with the fascinating psychopath before his execution: "At Carlisle I alarmed the whole Court... by hallooing to Wordsworth who was ... on the other side of the Hall—*Dinner!*... Then visited Hatfield, impelled by Miss Wordsworth—*vain*, a hypocrite/It is not by mere Thought, I can understand this man/". *CN* I 1432. This corrects De Q's impression that Hatfield had refused to see C and that this antipathy was what "could not be penetrated".

C never followed up the hints of his concluding paragraph, but he must have read the Hatfield correspondence (the "mass of papers") and may have recited to friends the whole story, not merely of the Keswick episode but of the earlier swindles and seductions—the ensnared natural daughter of Lord Manners-Sutton who bore Hatfield three daughters and was left to die of poverty and a broken heart; the faithful wife, Michilli Nation, a warden's daughter, who achieved Hatfield's release from her father's jail and still loved him, after Keswick. Stuart believed that "but for the exposure of private families, [C] would have given an account of Hatfield's baseness which would have shocked ... the world". Stuart x 126–7. During Nov–Dec 1802 at Crescelly, C took upon his knee young Katherine Byerley Thomson (1797–1862) and told her "with a plaintive voice... the story of Mary of Buttermere, then a recent subject of popular discourse", and she long remembered "his pallid face, his long black hair... the appealing tones of his voice—the earnest gaze", the tears running down his cheeks. *Recollections of Literary Characters and Celebrated Places* (1854) II 58; see *CL* II 900 and Litchfield 125–6, 139–40. Yet it was not Mary but Michilli, the Penelope of the story, who was to be the heroine in the prose or verse epic that C never wrote but had "planned out" by Feb. *CL* II 919. (Or perhaps the "long comic Poem" was an unrelated project.) By Apr it was taking the shape of a novel, we learn from a notebook memorandum listing Hatfield and a Penelope among "characters in my novel—". *CN* I 1395. In Apr 1804 he was thinking of the abundance of Hatfields as filling out, with Iagos, the many shapes that Vice could counterfeit. *CL* II 1121.

There followed counterfeit Hatfields and Marys in abundance—in farces, melodramas, and novels, most of them with little recourse to the tale of real life, the bare sensation of which inspired them. C actually supplied, perhaps unaware, the main narrative material for the earliest and fullest account of Hatfield, from which, with the trial records, most subsequent accounts have derived. The anonymous "Particulars of the Life of John Hatfield" published in two autumn 1803 numbers of R. S. Kirby's *Wonderful and Scientific Museum; or Magazine of Remarkable Characters* draws heavily upon *M Post* materials, possibly with Stuart's co-operation. It also preserves a Bond Street portrait of "The Famous Seducer &c. &c.".

The only interesting novel based on the affair is *James Hatfield and the Beauty of Buttermere: A Story of Modern Times*, with illustrations by Robert Cruikshank (3 vols 1841). The fictional parts make much of the scenery and of C and WW and RS; and "we have sought to embody [the Ancient Mariner] in one of the characters..." (p vii). There is a poet named Golefield intended to resemble C. WW acquired a copy: see *Prelude* (1926) 546.

It is presumably only in C's imagination that Hatfield (or even Bonaparte and Pitt) became the subject of "Theses of the Universities of Oxford & Cambridge". *CN* II 2651.

1803

6 January–20 August

OUR FUTURE PROSPECTS

6 January 1803, Thursday, *M Post* title. New attribution, based on internal evidence that tightly links this to C's previous essays; *CL* II 912 proves that C still considered himself engaged in editorial writing. The metaphors of equilibrium and change, including avalanche and volcano passages, have links to *The Friend*.

AMBITION, of all the passions that actuate individuals, or states, is the least susceptible of restraint; the most likely to be carried to excess. But as every other passion weakens its force by unlimited indulgence, so does this, when it sets bounds at defiance, overthrow the means of the ultimate attainment of its objects. The individual, who raises himself to an envied superiority over his equals, no less certainly exposes himself to their detestation and jealousy, than the nation, which pursues a system of aggrandisement, and universal dominion, excites the hatred and suspicion of its surrounding neighbours. In both cases the rights and liberties of others are capriciously usurped, and forcibly withheld; the animosity, therefore, with which the invaders are regarded, will ever be commensurate with the value set on the rights violated. A people that has fought and bled for freedom, may be dazzled by the splendour of great exploits, and shut its eyes upon the object for which these exploits were undertaken, but cannot be eventually cheated into a tame submission to the feats of a despot. Neither can nations, though influenced by motives of policy, of interest, or of necessity to a temporary acquiescence, continue always quiet and unconcerned spectators, and objects of the insults and encroachments of an aspiring neighbour. The time will come, when the Powers of Europe, awakened to a sense of common danger, will unite for common security against the common invader; and perhaps their liberties and independence have no more solid pledge of existence, than the universal sense of peril and disgust which the undisguised and unqualified ambitious designs of France have excited.

Already has Europe been laid at her feet, and the vast projects conceived by Louis Le Grand, in all the plenitude of his power and ambition, fully and fatally realised in this quarter of the globe. With Austria prostrate, Italy subjugated, Switzerland new modelled, Spain and Holland at her disposal, the Northern Powers conciliated, the

Southern intimidated, with her enemies humbled, and her friends aggrandised, with a barrier impregnable, to secure her from attack, and a tremendous military establishment, to enable her to avail herself, with effect, of every opportunity of external aggression; what object does Europe at present afford, either interesting to her ambition or worth her pursuit? That balance has been weakened, which alone could operate as a check upon her enormous means, and the whole weight of which was at all times necessary to keep her within reasonable bounds. In destroying the equilibrium, she has taken the most decisive method; what she removed from the scale against her, she has applied to augment her own preponderance; so that, as by the diminution of the counterpoise she would be formidable, her own means remaining unaltered, by the accumulation of strength she has become, in a far higher degree, dangerous. Yet Europe still possesses resources for the restoration of this balance. There are still powers sufficient, by a cordial co-operation, to arrest the progress of the great nation. When the sense of common danger shall have stifled the narrow suggestions of a paltry and mercenary policy, when it shall have merged every other consideration in the great question of common security, then shall this mighty people be made sensible how little the vaunted pre-eminence of any (however great), community can avail against the claims of justice, and the determined resolution of nations, united for the maintenance of their rights, and the preservation of their independence. The mis-shapen mass of snow, agitated on the Alpine summit, descends at first harmless and unheeded; but accumulating, and accelerating in its progress, its track is marked by ruin and desolation. There is a limit, however, beyond which it cannot proceed. The same law that hurried it from its elevated situation, accompanies it through all the stages of its course, and conducts it, with unerring fidelity, to the spot where its impelling force is to be exhausted, and it is itself to vanish before a milder temperature.[1]

The present Government of France is well aware of the existence

[1] C first described this phenomenon in *Hymn Before Sunrise* (lines 61–2 in *M Post* version), published four months earlier. (He did not call it an "avalanche", line 71, until amplifying the poem for the revised 1809 *Friend*: see *CC* II 183.) In the *Hymn* "The silent snow-mass, loos'ning thunders God!" In the present passage the "mass of snow", loosened by being "agitated", is at first "silent". In the *Hymn* the snow obeys the bidding of God; in the essay the "same law that hurried it" is, of course, God's law. The passage on "equilibrium... scale... counterpoise", just above, has parallels in other *M Post* articles, e.g. 9 Nov 1802, the paragraph following n 7, above.

of a very sufficient counterpoise for its natural and acquired preponderance amidst the nations of Europe; if they should unite with zeal, and from a sense of universal danger, and mutual interest, to oppose it. The Rulers, or rather the Ruler, of France, is thoroughly sensible of the delicate part that is to be sustained, before the final accomplishment of universal empire. He knows that some Powers must be intimidated, some flattered, and some deceived. Intimidation has been carried as far as circumstances would admit; flattery has been essayed, but without any lasting effect; and imposture has been, and may be, made the instrument of domination on one hand, and of degradation on the other. Machiavel's maxim[2] was never better understood, nor more successfully practised. Yet, what has been effected by the scarcely interrupted chain of rapid successes, that have characterised the progress of the revolution? France has acquired a vast extent of territory, and a wider extent of influence; but with all her vaunted conquests, all her undisputed dictation, has she gained a single ally that would willingly second her views of aggrandisement, that does not apprehend danger from her ambition, and look upon her usurpations with jealousy and disgust? Will those cautious powers,[3] that kept aloof from the horrors and operations of war, in order more effectually to take advantage of the weakness and calamities of their neighbours in making incroachments upon their states, regard without interest or alarm the mighty projects of a Government, the basis of whose power is usurpation, the object of whose ambition is universal subjugation? Can it reckon with certainty upon the cordial co-operation of those states, that submissively bow to its authority? or was the wanton and insolent assertion of superiority ever known to produce a prompt, sincere, and irreluctant compliance? Yet, even if these questions could be answered in the manner most favourable to the designs of France, there still remain powers able, and no doubt, inclined to prevent her execution of them. For, though we cannot but contemplate the vast accumulation of strength, and the dangerous degree of influence which she possesses, with

[2] Cf *Prince* ch 18, "How Princes Should Keep Their Promises": "By no means can a prudent ruler keep his word—and he does not—when to keep it works against himself and when the reasons that made him promise are annulled. If all men were good, this maxim would not be good, but... they are bad and do not keep their promises...". The prince "who knows best how to play the fox comes out best, but he ... must be a great simulator and dissimulator". Tr Allan H. Gilbert (1963) 65.

[3] Cf Burke's account of the behaviour of the powers of Europe in *Two Letters ... on the Proposals for Peace with the Regicide Directory of France* (1796) 144.

apprehension and jealousy, yet we are not of the number of those who sink precipitately into despair from the absence of obvious or apparent circumstances, whereon to found expectations. Without intending disrespect to any government or state, we conceive, we may not improperly take up the subject in a speculative point of view; and, without arrogating to ourselves superior sagacity, or incurring the charge of wishing to accelerate the renewal of hostilities, we think, we may with propriety trace in the situation of Europe, and in the circumstances and conduct of France, the existence of such moral causes, and of such political facts, as, collectively considered, leave no room for alarm on the subject of common security and independence. A few pillars may have been displaced, but the main columns still sustain the weight of the balance.[4] Every thing in nature has its period. The French Revolution was a political eruption, its lava revolutionary principles, and the patriotic enthusiasm of its armies, fighting for liberty and independence, which marked its progress with desolation and terror; but it should not be forgotten, that, when the volcanic matter is exhausted, the effects of an eruption are surveyed with wonder and admiration, but cease to be objects of terror and dismay.[5]

[16 July 1803, Saturday]

We shall also commence (on Monday, perhaps) a series of Essays under the title of "THE MEN AND THE TIMES," *which we trust will likewise contribute to the welfare of the Empire at this important crisis.*

THE MEN AND THE TIMES

ESSAY THE FIRST[1]

18 July 1803, Monday; *M Post* title. New attribution, identified by the signature, confirmed by the style and an autograph ms of a first draft corresponding to the

[4] Cf "Observations on Egypt", App B, 1804, below, III 212.

[5] C is now subduing the metaphor of the volcano to that of the avalanche (see above, n 3), which is unable to recover its expended momentum. His view is radically different from the view implied in his question thirteen months earlier (3 Dec 1801): "But are we quite sure that the volcanic force of the Revolution has wholly spent itself?" He was not then sure, nor unsympathetic with that force; he is now both. For a later use of this imagery, see *Friend* No 11 (1809–10) *CC* II 147.

[1] As early as January (e.g. in editorials of 14, 27 Jan; 3 Feb) Stuart had been indirectly supporting Addington by accusing both the Old and the New

concluding paragraph; see App B, below. The numerous references to "The Men and The Times" in C's notebooks (e.g. *CN* I 1577 and 1646) and letters now are given substance.

THE first object, at the present moment,[2] the grand preliminary of all after objects, is this: to excite in every part of the British Empire, THE SENSE OF DANGER, WITHOUT THE FEELING OF FEAR. He who impresses despondency, prepares the mind for indifference. In the very outset of the contest, to bid a great nation look forward to a *Vendean* warfare, with an invading army—O misery! O shame![3] If these sentiments produce any other effect, than that of heaping disgrace and indignation on those, who have so industriously disseminated them, what effect can they possibly produce, except like the screams and croaking of ill-omened birds,[4] to inflict an apathy

---

Opposition of "undue despondency", an accusation qualified by conceding that the kind of fear Windham (of the New Opposition) encouraged was "a noble and manly despair". This was a quibbling position, easily laughed to scorn by Cobbett, whose *Political Register* of 29 Jan (III 126–8) attributed the *M Post* article of 27 Jan to one of the "small politicians" attached to Sheridan's "non-descript way of thinking"—an apt characterisation of the *M Post* when it lacked the confident tone of C.

2 Britain had renewed war with France at the end of May, and Stuart had called for editorial help from C (before 20 May: see *CL* II 945). Perhaps he waited before turning elsewhere; not until 1 Jul was he ready to announce a "series of Papers" on "the present Situation of the Country". But after four of these—on "The Invasion", i.e. the invasion supposedly threatened by France—Stuart was suddenly able to announce, probably as soon as received, and to print in his next paper, this first of a signed series by ΕΣΤΗΣΕ. (Stuart promised to continue "The Articles on the Invasion...Tomorrow", but they lacked power and C's were to be his big guns.) On 10 Jun C was "this moment...writing for Stuart, to whom I am under a positive engagement to produce three Essays by the beginning of next week". *CL* II 950. In a letter posted 2 Jul he advised RS to "expect certain Explosions in the Morning Post, Coleridge versus Fox—in about a week". *CL* II 954.

The week became a fortnight, and from the surviving ms we can see why. His first intention was to proceed to his explosions "at once, & by the shortest road", after a brief exordium. He then worked backward, inserting so much preliminary matter that his original exordium became the final paragraph of "Essay the First"; in it, moreover, he promises not to conclude before giving analyses of the leading men of both countries, including the long-promised Character of Bonaparte.

3 Windham in Parliament 6 Jun favoured fully disciplined troops to oppose the invading French, "more army" and "less militia". Debrett III (1803) 547. C would defend the Ministers' trust in Volunteers (in Mar 1804 in *Courier*), but when it came to the question of personal involvement C agreed that the regular army should bear the brunt. *CL* II 1017.

4 C now wished to dissociate himself from the "birds of warning" with whom he had identified himself in *Ode on the Departing Year* and *The Raven*.

of terror? There is a party among us (rather, let us say, a faction: for all *party* in the present awful exigence is faction in the worst sense of the word), there is a faction, who, from the hour of their dismissal from power, have adopted the language of despondency by system. Of these men hereafter. If there be honest men among them, their *end* must be honourable, and the same with ours, namely, to rouse the people to timely exertions; but their means are inappropriate, even to absurdity. He, who impresses despondency, prepares the mind for indifference. Patriotism and patriotic valour, like all other active virtues, are indissolubly wedded to hope.

An approaching enemy will always, and by an instinct of nature, inspire enough of fear to prevent carelessness or inaction: contempt of the enemy is an act of the rational soul, by which we limit and modify that natural instinct; and it is therefore the prelude, because it is one of the chief causes, of success. If our naval heroes, before each sea-fight, had addressed the crews in the spirit of that language, with which Mr. Windham has addressed the nation,[5] would our sailors have atchieved those victories, which have emblazoned on our national coat of arms the noble motto, Safety with Glory! The good old proverb says, "While there is life, there is hope." In all national concerns we may say with strict truth, while there is hope, there is life. For the life of a nation subsists in brave thoughts, which are the pre-existing souls, and vital essences of brave actions.[6] But in order to brave thoughts we must have pleasurable feelings, that is, hopes: for what is hope but a pleasurable feeling, which, connecting itself with definite images of future things, becomes at once both impulse and motive? If we would have great results, we must have great exertions: and how can we expect great exertions, unless there pre-exist in the minds of men in general high and confident hopes of answerable results? The most despondent orator of the alarmists cannot be more deeply convinced than we, that in the present state of society no substantial and efficient hope can be produced by

[5] C is in agreement with Addington's Secretary at War, Charles Yorke, who, in the debate of 6 Jun, refused to fear "those phantoms of invasion which Mr. Windham had conjured up" and who "expressed his dislike of the despondent tone in which Mr. Windham usually spoke both of peace and war". Debrett III 547–8; Windham's own words are briefly reported and do not convey his despondency of tone, but see Farington II 104.

Evidently the parliamentary reporters agreed that "the spirit of that language" should not reach the English public.

[6] Cf C's recipe against Dejection in his Ode of 1802; see also C on George Washington (27 Jan, 25 Mar 1800, above) and WW's Intimations Ode.

delusion. The people must see the whole of their danger; we will not diminish, they must not magnify it. The nation must know the truth, and the whole truth, and the whole will come to this; if we act as beseems a generous, brave, and unanimous people, we have nothing to fear; and if, in the present awful state of our country, we prove ourselves cowardly, selfish, and factious, we are already at the worst, that a good man can fear, we are already weltering in the lowest gulph of infamy, and even the infernal tyranny of the Corsican Liberticide would be a blessing, if it were likely to prove our PURGATORY. But so low we are not sunken. The nation is sound at heart. The worst disgraces have been the work, in great measure, of that very faction which is now dispiriting us. Perhaps we may have all Europe as an enemy; and no enemy is to be despised, or thought lightly of; but neither is it the nature of Englishmen to fear any, or all together, in a wise, just, and honourable cause.

These indeed we acknowledge, as the necessary conditions of a well-founded hope; first, that our cause is good; and secondly, that our means are proportionate to our cause. To prove, first the one, and then the other, will be the object of the succeeding Essays. We have two opponents, Mr. Fox, who asserts the injustice and impolicy of the present war; and the faction of Lord Grenville and Mr. Windham, who have been clamorous for hostilities against France; and now that hostilities are waged, have dared all things to perplex the ministry, and to dishearten the nation.[7] A war may appear expedient, that is not just; but it cannot be just, in an enlarged sense of the word, if it be not expedient. We shall attempt, therefore, to prove, that on the presumption of its expedience, the war is *morally* just; secondly, that it *is* expedient, and consequently, that the war is both just and wise, not only *morally*, but likewise *politically*, just.

Mr. Fox's famous speech is confessedly the best defence of the First Consul, the most powerful attack on the moral and political justice of the war, that has appeared hitherto either in England or in France.[8]—He has since then publicly set his seal and signature to the

[7] Examples are easily found. On 26 May, Grenville and Fitzwilliam in the House of Lords treated Secretary of State Pelham with what he took as "a sneering levity" (Debrett III 540); on 1 Jun Tom Grenville in Commons accused Ministers of "a sort of fraud on the public" in one clause of the Treaty (476); on 2 Jun Fitzwilliam introduced a resolution accusing them of having deceived the people (477–92).

[8] C must clear aside if he can the moral doubts raised by Fox's three-hour speech of 24 May 1803, which had been a last-ditch effort to turn a vote of congratulation to ministers for going to war into a vote urging them to make peace. C turns directly to Fox in Essay II (20 Aug).

opinions which he then avowed, by declaring at the Whig Club, that the present war was utterly destitute of common sense, and common policy.—Our first essay, therefore, will be an examination of this famous speech. The following essays will take up the conduct of the Ministry. 1. In that point of view, in which they had the approbation both of Mr. Fox and Mr. Pitt, and here our object will be to shew, that by those who approved of the Treaty of Amiens, the conduct of Ministers cannot be attacked wisely or consistently. 2. In a broad and philosophical view, in which we shall not hesitate to condemn many parts of their conduct; but by looking back to the conduct of their predecessors, and to the principles of those who are eager to step into their places, we shall find good reason, though in particular instances we condemn them *absolutely*, yet *comparatively* to acquit them, even in these.

The discussion of these questions we consider most important, as tending to impress on the public mind a double confidence—a confidence in the justice of its cause, and a confidence in the competency of its official servants, not as the best we *would* have, but as the best, we *can* have; and as fully adequate to perform, all that is necessary, in an exigency, where we must look to ourselves principally; and, where the measures to be adopted are so obvious, that if we have a zealous and honest ministry, we have all that is absolutely needful. Having considered these preliminary questions, we shall endeavour to state the real extent of our danger, and to prove, that it is not greater on the whole than at any former period of the war; and lastly, to ascertain what means, it is certain, will not preserve us; what means, it is not certain, will preserve us; and what means certainly *would*, if only the people have confidence in the Government, and the Government no jealousy of the people.

We have entitled these Essays, THE MEN and THE TIMES.[9] For we shall not conclude them without having given, to the best of our ability, a philosophical analysis of the characters of the leading men in England, of the leading man in France, and the national character of the English and French people. The evening twilight of a short and stormy winter's day of peace has closed in—a long and tempestuous night is to follow. History does not furnish a more momentous period; none in which it more behoved all classes of society to divest themselves of every party, nay, of every national prejudice, and calmly and disinterestedly to meditate ON THE MEN, AND ON THE TIMES. The writer of these Essays, withdrawing himself from more

[9] For C's ms draft of this paragraph, see App B, below.

congenial pursuits, has felt it his duty to offer his humble contribution to the formation of public opinion. It is the contribution of an individual recluse; but of one who has fixed his eye steadily on the whole series of those events, which have given to the last fifteen years so terrific an importance, and who has been in the habitual practice of attempting to connect them with analogous events of past times, yet watchfully solicitous not to be seduced by superficial resemblances to overlook inherent differences.—The writer has observed, that the common cause of the most dangerous mistakes is not so frequently any defect of understanding, as an excess of those passions by which the understanding is clouded.[10] He cannot, therefore, but feel a certain confidence in the results of his reason on the subjects, which at present interest the civilised world; for he has thought long and habitually on them,[11] and he is conscious that, even in his most secret feelings, he has not the remotest connection with any existing party, that he has no ambition which can be gratified, directly or indirectly, by vilifying or by flattering any man, or any body of men; no interests but those which are common to all independent Englishmen, to every honest man. His readers will not be offended by the solemnity and seeming egotism of this conclusion. The magnitude and importance of the subject, while it impresses a seriousness on the mind of the writer, communicates to him a small share of its own dignity. At all events, he who feels none, would be ill adapted to the present task, and touches the ark with unhallowed hands.[12]

ΕΣΤΗΣΕ

[10] On the bedimming mists of passion, see, early, *Religious Musings* and *Destiny of Nations* or, late, C's marginal comment on *The Conduct of the British Government* (by Vindex, 1831): "*War* is not forbidden by the Gospel; but only the Passions, whence alone come wars among men." *CM* (ms).

[11] Cf in the Preface to *LB* (1798) the poet who has "thought long and deeply".

[12] Can C have remembered his friend Dr Beddoes's strictures on Pitt? They are thus quoted in *M Post* 28 Jun 1796: "...we cannot help thinking, with Dr. Beddoes, that 'TO PREVENT, by every legal exertion, a man who has once stood in THIS predicament, from approaching the ark of STATE again,' ought to be engraved as a rule of SELF preservation on the heart of every inhabitant of a Free Country".

[8 August 1803, Monday]

By the approaching prorogation of Parliament, we are enabled to promise the early appearance of many valuable favours, among which we place first No. VI of "THE INVASION," *and No. II of* "THE MEN *and* THE TIMES." *Our poetical articles shall also come forth to gratify our readers.*

[15 August 1803, Monday]

The Second Essay of "THE MEN AND THE TIMES," *is intended for to-morrow.*... *Many Poetical Articles are on our list for insertion.*

[19 August 1803, Friday]

The Second Essay on THE MEN AND THE TIMES *to-morrow.*

THE MEN AND THE TIMES

NO. II[1]

20 August 1803, Saturday; *M Post* title. New attribution, signed. The first several paragraphs reappear almost verbatim in the Amiens chapter of *The Friend*—where the focus is on Malta and on expediency and both themes are expanded.

The subject's large:
Nor can we there too much dispute, where when
We err, 'tis at two nations' charges. Peace
And War are in themselves indifferent:
The time doth stamp them either good or bad.
Suckling's Tragedy of Brennoralt [2]

THE late Peace was negotiated by the Government, ratified by the Legislature, and received by the Nation, as an experiment. A majority of the thinking part of the Empire considered it as dearly purchased by the Treaty of Amiens; no small number thought it far too dearly purchased; but by all parties, who wished for Peace at all, the Peace was avowedly considered, as an *experiment*.—In proof of what? Of this: whether Bonaparte, devoting his ambition and activity to the re-establishment of the trade, colonial tranquillity, and social morals of France, *would abstain from insulting, alarming, and endangering the British Empire.*

[1] Announced 8, 15, and 19 Aug; undoubtedly delayed by much parliamentary business (the session continuing to 12 Aug). Probably written soon after the 1st essay, certainly before C's walking tour of August.

[2] In Feb or Mar C copied several short passages from Sir John Suckling's *Brennoralt* into his notebook (*CN* I 1363–5). Here he is quoting from King Sigismund's speech in Act III, with the words "two nations" in place of "a Kingdom's", to suit the present occasion. Suckling *Works* (1719) 357.

The First Consul lost no time in enabling us to *foresee* the result of the experiment; for he immediately enforced the hostile regulations against our commerce with an inhumanity which would have been disgraceful even during hostilities; and he soon *afforded* the result, and made the experiment decisive. He *insulted* us by indecent and pertinacious demands respecting the liberty of the press, and the rights of hospitality; by the official publication of Sebastiani's infamous report;[3] and by a direct personal outrage offered to our Ambassador, in the presence of all the foreign Ministers.[4] He *alarmed* us by a display of the most unprincipled ambition, in the subversion of the independence of Switzerland, in the avowal of designs against Egypt, Syria, and the Greek islands, and in the mission of military spies to this country. Lastly, he both *alarmed* and *endangered* us by forcibly maintaining a French army in Holland, and by demands relative to the immediate evacuation of Malta, when he had himself effectually done away the security of the independence of that Island, and when he had openly avowed such designs on Egypt, as not only in the opinion of our Ministers, but in his own opinion, and that of his own Ministers, made it of the last importance to this country, that Malta should not belong to, or be influenced by, the French Government.

The main cause, then, of the peace was the possibility, and consequent hope, that the French despotism would abstain from insulting, alarming, and endangering the British Empire. (Could the certainty of the contrary have been attained, without the peace, even Mr. Fox would have been among the foremost to have voted against the peace.) But if the hope, and the possibility of one event were the necessary condition of the peace, the failure of the hope, the certainty of the opposite event, is as necessarily the cause of the renewal of war.

[3] For the complicated *cause célèbre* of this report, see Farrer 132–6. Britain's failure to withdraw from Egypt according to treaty was the cause or pretext of a mission of the French Colonel Horace François Bastien Sébastiani (1772–1851, count of the empire 1807) in Oct 1802. The latter's Report, published in the *Moniteur* 30 Jan 1803 and translated in London papers, was felt by the French to be an answer to Sir Robert Wilson's recent book on the British expedition of 1801, full of atrocity tales of Bonaparte in Syria. But the British believed Wilson and read Sébastiani's account of the popularity of the French in Egypt, especially his observation that the British and Turkish forces there were too weak to withstand an army of 6000 French, as evidence of French imperial designs.

[4] In Feb 1803 when Bonaparte found that the British were unwilling to yield Malta, he summoned the ambassador Sir Charles Whitworth (1752–1825; Earl Whitworth from 1815), and railed at him for nearly two hours, with occasional oaths and shouting.

Now the facts themselves have not been denied, nor the nature of the facts disputed, by any speaker or writer in this kingdom. The true justifying cause of the war is therefore, in its *essence*, independent of all* treaties; it bears no other than an *accidental* relation to any treaty, namely, as far only as the breach of that treaty may have furnished one or more instances of insult, alarm, and endangerment. What can render a war just, presupposing it to be expedient, if insult, alarm, and danger do not? and how is it conceivable, that it can be expedient for a rich, united, and powerful Island-Empire to remain in peace with an insolent neighbour, who has proved to it, that to insult, alarm, and endanger it is both its temper, and its system?[5] This appears to me the true state of the quarrel between Great Britain and the First Consul. Is it the true state? To answer this question himself, and to enable others to do so, I contend, was the sole and whole business of a loyal English Senator in the first instance. Mr. Fox thought otherwise. As a Statesman, as a Patriot, he assuredly erred; but as an Advocate, as a Pleader at a Bar, he acted prudently. The grand secret of perplexing and silencing an adversary is to confuse the argument.[6] The conduct of the Ministry separately taken, and the conduct of Bonaparte separately taken, and there arises no difficulty in either question. The plainest *good* sense enables us to see what in the conduct of the Usurper ought to excite our alarm and indignation, what in the conduct of our own Ministry deserves praise, and what calls for censure, and again in the latter instance what it is *right*, and what it is *advisable*, to pardon. But this would not have answered the purposes of an Advocate. By linking the cause of the country with the cause of Ministers, he gained all the well-known advantages of *diversion*:—pressed hard by the cause of the country, and forced to retreat, he gives himself a mock victory by attacking the Ministry; and instead of honestly deciding the grand question by arguments, which his own judgment could furnish, he employs

* Unless indeed it could be proved, that our Government had by an express Treaty made over to the First Consul a right to insult, alarm, and endanger us; and even then it would be necessary to prove, in addition, that such a Treaty is morally binding upon the people, against whose *vital* interests it had been concluded.

[5] The essay up to this point reappeared in *Friend* No 22 (*CC*) II 301–2 (I 266–7).

[6] C prepared a point-by-point refutation of Fox (see ms in App B, below), but put it aside, possibly for use in a subsequent essay that was never written. Instead he chose a method of attack that consists in restating Fox's arguments in terms that can be shown up as equivocations.

his skill in overthrowing the false or doubtful arguments which mistake had drawn from his opponents, or their peculiar and official situation had forced from them.

But Mr. Fox commences his speech[7] by affirming, that the cause of the country, and that of the Ministry are *inseparable*.[8] Almost all the arguments of this celebrated oration are founded on *equivocations*, more or less obvious, and this is an equivocation. If by the phrase inseparable, Mr. Fox would say only, that the one question cannot be treated of historically or argumentatively, without frequent references to the other, he says what no one is disposed to deny. But it is too gross a sophism to infer, that two things, which are, or happen to have been, co-present in time and space, cannot be considered separately in the reason; and that whatever applies to the one must of necessity apply to the other.—Would Dr. Herschell allow this argument, if it were applied to the light and heat of the sun?[9] or to bring a more familiar instance, it was not possible to consider Hardy's case at the famous trials, without frequent reference to the case of Thelwall, Tooke, &c. what if on the strength of this argument it had been proposed to have tried them all in a bundle?[10] Admit for a moment, that we should not have gone to war with France but for Malta; and admit, that Malta is an insufficient and unworthy cause for war;[11] if nevertheless the war be just and necessary from other sufficient and honourable causes; does any thing else follow, than that good ends are often brought about apparently by low means?

[7] It is difficult to reconcile C's account with any report of Fox's actual speech (of 24 May). It is obvious, however, that he had in hand a pamphlet copy of the full shorthand report that subsequently became Debrett's source. The *M Post* report is sketchy—containing, for example, nothing germane to C's quarrel with Fox about Switzerland, and in general little fodder for C's interpretation. (Stuart would have sent C the pamphlet as soon as possible, perhaps with the suggestion that he write these essays to "explode" it.)

[8] Fox held that, since the ministerial excuse for war was France's refusal of "satisfaction and redress" for "indignities and provocations" (in the language of the ministerial address, which contained nothing to correspond with C's "endangered"), justification might rest entirely in the terms, times, and circumstances of demands and refusals of satisfaction and redress; that therefore it was impossible "to separate the two questions of the justice of the war and the conduct of Ministers". Debrett III 379–82.

[9] C had been reading William Herschel's "Thermometric *Spectrum*", in *Phil Trans*, in May 1801. *CL* II 727.

[10] See above, 3 Dec 1801 n 23, 4 Nov 1802 fifth paragraph.

[11] Fox had exclaimed: "And all this for what? For Malta! Malta! plain, bare, naked Malta, unconnected with any other interests." *Speeches* (1815) VI 526.

I have a plot of land that needed draining, both for health and for improvement; but it was not possible to drain it, unless my neighbour drained a field of his at the same time. He had turned a deaf ear to all my arguments, from the ague in both our families, from scanty produce, &c. but at last a thought struck him, that he would make a fish-pond in his field, and on the strength of this idle whim he sets about the drain, and permits me to do the same. No doubt, as a moral man, I must wish, that my neighbour had been actuated by better motives. If he were not merely my neighbour, but my uncle or my brother, I may be *ashamed* of him, and consider my own reputation as injured by his folly. But the *result* of his folly would remain unaffected by all this: and I should commence my draining with all imaginable alacrity, and should smile at any one, who wanted a better reason for my conduct, than that my health and my fortune made it expedient or necessary.[12]

I will run the risk of being tedious, rather than miss a chance of being clear. Different illustrations suit different minds. In the reigns of Elizabeth or Edward VI. a learned Protestant may be well supposed to have regretted deeply, that our most just, most necessary reformation had been effectuated by the adulterous lusts of an abandoned tyrant.—But surely he would only have smiled with contempt at Bellarmin or Suarez,[a][13] if in answer to the defences of our English Protestants, the Popish Divines had insisted on the conduct of Henry VIII. as decisive of the question concerning the merits of the reformation. "Talk as much as you will of the iniquity of the Catholic Clergy, of the absurdity and impiety of the Catholic Creed, still you would have had no reformation, if the Court of Rome had not persevered in its righteous refusal to permit an iniquitous divorce? In vain will you contend that this is an historical fact, not a theological argument; and that the two questions ought therefore to be carefully kept distinct. The one was the occasion of the other, and [they] *are*

[a] *M Post*: Suavey

[12] If C's readiness to argue that going to war with France is so obviously good for England's health and fortune as to justify the flimsiest *casus belli* is startling, C's unused notes are more unvarnished: "We have detected the Tyger...whether we fire at him... depends on the probability of the shot missing or hitting....Eng. Fully convinced that her prosperity & that of the human race depends...". For C's notes see App B, below.

[13] Roberto Francesco Romolo Bellarmino (1542–1621), great Catholic controversialist; Francisco Suárez (1548–1617), philosophical jurist; both Jesuits engaged in pamphlet warfare with the English Protestants. C had been reading Suárez in Aug 1801; see *CN* I 973, 975.

therefore in their nature inseparable; the distinction which you would require is impracticable; for it is impossible to enter into an examination of the justice and necessity of the war (*against the Catholic Church*) *without taking into view the proceedings which produced it; for such as the cause is, such must the effect be.*"

If our divine condescended to animadvert on so silly a statement, would he not answer at once—two questions may, from the co-presence of the facts, be inseparable in the page of the Historian, which are incompatible in the views of the Reasoner. You have confounded the cause with the occasion: the facts, which you state, formed only the *occasion*, that the blessed event took place at that particular time. The cause is to be sought for in the indignation of a people; beginning to be enlightened, at the iniquities, absurdities, and blasphemies, which had been so long imposed upon them by the Church of Rome; this indignation is the true *cause*, and being not only a permanent, but an encreasing cause, it must, in the nature of things, have found some other *occasion*, probably a better one. But why, most learned Catholic! do you thus skulk away from these genuine, national, essential questions? Has, or has not, the Court of Rome insulted, alarmed, and endangered, the reason, peace, and liberty of mankind? Admitting that our Government acted from insufficient or base motives, yet is it, or is it not true, that our Government, actuated by the purest principles of philanthropy as well as patriotism, would nevertheless have done precisely the same?

I declare solemnly, this appears to me strictly a case in point, and literally applicable to the whole of Mr. Fox's argument on this head. —Mr. Fox does not deny, nay, he expressly admits, that Great Britain has been insulted, alarmed, and endangered by France: he does not pretend (how indeed is it possible he could?) he does not pretend, that this insult, alarm, and endangerment, on the part of the First Consul, are only acts of reprisal for aggressions of a similar nature from our Ministers?[14] He knows what all men know, that the

[14] A conjuring trick. Fox had not "expressly admitted" that France endangered Britain. C was altering the ministerial protestation of "indignities and provocations" when he stretched the second term (here and above) into "alarming and endangering the British Empire". C inserts the "danger" and then takes it as admitted. The basic cause of alarm was the potential expansion of the French Empire; the British in choosing to destroy that empire before it grew larger were embarking on a "preventive" war rather than one strictly of self-defence. C's analogy of the draining of farm land is disingenuous but could be made to fit the situation by turning the question to alarm at a rival farmer's putting the plough to greater acreage.

Recurring to this debate in *Friend*

subversion of the independence of Switzerland, the maintenance of an army in Holland, the avowal of intentions against the Turkish Empire, and the *mission* and *conduct* of Sebastiani, if not the publication of his report,[15] did all in the strictest sense of the word *originate* in the temper and views of Bonaparte!

God be praised! the sense of the country is against Mr. Fox. Ninety-nine Englishmen in every hundred act at the present moment on the conviction that the two questions not only are not inseparable, but that they are almost incompatible. I have dwelt the longer on this argument, because I consider it as of the last importance, that in the present exigency Englishmen should feel in their hearts, and be convinced in their understandings, that they have a cause of their own; that they must think for *themselves*, and act for *themselves*: for by themselves alone, under the providence of the Supreme Being, must they be saved. Let them so think, so feel, and so act! Then let France

---

No 22 C takes it as "the great ultimate fact, that Great Britain had been insulted, alarmed, and endangered by France"—and brushes Fox's arguments aside by the simple (false) assertion that "Mr. Fox himself expressly admitted" it. *Friend* (*CC*) II 302 (I 267).

[15] Fox made a sharp distinction between "insults" and "actual injuries": the conduct of France in Switzerland was "oppressive and tyrannical" but "could not be taken as an act of hostility against" England —to go to war for "the restoration of Switzerland to her independence" could only be an act of hypocrisy, considering Austria's intentions; as for Holland, "worse treated" by France "than any other country whatever", Bonaparte had sent troops there not with any reference to Great Britain but to have them "fed and cloathed at the expense of Holland"—Britain *should* have protested on grounds of humanity, but Ministers had only "mentioned Holland to the First Consul" and received assurances. As for French intentions against Turkey and the report of Sébastiani, Fox refused to consider *desire* the same as *design* or to consider dangerous such things as Napoleon's saying that he "could have taken Egypt" with the troops he had sent instead to St Domingo.

It is significant that C does not repeat, and thus does not keep open for discussion, the charge made in his second paragraph above: Bonaparte's "inhumanity" in his enforcement of "hostile regulations against our commerce". Fox implied that the regulations themselves were the main cause of alarm; he reminded the British of their own commercial monopolies and pointed out that if his countrymen were primarily concerned about one nation's inhumanity to another they ought to be greatly concerned about French inhumanity toward the blacks of St Domingo, and he accused them of viewing St Domingo as "no affair of ours" because the result of French inhumanity to the blacks had been of military and commercial advantage to the British. C would have agreed with Fox that French conduct toward Toussaint formed "a material blot in the character of Bonaparte himself", but C does not cite St Domingo at all. He is concentrating on blots that can be seen as threats to the commercial and territorial prosperity of Britain.

bribe, or puzzle all Europe into a confederacy against us, I will not fear for my Country. I trust, that the words of Isaiah will be truly prophetic, and that, even of this people it will be truly said, "They trode the wine-press alone, and of the nations there was none with them.——They looked and there was none to help; they WONDERED that there was none to uphold. Therefore THEIR OWN ARM brought salvation unto them, and their INDIGNATION, *it* upheld them."[16]

There has appeared in the *Moniteur* (in three supplementary sheets to No. 263, *an* 11), an answer to our Manifesto, composed with no mean ability.[17] In my next Essay,[18] I propose fairly to state all the arguments, both in Mr. Fox's Speech, and in this counter-manifesto, which apply to the question, as it stands between France and England. The other, and in my deepest conviction, perfectly distinct consideration, I shall refer to a distant Essay. I have seen neither in Mr. Fox's speech, nor in the manifestoes of France, any one argument, that fairly controverts the simple statement with which I have introduced this Number; and, I trust, it will not draw the soundness of my after reasoning into suspicion (if even now I anticipate the result of the whole). As I have begun with an old dramatic writer, so I will conclude—and, I believe, that the quotation from the same obscure

[16] Isa 63.3, 5 (altered). Cf *Conciones: Lects 1795* (*CC*) 73, in which C quotes the same text of Isaiah, with similar alteration, but uses it in a quite different context.

[17] *Gazette Nationale ou Le Moniteur Universel* XXVI No 263 23 prairial an 11 (12 Jun 1803) 1189–99: "Déclaration du Roi D'Angleterre, et pièces officielles publiées par ses ministres, accompagnées de quelques observations". Some London papers presented abridged translations 17 Jun, e.g. the *Courier*, which called the observations "false and illiberal" and "neither remarkable for their justness nor their ingenuity".

Stuart published neither text nor translation but apparently sent it off to C to deal with, publishing only this thoroughly John Bullish paragraph on the 17th:

> Last night we received Paris Journals to the 14th. The *Moniteur* again contains a laboured justification of the conduct of France in entering on the war. It occupies three supplementary sheets, and is a copy of the King of England's Declaration, with notes upon, and in answer to, it far more extensive than the text. These notes are printed on a type larger than usual. Every circumstance shews they come from high authority, and are deemed of importance. The other Journals continue to be filled with little else than argument justifying France in the war. From all this detailed and anxious defence of the Chief Consul, we perceive the French Government feels the necessity of vindication; it seems to think there is a difficulty in persuading the people that the Grand Pacificator is blameless. In England the best essay on the subject has been Mr. Fox's speech against the war on the part of this country; in England there has been but little argument in support of the war, and yet the people fully feel its justice and necessity.

[18] No further essay appeared.

tragedy, will express the sentiments of the nation at large, as well as my own:

> Were, Sirs! the question simply Peace or War,
> It were no more than shortly to be ask'd
> Whether we would be well or ill:
> Since War the sickness of the kingdom is,
> And Peace the health;—but here I do conceive
> 'T will rather lie, whether we had not better
> Endure sharp sickness for a time, to enjoy
> A perfect strength, than let it languish on us,
> And wearily and slowly wear us out.
> Then, Sirs! as terrible as War appears,
> My vote is for it: nor shall I ever care,
> How ugly my Physician's face may be,
> So he can do the cure. *Tragedy of Brennoralt*[19]

ΕΣΤΗΣΕ

[19] C again quotes from Act III, this time from the speech of Miesla. Suckling *Works* 356–7. For his own purposes C reverses "War or Peace" to "Peace or War"; he invents line 9 ("And wearily and slowly wear us out") to cover an elision of fourteen lines—and to make a point not in Suckling; and he recasts line 12: in Suckling "How ugly my Physician's Face shall be" alludes to the face of War, when it shall come; in C "How ugly my Physician's face may be" alludes to the present minister, Addington, now widely known as "The Doctor" from his father's being a court doctor and from his own pride in a smattering of medical knowledge.

This reluctant acceptance of Addington as war minister was in the current *M Post* vein. When Addington took Tierney into the cabinet in "defiance of Pitt and Fox" Stuart praised him for being "no longer the Jackboot's Jack-boot" (which Fox had called him 5 May 1801 at the Whig Club) and also for his not having again suspended the Habeas Corpus Act (9 Jun). This return to sanity also impressed C (see *CN* I 1455), who yet continued to think Addington a "foolish, well meaning Driveller" (*CL* II 1011) and privately likened the combination of "Addington+Tierney" to the predatory collaboration of "the Seacrab & the Pinna" (*CN* I 1753).

Some time in Aug or Sept 1803 Stuart "sold and finally left" the *M Post*, leaving C's series unwanted and unfinished. Worse yet, the paper's editorials soon took on a bellicosity that shocked and alarmed him. For details, see above, I xcv.